D0899084

MUSIC THEORY AND THE
EXPLORATION OF THE PAST

MUSIC THEORY AND THE EXPLORATION OF THE PAST

Edited by

Christopher Hatch and
David W. Bernstein

The University of Chicago Press
Chicago and London

Christopher Hatch has retired from the Department of Music at Columbia University. David W. Bernstein is assistant professor of music at Mills College.

The University of Chicago Press, Chicago 60637
The University of Chicago Press, Ltd., London
© 1993 by The University of Chicago
All rights reserved. Published 1993
Printed in the United States of America

02 01 00 99 98 97 96 95 94 93   5 4 3 2 1

ISBN (cloth): 0-226-31901-6
ISBN (paper): 0-226-31902-4

Library of Congress Cataloging in Publication Data
Music theory and the exploration of the past / edited by Christopher Hatch and
    David W. Bernstein.
        p.   cm.
    Includes index.
    1. Music—Theory. 2. Musical Analysis. I. Hatch, Christopher, 1926–
II. Bernstein, David W., 1951–
MTG.M96205 1993   91-46985
781—dc20   CIP
                                                                        MN

IN HONOR OF
PATRICIA CARPENTER

Historians and theorists share the same data to some extent, musical works and documents. Perhaps the historian begins with the context; the theorist surely begins with the work. But for a good theorist the work is an instance, not an end. He should move from the structure of a work to that of a repertory, style, genre, or system, aiming ultimately to integrate the work into the intellectual activity of which it is a part. The historical attitude must be built into . . . theory.

PATRICIA CARPENTER

CONTENTS

ACKNOWLEDGMENTS

The editors of such a book as ours owe their primary debt to their fellow authors. We greatly appreciate the thoughtful care and individual acts of helpfulness that came from each and every contributor to this volume. Beyond this we want particularly to thank Murray Dineen, who gave us the idea that set this project going, and Mills College, from which a Faculty Development Grant provided generous financial aid. We also cannot begin to count the ways in which Lois Hatch and Jamie Howell participated in the making of this book. Finally there remains the gratitude we both feel toward the book's dedicatee, Patricia Carpenter. Here our profound intellectual obligations blend inextricably with affection.

Some of the authors have given us the following information about their essays:

"Finding the *Soggetto* in Willaert's Free Imitative Counterpoint: A Step in Modal Analysis" by Benito V. Rivera. This essay is a revision and expansion of a paper read at the Annual Meeting of the American Musicological Society in Baltimore, 1988. The author wishes to thank Professors Howard M. Brown and James Haar for sharing with him their valuable observations.

"Mode and Counterpoint" by Peter N. Schubert. This essay was prepared with the help of a grant from Barnard College. The author wishes to thank the members of his seminars in music theory at Columbia University for their helpful comments on this study.

"The Cavalier Ercole Bottrigari and His Brickbats: Prolegomena to the Defense of Don Nicola Vicentino against Messer Gandolfo Sigonio" by Maria Rika Maniates. A version of this study was read during "Music and Science in the Age of Galileo, an International Symposium," University of Calgary, 26–29 April 1989.

"Theory as Polemic: Mutio Effrem's *Censure . . . sopra il sesto libro de madrigali di Marco da Gagliano*" by Edmond Strainchamps. In a different form this study was presented at the Fourth Biennial Conference on Baroque Music at Royal Halloway and Bedford New College (University of London), Egham, Surrey, England, and as part of the Music Lecture Series for 1989–90 at the State University of New York at Buffalo.

"The Contrapuntal Combination: Schoenberg's Old Hat" by P. Murray Dineen. Funds for research presented in this essay were provided by a doctoral fellowship from the Social Sciences and Humanities Research Council of Canada.

"Harmony as a Determinant of Structure in Webern's Variations for Orchestra" by Graham H. Phipps. The findings in this study are derived from the author's work in the Webern Archives at the Paul Sacher Foundation in Basel, Switzerland. He wishes to thank the University of North Texas and the American Council of Learned Societies for grants that permitted him to work in the archives for two periods in 1987 and 1988. He also wishes to thank the staff of the Paul Sacher Foundation for their gracious assistance in making the Webern sketch materials accessible to him.

"'The Fantasy Can Be Critically Examined': Composition and Theory in the Thought of Stefan Wolpe" by Austin Clarkson. Permission to reprint an excerpt from Stefan Wolpe's *Form for Piano* (1962) has been kindly granted by Seesaw Music, New York, in behalf of Tonos Musikverlag.

MUSIC THEORY AND THE
EXPLORATION OF THE PAST

INTRODUCTION

CHRISTOPHER HATCH AND DAVID W. BERNSTEIN

In recent years the discipline of music theory has developed into a diverse field of inquiry encompassing a variety of subdisciplines. What is particularly striking about the present state of the discipline is its independence from the other principal branch of musical scholarship—historical musicology. This situation is quite unlike the original conception of the founding fathers of *Musikwissenschaft* at the turn of the twentieth century. For them scholarship in music was to constitute an organic discipline that incorporated systematic and historical concerns, all of which could and should intersect on many levels.

The isolation of theoretical studies from other avenues of musical research was as much a necessary condition for their emergence as a discipline as it was a result of the positivistic spirit of the twentieth century. In many areas music theory has emulated science and mathematics—disciplines that only rarely address historiographical issues. It is thus not surprising that over the past few decades theorists have to a great extent divorced themselves from historical questions, creating a barrier (institutionalized in many universities) that separates music theory and historical musicology into two camps. This situation should not be lamented, for theoretical research in its autonomy has developed into a sophisticated art. Indeed, the present-day diversity of the field as well as the technical finesse of its methodologies could never have been imagined a century ago.

Now, however, the time may have come to encourage the dialectical process and to test the value of merging the two disciplines. Of scholarly undertakings that have already moved in this direction, few if any are more notable than the pioneering studies written by Patricia Carpenter, a distinguished member of the Columbia University music department. Her achievement as both teacher and scholar has been to make the historical and theoretical approaches inseparable, and such divergent subjects as Renaissance modal theory and Arnold Schoenberg's theoretical concepts have successfully responded to her

1

methods.[1] Since her retirement in 1989 she has continued to provide exemplars showing how the theory and analysis of music become most meaningful when placed in a historically defined intellectual context. Scholars who have strongly and directly felt the influence of Patricia Carpenter are well represented in *Music Theory and the Exploration of the Past*, and the remaining contributors are clearly in sympathy with her views, which have inspired the underlying theme of this book. Each author was asked to discuss historical situations as they impinge on music theory, or to scrutinize theoretical concepts as they in turn relate to historically determined circumstances and objects. Thus in this volume theory lays claim to its historical habitations.

By assembling this collection we have endorsed a particular position with regard to the relationship between music theory and music history. It is not our intent, however, to adopt a polemical stance, to set forth a prolegomenon to a new, historically tempered music theory designed to replace theory as it is currently being practiced. The excellence of the many monographs, articles, and papers produced in the past twenty years or so attests to the indisputable worth of contemporary theoretical research. Rather, with this book we hope to demonstrate that introducing a historical matrix into theoretical research can yield additional insights into musical works and documents.

Although the nineteen scholars who have contributed to this collection stand on common ground, they represent widely differing areas in the field of music. The theorists among them share no single systematic or analytical allegiance, and their fellow musicologists command a broad array of historical methodologies. Moreover, diverse epochs and highly contrasting repertories have figured in their prior work. The reader of *Music Theory and the Exploration of the Past* should thus expect to meet a great variety of approaches to the intersection of history and theory. And of course no author has had to confine his or her study to a single approach. Some essays include pages that would be completely at home in a traditionally conceived history of theory. For instance, the modal theories of Illuminato Aiguino, the intervallic classifications of Jérôme-Joseph de Momigny, and the idea of symmetry in the writings of German theorists around 1900 are each given straightforward expositions. Such passages, however, are always environed in musical, intellectual, or circumstantial contexts. The case of Momigny is a model in this respect, for from it the reader can learn how certain publishing procedures let the theorist revise his arguments, and so appear to contradict himself, within the confines of a single treatise.

Social forces and biographical facts are vital components of any historical situation, and a few authors in the collection have investigated the specific conditions from which theoretical pronouncements arose. They demonstrate how pedagogical commitments and philosophical positions, patronage and career opportunities, along with subjects like attribution and publication, may influence the formulation of a given theory. Controversy and the urge to rebuke and condemn often come to the fore, since theorists over the years have not been averse to wrangling with their peers. *Music Theory and the Exploration of the Past* details two sustained quarrels that engaged certain Italian musicians and scholars around 1600. And the way in which social attitudes later affect theory is clearly illustrated in a study of August Halm's and Ernst Kurth's theoretical views early in the twentieth century. Such essays reveal how not merely the occasions for theory but also its inner workings, its very substance, can be determined by external forces.

In several essays one can see how music theory interweaves itself with more encompassing intellectual trends and traditions, particularly Renaissance humanism and nineteenth- and twentieth-century positivism. But perhaps Schoenberg's dependence on Goethe's thinking constitutes this volume's prime example of theoretical notions being generated from nonmusical sources. By contrast, the connection between theory and its musical surroundings is most direct when theoretical discourse treats such practical matters as notation, tuning, and intonation. In an essay that focuses on a problem of this sort, one author demonstrates how a close reading of medieval treatises can greatly clarify the rhythmic interpretation of Notre Dame polyphony. Another essay deals with the relationship between a composer's thoughts on theory and his actual compositions. Here the arresting figure of Stefan Wolpe is the object of inquiry.

Theorists today tend to devote their time as much to analysis as to systematic theory. Already existing theories are often easy to convert into analytical methods, and on occasion a theory is framed chiefly to serve as a tool of analysis. Thus the fact that analysis occupies the limelight in the present volume should come as no surprise. Naturally, analytical documents from the past are examined here and there as objects of historical study. Most of the authors, however, have gone in a different direction by undertaking fresh analyses infused with historical thinking. In these the historical component varies. The analyst may choose to found his methods entirely on contemporaneous theoretical sources, as is the case in several of the modal studies contained in the collection. Or, again, the analyst may use contemporaneous sources to temper modern analytical techniques.

Further comment here on individual essays can wait until we have taken a broader look at the status of analysis in relation to history and then to theory. Historically derived analysis, no matter the extent to which it respects historical contextuality, poses problems to present-day musicologists and theorists alike. An orthodox historian might observe that a historically inflected analysis receives no legitimation from the discipline of history, strictly defined. Were a scholar to derive his analytical method directly from the same time, the same place, even the same person as those from which the work under discussion springs, the result would be only a re-creation or, more accurately, a fabrication vis-à-vis the past. Such historically based analysis, when judged by the criteria of historical investigation, is insupportable. Moreover, analysis, aside from a handful of interesting yet isolated cases, is a relatively recent phenomenon. Historically oriented analyses are frequently forced to assume a connection between specific theoretical documents and a musical work.

At the same time, "historical" analysis cannot meet the standards imposed by current systematic theory. Today we favor analyses that apply existing systems, however anachronistically. Our fascination with systems and system-building emphasizes the most modern analytical tools. As the author of the opening essay notes, theorists are often inclined to see the history of theory as an evolutionary process culminating in their own theoretical concepts and "state-of-the-art" analytical techniques. Earlier theory, according to this view, has merely antiquarian interest and possesses little power to explicate musical works.

If analysis has to be validated on other than historical or systematic grounds, perhaps elementary and practical tests would suffice. A set of queries might be put to each analysis. Does it tell us something about the piece that we did not know before? Is that "something" a recognizably important component in the piece? Does the analysis explain anomalies? Does it provide intellectual justification for what we have already felt about the piece? And does it use a method that can be fruitfully applied to other pieces? These tests accord with simple reasonableness, satisfying certain pragmatic proof-of-the-pudding standards, though they fail to establish analysis as a discipline in its own right or even as a quasi-independent branch of theory. Rather, they rest on the notion that analysis, which deals with works of art, must in some way be true to these works. The presence of such truth in an analysis will be as open to debate as is the meaning of the analyzed work itself. Accepting this idea deflates analytical pretensions, but then to recognize where imponderables hold sway is one sign of rationality. The potential value of rigorous and complex analytical systems is not in the least threatened by these concessions, though the worth of a system must be gauged by factors external to it.

A choice of analytical techniques can be motivated, but certainly not determined, by these broad generalizations. In making the choice, an analyst could do worse than canvass the methods that would be congenial to the underlying musical mentality of a work's composer and to that of his intended audience. The chances are strong that at any given time and place the natures of thinking *in* music and thinking *about* music will correspond in many respects. Thus as a basis for selecting one or another mode of analysis historical considerations, having been dismissed at the front gate, gain entrance by the back door.

The analyses in the present collection exhibit a wealth of historical knowledge. Some authors reconstitute little-known systematic theories, while others use more familar procedures and occasionally cross the contested boundary between analysis and criticism. The essays' historical angle is not limited to theories formulated during composers' lifetimes. The implications of a comment written years after a work's first performance, an awareness of how a piece reinterprets its composer's earlier output—these too allow the past to make its contribution.

Where analysis is guided by historical consciousness, it may help to resolve some problems that current thinking about theory and analytical methods has brought to the fore. Analytical formalism is under attack nowadays, being caught in the same line of fire as positivism in historical musicology. The significance of the hard evidence on which these methods rely has been put in question, and as a result compensatory measures are being advocated. Both the subversion of entrenched assumptions and a yielding to subjectivity are now urged upon scholars. Yet many resist these counsels, for they envisage a hurtful loss of rigor if such recommendations are accepted. The full-scale analyses in *Music Theory and the Exploration of the Past* speak to these fears and yet to some degree follow the advice of those who would go beyond formalism. The analyses themselves are carried out with all the marshalling of concrete detail that any systematic, a historical analysis might boast, so the tests of objectivity are met. But the authors of these analyses are unusually skillful in showing the reader where they stand and what conscious choices regarding analytical preconceptions they have made. By recognizing the temporal and circumstantial provenance of the music they examine, they create analyses that are fictive transactions. That is to say, their analyses represent exchanges between scholars who are at home in the 1990s and compositions to whose secrets historical imagination alone may hold the key.

These essays can also remind the reader that analysis is in another sense bipolar, since it takes place in a field between theoretical precepts and musical artifact. The pull of these poles is seldom even. In general it can be said that analyses are of two sorts; some intend especially to display the power of a particular analytical approach, while others are chiefly motivated by a wish to explain the extraordinary traits of the composition being studied. Such a difference in emphasis is neatly illustrated by the book's three modal analyses. All three use contemporary theories of mode as a base of operations, but whereas the studies of Palestrina's *Dies sanctificatus* and Willaert's *O invidia* stress a finely articulated analytical system in part for its own sake, the analysis of Okeghem's *Missa cuiusvis toni* seems designed first and foremost to explain the distinctive characteristics of that composition in terms of the prevailing modal norms.

The contributions dealing with Beethoven and Mozart create their own contrast. On the one hand, in each Beethoven essay the author closely studies an individual composition in an ad hoc fashion and with a minimum of theoretical apparatus, drawing on near-contemporaneous theory or criticism. On the other hand, the Mozart essay sets about scanning many works with an eye to delineating a definitive view of chromatic technique in the music of the Viennese Classical composers. In this endeavor eighteenth-century theoretical sources are supplemented by the writings of Schoenberg and Schenker, whose theoretical concepts are inseparable from their profound understanding of the Classical repertory. The result is a synthesis of older theory with a more modern analytical perspective that approaches the hermeneutic resolution to the schism between historicism and "presentism" called for in the opening essay of the volume.

Two analyses that treat Webern's Variations for Orchestra and Stravinsky's *Requiem Canticles*, respectively, show how rewarding a historical—or, better, contextual—reading of twentieth-century music can be. Both compositions lend themselves to the standardized methods of serial and set analysis but, advancing beyond this, the authors place these works under a new light. The Webern piece is made to disclose a tonal and tertian substructure that in other forms would have been familiar to the work's first audiences. Then the *Requiem Canticles*, for all its serial complexity, is shown to contain Stravinsky's accustomed octatonicism. An ahistorical serial treatment could never uncover the ways in which the *Requiem Canticles* is retrospective and referential with respect to the composer's earlier works. (Just as these studies suggest alternatives to purely serial- or set-analytical methods, one of the Beethoven essays reveals the limitations of another abstract, ahistorical perspective by rejecting the restrictive application of "sonata form" axioms to the "Eroica" Symphony.)

In three essays that appear together toward the close of this volume, distinctive facets of Arnold Schoenberg's thought are addressed. These studies establish that Schoenberg was the legatee of a long-standing theoretical tradition as well as being Goethe's heir, that his theories explicate concepts embodied in Bach's music and his own alike, and that his analytical methods are well suited to early nineteenth-century music. *Mutatis mutandis*, these conclusions regarding the origins and uses of a theorist's work have parallels elsewhere in the book.

At the beginning and midway through the volume stand two philosophically inclined essays. In different ways they embrace the history of theory as their subject. Proceeding in a mostly nonhistorical way, the initial essay strives to define the *history* of theory; the other, proceeding historically, delves into the meaning of *theory*. Whereas the first author presents some persuasive solutions to the historiographical problems he sets forth, the second author, very much attuned to the lessons of history, implies some unanswerable questions about the entanglement of theory in aesthetics. In short, the first essay addresses issues of methodology, and later in the course of the book another offers a reminder of theory's problematic status.

Apart from these two studies, the essays in *Music Theory and the Exploration of the Past* are arranged chronologically. Yet each reader can feel free to regroup them by seeking out the alliances that connect their methods, styles, or subjects. This introduction has, after all, indicated several different threads that help to unite the volume. In whatever order the book is read, we trust that it demonstrates the merits of investigating the roles that history can and should play in the study of music theory.

Note

1. Patricia Carpenter, "Tonal Coherence in a Motet by Dufay," *Journal of Music Theory* 17 (1973): 2–65; idem, "Musical Form and Musical Idea: Reflections on a Theme of Schoenberg, Hanslick, and Kant," Edmond Strainchamps, Maria Rika Maniates, and Christopher Hatch, eds., *Music and Civilization: Essays in Honor of Paul Henry Lang* (New York, 1984), 394–427.

ONE

Music Theory and Its Histories

THOMAS CHRISTENSEN

At first glance there seems to be an ineluctable dilemma inherent in any history of music theory. The dilemma arises in trying to determine the proper context for interpretation: Are we to read any given theory as a theoretical text or as a historical document? Neither choice alone seems particularly satisfying. Yet it is not immediately obvious how the two can be reconciled in any straightforward manner. If we follow the first course and consider solely the theoretical "content" of some past theory, we are presuming that this content can be extracted from—and rationally analyzed outside of—its historical and biographical contexts. Theories, simply put, make normative claims that are temporally immutable.

Such an interpretation, however, seems to deny, or at least suppress, the contextual aspects of the theory. If we choose instead to take the second course and consider the historical and biographical contingencies of the same theory, its "immutable" nature might seem to possess far less tenacity. We might find that the theory cannot be easily analyzed outside its historical boundaries; the problems the theory addresses may be culturally peculiar, its language of discourse alien to ours. There is indeed a real question as to whether the theory can be "translated" into anything meaningful to those of us living in differing musical and intellectual cultures. Yet if we accept such historical circumscription, then theory texts become reduced to mere antiquarian documents. "Historicizing" music theory conflicts in a fundamental sense with the ontological claims of theory to historical transcendence. In characteristically dialectical fashion, Carl Dahlhaus expresses this thought succinctly:

> Theory . . . stands in an almost unavoidably discrepant relationship with history—history as a mode of thought, not as a collection of facts: musical phenomena are, as it seems, either given from nature or historically grounded; and as soon as the model of historical interpretation dominates,

theory suffers a loss of its substance and fades, so to speak,
to a shadow of itself. Strictly speaking, to explain theory
historically means to take away the very claim upon which
it as theory had been based.[1]

Of course this is an intractable quandary only insofar as we hold to
a strict dichotomization between history and theory. Dahlhaus, I should
point out, does not ultimately accept its validity; in the pages following
the excerpt I have quoted, he goes on to explore the subtle interrelation-
ship between music theory and historical interpretation. Any residual
contradictions between the two are revealed to be far less fearsome
than his initial portrayal suggests, dissolving as they do under his sophisticated dialectical critique. Now in the intellectual tradition of
German *Musikwissenschaft*, where both history and theory can be seen
as related idealist constructs, Dahlhaus's dialectical resolution should
be congenial. However, for contemporary American musicologists, for
whom the disjunction between history and theory has traditionally
been much stronger, the possibilities for mediation that Dahlhaus outlines are perhaps not as apparent.

In this essay I would like to reexamine the putative dilemma between "historical" and "theoretical" readings of music theories and
analyze its conceptual and empirical ramifications in practice. I will
retain the basic polarity Dahlhaus sets up between theoretical and historical ontologies, but recast his arguments in terms that better address
current issues in American musicology. I will call these two poles "presentist" and "historicist" positions, respectively, where "presentism"
corresponds roughly to the theorists' ahistorical perspective, and "historicism" the historians' atheoretical perspective. I concede at the outset that this inelegant formulation presents a stark and oversimplified
polarization to which few American musicologists, be they historians
or theorists, would subscribe. But I suggest that in practice we still often
fall into the trap of writing predominantly from one side or the other
without realizing the full implications of the position we have chosen.
By retaining a strong distinction between presentism and historicism,
we will have a useful heuristic by which to ferret out these less overt
allegiances.[2]

Finally, in the last section of this essay I shall consider ways in which
the apparent incompatibility between presentist and historicist interpretations of music theory can be mediated. Drawing upon Hans-Georg
Gadamer's sophisticated philosophical hermeneutics, I hope to show
that any discrepancy between analytical and historical modes of understanding need not constitute an irresolvable conflict. Indeed, for
hermeneutics it is precisely through the tension between the presentist

and historicist perspectives that real understanding can take place. But before exploring this suggestive possibility, I want to examine the individual positions separately. I shall begin by considering the presentist ideology.

The Presentist's Myopia

By "presentism" I understand any perspective whereby an object is studied in light of present knowledge and norms. Music theory is avowedly presentist when it interprets music from the past using contemporary analytical tools and modes of classification. Much formalist and structuralist literary criticism can also be labeled as presentist, in that literary texts are treated as autonomous objects severed from their historical contexts and authorial intentions. But it is also possible to practice history in a presentist manner as, for example, when we analyze the past in terms of some ideal process or structural grid that we superimpose and measure from the present.

Perhaps the most notorious—and persistent—strain of presentist historiography is teleology, wherein the past is seen as part of some determinist process directed to, and culminating in, the present. This process is usually considered to be progressive, with the entailed judgment that the present is at a qualitatively more advanced stage of development than the past. Herbert Butterfield described such teleological history as "Whiggish" after those nineteenth-century British historians whose narrations served as glorifications of Protestant, parliamentarian democracy.[3] The history of science, too, was depicted in the nineteenth century in a teleological manner. Science was seen as a fully progressive enterprise confirming the Enlightenment's optimistic faith in human reason and the never-ending advancement of knowledge.[4]

Since music theory has long turned to science for heuristic models, it is not surprising that the first real histories of music theory from the nineteenth century reflected the Whiggish biases of contemporaneous histories of science.[5] Both genres were permeated with the spirit of progress. Music theory, like science, was seen as evolving inexorably toward higher levels of sophistication and truth, and—depending upon the temerity of the author—attaining its final perfection in his own writings.

In arguably the earliest bona fide history of music theory, François-Joseph Fétis sought to examine "The Principal Systems of the Generation and Classification of Chords."[6] Inspired by the writings of Auguste Comte, Fétis depicted the history of music theory (just as he did the history of music itself) in progressive stages of evolution that culminated in his own theory of *tonalité*. Fétis was convinced that his recognition of tonality was a historical necessity. Concluding his survey of this progress, he confidently asserted:

> The theory of harmony has reached the final limit of art and science. It is complete, and nothing more can be added. . . . I have completed it by placing it upon the unshakable base of tonality. What invincibly demonstrates the excellence [of my system] is that it is at once a history of the progress of art and the best analysis of the facts that it manifests.[7]

In a more rigorously Hegelian narration, Hugo Riemann portrayed the historical development of music theory as a relentless dialectical process. Writing in 1908, he claimed that "the development of theoretical knowledge concerning the essence of music convincingly demonstrates continuous progress up to the present standpoint. . . . [It] reveals the gradual discovery of all the laws that are valid today."[8] Of course Riemann believed that these "valid" laws were embodied in his own theories of functional harmony and dualism. Thus the third book of his monumental *Geschichte der Musiktheorie*, which details the development of harmonic theory beginning with Zarlino, reads almost like a military narrative. Riemann's story recounts an epic intellectual battle between foresighted progressives (such as Zarlino, Johann Friedrich Daube, and Moritz Hauptmann) and obstinate conservatives (including most thorough-bass theorists and such monists as Gottfried Weber and Ernst Richter).[9]

The idea of progress has come to ring hollow in our age. Hence it is rare to find such uncompromising faith in teleological history anymore. But if the Whiggish virus is now in remission—countered as it seems by the equally infectious strains of historicism that I will discuss in the next section—another form of presentism that has proved to be even more tenacious soon took its place: positivism. The positivist, it will be remembered, holds allegiance to universal standards of rationality and method through which any systematic theory (scientific, philosophical, or musical) can be evaluated—for example, by criteria of logical rigor, economy, empirical adequacy, or falsification. If theories cannot be confidently ordered in a strictly progressive and evolutionary process, they can at least be individually weighed according to the degree to which they meet, or fail to meet, these standards.

An example of positivist history of science that intersects at important points with music theory is the history of rational mechanics written by Clifford Truesdell.[10] Truesdell has defined "rational mechanics" as the axiomatized mathematical science of elastic and flexible bodies, such as vibrating strings, bars, and membranes. It provides, then, a foundation for understanding the physics of sound production in all musical instruments and, not of less consequence, any acoustical theory of tonality.

The most significant advances of rational mechanics occurred in the course of the eighteenth century, so this is naturally the period upon which Truesdell concentrates his attention. But the full development of the mathematical tools necessary for the complete axiomatization of this science did not take place until recently. Truesdell writes his survey from the perspective of a twentieth-century scientist who already knows the answers. In an unabashedly presentist mode he translates the mathematical formulations found in the canonical treatises of eighteenth-century rational mechanics into modern scientific notation. He then proceeds to analyze and judge the results using tools and standards entirely unknown to the authors of these texts. The resultant picture he creates is highly skewed, occupied on the one side by fore-sighted scientists whose work can retrospectively be seen as coming closest to meeting the standards of contemporary rational mechanics (such as Euler and Jakob Bernoulli), and on the other side by conservatives (such as d'Alembert) who are chided by Truesdell for their near-sighted and inept work. This is not the place to analyze Truesdell's historiography in detail, as relevant as that might be to the history of music theory.[11] I only cite it as an example, albeit an extreme one, of a bias that can be found to this day in much of the literature on the history of science.

Many music theorists today also seem to subscribe to the positivist historiography exemplified by Truesdell. For instance, Allen Forte has vigorously defended a presentist approach in the face of what he perceives to be the specious dogmas of historicism. Writes Forte:

> My view . . . is that a knowledge of history is totally inadequate for understanding musical documents, including musical scores as well as treatises on music. It is only now, with the development of contemporary modes of theoretical thought, that scholars are beginning to understand more fully many of the classic documents of music theory.[12]

Forte certainly would not deny that music theories have historical origins and contexts. (He has, after all, amply demonstrated knowledge of the history of theory in many of his writings.) Rather, he asserts that historical factors in and of themselves cannot provide complete understanding or logical validation of theory. This is, of course, the position of the positivist.

A "history of theory" written in a presentist mode will be a traditionalist one that recounts the genealogy of a particular structural parameter, analytical approach, or theoretical question in which the author takes an interest. The basic form of such a history is predetermined, since the goal of the narrative is already known: the present. All that remains is for the historian to work backwards and retrace the events and ideas that led up to his own time.

This points to the reverse side of the teleological coin: geneticism. Once the historian has decided that a given theoretical concept is to be reified, the search for its initial conception and earliest manifestations becomes as important as the study of its maturation. Such an approach might impel the historian to ask, like Riemann, who the first theorist was to "recognize" the inversional relation between major and minor triads. Or we might seek, along with Fétis, to discover the first composer to exploit the appellative character of the dominant seventh chord.

Among those who today approach the history of music theory in a presentist manner, Schenkerians are perhaps the most prominent. In their readings of theory texts Schenkerians frequently focus upon a limited number of theoretical traditions on which they place particular value (*Figurenlehre* of the seventeenth century, thorough-bass practice from the eighteenth century, techniques of harmonic reduction from the nineteenth century) at the expense of other, competing theoretical traditions (generative derivations of harmony, theories of melody and form, motivic analysis). Their "history of music theory," like those by Fétis and Riemann, discerns a teleological progression of theoretical thought—here one that culminates in Schenker's formulations. In their crudest forms, their histories judge past theories only to the extent to which they most closely adumbrated Schenkerian ideas.

But no such tidy and directed historical narrative is without cost. The problem is not that this history is selective. (Selectivity, after all, is an essential part of writing history; one cannot say *everything* about the past.) The problem is that it is myopic and reductive. Presentist historians impose upon the past their parochial concerns regarding what constitutes the essential issues of music theory, whether or not in fact these issues held a commensurate position of importance or meant the same thing in their own day. The past, in other words, is interpreted so as to validate the present. And this can only lead to anachronism.

For example, Schenkerians often point to the *Figurenlehre* codified by the seventeenth-century composer Christoph Bernhard as constituting part of a broader tradition of diminution merging seamlessly with eighteenth-century *General-Bass* practice and beyond to Schenker.[13] But in focusing upon this singular element of Bernhard's theory—or put another way, by interpreting it solely in light of the ideal of diminution—the Schenkerians miss the rich scholastic-rhetorical tradition in which

Bernhard's figures were rooted, one that cannot be reduced to a technical compositional device.

Presentist historians of music theory also risk conflating the varied pedagogical functions of differing theoretical and compositional traditions. In other words, they fail to recognize the distinctions between genres of music theory. Yet one cannot expect the same degree of empirical correlation to practice, for example, in a medieval theory treatise on "harmonics" as one would in a counterpoint text. The kind of practice-oriented descriptions of figured bass given by Carl Philipp Emanuel Bach that Schenkerians find so congenial cannot be used as a measure to evaluate the speculative arguments of someone like Rameau who worked within an entirely unrelated pedagogical and heuristic paradigm. This is not to say that there are no filiations between Bernhard and Jean de Muris, Sylvestro Ganassi, and Simon Sechter (to name some of the contrasting theorists whom Robert Morgan has grouped together as espousing related theories of diminution).[14] It is to say, rather, that any connection we draw must be sensitive to the unique historical contexts of each theory and not forced into molds meant to validate our own interests.

For another example of anachronistic historiography in music theory, let us consider the paradigmatic problem of "sonata form" and its origins. As we know, "sonata form" was a concept reified only in the nineteenth century by theorists such as Reicha and Czerny, although the musical repertory from which it was induced stemmed largely from the eighteenth century. The discrepancy between practice and the belated "recognition" of sonata form has led some historians to scour the eighteenth-century theoretical literature for the earliest antecedents of sonata-form theory. The danger here is that we are looking for something in light of a later morphology that may have little to do with the concerns and meanings of the eighteenth-century theorists. (Quentin Skinner aptly calls this the "mythology of prolepsis.")[15] Why should we view, say, Scheibe's analysis of the rhetorical process of "symphonic composition" as an embryonic form of Reicha's *grande coupe binaire* any more than we see Giuseppe Torelli's *Concerti musicali* as but underdeveloped symphonies of Mozart? Such caution certainly does not preclude the drawing of historical connections, provided it is done without the implications of causality or teleology.[16]

Many theorists may defend presentism, as Forte has, by claiming that the sophistication and advanced state of our present theoretical thought allows us to see further and deeper than past theorists could, and hence to be capable of normative evaluations and analysis. But such positivist claims on behalf of an objective (and ahistorical) method have been strongly challenged in the last quarter-century. Nowadays few philosophers of science accept that all scientific theories can be comparatively analyzed and evaluated with invariant rational criteria; past scientific theories have been shown to be incommensurable with one another in fundamental ways.[17] Thus no single "scientific method" or "logic of discovery" by which to test all theories can be laid down.

In the face of these lessons from a cognate field, why does presentist/ positivist historiography continue to occupy such a comfortable home in the current music-theoretical environment? One answer suggests itself: the dominance of analytical formalism in our profession. Just as we so often analyze musical works as autonomous pitch structures severed from their historical and authorial contexts, so too do we tend to abstract theories. It is surely not surprising in this regard that we see Schenker's theory—the current paradigm of tonal formalism in America—so frequently severed from its historical contexts and rein-terpreted, axiomatized, and redacted within a Platonic tonal universe occupied by diminutions, *Urlinie* progressions, unfoldings, and the like. Not only, it seems, is it unnecessary to know the historical, cultural, and biographical context of Schenker's ideas; such understanding is even faulted for distracting our attention from the essence of his theory.[18] Thus John Rothgeb admonishes the reader of Schenker's *Kontrapunct*

> to recognize that however much Schenker may have regarded
> his musical precepts as an integral part of a unified world-
> view, they are, in fact, not at all logically dependent on any
> of his extramusical speculations. Indeed, no broader philo-
> sophical context is necessary—or even relevant—to their
> understanding.[19]

The implication of Rothgeb's assertion seems to be that Schenker's theory can be divorced from the musical, cultural, and biographical environment in which his ideas germinated and developed over some fifty years. But Schenker was a theorist fully aware of his own historic-ity—alarmed about the seemingly lamentable state of German musical composition and pedagogy, and fearful above all for the perilous sur-vival of a musical tradition for which he felt himself an expositor and guardian. With the possible exception of Schoenberg, Schenker was the most historically conscious of any twentieth-century theorist. He would surely have found it astounding that his theory might come to be un-derstood or applied in anything other than the context of the "unified world-view" he held.[20]

Another theorist whose writings can be fully understood only within their rich historical and biographical contexts is Jean-Philippe Rameau. His annunciation of the *basse fondamentale* is invariably cited as a watershed in the development of tonal theory. Unfortunately Rameau's writing style is prolix and discursive; his arguments seem to constitute an eclectic and not always coherent mix of scientific, scholastic, and mystical reasoning that changed erratically in the course of his lifetime. In the past, most theorists have been content to ignore the verbiage and focus upon the pure "theoretical content" of his system.[21] But Rameau's varying heuristic and rhetorical strategies are not simply annoying overgrowth that one must cut through in order to get to the heart of his thought. They are in fact essential constituents of it. (If the linguistic turn has taught us anything, it is that language may constitute as much as convey meaning.) And these varying heuristic and rhetorical strategies can be understood only within the specific (and changing) musical, intellectual, and social environments that impinged on their formulation.

One can thus not hope to capture the full meaning of Rameau's theory simply through an analysis of the text as an autonomous artifact. We need instead to view his *oeuvre* synoptically and contextually. To understand Rameau's conception of the fundamental bass in the *Traité de l'harmonie* means reconstructing the musical conditions of his time that impelled his discoveries, reconstituting the varied pedagogical traditions to which Rameau was heir (monochordist [or canonist] theory, French thorough-bass practice, late seventeenth-century contrapuntal theory, etc.), and identifying the intellectual ideas with which he came into contact (Cartesian mechanistic philosophy, Newtonian empiricism, Lockean sensationalism, etc.). The changing arguments he gave to his theory, the variegated rhetoric he employed, and his shifting pedagogical strategies make sense only when viewed against the many *mise en scènes* of his life; we must see Rameau as the temperamental composer working in the charged political world of the Paris Opéra, the sycophantic aspirant to the Royal Academy of Sciences, the jealous rival to the Encyclopedists. In short, Rameau's music theory cannot be fully understood unless placed and analyzed within its total historical context.[22]

Indeed, any history of music theory risks gross anachronism by extracting some individual problem from its historical contexts and studying its development in order to form a continuous diachronic narrative that crosses the ages. (An example of this might be a study of "changing derivations of the minor mode," or of "evolving theories of the downbeat.") This is the problem that has plagued intellectual historians over the years and has led to a noticeable discrediting of the general "history of ideas" school of intellectual history, with all its attendant immutable "unit ideas" and "timeless questions" that putatively run through all cultures and periods.[23] Gadamer reminds us that "there is no such thing, in fact, as a point outside history from which the identity of a problem can be conceived within the vicissitudes of the history of attempts to solve it."[24] And Quentin Skinner writes:

> Any statement . . . is inescapably the embodiment of a particular intention, on a particular occasion, addressed to the solution of a particular problem, and thus specific to its situation in a way that it can only be naive to try to transcend. The vital implication here is not merely that the classic texts cannot be concerned with our questions and answers, but only with their own. There is also the further implication that—to revive Collingwood's way of putting it—there simply are no perennial problems in philosophy: there are only individual answers to individual questions, with as many different answers as there are questions, and as many different questions as there are questioners. There is in consequence simply no hope of seeking the point of studying the history of ideas in the attempt to learn directly from the classic authors by focusing on their attempted answers to supposedly timeless questions.[25]

If Skinner's conclusion is a bit too pessimistic (and I shall shortly explain why I believe it is), I think his essential observation is still valid and potent with implications for the historian of music theory: every music theory must first be understood as a creative intellectualization of music that is informed by a unique complex of culturally specific parameters. And this is precisely what a presentist approach fails to do by seeing some past theory only on the basis of *our* concerns, *our* models or, in other words, *our* theories. It is myopic of us, if not a bit narcissistic, to imagine that past theorists were necessarily talking about (or worse, adumbrating) the same topics with which we are concerned today. Too often the continuity and cohesion we discover in the past were projected there by ourselves. And however comforting it is for us to imagine music theorists conversing across cultures and time (let alone disparate musical repertories) in some imaginary Peripatetic Lyceum, the fact is that more often there is, as Michel Foucault has shown, discontinuity, incommensurability, and ruptures in discourse.

This is not to deny that there can be filiations, continuity, or homology in music theory, that theorists share musical repertories, face common problems, and ask similar questions, that theorists, in other words, participate in various kinds of tradition. Nor do I mean to suggest a position of extreme relativism wherein we have no access—no rational "bridgehead"—through which we may penetrate and evaluate alien systems of thought. I only want to suggest here that greater insight will be gained when we look first at theories (like artworks) for what is unique and defining about them, not for what is common and invariant. Put another way, real historical understanding presupposes discovering relations *within* a cultural context before relations *across* cultural boundaries, although both are ultimately indispensable to the historian. I shall develop this program in more detail in the last section of this essay.

The Historicist's Naivety

It is hardly surprising that the coarser forms of presentist historiography just described would eventually engender strong opposition. Indeed, as early as the mid-nineteenth century, historians such as Leopold von Ranke, Johann Gustav Droysen, and Jacob Burckhardt were decrying the various idealist histories of their compatriots and advocating a more "objectified" and empirical attitude.[26] This is the position that has come to be known as "historicism" and is epitomized in Ranke's catchphrase that history should be written "as it really was."

For the historicist, the past is too multifarious and complex to be reduced to a series of moments within some determinist historical process or structure; it demands rather to be revealed in its full richness and uniqueness.[27] This is why the orthodox historicist rejects every form of presentism in historical inquiry, whether it be the introduction of contemporary standards of rationality or the superimposition of structuralist models and idealist historical forces. Instead, the historicist studies the past "on its own terms." Any portrayal or analysis of the past, in other words, must be commensurate with the norms of the time, not the present. The historicist approach is thus more empathic than explanatory. It corresponds to what an anthropologist would call "emic" analysis, and traditional hermeneutics the *subtilitas intelligendi*.

For the twentieth-century historicist R.G. Collingwood, real historical understanding of the past can transpire only by means of a "historical imagination" in which we abandon our presentist position and "re-enact" the past in the shoes of those historical actors we are studying. "History," he tells us in his *Autobiography*,

> did not mean knowing what events followed what. It meant getting inside other people's heads, looking at their situation through their eyes, and thinking for yourself whether the way in which they tackled it was the right way. Unless you can see the battle through the eyes of a man brought up in sailing-ships armed with broadsides of short-range muzzle-loading guns, you are not even a beginner in naval history, you are right outside it. . . . You have for that mo-

ment allowed yourself to drift outside the region of history altogether.[28]

An ideology closely related to historicism is "intentionalism," which holds that any action or text is the product of a unique—and historically specific—intention on the part of the actor or author. (This is the gist of Quentin Skinner's argument quoted earlier.) It follows from this that the historian's task is to reconstruct cultural and biographical contexts in order to retrieve these intentions. And this is best accomplished with a historicist method.

E.D. Hirsch has strongly argued for an "intentionalist" approach in the study of literary texts. Hirsch condemns as presentist and anachronistic virtually all structuralist readings of literary texts. Like Skinner, he advocates instead an approach through which the intentions of the author are recovered by reading a text "in its own terms":

> To understand an utterance it is, in fact, not just desirable but absolutely unavoidable that we understand it in its own terms. We could not possibly recast a text's meanings in different terms unless we had already understood the text in its own.[29]

Of course contemporary literary theory is by no means the only discipline with historicist critics like Hirsch. In almost any discipline that involves the interpretation of past human creations (whether texts, speeches, artworks, or actions) there can be found an active coterie of historicists and intentionalists.[30] And in our poststructuralist, postpositivist climate, with all the attendant distrust of theory, their numbers appear to be on the rise.[31]

In recent years a number of musicologists have also taken positions that intersect the historicist agenda. For the most part these are historians who are dubious of contemporary music theory because of its baleful penchant for anachronism. It is not that these musicologists altogether deny the legitimacy of contemporary analytical tools when applied to music of the past. Rather, they contend that music is most meaningfully understood in the context of its own culture and that music theories coterminous with the music under consideration have a better chance of decoding such culturally rooted meanings than do contemporary, presentist theories.

The historicist cudgel has been most recently taken up by Richard Taruskin in challenging the value of Allen Forte's theory of pitch-class sets when applied to the music of Stravinsky and Scriabin.[32] Taruskin is skeptical about such applications of Forte's theory, since in his view criteria for analytical statements on music "are historically delimited, and must be determined by historical methods."[33] Forte's theory,

Taruskin vigorously asserts, manifestly does not meet this demand. He advocates instead the use of alternative theories, ones that are rooted in the same cultural soil as the music. This means, at least in the case of Stravinsky and Scriabin, modified forms of tonal (but not Schenkerian) and octatonic analysis.

Gary Tomlinson would probably sympathize with Taruskin's critique. He accuses the presentist (or "ethnocentric") music analyst of succumbing to "a solipsistic and ultimately narcissistic aestheticism" by failing to take into account the "cultural web" (an expression he borrows from Clifford Geertz) of the music's historical contexts.[34] Although Tomlinson does not explicitly prescribe historical music theories as the antidote for current presentist ills of contemporary music analysis, I think he would favor the notion, given the implications of what he advocates:

> We study, or should study works of art as records of human aspiration, achievement, and meaning in contexts different from our own. We should cherish them for what they tell us about the diverse creative acts that gave rise to them. When instead we view them ahistorically—as aesthetic objects uprooted from some context that we believe engendered them and transplanted into our own cultural humus—then we forfeit the possibility of conversing meaningfully with their creators. With easy but all-too-familiar meanings we talk mainly among ourselves, reflected in the work, and not with the work's creators shining *through* it. The work is a mirror rather than a magnifying lens, so to speak. And by regarding it as a mirror we give up or at least drastically limit our ability to broaden our world of discourse.[35]

Joseph Kerman's rhetoric is similar to Tomlinson's, even going so far as to employ the same ecological metaphor:

> [The analyst's] dogged concentration on internal relationships within the single work of art is ultimately subversive as far as any reasonably complete view of music is concerned. . . . By removing the bare score from its context in order to examine it as an autonomous organism, the analyst removes that organism from the ecology that sustains it.[36]

Finally, Leo Treitler has complained how

> prevailing modes of structural analysis are anti-historical, in two respects: they decontextualize their objects in their rationalistic treatment of them; and they are taught and practiced without notice taken of their own historicality or, in

general, of the role that particular models play in the organization of understanding.[37]

In contradistinction to the ahistorical, formalist approaches of music analysis, Treitler recommends a hermeneutically inspired kind of historical understanding. The means by which such historical understanding may be gained, according to Treitler, is fully consonant with historicism: music analysis should be taught along historical lines.[38]

It seems fair to conclude that these critics are skeptical of almost every sort of music analysis that ignores the historical contexts of music, either by applying rigidly presentist methods (that is, contemporary analytical techniques) or by simply claiming to stand outside of history. Yet those of us who concur that music theories, like musical works of art, must be viewed as historically bounded and culturally rooted, may take exception to inferences that analytical techniques must therefore also be historically rooted. This reasoning is fallacious in that it conflates subject and method—ontology and epistemology.

To explain what is meant by this, I will draw upon some recent debates within the "authentic performance practice" movement. For I am convinced that the historicist ideology underpinning these musicologists' calls for "historical analysis" represents the same species of "authenticism" that the proponents of historical performance practice uphold, and consequently it suffers from the same logical and aesthetic difficulties. Here is how the parallel works: By reconstructing as closely as possible not only the original performance practice of a given musical work, but a historically rooted conceptual (i.e., theoretical) framework by which it was understood (either by the composer, the general public, or some ideal listener of the time), we presumably have better access to "authentic theoretical meaning." If we wish to undertake any kind of analysis of the music, then, we should do so using contemporaneous theories, vocabulary, and concepts as much as possible. Antiquarian theory texts thus become as much a part of the historicist's panoply as the sackbut, *notes inégales,* and 1/6 comma temperament.

A corollary to this authenticist orthodoxy is that the validity of a theory lies in inverse proportion to its historical distance from the object of its analysis. In other words, since historically rooted interpretations of an artwork are privileged, subsequent interpretations (whether they be performances or analyses) represent unavoidable declines in meaning. Ironically, the situation is the inverse of anachronistic presentism. For a rigid historicist, history entails a movement away from some original Arcadian state of cognition that we should try to recover, whereas for the anachronistic presentist, greater distance and perspective offer the promise of greater insight and understanding.

Of course a naive authenticist aesthetic is a vulnerable one. As critics have repeatedly pointed out, there can never be a single performance of a given musical piece that can be said to be definitive. There are inevitably subjective elements of performance that elude codification into a static performance dogma. Just so, there is no single "authentic" analytical or theoretical perspective that can be reified purely by historical evidence.[39] (Strictly speaking, the whole notion of analysis is anachronistic in relation to pre-Romantic musics.) "Theories," like performances, have always existed in multiplicity. Partisans of historical performance practice often proffer naive aesthetic and cognitive justifications for granting privilege to a putatively historical "authentic performance." Numerous critics have rightly demanded to know why we would want to—or, indeed, how we possibly could—suppress completely our own knowledge, values, and tastes for the sake of some distant and ultimately elusive literal replication except as a symptom of the alienation and malaise that besets the modernist aesthetic.[40] More than anyone else, Richard Taruskin has worked to expose the naive "authentistic" aesthetics of those performers who blindly seek historical objectivity in their performances. He has argued passionately for the rights, indeed the unavoidable necessity, of musicians to bring their own values, norms, and feelings into a performance. "Performers," he reminds us, "cannot realistically concern themselves with *wie es eigentlich gewesen*. Their job is to discover, if they are lucky, *wie es eigentlich uns gefällt*—how we really like it."[41]

Taruskin certainly does not mean to suggest that the recovery and replication of various historical modes of performance are not possible, at least in part. Nor does he doubt that historically informed performances have the potential to offer profoundly satisfying musical experiences. His primary arguments, as I understand them, are directed against the misplaced values of those who naively strive to resurrect some putatively authentic historical performance that could or should be insulated somehow from our present social and aesthetic conditions. Why, then, one wonders, is Taruskin not led to conclude that historical contextuality in music analysis is but another form of "authenticity"? The search for historically indigenous modes of analytical interpretation, after all, is based upon an "authentistic" aesthetic just as historical performance practice is.

Clearly, "objective" historicists are as much the victim of positivist mythology as are anachronistic presentists with their "objective" rational methodology. As critics ranging from the fields of philosophy of science to literary theory have amply shown, the perspectives all of us bring to our views of the world are conditioned by inescapable constraints of language, culture, profession, and our own unique and ever-changing historical position.[42] We can no more escape our own "theory-laden" perspective than we can pretend to immerse ourselves fully and empathically in some distant culture like a native. This means that the "historicist" ideal is unattainable, since there is no Archimedean point of objectivity and observation from which we can interpret history. Historical facts do not lie ready-made awaiting excavation. History is an active and subjective construction of the observer and presupposes, as Hayden White has argued, a kind of political commitment:

> There is no value-neutral mode of employment, explana-
> tion, or even description of any field of events, whether
> imaginary or real. . . . The very use of language itself implies
> or entails a specific posture before the world which is ethi-
> cal, ideological, or more generally political: not only all in-
> terpretation, but also all language is politically contami-
> nated.[43]

It is not surprising in this regard that Hirsch's strong program of authorial intention has received such criticism in the last few years. More and more evidence has accumulated in psychology, philosophy, and linguistics that renders suspect the existence of some straight-forward authorial intention, or at least one that can be recovered in any certain or immediate way.[44] (It is significant that Quentin Skinner, for one, has begun in his more recent writings to pull away from his earlier position of extreme intentionalism.)[45]

A certain degree of presentism is thus an unavoidable reality in historical inquiry. To deny the existence of our received prejudices and cognitive constraints is naive or disingenuous. All observation, whether analytical or historical, is filtered through culturally tinted lenses. But this need not be cause for consternation if we are sufficiently aware not only of the limitations it imposes upon us, but also of the liberating possibilities it offers. In fact, it is only when one recognizes and affirms (rather than denies and suppresses) one's "presentness" that true historical understanding arises.[46] "Historical consciousness," Gadamer tells us,

> fails to understand its own nature if, in order to understand,
> it seeks to exclude what alone makes understanding pos-
> sible. *To think historically means, in fact, to perform the transpo-
> sition that the concepts of the past undergo* when we try to think
> in them. To think historically always involves mediating
> between those ideas and one's own thinking. To try to es-
> cape from one's own concepts in interpretation is not only
> impossible but manifestly absurd. To interpret means pre-
> cisely to bring one's own preconceptions into play so that
> the text's meaning can really be made to speak for us.[47]

One might still argue that the essential goal of historicism is desirable. We could acknowledge a certain unavoidable degree of presentism in any historical reconstruction (the "theory-laden" nature of observation) but still strive to arrive at a relatively stable consensus of meaning. Otherwise we would seem condemned to extremes of either skepticism or relativism.

In acknowledging the inescapable constraints of observation, one need not be condemned to (as Karl Popper derisively calls it) the "Myth of the Framework" by which "we are prisoners caught in the Framework of our Theories; our expectations; our past experience; our language."[48] Acknowledging that language, culture, and history condition our perspectives does not mean that we can never focus clearly or with any consensus upon the past.[49] There exist rational criteria and critical mechanisms that, although less formal and more localized than those demanded by the positivists, still provide valid means by which we can understand and evaluate theories. (Such are exemplified by scientists who can coalesce within a given "paradigm" as Thomas Kuhn has shown, or "interpretive communities" that operate within the field of literary criticism as explained by Stanley Fish.)

But no consensus of interpretation among musicologists can be achieved through a naive and literal reading of historical music theories. I consider it a fallacy of proximity to measure the value of a given theory in direct proportion to its chronological contiguity with the musical repertory to which it is applied. Such prejudice presupposes a collective *Zeitgeist*, whereby coeval theories will necessarily be more "in tune" with the music of their time.[50] A rudimentary knowledge of both music history and music theory makes it abundantly clear that this is as much the exception as it is the rule.

The reason lies not in that worm-eaten romantic saw that great artworks are necessarily "ahead of their time." Nor has it anything to do with the corollary (often said derogatorily) that theory "lags behind" practice. It is rather that theory can be—and typically is—independent of practice, or at least of contemporaneous practice. *Theoria* in its most essential sense means a detachment of some observer from the object under scrutiny. There is no good reason to assume that contemporaneous observers within a culture will always be closer to the texts of their culture than present-day observers can be (or conversely that past observers might not in some ways be as alienated within a culture as we can be empathic across cultures). Otherwise we would have to claim that all cultures are incommensurable holisms and all attitudes are predetermined by some inescapable cultural *Weltanschauung*.[51]

We know in fact that many theorists are conservatives who do indeed "lag behind" practice and prefer instead to deal with music of previous generations (good examples being Schenker and Zarlino). But as our own century has amply illustrated, theorists can also be in the avant-garde; they may concern themselves, as do many serial theorists, with music that does not find empirical confirmation in the wider musical repertory. Simply put, practice and theory do not align in any chronologically predictable pattern.[52] Thus we cannot decide *a priori* that a given theory has greater potential for offering "historically authentic" insight when applied to music contemporaneous with it than has a noncontemporaneous theory.

The opposite can just as well be true. Many examples of twentieth-century music analysis are sensitive to the historical nuances of the music they treat even though they are not coterminous with it. For example, all but the most uncharitable of critics grant the profound insight and musical sensitivity of Schenker's analyses of the music of the Viennese Classicists. His theory, far from being anachronistically presentist, grew out of a lifelong immersion in—and identification with—a musical tradition that could be reasonably traced to Schenker's own day. In view of the breadth and depth of his analyses (covering everything from sketch studies to the music's pedagogical and performance traditions), Schenker was in some ways closer to his beloved German masterworks than any contemporaneous observer could have been. It is almost as if the single-minded passion he had for this repertory and his equally dogmatic refusal to consider any music standing outside it allowed him a kind of empathy and insight unavailable to more liberal and pluralistic theorists.[53] Prejudice, as Gadamer has shown us, can often be a surprisingly enlightening path.

Toward Hermeneutic Reconciliation

I have already had occasion in this essay to refer to the writings of Hans-Georg Gadamer. Much in my critique of both the presentist and historicist dogmas is drawn from the sophisticated analysis of philosophical hermeneutics he has elaborated. In this final section I want to increase my indebtedness to Gadamer and show how hermeneutics addresses—and convincingly overcomes—precisely the dilemma we have explored between the presentist and historicist positions.[54] Gadamer, of course, never addressed himself to the special problem of historical music theories. But because one of the central concerns of hermeneutics is the interpretation and application of historical texts, his writings can be seen to be acutely relevant to the problems we have considered in this essay.[55]

Let us begin by recalling the shared objectivist claims of the orthodox presentist and historicist. In each case, the observer seeks a fixed historical point from which a secure and stable interpretation of a text can be carried out. On the one hand, the presentist seeks to extract a music theory from its historical contexts and analyze it from a contemporary perspective while, on the other hand, the historicist seeks to suppress his contemporary position and understand a theory from its indigenous historical position. Neither dogma, as we saw, is tenable since theorists as well as theories each have a historical location that can never be fully transcended. We saw how the presentist, in uprooting a theory text from its cultural context and analyzing it only in light of contemporary knowledge, gains a limited and often severely distorted understanding of the text. Yet when the historicist attempts to remedy this by returning to just those historical contexts that the presentist has missed, we discovered that his viewpoint too was cloaked with prejudices and interests that cannot simply be shed like some worn overcoat. We thus seem to find ourselves back in the intractable dilemma outlined at the beginning of this essay. Historical understanding appears thwarted by an unbridgeable gulf.

It is here that hermeneutics can offer a way out. Far from constituting an unbridgeable gulf, the gap between presentism and historicism—or more properly, the present and the past—becomes an essential condition for understanding. This is possible by reifying a nonpositivist species of understanding (*Verstehen*) that transcends the Cartesian dichotomy between object and subject. Rather than looking at the relation between "text" and "reader" as binary, Gadamer (following Heidegger) sees interpretation as a single ontology. Interpretation, which is coextensive with understanding, is never achieved through the subjectification of a text, but rather by means of an ongoing and never-ending process of mediation. The analogy Gadamer invokes to describe this relation is that of dialogue. The reader engages the text in a kind of figurative conversation (or "play") and thereby mediates the cultural/historical opposition that separates them.

This may sound more mystical than meaningful. How, after all, can we engage a text in conversation? In what nonpsychic sense can we claim to converse with an author who is long dead? A solution becomes plausible when we understand that dialogue in the hermeneutic sense is a much richer concept than the narrow linguistic activity with which we normally associate it. A dialogue begins with the recognition that there is another voice "out there" (in the guise of a text) different from our own. Naturally we want to know where this voice originates. Like the historicist, we would want to orient the text in its cultural contexts. We attempt to reconstruct the thick "cultural web" in which the text originated: to discover the questions and problems to which it served as an answer, to uncover the many nuances of language and rhetoric through which the text resonated among its readers.

Yet in contradistinction to the historicist, a hermeneutic interpreter never forgets that he too is situated in a cultural context that inescapably prejudices his reception of that voice. Far from being a deplorable condition, Gadamer shows the holding of "prejudice"—pre-judgment—to be a necessary and even desirable condition for understanding.[56] It is not with the *tabula rasa* that we understand, but by having a text rub against meanings and ideas we already command. Dialogue does not occur if we suspend our beliefs and passively accept another viewpoint; it occurs only by confronting and testing our beliefs with the differing viewpoint.

This still does not tell us, though, how communication can take place over the historical gulf we have discussed. How can we begin to converse if the historical conditions separating ourselves from some past text are so wide as to seem to preclude any common language or rational discourse?[57] An answer opens up when we realize that one's contextuality consists of more than some fixed horizontal cultural position. There are also vertical cultural contexts. We are situated, in other words, in both a synchronic and a diachronic position. These diachronic relations are what we call tradition.

Gadamer spends a good deal of effort in relegitimizing the concept of tradition.[58] He shows that one's position in history necessitates the conscious and free participation in tradition. A tradition, it must be remembered, is not merely passive accumulation or something into which we are born; it is rather something we actively cultivate. It is "not simply a permanent precondition, rather we produce it ourselves inasmuch as we understand, participate in the evolution of tradition and hence further determine it ourselves."[59] Tradition is thus the awareness of those historical conditions that govern our present understanding. (Gadamer calls this the "wirkungsgeschichtliches Bewusstsein" or "consciousness of being affected by history.")[60]

Any interpretation of a text, then, takes place against a "horizon" that is plotted by synchronic and diachronic coordinates. But this interpretation is not necessarily static. Since we have free will to choose the traditions in which we participate, it follows that by engaging ourselves in new traditions, we can in effect broaden, if never entirely abandon, our own "horizons." We can become receptive to new meanings, new modes of understanding, by projecting ourselves against a new "horizon":

> Every encounter with tradition that takes place within historical consciousness involves the experience of a tension between the text and the present. The hermeneutic task consists in not covering up this tension by attempting a naive assimilation of the two but in consciously bringing it out. This is why it is part of the hermeneutic approach to project

a historical horizon that is different from the horizon of the present. Historical consciousness is aware of its own otherness and hence foregrounds [*abheben*] the horizon of the past from its own. On the other hand, it is itself ... only something superimposed upon continuing tradition, and hence it immediately recombines with what it has foregrounded itself from in order to become one with itself again in the unity of the historical horizon that it thus acquires.[61]

It is in the mutually defining relation between the past and present that the hermeneutic process of dialogue can take place and that the proverbial "fusion of horizons" may be achieved. Invoking Heidegger's famous hermeneutic circle, Gadamer shows how historical understanding is gained in a dialectical process. We begin the interpretation of any text with the prejudices and preconceptions implicit in our "horizon of expectations." As we begin to "read," however, our prejudices are subject to testing and modification, which in turn alter how we continue "receiving" the text. The process is essentially the relation between part and whole; we know a whole only through the parts, but the parts can only be interpreted holistically. Each affects the other in a constant dialogue.[62] The circular relation between part and whole, past and present, far from being tautological or vicious, captures the essential ontological condition by which all understanding takes place. By means of the hermeneutic circle, we see that real historical interpretation involves neither the domination of the historian over the past nor his submission to it. Rather it occurs by means of a dialogue carried on through the pathway of tradition. Gadamer thus concludes:

Time is no longer primarily a gulf to be bridged because it separates; it is actually the supportive ground of the course of events in which the present is rooted. Hence temporal distance is not something that must be overcome. This was, rather, the naive assumption of historicism, namely that we must transpose ourselves into the spirit of the age, think with its ideas and its thoughts, not with our own, and thus advance towards historical objectivity. In fact the important thing is to recognize the temporal distance as a positive and productive condition enabling understanding. It is not a yawning abyss but is filled with the continuity of custom and tradition, in the light of which everything handed down presents itself to us.[63]

It should be clear from all this how the tension between presentism and historicism that we have explored need no longer pose an intractable dilemma. Instead of seeing these as two opposing poles that we must choose between, we recognize them as codeterminant. A text has a double hermeneutic identity. It is, as the historicist insists, a historical document written by an individual living within a unique culture and addressing definite problems in a personal discourse. Yet this does not constitute its final meaning to us today, for meanings are never finished. A text is not like some archeological object that is to be excavated and preserved. A text is always open and subject to new readings and meanings by virtue of being read and interpreted in new contexts. We cannot deny that we live in a different world from that in which the text originated. The presentist is right in this regard. The time separating the text from our reading must necessarily alter its reception. We would be naive to think we can or should read the text ignoring the accumulated meanings and changes accrued to it over time, or denying the differing circumstances in which we are reading the text. But by saying that we read a text differently, it does not follow that all interpretations are relative, that the text possesses no immanent meaning. By virtue of the filiations of tradition and communality of language that connect us to the past, a text can still have a common meaning for us. Although we are distant from the past, we are not necessarily separated from it.[64]

All of this may seem terribly abstract and far removed from the problems facing music theory. If hermeneutics suggests solutions to the subtle interpretive problems posed by literary theory (or biblical and legal texts, the two paradigmatic subjects of classical hermeneutics), it is not at all clear that this is so with regard to music theory. After all, a text by Tovey is presumably not so opaque as one by James Joyce; a late eighteenth-century thorough-bass treatise, we would imagine, offers fewer interpretive problems than does, say, Talmudic law. But as we have seen, such complacency can be misplaced. It is precisely when we are confident that we understand the meaning of a past text because of its familiar resonance that we are most vulnerable to anachronism. Theory texts offer innumerable instances of terminology and concepts that have changed subtly over time, examples being "tonality," "mode," "phrase," and "cadence." We also face the problem of terminology that has largely gone out of current theoretical circulation: *Phthongos, repercussio, affinité, Zergliederung,* etc.[65] And certainly the arguments within the performance-practice community over the interpretation of performance prescriptions in theory texts (let alone the decisions as to which theory texts to privilege) suggest that the reading of historical music theory is by no means straightforward.

I could well imagine the writings of many theorists benefiting from a careful hermeneutic reading. Zarlino, Rameau, and Reicha are three who come immediately to mind. This is not only because their theories are sophisticated and filled with concepts and linguistic formulations that require sensitive historical exegesis, but because they are theories that impinge upon the present. Ideas first articulated by each of these theorists have filtered down to us and in the process undergone subtle (and sometimes not so subtle) transformations. Many of these ideas are so familiar (e.g., the distinctions between dissonance and consonance, the fundamental bass, sonata form) that extraordinary hermeneutic sensitivity is required to disentangle our received notions from their original expression. Again, this is not to say that we should privilege one over the other, but rather that we should recognize that our understanding arises from an ever-accumulating dialectic between past meanings and new interpretations.

Let me conclude with one final illustration: the *Gradus ad Parnassum* of Johann Joseph Fux, published in 1725. Fux's formulation of species counterpoint is one familiar to virtually all music-theory students today. But the rules of species counterpoint originated in a historical context quite different from ours; they were compiled with very specific stylistic and pedagogical intentions in mind and were themselves drawn from a long and distinguished tradition of seventeenth-century Italian compositional pedagogy. Nonetheless, generations of subsequent theorists (Mizler, Albrechtsberger, Cherubini, Bellermann, Schenker, Jeppesen, Salzer) have been able to recognize in Fux's rules a value that transcended his particular historical situation. Fux's ideas were found to be adaptable and relevant to changing musical environments, and thus capable of generating a tradition. Yet this tradition is not wholly congruent with the historical formulation articulated by Fux in 1725.

If any proof of this is wanted, one need only compare the rules and examples of, say, third species in two parts given by Aloysius with those by later interpreters who refined his strictures in order to adapt them to different musical repertories. The stylistic application as well as the pedagogical formulations of Felix Salzer and Carl Schachter differ greatly from those of generative interpreters such as Peter Westergaard and David Lewin. Likewise, these approaches are different from those of theorists who study Renaissance music such as Knud Jeppesen or Gustav Soderlund. Thus there is no immutable object called "Species Counterpoint" existing outside of the particular stylistic and pedagogical parameters within which it is applied. Fux's *Gradus ad Parnassum* is a theory with both a historical and a contemporary identity, one whose full meaning is revealed only when we take cognizance of its rich unfolding over time as a theoretical tradition.

In making a plea for the recognition of a hermeneutic dimension in the interpretation of music-theory texts, I want to emphasize again that I am not recommending the abandonment of current modes of analysis and history. As we have seen, hermeneutics is not a prescriptive method we can appropriate like some analytical theory; it is not a third alternative to the presentist and historicist perspectives. The point of hermeneutics is only to instill in the interpreter a critical historical consciousness—the "wirkungsgeschichtliches Bewusstsein." We can continue to read theory texts from both presentist and historicist viewpoints with the awareness of their complementary nature. There is nothing inherently pernicious in analyzing the logical validity of Rameau's arguments using current norms, or constructing traditionalist histories that look for "precursors to Schenker" when we are sensitive to the specific historical nature of such interpretations. Likewise, the historian can try to reconstruct the historical context in which a given theorist's ideas were formulated, as long as he too is aware of the specific parameters of his undertaking. If anything, hermeneutics provides the justification that any of these interpretive strategies would need in order to counter the more dogmatic arguments of its critics. Simply put, hermeneutics does not in any way impose limitations as to what interpretations we make; it only clarifies the conditions upon which those interpretations are made.[66]

There is one final relevant aspect of hermeneutics that I want to bring up here—the role of application. According to Gadamer, no understanding or interpretation of a "theory" can take place independent of its application.[67] (While the specific example Gadamer uses is legal theory, his arguments apply just as well to music theory.) Only by testing the empirical claims and heuristic value of a theory (or law) can it have any meaning to us. And such praxis necessarily arises in a contemporary perspective. (It makes no sense to speak of applying a law in a historicist sense, since any application must be made by a living judge to a contemporary situation.) Paradoxically, then, historical understanding of theory requires present application.

Once we have introduced the notion of present application as an essential feature of historical understanding, however, we begin to blur the boundaries between historical theory and contemporary music analysis. All analysis, as we have seen, presupposes some amount of "theory ladenness" framed by the traditions and prejudices that are ours. Yet we have also seen how these traditions and prejudices are historically rooted. The music analyst can no more escape the burden of the past that conditions understanding than can the historian.

From this view, then, the history of theory takes on a critical new responsibility that far exceeds its charge as custodian of tradition; it defines the very historical basis upon which present understanding— contemporary music analysis—takes place. From a hermeneutic perspective all analytical activity is fully historical. The positivist claim to immanence and transcendence made by formalist theorists can be seen to be a thoroughly historical prejudice. (Simply asserting that a method is ahistorical does not make that prejudice any less a historical one.) Music analysis cannot help being historical by virtue of the fact that it partakes in a legacy of musical repertories and intellectual traditions that together define the discipline of music theory.

This conclusion is surely not to be lamented. In dispelling the positivist myths surrounding music theory and revealing its contingent historical nature, hermeneutics in no way diminishes its importance and value. Indeed, much is to be gained. If we as music theorists are deprived of a transcendental observation base, we acquire an ultimately more resilient base in culture. Music theory can now be restored to its proper place, rooted in and nourished by the rich soil of our inherited musical and intellectual traditions. We find ourselves not as observers outside of and insulated from contemporary musical practice, but as a vital part of it; we find ourselves to be active and committed participants in a venerable and ongoing tradition of some three thousand years of musical contemplation to which we are heirs.

Notes

1. Carl Dahlhaus, *Die Musiktheorie im 18. und 19. Jahrhundert: Grundzüge einer Systematik* (Darmstadt, 1984), 57.

2. The tension between presentism and historicism is certainly not one peculiar to musicology. Any discipline that is involved in the interpretation of a "text" faces the same competing demands of Hermes and Clio. For example, anthropologists speak of "etic" (experience-distant) versus "emic" (experience-near) modes of analysis, and psychologists of "objective" and "phenomenological" analyses, while literary theorists often cite Roland Barthes's distinction between "analogical" and "homological" interpretations of texts. Not all of these polarities are identical, of course, but they all capture an essential hermeneutic tension between theoretical explanation and historical understanding.

A field in which the separation between history and theory is virtually institutionalized is philosophy. "Analytical philosophers" can be seen as representing the presentist position, while historians of philosophy (or "intellectual historians") tend toward the historicist position. A self-conscious collection of essays exploring this relationship is found in Richard Rorty, J.B. Schneewind, and Quentin Skinner, eds., *Philosophy in History* (Cambridge, 1984). See in particular the essays of Alasdair MacIntyre, "The Relation of Philosophy to Its Past," 17–30, and Lorenz Krueger, "Why Do We Study the History of Philosophy?" 77–101. But the discipline in which the gap between history and theory is perhaps the widest is science. Historians of science and philosophers of science often ask whether they share any common ground within their subjects. See, e.g., Thomas S. Kuhn, "The Relations between the History and the Philosophy of Science," in his *The Essential Tension* (Chicago, 1977), 3–20; Ernan McMullin, "The History and Philosophy of Science: A Taxonomy," in Roger H. Stuewer, ed., *Historical and Philosophical Perspectives of Science* (Minneapolis, 1970), 12–67; and John Losee, *Philosophy of Science and Historical Enquiry* (Oxford, 1987). I will have frequent occasion in this essay to draw upon appropriate parallels from all of these disciplines in order to elucidate the arguments that follow concerning the history of music theory.

3. Herbert Butterfield, *The Whig Interpretation of History* (London, 1931).

4. Helge Kragh, *An Introduction to the Historiography of Science* (Cambridge, 1987), 7–8.

5. I do not count as historians of theory those Renaissance humanists who assiduously recovered and attempted to interpret ancient Greek treatises on music theory and aesthetics. The impulse behind their efforts lay more in antiquarian fetishism coupled with a desire to revive ancient musical traditions than in a wish to historicize them (see Claude V. Palisca, *Humanism in Italian Renaissance Musical Thought* [New Haven, 1985]). I exclude also those eighteenth-century catalogues of theory treatises compiled by scholars such as Bontempi, Mattheson, Adlung, Hiller, and Martini, as again they constituted less a historicization of music theory than a parading of biblio-erudition.

6. François-Joseph Fétis, *Esquisse de l'histoire de l'harmonie considérée comme art et comme science systématique* (Paris, 1840); revised and expanded as book 4 of his *Traité complet de la théorie et de la pratique de l'harmonie* (Paris, 1844), 201–54.

7. Ibid., 254.

8. Hugo Riemann, *Grundriss der Musikwissenschaft* (Leipzig, 1908), 12.

9. And needless to say, it was often a hopelessly distorted reading of these theorists. As only one example: In his eagerness to have Zarlino stand as a precursor to his theory of dualism, Riemann grossly misinterpreted the Venetian's meaning of arithmetic and harmonic proportions. See Carl Dahlhaus, "War Zarlino Dualist?" *Die Musikforschung* 10 (1957): 286–90.

10. Clifford Truesdell, "The Rational Mechanics of Flexible or Elastic Bodies, 1638–1788," *Euleri Opera Omnia*, 2d ser., vol. 11, no. 2 (Zurich, 1960).

11. Before the innocent music theorist turns to Truesdell's problematic but nonetheless indispensable study, I would advise him to consult the trenchant critique and salutary correctives by Henk Bos, "Mathematics and Rational Mechanics," in G.S. Rousseau and Roy Porter, eds., *The Ferment of Knowledge: Studies in the Historiography of Eighteenth-Century Science* (Cambridge, 1980), 327–55, esp. 333–41.

12. Allen Forte, "Letter to the Editor." *Music Analysis* 5, nos. 2–3 (1986): 335.

13. This is the approach taken implicitly by Robert Morgan in his "Schenker and the Theoretical Tradition: The Concept of Musical Reduction," *College Music Symposium* 18, no. 1 (1978): 72–96. The nineteenth-century continuation of Morgan's teleological story can be found in Robert Wason's "Schenker's Notion of Scale-Step in Historical Perspective: Non-Essential Harmonies in Viennese Fundamental Bass Theory," *Journal of Music Theory* 27, no. 1 (1983): 49–73.

14. Morgan, "Schenker and the Theoretical Tradition," 75ff.

15. Quentin Skinner, "Meaning and Understanding in the History of Ideas," *History and Theory* 8 (1969): 22.

16. We might express the difference this way: asserting that a repertory of early Baroque binary compositions (along with other tributaries) *evolved into* the Classical symphony is not the same as saying that these compositions *evolved toward* the symphony. The former idea entails a plausible developmental diachrony, albeit a particularly rich and complex one, whereas the latter idea suggests simplistic teleological determinism.

17. The literature on this topic is overwhelming. The *locus classicus* is Thomas S. Kuhn, *The Structure of Scientific Revolutions* (Chicago, 1962). Since the publication of Kuhn's book, numerous other critics (such as Imre Lakatos, Paul Feyerabend, Larry Laudan, Jerome Ravetz, David Bloor, Michael Mulkay, and Dudley Shapere) have

continued the assault upon positivist presuppositions in science from many fronts, including the history, philosophy, sociology, psychology, and even rhetoric of science. The net result of these criticisms has been the virtual abandonment of the logical-positivist program by philosophers of science. For a concise summary of these developments, see Ernan McMullin, "The Shaping of Scientific Rationality: Construction and Constraint," contained in McMullin, ed., *Construction and Constraint* (Notre Dame, 1986), 1–47. A more technical, if somewhat conservative analysis of the rise and fall of logical empiricism in scientific philosophy has been written by Frederick Suppe, *The Structure of Scientific Theories* (Urbana, 1977), 3–231 and 619–730.

18. Leonard B. Meyer has made the provocative argument that the nineteenth-century aesthetic of Romanticism shares a number of affinities with twentieth-century formalism—the common rejections of historicity, contextualism, and convention in favor of "elite egalitarianism," originality, and individuality (*Style and Music: Theory, History, and Ideology* [Philadelphia, 1989]; particularly relevant is the epilogue, "The Persistence of Romanticism"). In this light, the transformation of the metaphysical Schenker of "organicism" into the positivist Schenker of "axiomatized hierarchies" by some recent interpreters is a perfectly logical and consistent development, and not at all the "unnatural confluence of two streams of thought which ought to, and inevitably will, reject one another because they represent mutually contradictory values," as William Benjamin gloomily forecast ("Schenker's Theory and the Future of Music," *Journal of Music Theory* 25, no. 1 [1981]: 171).

19. John Rothgeb, translator's introduction to Schenker's *Counterpoint* (New York, 1987), 1:xiv.

20. A recent excellent study that explicates some elements of Schenker's theory in the context of his "world-view" has been written by Kevin Korsyn, "Schenker and Kantian Epistemology," *Theoria* 3 (1988): 1–58. Although I think Korsyn has exaggerated some connections in his eagerness to find a Kantian precedent for many of Schenker's concepts, he does convincingly demonstrate how Schenker's theory was decisively shaped and guided by external influences and, more importantly, can only be understood fully in light of these factors. Korsyn's article is a model of the sophisticated and historically acute exegesis that future Schenkerians will need to emulate in order to counter the perils of historical myopia.

21. Typical of such a distilled historicization is Joan Ferris, "The Evolution of Rameau's Harmonic Theories," *Journal of Music Theory* 3, no. 1 (1959): 231–56. But the practice dates back to Rameau's own day in the redactions of Rousseau and d'Alembert.

22. I have tried to do something of the sort in a recent article ("Eighteenth-Century Science and the *Corps Sonore*: The Scientific Background to Rameau's Principle of Harmony," *Journal of Music Theory* 31, no. 1 [1987]: 23–50), where I show that some of the diverse mathematical and acoustical arguments Rameau borrowed from contemporaneous scientists to develop his theory of the fundamental bass and definition of mode were not (as often depicted) belated justifications added *a posteriori*, but were in fact integral to their discovery and formulations. A more detailed study of Rameau's theory in historical context will appear in my forthcoming book, *Jean-Philippe Rameau: The Science of Music Theory in the Enlightenment* (Cambridge University Press).

23. For a representative sampling of articles critical of traditional intellectual history, see Robert Darnton, "Intellectual and Cultural History" in Michael Kammen, ed., *The Past before Us: Contemporary Historical Writing in the United States* (Ithaca, 1980), 327–49; William J. Bouwsma, "From History of Ideas to History of Meaning," *Journal of Interdisciplinary History* 12, no. 2 (1981): 279–91; Dominick LaCapra, "Rethinking Intellectual History and Reading Texts" in his *Rethinking Intellectual History: Texts, Contexts, Language* (Ithaca, 1983), 23–71; Frank E. Manuel, "Lovejoy Revisited,"

Daedalus 116, no. 2 (1987): 125–48; and a fine survey of more recent approaches to intellectual history in John E. Toews, "Intellectual History after the Linguistic Turn: The Autonomy of Meaning and Irreducibility of Experience," *American Historical Review* 92 (1987): 879–907.

24. Hans-Georg Gadamer, *Truth and Method* , 2d ed., trans. and revised by Joel Weinsheimer and Donald G. Marshall (New York, 1989), 375.

25. Skinner, "Meaning and Understanding," 50. Another critic who has espoused a related position of "intentionalism" is E.D. Hirsch, Jr. (*Validity in Interpretation* [New Haven, 1967]).

26. Hans Meyerhoff, *The Philosophy of History in Our Time: An Anthology* (New York, 1959), 9.

27. Lest I cause confusion here, let me point out that there are two general meanings of the term "historicism" as commonly employed. The older and more widely used meaning of the term is rooted in the new empiricism of the nineteenth-century German historical school, analyzed by Friedrich Meinecke in his *Die Entstehung des Historismus* (Munich, 1936). (See the article "Historicism" by Georg G. Iggers in the *Dictionary of the History of Ideas*, ed. Philip Wiener [New York, 1973], 2:456–64.) "Historicism" in this sense emphasizes the complexity and irreducibility of all history and hence the fatuousness of historical "laws," "cycles," and other determinist processes. Some years after Meinecke, Karl Popper appropriated the term in his short but widely influential historiographical monograph *The Poverty of Historicism* (Boston, 1957). Idiosyncratically, Popper inverted the traditional meaning of the term. He labeled as historicist precisely those determinist ideologies that the nineteenth-century historicists rejected. (See John Passmore, "The Poverty of Historicism Revisted," *History and Theory* 14, no. 4 [1975]: 30–47.)

I mention all of this here because one can find the term invoked in current musicological literature in both senses. In the present essay I use the term in its original sense. I might have used some less confusing term such as "objectivism" or "literalism," but neither of these captures the peculiar sense of historical authenticity entailed by "historicism." Moreover, the tradition of nineteenth-century historicism dovetails nicely with the continental hermeneutic tradition that I discuss toward the end of this essay.

28. R.G. Collingwood, *An Autobiography* (Oxford, 1939), 58.

29. E.D. Hirsch, Jr., *Validity in Interpretation* (New Haven, 1967), 134. Hirsch, it should be pointed out, distinguishes his position from that of "radical historicism." The latter view holds that the past is so complex and alien from the present that the historian can never truly understand it, let alone depict it. Hirsch dismisses such skepticism as "cognitive atheism" (*Validity in Interpretation*, 40–44).

30. The most outspoken historicists seem to be found among intellectual historians and political scientists (many of whom are cited in note 23 above). But many historians of science have also expressed strongly historicist sentiments. See, for example, A. Rupert Hall, "Can the History of Science Be History?" *British Journal for the History of Science* 4, no. 15 (1969): 207–20; Arnold Thackray, "History of Science in the 1980s," *Journal of Interdisciplinary History* 12, no. 2 (1981): 299–314; and Nathan Reingold, "Science, Scientists, and Historians of Science," *History of Science* 19 (1981): 274–83.

31. One of the more recent instances is found in the polemical article by Steven Knapp and Walter Benn Michaels, "Against Theory," which appeared in *Critical Inquiry* 8, no. 4 (1982). While the issues Knapp and Michaels raise go far beyond those discussed here, their "anti-foundationalist" skepticism of theory accords with the historicist position as I have outlined it. Their article, along with a dozen or so lively responses that it engendered can be found in W.J.T. Mitchell, ed., *Against Theory: Literary Studies and the New Pragmatism* (Chicago, 1985).

32. Richard Taruskin, "Letter to the Editor," *Music Analysis* 5, nos. 2–3 (1986): 313–20; similar historicist biases are expressed in his review of James M. Baker's book on Scriabin's music, *Music Theory Spectrum* 10 (1988): 143–69.

33. Taruskin, "Letter to the Editor," 318.

34. Gary Tomlinson, "The Web of Culture: A Context for Musicology," *19th-Century Music* 7, no. 3 (1984): 358.

35. Gary Tomlinson, "The Historian, the Performer, and Authentic Meaning in Music," in Nicholas Kenyon, ed., *Authenticity and Early Music* (Oxford, 1988), 121.

36. Joseph Kerman, *Contemplating Music: Challenges to Musicology* (Cambridge, Mass., 1985), 73.

37. Leo Treitler, "'To Worship That Celestial Sound': Motives for Analysis," *Journal of Musicology* 1 (1982): 159. Also see his article "What Kind of Story Is History?" *19th-Century Music* 7, no. 3 (1984): 363–73.

38. Treitler, "To Worship That Celestial Sound," 170. I should add that Treitler by no means rejects all formalist modes of analysis. Indeed, the very illustration of interpretive criticism that he offers in his article (using the first movement of Beethoven's Ninth Symphony) constitutes a sophisticated synthesis of formalist and historicist approaches.

39. Carl Dahlhaus, *Foundations of Music History* (Cambridge, 1983), 159.

40. This Nietzschean critique has been developed recently in two provocative articles: Laurence Dreyfus, "Early Music Defended against Its Devotees: A Theory of Historical Performance in the Twentieth Century," *Musical Quarterly* 69 (1983): 306ff.; and Robert Morgan, "Tradition, Anxiety, and the Current Musical Scene" in Kenyon, *Authenticity*, 57–82.

41. Richard Taruskin, "The Pastness of the Present and the Presence of the Past," in Kenyon, *Authenticity*, 203. Also see his article "On Letting the Music Speak for Itself: Some Reflections on Musicology and Performance," *Journal of Musicology* 1 (1982): 338–49.

42. This Wittgensteinian thesis has been explored by, among others, Norwood Russell Hanson, *Patterns of Discovery: An Inquiry into the Conceptual Foundations of Science* (Cambridge, 1972); and Stanley Fish, *Is There a Text in This Class? The Authority of Interpretive Communities* (Cambridge, Mass., 1980).

43. Hayden White, "The Fictions of Factual Representation," *Tropics of Discourse: Essays in Cultural Criticism* (Baltimore, 1978), 129.

44. David Hoy has outlined a number of these "anti-intentionalist" arguments; see his *The Critical Circle* (Berkeley, 1978), 11–40. Note, however, that these arguments are not the same as those articulated some thirty-five years ago in the famous critique of the "intentional fallacy" by William K. Wimsatt, Jr., and Monroe Beardsley, in Wimsatt and Beardsley, *The Verbal Icon: Studies in the Meaning of Poetry* (Lexington, Ky., 1954). Their attempt to position a text independent of both author and reader shares the same illusive ideal of objectivism as does the presentist.

45. Quentin Skinner, "Hermeneutics and the Role of History," *New Literary History* 7 (1979): 209–32.

46. For a spirited critique of Skinner's intentionalist position, see David L. Hull, "In Defense of Presentism," *History and Theory* 18 (1979): 1–15. Similar positions are taken by Adrian Wilson and T.G. Ashplant, "Whig History and Present-Centered History," *Historical Journal* 31 (1988): 1–16; Rupert Hall, "On Whiggism," *History of Science* 21 (1983): 45–89; and Joseph Femia, "An Historicist Critique of 'Revisionist' Methods for Studying the History of Ideas," *Theory and Practice* 20 (1981): 113–34.

47. Gadamer, *Truth and Method*, 397.

48. Karl Popper, "Normal Science and Its Dangers," in Imre Lakatos and Alan Musgrave, eds., *Criticism and the Growth of Knowledge* (Cambridge, 1970), 56.

49. The specious antinomy between "objectivism" and "relativism" has been brilliantly exploded by Richard J. Bernstein in his *Beyond Objectivism and Relativism: Science, Hermeneutics, and Praxis* (Philadelphia, 1983).

50. A delightful but devastating critique of concepts such as *Zeitgeist* and the related Hegelian notions *Volksgeist* and *Lebenswelt* is offered by E.H. Gombrich in his monograph *In Search of Cultural History* (Oxford, 1969). An updated version of the *Zeitgeist* idea is invoked within the French *Annales* school, with the notion of *mentalités*; their approach, however, is no more successful in resolving the various ontological/empirical problems engendered by a socio-psychological approach than is that of their German idealist counterparts. See Roger Chartier, "Intellectual History or Sociocultural History? The French Trajectories," in Dominick LaCapra and Steven L. Kaplan, eds., *Modern European Intellectual History: Reappraisals and New Perspectives* (Ithaca, 1982), 13–46.

51. This need not contradict the situation I described earlier in which all of our views can be seen to be culturally and historically informed, for cultures can still provide room for competing viewpoints. Saying that a culture constrains interpretation is not saying it determines interpretation. Indeed, it is only by virtue of certain common constraints, as Stanley Fish has shown, that communications and disagreement within interpretive communities can take place. See Stanley Fish, "Demonstration vs. Persuasion: Two Models of Critical Anxiety," in his *Is There a Text in This Class?*, 356–71.

52. Another element in this complex equation ought to be considered, although I cannot pursue the topic here: the development of the proverbial "canon" and musical "museum" in the nineteenth century. As musical works began to be played and studied well past the time in which they were written, theoretical analysis of them could continue and evolve concomitantly even though the theories might have little or no connection to contemporary practice. This situation obviously complicates the relation between theory and practice, confounding any literally chronological mapping of one onto the other. (For example, when Reicha and Czerny were first codifying the principles of sonata form in the 1830s, its role in musical practice was on the decline. The pieces they analyzed were not by their contemporaries, but by Mozart, Haydn, and early Beethoven.) Yet as long as some musical works remain in the canon, theorists can rightly claim (as do their performing colleagues) that they form an inseparable component of their present musical culture and thus a legitimate and inexhaustible subject for fresh reinterpretation and analysis.

53. Of course, not all theorists who channel their energies within a delimited repertory need accept Schenker's chauvinistic normativism. One need only recall Knud Jeppesen's brilliant study of the music of Palestrina.

54. The following discussion depends fundamentally upon Gadamer's philosophical hermeneutics, but I am aware that there are hermeneutic positions differing in fundamental ways from that of Gadamer. (Above all I am thinking of Jürgen Habermas and Paul Ricoeur.) Obviously, any discussion of these differences would far exceed the practical boundaries of this essay. In any event, it would be unnecessary because I believe Gadamer's ideas satisfactorily address the particular issues I have raised here.

55. The *locus classicus* of hermeneutics is Gadamer's *Wahrheit und Methode* (1960), translated as *Truth and Method* (see note 24 above). Gadamer's treatise is a challenging work, demanding a wide-ranging knowledge of the many philosophical and historiographical traditions upon which he calls. For the uninitiated, I would recommend first consulting a few of the fine expositors of hermeneutics, particularly Hoy, *Critical Circle*, and Joel Weinsheimer, *Gadamer's Hermeneutics: A Reading of "Truth and Method"* (New Haven, 1985).

56. Gadamer, *Truth and Method*, 276ff.

57. Such is the position of Barry Barnes and David Bloor in their provocative essay "Relativism, Rationalism and the Sociology of Knowledge" in Martin Hollis and Steven Lukes, eds., *Rationality and Relativism* (Cambridge, Mass., 1982), 21–47.

58. Gadamer, *Truth and Method*, 280ff.

59. Ibid., 293.

60. Ibid., 301. Others have translated this as "effective-historical consciousness."

61. Ibid., 306.

62. For a related hermeneutic analysis of "conversation," see Richard Rorty, *Philosophy and the Mirror of Nature* (Princeton, 1979), 389. The feasibility of the literary critic engaging in conversation is explored by LaCapra in *Rethinking Intellectual History*, 64–65.

63. Gadamer, *Truth and Method*, 297.

64. To those readers acquainted with current issues in literary theory, the ideas in the preceding paragraphs will sound familiar. A certain hermeneutic dimension underlies much of the current interest in "reader response" and "reception history" (as developed, for example, by Gadamer's student Hans Robert Jauss in his *Toward an Aesthetic of Reception*, trans. Timothy Bahti [Minneapolis, 1982]). But hermeneutic ideas have been fruitfully incorporated in other disciplines, too, including intellectual history and philosophy. The writings of Bernstein and Rorty already cited are exemplary in this regard (see notes 49 and 62 above).

Even the history of science has benefited from hermeneutics, where critics have argued that sciences evince the same discontinuities of language and method as the humanities and therefore are subject to hermeneutic analysis. See Gyorgy Markus, "Why Is There No Hermeneutics of Natural Sciences? Some Preliminary Theses," *Science in Context* 1, no. 1 (1987): 5–51; Josef Bleicher, *The Hermeneutic Imagination: Outline of a Positive Critique of Scientism and Sociology* (London, 1982); and Thomas McCarthy, "Scientific Rationality and the 'Strong Program' in the Sociology of Knowledge," in McMullin, *Construction and Constraint*, 75–95.

Gadamer did not see hermenetics as relevant to the natural sciences in his earlier writings, granting the positivists the separation of natural science from the *Geisteswissenschaften*. Since then, however, he has modified his position. For citations, see the interesting chapter "Hermeneutics and the Natural Sciences," in Weinsheimer, *Gadamer's Hermeneutics*, 1–59.

65. Exemplary case studies of such transformations of meaning are found in Hans Heinrich Eggebrecht, ed., *Handwörterbuch der musikalischen Terminologie* (Wiesbaden, 1972–).

66. Hoy, *Critical Circle*, 139.

67. Gadamer, *Truth and Method*, 307ff.

TWO

The Earliest Phases of Measured Polyphony

ERNEST H. SANDERS

The exploration of the rise and evolution of Western polyphony requires of twentieth-century observers and narrators unceasing caution and historical empathy. In dealing with the evidence of the musical manuscripts and coordinating it with the pertinent treatises, they must be ever watchful for patterns and habits of thought lying just under the notational or verbal surface. Interpretive rigidity will often obscure nuances indicative of particular strands of thinking and will interfere with the historian's obligation to recognize evolutionary trends and phases suggested by the available evidence, while at the same time eschewing the twin traps of etiology and meliorism.

The inferences to be drawn from medieval commentaries on the practice of music—i.e., *ars musica* (*musica practica*), as opposed to *scientia* (*musica theorica* or *speculativa*)—depend to a considerable extent on their nature as prescriptive systematizations of the state of the art, on the one hand, or as reports of particular practices, often of individual composers, on the other. Hans Heinrich Eggebrecht and Fritz Reckow have illuminated the appearance of the latter phenomenon in the thirteenth century.[1] The former type, redounding to the benefit of lesser composers, is illustrated by such treatises as the *Musica enchiriadis*, Guido's *Micrologus*, much of Johannes de Garlandia's treatise (especially the onerously thorough theory of its eleventh chapter) or, for that matter, parts of J.-P. Rameau's *Traité de l'harmonie* and A.B. Marx's *Lehre von der musikalischen Komposition*. Representatives of the latter type, which more often than not is intended to instruct performing musicians, are the treatises of Anonymous IV and Robertus de Handlo (or, with far greater propagandistic intent, Giulio Monteverdi's *Dichiaratione*). Such authors are not theorists but reporters who gather their observations from the workshop, generally aiming to acquaint their readers with the latest advances of the decreasingly anonymous avant-garde.[2] They often turn out to be our most valuable informants regarding practices not—or not yet—standardized systematically. Contrariwise, incautious and often

anachronistic reliance on the theorists can account for serious misinter-
pretations of the practical sources.

Eggebrecht has rightly pointed out that "indeed, the history of medieval music is essentially history of notation: each compositional novelty—complemented by verbal theory—is largely the consequence of
notational advances, evident at first in practical sources (as in the case
of modal notation or of the *ars nova*)."[3] Regrettably, it is precisely the
issue of rhythmic modal notation, as transmitted by the "verbal theorists," that has often led to misunderstandings of flexibilities and idio-
syncrasies in the leading "Notre Dame" composers' music and its notation. Friedrich Ludwig has asserted, in a long, glowing passage
remarkable as much for intensity as for complexity, that it should not
surprise us that the music composed in France, primarily in Paris, during
the several decades around 1200 was incapable of theoretical reduction
to rules. He recognized that the rhythmic modes explained by the theorists, conveying points of view that reflected a more advanced stage of
motet composition, were "merely a few patterns that . . . give not even
the faintest notion of the wealth of Perotinus's rhythmic language, let
alone the still more flexible rhythmic idiom of Leoninus. The theorists
call these rhythmic patterns modi."[4]

As is so often the case, Ludwig's observations here have remained
unexceptionable. Aside from some stray remarks in the treatise of
Anonymous IV,[5] no treatise has come down to us that reflects the rhythmic modes and their notation as practiced during the first half of the
thirteenth century and as evidenced primarily in manuscripts W_1 and
F.[6] The earliest informant is Johannes de Garlandia, whose treatise[7] (ca.
1250), because of its introduction of the concepts of *proprietas* and *perfectio*,[8] exhibits a somewhat later orientation. New symbols indicating
the absence of propriety provide clarification of the second rhythmic
mode, which had begun to appear sometime in the first decade of the
century,[9] while the absence of perfection is signified by other new notational devices intended largely to facilitate the recognition of modal
rhythm in polyphony *cum littera*; for instance, an extension of the normal syllabic articulation of a modal pattern is to be indicated with an
imperfect ligature (ex. 2.1).[10]

Example 2.1

O   vir - go   Ma - ri - - a   O   vir - go   Ma - ri - - a

One anomaly of Garlandia's notational system is that the ternary ligature *cum proprietate et perfecta*, whose components are unequivocally said to signify long, breve, long,[11] is nonetheless read differently in certain modal situations.[12] In addition to demonstrating two methods of notating the sixth mode, by means of plicated ligatures, as subdivisions of and compatible with either the first or the second mode, Garlandia reports, with disapproval, an older method well known from the musical sources. It consists of a string of *ternariae cum proprietate et perfectae* attached to an initial *quaternaria*. Here no notes are conceived as plicated longs, but all are plain breves (except, in a first-mode context, the final one). The notation of the third mode also requires the first two notes of perfect ternary ligatures with propriety to be read as breves, albeit not *breves rectae* (of one *tempus* each), but in each case a *brevis recta* followed by a *brevis altera* (of two *tempora*). We do not know whether Garlandia was at all uneasy about this systemic irregularity, since he fails to acknowledge it, quite possibly because his notational system contains no symbol for a perfect (i.e., complete) ternary ligature whose first two notes are breves.[13]

In attempting to explain these irregularities, one must keep in mind that the first two notes of all *ternariae cum proprietate et perfectae* are short in both the third and the sixth modes. The older part of the anonymous *Discantus positio vulgaris*,[14] which affords a few glimpses into a premodal stage of measured discant and its notation, contains this relevant passage:

> Whenever two notes are bound in discant, the first is a breve and the second is a long. . . . When three notes are bound following a rest, the first is a long, the second is a breve, and the third is a long [i.e., ♩ ♪♩]. If the three notes follow a long, the first two are breves and the third is a long. The last of these is extra long if, in turn, it is followed by a long. If four notes are bound, all of them are short [except, presumably, the last one]. If, however, there are more than four notes, they are not, as it were, subject to rule, but are executed at pleasure.[15]

One remark in this passage is puzzling because from a modal point of view the two short notes of a ternary ligature preceded by a long would have either to be unequal (as in the third mode) or to become semibreves. The former alternative was unknown to the author, as modal patterns were yet to be formulated,[16] while the latter is contradicted not only by the use of the term *breves*, but also by the author's statement in a preceding paragraph that "beyond measure refers to those things measured by less than one tempus or more than two *tempora*. For example: semibreves, which are written like this: ♦♦♦."[17] It would seem, then, that somehow the combination of a long and two breves might at one time have been considered as equivalent in duration to that of a long and one breve, and that in such cases the two breves were not precise semibreves.

In order to clarify this puzzling inferential proposition it will be helpful to recall later instances of flexibility and imprecision in the articulation and notation of short note values. It is well known that until the early 1270s either two or three equal semibreves, at first terminologically undifferentiated from the concept of breve, could subdivide a breve. Triple subdivision of the breve, becoming fairly common in the second half of the century (e.g., in manuscript *Cl*), is still rare in the motet fascicles of *F* and *Ma*; it appears somewhat more frequently in the third and fourth motet fascicles of W_2.[18] The only writer to report the division of the breve into either two halves or three thirds is Anonymous IV, though he applies the term *semibrevis* only to the bipartition of the breve.[19] A few years later this ambiguity is eliminated by the new notion of the *semibrevis minor* and *maior*.[20] Similarly, the newly codified semibreve soon spawned its progeny, the minim, as composers gradually increased the equal subdivisions of the breve (*brevis recta*) from three to four and more. This process finally reached a maximum of nine and thereby, in effect, produced prolation, though the ingredient notes were at first still referred to as semibreves, just as in the thirteenth century semibreves had at times been called breves.[21]

The passage in the *Discantus positio vulgaris* cited earlier seems comprehensible only if analogous circumstances are seen to have obtained for some time after durational differentiation of notes had begun to arise in discant. Evidently the didactic codification of discant permitted each of the isochronous cantus-firmus notes to sustain two or, secondarily, three notes in the upper voice. In either case the note that coincided consonantly, as a rule, with a given note of a chant melisma was long, i.e., longer than short. If one note intervened between two such consonances, its brevity constituted half of the preceding note. If two notes intervened between two consonances, each of them apparently was worth half of the first note. Either way the long was twice as long as the breve. (Occasionally, three equal breves could be set over a note of chant by means of an initial *quaternaria* or an equivalent *coniunctura*.) This relatively flexible system is superimposed on and sustained by the immeasurably even notes of the chant. Modern performances of such discant that resort to precisely measured semibreves would cause the rhythmic progression of both voices to be too sharply defined. The likely tempo of performance (ca. MM=108 for each note of chant) would, in any case, have made the notion of the semibreve redundant and excessive.[22] To be sure, the author of the *Discantus positio vulgaris* mentions and briefly describes the semibreve in a closely preceding passage. But in view of the cited definitions of ligatures consisting of three or more notes, this notice of the semibreve seems curiously inorganic and inconsistent with the stipulations that the values contained in all ligatures of up to four notes are either long or short as indicated, and that ligatures containing more than four notes are performed ad libitum.[23]

Apparently, then, discant sections in such sources as the Codex Calixtinus[24] or, quite possibly, the W_1 version of the *Magnus liber organi* would at one time have been performed as given in examples 2.2 and 2.3.[25] The organa appended to the Vatican organum treatise also contain applicable discant polyphony.[26] In this connection the occasional notation of continuous breve motion in manuscript *F*, though differing from the traditional irregular notation of the sixth mode reported by Garlandia, is particularly suggestive (exx. 2.4a and 2.4b).[27]

Example 2.2   Codex Calixtinus, fol. 189 v

Bo - - a - - - - - - - [- ner-ges]

Example 2.3 W_1, fol. 43 (37)

[angelo -] - - - - - [- rum]

Example 2.4

a. F, fol. 128 v (Dp. 2278)

b. F, fol. 345
(from conductus by Perotinus, *Dum sigillum*)

fi - - - - - [- li - a]   [Dum] _____

Like other treatises,[28] however, even the first half of the *Discantus positio vulgaris*, in the less than pristine version Hieronymus de Moravia has transmitted, seems in some ways heterochronically inconsistent. Thus the text stipulates that "all of the notes of the discant are measurable in terms of the correct breve and the correct long," but it then continues: "Thus for every note in the cantus firmus there must be at least two notes, a long and a breve—or some equivalent of these, such as four breves or three breves with a plica."[29] Indeed, the equivalent of a long note is two breves, which in the absence of semibreves are followed by two breves (or one).[30] On this basis the passage in example 2.5 might be hypothesized for a discantus voice. This kind of phenomenon cannot have survived past the time when Perotinus began writing polyphony for three voices (presumably the 1190s). The notation given in example 2.5 would then have had to be conceived for performance in either of the two solutions given in examples 2.6 and 2.7.

The rhythms of example 2.6 evidently are earlier than those of example 2.7, which includes the *longa ultra mensuram*.[31] Discant passages exhibiting these newer rhythms in the upper voices usually are supported by double longs in the tenor. Such discants are exceedingly rare in the generally oldest stylistic version of the *Magnus liber* preserved in W_1.[32] That these more "measured" passages represent a relatively modern (post-Leoninian) style is also indicated by their frequent occurrence among the substitute snippets collected in *F* (fols. 178–83v). Furthermore, a good many organal passages as well as discant portions whose tenor moves in single longs in W_1 exhibit double long tenor notes in *F*

Example 2.5

Example 2.6

Example 2.7

and W_2 , sometimes involving variation technique in the duplum (ex. 2.8a). Often the modernizations also concern changes in the counterpoint in order to eliminate unsupported fourths over the tenor (see *F* and W_2 in ex. 2.8b). More extended specimens of such variational revision occur in O 1 ("et Jherusalem") and O 10 ("paraclitum dabo"). The same technique, which also crops up in the abbreviate substitutes,[33] is most strikingly displayed in a Cambridge concordance of the Alleluia *Dies sanctificatus a3 (GB-Cu Ff. 2. 29, fol. 1v).*[34] The presumably earliest appearances of the modern rhythms occur in the organa tripla, only a handful of whose tenors do not contain double longs or rhythmic patterns, and in Perotinus's two organa quadrupla. At times both the older and the more recent rhythms, involving the same or similar ligations, appear in the same composition, as, for instance, in Perotinus's *Sederunt* (exx. 2.9 and 2.10).[35] The two organa quadrupla (*Viderunt* and *Sederunt*) are premodal; and in transcription of repertories such as the organa tripla, rhythmic patterns other than what Franco ultimately called the first and fifth modes (i.e., first, alternate third, and sixth) must also be eschewed, unless the ligature notation consistently and ineluctably indicates the second mode. (For instance, a constellation of one *binaria* at the beginning of a phrase followed by several others should not be taken to indicate the second mode, unless a *ternaria* forms its conclusion.)

It is particularly significant that the rhythm ♩. ♩♪♩. , written as a single note followed by a *ternaria*, as at the beginning of each of the phrases in example 2.10, was defined in the years around the turn of the

Example 2.5 (cont.)

Example 2.6 (cont.)

Example 2.7 (cont.)

Example 2.8

a. W₁, fol. 21 (17); *F*, fol. 81 and W₂, fol. 55v

b. W₁, fol. 30 (26); *F*, fol. 107; W₂, fol. 70

Example 2.9 *Ma*, fol. 17

began to write his *Magnus liber*. The somewhat flexible values of long and breve were subsequently replaced by a system in which only one *brevis* (*recta*) could be half of one *longa* (*recta*); this must have happened no later than the 1190s and probably earlier, though it is impossible to say whether it was reflected by the earliest version of the *Magnus liber*. Its pre-Perotinian organal style doubtless continued to be fundamentally free in its rhythmic flow, though later interpretations and redactions increasingly reshaped organal *dupla* toward the mensurability characteristic of discant.[59] With the further rhythmic development of discant, both the third and sixth modes of the new system, which arose in the first decade of the thirteenth century, reflect in their ambiguous notations (especially in Garlandia's system) the difficulties of assimilating the earlier flexibilities. (On the whole, modal rhythm, an aspect of discant elaboration of chant melismas, did not affect the syllabic portions of most conducti[60] until the second half of the century, when the genre was beginning to decline.) The Franconian codification of the semibreve and its subsequent proliferation, the neutralization of the modal system by Franco's concept of the perfection and by his notational reform, and the appearance in the later thirteenth century of imperfect mensuration and its subsequent didactic recognition led to the modern binary as well as ternary system of integrated, hierarchically ordered durational values established in the 1320s—truly an *ars nova*.

Notes

1 See Fritz Reckow, ed., *Der Musiktraktat des Anonymus 4*, Beihefte zum Archiv für Musikwissenschaft, nos. 4–5 (Wiesbaden, 1967), 2:11–15, and the references given there. On an earlier occasion I had referred to them as "teacher-reporters ('theorists')"; communication in *Current Musicology* 9 (1969): 213.

2 Hans Heinrich Eggebrecht, "Gedanken über die Aufgabe, die Geschichte der Musiktheorie des hohen und späten Mittelalters zu schreiben," in Frieder Zaminer, ed., *Über Musiktheorie*, Veröffentlichungen des Staatlichen Instituts für Musikforschung, Preussischer Kulturbesitz, vol. 5 (Cologne, 1970), 17. Of course, whether compositional advances are consequences of notational advances or vice versa is highly debatable. For this reason the warning should be emphasized that since the later twelfth century the term "history of notation" must be qualified as "history of the notation of rhythm."

3 Friedrich Ludwig, *Repertorium organorum recentioris et motetorum vetustissimi stili*, vol. 1, *Catalogue raisonné der Quellen* (Halle, 1910), 50. Ludwig does not explicitly recognize premodal rhythmic notation. Though it is a truism, the warning should be emphasized that neither later sources nor later commentaries must be used uncritically in reading of earlier compositions or versions of compositions.

4 Reckow, ed., *Der Musiktraktat* 1:49–51.

5 Wolfenbüttel, Herzog-August-Bibliothek, 677; and Florence, Biblioteca Medicea-Laurenziana, Pluteus 29.1. W₂ (Wolfenbüttel, Herzog-August-Bibliothek, 1206), the third of the major "Notre Dame" manuscripts, already evinces a few more progressive notational features.

Example 2.10   *Ma*, fol. 19

[Ad - iu -]va

century as a *longa ultra mensuram* plus two breves plus a long.[36] The crucial question why the second note, the first of the *ternaria*, was not considered a long, like the first and third notes in the configuration ♩ ♪♪ ♪♩ , is answerable only if one recognizes that originally it must have had less length (as shown in examples 2.2 and 2.3) than it was bound to begin to receive (except in passages like that of example 2.10) by the last decade of the twelfth century. The patent illogic of designating and writing a long as a breve (even in isolated remnant cases of syllabic notation in so late a source as the Montpellier manuscript), the way the antepenultimate and penultimate notes in certain *coniuncturae* were performed, and the rise of the second mode must account for the gradual conversion of the two "breves" to the paired breves (*brevis recta* and *brevis altera*)[37] characteristic of the next, the third mode. Gradually replacing the "alternate third mode," it presumably became standardized in the clausula repertory, in which by ca. 1210 the pre-Garlandian (Perotinian) modal system can be seen to be completely represented (except, of course, for the fourth mode).[38] In the third mode the succession of the durational values of one *tempus* and two *tempora* could and, in fact, had to continue to be conceived as two breves, the second of which could not in any case be a long, since its position before another long would require it to be *longior longa*. (These circumstances, arising from the beginnings of measured discant, explain the curious nature of the third mode as well as the more than tercentenary notational tradition of alteration.) Apparently Garlandia's notation of the third mode was due not only to his system's inability to provide for a "proper" ligature (breve, breve, long), but also to the prehistory of the third mode,[39] which had made the attendant, premodal *ternaria* notation as strict a convention as that of the *binaria* (short, long).[40] By the 1190s a ternary framework for the rhythmic values of polyphony had necessarily come into being, and it accommodated the traditional concept of a *longa* followed by two breves either with the *longa* reduced to brevity (irregularly notated sixth mode) or with the three notes protracted to twice their previous value.[41] In both cases the ligature notation remained unchanged,[42] and the ternary long of the new third mode continued to be regarded as the element *ultra mensuram*. Only Franco, aiming at precision and fixity, definitively extended mensurability from one *tempus* and two *tempora* to three, making his concept of the perfection the new standard.

*   *   *

The practices inferred here from the *Discantus positio vulgaris* would seem to have arisen sometime in the third quarter of the twelfth century. The matrix from which they evolved can be found in the stylistic conventions of the polyphony described in the "London" treatise and particularly in the "de LaFage" treatise.[43] Both discuss discant and organum in terms of strict note-against-note style on the one hand, and a melismatic upper voice on the other. The latter technique is also described in the prose part of the earlier "Milan" organum treatise, though only in its function as a modest cadential flourish in traditional note-against-note counterpoint.[44] The anonymous author of the de LaFage treatise is particularly emphatic in his assertion that, with the exception of such cadential situations, discant must be note against note. As Eggebrecht suggests with his customary acumen,[45] the stringent prohibition against sullying the purity of discant with organal excesses could be seen as a conservative's caveat against the troublesome practice, evident well before early Notre Dame discant, of setting two or more notes in the discant against any given note in the chant,[46] the more so as his description of organum recalls the ornate style of the *Magnus liber*, to be reined in by subsequent revisions.[47] The contrapuntal practices discussed by the author must have arisen during the first half of the twelfth century.

The indications that the de LaFage treatise reflects polyphonic conventions of ca. 1150 are contradicted by the argument that the author, evidently a Cistercian, could not have written it before the early thirteenth century and that it functioned "as a theoretical source for Cistercian ideas about two- and three-part polyphony, discant, and organum during the thirteenth and fourteenth centuries."[48] The main rationale for these conclusions, apart from the lateness of the sources, is the fact that the treatise mentions three-part polyphony once as note-against-note discant for three voices (chant and two discants), and another time

as a mixed genre, i.e., discant with an added organal
Eggebrecht has observed, the kinds of three-part polypho
by the de LaFage Anonymous are the only ones that neith
reflect mensuration,[49] which, as a French author,[50] he woul
commented upon if he had written in the thirteenth cent
known description of organum—*mira quadam flexibili*
confirm the nonmensural nature of polyphony compo
time. His three-part polyphony is therefore pre-Perotir
probability, given the notational evidence of the practi
description of two-part polyphony predates Leoninus
which is likely to have been written ca. 1180,[51] some yea
appearance of Parisian (Notre Dame) polyphony.[52] On
sion I mistakenly assumed that the recently proposed
treatise was at least in part based on the apparent Cist
of ornate polyphony,[53] for which the earliest practi
Meaux Abbey in Yorkshire) comes from the late thir
and also on the unlikelihood that any sort of polyph
by the Cistercians in the first half of the century.
certainly, many of the original Cistercian austerities
disregarded.[55] But while in the third quarter of the t
probable period in which the de LaFage treatise was
was surely still seen as incompatible with Cistercia
after the reforms of Bernard de Clairvaux,[56] no evide
view that the original manuscript, though belongi
chant tradition of the mid-twelfth century and cor
on polyphonic elaboration of chant, could have
non-Cistercian community.[57] Not only does the
Leoninian practices, but no known facts compel a
not be cited, therefore, to support statements be
sive evidence of "the progressive development
lyphony."[58]

Quite to the contrary, the development of *mu*
beginnings to the early fourteenth century pre
evolutionary consistency that it would seem t
to deny. Evidently, once the restriction of disca
counterpoint was relaxed, the steady progres
was durationally defined by two or three no
either a long and a short or a long and two she
taking up the same amount of time. (It could
longa [*longa ultra mensuram*] or three equal bre
the *Discantus positio vulgaris* quoted on p. 43 a
would have occurred before the 1170s, wh

7. Johannes de Garlandia, *De mensurabili musica*, ed. Erich Reimer, Beihefte zum Archiv für Musikwissenschaft, nos. 10–11 (Wiesbaden, 1972).

8. Actually, the noun *perfectio* appears only once; everywhere else the term Garlandia uses is the participial adjective *perfectus* (see Garlandia. *De mensurabili musica* 2:76; also Wolf Frobenius, "Perfectio," *Handwörterbuch der musikalischen Terminologie* [Wiesbaden, 1973], 1–2).

9. Cf. Reckow, "Proprietas und perfectio," *Acta Musicologica* 39 (1967): 123; Garlandia, *De mensurabili musica* 1:53; Ernest H. Sanders, "Conductus and Modal Rhythm," *Journal of the American Musicological Society* 38 (1985): 449 and n. 54.

10. Cf. Reckow, "Proprietas und perfectio," 127–28. The example is designed in accordance with applicable Garlandian precepts, since there are no sources exhibiting Garlandian notation. The manuscript most closely related to it is *Ba* (Bamberg, Staatliche Bibliothek, Lit. 115 [olim Ed. IV.6]). Not only the rests, however, but also the writing of the *binaria cum proprietate et imperfecta* as if it were a *binaria sine proprietate et perfecta* (e.g., fol. 14v, penultimate staff of the motetus voice) differ from Garlandia's system. The notation of rests is taught only by Lambertus. Cf. Garlandia, *De mensurabili musica* 2:65–66.

11. Garlandia, *De mensurabili musica* 1:50 and 52.

12. For a detailed treatment of this issue, see Sanders, "Consonance and Rhythm in the Organum of the Twelfth and Thirteenth Centuries," *Journal of the American Musicological Society* 33 (1980): 275–77.

13. It cannot, since the *ternaria sine proprietate* denotes breve, long, breve, in contrast to the rhythm of the proper *ternaria*; cf. Reckow, "Proprietas und perfectio," 122. The Sowa Anonymous, who, like Anonymous IV (Reckow, *Der Musiktraktat* 1:54 and 56), follows Garlandian precepts, applies the principle of imperfection of ligatures exceptionally to the melismatic notation of the sixth mode (Heinrich Sowa, ed., *Ein anonymer glossierter Mensuraltrakt 1279* [Kassel, 1930], 88–89). Only Franco's system finally eliminates all these incongruities.

14. Hieronymus de Moravia, *Tractatus de musica*, ed. Simon Cserba, Freiburger Studien zur Musikwissenschaft, no. 2 (Regensburg, 1935), 189–92; cf. Sanders, "Consonance and Rhythm," 266 n. 2.

15. "Quandocumque due note ligantur in discantu, prima est brevis, secunda longa, ... quando autem tres, si pausa precedit, prima est longa, secunda brevis, tercia longa; si nota longa precedit, prime due sunt breves, tercia longa, quam si nota longa sequitur, tercia erit longior longa. Si vero quatuor ligate fuerint, omnes sunt breves. Quodsi plures quam quatuor fuerint, tum quasi regulis non subiacent, sed ad placitum proferuntur" (Moravia, *Tractatus de musica*, 190). With the exception of the bracketed insertions, the English translations of all quoted passages are taken from Janet Knapp, "Two Thirteenth-Century Treatises on Modal Rhythm and the Discant," *Journal of Music Theory* 6 (1962): 203.

16. See also his statement, quoted more fully below (note 29), that "all notes of discant are measurable by means of the simple breve and the simple long."

17. "Ultra mensuram sunt que minus quam uno tempore et ampliori quam duobus mensurantur, ut semibreves, que sic figurantur: ♦♦♦ (Moravia, *Tractatus de musica*, 190). The fact that three semibreves happen to be given must not, of course, be taken to indicate a Franconian subdivision of the breve.

18. For *F* and *W₂* see note 6 above. *Cl* = Paris, Bibliothèque Nationale, n.a. fr. 13521; *Ma* = Madrid, Biblioteca Nacional, 20486.

19. Reckow, *Der Musiktraktat* 1:45.

20. For the most thorough discussion of this topic, see Wolf Frobenius, "Semibrevis," *Handwörterbuch der musikalischen Terminologie* (Wiesbaden, 1972). Max Haas's doubts that Franco "means precisely discernible [*fassbare*] differences of semibreve lengths"

("Die Musiklehre im 13. Jahrhundert von Johannes de Garlandia bis Franco," in Frieder Zaminer, ed., *Die mittelalterliche Lehre von der Mehrstimmigkeit*, Geschichte der Musiktheorie, vol. 5 [Darmstadt, 1984], 141–42 and n. 210) seem incomprehensible. Franco treats semibreves, melismatic and syllabic, precisely in analogy to the significance of breves in third mode.

21. See Sanders, "Petrus de Cruce," *New Grove Dictionary of Music and Musicians* 14:598–99.

22. See also note 16 above.

23. As Fritz Reckow has pointed out ("Proprietas und perfectio," 137 n. 81), the passage defining the rhythmic meanings of ligatures, more than any other in the treatise, is likely to reflect the earliest, i.e., premodal, state of rhythmic notation.

24. Santiago de Compostela, Biblioteca de la Catedral (unnumbered).

25. These circumstances, as well as the variancy of the sources, explain the diffidence with which scholars generally have approached the notion of producing a critical edition of the *Magnus liber organi*. For a *Gesamtausgabe*, which would rightly be regarded as binding, we know both too little and too much. We cannot even tell to what extent the original organa are accurately represented in the manuscript copies. There is no reliable way to bring the totality of these chant settings into focus as an opus.

26. See Frieder Zaminer, *Der vatikanische Organum-Traktat (Ottob. lat. 3025)*, Münchner Veröffentlichungen zur Musikgeschichte, vol. 2 (Tutzing, 1959); Irving Godt and Benito Rivera, "The Vatican Organum Treatise—A Colour Reproduction, Transcription, and Translation," in *Gordon Athol Anderson (1929–1981) In Memoriam*, vol. 2 (Henryville, Penn., 1984), 264–345. Style and technique of these organa represent a stage of polyphony developed further in Leoninus's *Magnus liber organi*; cf. Hans Heinrich Eggebrecht, "Die Mehrstimmigkeitslehre von ihren Anfängen bis zum 12. Jahrhundert," in Zaminer, *Die mittelalterliche Lehre*, 67–68.

27. See also the excerpt from *Benedicamus* no. 3 quoted in Sanders, "Consonance and Rhythm," 273.

28. E.g., that of Garlandia; cf. Sanders, "Consonance and Rhythm," 274–85.

29. "Omnes autem note discantus sunt mensurabiles per directam brevem et directam longam. Unde sequitur quod super quamlibet notam firmi cantus ad minus due note, longa scilicet et brevis vel aliquid his equipollens, ut quatuor breves vel tres cum plica brevi proferri debent" (Moravia, *Tractatus de musica*, 190–91).

30. The statement that four breves can take the place of a long plus a breve is not strictly consistent with the assertion that all notes of discant are measurable by means of the regular breve and the regular long.

31. Sanders, "The Medieval Motet," in Wulf Arlt, Ernst Lichtenhahn, and Hans Oesch, eds., *Gattungen der Musik in Einzeldarstellungen: Gedenkschrift Leo Schrade* (Bern, 1973), 501–2.

32. There are at most five (only one of them in the *Magnus liber de antiphonario*, which may well have been the first of the two books Leoninus composed): O 28 ("vester venturus"); M 23 ("[Ascen]dens; in altum; dona"); M 32 ("quem to[tus]"); M 42 ("[Judi]ca[bunt]") and almost certainly M 54 ("mea"), William G. Waite's transcriptions notwithstanding (*The Rhythm of Twelfth-Century Music* [New Haven, 1954]). Through a fluke in transmission the tenor of the cited discant passage in M 32 employs double longs in W_1 (fol. 38v [31v]), but single longs in F (fol. 123) and W_2 (fol. 77v). As Craig Wright has shown, manuscript F reflects the earliest state of the *Magnus liber organi* with respect to liturgical repertory, but not to musical style (*Music and Ceremony at Notre Dame of Paris, 500-1500* [Cambridge, 1989], 271); as to the latter, the priority of W_1 among the extand versions is unchallenged.

33. See Sanders, "The Medieval Motet," 505–6, and, especially in idem, *"Sine littera*

and *cum littera* in Medieval Polyphony," in Edmond Strainchamps, Maria Rika Maniates, and Christopher Hatch, eds., *Music and Civilization: Essays in Honor of Paul Henry Lang* (New York, 1984), 216 n. 3 and 218 n. 6, regarding matters of chronology and evolution of styles and techniques in this repertory. The tendency toward a more "measured" tightening of style is also demonstrated by the abridgment, through omission and revision, of the organum triplum *Sancte Germane* (possibly by Perotinus) in *Mo* (Montpellier, Faculté de Médecine H 196) and by the abridged dupla of the *Magnus liber* in a manuscript first reported by Kurt von Fischer, "Neue Quellen zur Musik des 13, 14, und 15 Jahrhunderts," *Acta Musicologica* 36 (1964): 79–97, specifically 80–82. At the conference on Medieval and Renaissance Music held in London in August 1986 John Bergsagel presented evidence of a similar manuscript, fragments of which are preserved in the Royal Library in Copenhagen.

34. Heinrich Husmann, failing to recognize the import of the unambiguous notation, squeezed his transcription of the passage ("nobis") into the time frame it fills in the versions preserved in W_1 and F (*Die drei- und vierstimmigen Notre-Dame-Organa*, Publikationen älterer Musik, vol. 11 [Leipzig, 1940; reprint ed., 1967], 23–24).

35. Example 2.9: The other two concordances (W_1, fol. 3v [1v]; F, fol. 4–4v) are identically notated. Similar passages occur in Perotinus's conductus *Salvatoris hodie* and in many of the presumably Perotinian abbreviation substitutes (cf. Sanders, "The Question of Perotin's Oeuvre and Dates," in Ludwig Finscher and Christoph-Hellmut Mahling, eds., *Festschrift für Walter Wiora* [Kassel, 1967], 242).

Example 2.10: The first four notes of the duplum and quadruplum voices are written as *quaternariae* in two of the three concordances (W1, fol. 5 [3]; F, fol. 6; W2, fol. 2), and those of the triplum in one of them. The first ligature of each of the last three *ordines* of the quadruplum is written as a *quaternaria* in two or three of the concordant manuscripts; the scribe of W_2 even wrote its last phrase as a plicated *quaternaria* followed by a *binaria*. (Ludwig's reason for his relatively late dating of *Ma* [*Repertorium*, 138–39] was, in effect, refuted by Husmann; see Sanders, "The Medieval Motet," 524 and n. 89.) Another example of Garlandia's irregular notation of the sixth mode is a passage in Perotinus's Alleluia *Posui adiutorium*, cited by both Johannes de Garlandia (*De mensurabili musica* 1:56) and Anonymous IV (Reckow, *Der Musiktraktat* 1:56). It is well known that there are many such passages in the discant portions of the *Magnus liber organi*, especially the version in W_1 (cf. Sanders, "Consonance and Rhythm," 275).

36. For the evidence, see Sanders, "Duple Rhythm and Alternate Third Mode in the Thirteenth Century," *Journal of the American Musicological Society* 15 (1962): 278–82.

37. Though, as Garlandia puts it, the third, fourth, and fifth modes are "ultramensurabiles," the expression "brevis in ultra mensuram" for the second breve in each pair of breves in this mode (Haas, "Die Musiklehre," 138) does not occur in the treatises. Garlandia (Paris version; see *De mensurabili musica* 1:92), Anonymous IV (Reckow, *Der Musiktraktat* 1:26, 38, and 44), Anonymous VII (both versions; for the Paris version see Charles-Edmond-Henri de Coussemaker, *Scriptorum de musica*, vol. 1 [Paris, 1864], 379a), and the Sowa Anonymous (Sowa, *Ein anonymer glossierter Mensuraltrakt*, 26, 28, 63, and 86) specifically assert that it contains two time units, though Garlandia (*De mensurabili musica* 1:38), Anonymous IV (Reckow, *Der Musiktraktat* 1:76), and the Sowa Anonymous (Sowa, *Ein anonymer glossierter Mensuraltrakt*, 76), like the author of the *Discantus positio vulgaris* (see p. 43 above), also still regard anything other than the *longa recta* and the *brevis recta* as "beyond measurement." Obviously, however, the notion of a value of three time units being "ultra mensuram" is, in effect, residual terminological baggage for all commentators after the *Discantus positio vulgaris*. This is most strikingly apparent in the case of Garlandia, who gives numerous examples of the mensural and contrapuntal compatibility of "rectus modus ad modum

per ultra mensuram" (Garlandia, *De mensurabili musica* 1:84–88). Clearly, ever since the appearance of Perotinian discant for tenor and two upper voices nothing is in fact any longer beyond measurement in discant.

38. See also Sanders, "Consonance and Rhythm," 277–80. The continued cultivation of the rhythms of the "alternate third mode" in some circles—especially in England, where composers largely rejected the second and third modes until the time of Franco's treatise (presumably 1280)—must account for his particular modal system. The English likewise began around this same time to replace the paired breves in their notation of the "alternate third mode" with a long and a breve (English breve), thus finally relegating this conventional reading of two successive breves to historical oblivion and, from Franco's modal point of view, converting it into a subspecies of the first mode; cf. Sanders, "Duple Rhythm," 263–86; idem, "*Sine littera*," 219 n. 7. The origin of the lozenge-shaped English breve may well lie in the kinds of *coniunctura* notation posited in example 2.5 above.

39. In view of the passage from the *Discantus positio vulgaris* cited on p. 43 above, it is obvious that there is no prehistory for the fourth mode, an unreal construct said by "Dietricus" (the name of the scribe) to be "not in use" (cf. Sanders, "Conductus and Modal Rhythm," 467 n. 101); this is in contrast to the second mode, which may owe its codification to the conversion of the tradition of "upbeat" premodal phrases.

40. Significantly, the long-short-long rhythm is at times notated as a *longa* followed by a *binaria* in W_1 even though no repeated notes are involved; for instance, O 2, fol. 17v (13v): "de (celis)"; M 17, fol. 33v (29v): "a(ve)"; M 40, fol. 44 (38): "non de(ficient)," twice; M 49, fol. 46 (40): "(et spe)ra(bit)." In F each of these passages has a *ternaria*.

41. Peter Wagner insistently (in three journals) called attention to an analogous melodic phenomenon in conjunction with the rise of diastemic notation; see Willi Apel, *Gregorian Chant* (Bloomington, Ind., 1958), 108 n. 13.

42. In the first case the contraction of the first four notes into a *quaternaria* became a frequent practice, especially in the later sources (F, *Mü A* [Munich, Bayerische Staatsbibliothek gallo-rom. 42, and Berlin, Bibliothek Johannes Wolf; the latter is lost but photographically preserved in Paris, Bibliothèque Nationale, Département de Musique, Vma 1446], and W_2). Thus the first seven notes of example 2.3 appear in the F and W_2 concordances in regular sixth-mode notation, i.e., as a plicated *quaternaria* followed by a *binaria*. Other such passages are notationally revised to produce the irregular sixth-mode pattern reported by Garlandia (see p. 43 above), as, for instance, in the setting of "manere" in M 5. All three notations appear in one passage from Perotinus's *Sederunt* (ex. 2.10; see note 35 above).

43. Two versions of the London treatise are preserved: in London, British Library, Egerton 2888, and in Naples, Biblioteca Nazionale "Vittorio Emanuele III"; VIII, D. 12. They date from the "second half of twelfth century" (*Catalogue of Additions to the Manuscripts in the British Museum in the Years 1906–1910* [London, 1912], 274) and from the "late Twelfth century" (*The Theory of Music from the Carolingian Era up to 1400*, vol. 2, ed. Pieter Fischer [RISM B III², Munich, 1968], 70). Each of these versions of the treatise, which probably dates from the mid-twelfth century, has been published: see Marius Schneider, *Geschichte der Mehrstimmigkeit* (Berlin, 1934–35; reprint ed., Tutzing, 1969), 2:106ff., specifically 115–20; and Guido Pannain, "Liber Musicae. Un teorico anonimo del XIV secolo [*sic*]," *Rivista Musicale Italiana* 27 (1920): 407–40. For details on the de LaFage treatise, see Sanders, "Consonance and Rhythm," 265–66 n. l, and Eggebrecht, "Die Mehrstimmigkeitslehre," 59 and n. 61. No manuscript source predates the fourteenth century. Like most others (see Sanders, "Conductus and Modal Rhythm," 452–53 and 446), the London and de LaFage treatises deal with the polyphonic elaboration of chant melodies. This is indicated not only by the musical examples given (or referred

to, but omitted) in the sources of the de LaFage Anonymous, but also by the fact that both are chant treatises that end with discussions of nonmonophonic aspects of chant. The absence of the fundament of a *cantus ecclesiasticus* in the polyphonic settings of *versus* and *conducti* militates against modern exemplifications of the writings by such authors with specimens taken from those repertories, which are not strictly bound by laws and rules.

44. See Eggebrecht, "Die Mehrstimmigkeitslehre," 50; edition, translation, and exhaustive commentary in Hans Heinrich Eggebrecht and Frieder Zaminer, eds., *Ad Organum Faciendum: Lehrschriften der Mehrstimmigkeit in nachguidonischer Zeit*, Neue Studien zur Musikwissenschaft, vol. 3 (Mainz, 1970), 43–108.

45. Ibid., 61.

46. The pertinent passage reads as follows: "And one must beware with all care and the greatest caution that the discant have no more notes than the chant" ("Et hoc etiam omni cura maximaque cautela cavendum est ne discantus plures punctos habeat quam cantus"; quoted from Jacques Handschin, "Aus der alten Musiktheorie," *Acta Musicologica* 14 [1942]: 24).

47. Eggebrecht, "Die Mehrstimmigkeitslehre," 65.

48. Sarah Fuller, "An Anonymous Treatise *Dictus de Sancto Martiale*: A New Source for Cistercian Music Theory," *Musica Disciplina* 31 (1977): 23 and 27.

49. Eggebrecht, "Die Mehrstimmigkeitslehre," 65.

50. Fuller, "An Anonymous Treatise," 24.

51. Cf. Sanders, "Consonance and Rhythm," 268 n. 8. In the absence of any evidence it is apposite to propose that the gold ring set with rubies Leoninus received, probably in May 1182, from Pope Lucius III's legate to France (cf. Craig Wright, "Leoninus, Poet and Musician," *Journal of the American Musicological Society* 39 [1986]: 25–27) constituted a reward or token of appreciation for his *Magnus liber organi*. In the last four lines of Leoninus's poem of gratitude, which consist of a strikingly emphatic expansion of the fleeting expression "parvum munus" in the Ovidian model, there may be a hint (the topical nature of the flourishes notwithstanding) that he regarded himself as worthy of a significant present, perhaps greater than the ring he acknowledged in his poem:

> Tu quoque ne queso reputes te parva dedisse
>   Esse nichil parvum quo mihi dante potest.
> Nec iam parva forent; etiam si parva fuissent
>   Magna facit magnus munera parva dator.

> I beg you not to consider yourself as having given too little;
>   There can be nothing small in your giving to me.
> And indeed your gift was not small; and even if it had been small,
>   Given by a great giver a small gift becomes large.

In an earlier poem, by contrast, he referred to a "splendid gift" ("preclarum munus") he had received from King Louis VII at the request of Alexander II, Lucius's Francophile predecessor.

52. For the evidence furnished by the conductus repertory, see Sanders, "Style and Technique in Datable Polyphonic Notre-Dame Conductus," in *Gordon Athol Anderson*, 521.

53. See "Communications" in *Journal of the American Musicological Society* 34 (1981): 590 n. 1; and 35 (1982): 586–87.

54. Richard L. Greene, "Two Medieval Musical Manuscripts: Eggerton 3307 and Some University of Chicago Fragments," *Journal of the American Musicological Society* 7 (1954): 27–28. This Cistercian source of polyphony seems to have remained largely

unknown or disregarded; cf., for instance, Gilbert Reaney, "The Social Implications of Polyphonic Mass Music in Fourteenth Century England," *Musica Disciplina* 38 (1984): 164. Mark Everist has recently published evidence for the nearly certain Cistercian origin of an even earlier continental source of polyphony, dating from "between 1230 and 1260" ("A Reconstructed Source for the Thirteenth-Century Conductus," in *Gordon Athol Anderson*, 97–118, esp. 110–14).

55. For details regarding the situation in Yorkshire at that time, see Sanders, "Duple Rhythm," 274–75 n. 132.

56. The treatise should probably be dated within a decade or so of the reform of Bernard de Clairvaux, which "must have been effected sometime between 1142 and 1147" (Chrysogonus Waddell, OCSO, in *The Works of Bernard of Clairvaux*, vol. 1, Cistercian Fathers Series, no. 1 [Spencer, Mass., 1970], 154).

57. The legitimacy of this view was confirmed in a personal communication from Father Waddell. See also his informative "The Origin and Early Evolution of the Cistercian Antiphonary: Reflections on Two Cistercian Chant Reforms," in *The Cistercian Spirit: A Symposium*, Cistercian Studies Series, no. 3 (Shannon, 1970), 190–223.

58. Cf. Fuller, "An Anonymous Treatise," 28.

59. The transcriptions in Sanders, "Consonance and Rhythm," 272–73, may well be seen to be supported by the post-Garlandian view of the comparatively late Sowa Anonymous, who comments that *organum speciale* "est reducibilis ad numerum [i.e., rhythmic measure; foot] recte vocis" (Sowa, *Ein anonymer glossierter Mensuraltrakt*, 128).

60. See Sanders, "Conductus and Modal Rhythm." The fact that the conductus poems are *rithmi*, not *metra*, is additional and fundamental evidence that the patterns of the rhythmic modes are irrelevant; see Sanders, "Rithmus," in the forthcoming festschrift for David G. Hughes, ed. Graeme M. Boone, Isham Library Papers (Cambridge, Mass.), vol. 4.

THREE

Modal Strategies in Okeghem's
Missa Cuiusvis Toni

Leeman L. Perkins

The last couple of decades have brought a growing awareness of the significant role played by modal concepts in what may be loosely called the "tonal" organization of fifteenth- and sixteenth-century polyphonic music. The work of such scholars as Bernhard Meier and Harold Powers[1] has made it increasingly evident that the factors governing the shape of opening motives, the range of individual parts, points of internal closure, and cadential finals (some of the most obvious hallmarks of any musical structure) were not then defined primarily in terms of chordal progressions as they came to be after Rameau, but rather with respect to the prevailing norms for melodic facture. It is clear that those notions of order derived directly, on the one hand, from the current theoretical concepts of mode and, on the other, from the practical experience of the musician. The latter eventually included the application of modal criteria to polyphonic composition. But it began, of course, in childhood through contact with the plainchant of the liturgy.

As is now well known, the professional singers of the period, from whose ranks came the composers of polyphony, generally received their training almost entirely within the educational institutions established by the Christian Church. They usually started the process at seven or eight years of age, serving as choirboys and learning, together with their Latin, first the psalm tones and then an increasing repertory of chants in other categories: antiphons, responsories, and ultimately both ordinaries and propers for the Mass. The psalms, in most instances, were to be memorized in order that they might be sung even in the dark,[2] and many of the chants that were repeated a number of times in the course of the year—such as the four great Marian antiphons—were probably soon committed to memory as well. As a result of this intimate and ongoing familiarity with plainchant, the musician's melodic sense had to be deeply influenced by the recurring patterns and organizational principles of that large body of music long before he had occasion to reflect consciously upon modal criteria as a guide to melodic facture.

The careful and detailed treatment given questions of mode by author after author from the fourteenth century through the sixteenth is ample evidence of the importance the Western world attached to that aspect of the theoretical tradition.[3] Moreover, the attention directed by humanist scholars to the discovery and study of the ancient Greek musical treatises helped to make modal theory an increasingly central concern of theorists during the fifteenth and sixteenth centuries. The theorists' attempts to compare Greek modal systems with those that had been developed during the Middle Ages, primarily in order to deal with liturgical plainchant, stimulated critical examination of current theory and practice. One reflection of that activity is to be seen in the efforts of Glarean and Zarlino to resolve some of the anomalies of the medieval system through its expansion from eight modes to twelve.[4] If their success in supplanting the older system was limited, it was undoubtedly because, as we shall see, the very ambiguities and inconsistencies that they were trying to eliminate had become an important part of the way in which the modes had come to be understood and used.

Ostensibly, modal theory was primarily concerned with the classification of existing melodies for both practical and didactic purposes. For example, the combination of antiphons and psalms for liturgical ends had to be accomplished in some orderly manner in order to avoid undue difficulties in performance while achieving the greatest possible euphony. Similarly, the grouping of chants into families on the basis of well-defined musical relationships facilitated the task of learning the enormous repertory of the liturgical year. It has long been noticed, however, that the principles of classification could serve equally well as a kind of theory of melody.[5] That has clearly been the underlying assumption for a good deal of the critical stylistic analysis done in recent years, but there may have been a tendency to take the theoretical definitions of mode a bit too literally and to devote insufficient care to examining their relationship to modal practice as evinced first of all by the chant itself.

As we all know, the criteria for modal determination expounded by the theorists were threefold: first to be considered was the final, then the range or ambitus, and lastly the species of fourth, fifth, and octave defined by the first two factors. However, this systematic approach was apparently affected powerfully and fundamentally by the musician's actual experience with liturgical monophony. Regular finals were allowed on only four of the seven steps constituting the "grave" octave (from A to a) of the medieval gamut—D, E, F, and G. On these were based only four pairs of modes, each of which could be distinguished in principle by the placement of its central octave with respect to its final and by the characteristic species of fourth and fifth of which that octave was composed. In both authentic and plagal modes the characteristic species of fifth was located between the final and the confinal above it. To this was added the characteristic species of fourth, ascending from the confinal in the authentic modes and rising from its replication at the lower octave to the final in the plagal ones (see ex. 3.1).

Example 3.1

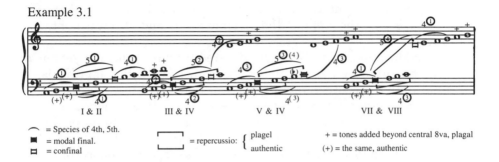

⌒ = Species of 4th, 5th.
■ = modal final.
□ = confinal

⌐⌐ = repercussio: { plagel / authentic

+ = tones added beyond central 8va, plagal
(+) = the same, authentic

I & II   III & IV   V & IV   VII & VIII

However, the chants themselves did not fall neatly into the clearly defined octave of the theoretical ambitus. The incontrovertible fact that virtually every authentic chant used at least one step below the final prompted the addition of a step or even two below the final as part of the "normal" range of the authentic modes. Similarly, the tendency of plagal chants to reach a step or two above the confinal led to a corresponding extension of the plagal modes.[6] A great many chants departed from even these revised theoretical norms, either because they failed to use all of the regular ambitus or because they actually went beyond it.

Further theorizing therefore followed in an attempt to deal systematically with such irregularities. A mode was described as perfect if the chant being classified just filled out the range theoretically allowed, imperfect if the melody failed to touch the recognized limits, and pluperfect if it exceeded them. And if the ambitus of the chant was so wide as to replicate the entire species of fourth characteristic of a modal pair, either above the confinal in a plagal mode or below the final in an authentic one, the result was seen as a combination of the two and the mode was termed mixed.

Since there were four different species of fifth, each pair of modes could be identified in principle by a unique sequence of tones and semitones above the final. In reality, however, by the fifteenth century the pair on F almost invariably carried B-flat as a signature. The reasons for the alteration are readily understood; the mutation of the species of fifth theoretically characteristic of the modal pair was seen as preferable to the tritone that otherwise occurred. Still, the result was to make the species of fifth from F to c identical with that from G to d and therefore to blur the distinction between modes 5 and 7, on the one hand, and 6 and 8, on the other.[7] Moreover, other ambiguities were possible with the modes on G. Because there are but three species of fourth, the one (from d to g or D to G) required to complete their central octave duplicated the first species associated with the modes on D, while the ambitus of mode 8 was exactly the same as that of mode 1, even if the point of division into fourth and fifth was not the same.

The Mixolydian pair of modes differed from the others in yet another important respect. In all but the modes on F with b-mi (that is, b-natural), the characteristic species of fourth fell in two separate locations: it stood alone either above the confinal (in the authentic member) or below the final (in the plagal one), and it was also to be discerned in the intervallic progression of the characteristic species of fifth ascending from the final. The same was true, obviously, of the modes of the third pair when b-fa apparently came to be used as a matter of course from the late fourteenth century on. Because it shared this location and its constituent scale degrees with the overlapping fifth, that fourth was designated *communis*,[8] and a desire to extend that congruence and, hence, the symmetry of the theoretical construct may have contributed to the routine adoption of B-flat for modes 5 and 6 on F. The pattern breaks down finally and inevitably, however, with the modes of the fourth pair, since the fifth above G opens with two whole tones and a semitone, while the fourth ascending from d has first a tone, then a semitone and another tone. The two constituent parts of the octave do not match, therefore, as they do in the remaining modal pairs.

A similar discrepancy arose from the medieval practice of assimilating chants ending on a with the pair based on D. The fifth from a to e is of the first species, matching the one from D to a, but the fourth from e to a is of the second species, which was identified characteristically with the modes of the Phrygian pair. A related problem was posed by the traditional identification of chants closing on C with the two modes based on F. Although the fourths were the same in this instance, the species of fifth from c to g was the fourth, that associated with the modes on G, whereas the third species of fifth was regarded, theoretically at least, as characteristic of modes 5 and 6. If b-fa is adopted for the Lydian octave, however, this divergence disappears and the two scales become identical. (Incidentally, that circumstance may also have contributed to the acceptance of the flat as "regular" for the modes with F as a final.)

Yet another practical element that disturbed the tidy theoretical construct of four pairs of modes on successive finals and instead distinguished them from one another in real musical terms was the characteristic interval of the melodic formulae used for the corresponding psalm tones. That interval, which Meier conveniently designated as the *repercussio*,[9] was defined at the lower end by the modal final and at the upper by the reiterated reciting pitch, variously known as the *repercussa*, *tuba*, or tenor. Had the modes been truly symmetrical, the unvarying pattern would have been that the *repercussa* of the authentic psalm tone coincided with the confinal a fifth above the final, and that of the plagal tone occurred a third lower.

In practice, however, that was so only in the modal pairs on D and on F. The confinal of modes 3 and 4, which was b-mi, was apparently rejected as a *repercussa* early on because of its tritone relationship with the F below and was replaced by c. Consequently, for the authentic mode on E the characteristic interval from final to *repercussa* came to be a minor sixth rather than a perfect fifth; and since the *repercussa* for its plagal companion was a third lower, its *repercussio* spanned not a third, as in mode 2, but rather the fourth from E to a. For similar reasons the *repercussio* of mode 8, which should have spanned the third from G to b, was also expanded to a fourth when the *repercussa* was shifted up a semitone to c.

When examined in light of these anomalies and exceptions, the modal system of the fifteenth and sixteenth centuries proves to have been considerably more complex in practice than in theory. Only the modes of the first pair are completely regular in all important respects, and even there the tendency to use b-fa instead of b-mi when the melody ascended but one step above the confinal introduced a variable element that could impinge upon the characteristic first species of fourth, implying an alteration to the second species, which was traditionally associated with the Phrygian pair. In every other modal pair there were similar ambiguities, as has been seen, most of them more marked and more explicit. Let us summarize briefly some of the practical implications of the inconsistencies noted.

If, for instance, a melody of the third mode were to begin from the step below the final and to ascend at first only to the fourth above, one would hear the first species of fifth characteristic of the first modal pair. Or if the initial pattern turned between g and c, like the intonation of the third psalm tone, the fourth heard would be of the third species, that linked with the modes on F. And if the melodic line were to span the complete *repercussio* from E to c, this sixth could be perceived as the third species of fifth with the customary semitone below. For the pair of modes from F, the introduction of b-fa changed the species of fifth immediately above the final from the third to the fourth, which was theoretically proper only to the modes of the fourth pair. The plagal member of the latter pair embodied in practice two distinct sources of ambiguity: an ambitus identical with that of mode 1—with which it also shared, like its authentic companion, the characteristic first species of fourth—and a *repercussio* spanning the fourth from G to c, whose third species was that associated with the modes on F.

It was undoubtedly the presence within a single modal octave of such intervallic progressions with potential affiliations to more than one final that gave rise to the theoretical notion of modal commixture—that is, the intentional juxtaposition within a single melody of the species of fourths and/or fifths characteristic of more than one mode. That is undoubtedly why Tinctoris gives as examples of commixture the first mode and the seventh (with the common octave divided both at a and at g; see ex. 3.2a), the second and the eighth, perhaps in part for the sake of symmetry (where the third species of fourth from g to the top of the permissible range of mode 2 is construed as part of the fourth species of fifth characteristic of the Mixolydian modes; see ex. 3.2b), the third mode and the seventh (with the first species of fourth from d to g added above the regular repercussio from E to c; see ex. 3.2c), the fourth with the sixth (juxtaposing the characteristic second species of fourth of the *repercussio* from E to a with the third species of fourth from F down to C; see ex. 3.2d), and the seventh with the fifth and the sixth (by dividing the octave from G to g at c and then adding the fourth species of fifth from C to G below; see ex. 3.2e).[10]

In every instance the departure from theoretical modal norms can be seen as reflecting the importance of the repercussio to the melodic sense of the author. It would seem, moreover, that if we are to understand fully the modal practice of the fifteenth and sixteenth centuries as well as its theory, it is essential that the role played by the *repercussio* be much more carefully and completely defined than it has been thus far, not only for the psalm tones and related formulae where it presumably originated, but also—and perhaps more importantly—in melodic facture of all kinds, both monophonic and polyphonic.

Although much of the evidence has yet to be carefully examined, it is nonetheless already clear, then, that the *repercussio* was regarded during the fifteenth century as an integral and distinctive feature of

Example 3.2 Tinctoris

a. Tonus primus septimo commixtus

b. Secundus tonus octavo commixtus

c. Tertius tonus commixtus septimo

d. Quartus commixtus sexto tono

e. Septimus tonus quinto

et sexto   commixtus

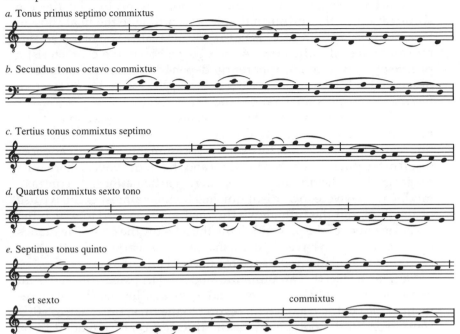

the mode, often taking precedence over its characteristic species when the two did not coincide. Support for this assertion has been emerging steadily from studies, such as those already cited, of the polyphonic repertories of the fifteenth and sixteenth centuries.[11] But if this is so, how is one to account for a work such as the four-voice setting of the Ordinary of the Mass attributed in fifteenth-century sources to Johannes Okeghem and bearing the descriptive title *Missa cuiusvis toni*?[12] The implication of such a designation is generally believed to be that the composition was so conceived that in performance knowledgeable singers would be able at will to lend to the music the characteristics of any of the modes based on the four finals that were conventionally used for classification at the time. That this was the composer's intention is further suggested by his replacement of the usual clefs by a special symbol apparently derived from the so-called sign of congruence that indicates only the final of the mode. Support for this interpretation of the evidence can be found in the testimony of Glarean, who coined the term *catholicon* for compositions of this type and gave as examples only this and one other work attributed to Okeghem, the canon *a3* entitled *Prenez sur moi*.[13]

If in fact this Mass setting was conceived as a large polyphonic work that could be shifted from mode to mode simply by adjusting the solmization of the individual voices according to the final chosen: D-sol-re, E-la-mi, F-fa-ut, or G-sol-re-ut,[14] its realization involved significant practical difficulties. As has been shown, the characteristic profile of a given mode apparently depended in some instances as much on such features as an irregular *repercussa* and a distinctive *repercussio* as on its final, range, and species.

Also important—and variable, especially in a lengthy sectional work like the polyphonic Mass Ordinary—was the choice of pitches for internal cadences. Mode 3, for example, presumably allowed cadences on all of the pitches between the final and the sixth above, whereas its plagal avoided the fifth degree for internal articulations. By contrast, modes 5 and 6 were to be distinguished by their almost exclusive use of the third and the fifth above the final for cadences, to which the plagal member of the pair added the third below the final. The modes on D and on G also have distinguishable, if less markedly distinctive, patterns of cadential preference for internal articulation.[15]

Despite the fact that an authentic mode and its plagal differed from one another not only in *repercussa* and *repercussio* but also in the placement of the central octave with respect to the final, the range of adjacent voices in the polyphony of the fifteenth century tended to be about a fifth apart, thus covering alternately both authentic and plagal ranges. This anomaly was recognized, of course, in the common practice of designating the mode of a composition according to the range of the superius and tenor, which tended to be in adjacent octaves in four-part writing, and regarding that of altus and bassus, which were similarly paired, as subservient. However, modal mixtures—that is, a combination of authentic and plagal modes associated with the same final—could also arise when the ambitus of individual voices exceeded a ninth or a tenth, and this, too, could affect the perception of modal identity.

A careful examination of Okeghem's *Missa cuiusvis toni* suggests to me that Okeghem was aware of these problematic ambiguities. It is possible in fact to argue that his compositional choices involving the range of individual voices, the articulation of structurally significant intervals in the melodic lines, the selection of pitches for internal cadences, and the use of figures calling for the introduction of accidentals were determined in large measure with an eye to overcoming these difficulties, so that an experienced listener would in fact perceive reasonably characteristic examples of any mode the performers wished to follow in accordance with the point of departure taken for the solmization of the pitches around the final.

Obviously the underlying assumptions for such a line of reasoning are that the singers of the fifteenth century were aware, at least subliminally, of the distinguishing features of each of the modes and that they would have made adjustments, either consciously or instinctively, in changing from one final to the next in order to make the selected mode as clear as possible. In view of the manner in which church musicians were generally trained at the time, I believe that these assumptions can be safely made.

It was the composer alone, however, who determined the pitch of resolution for the internal cadences, and it is striking that the greatest number of these close on the fourth degree of the octave associated with the final. In all there appear to be approximately twenty-nine cadential formulae that resolve in this manner, including those that end major subsections in the Credo and the Sanctus.[16] By comparison there appear to be no more than twenty-five cadences to the final itself,[17] only three to the fifth degree,[18] two to the third,[19] and three to the sixth.[20]

The obvious question, then, is why was the preponderant cadential role given to the fourth degree above the final rather than the fifth, for example, which tends to predominate in the modes on D and on F? The answer seems to be not only that the fourth degree was a conventional cadential pitch for all of the modes except 5 and 6 but also, and perhaps more importantly, that it was the one most characteristic for the modal pairs on both E and G. It had the advantage for mode 3 of avoiding the problematic tritone above the confinal B, and for mode 4 of defining the *repercussio*. Similarly, for modes 7 and 8 it pushed into the background the fifth degree (D) with the ambiguity resulting from its implicit reference to the first species of fourth (and fifth) and hence to the first pair of modes, and for the plagal member of the pair it helped once again to define the *repercussio*. At the same time it brought into prominence the fifth above C, which was of the same species as that above G.

But how can one justify the fourth degree as the primary cadential pitch for the modes on F, in which it was not normally used? Perhaps by analogy with the modes on G, with which they shared the characteristic species of fifth when b-flat was used as a signature with F as a final. The fourth degree of the resulting scale is, of course, that very pitch, b-fa, and when taken an octave lower it implied a replication of the third species of fifth that was theoretically the one proper to the third modal pair, even though it was normally avoided in practice because of the tritone contained within it. If it was in fact Okeghem's intention to give prominence to that relationship, it would help to explain the notable emphasis given in the bass part to the fifth below the final. For the modal pairs on both F and G the result is simply a transposition of the characteristic species to the fifth below the final.

For the modes on E the consequence is more ambiguous: the fifth upward from A does not normally contain the semitone immediately above the final that characterizes the species (of fourth and fifth) associated with modes 3 and 4. There are, nonetheless, a fair number of compositions of the fifteenth and early sixteenth centuries with an A final explicitly designated as "quarti toni."[21] Such works offer some evidence that the juxtaposition of E and A as the pivotal pitches for melodic and cadential organization was enough to identify the mode even though the B above the confinal A was generally sung as mi rather than fa. A similar problem arises from the emphasis in the bass on the fifth degree below the final when the latter is on D, but in that case—as will be seen presently—a use of "accidentals"[22] characteristic of the modal pair must also be considered.

The pitch inflections in question are generated first of all by the melodic profile given to the superius, which is striking in its consistent emphasis on the sixth above the final as a primary structural entity. With the exception of the Credo, which gives greater prominence to the fourth degree of the modal scale—perhaps in deference to the melodic patterns associated with the plainchant setting—each section of the Mass opens with a melodic line that turns between the final and the sixth degree above. The result, of course, is to accommodate the characteristic features of each of the authentic modes; it encompasses the *repercussio* of mode 3 and adds to the characteristic fifth of modes 5 and 7 the tone that helps to distinguish them not only from the pair on E but also from the pair on D. For in the latter modes, the sixth degree is b, and when that pitch was linked by itself to the fifth below, as it was by Okeghem, it was usually sung as fa rather than mi. The consequence, in many passages of the *Missa cuiusvis toni*, is to imply a B-fa in the bass part as well, thus making the fifth from G to D identical in species to that ascending from the final itself.

The prominence given in the superius to melodic figures cast within the sixth above the final would suggest that the mode of the work overall should be considered to be authentic. There are other aspects of the composer's use of range that point to a different conclusion, however, such as the previously noted emphasis given to the fourth above the final in the Credo. We can further observe that in the Kyrie, although the tenor rises only to the sixth above the final and takes but one step below, the superius rises to a sixth above the final but adds a fifth below. The tenor has a normal range in the Gloria as well, but the superius covers the total ambitus from the octave above the final to the fourth (and in one instance the fifth) below.

In the Credo both the tenor and superius again venture no higher than the sixth above the final, but in this section the tenor descends as far as the fourth and the superius to the sixth below. In the Sanctus and the Agnus Dei the ranges used for superius and tenor are like those in the Kyrie and the Gloria, with the superius rising to a sixth or octave above the final and adding a fourth or a fifth below, whereas the tenor makes use of an ambitus that could be considered normal for the authentic modes. At the same time the altus and bassus parts generally straddle the plagal octave, with the one or two added pitches for which allowance was made by the theorists of the period.

What conclusion is then to be drawn from these ambital circumstances? Perhaps, if one were to rely on Tinctoris's rule of thumb and identify the mode of a polyphonic work by that of its tenor, it would be that the *Missa cuiusvis toni* essentially lies in the authentic mode based on each of the four traditional finals. It may be, nonetheless, that it was also Okeghem's intention to illustrate modal mixture, combining authentic and plagal ranges in the superius, on the one hand, and placing the plagal Credo as a pivot of sorts between the authentic sections on either side. (This would help to explain the frequent use of the fourth degree as a cadential final in that section in particular.) If so, his title may have an even larger meaning than has generally been understood, in offering the singers the liberty of employing any mode they wished, in both its authentic and plagal configuration, depending upon their choice of final.

Notes

1. Meier's most imposing of many contributions in this area is his *Die Tonarten der klassischen Vokalpolyphonie* (Utrecht, 1974). (An English translation by Ellen S. Beebe with revisions by the author is now available under the title *The Modes of Classical Vocal Polyphony* [New York, 1988].) Powers has made the findings of recent scholarship readily accessible in his admirable article "Mode" in *New Grove Dictionary of Music and Musicians* 12:376–450. See also Leeman L. Perkins, "Mode and Structure in the Masses of Josquin," *Journal of the American Musicological Society* 26 (1973): 189–239, and other items included in Powers's bibliography.

2. For example, according to J.-A. Clerval, *L'ancienne maîtrise de Notre-Dame de Chartres* (Paris, 1899; reprint ed., Geneva, 1972), 105, the "heuriers matiniers" who sang for both the Office and Mass on a regular basis at the cathedral of Chartres were expected to be able to sing Matins in the dark and were subject to fine if unable to sing the Psalter from memory.

3. See the bibliography included by Powers in "Mode," 448.

4. Heinrich Glarean, *Dodecachordon* (Basel, 1547; reprint ed., New York, 1967; an English translation by Clement Miller is available in Musicological Studies and Documents, vol. 6 [Rome, 1965]), and Gioseffo Zarlino, *Le istitutioni harmoniche* (Venice, 1558 and, revised, 1573; reprint eds., New York, 1965 and 1966, respectively; an English translation by Guy A. Marco and Claude V. Palisca of part 3 has been published

as *The Art of Counterpoint* [New Haven, 1968] and by Vered Cohen and Claude V. Palisca of part 4 as *On the Modes* [New Haven, 1983]).

5. By Lucie Balmer, for instance, in her study of *Tonsystem und Kirchentöne bei Johannes Tinctoris* (Berne, 1935), 280.

6. Marchetto da Padova, writing in the second decade of the fourteenth century, allowed no more than a tone below the final for the authentic modes and a tone above the confinal for the plagal ones (see his *Lucidarium*, "treatise" 11, chap. 2, "De tonis quot sint et qui," nos. 378–81, in the edition with English translation by Jan W. Herlinger [Chicago, 1985]), whereas Tinctoris, who was writing about a century and a half later, was willing to add a third to the central octave of the theoretical modes—below it for the authentic modes and above it for the plagal modes (see his *Liber de natura et proprietate tonorum*, chap. 26, "De perfectione, imperfectione, et plusquam perfectione tonorum," 87 in the edition by Albert Seay, Corpus Scriptorum de Musica, vol. 22 [Rome, 1975]; an English translation, also by Seay, is *Concerning the Nature and Propriety of Tones* [Colorodo Springs, 1967]).

7. See, for example, Tinctoris, *Liber de natura et proprietate tonorum*, chap. 11, "De similitudine formationis quinti toni et sexti ac septimi et octavi," 77 in the Seay edition cited above.

8. By Marchetto, for example, in his *Lucidarium*, "treatise" 11, chap. 4, "De formatione tonorum per species," nos. 432–35 in Herlinger's edition cited above.

9. Although the expression is not found with that meaning in the theoretical treatises of the fifteenth century, it conveys a concept of critical importance, and Meier's consistent use of it in *Die Tonarten der klassischen Vokalpolyphonie* and elsewhere is surely justifiable on those grounds.

10. See Tinctoris, *Liber de natura et proprietate tonorum*, chaps. 8–15, 78–80 in the Seay edition.

11. One instructive and relatively early example is Leo Treitler's article on "Tone System in the Secular Works of Guillaume Dufay," *Journal of the American Musicological Society* 18 (1965): 131–69.

12. This title was used in the majority of the sources for the composition: Rome, Biblioteca Apostolica Vaticana, MSS Cappella Sistina 35 and Chigi C.VIII.234; the Petreius print *Liber quindecim Missarum* of 1547; and the treatise *Erotemata musices practicae* of 1563 by Ambrosius Wilphlingseder. Similar but different titles are found in the Wolfheim fragment formerly in Berlin at the Preussische Staatsbibliothek, Mus. MS 40.634 (*Omnium tonorum*) and in Glarean's *Dodecachordon* of 1547 (*Missa ad omnem Tonum*). See the second corrected edition of the *Collected Works*, ed. Dragan Plamenac (New York, 1959), 1:xv–xviii and xxvi; Plamenac also included as plate 5 a facsimile from the Chigi Codex showing the special sign used to indicate the final of the mode.

13. The relevant passage from the *Dodecachordon* (Basel, 1547), 454, was cited by Plamenac in his edition of the *Collected Works* 1:xxx.

14. Plamenac has given a combination of clefs that can be used to achieve the solmization desired, but for the modes on E and on G their use requires a B-flat key signature and a transposition of a fourth upward. It is possible to doubt that singers of the fifteenth century were so completely dependent upon clef signs and to suggest that the location of the final was enough to guide their solmization of the written notes.

15. See table 1 in Perkins, "Mode and Structure in the Masses of Josquin," 200ff.

16. The first subsection of the Credo, for example, ending in m. 33, and the "Pleni sunt" and the "Qui venit" of the Sanctus. Other cadences to the fourth degree include those concluding in mm. 27 and 30 of the Kyrie; in mm. 70 and 82 of the Gloria; in mm.

12, 15, 20, 31, 56, 87, 115, 122, 155, 164, and 174 of the Credo; in mm. 7, 11, 20, 32, 50, 66, 83, and 105 of the Sanctus; and in mm. 4, 12, and 29 of the Agnus Dei. (All references are to the Plamenac edition.)

17. Cadences to the final, in addition to those found at the end of each of the five major sections of the Mass, include those in m. 7 of the Kyrie; in mm. 9, 11, 31, and 50 of the Gloria; in mm. 8, 22, 44, 49, 93, 124, 126, and 130 of the Credo; in mm. 4, 16, 26, 74, and 86 of the Sanctus; and in mm. 16 and 23 of the Agnus Dei.

18. Cadences to the fifth degree are found at m. 15 in the Gloria; at m. 181 in the Credo; and at m. 28 in the Sanctus.

19. Cadences to the third degree are to be seen in m. 6 of the Gloria and in m. 144 of the Credo.

20. Cadences to the sixth degree may be seen at m. 18 in the Gloria; at m. 26 of the Credo; and at m. 102 in the Sanctus.

21. See, for example, the two *Magnificat quarti toni* by Johannes Lhéritier in his *Opera Omnia* (1969), 1:20 and 25, and my comments in the introduction, xxx.

22. Since the choice of pitch in question involves B, mi or fa, both of which were regularly found in the Guidonian hand, and were consequently considered to be *musica recta*, I shall not refer to them here as *musica ficta*. Genuine *ficta* inflections are, in this context, truly accidental with regard to the identity of the modes and would generally have had little bearing on the identification of the mode.

FOUR

Finding the *Soggetto* in Willaert's Free Imitative Counterpoint: A Step in Modal Analysis

BENITO V. RIVERA

Modal procedure in Renaissance imitative polyphony has long resisted definitive explanations. While the theory of mode may sound systematic and logical, its true applicability to sixteenth-century practice continues to be a debated issue. Those who study the repertory often fail to agree in their interpretation of the dense and seemingly uncoordinated modal signals that crowd so many measures of free imitative counterpoint. Indicative of the problem's complexity is the fact that Harold Powers, a leading authority on the history of modal theory, recently raised the question: "Is mode real?"[1]

It seems fair to say that we feel more secure and less hampered by theoretical preconceptions when we deal with the melodic procedure of medieval plainchant. Aware that the chant repertory was in existence prior to the medieval theory of the modes, and aware that the theorists themselves had acknowledged notable discrepancies between precept and practice, we are not surprised or uncomfortable when a chant gradual classified under mode 2 seems to touch many other regions before settling on one firm base.[2] But in Renaissance polyphony we are bothered when we find similar irregularities in its modal procedure. We want to be able to explain every passage in terms of an all-encompassing, consistent modal system. Perhaps we should take more seriously the likelihood of a correlation between the widely ranging modality of some chants and the widely ranging modality of Renaissance polyphony.

One further preliminary observation should be made here that bears directly on the analytical strategy to be proposed in this essay. When a polyphonic composition is based on a recognizable cantus firmus, analysts generally agree that the overall modal procedure of the piece will depend on the modal procedure of that cantus firmus, which in

turn may be influenced by the grammatical and rhetorical idio-
syncracies of the text. In other words, the text can account for modal
irregularities in the cantus firmus, and the cantus firmus can account
for modal irregularities in the polyphonic complex.

Cantus-firmus composition is not the focus of this study. Free imitative polyphony is. But it is well to take cognizance of the former,
because there exists an important analogy between the two. The influential theorist Gioseffo Zarlino tells us that every composition must
have a *soggetto*, which functions like a cantus firmus in some significant ways. Many *soggetti*, those that are not cantus firmi, are generally
not recognizable as familiar melodies; they do not stand out in distinc-
tively long notes, and they are not presented in conspicuous canonic
imitation. They are newly composed, divided into separate phrases,
dispersed, and, we might say, buried to blend into the dense polyphonic complex. They can, however, be brought to the surface through
careful analysis, and I would argue that for a better understanding of
modal procedure they must indeed be brought to the surface and
studied.

Zarlino's observations regarding the nature of the *soggetto* are scattered in several chapters of his treatise, and sometimes they tend to be
confusing and downright contradictory.[3] Nevertheless he is unequivo-
cal about the importance of the *soggetto* in every composition. He writes:

> Before beginning, it is necessary to establish what are the
> essentials of every good composition, those features whose
> omission would result in an imperfection. The first is the
> *soggetto*, without which nothing can be made. . . . The poet's
> *soggetto* is [an incident of] history or a tale. Whether the
> story is of his own invention or borrowed from others, he
> adorns and polishes it with various embellishments as it
> pleases him. . . . The musician . . . also has a *soggetto* upon
> which to construct his composition, which he adorns with
> various movements and harmonies.[4]

The analyst will have no difficulty in identifying the *soggetto* if it is a
borrowed melody, such as the chant *Veni Sancte Spiritus*. But what if
it is a newly invented hidden melody, designed uniquely for a particular motet or madrigal? We can infer from Zarlino that a hidden *soggetto*
will have the same melodic coherence as any cantus-firmus melody.
He has compared the *soggetto* to a story, presumably one that has a
coherent beginning, middle, and end. According to him the hidden
soggetto will proceed in a mode, and the other voices will interact with
that mode:

> When I speak of *soggetto*, I mean the part that is the princi-
> pal one and leader of all the others. . . . It is not necessarily
> the first voice to sound but *that which sets and maintains the*
> *mode and to which the other voices are adapted.*[5]

While Zarlino writes a great deal about canonic *soggetti*, his guidelines apply to a broader field than just canons. He cites as models for
study some of his own motets that display only free imitation, and he
asserts that his observations apply also to canzoni, madrigals, and
"other songs."[6] In all such works he underscores the importance of the
mode of the *soggetto*. When contrapuntal imitation occurs at the distance of a perfect fifth or perfect fourth, where the intervallic structure
of the melody remains unchanged as in the case of a canon, he stresses
a distinction between what he considers the true *soggetto* and what he
considers a subordinate imitating voice, regardless whether this precedes or follows the *soggetto*. The true *soggetto* may only be found in
the voice that presents the mode at the proper pitch level (or its octave
transposition). If a composition is in G Hypodorian and the *soggetto* is
presented canonically at two pitch levels, say in G Hypodorian and a
fifth above in D Hypodorian, the true *soggetto* will be the one in G
Hypodorian. The voice in D Hypodorian will be identified as a distinct accessory and should not be mistaken for the former. To emphasize the importance of this separation, Zarlino cites his seven-voice
setting of *Pater noster/Ave Maria*, partly given in example 4.1. Here, he
explains, the true *soggetto* of the canon lies in the septimus, not the
quintus or sextus.[7] In summary: some voices imitate the *soggetto*, but
strictly speaking they are not the *soggetto* because they do not proceed
at the pitch level of the governing mode.

We can observe how Zarlino's revered teacher, Adrian Willaert,
uses a *soggetto* in free imitative counterpoint. The first forty-seven
measures of his *Veni Sancte Spiritus* (ex. 4.2) will serve as a good model,
in that the underlying chant melody (marked in the example with
dashed slurs) is already established as the *soggetto* of this motet. What
we learn from Willaert's treatment of this chant may be applied eventually in analyses of works with newly composed, hidden *soggetti*. The
following are some fundamental observations:

1. The *soggetto* is divided into complete phrases, and the phrases are
deployed among different voices. Any voice is eligible to be the carrier
of any given phrase of the *soggetto*.

2. Phrase overlaps are avoided. No phrase of the *soggetto* enters
until the previous one has been stated in full.

3. Some phrases of the *soggetto* may be displaced to a different oc-

tave position. See the migration of the *soggetto* to the bass at m. 27. An even more striking instance, not shown in example 4.2, occurs later in this motet when the *soggetto* migrates from mm. 65–69 in the alto, "In labore requies," to mm. 71–76 in the cantus, "In aestu temperies."

4. Text segments are not repeated in the *soggetto*. A phrase such as that in mm. 17–23 of the alto, "Lucis tuae, lucis tuae, lucis tuae radium," is automatically eliminated as a possible *soggetto* phrase.

5. When imitation occurs in some but not all voices, the *soggetto* is generally among the voices involved in imitation. There are interesting rare exceptions to this rule in the present motet, for a good reason. One will notice that the melody of the chant consists, remarkably, of sequentially repeated phrases. The first six phrases follow the pattern *A A' A, A A' A*. If Willaert had subjected each of these *A*'s to imitative development, an intolerable redundancy would have resulted. His solution for the second, third, fifth, and sixth phrases was to forgo imitating the *soggetto* and to treat imitatively the accompanying free material instead. Such exceptions are so special that they do not affect the validity of our general observation.

6. The *soggetto* proceeds in a specific mode, D Dorian in our present example. The accessory counterpoint, such as the tenor at m. 1, transposes the mode to a different pitch level. In analysis the distinction must be maintained between the mode of the *soggetto* and its transposition in the accompanying counterpoint.

7. The *soggetto* may digress to other modes or employ modal irregularities as it unfolds. This is of course a basic license in chant theory, and it in no way conflicts with the preceding sixth observation. Modal displacements in the accompanying counterpoint are one thing, and modal digressions in the *soggetto* itself are another.

Willaert composed a great number of motets that are based on chant melodies. Most of them tend to be more conservative than the four-voice *Veni Sancte Spiritus*, in that they present the chant melody in nonmigrating fashion. There are three works, however, where the chant melody does migrate, albeit only occasionally. In *Magnum haereditatis mysterium* (for four voices) the chant melody appears mostly in the cantus except at the words "nesciens virum" and "omnes gentes venient dicentes," where the tenor takes over. In *Ave Regina coelorum* (for four voices) there is a bit more interchange between cantus and tenor. In *Pater noster* (for four voices) sometimes the chant is treated canonically in the cantus and tenor, and sometimes it appears only in the cantus ("fiat voluntas tua," "da nobis hodie," and "sed libera nos a malo") or the tenor ("debitoribus nostris, et ne nos inducas in tentationem"); the phrase "sicut et nos dimittimus" is treated canonically in the cantus and altus.

Example 4.1   Zarlino, *Pater noster*

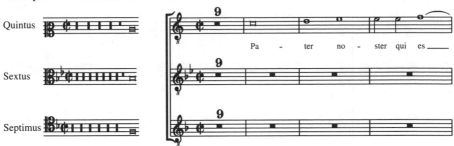

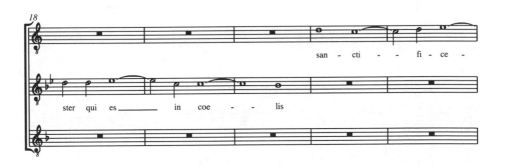

Example 4.2   Willaert, *Veni Sancte Spiritus*

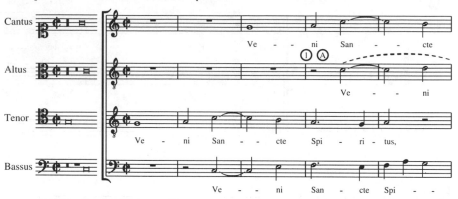

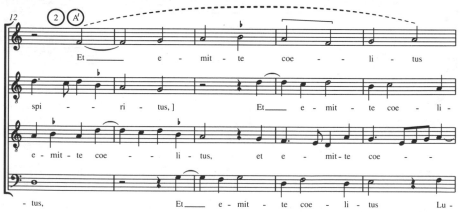

The central object of our analysis is Willaert's five-voice madrigal setting of the sonnet *O invidia* by Petrarch. A brief perusal of the text of the sonnet will reveal its highly emotional and vehement tone:

(1) O invidia, nemica di virtute,
(2) Ch'a bei principi volentier contrasti,
(3) Per qual sentier così tacita intrasti
(4) In quel bel petto, e con quali arti il mute?

(5) Da radice n'hai svelta mia salute:
(6) Troppo felice amante mi mostrasti
(7) A quella, ch'i miei prieghi humili e casti
(8) Gradì alcun tempo, hor par, ch'odi'e refute.

(9) Né però che con atti acerbi e rei
(10) Del mio ben pianga, e del mio pianger rida,
(11) Poria cangiar sol un de'pensier miei.

(12) Non perché mille volte il dì m'ancida,
(13) Fia, ch'io non l'ami, e ch'i non speri in lei:
(14) Ché s'ella mi spaventa, Amor m'affida.

O Envy, enemy of virtue,
you who gladly fight against good beginnings,
by what path did you so silently enter
that lovely breast, and with what art do you change it?

By the roots you have snatched my salvation;
you made me appear too fortunate a lover
to her, who in my prayers humble and chaste
took pleasure for some time, and now seems to hate and
    refuse them.

But no, though with gesture bitter and cruel
at my luck she weep and at my weeping laugh,
she cannot change even one of my thoughts;

no, though a thousand times a day she kill me,
it will not be that I will not love her and not hope in
    her;
for if she terrifies me, Love gives me confidence.

In the first quatrain the desolate lover addresses Envy, complaining

that she has vitiated the affection of his beloved. He then recounts, in
the second quatrain, how the beloved has spurned his supplications.
But in the final sestet he affirms his resolve to endure her cruelty and
continue to love her.

To make the music analysis easy to follow, I first present in example
4.3 what I believe to be the complete *soggetto* of Willaert's polyphonic
madrigal. Only after we have examined this example will we then
proceed to explain the method of reconstructing the *soggetto* through
a study of the polyphonic setting.

As it stands, example 4.3 might at first seem to be in the transposed
Aeolian mode, with the final on D, and with a B-flat signature. In
support of this we notice that in mm. 1–22 a noticeable prominence is
given to the notes D and A, and at m. 69 the first part of the madrigal
closes on the note A. These details all seem to confirm a D-Aeolian
modality. However, Zarlino explicitly singles out this madrigal as an
example of the transposed Hypodorian, that is, G Hypodorian with a
B-flat signature. He maintains that the ending on D should not surprise us because it is possible for a piece to end irregularly on the fifth
scale degree above the true final.[8] A closer look at example 4.3 will
explain Zarlino's classification. As we will soon see in greater detail,
the first part of the madrigal does display a conflict between two modal
areas, one based on D and the other based on G. In the second part of
the madrigal, beginning at m. 70, G becomes the prevailing modal
determinant. This is especially clear in the last three staves of example
4.3, where the *soggetto* peaks on the high G. These three staves by the
way, display a shift upwards to the authentic G-Dorian ambitus. Their
ascent to a higher register is appropriately in keeping with the defiant
tone of the text at this point: "No, though a thousand times a day she
kill me, it will not be that I will not love her and not hope in her; for
if she terrifies me, Love gives me confidence." Thus the madrigal is in
G Hypodorian, with a mixture of G Dorian at the end and a commixture
of D Aeolian in the beginning.

We turn now to analyze example 4.3 in sequence. (The boxed numbers in the example refer to the lines of the sonnet.) In line 1a, which
is sung by the quintus in mm. 3–5, the direct address to "invidia"
suggests D Aeolian by means of a declamation on the notes D and F.
The initial note A of line 1b, though brief and unaccented, can nevertheless be perceived prominently, and this together with the two F's
in m. 9 continues to evoke the modal *harmonia* D–F–A. This does not
last long, however, for at the end of line 1b the downward leap from
G to C introduces a modal contradiction that aptly punctuates the idea
of "nemica" (enemy [of virtue]). Line 2 quickly brings us back to D
Aeolian by outlining the notes D–F–A, but the unstable ending on the

Example 4.3 Soggetto in Willaert, *O invidia*

note E again serves to highlight the hostile word "contrasti." (Although
I am acutely aware of the risk involved here in proposing subjective,
rhetorical interpretations, I do not see how this can or should be
avoided, given the nature of the work and the rhetorical tradition it
stems from.) Whatever the textual interpretation, the cadential pitches
C (m. 10) and E (m. 17) are perceived as the lower and upper neighbors
of the D's in mm. 5 and 19.

Although the text in line 3b clinches a rhyme with line 2 ("contrasti"–
"intrasti"), the grammatical sense of line 3b is not completed until it
reaches the end of line 4a ("così tacita intrasti / In quel bel petto").
Hence Willaert had to find a way of linking the two phrases musically. This he achieved by means of a partial melodic sequence: the
last four notes of line 3b are echoed a step higher in the last four notes
of line 4a.

The high point of the first quatrain is reached in line 4b—Envy has
succeeded in reversing the disposition of the beloved. The musical
soggetto depicts this first climax by reaching the high D for the first
time. Notice the gradual ascent from the B-flat in line 3b, to the C in
line 4a, to the D in line 4b. The modal shift at the end of line 4b from
D Aeolian to G Hypodorian may also be rhetorically linked with the
word "mute" (change).

One more detail in the first four lines deserves to be pointed out.
Line 1b rhymes both verbally and musically with line 4b: "virtute" on
a downward leap of a perfect fifth from G to C, matched by a similar
leap from D down to G on "mute." Likewise notice the verbal and
musical rhymes between lines 2 and 3b: "contrasti" and "intrasti,"
with matching cadences that descend by half step. In the next section
Willaert will not bring out the rhymes in this same way, but he will
design something equally text related.

One aspect that musically unifies the next quatrain, lines 5 to 8, is
that all the phrases end with the note A. This can perhaps be explained
by the fact that these lines have the character of a narrative, wherein
the poet is recounting, or reciting, the events that have caused his
misery. From line 5 to line 7b, the note D occurs repeatedly in the
manner of a reciting tone, and the high tessitura intensifies the deliv-
ery. At the same time lines 5 and 6 continue to undermine the original
D Aeolian by again employing the G that was first raised to challenge
it at the end of line 4b. Consequently the phrase endings of lines 5 and
6 on the note A no longer sound related to D Aeolian, but rather sound
like the unstable second degree of G Hypodorian. It is only at lines 7
and 8, where D and A are emphasized and G is minimized, that D
Aeolian regains prominence.

The second half of the madrigal illustrates an even more volatile psychological situation. Here the lover envisions himself assaulted from every side and has to struggle to prove his constancy. The music accordingly shifts twice from one tonal center to another and back: G (mm. 70–75), F (mm. 81–93), G (mm. 93–111), B-flat (mm. 112–20), and finally G (mm. 120–23). Also, the ambitus of the prevailing Hypodorian mode is again ruptured to include the upper region of the Dorian. Through all this, however, it is remarkable that when the *soggetto* is viewed as a single line of melody, the modal irregularities reveal themselves to be quite sensible. The digression to F in mm. 81–93 is achieved through a perfectly understandable motion to the lower neighbor of the G in the preceding phrase, which subsequently returns to G in m. 93. The shift to B-flat in mm. 112–20, besides constituting a theoretically acceptable emphasis on the third degree above the modal final, is also made plausible by the preceding D's, B-flats, and F in mm. 105–11; and the return to G in the final phrase, which was prefigured in m. 110, requires nothing more than one added step above F.

* * *

After this demonstration of the *soggetto* as a repository of rhetorical and modal meaning, we now turn to a discussion of how the *soggetto* has been reconstructed from the polyphonic setting. In example 4.4 the *soggetto* is again marked with dashed slurs, and the boxed numbers refer to the lines of the poem as in the previous example. The smooth slurs indicate passages that bear an imitative resemblance to the *soggetto*, including rhythmic resemblance or resemblance by melodic inversion. All other markings in the score may be momentarily disregarded.

Phrase 1a in the quintus is identified as the beginning of the *soggetto*, because the pattern of initial entries in all five voices suggests that D Aeolian is the opening mode, and this mode is projected most clearly by the D–D–F–F–D motive. One should of course take note of this motive's appearance in the cantus at mm. 2–4. It was in part for simplicity of analytical presentation that no reference to it was made in example 4.3, where the primary concern was to map out a coherent melodic line. Nevertheless, it is plausible to believe that the cantus entry at m. 2 is compositionally subordinate to the quintus, whose vocal line is the predominant carrier of the *soggetto* in the next few phrases.. Phrase 1b in the quintus is prefigured in the alto starting at m. 6; observe how the rhythm of the alto at the words "nemica di virtute" is identical with that in the quintus.

Phrase 2 at m. 14 in the quintus ("Ch'a bei principi") is also prefigured, this time by the cantus, tenor, and bass starting at m. 10. I did not
identify mm. 10–13 of the cantus as the *soggetto* because the version in
the quintus seemed more melodically satisfactory; the cantus cannot
reach up to an A because of the constraint of its ambitus. Furthermore,
the cantus phrase overlaps with 1b in the quintus. This is not to say
that phrase overlap automatically disqualifies a possible candidate
for *soggetto*. Had a version of the quintus in mm. 14–17 not existed, one
would have been justified in settling for the cantus in mm. 10–13.
(Here I must warn the reader that absolute certitude cannot be a goal
in interpretive analysis; plausibility is.)

Phrase 3a at m. 17 in the quintus is prefigured by the alto and immediately imitated by the cantus. The cantus at m. 17 cannot be the
soggetto; were it to follow phrase 2, it would either entail an awkward
upward leap of a seventh from E to D or, if transposed an octave lower,
bring the melody down to an implausibly low region. Phrase 3b at m.
19 is the most likely continuation of 3a, rather than the transposed
imitations in the other voices. Beginning at m. 26 with the phrase "In
quel bel petto," each of the five voices has a different melody; imitation is completely absent. However, as was demonstrated above, there
is a melodic sequence between the last four notes of 3b and the last
four notes of 4a, thus making 4a the likely *soggetto*.

Phrase 4b at m. 32 in the cantus finally breaks the hitherto unchallenged dominance of the quintus. Indeed, we should examine why the
soggetto is not likely to be among the quintus's three statements of "e
con quali arti il mute." The first, at mm. 29–32, does not bring to fruition the expectation of a climax that was begun in phrases 3b and 4a.
Instead of climbing up to a high D, the quintus here regresses to the
bottom region of the mode. Not only is the second statement, at mm.
32–34, more lifeless than the first, but it even lacks a motivic relationship with the imitative material. The third statement, at mm. 34–37,
can fulfill the function of an acceptable *soggetto*, but again it pales
when compared with its counterpart in the cantus. The initial melodic
shape of the quintus at mm. 34–35 shows a significant deviation from
the model found earlier in the bass at m. 28, in the first quintus statement at m. 29, and in the cantus at m. 32. Notice that in m. 35 of the
quintus the G on the first beat should really have been a C to match the
other voices. But a C at that spot was not possible because of the B-flat
in the alto, thus suggesting that the quintus at this point is a subservient rather than dominating voice. Also notice that in mm. 36–37 of the
quintus, at the words "il mute," the line leaps up a third and then
descends a half step, while in earlier thematic statements of "il mute"

ship within each group we add a value of 1. For example, around the area of m. 19 ("così tacita"), the entrance notes are G, G, F/D, A, four pitch classes, and among these four there are two dissonant relation-downward leap of a fourth.) In other words, the quintus in mm. 34–37 appears to be only a distant cousin, while phrase 4b in the cantus reveals itself as the most convincing continuation of phrase 4a and at the same time as the culmination of an intensification initiated by the bass in m. 28. By now the method of tracing the *soggetto* should be clear, and the remaining sections can be verified accordingly.

Charles Burney, writing in 1789, expressed a cynical dislike for Willaert's music. "The dexterity and resources of [Willaert], in the construction of canons, are truly wonderful, as is, indeed, his total want of melody; for it is scarcely possible to arrange musical sounds ... with less air or meaning, in the single parts."[9] Total want of melody. Little air or meaning in the single parts. Indeed this criticism will seem convincing if one were to examine in isolation each voice part of *O invidia*. Even the quintus tends to chase its tail when it is not actually involved in presenting the *soggetto*. But that is precisely the point that Burney and other critics of his persuasion have failed to appreciate. In Willaert's style a single voice part was never intended to carry a continuous melody. The continuity has purposely been fragmented and hidden, and part of the listener's pleasure lies precisely in finding it.

How does the interaction between the *soggetto* and the other voices affect the mode? Each analyst can of course deal with the topic from a great variety of perspectives. This essay will touch upon only one aspect in order to give an example of what can be done, now that we have the guiding presence of the *soggetto* to provide focus and a secure sense of direction. In the *soggetto* we found instances of modal conflict, especially between D and G as modal centers. One way that the five voices interact to enhance this phenomenon rests on their patterns of entrance at the beginning of every phrase. Medieval and Renaissance theorists appear to have been sensitive to the structural and perceptual importance of entrance notes, because they prescribed rather fastidious rules concerning them. Even when they are not sounded simultaneously, entrance notes seem to create a harmony of their own that affects the mode. In example 4.4 I have circled some text syllables that begin significant phrases of the poem and whose entrance notes have been listed in parentheses above the score. The number immediately following stands for the *level of modal stability*, which is reckoned by counting the number of different pitch classes within the parentheses. Thus in the first group of notes, A/D, D, D, A, there are only two pitch classes, and hence the number 2. The smaller the number, the

greater the modal stability. Furthermore, for every dissonant relation-
we find an upward leap of a fifth or a fourth followed by a descent of
a fourth or a fifth respectively. (The stepwise descent of the bass in
mm. 30–31 and of the first quintus statement in mm. 31–32 masks the
ships, F–G and G–A. Therefore four pitch classes plus two dissonances
give a total of 6. That this reflects Zarlino's view of dissonance in fugal
entries can be verified in part 3, chapter 28, of his *Le istitutioni harmoniche*,
where he warns of a consequent disturbance to the ear.[10]

If we are careful not to carry this quantitative analysis too far—for
it can only be an approximation—we can use it to help substantiate
evidence of a stable beginning and a subsequent rising and fluctuating
of modal dissonance in this madrigal. The area around mm. 53–54,
where all the voices except the cantus are singing "humili e casti," is
striking in its suddenly low index number. The phrase immediately
before that presents a bit of an analytical problem. In mm. 49–53, is the
entrance of "Troppo felice amante mi mostrasti" in the cantus to be
considered part of the group in mm. 44–49, or of the group in mm. 49–
54? In other words, will grouping depend on textual and melodic
affinity or on temporal proximity? I have chosen to heed both parameters and thus relate the passage in question to both groups because
I believe that the conflict between the text grouping and the temporal grouping creates a special type of dissonance that should not be
ignored.

In general the prevalence of entries on D, G, and A in this madrigal
confirms the rivalry between D and G as modal centers. At the end of
the first section, around mm. 65–66, the entries on D, D, B-flat/D/G
would seem to suggest the modal center to be G; and yet the subsequent cadence falls on A, thus strengthening the claim of D as the
center. This rivalry invites the analyst to examine the interaction between entrance and closure, a topic unfortunately beyond the bounds
of the present essay.

Modal analysis, as we have seen here, can be greatly facilitated
through systematic study of the *soggetto*. It clarifies our perspective on
fragmentary melodies and conflicting signals, while illuminating new
regions for exploration.

Example 4.4 Willaert, *O invidia*

92

96

* * *

As stated early in this study, Zarlino writes about the *soggetto* in various sections of *Le istitutioni*, and his scattered statements sometimes create problems in interpretation. Below is a collection of comments that need to be examined in light of one another. An observation is appended after each excerpt to summarize it and to highlight notable ideas.

> 1. (part 3, chap. 26) "The *soggetto* may be one of several kinds. It may be a creation of the composer himself, a product of his genius. It may be taken from a composition of another, fitted to his own and adorned by various parts, as he pleases to the best of his talent. Such a *soggetto* may be of several kinds: it may be a tenor or another part of a cantus firmus composition or polyphonic piece. Or it may consist of two or more parts, one of which may follow another in a fugue or consequence, or be organized in some other manner. Indeed the types of such *soggetti* are potentially infinite in number."

Observation: The *soggetto* may be found in any voice part of a cantus-firmus composition or polyphonic work. The *soggetto* may also be a canon of two or more voices.

> 2. (part 3, chap. 26, immediately following the above) "After a composer has found his *soggetto*, he proceeds to write the other parts in the manner we shall investigate. This process is called by musicians 'making counterpoint.' But should he not have a *soggetto* to begin with, the part that is brought to actuality first, or with which the composer begins his piece, whatever it may be and however it may begin—whether a high, middle, or low part—this shall always be the *soggetto*. Upon it he will adapt the other parts in fugue, consequence, or however he pleases, suiting the music to the words and to the meaning they contain."

Observation: This passage would seem to mean that when when there is no preexisting *soggetto*, the part that enters first will always be the *soggetto*.

> 3. (part 3, chap. 26, immediately following the above) "But when a composer derives his *soggetto* as he composes the parts of a composition, that is, when he derives one voice from another and arrives at the *soggetto* as he composes all the parts together, as we shall see elsewhere, then

that fragment that he derives from others and upon which he subsequently builds the [newer] parts of his composition will always be called the *soggetto*. Musicians call this 'composing by fancy.' It could as well be called counterpointing, or making counterpoint, as one chooses."

Observation: In the process of composition, ideas that arise in one phrase may serve as inspiration for the invention of the *soggetto* in the next phrase. Therefore there is no rule that says the complete *soggetto* must be determined from the very start.

4. (part 3, chap. 28) "When I speak of *soggetto*, I mean the part that is the principal one and leader of all the others accommodated to it in consequence. It is not necessarily the first part to sound but that which sets and maintains the mode and to which the other parts are adapted, whatever their distance from the *soggetto*. See for example my seven-voice setting of the Lord's prayer, '*Pater noster*,' and the angelical salutation 'Ave Maria,' wherein the *soggetto* of the three parts that sing in fugue is the second rather than the first to be heard."

Observation: The *soggetto* is not necessarily the part that enters first in a point of imitation. Here Zarlino seems to contradict what he had said in the second excerpt above.

5. (part 3, chap. 43) "If [the contrapuntist] chooses to write his own *soggetto*, he may find that one part helps him compose the other so that the *soggetto* and the composition are completed more or less together. Therefore, what I call the *soggetto*, as I said earlier, is either the part that is presented ahead of the other parts in the composition, or the part that the composer has conceived first." ("E ben vero, che volendo comporre il *Soggetto* da se stesso, potrà aiutato da una parte della sua compositione comporre l'altra, di modo che tutto in un tempo verrà a comporre il *Soggetto*, & a dar fine alla Cantilena: percioche (si come hò detto altrove) *Soggetto* io chiamo quella parte, che si pone avanti le altre parti nella compositione; overamente quella parte, che il Compositore si hà primieramente imaginato di fare.")

Observation: The *soggetto* is either the part that is presented first or the part that the composer conceives first. The either/or disjunction—I will admit that the Italian is not very clear—seems to resolve the contradiction between the second and fourth excerpts above. It leaves room for different possibilities. What the composer conceives first is not necessarily the voice that is presented first. Zarlino also restates what he had said in the third excerpt, namely, that the *soggetto* may be composed in stages, not necessarily all at once.

> 6. (part 3, chap. 58) "Therefore, any time one wishes to write a piece upon a given *soggetto*, whether a cantus firmus or *figuratus*, or to write a canzone, madrigal, or motet, in which case the composer must invent the *soggetto*, he must first consider in what mode the *soggetto* should be or in what mode he wishes to compose his work. In this way he will know the pitches on which the cadences should fall and can arrange the harmonies in a manner that will keep the end from being discordant with the middle and beginning. Having considered these things, he may begin to write any part he wishes, always beginning on a regular pitch of the chosen mode and observing all the rules given above."

Observation: Canzoni, madrigals, and motets also have newly composed *soggetti*. A *soggetto* must have a modally coherent beginning, middle, and end.

In my analysis of Willaert's madrigal I hypothesized the existence of a melodically coherent and continuous *soggetto*, analogous to the chant melody upon which the *Veni Sancte Spiritus* motet was based. This assumption does not contradict excerpt 1 on page 99. The *soggetto* may occur simultaneously in more than one voice, when there is a canon or imitation at the octave or unison. I have acknowledged such a situation in example 4.4, in mm. 2–4 and 10–13 of the cantus. But when imitation occurs at an interval other than the octave or unison, a distinction must be made between the true *soggetto* and the accessory imitation. This interpretation is clearly supported by excerpt 4. It should also be noted that the positing of a continuous *soggetto* does not necessarily imply that it had to be composed in its totality before anything else in the polyphonic setting. The *soggetto* may very well have been conceived in stages, one phrase in the polyphony serving as inspiration for the creation of the next phrase of the *soggetto*. But at the same time I maintain that in such a procedure the composer was also concerned about preserving the continuity of the complete *soggetto*.

Finally, it would be well to close with this reminder: No one can claim with absolute certainty to have discovered the very *soggetto* that the composer intended. Every interpretation can only aspire to the plausible. Therein, after all, lies the richness of every work of art.

Notes

1. Harold S. Powers, "Is Mode Real? The Arguments from Aron," unpublished paper presented during the Eighth Annual Meeting of the Society for Music Theory (Vancouver, November 1985).

2. Take, for example, the gradual *Deriventur fontes* for the Mass in honor of St. Jerome Aemilian, *Liber usualis*, 1561.

3. In the final part of this study I shall reckon with the complicated aspects of Zarlino's discourse.

4. Gioseffo Zarlino, *Le istitutioni harmoniche* (Venice, 1558), part 3, chap. 26. I am very much indebted to Guy A. Marco and Claude V. Palisca's translation of part 3 of Zarlino's treatise (New Haven, 1968). In subsequent citations I have occasionally taken the freedom of modifying their translation.

5. Zarlino, *Le istitutioni harmoniche*, part 3, chap. 28.

6. Ibid.

7. Ibid.

8. Ibid., part 4, chap. 30.

9. Charles Burney, *A General History of Music*, ed. Frank Mercer (London, 1935), 2:172.

10. "However, it is not praiseworthy when two parts enter at a distance from the *soggetto*, above or below, of a fourth and a fifth, for then they would form a second between themselves. The entrance would then sound dissonant, and one of the parts might begin out of the mode of the composition. Although generally inadvisable, such an entrance is acceptable when the principal *soggetto* of a composition is so written that one part sounds above the other in fugue or consequence. . . . There is some disturbance to the ear when the voices enter" (Zarlino, *Le istitutioni harmoniche*, part 3, chap. 28).

FIVE

Mode and Counterpoint

PETER N. SCHUBERT

The aim of this study is to present a method of analysis that relates counterpoint to mode in Renaissance polyphony. Counterpoint in this context must be understood as embracing the building of all types of interval successions; these in turn can be related to the modes through some kind of interval typology. Although for medieval and Renaissance theorists modes were largely a matter of interval typology, many ambiguities and contradictions exist in historical writings.[1] Concrete instances of the difficulties that can arise are shown in example 5.1. The diagonal G–D fifth (shown with one asterisk) and the melodic G–D fifth (shown with two asterisks) are easy to explain in modal terms as establishing or signifying the seventh or eighth (Mixolydian) modes. It is less clear what modal significance, if any, to assign to the melodic E–B descending fourth (at "?"), the A–D fourth (at "??"), and the C–G fifth (at "???"). If the E in the first of these is seen as an upper neighbor, then it is not part of the outline of an important interval at all. But if we assume that the E–B fourth is a member of the Phrygian pair of modes, does it refer to the third (authentic) or fourth (plagal)? The A–D fourth is a constituent of the first pair of modes and might indicate commixture with one of them. Finally, the C–G fifth can be associated with the fifth and sixth modes.[2] Thus it is possible, depending on the criteria used, to find reference in this brief example to any of the eight modes!

What is at stake here is a notion of modal coherence that goes beyond prescriptions for the last note, a few internal cadences, and the general behavior of melodic lines, as given by most Renaissance theorists. The theorist who came closest to making a system that would shed light on the significance of the puzzling intervals in example 5.1 is the Brescian cleric Illuminato Aiguino.[3] His theories are summarized below, then used to analyze the Palestrina motet from which this example is taken. Finally, Aiguino's principles are used as the basis for an analytical method that makes it possible to demonstrate a composer's control of melodic and vertical intervals throughout a piece.

Aiguino's System

Aiguino wrote two treatises, both on the modes: *La illuminata di tutti i tuoni di canto fermo* (Venice, 1562; hereafter cited as *LI*) and *Il tesoro illuminato di tutti i tuoni di canto figurato* (Venice, 1581; hereafter cited as *IT*). Although the first deals with monophonic chant and the second with polyphony, there is little difference in their treatment of the modes. Because most of the material in the following summary is drawn from the second source, book and chapter references in parentheses are to *IT* unless otherwise indicated.

The most basic principle driving Aiguino's system is that the species (I, 29), especially the species of fifth (III, 47), define the mode. Each of the four species of fifth is uniquely associated with one of the four pairs of modes as defined by the four finals on which they are built. Fifths not built on the four regular finals (D, E, F, and G) are said to be out of place ("estraordinarie"); these are built up only from A and C (since that above B is diminished and hence unusable), and they define the modes on the basis of the semitone positions within them (I, 37–39): the fifth on A signifies the first or second mode, and that on C the seventh or eighth.

Fourths work similarly, defining the modes associated with the finals below which they are built. Those built below A and C are again out of place, or extraordinary, and define the modes on the the basis of the semitone positions within them, the former signifying the third or fourth mode, the latter the fifth or sixth. One exception to this system is the first species fourth. When it falls between D and G it is a constituent of the seventh or eighth modes and signifies those modes when clearly in that context, but otherwise it is extraordinary to the first or second modes on account of semitone position (*LI* II, 21–22). The A–D first species fourth signifies the first or second modes, but can be extraordinary to the seventh or eighth. Thus the first species fourth does not have the same unambiguous meaning as all the other fourths and fifths, having two possible readings depending on context.

The distinction between plagal and authentic can be based not only on range, but also on the direction of the characteristic skips and scale spans. Aiguino presents the skips and scales of the authentic modes ascending, and those of the plagal modes descending (I, 20). He proposes that composers can write pieces with all the voices in the same mode if they use predominantly the skips of that mode, regardless of the range they occupy (II, 32). The use of direction to determine mode is important in situations involving commixture, where the direction of an isolated species helps determine its modal assignment regardless of the context in which it is found.

Thus in Aiguino's system a fourth or fifth unequivocally signifies a mode.[4] This axiom enables Aiguino to systematize commixture with an unprecedented degree of precision. There are two large categories of commixture: perfect, in which the entire octave of the foreign mode is present (*LI* III, 1), and imperfect. Of the latter there are two kinds: major, in which two fifths signify the foreign mode, and minor, in which three fourths signify the foreign mode (II, 25–26, and *LI* II, 18 and 21). Significant species are recognized as those that occur as the outer limits of skips or as turning points (i.e., high and low points).[5] One consequence of the turning-point criterion is that, for Aiguino, any instance of passing outside the octave of the mode results in commixture (II, 28) as long as the foreign mode is confirmed by the presence of its species (otherwise the mode is called superfluous). Note that foreign species are to be used only when the words call for them, and that commixture obtains only when these species occur in sufficiently large numbers in the voice from which the mode is to be judged (usually the tenor).

To return to the puzzling intervals in example 5.1: Aiguino would consider the E–B descending fourth ("?") an important outline, and would call it a species belonging to the fourth mode; the A–D fourth ("??") and the C–G fifth ("???") both would be called extraordinary to the seventh mode. The only important melodic intervals in the opening not yet discussed are the A–E descending fourth (mm. 3–5) and D–G fourth (mm. 5–6) in the lower line. These can be assimilated to the fourth and seventh modes, respectively. This opening duo in a motet by Palestrina thus emerges as a modally coherent whole, consisting of a principal mode, the seventh, and containing elements of the fourth.

Another contribution to an all-embracing modal theory is Aiguino's statement that the species cause the cadences (I, 34).[6] Consequently foreign cadences may be used, when the species associated with them

Example 5.1 Opening duo from Palestrina, *Dies sanctificatus* are present in the piece, because: the words call for them (I, 35); or there is commixture involving the species (II, 25); or the species arise through imitation (III, 38). This linking of the vertical (cadential) and melodic dimensions offers the possibility of a high degree of modal uniformity in a piece. The concept of commixture allows the integration of foreign material, both melodic and simultaneous, in a controlled, orderly way.

Thus Aiguino would permit Palestrina to use a cadence to E on the basis of the fourth mode intervals in the opening, and would insist that the foreign species result from reasons of text affect. What follows is a close Aiguinonian analysis of the whole motet, taking into account not only such species identification as has been done here, but the textual motivation for commixtures and the relation of foreign cadences to foreign species.

Example 5.2   Palestrina, *Dies sanctificatus*

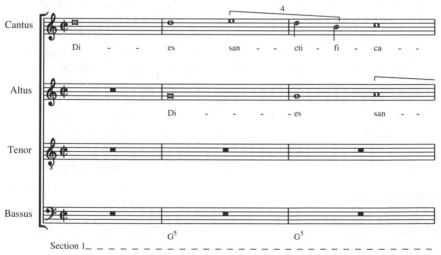

Section 1 (cont.)

Section 1 (cont.)

Section 1 (cont.)

108

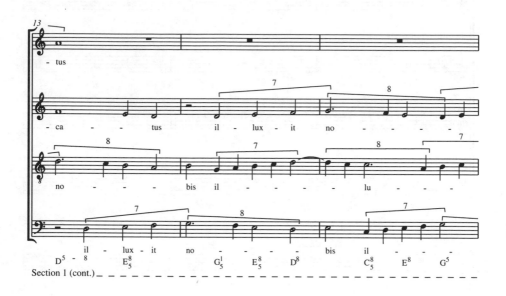

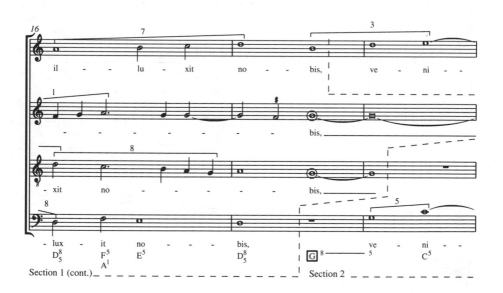

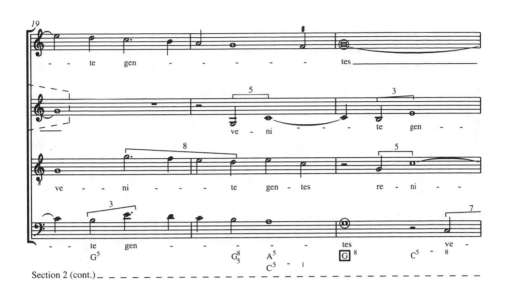

Section 2 (cont.) _

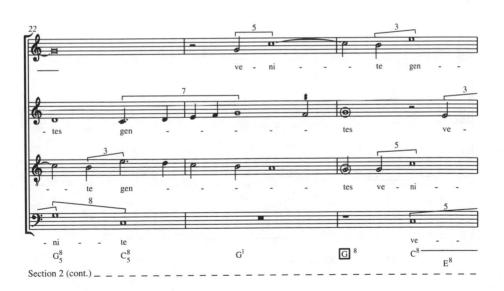

Section 2 (cont.) _

110

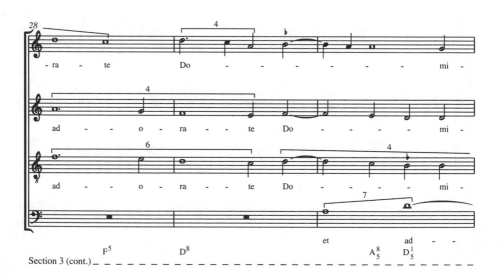

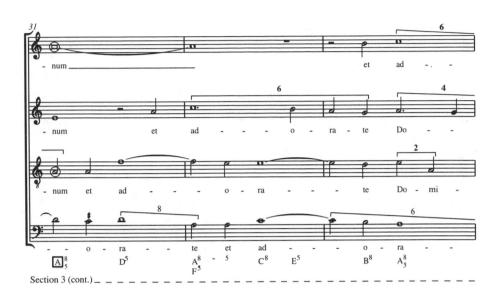

Section 3 (cont.) _

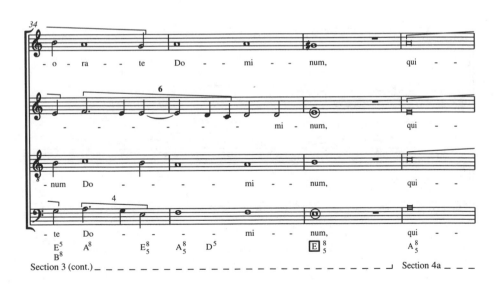

Section 3 (cont.) _ _ _ _ _ _ _ _ _ _ _ _ _ _ _ _ _ _ Section 4a _ _ _

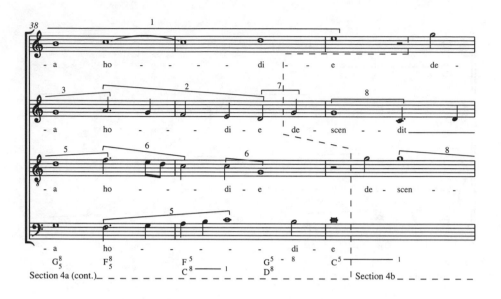

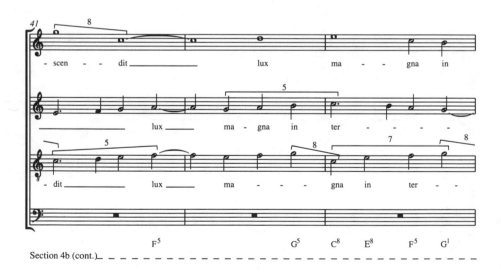

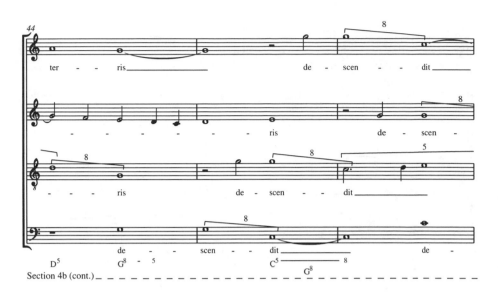

de - - scen - - dit ____ de -

D⁵ G⁸ - 5 C⁵ _____ 8
                    G⁸

Section 4b (cont.) _ _ _ _ _ _ _ _ _ _ _ _ _ _ _ _

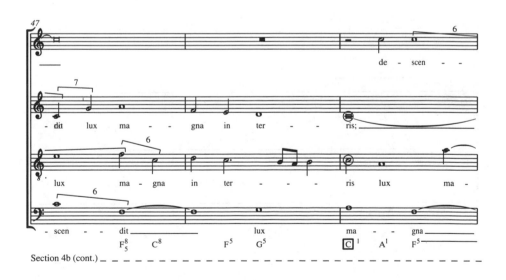

F⁸₅ C⁸   F⁵ G⁵   C¹ A¹ F⁵

Section 4b (cont.) _ _ _ _ _ _ _ _ _ _ _ _ _ _ _ _

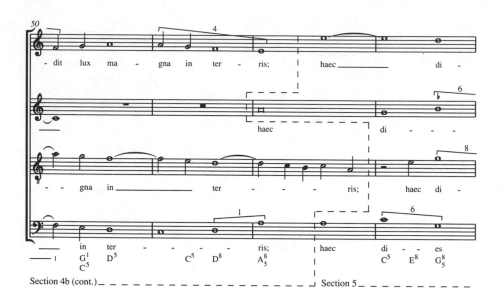

- dit lux ma - gna in ter - ris; | haec ___ di -

___ haec di - - -

- - gna in ___ ter - - ris; haec di -

___ in ter - - - - ris; haec di - - es

G¹ D⁵ C⁵ D⁸ A⁸₅ C⁵ E⁸ G⁸₅
C⁵

Section 4b (cont.) _ _ _ _ _ _ _ _ _ _ _ _ _ _ _ _ _ ⌐ Section 5 _ _ _ _ _ _ _ _

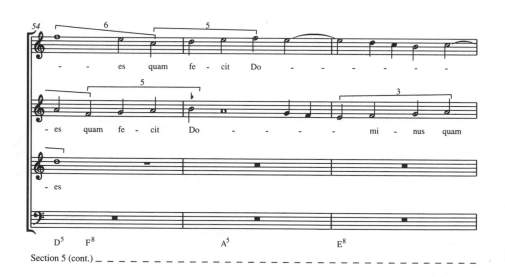

- - es quam fe - cit Do - - - - - -

- es quam fe - cit Do - - - - mi - nus quam

- es

D⁵ F⁸ A⁵ E⁸

Section 5 (cont.) _

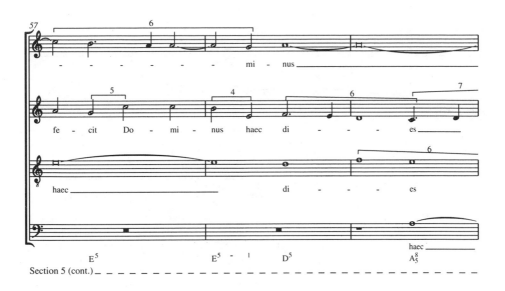

Section 5 (cont.)

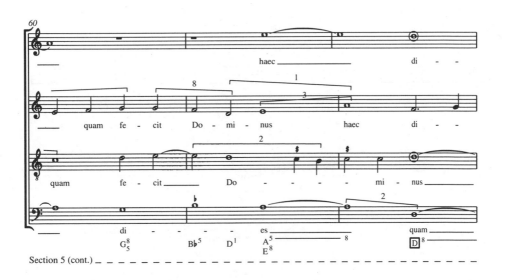

Section 5 (cont.)

Section 5 (cont.) ‒

Section 5 (cont.) ‒ ‒ ‒ ‒ ‒ ‒ ‒ ‒ ‒ ‒ ‒ Section 6 ‒ ‒ ‒ ‒ ‒ ‒ ‒ ‒ ‒ ‒

Section 6 (cont.) ‒

Section 6 (cont.)

Section 6 (cont.)

Section 6 (cont.)

The Motet According to Aiguino's Principles

Dies sanctificatus is the first in a collection of motets labeled with ferial indications but probably not intended for liturgical use.[7] It bears the indication "In Festo Nativitatis Domini," and its text is drawn from two sources: the verse of the alleluia at Mass on Christmas Day (*Liber usualis*, p. 409) and the gradual at Mass on Easter Day (*Liber usualis*, p. 778). The text juxtaposition, facilitated by the common word "dies" and the fact that both contain the word "alleluia," is striking in the contrast of the events that are celebrated. This juxtaposition, unique among the motets in this collection, will be called on to account for the commixture of the fourth (and/or third) mode with the principal mode, the seventh.

The motet is printed in its entirety in example 5.2. For the purpose of discussion, it has been broken into numbered sections on the basis of textual phrases and cadences, as shown below.

Sections	Cadences
(1) mm.1–17 Dies sanctificatus illuxit nobis,	m. 17: G
(A holy day shines upon us;)	
(2) mm. 18–27 venite gentes	m. 27: C
(come, people,)	
(3) mm. 26–36 et adorate Dominum,	m. 36: E
(and adore the Lord,)	
(4a) mm. 37–40 quia hodie	none
(for today)	
(4b) mm. 39–52 descendit lux magna in terris;	none
(a great light comes down to earth.)	
(5) mm. 52–67 haec dies quam fecit Dominus.	m. 67: G
(This is the day the Lord hath made.)	
(6) mm. 67–89 Exultemus et laetemur in ea.	m. 84: G
(Let us exult and rejoice in it.)	

When sections overlap the cadence or there is no cadence marking a section, a dotted line has been run through the parts to show the new text and point of imitation. Melodic interval species are indicated with brackets and labeled with the mode they signify (ascending intervals for authentic modes, descending for plagal). This procedure is modeled on Aiguino's examples of the modes, simple and commixed; species are deemed significant when they are articulated by skip or when they occur as upper or lower turning points. None of Aiguino's examples contains rests, and so no species is identified between the note before a rest and the one after it.

The tenor is contained within the G octave (except for the A in mm. 49–50) and ends "extraordinarily" on B. (In III, 38, Aiguino allows the tenor to end on B, D, or G in the seventh and eighth modes as long as the soprano takes the regular final, G, in its octave.) Such a tenor should be "made perfectly," that is, proceed with the correct species; if it does not, then the soprano must do so and the mode will be judged from it. Table 5.1 shows all the species in the tenor and soprano voices.

The species in the tenor confirm the initial impression of the piece as seventh or eighth mode. This is a tenor as Aiguino believed it should behave, progressing primarily with the species pertaining to the mode. Its range, not the direction of the species, determines that it is authentic. The high A could cause commixture if an important species were associated with it, but this is not the case. Therefore the mode must in fact be called superfluous (*IT* II, 28, and *LI* III, 1).

The cadences that separate sections of the text are indicated in example 5.2: the notes forming the cadential octave are circled, and their note name appears beneath the score in a box. Aiguino defines the cadence as a major sixth moving to an octave for the purpose of marking a textual completion (in the present case, such a completion need occur in only one of the two voices making the cadence).[8] For the time

Table 5.1.

	1st	2d	3d	4th	5th	6th	7th	8th
				Mode				
				Soprano				
5ths	1	1	0+	0+	0+	1	2	3
4ths	*	*	3	4	5	6	2	2
				Tenor				
5ths	1	2	0+	0+	0+	0+	7	8
4ths	*	*	4	6	6	6	2	5
Cadences		1D		1A♭				6G
				1E				3C

*In a seventh or eighth mode context, the first species fourth is interpreted as belonging to those modes. It is impossible to identify the transposed first species fourth in the tenor at m. 61.

+ It is not surprising that there are no fifths of the third through sixth modes in the tenor, since these only occur naturally as E–B and F–C and cannot fall within the G octave. The descending C–F fifth in the soprano (mm. 49–50) is made possible by that voice's excessive range.

being, the reader is to disregard the numerous unboxed letters and numbers printed beneath the score. Table 5.1 also lines up all the cadences of the piece below the appropriate column of species, permitting a correlation of species and cadences. The cadence labeled A(-flat) refers to a transposed Phrygian cadence (on A preceded with B-flat).

Many of the species in the tenor pertain to other modes; some of them cause commixture. Palestrina's tenor may be compared to some examples of commixture confected by Aiguino (see ex. 5.3).[9] These textless illustrative examples in *LI* are given in chant notation (brackets have been added here to designate species causing commixture; neumes are not indicated). Example 5.3a shows a melody with the same range as Palestrina's tenor, but the high A is associated with an ascending D–A fifth and so signifies perfect commixture with the first mode. Example 5.3b shows two ascending E–B fifths embedded in an eighth mode context, causing major imperfect commixture with the third mode, and example 5.3c shows three ascending D–G fourths in a third mode context, causing minor imperfect commixture with the seventh mode. Aiguino notes after this last example that fourths in the other direction would be sol–re and would cause commixture with the eighth mode.[10]

Example 5.3

a. Perfect commixture: the seventh mode with the first (*LI* III, 1)

b. Major imperfect commixture: the eighth mode with the third (*L I* II, 18)

c. Minor imperfect commixture: the third mode with the seventh (*LI* II, 21)

In *Dies sanctificatus* there is minor imperfect commixture with the third and fourth modes (caused by the presence of at least three second species fourths for each). Because the second species fourths occur often and at various points in the text, commixture here does not seem to be related to any specific words in the text, as Aiguino specifies it must be (II, 27). The commixture does cause the two cadences of the third and fourth modes—one the cadence to E with the full stop, and the other the cadence just preceding it on A (the *ficta* in m. 30 is plausible on the basis of imitation with the soprano, which has B-flat by necessity).

The two fifths signifying the second mode cause major imperfect commixture, resulting in the one cadence to D allowed by Aiguino (m. 62). There is also minor imperfect commixture with the fifth and sixth modes, but this commixture never results in a cadence. The single fifth of the first mode would be allowed by Aiguino, who accepts the occasional interval of a foreign mode in long pieces (II, 31).

The preceding brief analysis according to Aiguino's explicit principles shows Palestrina using melodic and cadential commixture of the third and fourth modes in the context of the seventh mode. It is reasonable to assume that this commixture reflects the juxtaposition of the two texts, because the third and fourth modes are associated with the species that can be built above the first notes of the "Haec dies" tune: A (with B-flat), as in the original chant tune, and transposed up a fifth to E. These pitches correspond exactly with the two cadences at the end of the second section (B-flat–A in m. 31, and F–E in m. 36).

It is difficult in the present case, however, to establish the necessary direct parallel between text affect and species so often insisted upon by Aiguino.[11] His definitions of the affects of the third and fourth modes, like those of most other Renaissance theorists, invoke anger and passivity, respectively,[12] emotions not reflected in the text. Furthermore, it is striking that Palestrina introduces the commixture at the beginning of the piece, not at the occurrence of any particularly "loaded" words.[13] The second species intervals in the seventh mode context of the opening do not "paint" a text, but rather foreshadow the middle of the piece (the cadence to E and the "Haec dies" tune). They are embedded in the opening and signify possible future events; in this way they may symbolize the immanence of Easter events in Christmas. The following discussion may help to explicate further the expressive function of the music.

Beyond Aiguino

The picture of the motet given above is like that of a bridge seen from afar: one long span (the tenor) and eleven piers (the major sixth-to-octave cadences at textual completions). All the details of the piece (many of them our favorite notes) are invisible at this analytical distance. However, principles extrapolated from Aiguino's system make it possible to "zoom in" on details that will not only confirm the accuracy of the big picture, but also reveal the extent of Palestrina's technical control over the vertical and horizontal dimensions.

One such extrapolation is to extend the search for species to all voices.[14] It seems likely that if a concern for unity, consistency, and homogeneity exists in the composer's mind, it will manifest itself in all parts. Examining them will reveal whether they corroborate the behavior of the tenor or behave differently in a modally significant way.

It is also possible to extend the notion of cadence. This can be done in two ways. One is to accept as modally significant all instances of movement from the major sixth to the octave, whether or not they occur at the completion of a text phrase. The drawback of this method is that some phenomena still remain invisible, most commonly the many long sections in which cadences are avoided and the so-called plagal cadences in which the final octave is approached obliquely. To find out how the composer controls details, it is necessary to include more types of musical event. The method adopted here is to recognize all mode-defining simultaneities as having weight regardless of how they are approached or where they occur with respect to the text. Thus in the following pages all perfect fifths and octaves are treated as meaningful.[15]

The problem with making a modal assignment to an octave, whether melodic or simultaneous, is that no theorist ever fully codified the many criteria that might be invoked for its assignment. For example, does the simultaneous octave on C denote the seventh or the sixth mode? The note C is an extraordinary final in the seventh and eighth modes because it is the lowest note of the characteristic fourth species fifth. It is also the irregular final of the fifth and sixth modes because it is the upper note of the characteristic third species fifth. Should notes be ascribed to modes on the basis of the species of fifth built above them or below them? It might be appropriate to distinguish types of perfect vertical interval in deciding how to assign them to modes. For instance, the fifth above D is unambiguously Dorian, but the octave can be Dorian or Mixolydian. In the present case, context has been used as a guiding principle, and ambiguous cases are noted.

Table 5.2.   Occurrences of Melodic Species per Mode

	Mode							
	1st	2d	3d	4th	5th	6th	7th	8th
Section 1	1	2		5			11	10
Section 2	1	1	7		6		2	2
Section 3	1	1		5	2	6	1	1
Section 4a	1	1	1		2	2	1	
Section 4b	1			1	3	3	2	10
Section 5	3	4	2	2	5	8	3	4
Section 6			7	7	2	4	10	11

The significant melodic motions in all voices are woven together with all the perfect fifths and octaves between all pairs of voices to form what may be called the "fabric" of the polyphony.[16] In example 5.2 the melodic species have been indicated by brackets and labeled with the number of the mode they signify.[17] The perfect vertical intervals (henceforth PVIs) in the polyphonic fabric are indicated by numbers preceded by the letter name of the lower note.[18]

The following discussion demonstrates that the fabric of each section of *Dies sanctificatus* is consistent and that it differs from that of other sections in some meaningful way. The consistency within sections results not only from the repetition of melodic intervals in the points of imitation, where it is expected, but in material that is appar-

Table 5.3.   Occurrences of PVIs per Pitch Class

	Pitch Class							
	A	B	C	D	E	F	G	B♭
Section 1	3		2	7	10	2	9	
Section 2	3		9	1	2	2	6	
Section 3	6*	2	1	4	4	2		
Section 4a	1		2	1		2	2	
Section 4b	2		6	3	1	5	6	
Section 5	6		4	5	7	2	5	1
Section 6	2	1	13	6	5	1	11	

*Three of these PVIs on A are in a context containing a B-flat.

Table 5.4.

Section	Principal Species (by mode)	Principal PVIs (by pitch class)	Remarks
1	7,8,4	G,D,E	Species and PVIs mixed, balanced
2	3,5	C,G	Few E and A; species and PVIs opposed
3	6,4	A,D,E	No PVIs on G, nor Mixolydian species
4a	None	None	
4b	8	C,G,F,(D)	Few E and A; species and PVIs match
5	6,5,8,2	E,A,G,D	Complex
6	8,7,3,4	C,G,(D)	Species and PVIs mixed and balanced until coda, where there are no PVIs on E

ently freely composed or accompanimental. The discussion below is based on the tallies shown in tables 5.2 and 5.3.[19]

Consistency within sections is manifested in the sharp dropping off of occurrences of certain types of both melodic and simultaneous intervals. Table 5.4 distills the tallies of tables 5.2 and 5.3 by eliminating all intervals occurring roughly less than half as often as those intervals occurring the most often in a given section.[20]

Section 1

Normally one may expect to find rests breaking up major text segments.[21] In the opening duo a surprising rest between subject and verb in the first line calls attention to the fourth mode: the high and low points in the first seven-note phrase outline the second species fourth. There is almost nothing in Renaissance theory about the modal significance of rests, but they are clearly important to the modal picture of this piece.[22]

The soprano and alto continuations over the entrances of the tenor and bass (mm. 10–13) cover octave ranges, but not those of the seventh or eighth modes. Rather, the soprano octave on E and the alto octave on A are instances of perfect commixture. The modes signified by these lines, however, are not perfectly clear. The A–E descending fourth on the word "sanctificatus" in the alto (mm. 12–13), sounded as in the opening duo, signifies the fourth mode, while the descending fifth skip E–A on "dies" signifies the second. The E octave of the soprano line seems divided at A by rhythmic features, with a fifth of the first mode above and a fourth of the third mode below. Rhythm, however, is not a melodic factor in any illustrations of commixture.[23] According to the doctrine of the dominance of the fifth, the soprano and alto octave ranges signify the second and first modes, respectively. It is important to note that these octaves are built on the notes of the point of imitation of "haec dies" (section 5), discussed below.

The PVIs in the opening duo (mm. 1–9) are the fifth and unison on G, the octaves on C and D, and the fifth on E. These are built on the principal notes of the two opposed modes—G, D, and C for the Mixolydian, and E for the Phrygian. (Context determines the ascription of the C and D octaves to the Mixolydian.)

The melodic material of the opening duo is the subject of invertible counterpoint in mm. 12–15. The appeal of invertible counterpoint at the twelfth is twofold for the Renaissance composer. First, it generates a line that is an imitation at the fifth of the original, and can yield melodic intervals of the same species. In this case the bass line in example 5.4b is the transposition down a twelfth of the soprano line in example 5.4a, while the alto is untransposed. The melodic intervals

Example 5.4

a. The original combination

b. The combination inverted at the twelfth

c. The tenor added to the alto and bass of *b*

in the bass are the same as those in the corresponding soprano part. Second, invertible counterpoint at the twelfth maintains the distinction between PVIs and the other vertical intervals that obtained in the original combination (octaves becoming fifths and fifths octaves, so PVIs map onto each other). The simultaneous intervals are labeled between the parts in examples 5.4a and 5.4b, and PVIs are circled, showing the succession 5–5–8–5–1 in the original becoming 8–8–5–8–12. Note the single alteration in the alto (marked with an asterisk). This alteration is made in order to avoid the unacceptable seventh (F to E) that results when the original interval of a sixth (E to C) is inverted at the twelfth.

The second feature allows Palestrina to reinforce the modal commixture by writing the inverted combination along with the original (the tenor and bass in mm. 12–15 repeat the opening combination beginning in m. 4 an octave lower) in such a way that fifths are added to octaves above E, a unison is added to the fifth on G, and an octave is added to the twelfth on C. Such doubled PVIs are circled in example 5.4c.[24]

The omission of the expected rest in the soprano (mm. 17–18) between textual phrases reveals another second species fourth. Like the unexpected rest in the opening phrase, the omission of a rest here points to the basic commixture of the piece.

To summarize: All the melodic intervals in section 1, except for three first species fifths, pertain to either the seventh and eighth modes or the fourth mode; so also do all the locations of the PVIs (G, D, and C for the seventh mode, and E for the fourth mode) except for three intervals on A. It seems that Palestrina is setting up an opposition between the seventh and eighth modes on the one hand and the fourth mode on the other, with a minor reference to the first and second modes.

Section 2

The sudden absence of seventh and eighth mode melodic intervals and third and fourth mode simultaneities sets section 2 apart from section 1 (see table 5.2). Ascending third species fourths (G–C and eventually C–F) are introduced here in a way that ties them in with the opening of the piece; the first one comes in the bass as an enrichment of the contrapuntal combination of the opening (soprano D–E over alto G). The D–E step in m. 18, however, is part of an ascending fourth from B, which is reduced to the simple B–E fourth in subsequent repetitions when sounded in parallel thirds with the G–C fourths (see examples 5.5a–c; note that example 5.5b can also be understood as the retrograde of example 5.5a). The third species fourths may account for the PVIs on F, especially as these are transposed down a fifth in mm. 24–25 (to C–F in the bass). While the modes represented by the species in parallel thirds are the fifth mode and the third, the PVIs are mostly on G and C (the C octaves and the single D octave have been assigned to the Mixolydian). The PVIs are thus predominantly Mixolydian in contrast to the Lydian and Phrygian species.

The presence of the simultaneities of the Mixolydian and the authentic (rising) species may be called for by the joyous affect of the cry "venite gentes."[25]

Example 5.5

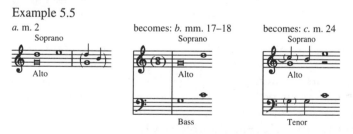

Section 3

The principal species here are the plagal (descending) versions of those in the preceding section; they may, along with the B-flat, symbolize adoration.[26] Some PVIs (those on A with B-flat and those on E) emphasize the Phrygian and transposed Phrygian modes; there are even two octaves on B, a fairly rare occurrence in this piece and in Renaissance music in general. Other PVIs (those on D and on A with B-natural) emphasize the Dorian mode. These PVIs do not readily fit into a scheme, but the complete absence of PVIs on G and of any seventh or eighth mode species marks the contrast between the joy in the previous section and the adoration here. The cadence to E is marked by rests in all voices, underscoring the importance of the Phrygian modes in this piece.[27]

Section 4a

This section functions as a link: no species or vertical intervals are stressed here. It may be thought of as a transition in which no mode reigns, but which is designed to regain the eighth mode.

Section 4b

Eighth mode fifths (descending on the word "descendit") dominate this section melodically, and the PVIs of this section are for the most part on G and C. Melodic species and PVIs both indicate the seventh and eighth modes. Not only is this section the most uniform in modal terms, but it contains the highest pitch of the piece, marking it as a joyful climax. The PVIs on F may be the consequence of the third species fourths observed earlier, or the "descendit" motive transposed down a fifth.

At the end of section 4b the soprano finally articulates a descending second species fourth, which links the octave on E noted in mm. 11–12 with the fourth mode. The first species fifth in the bass and the PVI on A anticipate the first and second mode intervals in mm. 62–65. The omission of the expected rests in m. 52 in these two voices reaffirms the importance of the pitches E and A.

Section 5

Palestrina uses the head motive of the chant but breaks off after the fourth note and composes his own continuation, de-emphasizing the second mode of the original chant and outlining several third species fourths.[28] This section is, in marked contrast to the preceding one, the most complex. More different pitch classes receiving PVIs are presented here than in any other section (their distribution also drops off more smoothly here than anywhere else, as shown in table 5.3). Third species fourths and fifths in the alto, fourth species fifths in the tenor and alto, and first species fifths in the bass give each voice a different thrust and the whole section a great density.

It is possible that the descending first species fifths refer to the original chant mode (the bass line is commixed with mode 2). Because of this, one might be tempted to consider the bass the voice from which the mode is to be judged.[29] The relatively large number of PVIs on A and D can be linked to this second mode influence, which is confirmed by the fact that there are more first and second mode melodic species in this section than anywhere else in the piece, and by the cadence to D in m. 62. Though there is no rest between sections 5 and 6, the mensuration change has been taken as an equivalent structural break. Consequently the A–E descending fourth in the bass (mm. 66–68) has not been tallied.

Section 6

The homorhythmic "et laetemur" exploits the same combinations that were used in "venite gentes" (section 2): the G–C fourths (or G–C descending fifths) in parallel against the B–E fourths. As in the opening section, the mix of species and PVIs is balanced between the Mixolydian and Phrygian modes. The cadential cliché of the tenor (a descending scale span from E to B) takes on special meaning in this commixed context. In the measures after the soprano cadence in m. 84 there are no PVIs on A or E: the coda confirms the Mixolydian mode.

Tables 5.2 and 5.3 show the six sections with the melodic intervals and PVIs that figure in each. From these tables it becomes apparent that Palestrina's control of the tiny elements discussed above (melodic and vertical species) serves not only to articulate sections, but also to reflect the juxtaposition of the texts; for example, the integration of the second species melodic intervals into the coda with no corresponding PVIs can be interpreted as a symbol for sadness overcome by joy.

An apparent anomaly is the notable presence of modes 5 and 6, at odds with the interpretation of the piece as a drama taking place between the Mixolydian and Phrygian modes. One way to integrate them would be to assign those fifth and sixth mode intervals that are G–C fourths to the Mixolydian through the notion of Marchetto's common fourth or that of the psalm-tone *repercussa*.[30] In both of these typologies, however, the G–C fourth is associated with the eighth mode; thus its assimilation would necessarily obliterate the distinction between authentic and plagal that has been successfully maintained. Further, accepting the G–C fourth as a definer of the Mixolydian modes means disregarding its species, a step totally at odds with the system.

Motives

The method of analysis suggested by Aiguino's theories and used above, permits the modal identification of all important intervals (whether vertical or horizontal) and their correlation within phrases. As we have seen, certain species of interval recur a great deal in *Dies sanctificatus*, suggesting an overall unifying idea: commixture of the seventh mode with the third and/or fourth modes. But this system of interval identification can lead even further. If vertical intervals are always presented through the same melodic motions or, conversely, if melodic motions always have the same intervallic accompaniment, they may be termed motivic.

A two-voice combination abstracted from the opening duo is shown in example 5.6a; this combination can be seen as the result of using the first two notes of the opening soprano melody both to precede and to accompany the second, as shown in example 5.6b. This combination occurs repeatedly in the opening duo, suggesting that the order of the two intervals is not as crucial to their identity as the voice-leading motions by which they are connected (a third up against a step down). Example 5.7 shows a reduction of the opening (the G unison is not part of the motive).

The opening can be viewed in two ways—as the combination of melodic lines whose species suggest the Mixolydian modes,[31] and as a succession of vertical intervals signifying two different modes, Phrygian and Mixolydian. The latter reading requires the elimination of many surface features, as demonstrated in example 5.7. Rhythmic features, including the rest in the alto voice, are not shown; the integrity of the phrases is dissolved, and even the outlines of melodic species disappear.

In this light, imitation is exposed as no more than a means of disjointing the surface of a contrapuntal combination. In the opening duo, for instance, the A–D fourth of the soprano and the D–G fourth

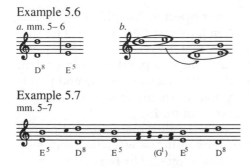

Example 5.6

a. mm. 5–6   *b.*

D⁸   E⁵

Example 5.7
mm. 5–7

E⁵   D⁸   E⁵   (G¹)   E⁵   D⁸

Example 5.8

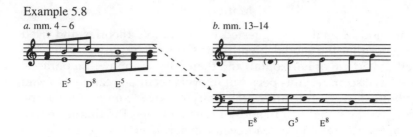

a. mm. 4 – 6   *b.* mm. 13–14

of the alto (shown beamed in example 5.8a) are merely ways into and out of the D–D octave and E–B fifth in mm. 5–6. The validity of this reading is corroborated by the fact that the corresponding notes in the two parts are not accompanied the same way: the first A of the soprano is sounded as part of an imperfect consonance, but the corresponding D of the alto makes a perfect consonance. The G of the alto is part of an imperfect consonance also, so both first species fourths have one end point de-emphasized. In this way of looking at counterpoint, the significance of any note in a melody may change with its accompaniment.

This may be the most important aspect of the horizontal-vertical relationship revealed in this study: when significant melodic end points and significant simultaneities are not the same, the notion of embellishing tones is called into question. The notes in example 5.8 between A and D do indeed "pass" in the sense of proceeding by step in one direction, but they are not "passing tones" in the sense of auxiliaries connecting harmonically supported principal tones. On the contrary, the A, by being harmonized with an imperfect consonance, is less important than the B, which is part of a perfect fifth. Horizontally the outline is of a first species A–D fourth with passing B–C; the succession of PVIs, on the other hand, emphasizes the second species E–B fifth, to which the A is auxiliary.

The same point can be made with respect to "neighboring" tones. The soprano E in m. 2 is like the A in the example above: it is harmonized with an imperfect consonance, making it a clear auxiliary embellishing the G–D fifth, but it is also the end point of an important species, the E–B descending fourth. Note that some of the end points identified in the motet as modally significant are in fact dissonances (e.g., the alto C in m. 11 or the tenor A in m. 15).

Since invertible counterpoint at the twelfth maintains all perfect intervals, it will leave undisturbed the conflict between the mode suggested by the melodic species and that suggested by the vertical intervals. Example 5.8b shows the positions of the fifth and octave reversed (the E^5–D^8 succession becomes E^8–G^5), and the imperfect intervals at the end points of the species are maintained as in example 5.8a. Example 5.8b is one of many variants and derived forms of the interval succession in example 5.6b to be found throughout the motet.

One such variant appears in the opening of the "haec dies" section, presented first transposed down a fifth in the alto and bass (ex. 5.9a) and then at the original pitch level in soprano and tenor (ex. 5.9b). Two other variants, which are like mirrors of each other, are the alto-bass combination shown in example 5.10a (the G octave "enclosed" between two A fifths in mm. 59–61) and the bass-soprano combination of mm. 10–11 (the A fifth "enclosed" between two G octaves) shown in example 5.10b. Finally, the same succession acts as a link into the last section (ex. 5.11). There is of course a great deal more to be said concerning Palestrina's motivic work in this motet, especially in terms of linear transformations, but the focus of this study is the two-voice combination that permeates the fabric of the piece and the commixture of the seventh mode with the third and fourth modes that it implies.[32]

Example 5.9

a. mm. 52–53

Alto

Bass

A^8 C^5

b. mm. 52–53

Soprano

Tenor

E^8 G^5

Example 5.10

a. mm. 59–61

Alto

Tenor

A^5 G^8 A^5

b. mm. 10–11

Soprano

Bass

G^8 A^5 G^8

Example 5.11

mm. 67–68

Tenor

G^5 E^8

Bass

Conclusion

The method of analysis presented here is rigorous and limited. It does not take into account any mode-defining intervals from other typologies such as those described by Meier as "Western-ecclesiastical" (psalm tones, the *octo beatitudines*, etc.), which clearly play a role in Renaissance music. It may not apply equally well to the music of other composers. The relationship between music and text, so important to this method, is compromised in cases where text underlay or *musica ficta* are in doubt, or where contrafactum or parody techniques are used. Finally, PVIs and melodic species are vitiated as mode-defining elements in cases of sequential procedures.

Nevertheless, the method makes it possible to observe the fine detail work that a composer may devise in order to differentiate sections within a piece or tie them together: he may use melodic species and PVIs to oppose each other (as in section 2 of *Dies sanctificatus*) or to reinforce each other (as in section 4b). Such analysis provides an objective means for discussing modal uniformity in pieces without text, it suggests that notes that first appear to be passing or neighboring tones may have modal importance, it establishes a clear relationship between mode and the technique of invertible counterpoint, and it shows how a contrapuntal combination, used motivically, can express a modal idea.

At its most general, this analytical technique exemplifies one way in which a single set of historically grounded principles can be used as the basis for a well-defined "modern" method of analysis that sheds light on hitherto unnoticed musical features.

Notes

1. While only fourths and fifths are used in abstract mode building, thirds and a sixth are used as well in defining psalm tones. Psalm-tone criteria are often interwoven with the fourths and fifths of the abstract modes, resulting in multiple identifiers for some modes. The "common" fourths of Marchetto da Padova are also sometimes added to the abstract fourths and fifths. The acceptance of B-flat in the Lydian modes further expands the number of types of interval used to define the modes.

2. The C–G fifth is a transposition of the F–C fifth using B-flat. Tinctoris explicitly mentions the use of the fourth species fifth C–G as a constituent of the "irregular" Lydian mode in *De natura et proprietate tonorum*, chap. 48 (Corpus Scriptorum de Musica, vol. 22, ed. Albert Seay [Rome, 1975], 100–101).

3. See Peter N. Schubert, "The Fourteen-Mode System of Illuminato Aiguino," *Journal of Music Theory* 35, no. 2 (Fall 1991). For more on Aiguino, see idem, "The Modal System of Illuminato Aiguino" (Ph.D. diss., Columbia University, 1987), esp. 4–11.

4. The exceptions to this neat formula are the first species fourths mentioned earlier (p. 104 above), and the unfilled-in F–C fifth with B-flat in the signature, which

can, under certain circumstances, be read as third species. See Schubert, "The Four-teen-Mode System."

5. The criteria of skips and turning points are not explicitly stated, but they are obvious from Aiguino's examples. In this respect his examples are like the examples of Marchetto da Padova and Johannes Tinctoris.

6. Cadences in psalms and canticles are treated separately by Aiguino (III, 1–6 and 28–32) and are not relevant to this study.

7. *Motecta festorum totius anni* (Rome, 1563); ed. Casimiri from the 1590 edition (Rome, 1939), 3:1. Anthony M. Cummings, in "Toward an Interpretation of the Six-teenth-Century Motet," *Journal of the American Musicological Society* 34 (1981): 43–59, cites the "marginal relevance" of many motets, especially those with "centonate texts," to the liturgy. He further points to the "complex polyphonic procedures inappropri-ate to some liturgical contexts" found in many motets. He concludes that motets were performed in the Mass or in nonritual contexts (e.g., the pope's dinner).

8. On Aiguino's definition of cadence, see Schubert, "The Fourteen-Mode Sys-tem."

9. The principal mode in each of these examples is expressed in the traditional way, by range and final, with the characteristic skips articulated both ascending and descending. The skips of the mode causing commixture, by contrast, are consistently ascending for authentic modes and descending for plagal modes. (It must be added that the first mode in the first of these examples is called "irregular," presumably because the octave on A suggests the irregular final A. Aiguino's concept of irregu-larity does not enter into this study.)

10. The full caption surrounding this example reads: "Dimostratione del terzo tuono commisto con il settimo, per i diatessaron re sol. [example] Et per contrario i diatessaron diranno sol re, & verrà commisto con l'ottavo"(*LI* II, 21).

11. Many references to the relation between text and music can be found in Schubert, "The Fourteen-Mode System."

12. Aiguino says that the third mode "increases animosity and wrathfulness, fright-ens enemies, inflames and kindles the spirit to rage." ("Il terzo tuono accresce animosità, & iracondia, spaventa l'inimici, infiamma & accende il spirito all'ira.") The fourth mode, on the other hand "is to be agreeable, because it is admirably suited to rest and tranquility." ("Il quarto tuono per appiaceri, perche si accomoda mirabilmente al riposo, & tranquillitade" [*IT* I, 30].) For other examples, see Harold S. Powers, "Mode," *New Grove Dictionary of Music and Musicians* 12:397–99. Zarlino says both the third and fourth modes are appropriate to lamentation because they are often used in conjunc-tion with the first species fifth A–E; see Powers, "Mode," 410.

13. Other motets in Palestrina's 1563 collection that have similar features are no. 2, which begins with the same 5–6–5 combination on G but with different conse-quences, and no. 35, which has a similar opening melody with different consequences.

14. Aiguino's uncertainty as to the voice from which the mode is to be judged is the cause of many chapters on the subject. He makes many prescriptions but does not say how to interpret an unclear situation. See Schubert, "The Fourteen-Mode System."

15. While Aiguino seems to believe that the octave is modally significant in both vertical and horizontal presentation (he uses the phrase "compositione del tuono" for both), he does not do likewise for the fifth. Fourths are not used here as meaningful simultaneities because in Aiguino's system they do not define modes as strongly as fifths, and they are not consonant.

16. The notion of the "fabric" of the piece is contemporaneous. See the essay by Edmond Strainchamps in the present volume, pp. 198 and 202, for the words "tela," "intrecciatura," and "tessitura."

17. The end points of melodic skips of a fourth or fifth are usually turning points

as well, but there are two cases of a fifth outline containing a second and a fourth (the alto in m. 61, and the bass in mm. 63–64); in these cases both the fifth and the fourth have been counted. Marchetto da Padova's lengthy discussion of significant intervals buried within the fifth in his *Lucidarium* (trans. by Jan W. Herlinger [Chicago, 1985]), "treatise" 11, chap. 4, no. 231ff.) invokes commixture and attests to the importance of skips that are not also turning points. When the outline of a sixth has been filled in with stepwise motion through a fourth and a skip of a third (e.g., "magna in terris" in the soprano, mm. 43–44), the fourth has not been counted, even though there is some argument for its being articulated by the skip at one end. Two fourths in the same direction, one filled in, the other by skip, occur in mm. 38–39 in the tenor. This is made acceptable in part by the repeated C; in the present case both intervals have been counted. Species of fourth or fifth wherein one end point is likely to be sharped to provide a leading tone and thus produce a nonharmonic interval (e.g., the alto in mm. 70–72) have not been counted. There are two intervals whose species are difficult to establish: a D–A descending fourth in the soprano (m. 29) has been read as second species on the basis of the B-flat that follows; and an E–B descending fourth in the tenor (m. 61) has been counted as first species on account of the C-sharp. Melodic stepwise motion through an octave (e.g., the alto in mm. 43–44) has not been counted because modal significance depends on how the octave is divided; a division may be apparent through durational or metric accent, but rhythm is not used as a factor in the present typology. A situation in which a metric factor might be invoked is that in which one of the end points of a fourth or fifth falls on a weak semiminim (e.g., the tenor in m. 15). Such species have been tallied in the present analysis, although it might be argued that their weak position makes them less significant (they are few enough that their omission would not skew the results). Species whose end points fall on durational values smaller than the semiminim are not counted.

18. All intervals larger than an octave are reduced, and duplications are not noted. (Thus, for instance, a fifth and a twelfth over a C would appear only as C^5.) Also not indicated are voice exchanges that duplicate an interval already noted (e.g., mm. 45–46, where fifths and octaves built on C are exchanged). PVIs lasting only a semiminim are counted if they fall on the strong part of the minim; otherwise (e.g., the alto and tenor D unison in m. 22) they are not counted.

19. The method of counting melodic species within sections is straightforward. There are three cases, however, in which a significant fourth crosses a sectional boundary: the soprano B–E fourth in mm. 17–18 (assigned to section 2), the alto D–G fourth in m. 27 (assigned to section 3), and the alto D–G fourth in m. 39 (assigned to section 4a). The numbers identifying these species have been placed on the side of the dotted line within the section to which they have been assigned.

The method of counting PVIs is simply to tally occurrences of letter-named notes as they appear beneath the score, regardless of whether the notes are the bases of fifths or octaves or both. Direct repetitions and the addition of one interval class (e.g., $C^{5–8}$ in m. 21) are not counted separately; PVIs on the same pitch class are only counted when another interval (perfect or imperfect) intervenes. There are instances of PVIs that act as eliding points between sections. If they are cadential, they are assigned to the previous section. The only PVI that elides and is not cadential is in m. 52, where the PVI on A is shared by both "-ris" and "haec"; this interval has been assigned to phrase 4b.

20. The exception to the "factor of two" rule is the first section, where the five fourths of the fourth mode lie closer in proportion to the intervals of the seventh or eighth modes than to those of the first and second modes. They have been included in table 5.4 because of their importance throughout the piece.

21. E.g., Gioseffo Zarlino, *Le istitutioni harmoniche* (Venice, 1558), part 3, chap. 50.

Aiguino warns repeatedly against the use of too many rests, saying that they cause "annoyance" ("fastidio") in singer and listener alike (e.g., I, 32, and III, 52).

James Haar, in his "Cosimo Bartoli on Music," *Early Music History* 8 (1988): 55, has found some other contemporaneous remarks on rests. In book 3 of his *Ragionamenti accademici* (Venice, 1567), Bartoli says that he greatly admires the compositions of Gombert because "they have been so arranged that all the parts sing continuously, with few rests, pressed together in close imitation, riveted together" ("ha tenuto uno ordine, che tutte le parti continoamente cantino, con pochissime pose, anzi fugate, strette serrate, inchiodate l'una nella altra" [fol. 36v]).

Nicola Vicentino, in *L'antica musica ridotta alla moderna prattica* (Rome, 1555), book 4, chap. 7, warns against singers breathing where they should not, in order not to "impoverish the harmony."

22. Guido d'Arezzo defines the *distinctione* as a phrase marked by a place to breathe, and says that the last note of a phrase should be the final or confinal. This remark in his *Micrologus* (ed. Joseph Smits van Waesberghe [1955]), chap. 15, is quoted by Franchino Gafori in *Practica musicae* (Milan, 1496), book 1, chap. 8. Aiguino, also referring to plainchant, says that the intervals occurring before the first rest are important enough ("hanno tanta forza") to determine whether the mode is authentic or plagal, regardless of what happens after the rest. The chapter is titled "Della dignità delle neume avanti la prima pausa come appare ne i libri Romani" (*LI* III, 19).

23. Examples of commixture in Marchetto, Tinctoris, and Aiguino (except his one example in *IT*) are all in plainchant.

24. The relationships in example 5.4c may be summarized as follows: the bass is to the alto as the soprano was to the alto in m. 3 (albeit inverted at the twelfth), but it is to the tenor as the alto was to the soprano in m. 4.

25. A theory that links affect with direction is Vicentino's classification of intervals as *incitato* (vigorous) or *molle* (weak). In his typology the ascending fourth is vigorous, especially the third species fourth, with the semitone at the top of the span. The second species fourth, because the semitone is at the bottom of the interval span, is mixed. The descending fourth, on the other hand, is weak (*L'antica musica*, book 1, chap. 32). See also Vincenzo Galilei's *Dialogo della musica antica e della moderna* (Florence, 1581), 76. Both are discussed in D.P. Walker's *Studies in Musical Science in the Late Renaissance* (London, 1978), 64–65.

26. Bernhard Meier, in his *The Modes of Classical Vocal Polyphony* (trans. Ellen S. Beebe [New York, 1988]), mentions *Dies sanctificatus* as an example of the cadence on mi used in connection with the affect of "servitude, humility, and lowliness," noting the attendant melodic descent as well (273–74).

27. Compare no. 36 in the same collection (1563) for another Palestrina motet containing a full cadential stop in the middle.

28. The interested reader will want to compare Palestrina's own *voci pari* setting of *Haec dies*, no. 15 in the *Motectorum liber secundus*, 4 voices (Venice, 1581; edited by Casimiri from the 1604 edition, Rome, 1941). This motet is based on the chant tune and Palestrina maintains the second mode.

29. Contemporaneous corroboration for choosing the bass as the voice from which to judge the mode can be found in Vicentino's *L'antica musica*, book 3, chap. 15, fol. 48r, and Galilei's *Dialogo*, 76.

30. References to ut–fa as definer of the eighth psalm tone can be found in Heinrich Glarean's *Dodecachordon* (Basel, 1547; reprint ed., New York, 1967), part 1, chap. 13, and Zarlino's *Le istitutioni harmoniche*, book 4, chap. 15, among many others. Marchetto discusses "common" G–C fourths in the eighth mode in *Lucidarium*, "treatise" 11, chap. 4, no. 197–99.

31. In a different context the D octave and the first species fourths could all be

called Dorian. The contextual elements of the opening are the notes G and D, which when paired define the seventh and eighth modes, and the G final.

32. Although the interval succession in which one voice moves by whole step and the other by minor third is constant in all the examples given, there are two exceptions to the statement that they all represent the same commixture. The fifth-to-octave motive transposed so that the fifth falls on A does not always signify the same modal commixture as the untransposed version. When there is a B-flat in the environment (as in m. 53 or m. 61), the A–E fifth does indeed signify the third or fourth mode. When, however, there is B-natural (as in mm. 10–11 or m. 52), the A–E fifth signifies the first or second mode. In the latter two instances the commixture is of the seventh mode with the first or second mode. It might be possible for the analytical method to absorb these species into the overall picture through the notion of some kind of "substitute interval" (akin to the notion of substitute chords), which is beyond the scope of the present essay.

SIX

The Cavalier Ercole Bottrigari and His Brickbats: Prolegomena to the Defense of Don Nicola Vicentino against Messer Gandolfo Sigonio

MARIA RIKA MANIATES

DRAMATIS PERSONAE

ERCOLE BOTTRIGARI (Bologna, 24 August 1531–San Alberto di Piano near Bologna, 30 September 1612). Bolognese patrician and learned humanist with a wide circle of literary and scholarly associates. Three published works on music, *Il Patricio* (1593), *Il Desiderio* (1599), and *Il Melone & Il Melone secondo* (1602), plus unpublished polemical tracts as well as translations of ancient classical sources. Friend and tutor of Anniballe Melone.

ANNIBALLE MELONE (d. Bologna, mid-April 1598). Dean of musicians ordinary to the Senate of Bologna and successful music teacher. Member of Bottrigari's domestic circle, his pupil in ancient Greek music theory. Copied nearly all his tutor's works. Contested authorship of *Il Desiderio* (1594 under the anagram "Alemanno Benelli," and 1601 posthumously under his own name). *Il Melone & Il Melone secondo* written at his request.

GIOVANNI MARIA ARTUSI (Bologna, ca. 1540-45–Bologna, 18 August 1613). Music theorist and canon regular of San Salvatore in Bologna. Polemicist on behalf of Gioseffo Zarlino, and against Vincenzo Galilei, Claudio Monteverdi, and Bottrigari. Attacked *Il Patricio* in the *Seconda parte dell'Artusi* (1603). Published *Il Desiderio* under the name of Anniballe Melone (1601), and threatened to do the same with "Gli Meloni." Heir to Melone's papers.

GANDOLFO SIGONIO (fl. Bologna, ca. 1570–1590). Brother of the renowned Modenese humanist Carlo Sigonio (1524–12 August 1584). Follower of Zarlino. Close friend of Melone. Unpublished letters written to Melone in Bologna (1571–74). Wrote the *Discorso* against Don Nicola Vicentino.

137

* * *

The above list hardly does justice to the complicated network formed by the friendships and animosities among the persons in this story. Because this network is responsible for the subtexts discernible in the main sources (Gandolfo Sigonio, *Discorso intorno à' madrigali e à'libri dell'Antica musica ridutta alla moderna prattica da D. Nicola Vicentino;* and Ercole Bottrigari, *Il Melone secondo overo, considerationi intorno al Discorso di M. Gandolfo Sigonio sopra i madrigali, e i libri dell'Antica musica ridutta alla moderna prattica da D. Nicola Vicentino*),[1] we begin with a detailed briefing of the main and the secondary characters in order to understand better the motivations, both explicit and implicit, behind the writing of these texts.

* * *

One of two sons sired by a cultivated Bolognese aristocrat, Ercole (along with his brother Giovanni Galeazzo) was recognized as legitimate in 1538 and taken into the Bottrigari household, where he received a very fine private education from the leading scholars and intellectuals of Bologna. In addition to classical languages, literature, law, mathematics, physics, astronomy, architecture, and perspective, the young Ercole also studied practical music under Bartolomeo Spontone (1530–92), choir director of San Petronio and family friend.[2] In 1542, the eleven-year-old Ercole, by all accounts a precocious youngster, was named a page to the papal legate in Bologna, the distinguished Venetian humanist and statesman Gasparo Cardinal Contarini (1483–1542), and elevated by the aged prelate to the rank of Knight of the Holy See and the Lateran Militia.[3] Man and boy, he proudly retained the title of cavalier until his death.

Ercole married a young woman from a rich family of Bologna in 1551 and settled down to a life of private humanistic study and public civic service. This mode of existence was interrupted in 1574 by a legal quarrel over some property rights with his wife's family, a squalid quarrel during which Bottrigari dueled with his adversary's son and was wounded in the arm. Having refused to cede an inch of ground or honor to settle the dispute, Bottrigari moved in 1576 to Ferrara, where he spent the next eleven years at the splendid court of Duke Alfonso II d'Este. Here Bottrigari began to amass his library and to study ancient Greek music theory. Though we have no documentary evidence, it seems likely that the Estense patronage of both Lodovico Fogliano (d. ca. 1539) and Don Nicola Vicentino (1511–ca. 1576-77) had something to do with the new emphasis in Bottrigari's catholic humanist interests.

Upon returning to Bologna in 1587, after an acceptable truce with his relatives was patched up, Bottrigari settled in the country estate of his family at San Alberto di Piano. At this point Anniballe Melone enters the picture. However one may assess Melone the man, it is clear that Melone the retainer prompted much of the written work on music theory produced by Bottrigari. There followed a quiet period of studying, tutoring, writing, and conversing with humanist friends, a period marred only by the aftermath of the mysterious publication of *Il Desiderio* in 1594 under the fictitious name "Alemanno Benelli." From 1598 to 1604 Bottrigari was embroiled in a nasty public argument with Giovanni Maria Artusi, at the center of which lay Melone's private papers. The dispute petered out in 1605, and Bottrigari continued his work on ancient source material until 1610, the date of his last manuscript.

* * *

Although it is true that Bottrigari almost always wrote in a sharply argumentative vein developed from his own perception of the Platonic dialogue,[4] it is possible to separate the purely polemical writings from all the rest. The former came into being because of the activities of Artusi, whom one scholar has called Bottrigari's archenemy,[5] and therefore they will be described later in the context of that controversy. But first let us divide Bottrigari's output into published and unpublished works, beginning with the nonmusical ones.

In the earliest published corpus are a translation of Ptolemy's description of the celestial sphere (1572) and an edition in 1576 of a little-known work on rivers by the great fourteenth-century jurist Bartolus de Sassoferrato.[6] About ten years later Bottrigari published a translation, mainly by Cosimo Bartoli (d. ca. 1572), of the works of the French mathematician Oronce Finé (d. 1555).[7] Among the surviving manuscripts there is a treatise completed in 1598 on the construction of theaters based on Vitruvius, an Italian translation of Pseudo-Aristotle's *De audibilibus* (1606), and a study (15 July 1609) of the Pythagorean legend of the hammers.[8] To this list we should add the less significant works on Italian literature, among them an anthology of poetry,[9] the fourth volume in a series initiated in Venice by Lodovico Domenichi (fl. ca. 1550) and whose editors included the printer Andrea Arrivabene (d. after 1570) and the *poligrafo* Ludovico Dolce (d. 1568). Bottrigari's collaboration in inventing a nine-syllable poetic line is documented in a treatise bearing his name and dedicated to him by his close friend, the poet and historian, and later cavalier, Ciro Spontone (d. after 1638).[10]

The single unpublished treatise on music is the erudite and virtually impenetrable study of the ancient and modern modes, "Il Trimerone de fondamenti armonici, overo lo essercizio musicale" (1599).[11] As noted above, the published corpus—and Bottrigari's troubles— began with *Il Patricio, overo de'tetracordi armonici di Aristosseno, parere, et vera dimostratione*, printed in 1593 in Bologna by Vittorio Benacci. The name that opens the title, in true Platonic fashion, alludes to the target of its contents, the illustrious Neoplatonic humanist and philosopher Francesco Patrizi da Cherso (1529–97).

Patrizi, though a staunch antiperipatetic, lived the peripatetic life of an itinerant humanist. After studying with Francesco Robortello (1516–67) in Padua, he shuttled between Venice and Cyprus in the 1560s. When Cyprus fell to the Turks in 1571, he went to Modena. And in 1578 he was invited to teach at the University of Ferrara, where he stayed until his death. Bottrigari was in Ferrara at this time and became good friends with Patrizi. The latter wrote and published on a wide spectrum of topics, and his firmly stated views made him stand out from the humanist herd of Aristotelians in the northern climes of Italy.

The particular work that interests us is *Della poetica*, printed in Ferrara by Vittorio Baldini in 1586. Patrizi's original intention was to publish ten "decades" on poetics, each decade divided into ten books. However, only "La deca istoriale" and "La deca disputata" were completed in time to be printed in 1586 under the omnibus title given above. The other five extant decades, written between 1587 and 1588, remained in manuscript.[12] This work, then, was a typically wide-ranging, indeed rambling treatment of ancient Greek poetic theory and practice. It may seem small-minded of Bottrigari to have zoomed in on one minor element—Patrizi's description of the Aristoxenian tunings in the seventh book, "Dell'armonia, compagna dell'antiche poesie," of "La deca istoriale."[13] But in Platonic fashion, at least in Bottrigari's interpretation of it, what may have been a minor fault became the pretext for a lengthy and learned disquisition on the divisions of the tetrachords into the three genera (diatonic, chromatic, and enharmonic) as described by various ancient writers. And though he criticized Patrizi's brief account of Aristoxenus, Bottrigari meant his correction to be taken with the good grace typical of a pupil of Plato.

Patrizi's reaction is not known. However, Artusi leapt, somewhat belatedly, into the breach in 1603 with the Venetian publication by Giacomo Vincenti of the *Seconda parte dell'Artusi overo delle imperfettioni della moderna musica*.[14] This is a treatise remembered today more on account of its ongoing criticism of the madrigals of Monteverdi (carried over from *L'Artusi* of 1600) and the related quarrel with "l'Ottuso Academico" (whose identity is still unknown) than for its main reason for existing.[15] The latter can be adduced from the second section of the

book, the fifteen "Considerationi musicali." It is indicative that in
these "Considerationi" Artusi spends more time reprimanding
Bottrigari, whom he constantly calls the author of "the opinion" ("il
parere"), and less in justifying Patrizi. And Artusi's original intent is
all too clear from the venomous sarcasm in the uncalled-for letter of
dedication and the letter to the readers. Having dedicated his book "to
the Most Illustrious Lord, the Cavalier Ercole Bottrigari, Most Worthy
Patron," Artusi goes on to explain why:

> Thus you and any other honest lover of the merits and very
> fine qualities of Mr. Patrizi could see, as if in a mirror, how
> deceived are they who, without cause, are impelled to cen-
> sure him so that the world discerns him as more ignorant
> than learned and esteems them as luminaries, although in
> the universal judgment of all intelligent people they are
> incapable of putting pen to paper.[16]

A little later Artusi enjoins Bottrigari to act as a true cavalier should
by protecting the cause he has placed in his hands for the sake of the
deceased (i.e., Patrizi, who died in 1597). Artusi also alludes to a letter
of rebuttal sent to him by Bottrigari entitled "Ante Artusi" ("Against
Artusi"). Artusi could not resist a pun, and in this case suggests un-
kindly that the letter should have been called "Post Artusi."

In the letter to the "friendly readers," Artusi launches into a defense
of Patrizi by pointing out that the humanist introduced the rigorous
subject of harmonic science only as an aside to his main topic, the
accommodation of harmony to poetry by the ancient Greeks. He goes
on to describe how Anniballe Melone, the author of that fine book *Il
Desiderio*, had perused Patrizi's work and pondered on the discrepancies with the "Demostrationi" (i.e., Zarlino's *Dimostrationi harmoniche*
[Venice, 1571]). Melone then resolved to contact his friends to learn
their opinion ("il parer loro"), among them Artusi. This sham digression goes directly to the point—a slighting reference to the author of
"the opinion," who responded to Melone's wishes by publishing *Il
Patricio* in 1593. Artusi of course gives the title in full in order to include Bottrigari's word "parere," and invites the readers to read his
"Considerationi" to find out how pardonable are the things said by
Mr. Patrizi and how base and false are those said by the author of "the
opinion."

At the end of this letter Artusi reminds the readers that, driven by
the love of truth, he has already told the world that *Il Desiderio* was
written by Melone and "not by others, who may bay the moon if they
wish."[17] Moreover, the author of "the opinion" insults not only Patrizi
but also Melone, whose service and friendship he has thereby slighted.

This man has no shame, for he insists that he is the author of *Il Desiderio* and of the exposition of some problems by Aristotle, "the original copies and sketches of which are still in the hands of Melone's heirs" (i.e., Artusi).[18] Artusi's final thrust has to do with the nasty and completely unwarranted things said of him by the author of "the opinion." Insofar as the said author claims that Artusi stole material from him in the first part of his treatise of 1600, Artusi must conclude that this unfortunate man suffers from a persecution complex. Compassion notwithstanding, Artusi warns the readers against him by quoting the proverb "Da mal Corvo mal ovo," a vulgar version of the biblical aphorism "By their fruits ye shall know them."

* * *

The material in Artusi's dedication and letter to the readers presents us with four issues that, under detailed scrutiny, take us into the wider context of events and personalities. First, we must not be misled into dismissing the acrimony of Artusi's prose as symptomatic of the received mode of public argumentation. True, quarrels often became quite violent; Artusi's manner, however, was considered vituperative even for adversarial decorum at that time. It seems that in one copy of this treatise the official censor signed his name at the end of the "Considerationi" with a notation to the effect that the author had to identify himself precisely on the title page; furthermore, "all the more personally offensive passages, including the entire sarcastic letter of dedication to Ercole Bottrigari and the letter to the reader, are struck out in this copy with a single stroke of the pen."[19]

Artusi seems to have had a penchant for bizarre and flamboyant humor and, like an eager pugilist, he was prancing in his corner even before the bell had rung—singular behavior in a priest, one might say. He joined the opulent order of San Salvatore as a youth in 1562 and took his solemn vows in 1563. He apparently came from a poor family. For this reason Bottrigari, in a fit of anger in 1604, made a snide remark about his vocation. This remark is dismissed by Gaetano Gaspari, a latter-day supporter of Bottrigari, though he does add that the sacerdotal virtues of "modesty, gentleness, and humility" were unfamiliar to Artusi.[20]

A devoted disciple of Zarlino (1517–90), Artusi felt it his duty to defend his master's voice against all comers, and he did so in no uncertain terms. In 1588 and 1590 he wrote two satirical pieces (now lost) against Vincenzo Galilei (ca. 1520–1591), whose *Dialogo della musica antica e della moderna* (Florence, 1581) sternly repudiated Zarlino and also insinuated that he had delayed the printing of Galilei's work and appropriated material from it.[21] The story of the hatred between Galilei and Zarlino, fascinating in its own right, is not part of the present inquiry, aside from the fact that Zarlino brought out his *Sopplimenti musicali* (Venice, 1588) to refute the accusations and criticisms leveled against him by his wayward pupil, and that Galilei replied to his erstwhile mentor's chiding in his *Discorso intorno all'opere di messer Gioseffo Zarlino da Chioggia* (Florence, 1589).

Is it an accident that Artusi should have published certain pamphlets in 1588 and 1590? Be that as it may, what is left of these missives shows Artusi on his mettle. The earlier of the two is called *Lettera apologetica del Burla Academico Burlesco al R.ᵈᵒ D. Vincentio Spada da Faenza.*[22] In the bits quoted by Bottrigari from the beginning and the ending, one can assess the general tenor of the whole. At the start, "il Burla" ("Prank") asks Galilei in mocking tones what he thinks he has accomplished and then supplies the answer: "A buzzing, a fracas, a rumbling so loud that finally my brains have been scrambled because of you."[23] The ending begins on a more serious note, in that the writer recommends the example of good composers (Willaert, Rore, Merulo, and Porta) and refined stylists (Cicero, Livy, and Caesar). But after warning Galilei against living in ignorance, Artusi fires his parting shot: "Rest assured that your lips have scarcely touched the waters of the Parnassian fountain. Well then, I leave you to God. From our Chancery, 14 January 1588. Your most cordial of friends, Prank."[24]

The second letter, *Trattato apologetico in difesa dell'opere del R.ᵈᵒ Zarlino da Chioggia*,[25] paraphrases the title of Galilei's 1589 polemic. This time there can be no doubt as to the recipient. Indeed, in a lengthy gloss on the title Artusi names both Zarlino and Galilei, refers to himself as the Lord Cabal and the "Academico Infarinato" ("floured academic"— i.e., academic with a sprinkling of learning), and graces Galilei with a multitude of quasi-honorific titles only to end with a list of the defects in his *Discorso*. In the letter proper, Artusi becomes more abusive, calling Galilei "ignorant, obstinate, and malicious" because in complete disregard of his just critics, he continues to propose the same "blunders, dreams, chimeras, and fantasies."[26]

So much for Artusi's polemical style. In the prefatory remarks to the *Seconda parte dell'Artusi*, he dwells on Bottrigari's insult to the dead. But we must temper our impression of Artusi's self-righteous indignation by recalling that in 1593, when Bottrigari published *Il Patricio*, Patrizi was still alive. Melone died in 1598, a year before the second edition of *Il Desiderio*. In order to cast Bottrigari's motives in the worst possible light, similarly unctuous sentiments about Melone's death were summoned up by Artusi in both the dedication and the letter to the readers in his edition of *Il Desiderio* in 1601. Artusi's accusation that Bottrigari took advantage of Melone's demise is the second issue that requires investigation.

Il Desiderio had three printings under three different names in Bottrigari's lifetime: "Alemanno Benelli" in 1594, Ercole Bottrigari in 1599, and Anniballe Melone in 1601.[27] How and why did this happen? It is impossible to say with any certainty because none of the extant relevant documents comes from disinterested parties. The best we can do is to follow the evidence as it pertains to the chronology of the events, bearing in mind that each writer has a vested interest in our favorable judgment.

In the 1599 edition of *Il Desiderio*[28] there is a third-person account of the events leading up to this printing and to that of 1594 in a letter to the readers written by Bottrigari. Here is what he has to say. Because it was Melone who instigated the writing of the dialogue and so enjoyed it, Bottrigari introduced him as an interlocutor under the anagram "Alemanno Benelli," the other speaker being Gratioso Desiderio, one of the characters in Zarlino's *Dimostrationi harmoniche*. After detailing the many other works he prepared for his friend, Bottrigari then resumes the narrative to relate how Melone was seized by the desire to become better known through the printing of this dialogue and the two *Melone* pieces as well. Though indifferent to the charms of publication, Bottrigari succumbed to Melone's pestering. Some details about a lost copy and a Venetian printer are inserted at this point to lend verisimilitude to the tale. We are given to understand that at first Bottrigari intended to stay behind the scenes ("star dietro la tavola") with an anonymous printing in order to gauge the reception of the work. But because the name of an author was mandatory, it was decided to publish under the disguise of the anagram.

After 1594 (says Bottrigari) Melone began to press him to reveal the identity of "Alemanno Benelli" and, before receiving his sanction, told the secret to some friends. When Bottrigari heard of this "he was rather disgusted and had an argument about it with Melone."[29] Melone apologized in some letters and again asked permission to come forward. Once more, Bottrigari procrastinated as tactfully as he could. But Melone nagged him until he gave in. The result was the 1599 edition of *Il Desiderio*. We are left with the impression that although Melone did not live to see it, his spirit is somehow embodied in this publication.

In 1601 Artusi brought out *Il Desiderio* posthumously under the name of Anniballe Melone. Though printed in Milan, this edition is dedicated to the Senate of Bologna,[30] an insult that Bottrigari could hardly ignore. In the dedication Artusi stresses the many years of service given by the late Melone to the Senate, and links these activities with the subject matter of the dialogue. Considering the temerity of those who dare to attribute the work to another author, thereby seeking to rob the dead man of his honor, he concludes that it would be both proper and pious of the Senate to defend the deceased.

The letter to the readers expands on this issue in a less formal and hence more pointed manner. Artusi describes the blameless, docile, and congenial personality of Melone, traits evident in his cultivation of and homage to many important learned persons, including the Illustrious Cavalier Ercole Bottrigari. It is not true, declares Artusi, that Bottrigari wrote *Il Desiderio*. He does not doubt that Bottrigari read every single page of it and corrected it in places, for Melone was so timid he would do nothing without Bottrigari's advice. As proof Artusi cites a letter written by Bottrigari to Melone, in which the writer acknowledges receiving the exposition of a problem by Aristotle and even gives his opinion of it. Moreover, Melone did not make two copies of the dialogue to send to Venice because both of the original sketches, in Melone's hand, now belong to his heirs (i.e., Artusi). Artusi concludes that these facts constitute irrefutable evidence for the authorship of Melone.

At this point Artusi examines the curious inconsistencies between the 1594 and 1599 printings. This passage deserves to be transmitted in full, for it poses questions that are still pertinent today:

> Now, if Bottrigari had written this dialogue (which is not true), why did he not print it himself the first time, but rather allowed it to be published under the name Alemanno Benelli? And if he had conceded this to his friend so as to please him, then why, no sooner had his friend died, a friend from whom he had received so much homage and so much service, did he allow it to be published under his own name, thus robbing his friend of his honor? Why should Bottrigari remain behind the scenes in order to hear what the world says about such a deed? For no other reason than that he knows it is Melone's labor and work, and not his own.[31]

Artusi closes the letter with a promise to ascertain exactly who made the translations claimed by others (i.e., Bottrigari in the 1599 edition) in his forthcoming defense of Patrizi (i.e., *Seconda parte dell'Artusi*, 1603). Artusi did not fulfill this promise but only repeated his suspicion about the authorship of the commentary on the Aristotelian problem. Perhaps he became absorbed in his dispute over modern music with "l'Ottuso Academico," or intended to prepare a separate tract on the translations. Or was he exercising caution? We cannot know. We can, however, conjecture about this turn of events. But in order to do so, we need to fit together some more pieces of the puzzle. One of these concerns the Melone papers and what they contained, another the role played by Melone, and yet another the polemical activities of Bottrigari.

To set the record straight, we need to know that there are two extant unpublished but undoubtedly circulated letters of rebuttal written by Bottrigari in the third person. The earlier of the two, finished 31 December 1602, is an indignant reply to Artusi's 1601 edition of *Il Desiderio*: "Lettera di Federico Verdicelli à'benigni, e sinceri lettori in difesa del Sig.ᵉ Caval.ᵉ Hercole Bottrigaro, contra quanto in pregiudicio della reputazione di lui ha scritto un certo Artusi in due sue lettere, una per dedicatoria all'Ill.ᵐᵒ Senato di Bol.ᵃ, l'altra à i cortesi lettori sotto la data di Milano à 12. di luglio 1601, & stampate in Milano appresso gli stampatori archiepis."[32] The other was completed 26 February 1604. Its title notwithstanding, it is an ill-tempered and tempestuous refutation of the *Seconda parte dell'Artusi* (1603): "Aletelogia di Leonardo Gallucio à benigni e sinceri lettori, per la difesa del M. I. Cav. Hercole Bottrigaro contra quanto ha scritto lo autore delle Inconsiderationi Musicali. Lettera apologetica."[33]

A third open letter, the "Antartusi," has been lost. As we have seen, Artusi ridiculed it in the prefatory material to the *Seconda parte dell'Artusi* in 1603. Bottrigari was thus impelled to discuss its contents briefly in the "Aletelogia di Leonardo Gallucio" in 1604. It seems likely from Bottrigari's description that the "Antartusi" was written between the appearance of the first part of *L'Artusi* in 1600 and the third edition of *Il Desiderio* in 1601. Bottrigari gives two reasons why he wrote this letter: first, to defend *Il Desiderio* against criticisms made by Artusi; and second, to disclose the thefts of material from "Il Trimerone," that is, Artusi's plagiarism of the portion at the end of the first dialogue and of most of the second dialogue as well.[34]

A glance at the contents of *L'Artusi* shows that there are only three allusions to *Il Desiderio*, one cited to corroborate a point and two treated as errors.[35] These cavils do not seem worthy of Bottrigari's perturbation, and surely not his use of the strong adjective "calunniose" (calumnious). Did Bottrigari indeed suffer from a persecution complex? This possibility seems plausible in light of the alleged thefts from "Il Trimerone," thefts that in Bottrigari's view amounted to an almost complete appropriation of this work. One eminent scholar has concluded that the charge of plagiarism is untrue, even though it is clear that Artusi had read "Il Trimerone" and emulated it. He concludes that Bottrigari was envious of Artusi's high level of scholarship.[36] Perhaps envy is too strong a word, and at any rate an emotion difficult to document. Vanity is another matter, for we find ample evidence of Bottrigari's intense pride in his nobility of birth, of spirit, and of intellect. After all, he was capable of starting a twelve-year feud over property rights by deliberately leaning against a disputed wall in the presence of his enemy, and of electing to live in exile rather than submitting to the peace bond exacted by the Bolognese authorities.

But the charge of plagiarism is not so easy to dismiss with respect to the section on the modes in the "Ragionamento secondo" of *L'Artusi*. Indeed, it is less likely that Bottrigari was prey to jealousy (a sort of *odium theologicum*) than to fear—fear that Artusi would continue to scavenge among his unpublished but not uncared-for works. The canon governing the propriety of citation and acknowledgment of sources was, to say the least, a flexible one at that time. Nonetheless, certain limits were recognized by almost everybody, and one of these was the unauthorized use of unpublished work by living persons.

Bottrigari's anxiety would perhaps be difficult to understand were it not for the matter of the Melone papers. This is the third issue raised by Artusi's remarks in 1603. That Bottrigari must have known about Artusi's possession of the papers before the latter declared it publicly in 1601 is shown by his recourse to legal action. He had Artusi's rooms searched after Artusi refused to return the disputed material, and when nothing incriminating was found, he collected about a dozen supporting statements between December 1600 and July 1601. One of these was from the widow, Lucia Melone, who testified that Artusi collected the bulk of her husband's manuscripts, except for a few pages of music, three days after he died. Another, submitted by Melone's student Lorenzo Righetti (d. after 1620), who was to edit *Il Melone & Il Melone secondo* in 1602, attested that Melone merely copied Bottrigari's works. Yet another is a rather touching testimonial by a bookseller who described Bottrigari's shock upon discovering Artusi's pilferage while browsing through *L'Artusi* in his shop.[37]

Bottrigari wrote the "Lettera di Federico Verdicelli" in the wake of these melancholy events. And we should bear in mind that the contents and tone of this letter are the result of his discomfiture at the lack of success in regaining the papers. Earlier in the same year (1602) he submitted a copy of the offending 1601 edition of *Il Desiderio* to the Senate of Bologna. The secretary, his friend Ciro Spontone, sent a formal acknowledgment to Bottrigari in January 1602, testifying to the Senate's positive reception of his claim to be the author of the dialogue.[38] Bottrigari appended the Senate's vindication to the 1602 letter he sent to Artusi. And Artusi retaliated by publishing the *Seconda parte dell'Artusi* in 1603 so as to humiliate Bottrigari in as many ways as he could devise, including what we must now see as the gloating reaffirmation of his possession of the Melone papers. Bottrigari responded with yet another open letter, the "Aletelogia" of 1604.

Both of these letters bristle with hostile remarks that betray an anger barely contained. The vocabulary becomes more abusive in the later of the two missives as Bottrigari fairly splutters in utter frustration. A few samples from the one page of the "Aletelogia" suffice. Artusi, observes the writer, should be treated with every civility since he has earned the following adjectives:

> malignant, slanderous, bad-mouthed, presumptuous, arrogant, imperious, . . . silly, ignorant, a detractor, a falsifier of the writings of another; a squabbler, impertinent, malicious, inconsiderate, a gossip, insolent, a quarrelsome fellow, along with such other preeminent titles as Pinhead, Dunce Cassock, Butt End, Twittering Blockhead, Gelding, Idiot, Scatterbrain, Freak, . . . a great Wiseacre, an Ogre, a Buffalo [Blockhead], an Elephant [Oaf], and so on.[39]

These are the "flattering words" of an exasperated man. There is little of substance in this letter, though some of the barbs are witty and well aimed. He counters Artusi's references to him in the *Seconda parte dell'Artusi* as the author of "the opinion" by consistently referring to Artusi as the author of the "Inconsiderations" and the "Imperfections." And with respect to the criticism of Monteverdi's music and the quarrel with "l'Ottuso Academico," Bottrigari asks "on what authority does he make himself out to be the public censor?"[40]

Other, more intemperate remarks, however, betoken fury. Bottrigari was particularly insulted by Artusi's condescending reference to him as "this poor little man" ("questo poveretto") who, in mistranslating Euclid into Italian, miscalculated the number of dieses in the chromatic tetrachord.[41] It is in this context that Bottrigari strikes back: How dare he, a man who took holy orders to escape poverty, snub a nobleman who lives his life nobly?[42] Such savage language tells us something of Bottrigari's character. But we must remember the circumstances, in this instance Artusi's allusion to one of his unpublished works.

Casting himself in the role of the innocent victim, Bottrigari insists that Artusi instigated this affair. Before this man published his two "Chatterings" ("Cicalamenti"),[43] says Bottrigari, the author of "the opinion" had paid no attention to him whatsoever—he did not speak or write of him, he had not read his "scribblings" ("scartafacci") on the art of counterpoint (*L'arte del contraponto* [Venice, 1586]), nor did he even know him by sight. Moreover, Artusi had the gall to shrug off

Bottrigari's previous letter, the "Antartusi." That Artusi ignored the "Antartusi" is a fact, but that Bottrigari had never heard of Artusi before 1600 is perhaps a disingenuous disclaimer.

One of the primary objectives of the "Antartusi" had been the recovery of the Melone papers. We know for certain from various comments made by Artusi that they contained copies in Melone's hand of *Il Desiderio, Il Melone & Il Melone secondo*, most of "Il Trimerone," and translations of and commentaries on ancient authors. In the letter to the readers for the 1599 edition of *Il Desiderio*, Bottrigari gives a list of his studies of classical sources, works made for the benefit of Melone. Most of these items had been already mentioned in the preface to an Italian translation of Boethius, finished 21 November 1597,[44] itself mentioned in the published list of 1599: from the Latin, the writings on music by Boethius, Martianus Capella, Censorinus, Cassiodorus, and Bede, plus a large part of the *Musica* [*Musica theorica* (Venice, 1529)] of Lodovico Fogliano; from the Greek, the *Harmonics* of Aristoxenus and of Ptolemy, the *Isagoge* and the *Harmonic Rule* by Euclid, *Problems*, 19, by Aristotle, the *Synopsis* or *Musical Compendium* of Psellus, the writings on music by Gaudentius and Alypius, plus the one by Plutarch.

Of this impressive corpus very little has survived.[45] That Bottrigari knew how to handle the Alypius tables for deciphering Greek notation is shown in his transcriptions of three Greek hymns, although he could have acquired this expertise from Galilei's *Dialogo*.[46] Except for Boethius's treatise, the Latin medieval material has disappeared, as has the Italian translation of Fogliano's work. But to this group we should add the translation into Italian of the section on cosmic harmony in Macrobius's *In somnium Scipionis . . . eruditissima explanatio*. In the same manuscript there is an Italian version of Plutarch's commentary on the generation of the soul in the *Timaeus* by Plato. These translations, the last from Bottrigari's pen, are dated respectively 12 February 1610 and 12 March 1610.[47] Among the Greek works the translations of Aristoxenus and Ptolemy, *Physical Problems*, book 19, by Pseudo-Aristotle (mentioned by Artusi), the *Synopsis of Music* by Michael Psellus, the *Sectio canonis* by Euclid, and the *Isagoge* by Cleonides (then attributed to Euclid) have been lost. However, there are two extant copies, both in Bottrigari's hand, of a codex consisting mainly of unidentified Latin translations of some Greek works, including Alypius, Gaudentius's *Harmonica introductio* (possibly by Johannes Baptista Augius [fl. ca. 1545]), and Plutarch's *De musica* by Hermannus Cruserius (fl. ca. 1540).[48] Bottrigari also translated Pseudo-Aristotle's *De audibilibus* into Italian (14 January 1606), not from the Greek but from the Latin version by Francesco Patrizi preserved in the same manuscript.[49]

We are beginning to form a more precise picture of Bottrigari's work as an antiquarian thanks to Claude Palisca's study of the Bolognese sources. From his research it would appear that in fact only one of the fifteen Italian translations mentioned by Bottrigari in 1599 has survived—Boethius's treatise on music, one of six from the Latin. There exists only one other Latin work, the commentary by Macrobius, and it comes from the post-1599 group. Of the nine Greek works listed in 1599, Palisca has found two in Latin translations copied by Bottrigari—Gaudentius and Plutarch. And there are also two Greek works from the post-1599 group. One of these is *De audibilibus*, then attributed to Aristotle, which Palisca believes was done from the Latin. The other, Plutarch's commentary on the *Timaeus*, has not turned up among Bottrigari's manuscripts as someone else's Latin version. However, this commentary is part of the *Moralia* (book 13), and the *Moralia*, along with the *Parallel Lives*, was printed in numerous Latin editions.

Although a comprehensive study of the available sources is needed to assess the Bottrigari *Nachlass*, one may use references by his contemporaries to corroborate the existence of specific translations in manuscript. We have seen several such references in the writings of Artusi. But these do not prove that the translations were made by Bottrigari from the original language. The crux of the matter is whether or not Bottrigari worked from the Greek. From the appearance of the documents cited thus far it appears that he did not; but this appearance is deceiving, and it warns us against too facile an assessment of circumstantial evidence. Palisca has concluded that Bottrigari was one of three music theorists in Italy who could read Greek.[50] This statement is based on his extensive examination of the fine critical study made by Bottrigari of the Latin translations of Aristoxenus's *Harmonic Elements* and Ptolemy's *Harmonics* by Antonio Gogava (fl. ca. 1550).[51] In Palisca's words, "Bottrigari's work marks the application of a text-critical method to the task of arriving at a Latin version of the fundamental texts of Aristoxenus and Ptolemy. His object may have been to use the emended Latin of Gogava as the basis for a set of Italian translations."[52]

It may be that these Italian translations had been completed, as suggested by the 1599 list, and subsequently disappeared, or that they were "works in progress," so to speak. If the latter, then the most damaging thing that can be said about Bottrigari is that he was somewhat cavalier about the status of his projects, exercising as a member of his class the *sprezzatura* of which Castiglione wrote. This attitude seems to run contrary to the punctilious treatment of the works themselves: he not only signed each piece, differentiated between an original and a copy, and indicated the day, month, and year, but also recorded the precise time of the day or night (often the wee hours of the morning).

It is evident that Bottrigari took great care with his manuscripts, and yet he allowed Anniballe Melone to copy them. He introduced Melone as a speaker in "Il Trimerone" under his proper name and, as we saw, in *Il Desiderio* under an anagram.[53] It is equally evident that Melone was in a position of great trust and did not always observe the punctilio required by his situation. Modern opinion on Melone is divided. Aside from the usual neutral comments, some scholars see him as a prominent musician in Bologna, a friend, inspirer, and amanuensis of Bottrigari who appropriated the authorship of *Il Desiderio* in 1594 with Bottrigari's consent. Others call him a modest Bolognese musician, a friend whom Bottrigari went out of his way to help and who repaid him by claiming the authorship of *Il Desiderio*, for which act he later apologized.[54]

Anniballe Melone was neither saint nor sinner. Rather it seems he was a good-hearted but somewhat self-serving man who liked to attach himself to persons of rank and consequence. This penchant is indicated by Artusi's comments in both the 1601 edition of *Il Desiderio* and the letter to the readers for the *Seconda parte dell'Artusi* of 1603. In the former Artusi lists four persons by name (Bottrigari included), and in the latter he mentions a group of persons (himself included). Melone's friendship with Artusi explains how the latter knew about the papers. He may even have examined them before 1598. He certainly set about procuring them with unseemly haste.

Here is Bottrigari's account of his relationship with Melone as given in the 1599 edition of *Il Desiderio*. He tells us that Melone, in his old age and after a successful career as a practical musician, decided to spend his time learning about music theory, since he no longer had any financial worries. He therefore sought out the society of anyone who was well versed in this aspect of music. Thus when Bottrigari returned to Bologna in 1587, Melone made it his business to become an intimate friend, one who "with all fondness, diligence, and solicitude, devoted himself to offering this nobleman [i.e., Bottrigari] honorable homage and service."[55] Bottrigari apparently enjoyed the companionship and discipleship of this affable man—that is, until Melone became obsessed with the idea of advertising his new status as a somewhat learned musician. This need for recognition apparently prompted him to write letters to distinguished persons, among them Zarlino. He also began at that time to badger Bottrigari to publish *Il Melone & il Melone secondo* and *Il Desiderio*. As we have seen, Melone's efforts led to the 1594 publication of *Il Desiderio* under the anagram "Alemanno Benelli."

Before going on to examine the evidence of the events subsequent to this printing, we should consider the wording of the 1599 account of it. First, Bottrigari warns the readers not to be surprised to see his name, even though *Il Desiderio* had been published recently "by a substitute author under a feigned name."[56] Bottrigari describes how, due to Melone's pleas, he decided to publish the dialogue "without the name of an author" and thus "to stay behind the scenes." But because it was necessary to have a name, the dialogue was published "under the credible name of an anagrammed person, and thus of some- one hidden by an emblem and a disguise." Bottrigari's inelegant syn- tax has been noted by several scholars.[57] And the truth is that it is not always possible to be absolutely certain about the reading of isolated sentences. In this instance, however, it is likely that the "someone" is Bottrigari hidden by a double mask: first, the emblem of the credible anagram itself (credible insofar as it refers to one of the interlocutors in the dialogue), and second, the disguise of the anagrammed person (his friend Melone). The point is that Bottrigari insists he was always the real author of *Il Desiderio*, and merely had indulged in a harmless subterfuge, a delightful game with Anniballe Melone and a certain Fulvio Codibò his willing playmates.

We have already read about Melone's actions after this printing. In the 1599 account Bottrigari rather quickly recounts the disclosure of the anagram to some persons, his displeasure, the altercation with Melone, Melone's letters pleading for permission to reveal the ana- gram, and his gentle but firm letters of refusal. Melone, however, was not to be refused and, of course, Bottrigari admits that in the end he gave in to his friend's fervor and longing. But something happened between the argument and the capitulation. Bottrigari's intriguing description is as follows:

> Afterwards, under a certain set of circumstances, he [Melone] tried through some letters, which are still in exist- ence, to gain the Lord Cavalier's assent and permission to divulge the anagram. In the letters of reply from the latter, he [Melone] was advised, for several reasons having to do with his honor, not to do so, and to keep quiet about it.[58]

When one sees what is obviously a skeleton, it is natural to wonder in whose closet it belongs. In the "Lettera di Federico Verdicelli," written in 1602 to refute the denunciation of Bottrigari by Artusi in 1601, the skeleton is fleshed out, so to speak. We are given to under- stand that it was not hidden in Bottrigari's closet, nor did it belong to Melone. Indeed, Artusi is to be blamed for exhuming the remains of an affair that had been better left to rest in peace.

Bottrigari maintains that Artusi's concern over the honor of the late lamented Melone is nothing but a fraud and a caricature. For he has forced Bottrigari, in defending his own honor, to dwell on Melone's pitiful attempts to camouflage the paucity of his knowledge and thus to masquerade as a learned musician.[59] In retelling the story, Bottrigari reluctantly fills in some of the details. He tells us that Melone first revealed the secret of the anagram to Claudio Achillini[60] when he went to his house to give him a singing lesson. This incident was reported at once to Bottrigari, who then became extremely disgusted ("grandamente sgustato"). His disgust only increased when Melone began showing the dialogue and disclosing the anagram to all and sundry because he was overcome by the ardent desire to obtain the position of *maestro di cappella* in the collegiate church of San Petronio, a post left vacant by the death of Andrea Rota in 1597.

So serious was he that he wrote forty-one letters to Bottrigari about this matter. Bottrigari quotes a little from the twenty-fifth letter of 29 August 1597. In it Melone relates that his friend Alfonso Ganassa[61] was chatting in the piazza with some gentlemen about possible successors to Rota. When the others claimed there was no Bolognese candidate fit for this post, Ganassa mentioned a few names, among them that of Melone. The others then asked how a man who had published nothing could possibly know anything. This incident, reported by Ganassa to Melone, and by Melone to Bottrigari, was reported by Bottrigari to Artusi as *prima facie* evidence of Melone's inordinate desire to appear qualified for a position beyond his true capacities. For Melone went on to say that if such people knew who Alemanno Benelli really was, they would have to treat him with more respect.

This, then, is the "certain set of circumstances" that set in motion the events between the two printings of *Il Desiderio*. Bottrigari's picture of persistent nagging on the part of Melone is supported by several pieces of circumstantial evidence. One of these is not the eventual appointment of Melone as *maestro di cappella* at San Petronio. He never got the post. Indeed, Ghinolfo Dataro (1540–1617), one of the singers, was acting choir director for two years, 1597 and 1598.[62] Whatever this fact may signify, it shows that the chapter was in some difficulty. One cannot help but wonder how much Melone and his partisans had to do with it. Bottrigari certainly gives the impression that Melone tried to enlist as many supporters as he could find, but his efforts proved futile. Don Pompilio Pisanelli (d. after 1606), a Bolognese citizen who was then *maestro di cappella* at the cathedral of Pisa, was appointed to San Petronio in 1599, the year after Melone died.

It is not, Bottrigari stresses, that Melone wanted to make himself out to be the author of *Il Desiderio*. He simply wanted the world, his world, to know that he was worthy and sufficiently erudite to be involved, and to be seen to be involved, in several of Bottrigari's writings (*Il Desiderio* and *Il Melone & il Melone secondo*).[63] We may infer that because Bottrigari seemed disinclined to publish the two *Melone* dialogues, whose titles would have given cachet to Melone's name, Melone became desperate to reveal the identity of the anagrammed person in *Il Desiderio*. It is also possible that some of those who already knew this secret had spread the rumor of Melone's authorship, a rumor Melone did not dispel firmly enough to salvage his honor when the truth finally was to be told. Bottrigari gave a sanitized version of these events in the 1599 edition of *Il Desiderio*, a version calculated to prove his own authorship of the work in question and to uphold his honor without impugning that of Melone, his misguided but still cherished friend. Some of the embarrassing details were omitted, some of the language toned down. In 1602, in the wake of Artusi's insults, Bottrigari had no alternative but to tell almost all. Still, one senses a reticence in treating this affair, especially in comparison with the language used in dealing directly with Artusi and his dastardly deeds.

Most of the 1602 letter deals with Artusi's "infamous, villainous, and very fallacious imputation"[64] that Bottrigari had stolen Melone's writings on music after the death of the latter. As for Artusi's threat to tell the world who was the true writer of the translations of ancient sources, Bottrigari in turn promises tit for tat. He announces his intention to publish incontrovertible evidence "that this fellow is a filthy slanderer, a flash in the pan"[65] who accuses Bottrigari of being what he actually is—an unprincipled plagiarist. Lest it be thought that Bottrigari was so touchy as to imagine poachers behind every page, let it be said that he could and did recognize the compliment of imitation when he saw it.[66]

In his letter to the readers in 1603 Artusi mentions Zarlino's *Dimostrationi harmoniche* as the catalyst for Melone's inquiry about the ancient genera and their tuning systems. This is the fourth and final issue we need to consider.[67] It would hardly do to sketch a "David-and-Goliath" scenario in which Bottrigari's defense of Vicentino and his views on chromatic and enharmonic music is pitted against the forces of conservatism impersonated by Zarlino. All the same, Bottrigari is virtually the only writer who has anything favorable to say about Vicentino's conception of the genera; this assertion does not take into account those writers who either quoted or pilfered the less outrageous material in his treatise, *L'antica musica ridotta alla moderna prattica* (Rome, 1555).[68] Furthermore, anyone seeking a reasoned critique and negation of Vicentino's tenets would have been directed to the writings of Zarlino.[69] From a cursory glance at what he wrote in *Le istitutioni harmoniche*, especially in the final chapters of part 3 (the best known of the four parts of this weighty treatise), it would appear that Zarlino did not take Vicentino too seriously. And this is exactly the mistake made by some of Zarlino's followers who reduced Zarlino's considered argumentation to silly commentary and gross dissection.

One such was Gandolfo Sigonio, whose little tract against Vicentino aroused Bottrigari's disdain and anger. Very little is known about Sigonio. He is mentioned as the brother of Carlo, who taught Greek in Modena, in a document of 1551 concerning the remarriage of their mother after their father died in the house of his mistress.[70] One of the few contemporary comments about him comes from the pen of Bottrigari, and it has been repeated both in full and in abbreviated form by modern scholars, but always out of context. In 1602 Bottrigari wrote:

> Melone was a great friend of Mr. Gandolfo Sigonio, from whose daily conversation Melone felt he acquired something very important to his desire [to learn about music theory]. For Sigonio was not only a good musical contrapuntist (whence he came to be called "Little Solfa," as if in playful disdain of this [skill], by his brother Carlo the humanist, a teacher of the most illustrious fame in the chief seats of the principal universities of Italy), but also very proficient in the teaching of Zarlino's *Istitutioni* and *Dimostrationi harmoniche*, though somewhat less so in the books on music, both Latin and vernacular, by other writers of our time.[71]

Other than this, the only trace of his activities comprises twenty-five letters written to Melone between 1571 and 1574.[72]

From the above description it would seem that Sigonio was some sort of music teacher in Bologna. However, in the *Discorso* he disclaims professional status in an ambiguous statement that could be true to fact or merely the rhetorical ploy of self-depreciation.[73] That he was one of Melone's tutors is clear, as is Bottrigari's emphasis on his ability to teach the works of Zarlino.

It is also indicative that in this passage Bottrigari should devote more space to Carlo. True, Gandolfo's brother was a very distinguished humanist known for his text-critical method in dealing with ancient writings on history. He was also notoriously belligerent. While teaching rhetoric at the University of Padua, Carlo Sigonio instigated a quarrel with Francesco Robortello, a Aristotelian and the teacher of Patrizi. So heated did matters become that one of Robortello's students, a certain Rhodigino, attacked Sigonio with a knife in 1562, wounding him in the face.[74] Sigonio then fled to the safety of the University of Bologna, followed by many of his students, including the young Torquato Tasso (1544–95). Tasso, in his maturity one of the great poets of the century, became a close friend of Bottrigari and wrote a number of poems in his honor. We have no evidence that Bottrigari and Carlo Sigonio had met in Bologna during the years 1563–76, the time they were both in Bologna. The anecdote, however, suggests that Bottrigari knew one of the brothers personally.

In any event, Bottrigari's glowing praise of Carlo and his repetition of the little joke at Gandolfo's expense suggest that Bottrigari identified with Sigonio the humanist rather than Sigonio the contrapuntist. One detects a hint of condescension in the comments that characterize Gandolfo Sigonio and his attempt at educating Melone. At the time of this writing, of course, Bottrigari had finished *Il Melone secondo* and had already formed his low opinion of Gandolfo Sigonio's abilities both as a music critic and as a scholar. The admission that Sigonio may have been a "good contrapuntist" was damning with faint praise inasmuch as Bottrigari, like so many humanists (Carlo included), had a low opinion of the art of counterpoint.

* * *

The publication of *Il Melone & il Melone secondo* in 1602 is part of the story that has been told on these pages. In the dedication to Count Francesco di Gambara,[75] Lorenzo Righetti informs Gambara that he found among the papers of his deceased teacher, Melone, two discourses addressed to him by Bottrigari. To honor both the sender and the recipient, he obtained permission from Bottrigari to publish this material. It is not clear whether Righetti actually used Melone's copy (which Artusi still claimed to own in 1603) or the original by Bottrigari. It seems, however, that Righetti found at the end of the text of *Il Melone discorso armonico* the first part of a chromatic madrigal for four voices by Bottrigari, *Il cantar novo* (Petrarch); the second part he located among Melone's miscellaneous papers.[76] Nor is it clear that Righetti initiated this project. It could very well be that Bottrigari, having heard gossip about Artusi's intention to publish these tracts, sought to forestall him and enlisted the help of one of Melone's former pupils, in particular one who had proved willing to testify that the papers in question were copies of Bottrigari's work.

This interpretation of events is to some degree corroborated by the prefatory material in the publication. Even in view of the contemporary penchant for deferential tributes and flowery encomia, the first five pages of *Il Melone discorso armonico* might strike one as a case of overkill. There is certainly a subtext running through these pages. The content of Righetti's dedication, dated 8 October 1602, was described above. It is followed by a poem dedicated to Gambara in praise of both the count and the cavalier by Melchiorre Zoppio (d. 1634).[77] The readers are then addressed in a two-page poem, also by Zoppio, where they find a pointed opening allusion to the futile efforts of detractors who only succeed in debasing themselves, and many praises of Bottrigari's integrity, nobility, and erudition in literature and music. Though of dubious literary merit, the poem shows Zoppio's particular intention to honor Bottrigari through exclusive use of the nine-syllable line. The fifth item is a letter addressed to Bottrigari by Paolo Marni, dated Bologna, 1 May 1602. Marni, a Mantuan by birth, was a minor composer of madrigals[78] with theoretical ambitions. In his letter Marni succeeds not only in eulogizing Bottrigari but also in advertising his own forthcoming treatise in defense of modern music, a work that was never published. Below this letter on the second page he appended an original, pompous Latin quatrain.

The prefatory material closes with a reprint of the letter originally written to Bottrigari on 28 May 1591 by the late Anniballe Melone. The letter recapitulates the main lines of the debate between Don Nicola Vicentino and [Don] Vicente Lusitano (fl. ca. 1550) that took place in Rome in 1551. Admitting that he was thoroughly confused by Vicentino's and Zarlino's treatises, Melone begs for clarification. There is no reason to doubt that Melone did write this letter. At the same time, the letter reads rather like a set piece. Perhaps Melone wrote it in 1591 at Bottrigari's suggestion, with the understanding that it would be published at the head of a treatise that would bear his name. Since the treatise languished in manuscript, by 1594 Melone was anxious, and by 1597 dismayed.

Between the third and fifth items there is a very fine woodcut, a portrait of Bottrigari in profile in a central medallion surrounded by a luxuriance of ornaments (see fig. 6.1). Among the shells, foliage, gargoyles, and architectural members are four female allegorical figures. On the upper right corner Arithmetica, seated on a cushion, flourishes a pen in one hand while clutching in the other a tablet with the numbers 1 through 6 engraved on it. The balancing figure in a mirror pose on the upper left corner, Geometria, has a ruler in one hand while trying, unsuccessfully, to grasp both a pair of compasses and T square in the other. Just below the middle on the left side we find Astronomia with an armillary sphere in one hand, standing in the

Figure 6.1 Portrait of Bottrigari.

guise of a caryatid, her feet poised on the head of a gargoyle and her head supporting an entablature on which stands an ornate vase of flowers. And on the right side, of course, is another caryatid, Musica, who performs the same design function as Astronomia while managing to play a large bowed string instrument, a viol of some sort.

These are "the four ladies" of the quadrivium, whose typical iconography in this woodcut forms an emblem familiar to the learned antiquarian. In the case of unfamiliarity with this sort of pictorial *topos*, very curious readings may result under certain circumstances. One such delightful interpretation comes from the pen of the eighteenth-century poet and librettist Apostolo Zeno. Zeno was an ardent numismatist, and he had in his collection one of two bronze medals minted to commemorate the death of Bottrigari. The medal in question had on the obverse a profile portrait of the cavalier. On the reverse there was an elaborate design that included several objects, two of which are described by Zeno—a sphere and a melon. The sphere must have been a version of the armillary sphere held by Astronomia in the woodcut; perhaps its details were not too clear in the cramped space of a medal, even a large one. But what was the melon? Zeno thought that Bottrigari had invented a melon-shaped string instrument which he described in a treatise entitled *The Melon, a Harmonic Discourse*. This object must have been a version of the viol held by Musica, but with its elongated shape reduced to a small oval that looked indeed very like a melon. Zeno's error did not go undetected for long, but some of the corrections are almost as entertaining as the mistake they sought to emend. One of them stated that the melon was an emblem for Bottrigari's eponymous friend (i.e., Anniballe Melone).[79]

* * *

The subject matter of *Il Melone & il Melone secondo* concerns two aspects of Vicentino's theory: first, his insistence that modern music was not purely diatonic, but rather a mixture of elements of the diatonic, chromatic, and enharmonic genera as defined by the ancient Greeks; and second, that it was possible, indeed desirable, to resurrect the latter two genera in modern polyphony. Bottrigari's abiding interest in Vicentino's theory, dating no doubt from his stay in Ferrara, can be detected in many ways. For instance, one of his friends was the antiquarian polymath Erycius Puteanus (1574–1646). That Puteanus should cite an insignificant detail from Vicentino's treatise in his *Modulata Pallas* can be attributed to Bottrigari's influence.[80] This observation is only important in that it indicates Bottrigari's touting of Vicentino, as does the information about him recorded in *Il Desiderio*. In short, Bottrigari took Vicentino seriously and placed his contributions to music theory on a par with those of Zarlino.

It is unfortunately not possible to date the writing of Bottrigari's and Sigonio's tracts with any accuracy. Since Melone's letter is dated 28 May 1591, we can thus assume that the two tracts were written sometime between 1591 and 1594. In 1599 Bottrigari states that up to 1594 he had been pressured by Melone to publish both *Il Desiderio* and the two *Melone* discourses. And as we saw, Bottrigari obliged with the printing of *Il Desiderio* under the anagram "Alemanno Benelli."

The dating of Sigonio's *Discorso* is more conjectural. In it Sigonio refers to two recently published booklets of four-voice madrigals by Vicentino.[81] Bottrigari in turn identifies them as the first and second books, but gives no dates. The only extant publications of music by Vicentino are Book One *a5* (Venice,1546), his first publication, and Book Five *a5* (Milan, 1572). This nearly thirty-year gap can be narrowed down somewhat. Among the specific compositions discussed in these writings is *I'vidi in terra* from Book Two *a4*. This madrigal features notes with superscript dots to indicate pitches inflected upwards by an enharmonic diesis, roughly the size of a quarter tone. If we bear in mind the secrecy with which Vicentino guarded his experimental music until the publication of his treatise, we can safely say that the second book appeared after 1555, perhaps in the 1560s or early 1570s. Vicentino died in Milan around 1576–77 from the plague. From Sigonio's wording, we may suppose that he wrote the *Discorso* in the 1570s or 1580s. This approximate date corresponds with the decades in which the elderly Melone became enamored of music theory. And though the lengthy title of *Il Melone secondo* does not help us decide whether or not Sigonio's diatribe was written for Melone, the context indicates that Melone is the unnamed person referred to in it.

Bottrigari's *Il Melone discorso armonico*, written in response to the letter by Melone mentioned above, deals with the issues raised by the famous public debate of 1551 between Vicentino and Lusitano.[82] Though Bottrigari vigorously championed Vicentino's position and declared the decision of the judges to be "wicked and unjust,"[83] he nevertheless roundly criticized Vicentino's faulty presentation and his theoretical inconsistency in its every excruciating manifestation.

The tone of *Il Melone secondo* is quite different. The objective was to rebut Sigonio, but in pursuing it Bottrigari simply passed over many of the shortcomings and merits of Vicentino's presentation. His irritation and contempt were such that all impartiality and composure went by the boards. It seems likely that Melone showed Sigonio's tract to Bottrigari after *Il Melone discorso armonico* had been written. Bottrigari did not take kindly to the remarks against Vicentino contained in it, especially from such a mediocre partisan of the traditional view of things. We cannot infer any ulterior motive to Bottrigari with respect to the nefarious influence of Artusi. Their quarrel did not erupt until after 1598 when Artusi came into possession of Melone's papers. But among these papers were the unpublished *Melone* discourses. That Artusi had read them is all too clear,[84] and what they contained by way of criticism of Zarlino may have contributed to Artusi's ire and disdain. There is no evidence that Artusi ever sought to take up the defense of Sigonio—a quixotic task at best. But whatever he may have thought of Sigonio, the mangled version of Zarlino's theories that Sigonio gives in no way invalidated the theories themselves. Nor did it excuse the errant ways of those who deviated from the Zarlinian canon.

Persons who dared to uphold any elements of Vicentino's theory of the genera, but especially those roundly condemned by Zarlino in the final chapters of his study of the art of counterpoint,[85] must have been anathema to Artusi. How else was he to receive notions such as the one Bottrigari advanced to crush Sigonio when the latter exclaimed in horror at the wildly irrational and disproportionate progressions recommended by Vicentino? Bottrigari's caustic rejoinder is that since the human voice is capable of producing an infinite variety of intervals, the composer is free to exploit its flexibility and to train singers with the aid of an instrument.[86] This claim flies in the face of Zarlino's closing argument against the musical eccentricities practiced by chromaticists.[87]

Bottrigari refers to Zarlino many times in the course of *Il Melone discorso armonico*, and these references show that he had read all of Zarlino's treatises. Though Zarlino is often cited to lend support to an argument, just as often he is cited for inconsistencies, errors, and misunderstandings—but always with the respect due to an outstanding theorist. The most extensive and most intriguing discussion occurs directly after Bottrigari's description and assessment of the Vicentino-Lusitano debate.

In order to defend his assertion that the music of his day was a mixture of all three genera and not purely diatonic, Vicentino had to convince his audience that any interval of a genus was sufficient to identify that genus. The crux of the matter was the status of incomposite minor and major thirds. Vicentino insisted that the minor third belonged solely to the chromatic genus (the other two intervals being the major and minor semitone) and that the major third likewise belonged to the enharmonic genus (the other two intervals being the major and minor diesis). Lusitano won the day by maintaining the traditional position that thirds were composite intervals made up of diatonic steps: the minor third composed of a whole tone and a major semitone, the major third of two whole tones. Both men cited passages from Boethius in their favor. Whatever else may be said of the conduct of the debate, Bottrigari's image of two blind pugilists flailing the air is both amusing and appropriate.[88]

The passage on Zarlino concentrates on Zarlino's attempt to show in very straightforward and practical terms how preposterous are Vicentino's claims.[89] Zarlino selects a plainchant and revises its contour in order to make it in turn a chromatic and an enharmonic melody. As one might expect, the chant becomes unrecognizable in the first revision and an apparent caricature in the second. To be fair to Vicentino, it must be said that he did not advocate enharmonic music for use in church, or in any public venue for that matter; this esoteric practice was reserved for private chamber music. He did, on the other hand, compose a fair number of chromatic religious works.

Bottrigari takes issue with Zarlino's method of superimposing the chromatic and enharmonic genera on the chant. And he offers his own reworking of this melody in order to show that it is indeed possible to achieve a less bizarre result (see ex. 6.1).[90] We can see, as he himself admits on the authority of custom, that Bottrigari has transposed the chant up a fifth. But this is not the only divergence from Zarlino's version. The ambitus of the melody is different, as are some of the interval species within it.

Before examining the reasons for these differences, we should review Vicentino's rules. The fourth, fifth, and octave are common to all the genera. For a melody in any one genus to remain pure, that is, to remain unadulterated by another genus, it must not include any intervals other than the ones proper to that genus. Thus, a purely diatonic melody may have neither a diesis (major or minor) nor a minor semitone nor a third (major or minor), a purely chromatic melody neither a minor diesis nor a whole tone nor a major third, and a purely enharmonic melody neither a semitone (major or minor) nor a whole tone nor a minor third.

The following diagram of the pitches used by Zarlino and Bottrigari allows us to compare the internal structure of the genera as each theorist conceived it. To facilitate analysis, Zarlino's version has been transposed up a fifth to match that of Bottrigari.

	Bottrigari	Zarlino
Diatonic	A–B–c–d–e	A–B–c–d–e
Chromatic	A–B–c–c-sharp–e	G-sharp–B–c–c-sharp–e
Enharmonic	A–B–B-double-sharp–c–e	G–B–B-double-sharp–c–e

First, it should be noted that the tetrachord from B to e is identical in the two schemes. In the parlance of antiquarian theory, with which both men were familiar, this is the tetrachord *diezeugmenon* (disjunct) of the Greater Perfect System. It is evident that they understood how this tetrachord changes shape in each of the genera. What is different is the pitch below this tetrachord. In Bottrigari's version, it remains a tone below the *paramese* (b), thus allowing him to retain the ambitus of the diatonic chant in the other two genera. In Zarlino's case this pitch falls a semitone in each of the genera respectively, forming a minor third with the *paramese* in the chromatic and a major third in the enharmonic. And as a consequence, the ambitus of the original chant widens first to a minor sixth, and then to a major sixth. The latter feature is one of the elements that contributes to the bizarre effect deliberately sought by Zarlino.

Indeed, the ancient Greek Greater and Lesser Perfect Systems are the key. Zarlino's example of this system in its generic mutations can be taken as the model of what both men believed was true of ancient Greek practice[91] (see ex. 6.2). Bottrigari has decided that the lowest pitch (a) of the transposed chant lies outside the controlling tetrachord (the disjunct), and therefore need not be included in the generic mutations. This decision permits him not only to keep both the fourth and the fifth intact, thus obeying one of Vicentino's rules, but also to retain the structural stability of the melody. However, in so doing he has also retained in the chromatic and enharmonic genera the step of a whole tone, a–b, (originally d–e) between pitches 1 and 2, 7 and 8, and 18 and

Example 6.1*

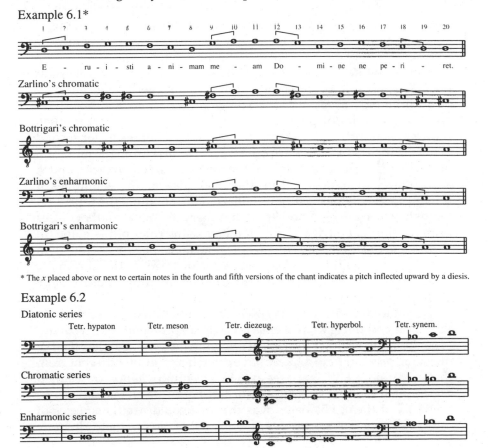

* The *x* placed above or next to certain notes in the fourth and fifth versions of the chant indicates a pitch inflected upward by a diesis.

Example 6.2

19.[92] This clearly contravenes Vicentino's rules. There is a way Bottrigari could have justified this anomaly—to shift the chant down an octave to the tetrachord *hypaton* (B–e) and thus claim that the A below, the *proslambanomenos*, is never altered in the genera because it lies outside all tetrachords. As it happens, the pitch below the disjunct tetrachord is the *mese* (a), and it belongs to the tetrachord *meson* (middle). As such, it is subject to the alterations effected by a genus. And this is precisely what Zarlino did in order to obey Vicentino's rules. Indeed, in his scheme each genus comprises only the intervals proper to it. And as a consequence, the ambitus of the chant must be widened by a semitone in each successive genus. There is but one option in this situation, and Zarlino seems to have taken it. Admittedly, Bottrigari is on shaky ground. He could not use the excuse of the *proslambanomenos*. The only other escape would have been to claim that the point of disjunction between the *mese* and *paramese* permitted him to disassociate the *mese* from the generic mutations effected in the tetrachord above it. In other words, it is the *mese* but, having no middle tetrachord below it, it functions as a quasi *proslambanomenos*. This kind of reasoning resembles the contortions of theorists when they try to decide how far below the final a chant may descend without changing mode.

Schemes of the genera, however, are like the abstract rules of grammatical logic. Just as the latter cannot explain everything that may occur in an individual sentence, so the former cannot do so with respect to the series of pitches in an individual melody. Let us then return to example 6.1. Disregarding for the moment the major second between pitches 13 and 14, we observe that in his chromatic mutation of the chant, Zarlino has retained the fourth between pitches 8 and 9, and arranged matters so that all other intervals are either semitones or minor thirds. Likewise with his enharmonic mutation: the fourth remains between pitches 8 and 9 and the other intervals are either dieses or major thirds. Bottrigari's version breaks the rules of the game. In addition to the three steps of a whole tone noted above, the fourth in the original (pitches 8–9) becomes a major third in the chromatic mutation and a minor third in the enharmonic mutation—both of these outlawed intervals.

Vicentino did not, to our knowledge, reply to Zarlino's attack. In this instance, Bottrigari's defense raises more problems than it solves. Had Vicentino been set the task of applying the genera to the chant in question, he would most likely have offered a solution different from that of Zarlino or Bottrigari (see ex. 6.3). Vicentino was not constrained by the pitches of the Greater and Lesser Perfect Systems, though he knew about them. His belief was that one could use the species of intervals (we might say classes of intervals) of the genera to alter any

Example 6.3*

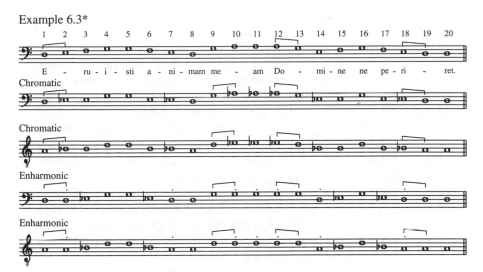

* The dots placed over certain notes indicate pitches inflected upward by a minor diesis.

pitch to become any other pitch; thus, B could become B-sharp, and A could become A-flat, which could become A-flat with a superscript dot (his way of notating the diesis), and so on. Needless to say, solmizating these pitches could become a nightmare.[93]

Example 6.3 shows the chant in the chromatic and enharmonic genera on both the original pitch used by Zarlino and the transposed pitch chosen by Bottrigari. The results are the same. The only outlawed interval is the major third that occurs between pitches 13 and 14 in the chromatic mutation.[94] There is no way to avoid this problem, Vicentino would surely have said. And he would have added that we need to look more closely at the original in order to see what is wrong. The chant is *not* purely diatonic; there lurks in it an interval from another genus. By now, the reader has undoubtedly discovered the offending interval—the minor third (a chromatic species) between pitches 13 and 14. This is precisely the spot where both Bottrigari and Zarlino had to admit the steps of a whole tone and a semitone in their chromatic and enharmonic mutations (see ex. 6.1). To conclude this discussion, it must be said that even if we were to choose Zarlino's version as the one closest to both Vicentino's rules and the Greater Perfect System, the one tiny flaw in his chromatic and enharmonic mutations supports Vicentino's original contention—namely, since that music in his day was a mixture of the genera, musicians did not understand the nature of the pure diatonic genus.

Why Bottrigari chose this particular solution to the problems posed by the task of imposing the genera onto the chant in question is a moot point. He certainly knew the Greater and Lesser Perfect Systems, and would have had no cause to disagree with Zarlino's explanation of them. This is made clear in his detailed criticism of anomalies in the compositions Vicentino wrote to exemplify the genera in polyphony. And to show how this ought to be done, Bottrigari appended to *Il Melone discorso armonico* the purely chromatic madrigal for four voices on a sonnet by Petrarch, *Il cantar novo* (see ex. 6.9, pp. 175–79).

In general, the linear contours of the piece hover around E and A, outlining the ancient Dorian mode. But the pitch content of the individual lines is restricted to the Dorian chromatic genus. A tally of the notes from the bass to the soprano shows that Bottrigari covers the entire ancient gamut from the *proslambanomenos* to the *nete hyperbolaeon* (A–a^1), with two extra pitches at the hyperbolic end, b^1 and c^2. Further, in part 1 the notes correspond to the chromatic pitches of the Greater Perfect System, that is, the first four tetrachords (plus the *proslambanomenos*) found in Zarlino's example (see ex. 6.2). One may not use the notes D and G in this system, and Bottrigari does not. In part 2 he adds to the previous pitch repertory two other notes, d (and its octave d^1) and b-flat. These are the two pitches necessary to complete the tetrachord *synemmenon* (hooked)—a, b-flat, c^1, and d^1—which is hooked onto the middle tetrachord to make up the three tetrachords of the Lesser Perfect System. The b-flat occurs but once in the tenor, whereas d and d^1 appear frequently in all parts except the bass. There is no discernible explanation for the frequent occurrence of these pitches.

As an antiquarian experiment in music practice, this madrigal is worthy of note. As a composition, it is not especially graceful. Besides the odd error, such as parallel fifths, there are many infelicities in voice leading and part writing. Whatever else may be said of Vicentino's compositions in his treatise, they are less stilted and show the hand of a man who knew his métier. However, there can be no doubt that in the antiquarian business, Vicentino was outclassed by Bottrigari.

In the one-way dialogue about Vicentino's theory, Bottrigari and Sigonio, but especially Bottrigari, wrote a great deal about the mathematical foundation of various ancient tuning systems for the genera. Sigonio's knowledge of this topic was negligible, Bottrigari's of course considerable—and he flaunted it. This aspect of the tracts, though of significant interest to historians of harmonic science, is irrelevant to the present inquiry.[95] It is in large part tangential to any examination of Vicentino's theory of the genera, for Vicentino, as Bottrigari correctly observed, was an Aristoxenian.[96] His geometric method of dividing intervals has nothing to do with any proportional system based on integer ratios. Vicentino himself paid lip service to harmonic science only insofar as it explained the syntonic diatonic tuning of Ptolemy, a tuning whose "pure" major and minor thirds were approximated by the meantone temperament of his archicembalo. Thus it is fair to say that in parading his erudition Bottrigari succeeded in making mincemeat of the hapless Sigonio, who could do no better than parrot a schoolboy's definition of the natural harmonic order of the *senario*.

Sigonio's little treatise is divided into two parts, one dealing with Vicentino's music and the other with his theory. Bottrigari follows suit, and so shall we. Though Sigonio admits that the novelty of Vicentino's melodies is pleasing, he faults the texture of his compositions for being overly homophonic and devoid of contrapuntal inventiveness. Bottrigari's rebuttal not only makes fun of Sigonio's opening admission (by asking what more one could ask), but also defends homophony and condemns contrapuntal devices as artifices that please composers but not listeners.[97]

Sigonio's more reasoned criticism of Vicentino's music concentrates on two elements, poor voice leading in consonant passages and inadmissible progressions in dissonant passages, each of these faults demonstrated in excerpts from madrigals in the first and second books. Bottrigari refutes the first accusation by pointing out that repetitive progressions of a similar sort can be found in the madrigals of many fine composers, among them Cipriano de Rore (d. 1565), "not only the most artful, but also the most delightful and polished composer of music in our time"[98] (*pace*, Sigonio).

The second element noted by Sigonio has to do with the presence of augmented and diminished fifths, as well as some very peculiar fifths that defy definition. Bottrigari dismisses the lot as cases of misprints.[99] Given the lack of a sufficient musical context, it is difficult to decide if Bottrigari's readings are correct. Vicentino, after all, admired the "marvelous effect" of the tritone and recommended its use to express the text.[100] For the most part, Bottrigari dwells on Sigonio's failure to examine all the voices of the disputed passages and enlarges the list of bad intervals that he ascribes to printing errors; in other words, Sigonio did not do his job properly. There is one exception. Bottrigari reprints all four voices of the excerpt from *I 'vidi in terra*, giving the original and his corrected version (see exx. 6.4a and 6.4b).[101]

This is a case where even a sympathizer failed to understand how Vicentino's system worked. Bottrigari was right in presuming a misprint in three notes of the tenor part (m. 2). The three E-flats are incorrect. But his solution, altering them to C with a superscript dot, produces a minor sonority in the measure in question. There is no reason to suppose that Vicentino did not want a major chord at this point (see ex. 6.4c). Moreover, it seems farfetched that the printer mistook C with a dot for E-flat. It is much more plausible that he copied these pitches one degree too high (E-flat instead of D-flat). The two solutions can be

Example 6.4   *I' vidi in terra*

tested against the first tuning of the archicembalo, the one that produced enharmonic inflections for every pitch in the octave.[102] According to this tuning, the values in cents of Bottrigari's intervals (ex. 6.4b),
upwards from the bass, are as follows: 309.7 (minor third) plus 387
(major third) plus 503.3 (tempered fourth). In the version suggested
by the present author (ex. 6.4c) they are: 387.1 (major third) plus 309.6
(minor third) plus 503.3 (tempered fourth). The original (ex. 6.4a), by
the way, is: 580.6 (tritone), 116.1 (major semitone) plus 503.3 (tempered fourth).

As for Sigonio's feeble conclusion to the first part of his tract,
Bottrigari is quite correct in pointing out errors of terminology and
applied harmonic science. And he defends Vicentino's right—indeed,
any composer's right—to use extravagant and uncomfortable intervals. If singers cannot produce them accurately, the fault lies not with
the intervals but with the singers. That a singer can be trained, with the
help of an instrument, to perform the most difficult and disproportioned
of intervals is shown in the improvised ornaments used by outstanding singers of his day.[103]

It is in the second part of his diatribe that Sigonio ventures into the deep waters of harmonic science where he founders. This problem aside, there are certain rapids to be negotiated, in the course of which neither Sigonio nor Bottrigari manages to keep his craft upright. The terminological wrangle over the proper name for the sharp accidental (chromatic diesis or sign of the minor semitone) is, to use Bottrigari's words for the entire discussion, "nothing but goat's wool [i.e., a futile argument]."[104] We might, however, take note of Bottrigari's withering comment on Sigonio's study on the etymology of *diesis* from the non-existent Latin verb *diesco*. Here and elsewhere Bottrigari ridicules Sigonio's mode of reasoning and of proving propositions, according an especially sardonic word of praise for his handling of the enthymeme.[105]

Sigonio begins his attack on Vicentino's theory by outlining the interval species of the tetrachord in each genus: major semitone, whole tone, whole tone in the diatonic; major semitone, minor semitone, semiditone in the chromatic; minor diesis, major diesis (the same size as a minor semitone), ditone in the enharmonic (see ex. 6.5). It is on the third (but not last) that Sigonio plans to concentrate before moving on to demolish what he thinks is a fourth tetrachord. He devotes more than a page to criticizing Vicentino for having placed the minor diesis before the major diesis in the enharmonic tetrachord, thereby deviating from the model furnished by Boethius. In his words, Vicentino, "the inventor of this division," was not aware that he had "overstepped the systems of the ancient philosophers."[106]

Bottrigari's response is devastating. First, he asks, which diatonic genus did Sigonio have in mind? And he offers five possible candidates, each with its mathematical description: the diatonic of Pythagoras, of Archytas, or any of the three collocated by Ptolemy (one of which duplicates that of Didymus). The matter of the chromatic genus becomes even more complex as Bottrigari goes into the details of the various sizes of *pykna* described by Aristoxenus, Pythagoras, Ptolemy, and Didymus—the last still in use in Bottrigari's time.[107] But when he gets to the enharmonic, Bottrigari reaches new heights of mockery. The following is a particularly eloquent reply to Sigonio's charge that Vicentino has overstepped the systems of the ancients:

Example 6.5

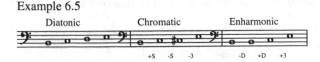

O audacious Aristoxenus, who first dared to go beyond the system of Olympus, the inventor of this enharmonic genus! O scorner of your predecessors, Archytas, [you] who did not fear to make another division of the enharmonic! O injudicious Didymus, and dissolute Ptolemy, more so than all other ancient philosophical musicians—for not only did you refuse to acquiesce to the venerable wisdom of your predecessors but you also wished, like them, to put your hand to this enharmonic genus and to form a species different from theirs! But above all, you, Ptolemy, introduced three new [species] into the chromatic and the diatonic [genera] from your own caprice! If then such great ancient musicians as these are worthy of reproof for having overstepped the previous systems, so indeed is the modern archmusician, Don Nicola [Vicentino]![108]

The matter of the fourth tetrachord is an intriguing puzzle (see ex. 6.6). After alerting his readers that such a tetrachord was unknown to the ancients, Sigonio describes the following set of intervals: major diaschisma (the same size as the minor diesis), minor diaschisma, and superfluous ditone (one diesis larger than the natural ditone). Bottrigari counters that Vicentino never described any such tetrachord. But this does not prevent him from carping on the precise identity of these ditones, dieses, and diaschismata.[109]

Vicentino did not propose a fourth tetrachord. However, he did admit the use of what Sigonio calls a diaschisma to subdivide the diatonic major semitone (see ex. 6.7).[110] On the archicembalo, this small interval is 38.7 or 38.8 cents. Thus, the linear progression from B to e in example 6.6 is: 38.7 (minor diesis), 38.7 (minor diesis), 425.8 (proximate major third, one diesis larger than the usual 387 third). Note that the dieses are equal in size, and not unequal as Sigonio supposes, a supposition that makes sense only if one is working with integer ratios as he did—hence the need for more terms to distinguish between the larger and the smaller subdivisions of the major diesis. Sigonio is blissfully unaware that Vicentino had six "comma" keys on his archicembalo (he wanted eight of them, but could not fit them in); these pitches did indeed split the minor diesis into two smaller steps of 19.3 and 19.4 cents (see table 6.1). But these extremely minute inflections were never used in unaccompanied vocal polyphony, and hence one would have

Example 6.6

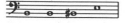

Example 6.7

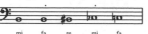

mi   fa   re   mi   fa

Example 6.8

Table 6.1. Vicentino's Archicembalo, First Tuning

Note		Cents		Note		Cents	
1F		1200		1B		580.6	
			38.8				38.7
3E♯		1161.2		5Ḃ♭		541.9	
			38.7				38.7
4Ė		1122.5		2B♭		503.2	
	19.3						38.7
6Ė̓		1103.2	} 38.7	3A♯		464.5	
	19.4						38.7
1E		1083.8		4Ȧ		425.8	
			38.7		19.3		
5Ė♭		1045.1		6Ȧ̓		406.5	} 38.7
			38.7		19.4		
2E♭		1006.4		1A		387.1	
			38.7				38.7
3D♯		967.7		5Ȧ♭		348.4	
			38.7				38.7
4Ḋ		929		3A♭		309.7	
	19.3						38.7
6Ḋ̓		909.7	} 38.7	2G♯		271	
	19.4						38.7
1D		890.3		4Ġ		232.3	
			38.7		19.3		
5Ḋ♭		851.6		6Ġ̓		213	} 38.7
			38.7		19.4		
3D♭		812.9		1G		193.6	
			38.7				38.8
2C♯		774.2		5Ġ♭		154.8	
			38.7				38.7
4Ċ		735.5		3G♭		116.1	
	[19.3]						38.7
[6Ċ̓]		[716.2]	} 38.7	2F♯		77.4	
	[19.4]						38.7
1C		696.8		4Ḟ		38.7	
			38.8		[19.3]		
3B♯		658		[6Ḟ̓]		[19.4]	} 38.7
			38.7		[19.4]		
4Ḃ		619.3		1F		0	
	19.3						
6Ḃ̓		600	38.7				
	19.4						
1B		580.6					

Letter names with superscript dots represent pitches enharmonically raised by one diesis. Letter names with superscript commas represent pitches that divide the enharmonic diesis in half.

to wade through the fifth book of *L'antica musica* to find them. Sigonio did not do so.

Furthermore, Vicentino entertained the possibility of vertical or linear proximate major thirds, and even notated the former (see ex. 6.8) to make sure the student of the archicembalo understood the possibilities of the instrument.[111] And although it is true that Vicentino did not claim that all of his microtonal inflections were found in the ancient genera, Sigonio is not far off the mark when he detects a "fourth tetrachord." If we were to follow the schema Sigonio himself proposes for the derivation of the chromatic and enharmonic genera from the diatonic, we could add the "fourth tetrachord" without violating the rules (see 4a in table 6.2).[112] However, to fulfill Sigonio's requirement of major and minor diaschismata, we must lower the third pitch (as in 4b of table 6.2). It is evident that Sigonio does not comprehend the nature of Vicentino's dieses. And it must be said that in all of his long-winded excursus on the problem of the fourth tetrachord, Bottrigari does not get to the core of Vicentino's complete system or of Sigonio's misunderstanding of that system.

He accuses Sigonio repeatedly of being carried away by disdain and contempt. True, but the same may be said of Bottrigari, who in his zeal to defend Vicentino calls Sigonio an ignoramus, a grammatical pedant, a blockhead ("un Buffalo"), a sick man prone to dreams and fantasies, and a calumniator.[113] Bottrigari was particularly aggravated by Sigonio's offhand references to Vicentino as "that fellow" ("costui"). And on his side, Sigonio was quite incensed by the title of "arch-musician" given to Vicentino by the friends and pupils who supervised the publication of the two madrigal books mentioned above.[114]

Bottrigari demolishes the arguments mustered by Sigonio, yet he fails to defend the substance of Vicentino's theoretical position. And although such a defense would encounter many obstacles because of Vicentino's shortcomings as a theorist, the task is not impossible. Bottrigari meant well, and he did insist on Vicentino's qualifications, his humility, and his worthiness of the title bestowed on him by his admirers.[115] But it is apparent that he was at his best when on the warpath. It is therefore fitting to close with the brickbat that introduces Bottrigari's mocking reaction to the "fourth tetrachord" fabricated by Sigonio:

> Now Sigonio is like the man who has a very bitter taste in his mouth (I can't imagine why), and so, as the proverb says, he cannot have a sweet tongue. He thinks he has discovered many errors "committed voluntarily," as he says, and—what is worse—"by the archmusician," whom he again calls "that fellow." And like the chap who has a tooth-

Table 6.2.   Tetrachords

1. (diatonic)

```
        +S                      T                      T
  ┌─────────────┐ ┌──────────────────┐ ┌──────────────────┐
  B             C                    D                    E
```

2. (chromatic)

```
        +S              -S                  -3
  ┌─────────────┐ ┌──────────┐ ┌────────────────────────────┐
  B             C            C♯                              E
```

3. (enharmonic)

```
  -D        +D(-S)                        +3
  ┌────┐ ┌────────┐ ┌──────────────────────────────────────┐
  B    Ḃ          C                                         E
```

4a.

```
  +DS(-D)  +DS(-D)                  Prox +3
  ┌────┐ ┌──────┐ ┌────────────────────────────────────────┐
  B    Ḃ        B♯                                          E
```

4b.

```
  +DS      -DS                      Prox +3
  ┌────┐ ┌──────┐ ┌────────────────────────────────────────┐
  B    Ḃ        B̈                                           E
```

Divisions of the Tone

```
  B        Ḃ        B♯      C        Ċ        C♯
  └────────┴────────┴───────┴────────┴────────┘
       -D       -D      -D       -D       -D
  └───────────────────────┘ └────────────────┘
            -S                       -S
  └───────────────────────┘ └────────────────┘
            +S                       -S
```

Legends: DS = diaschisma, D = diesis, S = semitone, T = tone, 3 = third, Prox = proximate.

   It should be noted that the major diesis is the same size as the minor semitone. Therefore, the major diaschisma should be the same size as the minor diesis in the hypothetical fourth tetrachord. To all intents and purposes, however, the minor diesis is the smallest discrete internal Vicentino expects his singers to be able to produce. For this reason, both the steps labeled as diaschismata by Sigonio are in effect minor dieses or major diaschismata (as in 4a). Sigonio fails to realize that an unequal division of the major diesis would result in something like tetrachord 4b.

ache and probes it with his tongue, with the utmost cruelty he states a third time that he is "completely stupefied at the thought that it was possible that he [Vicentino] could have had the utter temerity to accept and consent to be called archmusician."[116]

Bottrigari maintains throughout *Il Melone & Il Melone secondo* that Vicentino, his foibles notwithstanding, deserves the honor accorded him by his friends and disciples in awarding him the title of arch-musician. We know that Sigonio saw the matter otherwise, and that his views were transmitted to Bottrigari by Melone, who seems to have shuttled between the two camps. Zarlino would have been be-mused by Bottrigari's defensive posture. Artusi's opinion can be judged from a spiteful tale he tells at Vicentino's expense. In this story he compares Vicentino to the mascaron of Bologna, a silly old fool who, in order to win unending glory, goes to great expense and trouble to design a novelty—a short woolen cloak for summer wear—only to discover to his dismay that he is the only one who will wear it. Artusi ends by warning any would-be innovator of what the people of Bolo-gna will say to him: "It shall happen to you as it did to the mascaron."[117] Instead of an archmusician, Vicentino is a figure of amusement, a *commedia dell'arte* type, an archbuffoon.

* * *

One of the testimonials often cited in the literature on Bottrigari as evidence of his status is a comment made by the Monteverdi brothers in the "Dichiaratione" (Venice, 1607):

Even though he [Claudio] intends to explain his reasoning about how one uses consonances and dissonances in prac-tice, he has not called it Melodic Institutions, for he admits that it is not a subject for so lofty an undertaking. Instead, he leaves to Cavalier Ercole Bottrigari and to the Reverend Zarlino the composition of such noble writings.[118]

The "Dichiaratione," together with the original preface to which it is a gloss, was the famous rebuttal of Artusi's attacks on the madrigals of Claudio Monteverdi. Though mostly serious in tone, this rebuttal contains a fair number of ironic remarks. Given the animosity be-tween Bottrigari and Artusi, could we suspect that perhaps Claudio and Giulio Cesare Monteverdi wrote with tongue in cheek when they lumped Bottrigari, the champion of the archmusician, with Zarlino, the spiritual guide of Bottrigari's archenemy?

Example 6.9 E. Bottrigari, *Il cantar novo,* part 1

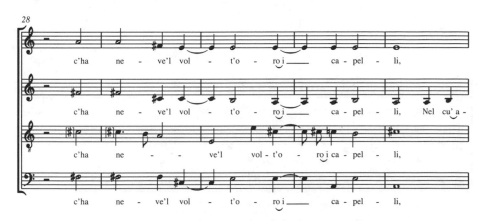

178

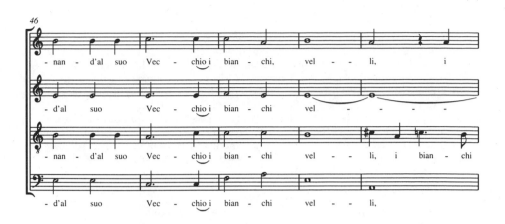

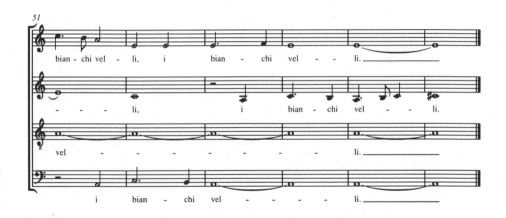

Notes

1. Bottrigari's treatise was published in Ferrara by Vittorio Baldini as the second part to *Il Melone discorso armonico*, though it has a separate title page. The first title page lists both parts as *Il Melone & il Melone secondo*. Henceforth this dual title will refer to the publication as whole, whereas *Il Melone discorso armonico* will designate the first part and *Il Melone secondo* the second part. Sigonio's work appears at the end of *Il Melone secondo* (pp. 32–39) after the table of contents and before the closing list of errata. See facsimile edition edited by Giuseppe Vecchi, Bibliotheca Musica Bononiensis, 2d ser., no. 29 (Bologna, 1969). For an English translation, see Maria Rika Maniates, "Bottrigari versus Sigonio: On Vicentino and His Ancient Music Adapted to Modern Practice," in Nancy K. Baker and Barbara R. Hanning, eds., *Essays in Honor of Claude V. Palisca* (New York, 1992).

2. Spontone dedicated two books of madrigals to Bottrigari: *Il primo libro di madrigali a quatro voci* (Venice, 1558) and *Libro terzo di madrigali a cinque voci* (Venice, 1583). The latter has a dedication written by Bartolomeo's son, Ciro Spontone.

3. See Gaetano Gaspari, *Musica e musicisti a Bologna: ricerche, documenti e memorie riguardanti la storia dell'arte musicale a Bologna*, Bibliotheca Musica Bononiensis, ed. Giuseppe Vecchi, 3d ser., no. 1 (Bologna, 1969), 270–71. The section pertinent to this article, 269–350, is reprinted from *Atti e memorie della Reale deputazione di storia patria per le provincie della Romagna* (Bologna, 1876) vol. 2, pt. 2:3–84.

4. See Ugo Sesini, "L'umanesimo musicale e Ercole Bottrigari," *Monumenti di teoria musicale tra Medioevo e Rinascimento*, La musica a Bologna, ed. Giuseppe Vecchi, A. Medioevo e Rinascimento, vol. 2 (Bologna, 1966), 44. (This is a posthumous reprint from *Convivium* 13 [1941].)

5. Carol MacClintock, "Bottrigari [Bottrigaro], Ercole," *New Grove Dictionary of Music and Musicians* 3:93.

6. *Trattato della descrittione della sfera celeste in piano di Cl. Tolomeo* (Bologna, 1572), and Bartolus Sassoferrato, *Tyberiades . . . tractatus de fluminibus tripartitus* (Bologna, 1576). Bottrigari's library passed largely intact into the hands of the famous eighteenth-century Franciscan musician and teacher Padre Martini, and it is now located in Bologna mainly in the Civico Museo Bibliografico Musicale, though some items can be found in the Biblioteca Universitaria.

7. *Opere di Oratio Fineo* (Venice, 1587). Bottrigari himself contributed the editing of the small treatise of optics.

8. The two treatises are "La mascara overo della fabrica de'teatri e dello apparato delle scene tragisatiricomiche" and "Enimma di Pitagora." For information on the Pseudo-Aristotle translation, see Claude V. Palisca, *Humanism in Italian Renaissance Musical Thought* (New Haven, 1985), 157 n. 52. Palisca points out that Bottrigari's translation was probably based on a Latin one by Francesco Patrizi. The topic of Bottrigari's translations is discussed below.

9. See Alfred Einstein, *The Italian Madrigal*, 2d ed. (Princeton, 1971), 2:626 and 629. The title of this publication is *Libro quarto delle rime diversi di molti eccellentiss. autori nella lingua volgare* (Bologna, 1551). This was the only volume published in Bologna, and it was not reprinted with the others later in the century.

10. Ciro Spontone, *Il Bottrigaro, ovvero del nuovo verso enneasillabo, dialogo del Sig. Ciro Spontoni* (Verona, 1589).

11. Bologna, Civico Museo Bibliografico Musicale, MS B. 44.

12. All seven "decades" are available in a modern edition. See Francesco Patrizi da Cherso, *Della poetica*, ed. Danilo Aguzzi Barbagli (Florence, 1969–71). The other five in order of completion are "La deca ammirabile," "La deca plastica," "La deca dogmatica universale," "La deca sacra," and "La deca semisacra."

13. Patrizi, *Della poetica*, vol. 1 (Florence, 1969), 344–48. Bottrigari's involuted excursus was clarified and mathematically exemplified by an unknown contemporary. See Remo Giazotto, "'Il Patricio' di Hercole Botrigari [*sic*] dimostrato praticamente da un anonimo cinquecentista." *Collectanea Historiae Musicae* 1 (1953): 97–112.

14. Both this part and the first (*L'Artusi overo delle imperfettioni della moderna musica ragionamenti dui* [Venice 1600]) have been published in facsimile in the Bibliotheca Musica Bononiensis, ed. Giuseppe Vecchi, 2d ser., no. 3 (Bologna, 1968).

15. See Claude V. Palisca, "The Artusi-Monteverdi Controversy." in *The New Monteverdi Companion*, ed. Denis Arnold and Nigel Fortune (London, 1985), 129 n. 2. Palisca cites one of Bottrigari's rebuttals as proof that "l'Ottuso" was a real person, but not Bottrigari himself (ibid., 135–37).

16. "acciche lei & ogni'altro Virtuoso amatore delle Virtù, & bellissime Qualità del Sig. Patricio, possi come in uno specchio vedere quanto si siano ingannati quelli che contra di lui senza occasione alcuna si mossero à Censurarlo, afinche il Mondo lo scopresse piu ignorante che Dotto; & essi per faccenti li giudicasse; se bene a giudicio universale di tutti gl'intelligenti, questi non erano sufficienti di portarlo dietro il Calamaio col paperio." *Seconda parte dell'Artusi*, fol. a2r. It cannot be determined if Artusi, a lover of puns, intended one on "il Giudizio Universale" in the eschatological sense of the "Last Judgment."

17. "& non d'altri abbagij alla Luna chi vuole." *Seconda parte dell'Artusi*, fol. a3v.

18. "li primi essemplari di cui & le prime abbozzature vivono ancora nelle mani de gl'Heredi del sodetto Meloni." *Seconda parte dell'Artusi*, fol. a4r. The allusion to the exposition must refer to the translation of Pseudo-Aristotle, *Physical Problems*, book 19, "On Harmony," which Bottrigari lists among the works he prepared for Melone's edification in the letter to the readers written for the 1599 edition of *Il Desiderio*.

19. Palisca, "The Artusi-Monteverdi Controversy," 136 n. 16. The copy belonged to Gaetano Gaspari, and in view of his outrage at Artusi's behavior, it is possible that the pen strokes are his own.

20. Gaspari, *Musica e musicisti a Bologna*, 309 and 322. Bottrigari's remark was made in the "Aletelogia di Leonardo Gallucio."

21. See the letter of dedication to Giovanni Bardi in the *Dialogo*, facsimile ed. (New York, 1967). Also D.P. Walker, *Studies in Musical Science in the Late Renaissance* (London, 1978), 15–19.

22. *Letter of Apologia by Prank, [the] "Burlesque Academic," to the Reverend Don Vincenzo Spada of Faenza*. This and the ensuing quotations can be found in Gaspari, *Musica e musicisti a Bologna*, 322–23. Gaspari, *Catalogo della Biblioteca del Liceo Musicale di Bologna* (Bologna, 1890), 1:66–67, reproduces the entire passage concerning Artusi (to whom Bottrigari refers by the somewhat provocative anagram "Usarti") from Bottrigari's "Aletelogia" of 1604 (Bologna, Civico Museo Bibliografico Musicale, MS B. 43, 119). Even though Galilei is not named in the excerpts from the actual letter, it is assumed on Bottrigari's authority that he was the recipient, for Bottrigari identifies the *Dialogo* of 1589 as the butt of Artusi's "public invective." Why Artusi waited seven years is not known.

23. "un bisbiglio, un fracasso, un romore tanto grande che m'ha per amor vostro hormai levato il cervello da luoco a luoco."

24. "et assicuratevi che à pena hanno le vostre labbra toccato le acque del fonte di Parnasso. Horsu vi lascio a Dio. Dalla nostra Cancellaria, il 14. Genaio 1588./ Vostro cordialliss.° Amico/Il Burla."

25. *Tract of Apologia in Defense of the Works of the Reverend Zarlino of Chioggia*; cited from Gaspari, *Catalogo*, 66. But see also Gaspari, *Musica e musicisti a Bologna*, 325. The ensuing quotations are also found in these two locations.

26. "ignorante, ostinato e malitioso" and "spropositi, sogni, chimere et fantasmi."

27. *Il Desiderio . . . Dialogo di Alemanno Benelli* (Venice, 1594); *Il Desiderio . . . Dialogo del M. Ill. Sig. Cavaliere Hercole Bottrigaro* (Bologna, 1599); *Il Desiderio . . . Dialogo di Annibale Meloni* (Milan, 1601).

28. Facsimile, ed. Kathi Meyer, *Veröffentlichungen der Musik-Bibliothek Paul Hirsch*, ed. Johannes Wolf, no. 5 (Berlin, 1924); English trans. by Carol MacClintock, Musicological Studies and Documents, no. 9 (1962). The 1599 edition is dedicated to Cardinal Aldobrandini by one Gratia Lodi Garisendi. One of two Cardinals Aldobrandini could have been the dedicatee: Pietro (1573–1610), the diplomat nephew of Pope Clement VIII who negotiated the takeover of Ferrara by the papacy in 1598, or his brother Cinzio (1560–1610), a man of letters who befriended Tasso and inherited his manuscripts. The Aldobrandinis were keen patrons of music, as can be seen from the list of the dedications to them in *The New Vogel*, ed. Emil Vogel, Alfred Einstein, François Lesure, and Claudio Sartori (Pomezia, 1977). About the Garisendi family little is known except that its members took part in the musical life of Bologna; Don Gaspari Garisendi was a singer at San Petronio (1575–82). See Osvaldo Gambassi, *La cappella musicale di S. Petronio: maestri, organisti, cantori e strumentisti dal 1436 al 1920*, Historiae Musicae Cultores Biblioteca, vol. 44 (Florence, 1987).

29. "ne sentì qualche disgusto, e n'hebbe ragionamento co'l Melone." Bottrigari, "A'benigni, e cortesi lettori," in *Il Desiderio* (Bologna. 1599), fol. a4r.

30. The dedication and the letter to the readers, discussed below, is reprinted in Gaspari, *Catalogo*, 70–71.

31. "Et se il Bottrigaro havesse fatto questo Dialogo (il che non è vero) perchè non lo fece stampar egli istesso la prima volta, ma sotto'l nome di Alemanno Benelli lo lasciò uscire al Mondo? Et se lo concesse all'Amico per gratificarlo, perchè subito morto l'Amico, dal quale ha havuto tanto ossequio, et tanta servitù, per levarle l'honore lo ha lasciato publicare sotto'l suo nome? Perchè stare il Bottrigaro dietro alla Tavola per sentire ciò che il Mondo dice di così fatto attione? Non per altro se non perche sa che questa è fatica, et facitura del Meloni, et non sua." Note the borrowing of "star dietro alla tavola" from the 1599 edition of *Il Desiderio*; see this article, p. 144.

32. "Letter by Federico Verdicelli, to kind and sincere readers, in defense of the Lord Cavalier Ercole Bottrigari, against that which was written about him, in jeopardy of his reputation, by a certain Artusi, in two of his letters, one by way of dedication to the Illustrious Senate of Bologna, the other to courteous readers, dated in Milan the 12th of July 1601, and printed in Milan by the archiepiscopal printers," 18. It is housed in Bologna, Civico Museo Bibliografico Musicale, MS B. 46, and in the Biblioteca Universitaria, MS 346.

33. "Flattering Words by Leonardo Gallucio, to kind and sincere readers, by way of defending the Most Illustrious Cavalier Ercole Bottrigari against that which was written by the author of the Musical Inconsiderations. Letter of apologia," 154. It is housed in Bologna, Civico Museo Bibliografico Musicale, MS B. 43, and Biblioteca Universitaria, MS 345. Both Leonardo Gallucio and Federico Verdicelli are *noms de guerre*.

34. Bottrigari, "Aletelogia," 18–19. See Gaspari, *Musica e musicisti a Bologna*, 308.

35. Artusi, "Ragionamento primo," *L'Artusi*, fols. 16v, 16v–17r, and 32v. The references, of course, are to Benelli, thus signifying Artusi's use of the 1594 edition and his repudiation of the 1599 edition. Bottrigari forgot to mention that Artusi also borrowed some material from *Il Desiderio* without giving any credit to its author, whoever he thought he was.

36. Claude V. Palisca, "Artusi, Giovanni Maria," *New Grove Dictionary* 1:647.

37. See Gaspari, *Musica e musicisti a Bologna*, 287 and 296; idem, *Catalogo*, 89; and Palisca, "Artusi," 647. Most of the statements are appended to the end of "Il Trimerone,"

though a few also appear in the "Lettera di Federico Verdicelli." Besides the "Antartusi," Bottrigari apparently wrote Artusi another letter demanding restitution of the Melone papers. One assumes that the search was done when Artusi did not comply.

38. The letter, written in Latin, is dated 29 January 1602. See Gaspari, *Musica e musicisti a Bologna*, 301.

39. "di maligno, di maldicente, di mala lingua, di prosuntuoso, di arrogante, di imperioso, . . . di sciocco, d'ignorante, di detrattore, di falsario degli scritti altrui; di zizaniatore, d'impertinente, di malitioso, d'inconsiderato, di cianciatore, d'insolente, di cattabrighe con altre preminentie tali, come Capocchio, Zimabue, Mozzicone, Zuccone da passarotti, Castrone, balordo, Cervello sventato, bizarro, . . . un gran Baccalare, un Gigante, un Bufalo, uno Elefante, e cotale." Bottrigari, "Aletelogia," 2. See Gaspari, *Musica e musicisti a Bologna*, 307–8.

40. "che autoritade egli habbia di fare il Censore publico?" Bottrigari, "Aletelogia," 72. See Gaspari, *Musica e musicisti a Bologna*, 308. Bottrigari goes on to say that "l'Ottuso" is quite able to defend himself. See note 15 above.

41. Artusi, "Duodecima consideratione," *Seconda parte dell'Artusi*, 42.

42. Bottrigari, "Aletelogia," 97. See Gaspari, *Musica e musicisti a Bologna*, 309.

43. That is, the two "Ragionamenti" in *L'Artusi* (1600).

44. "I cinque libri di musica di Anitio Manlio Severino Boethio." This translation is housed in Bologna, Civico Museo Bibliografico Musicale, MS B. 45.

45. Palisca, *Humanism*, 157 n. 51.

46. Bottrigari, *Il Melone discorso armonico* (Ferrara, 1602), 10–11. For a discussion of the various attempts to transcribe this material by Patrizi, Bottrigari, Galilei, Giovanni Bardi, and Girolamo Mei, see Palisca, *Humanism*, 417–18.

47. See Gaspari, *Catalogo*, 198.

48. They are housed in Bologna, Civico Museo Bibliografico Musicale, MS B. 46, and Biblioteca Universitaria, MS 595. For information on these codices, see Palisca, *Humanism*, 128 and 157. Very little is known about Augius and Cruserius. The latter collaborated with Desiderius Erasmus in translating the works of Galen and Hippocrates. He also translated Plutarch's *Parallel Lives* and *Moralia*.

49. It is housed in Bologna, Biblioteca Universitaria, MS lat. 326. See note 9 above.

50. Palisca, *Humanism*, 111. The other two were Fogliano and Francisco de Salinas.

51. Gogava's translations are *Aristoxeni . . . harmonicorum elementorum libri iii. . . . Cl. Ptolemaei harmonicorum . . . lib. iii. Aristotelis de objecto auditus fragmentum ex Porphyrij commentarijs* (Venice, 1562). These translations were commissioned by Zarlino. The Aristoxenian translation is reprinted in Rudolf Westphal, *Aristoxenos von Tarent: Melik und Rhythmik des klassischen Hellentums* 2 (Leipzig, 1893; facsimile ed., Hildesheim, 1965). Bottrigari's copy of this publication (Bologna, Civico Museo Bibliografico Musicale, MS A / 1) is the source scrutinized by Palisca (see *Humanism*, 157–59). There remains the task of identifying exactly what other books from Bottrigari's library are still located in Bologna, especially those with commentary in his hand. Mentioned in the modern literature are the following: Zarlino's *Le istitutioni harmoniche* and *Dimostrationi harmoniche*, Vicentino's *L'antica musica*, Galilei's *Dialogo* and *Discorso*, and Bartolomé Ramos de Pareja's *Musica practica* (Bologna, 1482).

52. Palisca, *Humanism*, 159.

53. Anagrams were a favorite form of amusement. In "Il Trimerone," Melone's interlocutor was "Alonso Cupino," the anagram for the Bolognese Paulo Consoni, a singer at San Petronio and friend of Bottrigari. In the "Aletelogia" Artusi becomes "Usarti" (see note 22 above).

54. See Palisca, "Artusi," 647; Karol Berger, *Theories of Chromatic and Enharmonic*

Music in Late Sixteenth-Century Italy (Ann Arbor, 1980), 84; MacClintock, "Bottrigari," 93; Oscar Mischiati, "Bottrigari, Ercole (Bottrigaro)," *Dizionario enciclopedico universale della musica e dei musicisti: le biografie* 1:636, as opposed to Sesini, "L'umanesimo musicale," 44; and D.P. Walker, "Bottrigari (Bottrigaro), Hercole," *Die Musik in Geschichte und Gegenwart* 2:156. Fétis makes reference to the appearance of some motets by Melone in Leonhard Lechner's *Mutetae sacrae* (1585); see François-Joseph Fétis, *Biographie universelle des musiciens et bibliographie générale de la musique*, 2d ed. (Paris, 1866–70), 1:74. If this 1585 publication ever existed, it is now lost. The motets in Lechner's *Motecta sacrae* of 1575 are all his own compositions; see his *Werke*, vol. 1, ed. Ludwig Finscher (Kassel, 1956). The present author was unable to verify the work attributed to Melone in Siegfried Wilhelm Dehn, *Sammlung älterer Musik aus dem XVI. und XVII. Jahrhundert* (Berlin, 1837–40).

55. "si diede con ogni affetto, diligentia, e solicitudine à far virtuoso ossequio, e servitù à questo Gentilhuomo." Bottrigari, "A'benigni, e cortesi lettori," *Il Desiderio*, fol. a3r. Now we know where Artusi got the words "ossequio" and "servitù" in his 1601 letter to the readers. See note 31 above.

56. "sotto un finto nome di supposititio Autore." For this and the ensuing three citations—"senza nome di Autore," "star dietro la tavola," and "sotto'l nome di Anagrammato verisimile, e di persona così in impreso e Mascarata"—see ibid., fols. a3r, a3v, and a4r.

57. Walker, "Bottrigari," 157; and Carol MacClintock, *Hercole Bottrigari: Il Desiderio*, Musicological Studies and Documents, no. 9 (1962), 7.

58. "che poi ad una certa occasione tentò per sue lettere, che anchora vivono, il Sig. Cavaliere assente, che li permettesse lo scoprimento dello Anagramma; Il che da lui per sue lettere in risposta fù per diversi rispetti concernenti l'honore di quello, consigliato à non lo fare, e tacerne." Bottrigari, "A'benigni, e cortesi lettori," *Il Desiderio*, fol. a4r.

59. Bottrigari, "Lettera di Federico Verdicelli," 226. See Gaspari, *Musica e musicisti a Bologna*, 301–2.

60. It is tempting to speculate that the Claudio Achillini in Bottrigari's letter was the man who would become the well-known Marinist poet (1574–1640). Achillini would have been about twenty-five years old and a recent graduate in law from the University of Bologna at the probable time of the incident; at the time of the writing of the letter he would have completed a four-year professorship of law in Bologna and just moved to Rome.

61. Alfonso Ganassa is listed as trombonist at San Petronio from 1576 to 1609. See Gambassi, *La cappella musicale di S. Petronio.*

62. See Gambassi, *La cappella musicale di S. Petronio.* Melone's appointment is accepted as fact by Meyer, facsimile ed. of Bottrigari, *Il Desiderio*, 10, and Walker, "Bottrigari," 156.

63. Bottrigari, "Lettera di Federico Verdicelli," 225. See Gaspari, *Musica e musicisti a Bologna*, 291.

64. "la infame, scellerata e falsissima sua imputazione." Bottrigari, "Lettera di Federico Verdicelli," 216. See Gaspari, *Musica e musicisti a Bologna*, 302.

65. "che costui è uno immondo, un detrattore, un vampalone." Bottrigari, "Lettera di Federico Verdicelli," 216. See Gaspari, *Musica e musicisti a Bologna*, 302.

66. See the discussion of his setting of Petrarch's *Come'l candido pié* and Filippo de Monte's subsequent reworking of both the poem and the music as *Amor che sol'i cor* in Book One *a3* (Venice, 1582) as set forth in "Il Trimerone," 131–32. The tone of the discussion, far from imputing plagiarism to de Monte, seeks only to establish who was imitating whom, contrary to what two scholars have said (see Sesini, "L'umanesimo musicale," 62, and Mischiati, "Bottrigari," 636).

67. Bottrigari makes no comment on Melone's reading of Zarlino. He does, however, ridicule Artusi's portrayal of Melone as a learned man by saying that Melone knew nothing of poetry or poetics (in contrast to himself, of course) and would never have even seen Patrizi's *Della poetica* if Bottrigari had not lent it to him, for he was a stingy man who did not spend his money on such books. Bottrigari, "Aletelogia," 9. See Gaspari, *Musica e musicisti a Bologna*, 320–21.

68. Facsimile, ed. Edward E. Lowinsky, Documenta Musicologica, 1st ser., no. 17 (Kassel, 1959). Annotated English trans. by Maria Rika Maniates, Music Theory Translation Series, ed. Claude V. Palisca (New Haven, forthcoming).

69. The only other extensive discussion of the issues raised by Vicentino is the unpublished and highly biased self-vindication written sometime between 1551 and 1556 by Ghiselin Danckerts, one of the judges of the public debate with Vicente Lusitano (Rome, 1551): "Sopra una differentia musicale," Rome, Biblioteca Vallicelliana, MS 56B.

70. See Ludovico Antonio Muratori, ed., "Vita Caroli Sigonii Mutinensis," *Caroli Sigonii Mutinensis opera omnia* (Milan, 1732–37), 1:6.

71. "Il Melone fu grande amico del messer Gandolfo Sigonio; per la giornale conversazione del quale il Melone sentì qualche maggiore acquisto per lo suo desiderio, essendo il Sigonio non solamente buon musico contrapuntista (ond'ei venisse, come per ischerzevole disprezzo di ciò, da suo fratello Carlo Humanista nelle prime catedre de'principali studij d'Italia lettore di chiarissima fama, detto Solfanino) ma versato molto nella lettione delle Istitutioni e delle Demostrationi armoniche del Zarlino, e qualche poco anchora ne'libri de gli altri scrittori di musica così latini come volgari della nostra etade." Bottrigari, "Lettera di Federico Verdicelli," 219. See Gaspari, *Musica e musicisti a Bologna*, 314 n. 2.

72. They are housed in Paris, Bibliothèque Nationale, MS Italien 1110. See Knud Jeppesen, "Eine musikhistorische Korrespondenz des frühen Cinquecento," *Acta Musicologica* 13 (1942): 9–11, and Edward E. Lowinsky, "Adrian Willaert's Chromatic 'Duo' Re-Examined," *Tijdschrift der Vereeniging voor Nederlandsche Muziekgeschiedenis* 18 (1956–58): 5–6.

73. "Although, Sir, I am the least [of musicians] and not so expert" ("Quantunque, Signor mio, io sia il minimo: E che non sia di tale professione"). Sigonio, *Discorso*, 32.

74. See Muratori, "Vita Caroli Sigonii," 7–8.

75. Count Giovanni Francesco di Gambara, a Bolognese aristocrat, was also the dedicatee of *La pazzia senile* (Venice, 1598) by Adriano Banchieri (1567–1634).

76. Bottrigari, *Il Melone discorso armonico*, 39–42. See example 6.9 in the present article. Bottrigari's copy survives in Bologna, Biblioteca Universitaria, MS 326. A somewhat inaccurate transcription is available in Sesini, "L'umanesimo musicale," 63–70. The sonnet is no. 219, *In vita di Madonna Laura*.

77. Though of minor importance in the literary history of Italy, Zoppio loomed quite large on the horizon of Bologna. He was the founder of the Accademia dei Gelati and wrote under his academic pseudonym, "Il Caliginoso Gelato." Besides several literary treatises, he wrote four tragedies. Only *La Medea* (Bologna, 1603) survives.

78. Two of his madrigals were printed in *Novelli ardore* (Venice, 1588) and *Madrigali . . . in soggetti di nozze* (Venice, 1590), respectively.

79. Zeno's description of the medal appears in *Biblioteca dell'eloquenza italiana di Monsignor Giusto Fontanini colle annotazione del sig. A. Zeno* (Venice, 1753). The story was reported by Fétis in his *Biographie universelle* 6:74. See also Meyer, facsimile ed. of Bottrigari, *Il Desiderio*, 25. According to Gaspari's description of the medal in question, the reverse side contained reliefs of an armillary sphere, a pair of compasses, a T square, a tablet with numbers, and a viol with six strings (*Musica e musicisti a Bologna*, 311).

80. Erycius Puteanus, *Modulata Pallas* (Milan, 1599), 97. The citation refers to information, obtained by Vicentino from some Venetian merchants, that in certain parts of Hungary musicians still used the old letters for sight reading instead of the Guidonian solmization system (Vicentino, *L'antica musica*, book 1, chap. 3, fol. 8v).

81. Sigonio, *Discorso*, 32.

82. Descriptions and documents of this debate are preserved in Danckert's unpublished treatise and in Vicentino's *L'antica musica*, book 4, chap. 43.

83. "iniqua, & ingiusta." Bottrigari, *Il Melone discorso armonico*, 19.

84. Aside from Artusi's references to them in 1603, his discussion of the Vicentino-Lusitano debate in 1600 reads suspiciously like a synopsis of Bottrigari's perspicacious comments. Compare Bottrigari, *Il Melone discorso armonico*, 16–25, and Artusi, "Ragionamento primo," fol. 20r–20v, and "Ragionamento secondo," fols. 37v–38r, in *L'Artusi*.

85. Zarlino, *Le istitutioni harmoniche* (Venice, 1558), part 3, chaps. 72–80. Part 3 is translated as *The Art of Counterpoint* by Guy A. Marco and Claude V. Palisca, Music Theory Translation Series (New Haven, 1968).

86. Bottrigari, *Il Melone secondo*, 9–12, and Sigonio, *Discorso*, 35–36. In these pages Bottrigari twice mentions three singers by name: Aledola, Fanello, and [Alessandro?] Merlo (ca. 1530–after 1594).

87. Zarlino, *Le istitutioni harmoniche*, part 3, chap. 80, 290. See *The Art of Counterpoint*, 288.

88. Bottrigari, *Il Melone discorso armonico*, 17.

89. The detailed discussion of the Vicentino-Lusitano debate occurs in Bottrigari, *Il Melone discorso armonico*, 16–25, and the discussion of Zarlino's transmogrification of the chant (*Le istitutioni harmoniche*, part 3, chap. 73, 281–82; see *The Art of Counterpoint*, 270–71) follows directly on pages 25–28. It should be noted that Zarlino never alludes to Vicentino by name.

90. The music for the enharmonic chants in *Il Melone* lacks the x sign that should mark the diesis. Zarlino's version is corrected after *Le istitutioni harmoniche*, part 3, chap. 73, and this version has been used to ascertain the placement of this sign in Bottrigari's version. In the latter case, the x signs have been put above the staff.

91. Zarlino, *Le istitutioni harmoniche*, part 3, chap. 72, 281. See *The Art of Counterpoint*, 269.

92. The step of a whole tone between pitches 13 and 14 in the chromatic and enharmonic mutations, common to Zarlino and Bottrigari, is another problem to be discussed below.

93. See Vicentino, *L'antica musica*, book 1, chap. 5.

94. The descending interval in the enharmonic mutation (G to D with a dot, or D to A with a dot) is a proximate fourth, and it is one diesis smaller than the tempered fourth.

95. For more information, see Sesini, "L'umanesimo musicale," and Berger, *Theories of Chromatic and Enharmonic Music*. Neither of these writers deals with the mathematics of the systems found in the sources. See also Maniates, "Bottrigari versus Sigonio."

96. Bottrigari, *Il Melone secondo*, 2.

97. Sigonio, *Discorso*, 32; Bottrigari, *Il Melone secondo*, 2–3. Bottrigari has a field day demolishing Sigonio's illogical linking of the pleasing novelty of the music and the rapid boredom of the listener.

98. "non solamente il più artificioso: ma lo più leggiadro, & polito Compositore in Musica de'nostri tempi." Bottrigari, *Il Melone secondo*, 5.

99. Sigonio, *Discorso*, 33; Bottrigari, *Il Melone secondo*, 4–7. This material is de-

scribed by Henry W. Kaufmann, *The Life and Works of Nicola Vicentino (1511–c. 1576)*, Musicological Studies and Documents, no. 11 (1966), 97–99.

100. Vicentino, *L'antica musica*, book 1, chap. 35.

101. Sigonio, *Discorso*, 35; Bottrigari, *Il Melone secondo*, 10.

102. See table 6.1. The numbers 1 through 6 before the letter names of the keys indicate on which of the six ranks each key is located. The first three ranks comprise the lower keyboard, and the second three the upper keyboard. For a more detailed exposition of the two tuning systems of the archicembalo, see the fifth book of my forthcoming English edition of Vicentino's treatise.

103. Sigonio, *Discorso*, 35–36; Bottrigari, *Il Melone secondo*, 9–12.

104. "de lana Caprina." Bottrigari, *Il Melone secondo*, 30; see also Sigonio, *Discorso*, 36 and 38. The same may be said of the disagreement over the propriety of using superscript dots to indicate enharmonic inflections, were it not for the intriguing examples from the Hebrew inserted by Bottrigari to refute Sigonio not so much by the relevance of this material as by the demonstration of his vast erudition (*Il Melone secondo*, 28–29). The truth is that Sigonio makes a botch of the comparison of the dot in music to the dot in geometry (*Discorso*, 39).

105. See Bottrigari, *Il Melone secondo*, 14, 17, 24, 25, 26, and 28.

106. "Inventore di questa Divisione"; "trapassato gl'ordini de gli antichi Filosofi." Sigonio, *Discorso*, 36–38; the examples of the B–e tetrachord in the three genera are on page 37. Bottrigari reproduces the chromatic and enharmonic tetrachords within his rebuttal (*Il Melone*, 15 and 18).

107. Botrigari, *Il Melone secondo*, 13–18. Of course, Bottrigari consistently and accurately cites chapter and verse from ancient sources: Aristoxenus, *Harmonic Elements*; Ptolemy, *Harmonics*; Pseudo-Euclid (Cleonides), *Introduction to Harmonics*; Boethius, *De institutione musica*. For good measure he throws in casual references to works by Guido d'Arezzo, Ramos de Pareja, and Nicolas Wollick.

108. "Ò troppo ardito Aristosseno; che primo osasti di passare oltre l'ordine di Olimpo; che fù l'Inventore di questo Genere Enarmonico. Ò sprezzatore de'tuoi Antenati Archita; che non temesti di fare altra Divisione Enarmonica. Ò poco giudicioso Didimo, & licentioso Tolomeo sopra tutti gli altri Musici filosofanti antichi, poi che ne anco voi voleste cedere alla veneranda autorità de'vostri Predecessori: Ma voleste non solamente, com'essi por mano in questo Genere Enarmonico formandone una specie diversa dalle loro: Ma nel Cromatico; & nel Diatonico sopra tutto ne introducesti tu Tolomeo trè nuove secondo il tuo capriccio. Se adunque sono degni di riprensione questi così gran Musici antichi per havere trapassato gli ordini primieri, ben n'è per ciò degno il Moderno Arcimusico D. Nicola." Bottrigari, *Il Melone secondo*, 19.

109. Sigonio, *Discorso*, 39; Bottrigari, *Il Melone secondo*, 25–28.

110. This example is part of a solmization pattern (Vicentino, *L'antica musica*, book 1, chap. 5, fol. 12v). Actually, B-sharp and C-flat with a superscript dot are two spellings for the same pitch. There are therefore only four notes in this example: B, B with a superscipt dot, B-sharp, and C, and the syllables "re-mi" would be sung to the same pitch. See Divisions of the Tone in table 6.2.

111. Vicentino, *L'antica musica*, book 5, chap. 21, fol. 111v.

112. Sigonio's hypothetical fourth tetrachord (4a) helps us to understand how the tone in Vicentino's system can be divided into five dieses. Table 6.2 illustrates this division with the whole tone between B and C-sharp.

113. "ingannato," "Grecastro," "grammaticuccio," "Buffalo," "quasi sogno d'infermo, & . . . di Romanzo rispetto," "malmenato." See Bottrigari, *Il Melone secondo*, 1, 2, 7, 16, 24, 27, and 30.

114. Bottrigari, *Il Melone secondo*, 22 and 25; Sigonio, *Discorso*, 32, 35, 36, 37, and 39.

This title also occurs in *Madrigali à cinque voci di l'arcimusico Don Nicola Vicentino pratico et theorico et inventore delle nuove armonie, nuovamente posti in luce da Ottavio Resino suo discepolo. Libro quinto* (Venice, 1572).

115. See Bottrigari, *Il Melone secondo*, 2, 8–9, 17, 19, 20, 22, and 26.

116. "Hora il Sigonio, come quello; che ha molto amaro in bocca (& io ne sò la cagione) ne perciò potendo egli com'è il proverbio, sputare alcun dolce: credendosi di haver scoperto molti errori, com'egli dice, *Commessi volontariamente*; che è peggio, *dallo Arcimusico*; ilqual'egli nomina di nuovo Costui, & a guisa di colui, à cui duole il Dente; alqual muove la lingua, molto infelonito soggiunge la terza volta, che si *stupisce grandamente pensando, come sia stato possibile, che habbia havuto tanto ardire di accettare, & consentire, che sia chiamato per Arcimusico.*" Bottrigari, *Il Melone secondo*, 25.

117. "A te intraverà come fece à Mascarone." *Seconda parte dell'Artusi*, fol. 4.

118. "perciò che intende versar le sue ragioni intorno al modo di adoperar le consonanze e dissonanze nel atto prattico, non ha detto Istitutioni Melodiche, perciòche egli confessa non essere sogetto di così grande impresa, ma lascia al Cavaglier Ercole Bottrigari e al Reverendo Zerlino il componimento di sì nobili scritti." "Dichiaratione," *Scherzi musicali a tre voci* (Venice, 1607), in *Tutte le opere*, ed. Gian Francesco Malipiero, vol. 10 (Vienna, 1930). This is a gloss written by Giulio Cesare on Claudio's famous preface to his fifth book of madrigals (Venice, 1605).

SEVEN

Theory as Polemic: Mutio Effrem's
Censure . . . sopra il sesto libro de madrigali di Marco da Gagliano

EDMOND STRAINCHAMPS

July 1617 is when all the trouble began, for it was then that the renowned Florentine composer Marco da Gagliano published his sixth book of five-part madrigals.[1] Dedicated to the Florentine patrician Cosimo del Sera (for whose *camerata* the pieces had been written in the previous year, as Gagliano indicates in his dedication), the book contains sixteen compositions by Gagliano, one madrigal by Lodovico Arrighetti, and a setting of a Petrarch sonnet in three anonymous madrigals, probably composed by Cardinal Ferdinando Gonzaga, as Emil Vogel argued.[2] The book was apparently well received and still in demand three years later when an unaltered reprint was issued by the same Venetian publisher.[3]

Notwithstanding the fact that his reputation as a composer had been established by his publication of five-part unaccompanied madrigals, Gagliano had produced none during the ten years preceding the appearance of this sixth book. He had instead occupied himself with music in other genres, extending the range of his mastery as well as his fame: his opera *Dafne*, published in 1608; a book of songs for one, two, and three voices with continuo (1615); and two books of sacred music—his responses for the Office of the Dead (1608), and a volume of masses and motets from 1614.[4] All of this production spread Gagliano's name throughout Italy and beyond; indeed, his music—most often his madrigals—reached as far as England, Denmark, Germany, Poland, and Portugal. Gagliano had a truly international celebrity, one that placed him among the most respected composers of his day.

Of more significance for Gagliano's standing in Florence itself, however, was the position he held from 1608 until his death in 1643 as the official leading musician of the city. This, the result of his dual appointment as *maestro di cappella* to the grand duke of Tuscany and at Santa Maria del Fiore, the Florentine cathedral, gave Gagliano from the age of twenty-five the heavy responsibilities of overseeing (and in part composing) the music required for the great variety of events sponsored by the Medici court and that used in services at the city's cathedral and occasionally in other churches. He had an important role, too, in the musical life of the most prestigious religious confraternity in the city, the Compagnia dell'Arcangelo Raffaello.[5] And he was the leading teacher of composition in Florence in his day, with students from among the nobility and the wealthy merchant class as well as from among those who would become professional musicians. He was active in the church of San Lorenzo, where the Medici had him appointed a canon, and he was recognized in Florence as a devout and pious man and, as a musician, in the words of one of his contemporaries, a man "as amiable as [he was] learned."[6] Eventually his administrative abilities within the chapter of canons at San Lorenzo led to the special distinction of his being elected an apostolic protonotary in 1614.[7]

But a full seven years before, he had already shown remarkable administrative skills. In the spring of 1607 these, complemented by the standing his musical attainments had earned for him among Florentine musicians, both professionals and dilettantes, gave him the authority to found an academy of music. His Accademia degli Elevati may be recognized as the formal successor to the salons or *camerate* of Giovanni de' Bardi and Jacopo Corsi that flourished in Florence during the several decades before. Notwithstanding its short life, Gagliano's academy stands as a significant institution in the history of late Renaissance music.[8]

Locally and even internationally Gagliano's fame was great; yet despite the respect in which he was held by the Medici court and, seemingly, by the entire city of Florence, and despite his recognized superiority, his attainments, and the remarkable authority that they had given him—or perhaps, rather, because of all these—he was the subject of a vicious campaign that sought on theoretical grounds to discredit his music and, by extension, to condemn him. First knowledge of the attack comes from Gagliano himself: in his publication of a new collection of sacred music, his *Sacrae cantiones*, the first of whose part books appeared in August 1622,[9] Gagliano inserted an open letter in which he complained of a document being circulated that denounced him and the madrigals of his sixth book. Gagliano's letter is as follows:

To my gracious readers:

On the occasion of publishing the present work, I have resolved, most gracious readers, to free myself from an extremely tiresome annoyance by making clear my arguments against some who, as perhaps you will have heard, have for a long time been busy vilifying my works and muttering about them openly. And although in the opinion of some I ought to have decided upon such an exposition before now, I have wanted, nevertheless, to refrain from it, having always held that whoever would have heard my case without animosity would not have needed any justification for my side; hoping at the same time, as often in similar cases it usually happens, that because of its flimsiness such a commotion must soon fade away. But having already seen the thing, contrary to my belief, spread so widely that my reputation was running some risk of suffering from it, I have been unable to restrain myself any longer from moving to defend said reputation of mine as something which must be considered equal to one's own life, and it is the most valuable thing that makes men honored in the eyes of the world. Wherefore I am obliged to entreat all those who want to honor me by spending some time with these musical works to give a glance at this brief written statement of mine wherein, if I am not mistaken, they can see how far beyond reason has gone the desire of those in whom passion prevails, and at the same time can be satisfied as to whether I have rightfully tolerated till now, as being of little quality, the accusations made against me.

When, then, at the end of the year 1617 I gave to the press my Sixth Book of Madrigals for five voices, Mutio Effrem, *musico*, now stipendiary of these Most Serene [Medici] Highnesses, according to what was subsequently reported to me, felt obliged to denigrate them extensively and to note various errors in them. And so that he could disclose even more of his animus against me, he formed from it an ample document that furnished no small pleasure to some who did not greatly love my things. This document was immediately made known in various places, both among professional musicians and among various gentlemen of the city. And since those who wish to know more in this art [of music] than the practice of singing are very few, so too were those very few who could correctly judge if Effrem was justified in what he had written on this matter. Therefore my adversaries found a clear field in which to elevate, to praise, to magnify, to exalt to the stars as something divine and never before experienced in the world, the worth and refinement of Mutio Effrem; suppressing, on the other hand, anything good that might have come from me, only preaching with all their strength my ignorance and shortcomings.

I was, in the fullness of time, advised of such odious behavior, and in particular of this document, wherefore I, [becoming] extremely disgusted and indignant, more by the way in which it was done than by the deed itself, began with all diligence to endeavor to see it. And reasoning that since I was certain that those who behaved in this way with me were hardly friends of mine (on other occasions they had let themselves be carried away and revealed themselves [as being] against me), [I concluded that] it could be that this piece of writing would have also the same character. I was quite confident that having [the document] in my hands, I would find it very easy to exonerate myself from what had been wickedly thought about my works because of it. But such a desire proved vain for me: by neither entreaty nor diligence nor artifice that I myself might have used, or that I might have had my friends use, has it been possible for me even to have a copy of it. On the contrary, those who had it in their hands, when they discovered my desire, greatly restricted the opportunities for it to be shown, and particularly in those places where one might find my confidants, who might be suspected by them of making me party to its contents.

For this reason, I grew increasingly convinced that those criticisms must be empty and of no importance and were only produced by the desire to spread the idea, be it right or wrong, that I knew little. For what would have been the purpose of Mutio Effrem and his followers, having discovered true and manifest errors in my music (on the basis of the accepted rules), to want then to keep them hidden from me so strictly? How much better they would have realized their intention of showing me poorly qualified for my art if they had thrust before my face a great handful of errors whence, wishing to defend myself, I would have been forced to defend error or to think myself worthless and bow before their thus heightened and enlarged intelligence. Acting, therefore, according to this way of thinking, I persisted in my view, as I am [persisting] at present, that Mutio went too far, and his adherents undertook, in order to bring me down, such a study that, when it would be seen and examined, would not be possible for them to support.

And in truth, if one probes more deeply into the origin of this document, why is it not also quite possible that one who is like Mutio Effrem, who, according to what one knows of him, has never put himself to the task of composing too many pieces, and who has never had the courage to show in print anything save one madrigal—is it not likely, I say, that he, being greatly deceived in judging my compositions and not really sure of the truth of his view, has tried in every way possible not to have me ever see [the document], fearing perhaps that I might discover its fallacies and that I could give a good reckoning of them?

Music is one of those arts that does not make men eminent without the practice of it, and just as one will never be a great doctor without experience and the practice of having treated and cured many infirm people, just so is he not to be considered a great musician who has not given proof of himself with many and perfect compositions in the ranks of competent men. In practice one encounters such difficulties as were never imagined, and sometimes a thing is thought perfect whose subsequent application is worthless; just as the opposite also often happens. Again, it happens that sometimes going outside the rules increases not a little the beauty of a work, and they tell me there are many examples of this in excellent architecture, and in the music of those great men whom we esteem highly they are most frequent; by him who has not gone very far in experience, these rule-breaking beauties [sregolate bellezze] can be held to be very gross oversights and beginners' errors. Effrem, then, as one not much experienced in composition, although otherwise he might be exquisite, being able to be in this and in other similar details easily deceived, I have always held—and with all the other reasons, as I have already said, I still hold—that this document [directed] against me was created without basis, and since I held it to be an empty thing, I believed surely that it would soon disappear of its own accord, having provided with itself much gossip. But finding myself mistaken in my opinion, I have seen it yet constantly gain strength instead of weakening, and my adversaries, not content merely to fill Florence with it, have made it go out to many places in Italy, to which places comes not the document, but very indistinct and confused news of it. There have not failed to take hold in some doubts concerning my works. And unable to suffer this any longer, I moved to defend my reputation, my honor, my labors after keeping silent so long. After having endured so much, I am expressing my indignation with this document. And my resolve is all the more spirited since I was earlier considering only the probable conjectures through which I perhaps could be affected by being misunderstood, but for some time now I have by sure means come to know some details of this criticism from which, if it is as it is said to be (evermore confirming me in my opinion) I have nothing to fear.

I wish, therefore, to make known to all those who might be against me in this matter, and to Mutio Effrem in particular, that I have not until now expressed resentment over this document because I have not seen it, and I have not judged it; and I shall never judge it until I do see it. And were I to see it, I think that I would be of the same opinion. Therefore, if he wants me to evaluate it, and if he thinks that he has persuaded me with his arguments and has caused me to be considered for the future what he has sought to have me considered [to be] up to now, let him publish his writing, let him act in such a way that I may see it, for otherwise, if he keeps himself under cover, reason is against him. And if I am not mistaken, the truth of the situation having been revealed through this declaration of mine, I shall assume that I am fully exonerated and have turned against him whatever misapprehension his words and the words of his followers may have spread about me.[10]

Even though Gagliano's letter is temperate and judicious in both its tone and its remarks, his indignation at the meanness and the spitefulness of what he reports as having transpired is apparent. It is startling that he names so forthrightly Mutio Effrem as the source of the campaign against him, and that he indicates so plainly that he believes Effrem's personal hostility toward him underlies the attack. Gagliano cannot properly defend himself, of course, since, as he indicates, he has not been able to discover the specific criticisms of his madrigals. But his dismissal of Effrem as a qualified judge of his work on the grounds that his lack of direct experience with the exigencies of the craft of musical composition is telling. And the additional suggestion of cowardice on the part of Effrem, who "never had the courage to show in print anything save one madrigal," is all the more damaging, this time to Effrem's honor as well as his authority.

In further justification of his music, Gagliano makes an aesthetic statement of particular significance with his remark that "going outside the rules increases not a little the beauty of a work," a declaration that calls to mind Monteverdi's rejoinder to canon Artusi. Extending the idea and pointing it more directly at Effrem, Gagliano continues by observing that "rule-breaking beauties can be held to be very gross oversights and beginners' errors" by one "who has not gone very far in experience." Indeed, in like manner with Monteverdi's *seconda prattica* statement, this is the best defense that Gagliano could have made: whatever the criticisms of his music may be, they are unjustified and irrelevant because they apply outmoded rules to a progressive musical language—a language that evolves by practice, not by theory.

Surprised and dismayed at the vitality and continuing spread of the vilification of his works, Gagliano had finally responded in August of 1622. As he indicates in his open letter, the criticism, first beginning as talk, then made more substantial in a circulated document, had commenced shortly after the publication of his sixth book of madrigals in mid-1617 (its dedication is dated 2 July), which means that he had endured the campaign of abuse for a full five years. Indeed, it may be that the reprinting of his sixth book in 1620, halfway through the period, was both a result of the interest in and a restimulation of the continuing denigration of its madrigals and their composer. What lay behind the unexpected longevity of the controversy was the increased importance music acquired as a subject of speculation and discussion in Florentine society during the late sixteenth and early seventeenth centuries. A number of avenues of traditional intellectual inquiry— most especially those of history, political thought, and moral philosophy, but also those touching on the fine arts and literature—were closed just at this time. Educated Florentine laymen acquiesced in a stagnation of thought in these old humanist areas of concern and instead shifted their interests notably to music and science.[11] It was Gagliano's misfortune that his madrigal collection of 1617 and the criticism of it should have served so well the impulse for theoretical analysis and intense (if misguided) scrutiny on the part of music-loving dilettantes and intellectuals, perhaps along with a few professional musicians, that characterized Florentine society of the day.

Mutio Effrem himself wasted no time in responding to Gagliano's open letter with its challenge to make public the document written against him. In January 1623 there appeared from the Venetian presses the *Censure di Mutio Effrem sopra il sesto libro de madrigali di M[esser] Marco da Gagliano, maestro di cappella della cattedrale di Fiorenza*,[12] the title page of which significantly omits the more important part of Gagliano's dual appointment, that of *maestro di cappella* to the grand duke of Tuscany. (See fig. 7.1.) The small volume, fifty-nine unnumbered pages in length, contains fifteen madrigals, all in score form; fourteen of them are by Gagliano (from his sixth book) and one is by

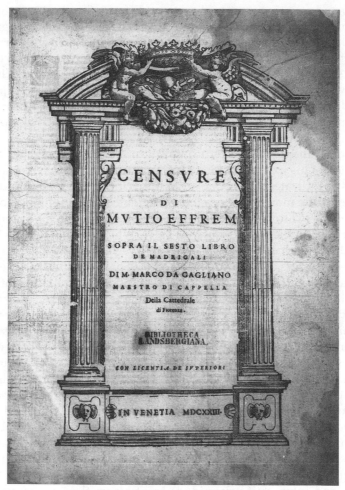

Figure 7.1   Title page of Effrem's *Censure*.

Effrem himself. The volume begins with a republication of Gagliano's open letter of 1622 and is directly followed by a letter from Effrem in response. Effrem's letter reads as follows:

> Very Reverend Messer Marco da Gagliano:
> If the service to the Most Illustrious and Most Excellent Prince of Venosa for the space of twenty-two years, accompanied by the favor shown to me by the Most Serene Highness of Mantua in having honored me with the position of *maestro di cappella* of his most serene chamber, and recently my having been favored by these Most Serene Highnesses of Tuscany by being enrolled in the number of their worthy musicians have

not convinced you, O Messer Marco, to believe that I am a musician, certainly you will be moved by these errors which are cited below, [errors] that have been found in your madrigals, with my approval, by young men desirous of learning from me the true rules of counterpoint—[young men], moved by a righteous indignation against you because clearly you mangled [through plagiarism] the fifth and sixth book[s] of madrigals of the aforesaid Most Excellent Prince [Gesualdo], who is so celebrated and admired, and because you did not hold me to be a musician.

Concerning the errors: In this letter of yours you say that a document was written and that a copy of it was given out not only in the city of Florence but throughout Italy as well, and yet how is it that you alone, who in that time were dying from the desire to have it, could not manage to unearth it? And why do you not add that having had [the document] offered to you by a gentleman and a knight, a common friend—[it] along with many madrigals, motets, masses, and other works of mine, together with his hospitality, when you were lamenting at length to him about it, so that confronting me in an honest trial you could free yourself from this censure—you did not want to accept it? This you cannot deny, both because it is known throughout the city and because I am told you are a person of good conscience.

I recall clearly, for I have not completely lost my memory, that a few months after said offer, you set about looking for [the document] with the greatest anxiety. But this was, you will allow me to say, at a time when, upon your entreaties, it was commanded with the greatest strictness by one who could [command] that it should not even be shown, let alone that a copy of it be given out.

But if only he must be called a true musician who with many and perfect compositions (to use your words) has given a good account of himself, how then, because of your works, many in truth, but imperfect for being full of errors, do you dare to attribute the title of musician to yourself? And as for [works of] mine, although of smaller quantity, yet perfect and good, would you have it that I am completely unworthy of [the title of musician]? It has to be understood, Messer Marco da Gagliano, that a good *madrigale* is worth more than a hundred *madrigalesse*. Being excellent in medicine does not consist in having a quantity of sick people and through ignorance and bad care crippling them or making them die, but in knowing how to apply the remedies well and with these to bring them back to perfect health, which cannot be done solely by practice and without the theory, because practice alone is often the cause of making very grave errors, as has befallen you, who are quite practical and not at all theoretical. Similarly, good architects do not go beyond the rules and measures, and therefore in their work you never find caprices, which you term "rule-breaking beauties." Be careful, Messer Marco, that you, as one with little knowledge of such a profession, have not been led to believe that what is the work of a simple mason is the creation of a good architect.

Now then, profit from this warning of mine so that you do not again fall into such failing, and in the future walk along the Common Road of Rules. And believe me, you will have done much if you do not stumble on that road, and do not worry about having things printed, because your works (as anyone can judge from this [following] score) deserve rather to be buried in the shadows than to enjoy the light. And so that you know that these Criticisms are not empty things that cannot come into your hands, I print them, at your demand, and I would have satisfied your desire in this manner sooner if you had indicated it to me sooner. These [Criticisms] I shall maintain to you and your followers eternally are true and real, and in my absence my adherents will fill in for me; they, with the guidance of good rules, will make you know how much you have strayed from the right path and will direct you to perfection with their teachings. I hope that as soon as you have examined them [the Criticisms] well, you will change your way of thinking, and that you will not be of the same mind as [you are when] you too arrogantly vaunt yourself. And with them, I also print this madrigal of mine so that by studying it you may come into knowledge of what the regulated beauties [*regolate bellezze*] are and learn the fabric [*tela*], the interweaving [*intrecciatura*], and the good use of foreign notes. In so doing, it will become clear to you that it is I who am worthier of the title "true musician" than is your Reverence, to whom may our Lord grant in the future greater proficiency in music than He has done in the past.

Live happy. Mutio Effrem.[13]

Unknown to historians as a composer, and remembered mostly for his *Censure*, Effrem is shown by this letter to have been a man of spectacular bad temper. Such scornfulness and abusiveness as are found not only in the letter but in Effrem's remarks on individual madrigals by Gagliano that follow in the *Censure* are perhaps without parallel in the theoretical literature. Indeed, considering the politics of the situation—the position of Gagliano in the grand ducal establishment and the concomitant insults to the Medici court that would therefore result—the *Censure* takes on a reckless character that must have been alarming to readers of the early Seicento.

The facts that are known about Effrem beyond what he himself relates in his letter to Gagliano are few. His musical production, more than Gagliano knew of, is nevertheless still slight, with a total of eight small compositions, most of them madrigals, including the one he printed in the *Censure*.[14] Even the broader facts of his life are only sketchily known. He was apparently Neapolitan in origin, born about 1555. His service with Carlo Gesualdo, according to his statement, must have run from 1591 to 1613 (the year the prince died), and he seems to have begun his service in Mantua in December of 1615. His appointment in Florence ran from June 1619 until October 1622, after which he returned to Naples, where he died sometime after 1626 (the last year in which there was a contemporary reference to him).[15] His official appointment to the rolls of the court musicians in Florence is misleading, though, because it is clear that he spent a good deal of time there before 1619. Among the indications of this is a letter Effrem wrote to the duke of Mantua from Florence on 11 July 1617, which makes clear his sojourn there during at least the summer of that year, the very summer in which Gagliano's sixth book appeared.[16]

In the course of his *Censure* letter Effrem makes several points that should be examined more closely. One of these occurs with his reference to "a gentleman and a knight, a common friend" who offered to show Gagliano the censorious document along with "many madrigals, motets, masses, and other works" by Effrem (only a few of which works Effrem ever "had the courage to show in print," as Gagliano put it). Only one man in Florence in this period fits the description of a music-loving gentleman and knight, a friend of Gagliano's: the dilettante composer Giovanni del Turco, Knight of the Order of Saint Stephen, as he styled himself on the title page of his second book of madrigals.[17] Gagliano's contacts with Del Turco extended over a very long period and include Gagliano's having been his teacher, Del Turco's having been the secretary of Gagliano's academy, Del Turco's having been the dedicatee of Gagliano's second book of madrigals, and Gagliano's having printed madrigals composed by Del Turco in each of his first four books of madrigals. Perhaps in the *Censure* affair Del Turco was neutral, a "common friend" to both parties, but it is possible that he sided with Effrem. A scurrilous poem against Gagliano is extant in the Del Turco family archive (see pp. 211–22), which must encourage speculation that Del Turco turned against his long-time friend and mentor over the controversy.

Other points of the letter to be noted bear on the Medici themselves. That Effrem refers to the document's having been suppressed, "commanded with the greatest strictness by one who could [command] that it should not even be shown, let alone that a copy of it be given out" (as a result of Gagliano's entreaty, Effrem claimed), indicates that the court had entered into the affair. The unnamed figure who could command was likely one of the duchesses, the mother and grandmother of Duke Ferdinand II, who acted as joint regents during his minority, or a principal court secretary. In this regard it is all the more significant that no mention of Gagliano as *maestro di cappella* to the grand duke of Tuscany appears on the title page of the *Censure*—that is, that the Medici are not connected to the document or the subject of its attack. Despite these cares taken, however, Effrem seems to have lost his position in Florence over the matter. He no longer appears on the court payrolls after October 1622, and it will be recalled that Effrem says that his adherents will represent him in his absence. The publication of the forbidden *Censure*, printed in Venice after his removal from Florence, may be rightly regarded as the last twist in the downward spiral of the kamikaze flight that Effrem took in his hatred of Gagliano, of his superiority, and of his achievements.

Effrem turns to Gagliano's madrigals in the pages that follow his letter, printing them in score form across facing pages. He prefaces each madrigal with his critical remarks on it, and in addition crosses are introduced into the scores themselves to mark mistakes, as Effrem recognizes them, in voice leading, dissonance treatment, harmony, etc. (See fig. 7.2.) About some of the madrigals Effrem has much more to say; in general, he has the most to say about the early ones and less to say about each successive work. Perhaps this accounts for Effrem's scrambling of the order of the madrigals as they appear in Gagliano's book. He also omits two of Gagliano's compositions published in the sixth book, but that is understandable in that they are different kinds of pieces, not really madrigals at all (one is the eight-voice concluding chorus of an intermezzo from Ottavio Rinuccini's *Mascherata di ninfe di Senna* of 1611, a piece in praise of Grand Duke Cosimo II, the other a drinking song—"musica da concertarsi co'l bicchiere," it is headed— that alternates between a five-voice homophonic refrain and imitative duets).

For the first madrigal, the first of a two-part composition that uses as a text for the two together a poem by Torquato Tasso, Effrem at once takes up two of his chief complaints with Gagliano's work: that he

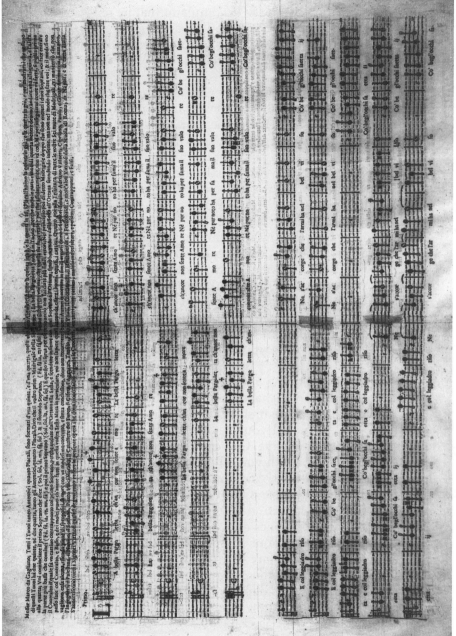

Figure 7.2 Gagliano's madrigal *La bella Pargoletta* as published in Efrem's *Censure*, with critical remarks above.

does not keep within the mode (a complaint that he reiterates in his comments on madrigals 2, 12, 13, and 14) and that he allows parallel octaves and fifths between two voices. The manner in which he couches his remarks is demeaning to an extreme.

Messer Marco da Gagliano:
   All the modes, the authentic as well as the plagal, are formed by a fifth and by a fourth. Those that are authentic have the fifth up and the fourth up; the plagals have the fifth down and the fourth down. And in pointing out to you that none of these modes has two fifths or two fourths, neither the authentic nor the plagal, I am indicating that your first madrigal from the sixth collection (*La bella Pargoletta*) is not in mode because all the parts move by a fourth while they should go one by a fifth and the other by a fourth. You start the first soprano who says sol–sol–la–mi–fa–sol; and the second soprano, fa–fa–la–mi–fa–sol. How will you ever maintain that this is correct imitation since [a correct point of imitation] certainly does not go in this way? But in order to teach you how it is to be done: first one takes the lower part, which might begin fa–fa–la–re–mi–fa, and then the first soprano, sol–sol–la–mi–fa–sol. And let this serve as an example to you so that you will not make such errors anymore.
   Then, at the beginning of this madrigal, after the two sopranos have entered, you have the contralto enter with a bad counterpoint against the first soprano because you go from the octave to the sixth, and you [have it] descend, together with that soprano, to the octave. One can perfectly well go from the sixth to the octave, [both voices] descending together, but not in the way that you do it. And you make the same passage with the contralto and the bass. And of the many *punti* that you have made in this sixth collection of yours in particular, you do not know which are good ones and which are bad. And as for the texture [*tessitura*] of all your six collections of madrigals, I shall insist to you that they are not worth a thing, being full of mistakes, always monotonous and ineffectual, whereas you will not find the good composers falling into similar errors— such gentlemen as the divine Adriano Willaert, Cipriano, Paolo and Giovanni Animuccia, Luzzaschi, Ingegneri, Palestrina, Nanino, Soriano, Pietro Vinci, Morales, Cavalier del Turco, Cifra, Agazzari, Teofilo, Filippo Vitali, Giovannelli, Monteverdi, Frescobaldi, and many other virtuosos of the schools of Rome, of Naples, and of all Italy. May all the gentlemen virtuosos who will deign to see the present work be advised that where they

find the signs of the crosses are bad *punti*, terrible textures, and abysmal counterpoints and *falsi*.[18]

According to Effrem's instruction, Gagliano's opening for soprano 1 and soprano 2 (quinto) in the first madrigal (see ex. 7.1) would be corrected as in example 7.2. Effrem's correction would result, however, in a leap to a seventh if the half-note distance between the soprano entrances as used by Gagliano is maintained (see ex. 7.2); it is only by delaying the entrance of soprano 2 by another half note that Effrem's correction would work. It should be noted as well that the descending fifth (la–re) and the answering descending fourth (la–mi) as given by Effrem do not serve to define a mode on F, the mode both of the opening phrase and of the pair of opening madrigals. Effrem's complaint at voice leading—the first of a great number of such in the course of the *Censure*—occurs in m. 3 for soprano and alto (see ex. 7.3) and again in m. 5 where the alto and bass repeat the same counterpoint an octave lower. In subsequent madrigals (for example, madrigals 4, 9, 11, and 12), Effrem marks other similar instances of parallel and hidden octaves as well as parallel and hidden fifths.

Example 7.1 *La bella Pargoletta*, opening

Example 7.2 Effrem's correction

Example 7.3 *La bella Pargoletta*, mm. 3–4

For Severo Bonini, a contemporary theorist writing somewhat later, who was an avowed admirer of Effrem, the *Censure* remarks on Gagliano's first madrigal were very problematic.[19] Turning to the very passage cited in example 7.3 above, Bonini wrote:

> The same [i.e., rendering judgment without real knowledge] will happen to mordacious ones such as these as has happened to some men who were otherwise universally and much respected—in particular Muzio Effrem, the Neapolitan. Overly confident in himself, he attacked a book of madrigals for five voices by Messer Marco da Gagliano, *maestro di cappella* of our Duomo in Florence. In the beginning of his published *Censures*, he cited as an example Messer Marco's setting of a sonnet so that, as he wrote, one might learn from it. Among his criticisms was this: that [Gagliano] had avoided parallel octaves [within] the space of a quarter-note, and not [within] the space of a half-note as the common rule requires.
>
> A few months ago this book came into my hands in the shop of the bookseller Signor Cortesi, and diligently I read through it all. I was completely astonished when I noticed that in about three places [in Effrem's own model madrigal] he had avoided parallel octaves by the space of an eighth-note, which is worse than that of a quarter-note; moreover, I found parallel fifths and more parallel octaves.[20]

Indeed, it is true that Effrem's own madrigal *Tu miri o vago et amoroso fiore* (his model for "regulated beauties") from the *Censure* is full of the same, and worse, kinds of errors in voice leading and dissonance treatment for which he excoriates Gagliano. (In one of the extant copies of the *Censure* such errors have been indicated. See fig. 7.3.)[21]

References to dissonance treatment—its preparation, its placement, its resolution—occur frequently in the *Censure*. In his critique of Gagliano's second madrigal, *Qual colpa ha del morire* (the second part of Tasso's poem *La bella Pargoletta*), after stressing the frequency with which Gagliano breaks the mode and, in this case, exceeds the vocal range established by the mode as well, Effrem marks several instances of unacceptable dissonance treatment. In mm. 6 and 9 (see exx. 7.4 and 7.5) he indicates without comment two improper treatments of seconds created by suspensions. The first of these is accompanied by a leap in the tenor to a dissonant fifth with the alto. One can only speculate as to whether Effrem faults the suspension because of its length or because its resolution is on a stronger rhythmic position than is its impact.

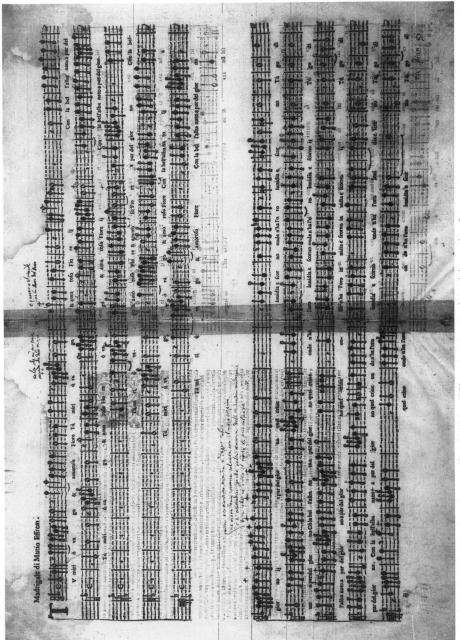

Figure 7.3   Effrem's own madrigal from the *Censure*.

Effrem points out many other instances of dissonance misused, according to him, in other madrigals. In madrigal 4, *Che non mi date aita* (see ex. 7.6), Effrem marks a leap to a dissonance in the bass (at mm. 26 and 28), accented passing tones in the alto, quinto, and soprano (mm. 25 and 28), and the same combination of tones as in example 7.4 (at the third chord in example 7.6). In madrigal 9, *Filli, mentre ti bacio*, a madrigal about which Effrem tells Gagliano "all the ideas are very poor, and you have used them so many other times,"[22] mm. 17–18 and 30 are singled out and commented on.

> That fa [in the alto at m. 17] that makes a ninth with the soprano and a second with the tenor, tell me, who can excuse it? And while the soprano makes a diminished fifth with the bass by means of a tie [= suspension] with the bass, to which you add a [diminished] fourth immediately afterwards—these are two ugly things that cannot stand because one bad thing does not save another. And the two fifths that are there [in the alto and tenor at m. 30]—I make a gift [of them] to you.[23] [See exx. 7.7 and 7.8]

Not only is none of these passages Effrem cites outside the harmonic idiom of Gagliano and his contemporaries, but Effrem, like Artusi,

Example 7.4   *Qual colpa ha del morire*, mm. 6–7

Example 7.5   *Qual colpa ha del morire*, m. 9

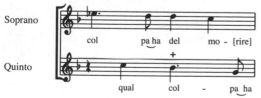

Example 7.6   *Che non mi date aita,* mm. 24–30

fails to take into account the crucial factor of the words the music sets. In the case of the last two examples, the power of the textual images, dying bitterly (ex. 7.7) and killing with honey (ex. 7.8) are, of course, pertinent to any proper discussion of the harmony and part writing.

More condemnation is heaped on Gagliano for his use of chromatic tones. In further commentary on the second madrigal, Effrem expands a specific reprimand into a general disapproval of Gagliano's use of flats and sharps. "You have no idea of how to employ them," he tells him, "notwithstanding [which], you proceed anyway, breaking the rules."[24] He goes on to recommend Gesualdo's music as a model for the use of chromatic tones and, by implication, all aspects of the com-

Example 7.7   *Filli, mentre ti bacio,* mm. 16–19

Example 7.8   *Filli, mentre ti bacio,* mm. 29–31

positional craft. Quite apart from the incredulity one feels at Effrem's having made such a remark—thereby exalting Gesualdo, who exhibits much more markedly the freedoms of voice leading and chromaticism for which Gagliano is so scathingly denounced—it should be pointed out that Gesualdo is the only composer mentioned in the *Censure* except for those listed in the prefatory letter quoted above. References to Gesualdo come up again in remarks on madrigals 6, 10, 12, and 14, and in these instances Gagliano is even accused of plagiarism, which was alluded to in Effrem's opening letter. Effrem declares that Gagliano stole passages from specific madrigals of Gesualdo's fifth and sixth books: in sections of *Chi sete voi che saettate* (madrigal 10 in the *Censure*) he decries Gagliano's dependence on Gesualdo's

Felicissimo sonno, and Gagliano's *Oime tu pianti, o Filli* (madrigal 14) is, according to Effrem, derived from Gesualdo's *Tu piangi, o Filli mia*. In both cases the resemblances are insignificant.

In addition to complaints of failure to preserve the mode, faulty voice leading, and the misuse of chromaticism, Effrem objects to Gagliano's cadences, terming them poor and accusing him, in his commentary on the third madrigal, of writing the same one in every piece. Some of Effrem's remarks are more general and address the style of the music. These range from a criticism of ornamentation (in madrigal 3) to, more pointedly, a derisive remark at madrigal 10 that labels Gagliano's use of decorative, filled-in thirds in quick rhythm as imitative of instruments or, in Effrem's words, as being like the little thirds (or thirdlets) played by shepherd bagpipers ("terzine da Zampogne"). In the comment on madrigal 7 Effrem rebukes Gagliano for the pacing of the musical matter, saying that the madrigal's passages wander; they are, in Effrem's words, "passi da Romei" (literally, pilgrims, in the sense of those who quest without knowing the precise route).

At the conclusion of his long commentary on the second madrigal Effrem makes most apparent the reactionary stance from which he views musical style and technique when he tells Gagliano:

> All those who compose madrigals, motets, masses, ricercars, canons, and cantus-firmus compositions must compose these types of music with every precision of counterpoint and accuracy and observation of rules, and not like you who, giving the impression that you are creating a beautiful passage, go outside the mode, make innumerable false *punti*, and ties that do not work, horrible textures, poor cadences, and, in a word, madrigals that are more like canzonettas than anything else. I advise you that there is a difference between composing the above-mentioned things and [composing] airs, canzonettas, and balletti, for in such things [as these latter] a man can take some liberties—though each one of these types of things has its limits.[25]

From a conservative view the late Florentine madrigal—and not only those in the genre by Gagliano—is marked by extraordinary concision and brevity, a less "vocal" style in which directness of utterance replaces melodic graces that at first glance might be seen as contradicting the basic aesthetic ideals underlying the musical-textual genre.[26] But students of the madrigal, and more especially of music in Florence at that time, recognize the logic and the naturalness of the evolutionary process in music and thought that led to this style. There is no contradiction of the genre, no unmadrigal-like composition among the fourteen examples in the *Censure*. The statements on style made by Effrem, at once an ultraconservative and a champion of Gesualdo, reveal again the limitations and the contradictions of his thinking.

Muzio Effrem, then, the devotee and sometime editor of Carlo Gesualdo's music, savaged Gagliano's madrigals for technical and stylistic liberties that are carried very much further in the prince of Venosa's work. By conservative standards some of the technical criticisms of Gagliano's music are justifiable, although there are many other progressive composers of the time who might more reasonably have been censured on those grounds. The critique of Gagliano's work, written by a man who cuts a poor figure as a theorist and who cannot even conform to his compositional principles in a madrigal of his own penning, is so furious and confused as to lead to the conclusion that Gagliano was attacked for personal reasons and that theory was a handy stick with which to beat him. How unlike Giovanni Maria Artusi with his criticism of Monteverdi's madrigals are Effrem's censures of Gagliano's, though they are frequently mentioned in the same breath. And Effrem was no doubt inspired by *L'Artusi overo delle imperfettioni della moderna musica* and the several subsequent publications in which Monteverdi was taken to task by Artusi. One ends with a grudging respect for the thoughtful, if reactionary, criticisms of Artusi, but there can be no respect for Effrem and his polemic masquerading as a theoretical tract.

Marco da Gagliano, so far as is known, made no reply to Effrem's *Censure*. Perhaps he thought it impossible to make any sensible response to such a document. Or perhaps he felt Effrem's violent document, finally published, made any response unnecessary, since its insupportable assertions were likely to alienate most of those who, on hearsay, might have given some credence to it. Alfred Einstein suggested that Gagliano may not have responded because he "didn't attach much value to the defense of works in an outmoded form."[27] Despite the lack of proof in the form of an extant reaction from Gagliano, there can be little doubt that the *Censure* must have been a traumatic event for him, and it may be that it affected him seriously as a creative artist. In the twenty years that remained of his life after 1623, he published only twice more—his opera *La Flora* in 1628 and his Responses for Holy Week in 1631. There were, perhaps significantly, no more madrigals by this "master madrigalist," as Einstein called him,[28] the best native-born composer Florence ever had.

Despite the seeming end of the affair with the departure of Effrem from Florence, it appears that some unpleasantness lingered. The *Censure* encouraged at least one other person to vent resentment of

Gagliano, though with only a trace of the ugliness of Effrem's polemic. Extant in the Rosselli-Del Turco family archive in Florence is a poem inspired by the *Censure* affair by Jacopo Cicognini, the Florentine poet and playwright, author of a number of librettos of the day, some of which were set by Gagliano. The poem is addressed to Francesco Ruspoli and models itself in tone and style on sonnets by Ruspoli that ridicule various important Florentines of the time. Cicognini's poem is as follows:

By Doctor Cicognini against Marco da Gagliano

My Ruspoli, day before yesterday, under a porch,
In that weather so dark, horrendous, and strange,
I sought refuge, shaking out my mantle
And that fashionable hat that I had made.

And to dry myself I entered that place where dwells
Mister Dickhead from Moncegli da Foiano,[29]
Because I was so far from my own house
And the sky, turned into rain, was pouring down.

I found him at the beginning of his meal,
Among tasty foods and the best wines,
And I related my misfortunes to him.

I felt the need to make many bows,
And he, grim and never uttering a word,
Seemed like the chief of assassins.

    I, who was about
To faint from hunger,
Held back my anger and my words.

    Then, full of just rage,
Seeing a man so barbarous and so evil,
I turned my ass to him without even saying goodbye.

    Wherefore, I said to myself,
Why give any more rhymes to this stingy face
—[the face] of an anatomist and a pirate.

    Today I learned through experience
That he who has not a decent form
Cannot make things with just measure.

    Thereupon, and with a *Censure*
Sent to him in printed form, it made him go crazy,
[He] not finding a way to reply to it.

How can Mister Dickhead
Demonstrate that he is in tune with harmony
When he is out of tune with courtesy?

But you will say that
It is a rule-breaking behavior of his, and that
He keeps the same manner in composing.

In this way he proceeds in
Marrying ugly notes to said verses,
But the good ones all belong to other composers.

Nor does he mind seeing himself
Whipped by Muzio with B *duri* and *chiave*,
Nor does he look at parallel fifths and octaves.

It is enough for him to walk gravely,
Act knowing and, while being ignorant,
Seem like an expert.[30]

Gagliano's life after the *Censure* episode seems certainly to have altered in external regards. There is no more evidence of his being involved in the *camerate* of the patriciate and their private music making, and his activities at the Medici court became both less frequent and less important.[31] Documents from the chapter of canons at San Lorenzo show Gagliano instead more involved in the affairs of the church.[32] From the vantage point of three and a half centuries both the theorist and the historian must feel disheartened in contemplation of the events that transpired. As a source belonging to the history of theoretical thought and understanding, Effrem's *Censure* is a document nearly devoid of any but curiosity value, a document that is almost an insult to the concept of theoretical speculation and criticism. In the last analysis, the wantonness and futility of the entire affair engender only dismay, since no one seems to have gained in the episode; rather, everyone appears to have been diminished by it.

Notes

1. *Il sesto libro de madrigali a cinque voci di Marco da Gagliano maestro di cappella del Serenissimo Gran Duca di Toscana . . . novamente stampati* (Venice, 1617).

2. Emil Vogel, "Marco da Gagliano: zur Geschichte des florentiner Musiklebens von 1570–1650," *Vierteljahrsschrift für Musikwissenschaft* 5 (1889): 518.

3. *Il sesto libro de madrigali a cinque voci di Marco da Gagliano . . . novamente ristampati* (Venice, 1620).

4. Details on all of Gagliano's publications may be found in Edmond Strainchamps's article on Gagliano in *New Grove Dictionary of Music and Musicians* 7:85–86.

5. Gagliano's activities in the sodality are partially detailed in Edmond Strainchamps, "Marco da Gagliano and the *Compagnia dell' Arcangelo Raffaello* in Florence: An Unknown Episode in the Composer's Life," in Sergio Bertelli and Gloria Ramakus, eds., *Essays Presented to Myron P. Gilmore* (Florence, 1978), 2:473–87. See also idem, "Music in a Florentine Confraternity: The Memorial Madrigals for Jacopo Corsi in the Company of the Archangel Raphael," in Konrad Eisenbichler, ed., *Crossing the Boundaries: Christian Piety and the Arts in Italian Medieval and Renaissance Confraternities* (Kalamazoo, 1991), 161–78.

6. The words "musico . . . così gentil come dotto" are those of the Florentine physician Lorenzo Parigi, who describes Gagliano thus in his *Dialogo terzo, ove d'alcuni cose di medicina si discorre* (Florence, 1618), 19. A portrait bust of Gagliano, still housed in the chapter room of the canons in San Lorenzo, shows a man of gentle as well as amiable countenance. The bust may be seen in *New Grove Dictionary* 7:82.

7. The official record of the election is in Florence, Biblioteca Medicea Laurenziana: Basilica di San Lorenzo, Archivio Capitolare, "Libro di Partiti G (1611–29)," MS 2635, at the date 2 January 1614. See also Domenico Moreni, *Continuazione delle memorie istoriche dell'Ambrosiana imperial basilica di S. Lorenzo di Firenze* (Florence, 1816–17), 2:3.

8. For the history of the academy and Gagliano's role in it, see Edmond Strainchamps, "New Light on the Accademia degli Elevati of Florence," *Musical Quarterly* 62 (1976): 507–35.

9. . . . *Sacrarum Cantionum unis ad sex decantandarum vocibus Marci a Gagliano insignis, & collegiatae ecclesiae Sancti Laurentij canonici, & musices Sereniss. Magni Etruriae Ducis Praefecti* . . . (Venice, 1622–23). Only the Bassus generalis, which appeared in August 1622, is extant; information about the vocal partbooks, including their publication date, January 1623, is known from Vogel ("Marco da Gagliano," 521 and 549), who saw the complete set at the Royal Library in Berlin. The set seems to have been lost in World War II.

10. The Italian text of the letter is printed in Vogel, "Marco da Gagliano," 565–67. The translation here has been made from the original text in Gagliano's 1622 publication and not from Vogel's transcription, which contains a few misreadings.

11. These points are thoroughly discussed in Eric Cochrane, *Florence in the Forgotten Centuries, 1527–1800: A History of Florence and the Florentines in the Age of the Grand Dukes* (Chicago, 1973), 116–48; and in Cochrane, "A Case in Point: The End of the Renaissance in Florence," in idem, ed., *The Late Italian Renaissance, 1525–1630* (New York, 1970), 43–73. See also Charles Stinger, "Humanism in Florence," in Albert Rabil, Jr., ed., *Renaissance Humanism: Foundations, Forms, and Legacy* (Philadelphia, 1988), vol. 1, *Humanism in Italy*, 175–208, esp. 198–202.

12. Information concerning the date of publication appears on the last page, [59], of the *Censure*.

13. The Italian text of the letter is printed in Vogel, "Marco da Gagliano," 567–68. The translation here has been made from Effrem's *Censure* and not from Vogel's transcription, which contains some misreadings.

14. A listing of all of Effrem's publications is in the article on Effrem by Edmond Strainchamps in *New Grove Dictionary* 6:61–62.

15. Ibid. also contains the known facts of Effrem's life. See also Antonino Bertolotti, *Musici alla corte dei Gonzaga in Mantova dal secolo XV al XVIII: notizie e documenti raccolti negli Archivi Mantovani* (Milan, 1890; reprint ed., 1969 and 1978), 96f. for Effrem's Mantuan period. Angelo Solerti, *Musica, ballo e drammatica alla Corte Medicea dal 1600 al 1637: notizie tratte da un diario* (Florence, 1906; reprint ed., 1968), 149, 155, and 157f., provides glimpses of Effrem, as he appears in Cesare Tinghi's diary of the Medici court, in his duties as *musico* during the years 1619–22 in Florence.

16. Effrem's letter begins: "While [I was] passing through Florence, the Most Se-

rene Grand Duke let me know that he would like me to stay the present summer in this city to serve him in some music for two festivities he has ordered to be made" ("Nel passare di Fiorenza mi fece sapere il S.mo Gran Duca che averebbe gusto ch'io mi fusse trattenuto la presente state in questa città per servirlo in alcune musiche in due feste che ha ordinato di fare"). The letter is in Mantua, Archivio di Stato: Archivio Gonzaga, Busta 1129, at the date 11 July 1617.

17. *Il secondo libro de madrigali a cinque voci di Giovanni del Turco, Cavalier di S. Stefano* . . . (Florence, 1614).

18. The original text of this passage is as follows: "Messer Marco da Gagliano: Tutti i Tuoni tanto Autentici quanto Placali, sono formati d'una quinta, e d'una quarta, quelli che sono Autentici hanno la quinta in su, e la quarta in su, i Placali hanno la quinta in giù, e la quarta in giù, e per mostrarvi che nessuno di questi Tuoni ha due quinte, né due quarte, tanto gli Autentici, quanto i Placali, Dico che il vostro primo Madrigale della Sesta muta (*La bella Pargoletta*) non è in Tuono, perché tutte le parti vanno di quarta mentre devono andare una alla quinta, e l'altra alla quarta; Voi cominciate il primo Soprano che dice (Sol, sol, la, mi, fa, sol) & il secondo Soprano (Fa, fa, la, mi, fa, sol) Come sosterrete voi mai, che questa sia fuga reale? poi ché assolutamente, non va così; Ma per insegnarvi come va fatta, si piglia prima la parte più bassa che cominci (Fa, fa, la, re, mi, fa) e poi il primo Soprano (Sol, sol, la, mi, fa, sol) E questo vi serva per esempio acciò non facciate più simili errori: Nel principio poi di detto Madrigale doppo che sono entrati i duoi Soprani, voi fate entrare il Contralto il quale fa un cattivo contrappunto col primo Soprano, perché andate dall'Ottava alla Sesta, e scendete insieme con quel Soprano all'Ottava; si può ben andare della Sesta all'Ottava scendendo insieme, ma non nel modo che fate voi; & il medesimo passo fate col Contralto, e Basso, e dei molti punti ch'avete fatti in questa vostra Sesta Muta in particulare, voi non sapete quali hanno da essere i buoni, e quali, i cattivi; Quanto poi alla Tessitura di tutte le vostre Sei mute di Madrigali, vi manterrò che non vagliono cosa alcuna, essendo piene di spropositi, sempre con un medesimo concetto, e senza conclusione, dove non troverrete i buoni Autori incorrere in simili errori, come li Signori il divino Adriano Villaert, Cipriano, Paulo, e Gioan Animuccia, Luzzasco, l'Ingegneri, il Palestrina, il Nanino, il Soriano, Pietro Vinci Morales, il Cavaliere del Turco, il Cifera, l'Agazzari, Teofilo, Filippo Vitali, il Giovannelli, il Monteverde, il Frescobaldi, e molt'altri Virtuosi della Scuola di Roma, di Napoli, e di tutta Italia. S'avvertiscono tutti i Signori Virtuosi quali si degneranno vedere la presente opera che dove troverranno segnate le Crocette, son tutti punti cattivi, malissime tessiture, e pessimi Contrappunti, e Falsi."

19. Severo Bonini, "Discorsi ed Regole" (Florence, Biblioteca Riccardiana, MS 2218); trans. and ed. by MaryAnn Bonino, *Severo Bonini's Discorsi e Regole: A Bilingual Edition* (Provo, 1979). Bonino believes the *Discorsi* was written over some years in the decade 1640–50.

20. Translation by MaryAnn Bonino, in *Severo Bonini's Discorsi*, 170. The first bracketed phrase and the bracketed word "within" have been added by the present author.

21. The copy of the *Censure* held by the Deutsche Staatsbibliothek (the only other extant printed copy is in Brussels) has in its score of Effrem's own madrigal crosses penned in to identify errors in the same manner as that used by Effrem in his criticism of Gagliano's works. In addition, Effrem's errors are remarked upon in seventeenth–century marginalia written in Italian (see fig. 7.3). One can imagine such a copy having been prepared by Severo Bonini, who, as he indicated, made such a careful study of the piece. Excerpts from Effrem's madrigal, with some of its errors, may by seen in Vogel, "Marco da Gagliano," 529f. These pages occur within Vogel's broader discussion of the *Censure* affair.

22. "In questo Madrigale tutti i concetti sono poverissimi, e gl'havete fatti molt'altre volte al vostro ordinario." The complete madrigal is printed in Edmond Strainchamps, "Marco da Gagliano, *Filli, mentre ti bacio,* and the End of the Madrigal in Florence," in Edmond Strainchamps, Maria Rika Maniates, and Christopher Hatch, eds., *Music and Civilization: Essays in Honor of Paul Henry Lang* (New York, 1984), 323–25.

23. "quel fa, che fa una nona col Soprano, e una seconda col Tenore, ditemi chi lo salva? E mentre il Soprano fa una quinta falsa a modo di legatura col Basso, alla quale aggiungete [*sic*] una quarta appresso, queste sono dua cattive che non possono stare, perch'una cattiva non può salvare un'altra, e dua quinte che ci sono di nuovo ve le dono."

24. "non sapete come s'hanno da fare che però il fate senza proprietà."

25. "tutti quelli che compongono Madrigali, Mottetti, Messe, Ricercari, Canoni, & obblighi sopra canti fermi, devono comporre queste sorte di Musiche con ogni squisitezza di Contrapponto, e politia, e osservanza di Regole, e non come voi che dandovi ad'intendere di fare un bel passo, uscite di Tuono, fate infiniti punti falsi, e Legature che non possono stare, pessime tessiture, cattivi termini, & in somma Madrigali che hanno più della Canzonetta ch'altro; avvertendovi che è diferenza da comporre le cose sopradette dall'Arie, Canzonette, e Balletti, dove in simili cose l'huomo si può pigliare qualche licentia havendo tutte queste sorte di cose ogn'una i suoi termini."

26. For more on this point as it is borne out in a specific madrigal, see Strainchamps, "Marco da Gagliano, *Filli.*" More inclusive remarks on Gagliano's madrigal style are in *New Grove Dictionary* 7:83–84.

27. Alfred Einstein, *The Italian Madrigal* (Princeton, 1949), 742. For more on this notion, see Strainchamps, "Marco da Gagliano, *Filli,*" 317.

28. Einstein, *Italian Madrigal,* 730.

29. About "Ser Fava de' Moncegli da Foiano": "fava" (literally, broad bean) is in Tuscan slang an obscene term for the male member (thus, "prick" or, better and more modern, "dickhead," the latter used in the translation here to catch Cicognini's obscene and scornful intent). "Foiano," the name of the Tuscan village in the Val di Chiana that was chosen to rhyme with the last word of line 7, "lontano," rhymes as well with "Gagliano," the name of a Tuscan village in the Mugello valley whence Marco da Gagliano's family emigrated to Florence a generation earlier. "Moncegli," undoubtedly chosen for a particular allusion, has no meaning to me.

30. I am grateful to the late Marquis Roberto Rosselli-Del Turco, who graciously allowed me access to the private family archive in his palace in Florence and permission to copy out and to publish Cicognini's poem. The Italian text is as follows:

Del Dottor Cicognini contro Marco da Gagliano

Ruspoli mio, l'altr'hier sotto una loggia
a qual tempo sì oscuro, orrendo e strano,
mi ritirai, scotendo il mio gabbano
e quel cappel, ch'io mi son fatto a foggia.

E per sciugarmi entrai là dove alloggia
ser Fava de' Moncegli da Foiano,
perché da casa mia ero lontano
e rovinava il ciel, converso in pioggia.

Al principio di mensa il ritrovai
fra gustose vivande e miglior vini,
e le sventure mie li raccontai.

Mi fe' il bisogno far di molti inchini,
et egli torvo e senza parlar mai
il consolo parea degl'assassini.

Io che sentìa vicini
pel digiuno, li spiriti venir meno,
tenni la rabbia e le parole a freno.

Poi di giust'ira pieno,
vedendo un huom sì barbaro e sì rio,
li volsi il cul senza pur dirli a Dio.

Onde tra me diss'io:
A che donar più rima a questo avaro
viso di notomista e di corsaro.

Oggi per prova imparo
che chi non ha civile architettura
non può far cosa con giusta misura.

Quindi e con una Censura
mandata in stampa, l'ha fatt'impazzare
non trovando ragion da replicare.

Come potrà provare
ser Fava d'accordar con l'armonia
se discorda dalla cortesia.

Ma dirai che la sia
una disregolata sua creanza
e che tien nel compar la medesima usanza.

Così quella avanza
sposando triste noti a detti versi.
Ma le buone son tutte di diversi.

Né cura di vedersi
frustar da Muzio con B duri e chiave
né la guarda in due quinte e due ottave.

Basta passeggiar grave,
far del saputo, et con ignorante
e visu verbo e opere furfante.

31. Cesare Tinghi's diary of the Medici court (see note 15 above), supplemented by other contemporary (and longer-running) diaries extant in the manuscript holdings of the Archivio di Stato in Florence, supports this point.

32. Principal among the documents are the volumes of the "Partiti" series belonging to the chapter of canons at San Lorenzo: "Libro G," MS 2635, of 1611–29 (see note 7 above) and "Libro H," MS 2, of 1629–57.

EIGHT

The Place of Aesthetics in Theoretical Treatises on Music

EDWARD A. LIPPMAN

The distinction between music aesthetics and music theory, which seems today to be unproblematic, is nevertheless fundamentally dependent on historical contexts of thought. The relationship between aesthetics and theory will clearly vary with the nature of the ideas considered to belong to each of the two areas of thought, with the prevailing conception of what each field is properly devoted to, and with the genre of theoretical treatise that is studied. Indeed we cannot even assume that the two fields have always existed or that they have always had a defined subject matter. Thus the problem we have posed can be answered only within a historical framework that takes into account the character of each field at a given time and the various types of writing found in each. Since these preliminary questions have not yet received definitive answers, however, our study cannot go beyond a number of examples that seem to permit generalizations within certain areas of theory. One basic consideration that can nevertheless be treated at the outset is the ambiguity that attaches to the term *aesthetics*. For the field of aesthetics, which deals with beauty and art and the expressiveness of art, ultimately concerns epistemology and metaphysics or, in a word, philosophy as a whole; *but only insofar as these matters bear on art*—on the experience of art and the nature of beauty. In treatises on music theory, on the other hand, we meet with discussions of cosmic harmony, ethics, mathematics, science (acoustics, physiology, psychology), ontology, theology, and still other matters, most of which are clearly philosophical, but from our present-day viewpoint, hardly involved in the experience of art. As a result, the concept of "the philosophy and aesthetics" of music, or of art, has gained currency, and I have had recourse in this essay to the term *philosophic-aesthetic*.

These introductory considerations immediately and inevitably come to the fore when we turn to the extant treatises of antiquity. As a quadrivial treatise, for example, Euclid's *Sectio canonis* (ca. 300 B.C.) deals with a branch of mathematics that has its basis in aesthetic and philosophical principles. Little space is given to these, yet they are an intrinsic part of the subject. The bulk of the treatise is devoted to demonstrating a series of theorems in mathematics and acoustics. But the preliminary considerations have a different status and belong to the presuppositions of the science. If anything is to be heard, Euclid asserts, pulsation and motion must exist.[1] Motions, however, are greater, or more frequent—producing higher notes—and lesser, or less frequent ("more intermittent")—producing lower notes. It follows, then, since motions are made up of parts, that notes are made up of parts. But all things made up of parts, and therefore notes in particular, are related to one another in numerical ratios. Whereupon Euclid proceeds to a consideration of the nature of consonance and dissonance. In this treatise, clearly, philosophic-aesthetic considerations are an essential foundational component of the whole.

This is still more the case in the *Harmonic Elements* of Aristoxenus (ca. 350 B.C.), even though this treatise is not quadrivial, but technical. In undertaking to ground the science of harmonics, Aristoxenus seeks to determine—in Aristotelian fashion—the laws that are intrinsic to melody. He rejects any derivation of principles from sources that lie outside melodic experience per se. Here is an expression of his powerful new approach:

> Continuity in melody seems in its nature to correspond to that continuity in speech which is observable in the collocation of the letters. In speaking, the voice by a natural law places one letter first in each syllable, another second, another third, another fourth, and so on. This is done in no random order: rather, the growth of the whole from the parts follows a natural law. Similarly in singing, the voice seems to arrange its intervals and notes on a principle of continuity, observing a natural law of collocation, and not placing any interval at random after any other, whether equal or unequal. In inquiring into continuity we must avoid the example set by the Harmonists in their condensed diagrams, where they mark as consecutive notes those that are separated from one another by the smallest interval. For so far is the voice from being able to produce twenty-eight consecutive dieses, that it can by no effort produce three dieses in succession. . . . It is not, then, in the mere equality or inequality of successive intervals that we must seek the clue to the principle of continuity. We must direct our eyes

to the natural laws of melody and endeavor to discover what intervals the voice is by nature capable of placing in succession in a melodic series.[2]

In Ptolemy's *Harmonics* (second century A.D.),[3] a large technical work that modifies and in many ways exceeds the scope of the traditional quadrivial conception from which it seems to have developed, philosophic-aesthetic concerns of various kinds are a prominent feature. Some of these are foundational and clearly intrinsic, such as those to which the first four chapters of the first book are devoted: criteria in harmonics, the task of the music theorist, the highness and lowness of sounds, and tones and their differences.

Chapter 1, for example, is based on the following consideration, which applies equally to hearing and vision:

> The criteria in harmonics are hearing and reason, but they judge different things: hearing, the material and the condition, reason, the form and the cause. For it is generally characteristic of sense perceptions that they produce only a coarse impression, taking an exact understanding from the other criterion. Reason, on the other hand, though it takes over from outside of itself a coarse notion, itself achieves an exact understanding. For since the material is limited and defined by the form, and the conditions by the causes of the motions, and of these concepts, the first of each pair belongs to sense perception and the second to reason, it follows obviously that the perceptions of the senses are limited and defined by the judgment of reason. Namely, sense perceptions at first present reason with their approximate impressions—insofar as these are in fact perceptible by the senses—but are led by reason to exact and recognized conclusions.

In addition to such foundational and methodological concerns at the beginning of the treatise, most of the third and last book is devoted to the human soul and the movements of the stars—to ethics and astronomy—in particular to the relationship these studies bear to the tonal system. The discussion is opened by chapter 3: "In What Context Should We Place Harmonic Power and the Theories Pertaining to It?"

These are philosophical matters that are obviously of a very different nature than what we have come upon so far; they are part of music theory only if "music theory" extends its range well beyond the technical structure peculiar to music. But how can we define such a larger scope of the field? The relationships that the soul and the stars bear to the musical system are relationships of structure; they have this much in common with music theory as ordinarily conceived. But if they are taken to be musical in themselves, if "music" is understood to encompass, along with tonal phenomena, both the soul and the stars, even though these are not literally manifested in tone, then it is clearly the breadth of the ancient conception of music that is responsible for a correspondingly broad conception of music theory.

Alongside this cosmic and metaphysical conception of music in antiquity, there was a comparably large view of music as an art of dance, poetry, and melody, which gave rise—in the field of music theory—to the disciplines of rhythmics, metrics, and harmonics. It is clearly the wide significance possessed by music that is responsible for the diversified contents and almost universal scope of musical treatises. Perhaps the single most striking example of this is the treatise *On Music* (second century A.D.) of Aristides Quintilianus, which belongs to the Aristoxenian tradition. This work, roughly contemporaneous with that of Ptolemy, has in fact been considered to represent the philosophy and aesthetics of music, or music ethics, rather than music theory. There is support for this view in the suggestion of dialogue form at the opening of the work and in the absence, or at least the subordination, of the discussion and elucidation of musical structure. Aristides marvels at the effort of the ancient philosophers, he tells his friends at the outset:

> I most especially admire the elevation of thought of these men whenever—as is our custom—we have a dialogue about music. For with them, this was not the pursuit of common men—as many of those ignorant of the subject, and especially our contemporaries, conjectured—but rather it was valuable in itself; and as it was useful in relation to the remaining sciences, presenting—so to speak—an expression of the beginning and the end, it was marveled at exceedingly. To me, there is especially apparent a specific good in the art, for its utility is considered not like the rest of the subjects that respect one matter or a small interval of time, but every age and the whole of life, every action should at last be set in order by music alone.[4]

After disposing of other individual liberal arts he turns again to music:

> Only the aforesaid, music, is extended through all matter—so to speak—and reaches through all time, adorning the soul with the beauties of harmonia and composing the body with proper rhythms, suitable for children because of the good things deriving from melody and for those advancing

in age because it transmits the beauties of measured diction and, simply, of discourse as a whole. But for those still older, it explains both the nature of numbers and the variety of proportions; it gradually reveals the harmoniai that are, through these, in all bodies; and most important and most perfect and concerning a thing difficult for all men to comprehend, it is able to supply the ratios of the soul—the soul of each person separately and, as well, even the soul of the universe.[5]

Here we have reached an instance, we might well maintain, not of the place of aesthetics in music theory, but of the place of music theory in aesthetics—and conspicuously also in metaphysics and in ethics and education.

What is true of Ptolemy and Aristides is also true of Boethius and Martianus Capella, who have conveyed the substance of the Greek authors into Latin. Saint Augustine represents a special case, for the combination of music theory (rhythmics) with aesthetics—or really theological aesthetics—in his *De musica* (ca. 400) is a special circumstance connected with his conversion to Christianity.

An examination of medieval theory will reveal a number of different ways in which philosophy and aesthetics find a place in works on music. Polyphony, for one thing, which seems to show an intrinsic tendency to invite speculation, is naturally receptive to philosophical excursus. In the *Scholia enchiriadis* (ca. 900), for example, it seems entirely natural when an exchange takes place concerning the nature of consonance. The Disciple asks, "But will you give now the reason why at some levels sounds are thus consonant, while at others they are either discrepant or not so much in agreement?" Whereupon the Master answers:

> Certainly one is at liberty to consider what reasons God has assigned, and thus in a delightful way we perceive a little the causes of the agreement and discrepancy of sounds, as well as the nature of the different tropes and why in transposing they pass over into other species or revert again to their own. For just as in counting absolutely the numerical series used (that is, 1, 2, 3, 4, and so forth) is simple and by reason of its simplicity easily grasped, even by boys, but when one thing is compared unequally with another it falls under various species of inequality; so in Music, the daughter of Arithmetic (that is, the science of number), sounds are enumerated by a simple order, but when sounded in relation to others they yield not only the various species of the

delightful harmonies, but also the most delightful reasons for them.[6]

And in considering the subject matter of mathematics, the Disciple asks what abstract quantities are. The Master answers:

> Those which being without material, that is, without corporeal admixture, are treated by the intellect alone. In quantities, moreover, multitudes, magnitudes, their opposites, forms, equalities, relationships, and many other things which, to speak with Boethius, are by nature incorporeal and immutable, prevailing by reason, are changed by the participation of the corporeal and through the operation of variable matter become mutable and inconstant. These quantities, further, are variously considered in Arithmetic, in Music, in Geometry, and in Astronomy. For these four disciplines are not arts of human invention, but considerable investigations of divine works; and by most marvelous reasons they lead ingenious minds to understand the creatures of the world; so that those who through these things know God and His eternal divinity are inexcusable if they do not glorify Him and give thanks.[7]

The *Micrologus* (ca. 1027) of Guido d'Arezzo is particularly rich in aesthetic discussion. One has the feeling in this case that the reason can be ascribed to his unusual intelligence and his personal interest in general ideas. There is a characteristic discussion of the ending of melodies that testifies to Guido's understanding of the importance of an ending and his insight into the mysterious way in which it informs the melody with meaning retroactively:

> Though any chant is made up of all the notes and intervals, the note that ends it holds the chief place, for it sounds both longer and more lasting. The previous notes, as is evident to trained musicians only, are so adjusted to the last one that in an amazing way they seem to draw a certain semblance of color from it.[8]

Guido continues with the principles of this melodic adjustment:

> The other notes should have a harmonious relationship with the note that ends a neume by means of the aforesaid six melodic intervals. The beginning of a chant and the end of all its phrases and even their beginnings need to cling close to the note that ends the chant.[9]

He then concludes his discussion with additional explanations and justifications of the unique importance of the ending:

> Furthermore, when we hear someone sing, we do not know what mode his first note is in, since we do not know whether tones, semitones, or other intervals will follow. But when the chant has ended, we know clearly from the preceding notes the mode of the last one. For at the start of a chant you do not know what will follow, but at its end you realize what has gone before. Thus the last note is the one we are better aware of. So if you wish to add to your chant either a verse of a psalm or anything else, you should adjust it most of all to the final note of the former, not go back and consider the first note or any of the others. This too we may add, that carefully composed chants end their phrases chiefly on the final note of the chant.
>
> It is no wonder that music bases its rules on the last note, since in the elements of language, too, we almost everywhere see the real force of the meaning in the final letters or syllables, in regard to cases, numbers, persons, and tenses. Therefore, since all praise, too, is sung at the end, we rightly say that every chant is subject to, and takes its rules from, that mode which it sounds last.[10]

In the *De musica* (ca. 1300) of Johannes de Grocheo, so interesting for its comprehensive picture of musical genre, philosophical considerations are situated, more traditionally, among the introductory material, notably in a discussion of the source of consonance and of how the consonances are related. About these "difficult" matters Grocheo can only "attempt to say something that is probable":

> There is a basic harmony like a mother, which has been called a diapason by our ancestors, and another like a daughter contained within it, called a diapente, and a third derived from these, which is named a diatesseron. And these three sounded at the same time give the most perfect consonance. Perhaps certain followers of Pythagoras, influenced by a natural inclination, sensed this, not having dared to admit it in these very words, but spoke of it in numbers in a metaphorical way. Let us say therefore that the human soul immediately created from its principle retains the type or image of its Creator. This image is called by John of Damascus the image of the Trinity, by whose

means natural awareness is innate within it. And perhaps
by this natural awareness it perceives a triple perfection in
sounds, something not possible to the soul of brutes because of its imperfection.[11]

In its location and its invocation of the Trinity, this suggests a traditional introductory *topos*, but it is notable in its concern with perception, reflecting, incidentally, the tonal ideal of its time rather than the
later sensuous ideals attached to the triad—of harmony, blending,
and fusion.

Like the medieval concern with polyphony, the new examination of
rhythm in the fourteenth century also provoked its own type of philosophical speculation, most conspicuously in the treatises of Marchetto
da Padova and Jean de Muris. In the discussion of imperfect time in
the second book of his *Pomerium* (1318), Marchetto is almost obses-
sively concerned with the secure grounding of the new species of
rhythm. He tries to construct an absolutely conclusive argument, using principles and distinctions derived from Aristotle, in which a central purpose is to define the difference between perfect and imperfect
time. The following discussion, for example, appears at the outset:

> In the first place we say that imperfect musical men-
> surable time is that which is a minimum, not in fullness, but
> in semi-fullness of voice. This definition we demonstrate as
> follows. It is certain that just as the perfect is that which
> lacks nothing, so the imperfect is that which lacks some-
> thing. But it is also certain, by the definition of perfect time
> already demonstrated, that perfect time is that which is a
> minimum in entire fullness of voice, formed in the manner
> there expounded. It follows, therefore, that imperfect time,
> since it falls short of perfect, is not formed in entire fullness
> of voice.
>
> But someone may say: You ought to derive the deficiency
> of imperfect time with respect to perfect, not from fullness
> of voice, but from lessness of time. Whence you ought to
> say that both times, perfect as well as imperfect, are formed
> in fullness of voice, but that fullness of voice is formed in
> less time when it is formed in imperfect time than when it
> is formed in perfect. Whence (our opponents say) that mini-
> mum which is formed in fullness of voice is imperfect time,
> not perfect.
>
> But to this we reply that to be in fullness of voice and to
> be a minimum is necessarily perfect time, for perfect musi-

cal time is the first measure of all, for which reason also the measure of imperfect time is derived from it by subtracting a part, as will presently be explained. Therefore, since the minimum in any genus is the measure of all other things in it, as previously observed, we conclude that minimum time is always perfect of itself, provided it be formed in fullness of voice, for as soon as we subtract from the quantity of perfect time we constitute imperfect.[12]

The mathematician Jean de Muris discusses musical rhythm in the second book (the *musica practica*) of his *Ars novae musicae* (1319). Although certain foundations of rhythm are treated in the first book of the treatise, the "practical theory" of rhythm is highly philosophical, concerned conspicuously both with the basis of the rhythmic system and with its coherence and completeness. After considering the difference between ternary and binary number, Muris continues:

> Seeing, on the other hand, that sound measured by time consists in the union of two forms, namely the natural and the mathematical, it follows that because of the one its division never ceases while because of the other its division must necessarily stop somewhere; for just as nature limits the magnitude and increase of all material things, so it also limits their minuteness and decrease. For it is demonstrated naturally that nature is limited by a maximum and a minimum; sound, moreover, is in itself a natural form to which quantity is artificially attributed; it is necessary, therefore, for there to be limits of division beyond which no sound however fleeting may go. These limits we wish to apprehend by reason.[13]

Muris then proceeds to deduce the whole elaborate system of musical rhythm from the principles of perfection and the properties of number. His discussion, however remarkable in its fusion of abstract thought and musical practice, is anything but unique in the history of music theory; rather, it is an instance of a pervasive feature of the field.

Something similar is found again in the theory of polyphony, for in the fourteenth and fifteenth centuries the rules for the contrapuntal succession of intervals rest at times on aesthetic value as well as on reason. The role of beauty was acknowledged for *musica ficta* in general, and it can be found in a polyphonic context in the rules for the motion of an imperfect to a perfect consonance, when the imperfect consonance must be inflected as major or minor to bring it as close as possible to the consonance that follows. Prosdocimo de' Beldomandi, for example, offers the following explanation in his *Contrapunctus* (1412):

> There is no other reason for this than a sweeter-sounding harmony. Why the sweeter-sounding harmony results from this can be ascribed to the sufficiently persuasive reason that the property of the imperfect thing is to seek the perfect, which it cannot do except through approximating itself to the perfect. This is because the closer the imperfect consonance approaches the perfect one it intends to reach, the more perfect it becomes, and the sweeter the resulting harmony.[14]

Marchetto and Ugolino also explain this principle, although in their account perfection is a more prominent consideration than beauty.[15]

In spite of Tinctoris's concern with the new sensuous properties of the music of his time and of the decades immediately preceding him, most of his theoretical treatises (all of which seem to date from the decade 1474–84) adhere closely to their technical subject matter. They include, however, aside from his dictionary of musical terms (*Terminorum musicae diffinitorium*), two works concerned not with structural theory but with matters more or less aesthetic in nature, namely with the effects of music (*Complexus effectuum musices*) and with the invention and practice of music (*De inventione et usu musicae*). His works as a whole, then, seem to represent a piecemeal version of the all-encompassing medieval *summa*, although his rejection of the larger, nonsonorous conception of music excludes any adequate treatment of metaphysical ideas.

While a variety of philosophical and aesthetic considerations is understandably always present in *musica theorica, musica practica* also often contains aesthetic ideas. Indeed, in the sixteenth century these are sufficiently frequent and striking to point to the eventual development of aesthetics as an independent concern, although the Renaissance ideas are still not characteristically directed to a middle-class audience that is concerned specifically with the experience of listening and that is largely untrained musically. Rather, aesthetic values appear in intimate conjunction with mathematical and structural interests, and it is only in writings on monody and the later madrigal that this Renaissance tradition is broken by a more exclusively aesthetic purpose.

A well-known Renaissance passage dealing with aesthetic matters appears in Heinrich Glarean's *Dodecachordon* (1547):

No one has more effectively expressed the passions of the soul in music than this symphonist, no one has more felicitously begun, no one has been able to compete in grace and facility on an equal footing with him, just as there is no Latin poet superior in the epic to Maro. For just as Maro, with his natural facility, was accustomed to adapt his poem to his subject so as to set weighty matters before the eyes of his readers with close-packed spondees, fleeting ones with unmixed dactyls, to use words suited to his every subject, in short, to undertake nothing inappropriately, as Flaccus says of Homer, so our Josquin, where his matter requires it, now advances with impetuous and precipitate notes, now intones his subject in long-drawn tones, and, to sum up, has brought forth nothing that was not delightful to the ear and approved as ingenious by the learned, nothing, in short, that was not acceptable and pleasing, even when it seemed less erudite, to those who listened to it with judgment.[16]

Glarean's obvious sensitivity to the expression of the passions, to individual genius, and to the aesthetic equivalence of the arts is combined in this passage and in this chapter of the treatise (book 3, chapter 24) with a discussion of the combination of the modes and thus set into a technical context.

Much the same characteristics are found in the "practical division" (parts 3 and 4) of Gioseffo Zarlino's *Le istitutioni harmoniche* (1558):

For just as the builder, in all his operations, looks always toward the end and founds his work upon some matter which he calls the subject, so the musician in his operations, looking toward the end which prompts him to work, discovers the matter or subject upon which he founds his composition. Thus he perfects his work in conformity with his chosen end. Or again, just as the poet, prompted by such an end to improve or to delight (as Horace shows so clearly in his *Art of Poetry*, when he says:

Aut prodesse volunt, aut delectare poetae
Aut simul et iucunda et idonea dicere vitae),

takes as the subject of his poem some history or fable, discovered by himself or borrowed from others, which he adorns and polishes with various manners, as he may prefer, leaving out nothing that might be fit or worthy to

> delight the minds of his hearers, in such a way that he takes on something of the magnificent and marvelous; so the musician, apart from being prompted by the same end to improve or to delight the minds of his listeners with harmonious accents, takes the subject and founds upon it his composition, which he adorns with various modulations and various harmonies in such a way that he offers welcome pleasure to his hearers.[17]

Here rhetorical conceptions dominate, but the passage is followed immediately by structural rules and an appeal to mathematics, which of course preponderate in part 3 as a whole.

Chapter 71 of part 3 devotes substantial attention to principles of perception and emphasizes the importance of specifically auditory values. In the elaboration of this point moral values are joined to aesthetic ones, evoking the tradition of which Horace became the classic instance:

> For since music was indeed discovered to improve and to delight, as we have said at other times, nothing in music has validity except the voices and the sounds which arise from the strings. These, as Aurelius Cassiodorus imagines, are so named because they move our hearts, a thing he shows most elegantly with the two Latin words *chordae* and *corda*. Thus it is by this path that we perceive the improvement and delight that we derive from hearing harmonies and melodies.[18]

Aesthetic matters continue to be prominent in part 4 of the treatise, especially in connection with the appropriateness of melody, harmony, and rhythm to the text of a composition (chapter 32).[19] Zarlino's discussion here, while exemplifying the rhetorical conception of appropriateness, is grounded in the theories of Plato, and also adumbrates major concerns of aesthetics in coming centuries, notably the nature of musical imitation and the ideal of the unity of the musical work.

Philosophical or, more properly, theological conceptions are conspicuous in German triadic theory of the early seventeenth century in the work of Johannes Lippius. His *Synopsis musicae novae* (1612) deals extensively with the triad, defining its properties exhaustively and extolling it as the fundamental source of both music and universal harmony. The ethical and religious aspect of Lippius's thought easily suggests the luminous aura of mystery and revelation that surrounds the triad in Bruckner and in post-Romanticism, creating a bond that seems to span the three centuries of the "modern" era:

The harmonic, simple, and direct triad is the true and uni-trisonic root of all the most perfect and most complete harmonies that can exist in the world. It is the root of even thousands and millions of sounds, because each of them should ultimately be reducible to the image of that great mystery, the divine and solely adorable Unitrinity (I cannot think of a semblance more lucid). All the more, therefore, should theologians and philosophers direct their attention to it, since at present they know fundamentally little, and in the past they knew practically nothing about it. Recently some have had intimations of it in a somewhat confused manner, although (very strangely) it is much employed in practice and, as will soon be seen, stands as the greatest, sweetest, and clearest compendium of musical composition. It draws a happy limit to other musicians' infinite and loosely scattered considerations regarding complete harmony.[20]

As Lippius's writings reveal, his notion of the triad as the foundation of music is more than an automatic ingredient of a universal eulogy; for the triad at that time was the center of both the music and the music theory of Germany, a position that it continued to occupy in western Europe until about 1900.

Both philosophical and aesthetic conceptions are integrally bound up with music theory in the treatises of Jean-Philippe Rameau. The interpenetration of these three areas of thought is especially evident in his *Observations sur notre instinct pour la musique, et sur son principe* of 1754. "The full enjoyment of the effects of music," Rameau maintains,

calls for a sheer abandonment of oneself, and the judgment of it calls for a reference to the principle by which one is affected. That principle is Nature itself; it is through Nature that we possess that feeling which stirs us in all our musical *instinct*.[21]

Thus our instinctual feeling in response to music will guide us to the principle on which it rests, which is grounded in nature. This principle is one of broad applicability. Indeed, in a type of Pythagoreanism, Rameau eventually finds that music gives the law to every manifestation of human thought and creativity. And as we can see in the following passage, the structure of music is indissolubly connected with its expressiveness: its technical theory, that is, with its aesthetics, but also with its metaphysical foundation.

It is necessary first to sing this music with the motion the
words require, without adding to them and without concerning oneself with any other feeling but that which the
melody is able to give rise to of itself, while remarking in it
the aspect towards which one will feel more inclination to
softness or to pride: and then, all bias aside, the new *flat* that
derives from the sphere of the subdominant, either in descending or in ascending, will be inclined naturally towards
softness: whereas the new *sharp*, given by the resources of
harmony from the sphere of the dominant, will demand the
animation of the melody, and render it susceptible of all the
pride with which one would wish to accompany it.[22]

During the course of the eighteenth century an independent aesthetics arose with its own circle of problems, directed to an audience
that was to a considerable extent unversed in music. Theory limited to
technical matters seems to have become more common as a result.
Speculative theory—*musica theorica*—did not disappear, although it
became relatively uncommon. It continued also to contain a variety of
philosphical matters concerned mostly with mathematics, cosmic
harmony, and ethics, and often with music history as well, which had
long since outgrown its mythic and legendary character. But philosophy and aesthetics were by no means drained even from practical
theory and from *musica poetica*. They play a role of one kind or another
with a persistence that argues their intrinsic relevance to music theory
as it is normally understood: to the study of harmony, counterpoint,
and form, that is, to treatises on musical structure and on composition.
    In addition, since scientific ideas of various kinds enter into
theoretical works—ideas belonging to acoustics, physiology, and
psychology—the fields that are found relevant by music theorists are
numerous as well as diverse. But music theory as a modern discipline,
entirely apart from the technically oriented treatises in the tradition of
musica practica and *poetica*, has also laid claim to music philosophy and
aesthetics as such, and essays and studies belonging to this area of
thought are now often considered to belong to theory instead. Articles
purely philosophical or aesthetic, for example, are frequently published in American periodicals that are designated as journals of music
theory. They have come to be "music theory" rather than "musicology" or "music aesthetics," in part for cultural and socio-political
reasons—music theory is an expanding field with a huge appetite for
material of all kinds—and in part because American musicology has
not developed organs of publication for essays devoted to aesthetics.

But yet another reason would be that there is a new conception of music theory that has come to exist alongside its traditional definition as a field dealing essentially with musical structure in all its forms. This new conception, however, has an old ancestry, for it goes back to the Greek meaning of theory as intellectual contemplation, a broad category that Aristotle contrasts with doing and with making. In this sense, music theory would encompass all ideas that deal with music, and would stand opposed, being philosophical, to performance and to composition as activities, but not to the theory of these activities. We may speak, then, of a circle that has closed in the history of music theory and left behind the traditional divisions of music study that belonged to the general and still evolving fractionation of the intellectual world.

A factor, finally, that brings the two conceptions of theory together to some extent is derived from the efflorescence in this century of the idea of "analysis," an idea, as is known, that has permeated Anglo-American intellectual culture in general and given rise to an endless succession of analytical techniques. Thus not only formal dissection and the interrelating of formal constituents is music analysis, but also the uncovering of encompassing linear features of a musical composition, and—what is of peculiar interest—the careful characterization of musical experience and perception. But "phenomenological analysis," which has appeared in recent years, is hardly analysis in a literal sense, just as Schenkerian analysis is less analysis than a type of subterranean synthesis. The notion of analysis, nevertheless, effects a certain appearance of unity in the motley makeup of present-day "music theory."

Notes

1. For the translation on which my discussion of the *Sectio canonis* is based I am indebted to Professor André Barbera of St. John's College, Annapolis. There is a conveniently available English translation by Thomas J. Mathiesen in the *Journal of Music Theory* 19 (1975): 236–58.

2. *The Harmonics of Aristoxenus*, ed. Henry Macran (Oxford, 1902), 184–85.

3. I am indebted to Thomas W. Baker for the English version of Ptolemy on which this discussion is based. There is a published German translation of the treatise by Ingemar Düring in "Ptolemaios und Porphyrios über die Musik," *Götebergs Högskolas Årsskrift* 40 (1934).

4. Aristides Quintilianus, *On Music*, trans. Thomas J. Mathiesen (New Haven, 1983), 71.

5. Ibid., 72.

6. Oliver Strunk, ed., *Source Readings in Music History* (New York, 1950), 134.

7. Ibid., 134–35.

8. *Hucbald, Guido, and John on Music*, trans. Warren Babb, ed. Claude V. Palisca (New Haven, 1978), 6.

9. Ibid.

10. Ibid., 67.

11. Johannes de Grocheo, *Concerning Music*, trans. Albert Seay (Colorado Springs, 1967), 6.

12. Strunk, *Source Readings*, 161.

13. Ibid., 174.

14. Prosdocimo de' Beldomandi, *Contrapunctus*, trans. Jan W. Herlinger (Lincoln, Neb., 1984), 83 and 85.

15. Ibid., n. 13 on 85 and 87.

16. Strunk, *Source Readings*, 220–21.

17. Ibid., 229.

18. Ibid., 250.

19. Ibid., 255–59.

20. Johannes Lippius, *Synopsis of New Music*, trans. Benito V. Rivera (Colorado Springs, 1977), 41.

21. Edward A. Lippman, ed., *Musical Aesthetics: A Historical Reader*, vol. 1 (New York, 1986), 339.

22. Ibid., 355.

NINE

Chromaticism in Classical Music

JAMES M. BAKER

This essay advances a new approach to the analysis of chromaticism in music of the Classical period, an approach based on the premise that chromaticism is an integral part of the structure of tonal music in ways that have not been heretofore recognized. To this day, chromaticism has been regarded as a rather special technique used mainly in a limited number of styles or genres—for example, Bach's Chromatic Fantasy and Fugue or the B-minor fugue from book 1 of his *Well-Tempered Clavier*. I intend to show that even in music that we have tended to associate with a straightforward, diatonic style—for instance, Mozart's early piano sonatas—there is often evidence of a systematic control of each and every pitch in the chromatic universe.

My view of chromaticism has been derived from a variety of sources—for one, the writings of theorists contemporary with Haydn and Mozart, who often expressed an acute sensitivity to chromatic differentiation. While these theorists did not discuss chromaticism in precisely the terms to be developed here, their refined sensibilities would certainly have made them aware of the chromatic phenomena I describe, and indeed they discussed many of these phenomena as best they could within the theoretical frameworks available to them. Another significant influence has been the writings of theorists who wrote at the end of the tonal period, particularly Arnold Schoenberg and Heinrich Schenker. Having been brought up in the era of Wagnerian harmony, these theorists added considerably to our appreciation of the potential structural uses of chromaticism within tonal structure.

I believe that the approach offered here may apply to a large body of tonal music, including music of the Baroque and Romantic periods. However, because chromatic techniques are especially well defined in Classical music—with its relatively clear-cut periodic structure and frequent strong contrasts between diatonic and chromatic materials—

this music seems to offer the ideal environment in which to begin to investigate the structural functions of chromaticism. In this essay I offer analyses of works by Mozart, in the conviction that his music most fully encompasses the range of chromatic techniques in use in his day and that it displays the most artful, subtle, and complete exploitation of the potential of these techniques in the creation of musical structure.

* * *

One of the most striking features of Mozart's style, yet one that has received scant analytical attention, is the element of diatonic-chromatic contrast. Examples 9.1–9.6 show several instances of such contrast, employed with varying degrees of subtlety. The second thematic group from the first movement of the Piano Sonata in F Major K. 280 (ex. 9.1) comprises two juxtaposed and highly contrasted ideas. The first (mm. 27–34) is a purely diatonic, symmetrically divided eight-measure phrase. The second (mm. 35–43) is an asymmetrically organized nine-measure phrase consisting of a five-measure ascent by sequence completed by a four-measure closing phrase. The latter phrase encompasses all twelve tones of the chromatic scale. Although both ideas entail sudden dynamic shifts from *forte* to *piano*, they project entirely different affects, the first light and jocular, the second a good deal more serious and passionate. These changes in mood link this relatively early work of Mozart with the *emfindsamer Stil* of C.P.E. Bach.

Examples 9.2 and 9.3 contain two passages from the Piano Sonata in A Minor K. 310. The first, mm. 159–74, is the latter half of the wholly symmetrical thirty-two-measure middle section of the last movement, an area of relative repose in the tonic major that provides momentary respite from the relentless main material in A minor. The fourth and final melodic phrase of this contrasting section (mm. 167–74) descends the major scale from the high A—the highest note of the section—set over a tonic pedal with pure diatonic harmonies. (The first two phrases of the middle section are diatonic as well, with the slightest chromaticism occurring in mm. 156–58 in conjunction with a modulation to the dominant.) The third phrase (mm. 159–66) provides the contrast within the middle section, involving a serpentine chromatic melody with only intermittent accompaniment. This phrase uses both major and minor modes (in fact, it embraces all twelve tones), introducing a note of unquiet in the seeming calm.

Example 9.3 shows a phrase toward the end of the second movement of the sonata, one in a series of phrases that confirm the F-major tonic. What is distinctive here is the progression used in conjunction with the *crescendo* on the second and third beats of m. 78, a rapidly paced chromatic progression consisting of an ascending melodic pattern supported by applied dominants and diminished sevenths. The chromatic aggregate, framed on either side by simpler and more regular progressions, generates tension that culminates with the arrival of the diatonic cadential six-four chord.

Examples 9.4 to 9.6 are from the opening phrases from the first two movements of the Quartet in E-flat Major K. 428. The first movement opens with a mysteriously subdued and poignant chromatic statement, a four-measure idea that is answered by a diatonic four-measure phrase closing on the tonic (see ex. 9.4). The antecedent is stated in octaves by all four instruments and contains nine of the twelve pitch classes, including three of the five nondiatonic elements, featured as metrically accented lower neighbors. That this phrase aspires toward completion of the chromatic aggregate is made clear when the phrase is reasserted *forte* in mm. 12–15, now harmonized so that all twelve pitch classes are encompassed within the phrase (see ex. 9.5). The heretofore missing F-sharp and D-flat enter for the first time in mm. 13 and 14 respectively, both occurring as metrically accented neighbors.

The theme of the second movement of the quartet presents an entirely different spatial disposition of diatonic/chromatic contrast (see ex. 9.6). Here both the melody and the accompaniment are purely diatonic for the first two bars. In m. 3, however, the cello begins to weave chromatically. Ultimately the viola and second violin are drawn into the chromatic web, so that by the end of the six-measure phrase—completed with a cadence to the tonic—all twelve tones have sounded. (Perhaps the chromatic digression accounts for the unusual length of the phrase.)

The variety and subtlety in Mozart's employment of chromaticism evident in the above examples suggest that chromatic strategy could well be a critical aspect of structure in certain of his works, and perhaps more broadly in music of the Classical style in general. The analytical literature to date has not focused directly on chromaticism in this music, at least not from the vantage points taken in our observations of the examples cited above. In order to develop a framework for examining chromatic usage in Classical music, we shall survey the theoretical literature on the subject, beginning with the work of theorists contemporary with Mozart and proceeding to some more modern notions of chromaticism within tonal structure.

Example 9.1   Mozart, Piano Sonata in F Major K. 280 (1775), i, mm. 27– 43

Example 9.2   Mozart, Piano Sonata in A Minor K. 310 (1778), iii, mm. 159–74

Example 9.3   Mozart, Piano Sonata K. 310, ii, mm. 76–81

Example 9.4   Mozart, Quartet in E♭ Major K. 428 (1783), i, mm. 1– 8

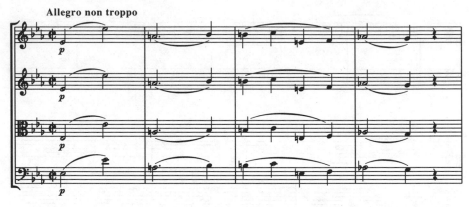

Example 9.5   Mozart, Quartet K. 428, i, mm. 12–15

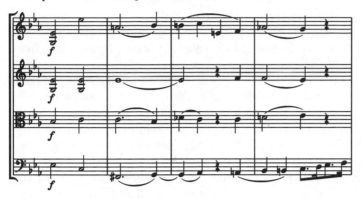

Example 9.6   Mozart, Quartet K. 428, ii, mm. 1– 6

* * *

Eighteenth-century theorists considered the diatonic major scale, whose intervals are associated with simpler numerical ratios, to be the fundamental pitch collection. J.P. Kirnberger stated that the origin of the scale "is not fully known. . . . We know only that the diatonic system of the ancient Greeks . . . can be derived from a series of pure fifths."[1] Kirnberger advocated a system of temperament in which nearly all fifths are pure, and in which the proportions of relations of scale degrees to the root (C) are formed, with one exception, among integers from 1 to 15. The ratios of the chromatic elements to C, on the other hand, employ integers from 9 to 256.[2] Abt Georg Joseph Vogler derived the diatonic major scale from the simpler proportions of the major triad, describing the scale as the collection of the pitches of major triads constructed on C and on the pitches a fifth below (F) and a fifth above (G). Vogler then derived the minor scale from the diatonic major by measuring intervals a major third below G, C, and D, introducing the chromatic elements E-flat, A-flat, and B-flat. He described the complete chromatic scale as the combination of major and minor with the addition of two chromatic tones: C-sharp acquired by measuring a major third above A, and G-flat a half step below G.[3] In his *Versuch einer Einleitung zur Composition*, Heinrich Christoph Koch adopted a more practical stance, showing how the chromatic elements are systematically introduced in moving from key to key around the circle of fifths, always the most important gauge of tonal relationships in the Classical period.[4] From this sampling of explanations of the origins of the chromatic scale, it is evident that theorists understood the diatonic major scale to be the basic tonal resource. Chromatic elements were considered derivative and removed from what is simplest and most natural.

Although eighteenth-century theorists often described an enharmonic scale with as many as twenty-one tones within the octave,[5] the premise of Classical tonality that each and every key be available dictated that the chromatic scale was in fact the basic frame of reference for pitch structure. The prevalence of the chromatic scale over the so-called enharmonic scale was most evident in the twelve fixed pitch classes of the keyboard, but was also borne out by the simultaneous enharmonic equivalencies frequently encountered in music for ensembles with no instruments of fixed pitch, such as the string quartet. Even in instances when enharmonic equivalents may be accorded different pitch inflections—A-sharp and B-flat, for instance, may ordinarily be played as two different frequencies in ensembles without fixed-pitch instruments—such equivalencies nevertheless share a basic function with respect to the definition of tonal space. As the following discussion will show, the totality of the tonal universe has been viewed traditionally as based on the containment of twelve (not twenty-one) tones. This was certainly the view of early twentieth-century theorists, but it may often be inferred from the writings of their eighteenth-century predecessors as well. In this universe, enharmonic inflection of chromatic elements does not jeopardize their functional identities. On the contrary, enharmonic variation often enhances chromatic procedures, as is the case in chromatic "liquidation," to be illustrated later.

One cannot infer, however, that the chromatic scale was necessarily tuned in equal half steps during the Classical period.[6] In 1802, Koch stated in his *Musikalisches Lexikon* that most theorists were in favor of systems of tuning other than equal temperament, such as Kirnberger's, in order to preserve the traditional characters of the individual keys.[7] Vogler's tuning system, which entailed expanding the major thirds constructed above white keys and contracting those built on black keys, resulted in the differing qualities of keys that he described as follows:

> C is . . . perhaps the most appropriate key for a painting, for pure water arias, for pure subjects. G is already livelier, but surely not boisterous. . . . D ignites fire in the heart. Now the entire body is animated, the spirit soars to heroic deed, is incited to bold, joyful, even rather exuberant songs of praise. Even the god of thunder has claims to this key. A is sharper yet. . . . It depicts more successfully the fire of an amorous and thus tender passion than of an impetuous [passion]. E can depict fire best of all insofar as it catches the eye through the intensity of its most piercing flames. F serves for a dead calm; B-flat for dusk; E-flat for night; A-flat for Plutonian realms.[8]

Chromaticism was most often discussed by theorists of the Classical period in conjunction with the subject of modulation. A chromatic element was recognized as signifying a leading tone in a foreign key. Thus C.P.E. Bach called the chromatic half step "the pivot and token of all natural modulation,"[9] and Kirnberger asserted that any chromatic element is a leading tone (a half step below either the tonic or the fourth degree) in a foreign key.[10]

Modulation was usually measured in terms of the relative proximity or remoteness of the departure and goal harmonies, typically gauged by the circle of fifths.[11] Most theorists endeavored to demonstrate the accessibility of the full range of twenty-four keys in one way or another—C.P.E. Bach and Kirnberger by means of the enharmonic reinterpretation of the diminished seventh chord, Vogler by more daring enharmonic equivalencies and linear progressions, which he categorized as instances of *Mehrdeutigkeit* (multiple function).[12] Yet all theorists clearly accorded greater structural significance to the diatonic modulations, that is, to modulations among the natural harmonies built on diatonic scale steps. This preference is clearest in the writings of theorists of the older generation like Kirnberger, but is equally characteristic of the younger generation.[13] Even the radical Vogler, who took pains to demonstrate modulation between every possible pair of chromatic half steps, stated that modulation to remote keys (which he specified by the term *Ausweichung*) was mainly a concern of church organists, who were required to improvise links between pieces in different keys.[14] In fact, in Vogler's earlier writings his overriding concern was for tonal unity, which he feared would be jeopardized by modulations to remoter key areas. Accordingly, the modulations that he allowed under normal circumstances amount to what we would call tonicizations of diatonic scale steps, each of which should retain its functional identity with regard to the single prevailing tonic. By the time of his *Handbuch zur Harmonielehre* (1802), however, Vogler seems to have been less concerned with tonal unity than with demonstrating exhaustively the possibilities for modulation among all keys—perhaps in response to the dramatic developments in harmony and style that had taken place in the twenty years preceding.[15]

Eighteenth-century treatises are full of cautionary statements concerning the use of chromaticism. C.P.E. Bach stated that "there are keyboardists who understand chromaticism . . . but few who know how to employ it agreeably, relieved of its crudeness."[16] He stated that "chromatic progressions are to be played only occasionally, with artistry, and broadly."[17] In remarks reflecting concerns similar to those of Vogler, Bach advised that, although the deceptive chromatic progressions associated with the fantasia are attractive, "they must not be excessively used, or natural relationships will become hopelessly buried beneath them."[18] Citing Bach's remarks, Kirnberger noted with approval that contemporary composers shunned the outlandish chromatic progressions of their predecessors: "[Enharmonic progressions] were very much in use at the time of Marcello and sometimes may have been used in such abundance only for the purpose of making it difficult for even connoisseurs of harmony to guess their proper treatment and to reduce certain chords to their true fundamental harmony."[19] For effects of sudden surprise Kirnberger favored the straightforward abrupt shift to a remote key— a practice then in vogue—over the elaborate enharmonic transitions of the older style. Excessive chromaticism was to be avoided because it obscured the meaning of the music. He stated, for instance, that "many minor seconds and augmented primes can follow one another in a slow tempo and in the expression of sad feelings; but they are comprehensible only to trained ears."[20]

As is evident from his comment, Kirnberger associated chromaticism with expression of the stronger emotions and passions, which he considered a deviation from the affective norm within the current style. He declared that "the rules of progression are based on the premise that the melody should be gentle and pleasant," stating further that "the simplest and most pleasing melody is without doubt one that proceeds only through the pure diatonic steps of the chosen key."[21] He quite willingly allowed for exceptions to the rules for expressive reasons, however: "What is forbidden in the strict style is not only permissible in the freer style but often sounds very good because the expression is often assisted by such deviations from the rules. This is particularly true in situations where disagreeable passions are to be expressed."[22] Kirnberger argued that harmony as well as melody was capable of expression. He demonstrated this phenomenon in a remarkable example containing twenty-six different harmonizations of a chorale tune, along with a commentary on the affective purpose of each, with special attention to the setting of the text.[23] He advised that modulations to remoter keys, which often require intermediate modulations, be used "only where the expression demands it, that is, where the feelings are to be led rapidly from one sentiment to another."[24]

Although eighteenth-century theorists valued chromaticism primarily for its affective power, they did not naively equate its use with an attempt to move the passions. Favoring diatonic melodies in theory, they nevertheless recognized the risk of monotony if music is not seasoned with a bit of chromatic spice. Kirnberger admitted that "a melody that has no notes other than those in the scale over a long span of time can easily become dull, since there is a short step from smoothness to dullness. To prevent this, there is nothing more effective than to use a note that does not belong to the scale, particularly when it falls on the main accent of the phrase." He felt that chromatic notes "can be used in the melody without reducing its pleasant or light character, if they are used sparingly and in such a way that they are easy to sing and comprehend."[25] Koch noted that an occasional chromatic note may be used simply to contribute "gracefulness and liveliness" to a melody.[26] Nonetheless, the generally cautious stance that theorists took toward chromaticism would indicate a sensitivity to even the slightest foreign element. As noted earlier, Kirnberger stated that any foreign pitch functions in some sense as a leading tone.[27]

With regard to current practice, theorists of the Classical period most often discussed chromatic effects as they occurred in the setting of a text or in articulating an area of contrast in a composition. As such, these effects were considered deviations from the diatonic norm. Although the examples that Koch offered from his own compositions are almost without exception purely diatonic (admitting only the minimal alterations necessary for modulation to closely related keys), his examples of music by other composers indicate that he was fully aware of contemporary chromatic practice.[28] Those examples taken from Pleyel and Benda feature chromatic progressions typical of the mature Classical style.[29] The passage from Benda provides a fitting setting of a text depicting love's pain: "Love's sweet flirtations pass away with the honeymoon,/and discontent and sorrow enter in the new household."

Because of the importance of the symphony in contemporary practice, Koch cited a lengthy passage from an article in Sulzer's *Allgemeine Theorie der schönen Künste* that stressed the value of dramatic gestures and contrasts in this genre. Chromatic modulation was one of the chief means for obtaining these effects—"sudden transitions and digressions from one key to another, which are more striking the weaker the connection is."[30] Koch located two areas in a symphonic first movement where chromaticism was most likely to occur. The first and primary area was the beginning of the second main period, where harmony "may modulate very arbitrarily, sometimes into this, sometimes into that related key."[31] The second was the slow and serious introduction to the Allegro, an optional section featured in some of the newer symphonies, which Koch viewed as remaining in the tonic key while employing passing modulations.[32]

While the examples of chromaticism discussed by eighteenth-century theorists often entailed an exhaustive use of the chromatic aggregate (see, for instance, Koch's examples from Pleyel and Benda cited above), theorists did not directly or explicitly describe structure in terms of chromatic saturation. A rare instance from the literature that appears to indicate the specific aim of encompassing the chromatic aggregate is Koch's description of a sequence of applied dominant seventh chords. Koch stated that this progression, shown in various inversional forms in example 9.7, was "a chromatic progression well known in the galant style."[33] Later in this essay we shall observe instances of this progression in passages from Mozart's works that immediately juxtapose fully chromatic and purely diatonic phrases.

Although theorists contemporary with Mozart may not have thought of the completion of the chromatic aggregate as a structural device or method, their writings often reflect a consciousness of the varying

Example 9.7

degrees of what could be called chromatic density. Vogler's discussion of his concerns in setting the text of a duet from his opera *Der Kaufmann von Smyrna* is evidence of this awareness (see ex. 9.8).[34] The lines "Fate has brought us here/perhaps only more cruelly to separate us!" inspired Vogler to introduce several chromatic effects.[35] In the second line of text, "vielleicht" (perhaps) is harmonized by the Neapolitan sixth, introducing the lowered second scale degree. Vogler then set "grausamer" (more cruelly) with two chromatically ascending diminished seventh chords, which of course incorporate eight of the twelve tones. The passage culminates with scales in contrary motion

Example 9.8

in the violins, expanding the dominant. These scales, which vividly depict the notion of separation, embrace eleven notes of the chromatic scale—all except the lowered second degree featured earlier. The drama of the phrase depends to a large extent on the process of motion from pure diatonicism to chromatic saturation. While Vogler did not refer directly to this process, he was clearly intent on exploiting the dramatic potential of the text, and he chose chromaticism to do so. He was particularly proud of the device of scales in contrary motion, fully aware that they served to "clinch" the phrase.

Theorists of the Classical period did not seem to take note of the sorts of local diatonic-chromatic juxtapositions illustrated in the excerpts from Mozart at the beginning of this essay. In fact, the more conservative theorists were apt to advise, like Kirnberger, against abrupt shifts from one scale to another, "since this can easily make the whole mottled and can completely destroy the unity of expression."[36] Kirnberger's cautious attitude seems dictated by a preference for the older style, in which unity of affect was a central concern.

Neither did these theorists directly address the relationship between chromaticism and the temporal aspect of music (rhythm, meter, and periodicity), but their writings nonetheless often show that they inferred a connection. Indeed, the words they chose to describe modulation to remote keys indicate that they viewed such modulations as interpolations subsidiary to more fundamental materials. "Ausweichung," the most frequent choice, connotes evasion or deviation, while the more descriptive "Ausschweifung" carries associations of extravagance, excess, and aberration.[37] One occasionally finds discussion of durational treatment of chromaticism at the local level, such as Kirnberger's rules for metric placement of chromatic elements.[38] On the other hand, theorists sometimes offered advice on chromaticism and overall periodic structure. Kirnberger remarked, for instance, that "a period must be all the shorter the more distant is its key from the main key," for "if one remains for too long in such a key, the feeling for the main key would be completely lost."[39]

Koch, whose theories of periodicity and form were the most perceptive and sophisticated of their time, rarely devoted specific comments to the impact of chromaticism on periodicity. In his treatise one only occasionally finds observations such as the following:

> Passing modulations in the minor key of the third appear in short compositions just as seldom as the alternation of the minor mode with the major mode of the main key. If they are used, the phrase must, for the most part, be extended so that the V-phrase [that is, the phrase that ends on the domi-

nant] of the main key can be heard at the end of it before the
closing phrase begins.[40]

Most of his examples of phrase extension are quite diatonic, but
Koch did include examples of contrasting chromatic segments interpolated into diatonic phrases.[41] He allowed such examples to speak
for themselves, however, by withholding any comment on the aspect
of chromaticism. As noted earlier in this essay, Koch was acquainted
with contemporary chromatic practice as demonstrated in excerpts he
cited from Benda and Pleyel.[42] These examples illustrate chromatic
saturation of the sort that Mozart employed (as will be discussed later),
although Koch would not have thought of their structure in precisely
these terms. Koch seems to have assumed that the listener would readily
grasp chromatic effects. One indication of this can be found in his
reference to a passage from his teacher, Christian Gotthelf Scheinpflug,
in which the meter is interrupted by a phrase in a slower tempo. Koch
made no mention of the chromaticism of the interpolated phrase, introduced in conjunction with a shift to the parallel minor. He simply
stated that "the beginner can, without difficulty, explain the reasons
for [the interrupting phrase] himself from the contents of the poetry"
(at the words "long, long lamenting"). He admitted that, especially in
instrumental music, it was easier to feel the reasons for such interpolations than to explain them.[43] Thus one forms the impression that
Koch was certainly sensitive to their effects, but he was not inclined to
seek an explanation for these effects in the realm of pitch structure,
particularly chromaticism.

Vogler was equally aware of the association of chromaticism and
interpolation. In his *Betrachtungen* he offered an analysis of a remarkable chromatic passage from the finale of his Concerto No. 2 in B-flat
Major, the Rondo alla polacca. The passage is a fanciful, highly impro-
visatory takeoff on the main theme of the rondo—a cadenza-like bridge
to the cadenza itself—based on a chromatically rising bass that fills in
the dominant octave. The fact that he did not indicate fundamental
bass tones for the passage as in other analyses in his treatise apparently signifies that the interpolation is of only secondary structural
significance.[44]

As has been demonstrated in the above overview, eighteenth-
century theorists were certainly keenly aware of chromaticism in the
music of their time, but their theories do not explicitly and systematically account for the structural uses of chromaticism, especially with
regard to periodicity and form. They were predominantly concerned
with practical matters, and most would never have dreamed of claiming that theory could account for everything that transpires in a work

of genius. Koch, with characteristic frankness and humility, ends the first chapter of the last volume of his *Versuch* with the remark that the beginning composer must make up for the shortcomings of theory by studying good scores.[45]

Thus, although the writings of Koch, Vogler, Kirnberger, and their contemporaries provide us with an excellent starting point, it is also useful to consider how notions of musical structure contributed by later theorists might enhance our appreciation of Classical music. In particular, certain theorists at the beginning of the twentieth century, most notably Arnold Schoenberg and his followers, developed an understanding of chromaticism that not only pointed the way to new compositional methods but also had the potential of shedding light on the music of their predecessors. Viewed in many quarters as a radical who had broken away from the natural laws that had governed music for centuries, Schoenberg insisted all his life that, in creating the method of composition with twelve tones, he was simply carrying forward an evolutionary process that linked him with previous generations of German masters.[46] Anton Webern, who adhered quite strictly to Schoenberg's teachings, succinctly described this progression in a lecture he gave in April 1933:

> Just as the church modes disappeared and made way for major and minor, so these two have also disappeared and made way for a single series, the chromatic scale. Relation to keynote-tonality has been lost. . . . The relationship to a keynote gave those structures an essential foundation. It helped to build their form, in a certain sense it ensured unity. This relationship was the essence of tonality. As a result of all the events mentioned, this relationship first became less necessary and finally disappeared completely. A certain ambiguity on the part of a large number of chords made it superfluous. . . . Harmonic complexes arose, of a kind that made the relationship to a keynote superfluous. This took place via Wagner and then Schoenberg, whose first works were still tonal. But in the harmony he developed, the relationship to a keynote became unnecessary, and this meant the end of something that has been the basis of musical thinking from the days of Bach to our time: major and minor disappeared. Schoenberg expresses this in an analogy: double gender has given rise to a higher race![47]

Schoenberg took pains to minimize the differences between tonal and twelve-tone music, stressing that in the evolution from diatonic to chromatic there had been no break from natural musical laws: "Five tones have been drawn into composition in a way not called upon before—that is all, and it does not call for any new laws."[48]

For Schoenberg and Webern, the materials of music originated in the natural phenomenon of the overtone series—the notes of the diatonic scale being found among the lower overtones and the chromatic notes occurring as higher overtones. Webern regarded the development of Western music over the centuries as "the ever-extending conquest of the material provided by nature," and he saw no reason why the quarter tones and microtones formed among still higher overtones would not someday be used.[49] Viewing the overtone series as a continuum, Schoenberg saw no essential difference between intervals that formerly were differentiated as consonances and dissonances:

> What distinguishes dissonances from consonances is not a greater or lesser degree of beauty, but a greater or lesser degree of *comprehensibility*. In my *Harmonielehre* I presented the theory that dissonant tones appear later among the overtones, for which reason the ear is less intimately acquainted with them. This phenomenon does not justify such sharply contradictory terms as concord and discord. Closer acquaintance with the more remote consonances—the dissonances, that is—gradually eliminated the difficulty of comprehension and finally admitted not only the emancipation of dominant and other seventh chords, diminished sevenths and augmented triads, but also the emancipation of Wagner's, Strauss's, Moussorgsky's, Debussy's, Mahler's, Puccini's, and Reger's more remote dissonances.[50]

In tracing his musical ancestry, Schoenberg identified two composers as his primary teachers: Bach and Mozart.[51] The comments on Mozart scattered sporadically throughout his writings indicate that Schoenberg esteemed Mozart for his ability to invent and develop contrasting materials and for the succinct elegance and continual variety of his forms—his "unique capacity of combining heterogeneous elements in the smallest space."[52] He valued what he called the "prose-like" quality of Mozart's style—"a direct and straightforward presentation of ideas, without any patchwork, without mere padding and empty repetitions"—noting particularly "the unexcelled freedom of its rhythm and the perfect independence from formal symmetry."[53] Demonstrating an astute awareness of factors emphasized in eighteenth-century theory, Schoenberg admired Mozart's variation of phrase length "by extension of a segment, by internal repetitions or by reductions and condensations."[54] Nevertheless, he did not directly

cite Mozart as an influence on his harmonic practice, usually acknowledging Wagner most openly in this regard.[55] Schoenberg did refer
occasionally, however, to Mozart's courage on the battlefield in the
historical struggle over the use of dissonance, and was especially fond
of citing the opening of Mozart's "Dissonance" Quartet K. 465 (an
excerpt we shall examine later).[56]

Schoenberg identified more closely with Bach than with any of his
other predecessors, seeing himself and Bach as performing comparable tasks at two critical junctures in the evolution of Western music.
Claiming special insight into the work of the Baroque master,
Schoenberg described Bach's contribution as follows: "He carried over
perfectly—a fact not yet discovered—the secret of the old contrapuntal art of former periods, from the church-modes to major and minor,
from seven to twelve tones."[57] Schoenberg sought likewise "to find the
form in which the laws of earlier art can be applied to the new."[58]
Bach's music represented for Schoenberg not so much the culmination
of an era as the forging of a new practice based on the availability of
all twelve tones, a development made possible by equal temperament.[59]
He went so far as to describe Bach (only partly in jest) as "the first
composer with twelve tones."[60] Schoenberg cited the B-minor fugue
from the first book of the *Well-Tempered Clavier* as anticipating twelve-
tone technique, because in this work "the chromatically altered tones
are neither substitutes nor parts of scales. They possess distinctly an
independence resembling the unrelated tones of the chromatic scale
in a basic set of a twelve-tone composition."[61] Anton Webern echoed
his teacher's adulation of Bach, finding in the latter's harmonization
of the chorale *Christ lag in Todesbanden* "the emergence . . . of the world
in which the twelve notes hold sway. Here already is a piece wholly
based on what we call chromaticism."[62] Webern remarked that Bach's
harmonic thinking "wasn't superseded by the later classical composers, nor even by Brahms" and thus implied an almost direct linkage
between Bach and Schoenberg.[63]

As the heirs to late nineteenth-century chromaticism and, especially, as the founders of an art in which the twelve tones of the
chromatic scale were emancipated from traditional distinctions of
consonance and dissonance, Schoenberg and Webern were no doubt
as keenly sensitive to chromaticism as any composers ever. What is
perhaps most interesting in their discussions of Bach and other masters is their assumption that older generations of composers could
have been fully in control of the universe of twelve tones within the
context of tonality. They hardly assumed that chromatic thought pre-
cluded or disturbed tonality. In fact, precisely to the contrary,
Schoenberg asserted that "rich, varied use of the degrees"—referring

here to the exploitation of the full range of chromatic variants within the scale—"is . . . the most essential feature of the harmonic art."[64] And Webern insisted that even Schoenberg's Piano Piece Op. 11, no. 1, which he characterized at one time as one of the first "atonal" pieces, has a tonal center.[65]

Webern's remarks on Schoenberg's Op. 11, no. 1, are particularly illuminating with regard to the function of aggregate completion as a formal device: "No. 1: ends on E-flat—it doesn't close in any key. The final bass note is the fundamental. How does the piece come to have E-flat as tonic? Let's look at the opening; up to bar 13 [recta bar 12] every note in the chromatic scale occurs, except E-flat!"[66] Although Webern's meaning has been somewhat obscured in the shorthand notes that are the source of these remarks, we can neverthess infer a good deal from their content. He attributed a significance to E-flat simply by virtue of the fact that it is the last pitch class to appear. He was no doubt also aware of the compositional context of this first presentation of E-flat. It occurs as the effective bass tone of a fleeting passage in thirty-second notes covering a vastly broader range than anything heard previously. The *ppp* dynamic level and much faster tempo also help mark this moment as the beginning of a new section. Many aspects of the music thus coincide to signal the entry of the twelfth chromatic element. Even so, one doubts that Webern would have considered this special treatment of E-flat sufficient to make it the tonal center of the composition. He seems to have based this judgment on a correspondence between the close of the piece and m. 12—and indeed one finds that the final tetrachord of the piece, based on E-flat, is a conspicuous segment of the arpeggio in m. 12, with the stacked fourths A–D–G-sharp appearing an octave lower at the end.

Aggregate completion of course became an important part of Webern's compositional method. As he described his early experience with the technique, he apparently came to it by intuition (presumably not consciously aware at the time of the structure of Schoenberg's Op. 11, no. 1, as he later described it):

> About 1911 I wrote the "Bagatelles for String Quartet" (Op. 9), all very short pieces, lasting a couple of minutes—perhaps the shortest music so far. Here I had the feeling, "When all twelve notes have gone by, the piece is over." Much later I discovered that all this was a part of the necessary development. In my sketch-book I wrote out the chromatic scale and crossed off the individual notes. Why? Because I had convinced myself, "This note has been there already." The inner ear decided quite rightly that the man who wrote out the chromatic scale and crossed off individual notes *was no*

fool. . . . In short, a rule of law emerged; until all twelve notes have occurred, none of them may occur again. The most important thing is that each "run" of twelve notes marked a division within the piece, idea, or theme.[67]

What is most intriguing about Webern's account is that he described his discovery of the principle of aggregate completion as a process of gradually becoming conscious of laws, already operative in his compositions, that reflected a "necessary development" in the evolution of musical structure. In a lecture delivered more than a year after he made the comments quoted immediately above, Webern extolled the music of Bach, and his words may well indicate that he had come to perceive Bach's chromatic practice as involving laws akin to those of the twelve-tone method of Schoenberg and himself. (One recalls Schoenberg's dictum that "the laws of the old art are also those of the new art.")[68] When Webern declared *"everything happens in Bach"*[69] and stated that in Bach's chorale harmonizations "it's already there, . . . the world in which the twelve notes hold sway,"[70] he was not simply justifying contemporary twelve-tone practice by way of historical precedent; he was at the same time intent on bringing his audience to a new understanding of Bach's own accomplishment. To be sure, Webern was hearing Bach with twentieth-century ears made sensitive through chromatic experimentation. Nonetheless, we should be willing to consider the opinion of a musician with such an incomparably refined ear. Webern, after all, was not asking us to discard our understanding of traditional tonal structure in favor of a radical nontonal perspective; rather, he seems to have been saying that in the works of the masters of the tonal period chromatic elements may participate more fully and significantly in structure than had previously been realized. His view would seem to call for an analytical method for tonal music that considers each chromatic element as important in its own right and that correlates chromaticism with the more familiar aspects of tonal structure. It is such an approach that I shall develop in analyzing music of Mozart in the latter part of this essay.

The Viennese atonalists were by no means the only theorists in the early twentieth century to focus on chromaticism in tonal music. Ernst Kurth's *Romantische Harmonik* (1920), with its detailed attention to the "Tristan chord," is the most notable example of the attempts at that time to consolidate late-Romantic harmonic practice. Not as widely known are the contributions of Heinrich Schenker to the theory of chromaticism. Because his later work focused on the diatonic foundations of tonal music, Schenker's earlier pronouncements on chromaticism, found chiefly in his 1906 book on harmony, have been generally overlooked.[71] Those who assume that Schenker ignored the musical

surface, relegating nonessential elements to the category of decoration, will be surprised at the amount of attention Schenker devoted to
chromaticism in his harmony treatise. There he put forward the theory
of the "urge to tonicization":

> Each scale-step manifests an irresistible urge to attain the
> value of the tonic for itself as that of the strongest scale-
> step. If the composer yields to this urge of the scale-step
> within the diatonic system of which this scale-step forms
> part, I call this process *tonicalization* and the phenomenon
> itself *chromatic*.[72]

Schenker actually broadened this definition in recognition of the feasibility that even individual tones—presumably any of the twelve tones
of the chromatic scale—may attain the status of a temporary tonic:

> It is not only the scale-step, as a comprehensive unit of a
> higher order, that strives to attain the value of a tonic; often
> it is an individual tone, even one of quite secondary impor-
> tance. . . . This shows the process of tonicalization in the
> narrowest confines, *en miniature*. We should be careful not
> to overlook these almost microscopic phenomena; they
> enhance the liveliness and activity of the tones on the level
> of the minimal, which often reveals relationships we might
> otherwise miss. In any case we should admire in these
> phenomena the omnipotence and omnipresence of the
> yearning for the tonic, which manifests itself more and more
> as a veritable miracle of Nature in our art.[73]

He referred to this process as microtonicization.

Schenker's theory of the urge to tonicization actually was directly
linked with the ideas of eighteenth-century theorists, such as C.P.E.
Bach and Kirnberger, who recognized any chromatic tone as in some
sense a leading tone in a foreign key. And in fact Schoenberg likewise
stated that the purpose of a chromatic alteration is to create a leading
tone, ascending or descending.[74] Although Schoenberg quibbled with
aspects of Schenker's theory of tonicization, he admitted that Schenker's
conception "is in fact rather similar to mine"; his assertion that "a bass
tone strives to impose its own overtones, thus has the tendency to
become the root of a major triad" resonates strongly with Schenker's
notion of the will of each tone to become a tonic.[75] Indeed, Schenker
and Schoenberg were generally very much in agreement in their presentations of the origins of chromaticism and their notions of its purposes, and their theories coincided with eighteenth-century teachings
in many respects.

Both theorists recognized the origin of chromaticism in the mixture of major and minor modes. While Schenker, like the theorists of the Classical period, based his theory on the notion of the primacy of the diatonic scale, Schoenberg's more practical attitude led him to observe that "the art of music was never really in possession of a tonality wholly limited to the seven diatonic tones of the scale."[76] Of the two theorists, Schenker was the more rigorous in accounting for the origin of nondiatonic elements. Like Schoenberg, he derived the lowered third, sixth, and seventh scale degrees from the minor mode. He demonstrated more concern than Schoenberg for supplying a theoretical explanation for the lowered second scale degree, which "arises in response to motivic challenges": that is, it is lowered in the minor mode in order to support consonant triads as do the other scale degrees.[77] (Schenker cited the opening of the first movement of Beethoven's "Appassionata" Sonata as an example of such a parrallelism.) The final chromatic element, the raised fourth scale degree, occurs in conjunction with the tonicization of the dominant.[78]

After he had developed his theory of the fundamental structure, Schenker took care to specify the level at which each chromaticism originated. Thus, while the Ursatz itself was purely diatonic, the first middleground level could feature the mixture of major and minor thirds as well as the lowered second scale degree. The lowered sixth scale degree, however, was introduced only at the foreground.[79] Schoenberg was less inclined to this sort of abstract speculation. Instead, like Vogler, he preferred to offer practical demonstrations of all possible chromatic chord connections.[80] In a chapter entitled "The Chromatic Scale as a Basis for Tonality," written for the revised edition of his Harmonielehre, Schoenberg went so far as to propose that harmonic theory be based "not on the seven tones of the major scale, rather, on the twelve of the chromatic scale," offering a brief outline as an initial step in this direction.[81]

Schoenberg and Schenker made strikingly similar statements concerning the purpose of chromaticism, echoing the eighteenth-century theorists' central concern for diversity (Mannigfaltigkeit) within a larger unity (Einheit).[82] Schenker wrote: "Chromatic change is an element which does not destroy the diatonic system but which rather emphasizes and confirms it. Its point of departure is the diatonic system, whence apparently it moves away; but through the byways of a simulated tonic it returns to it. The contrasts which chromatic change—apparently a purpose in itself—can conjure up illuminate the diatonic relationships all the more clearly."[83] Schoenberg also associated chromaticism with "coherent contrast," stating the paradox that, while "non-diatonic elements [tend] to form opposition to the fundamental tone," they nevertheless strengthen the tonal center by requiring "the application of strong means in order to verify the tonality, to paralyse eccentric effects."[84]

For Schoenberg chromaticism performed an essential function in the articulation of large-scale tonal forms:

> Whether something be a principal or subordinate idea, introduction or transition, episode, bridge, connecting link, embellishment, extension or reduction, whether independent or dependent, and, further, at which moment it begins or ceases to express one of these formal characteristics—all this is possible for masters of form to make manifest through harmony. . . . The degree of relationship allows a graduated removal of individual parts away from the tonal centre, according to the degree of their meaning: more remote digressions can thus be characterized differently from ideas that are closely related.[85]

In his discussions of musical form Schenker tended to focus on the most basic levels of structure and was thus inclined to de-emphasize the role of chromaticism in the determination of form, although he was clearly aware of its effects on periodicity. His remarks concerning the formal implications of mixture of diatonic and chromatic forms of the third scale degree near the background are indicative of his perspective: "The mixed third does not represent a linear progression or a neighboring note. It provides no occasion for a cadence, but can only give form the opportunity to set off two or three sections against one another. Certainly, this also means a delay, a tension, but, in a strict organic sense, mixture is less form-indicating, less form-generating than division or interruption."[86] Nearer the foreground, Schenker viewed chromaticism as even less important with regard to form, stating that "it usually enters the composing-out process only to embellish and extend."[87] While Schoenberg seems to have retained the eighteenth-century focus on periodicity, Schenker, probing deeper levels of structure, had come to a radically different understanding of musical form.

A most noteworthy contribution of twentieth-century theory that bears on the study of chromaticism, and one for which Schenker and Schoenberg must share credit, is the notion of the pitch relation as motive. For Schenker the motive is bound together with the phenomenon of diminution, the recurrence of a particular pitch relation or configuration at various levels of structure throughout a composition. The motivic identity is often based on a chromatic relation, as in the case of the motive that Schenker finds underlying the first movement of Beethoven's "Lebewohl" Sonata Op. 81a: "Here g-flat^2 and g^2 are engaged in a struggle with one another—only two single tones, certainly not a motive repetition in the usual sense. And yet the synthesis of the entire first movement circles around this conflict."[88] Schenker's idea of motive is closely related to Schoenberg's notion of *Grundgestalt*, the basic idea of a composition, which Schoenberg described as a unity based on a specific combination of melodic, rhythmic, and harmonic relations.[89] As Patricia Carpenter demonstrated in applying the *Grundgestalt* concept in an analysis of the first movement of Beethoven's "Appassionata" Sonata, Schoenberg would have viewed the D-flat–C semitone between the sixth and fifth scale degrees in F minor as the source of the overall tonal design, its many chromatic turns attained by extending this motive by analogy into other tonal regions. Although there are fundamental differences between Schoenberg's and Schenker's views of how a motivic pitch relation bears on the structure of an entire composition, the two theorists were in full agreement in their intuitions that tonal masterworks are based on such elemental relations. Their notion of the chromatic relation as motive will be a significant part of our approach in analyzing chromaticism in eighteenth-century music.

The analytical approach introduced here depends as well on the concept of musical space. This concept is most often identified with Schoenberg's dictum on the multidimensionality of compositional space in twelve-tone music: *"The unity of musical space demands an absolute and unitary perception. In this space . . . there is no absolute down,* no right or left, forward or backward. Every musical configuration, every movement of tones has to be comprehended primarily as a mutual relation of sounds, of oscillatory vibrations, appearing at different places and times."[90] While our analysis will not require attention to multidimensional treatment of ordered sets, the notion that musical materials may be combined in a variety of ways to define spaces within a composition will certainly be relevant. It is surely in this general sense that Schoenberg observed "Mozart's unique capacity of combining heterogeneous elements in the smallest space."[91]

Schoenberg and his followers were equally concerned with musical space in a more abstract sense. Webern discussed space most often in terms of the "conquest of the tonal field." Although on occasion he used this expression in discussing compositional space, more typically his phrase seems to mean "the full exploitation of the natural resource of the overtone series," which was for Webern the basic historical principle that brought us thus far to the equal employment of all twelve pitches of the chromatic scale.[92] In analyzing tonal music, Schoenberg thought in terms of the "domain of the fundamental"—a network of all possible pitch relations, the proximity of which he measured in terms of both the circle of fifths and the parallel and relative major/minor relations.[93] While the concepts of "tonal field" and "domain of the fundamental" are abstractions with no necessary connection to the use of compositional space as such, in fact for Schoenberg and Webern there was an intimate relation. They came to view the process of exhausting the available elements in an abstract domain as potentially form-defining. We are again reminded of Webern's statement: "The most important thing is that each 'run' of twelve notes marked a division within the piece, idea, or theme." In this regard, Schenker's theory of the "urge to tonicization," manifested by each pitch of the chromatic scale, reflects quite similar thinking, in that it points toward the potentially exhaustive use of tonal resources. While concepts of musical domain were most fully developed by twentieth-century theorists, this perspective was not foreign to theorists living two centuries before them. In discussing modulation (in ways that strikingly anticipate Schenker's notion of tonicization of scale steps), Vogler was fond of likening it to the conquest of territory, remarking for example that a tonicized note "immediately relinquishes the field to its rightful possessor."[94]

In closing this overview of theories of chromaticism, I wish to call attention to an important difference between the approach I shall put forward in this essay and attempts to apply the twelve-tone theories of Schoenberg in the analysis of earlier music. Under no circumstances do I deal here with ordered sets or multidimensional manipulations of materials of any kind. Although Schoenberg and Webern were the first to discuss the importance of aggregate completion as a compositional device in and of itself, this device bears no exclusive relation to twelve-tone technique and can be found to operate significantly and strategically in music written well before the twentieth century. In a well-known analysis where twelve-tone theories were misappropriated, Heinrich Jalowetz cited the chromatic unison passage which begins the development of the finale of Mozart's Symphony in G Minor K. 550 as a fleeting instance of atonality within a tonal structure.[95] While the overlapping sequences that he astutely identified may resemble imbricated trichords in serial music, and while the chromatic saturation of the gesture has a strongly disorienting effect, Jalowetz ventured too far when he asserted that there is "no diatonic point" of support for the progression and that the chromatic elements are thus "treated as of equal value." The fact that we hear the brief passage under examination only after the exposition has been performed and perhaps even repeated (not to speak of our having heard the preceding three movements) certainly provides a sufficiently strong frame of reference to enable us to interpret the chromaticism of the passage in tonal terms.[96] From the point of view of aggregate completion, the most interesting aspect of the passage is that it contains eleven of the twelve chromatic tones (not ten as Jalowetz stated)—all but G, the tonic. In beginning the development in this way, Mozart fulfilled two purposes: first, he heightened the dramatic effect of the chromaticism that is typically encountered in a development section by compressing it to virtually maximum density; second, in employing every note except G, he symbolically moved the greatest distance from the tonic and thus set up the strongest possible tension requiring a return to it. The force of tonality is such that we can never completely lose our bearings. Chromaticism may serve to enrich, expand, surprise, and confuse, but ultimately, as both Schenker and Schoenberg agreed, its purpose is to confirm the tonic. As Schenker wrote: "For the sake of the diatonic system itself we can never write too chromatically."[97]

* * *

The remainder of this essay will be devoted to an exploration of the ways in which chromaticism functions within the Classical style. We have already observed in examples 9.1 to 9.6 the use of chromaticism to create sharp contrasts with simple diatonic materials. Examples 9.4 and 9.5 also illustrate a device that I call reinforcement. In its most direct form, reinforcement involves the statement of a diatonic or only partially chromatic phrase, followed immediately by a repetition of the phrase, reharmonized so as to include all twelve chromatic pitches. The final phrase of the second movement of the Piano Sonata in F Major K. 280, shown in example 9.9, features a direct reinforcement. This phrase, an appendix expanding the F-minor tonic, consists of two very similar cadential phrases. The first of these is relatively diatonic, employing nine of the twelve tones. The second phrase, a varied repetition of the first and one that arches poignantly to a higher melodic register, incorporates the full chromatic aggregate. (On a broader level this four-measure phrase reinforces the comparable phrase that closes the first part of the movement, since the latter contains only eight

Example 9.9 Mozart, Piano Sonata K. 280, ii, mm. 57–60

tones.) Reinforcement may be used for a variety of expressive purposes, but always to some rhetorical effect. In example 9.9 the reinforcing phrase seems at first to probe more deeply a feeling of tender
sadness (in the *piano* parts of the statement), then to summon the resolve necessary for a firm close. (The addition of B-natural in the bass
seems particularly important in directing motion to the dominant,
creating a strong cadence.) In example 9.5 the reinforcing phrase is a
gesture of clarification and confidence following the rather tentative
initial statement of the idea (ex. 9.4).

　　Examples 9.10 to 9.13 illustrate other ways in which reinforcement
is likely to occur. Example 9.10 shows part of the closing section of the
first movement of the Quartet in E-flat Major K. 428. In this material
a fairly diatonic four-measure phrase is followed by a fully chromatic
reinforcing phrase (overlapping at m. 155) unusual in both its
harmonies and its six-measure length. The process here clearly
alludes to the opening of the movement, discussed in examples 9.4

Example 9.10　Mozart, Quartet K. 428, i, mm. 152–60

Example 9.11 Mozart, Piano Sonata in G Major K.283 (1775), iii, mm. 244–60

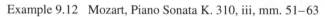

Example 9.12 Mozart, Piano Sonata K. 310, iii, mm. 51–63

Example 9.13   Mozart, Piano Sonata K. 310, iii, mm. 224–33

and 9.5: A-natural, the sole chromatic element in the first phrase (mm. 152–55), was in fact the critical first chromaticism in the piece (m. 2), and the reinforcing phrase (mm. 155–60) performs a function analogous to the original reinforcement of the antecedent of the theme (mm. 12–15). What is perhaps most interesting about the reinforcement in mm. 155–60 is that, in the course of the rich counterpoint of lines forced downward by lowered scale degrees, Mozart avoids the second and fourth diatonic scale degrees. These he adds only with the arrival of the dominant at the cadence (m. 159), thereby completing the aggregate at the same time.

Example 9.11 shows a remarkable chromatic passage from the third movement of the Piano Sonata in G Major K. 283, a sixteen-measure interpolation that breaks up and contrasts with the basically diatonic cadential gestures closing the piece. This passage is based on an eight-measure phrase that is repeated with parts inverted at the twelfth. The initial phrase contains eleven of the twelve tones, all but A-sharp. The invertible counterpoint yields all twelve tones, with A-sharp prominent in the right hand at the beginning of the repetition (m. 253).

Although reinforcements most often occur in close proximity to the phrases from which they originate, they may also be separated by large spans of time and even placed in opposing formal divisions—for example, in the exposition and recapitulation sections of a sonata form. Examples 9.12 and 9.13 show respectively a chromatic passage from the first *A* section of the third movement of the Piano Sonata in A Minor K. 310 and the chromatic reinforcement of this material that occurs when the *A* section returns after the contrasting *B* section. The first appearance of the chromatic idea in m. 52 is highly conspicuous,

since it deceptively replaces the expected tonicized C-major chord.
The passage is also significant because it introduces B-flat, the last of
the twelve tones to be used in the movement. In mm. 56–59 this deceptive gesture is repeated and then extended by sequence a whole step
higher, thereby encompassing every chromatic pitch except G-sharp
in a four-measure phrase. As can be seen, when this material is heard
again in mm. 226–32, it is modified so as to include G-sharp as well,
with a further extension that calls attention to G-sharp as the leading
tone of A minor. The addition of the G-sharp creates a dramatic change
that reinforces the original material and effects a completed aggregate
over a considerable span of time. What is most unusual here is that
Mozart uses this material at the same transposition level in both sections of the piece, but to different harmonic purposes. In the initial
section, the material is used to modulate from the mediant C major to
the minor dominant on E, whereas in the final section the material
serves to prepare one of the last and most significant cadences on the
tonic.

As is evident from the above examples, an essential factor in reinforcement is completion of the chromatic aggregate. Mozart's music
is filled with passages in which the various chromatic elements are
added in strategic ways until the entire chromatic aggregate has been
attained, and generally the introduction of the final chromatic element coincides with an important moment in the musical form. Indeed, his music is so full of such passages that one may deduce that
this process is fundamental to his style. Some instances of strategic
aggregate completion are shown in examples 9.14 and 9.15.

We have previously observed that theorists generally treated chromaticism as arising from the mixture of major and minor modes. While
technically mixture does not account for all twelve pitches, in practice
the shift to the minor mode provides an occasion to admit all nondiatonic elements. Example 9.14 is taken from the second movement
of the Piano Sonata in F Major K. 280—a rare instance of a middle
movement in the key of the parallel minor (the only such case in the
piano sonatas). At the broadest level this movement can be regarded
as the complement of the outer movements in that its key, F minor,

Example 9.14 Mozart, Piano Sonata K. 280, ii, mm. 43–46

incorporates A-flat, D-flat, and E-flat—nondiatonic elements of the main key, F major. The poignant phrase shown in the example contains all the nondiatonic tones of F major highlighted in the voice leading of the outer parts:

C	C	B♭	A♭	G♭	F	E♮
F	E♭	D♭	C	B♭	B♮	C

Example 9.15 Mozart, Piano Sonata K. 280, iii, mm. 78–108

The phrase in example 9.14 contains eleven tones; the twelfth—D-natural—is added in the expressive extension of this phrase (m. 49). The significance of this tender phrase transcends its immediate context in the middle movement; it appears to respond directly to the outer movements, filling in the gaps within the tonic major key and resonating with phrases of comparable chromatic density from those movements, such as the phrase from the first shown in example 9.1 (mm. 35–43).

The very brief development section of the finale of the Sonata K. 280 (ex. 9.15) is a fine example of the strategic placement of nondiatonic elements, each phrase introducing a new chromatic pitch. The lowered seventh scale degree, E-flat, prominent at the outset of this section (m. 79), is associated motivically with the beginning of the first movement. (There it was the first chromatic note to enter, occurring in m. 3 as part of the theme itself.) The second chromatic element, F-sharp, is introduced in the second phrase of the development (mm. 82–85). When the first eight-measure phrase is repeated down a whole step in mm. 86–93, D-flat enters, followed by B-natural in mm. 94–97, also the product of sequential repetition. The last chromatic element, G-sharp, enters at the climax of the development (m. 102) in conjunction with the augmented sixth chord preparing the applied dominant (A major) of the relative minor. (This particular applied dominant, a typical concluding chord in Mozart's development sections, might more properly be considered the major mediant in the overall key, functioning in this context as an intermediate harmony connecting a large-scale dominant with a structural tonic.) In fact, the climactic augmented sixth chord features the first important appearance of G-sharp in the last movement; G-sharp has occurred just once before, as an auxiliary sixteenth note in m. 30. Thus, on the basis of aggregate completion the arrival of G-sharp marks the climax not only of the development, but also of the movement up to this point. Accordingly, this chromatic completion conforms precisely with Webern's formal and aesthetic criterion that "each 'run' of the twelve notes [should mark] a division within the piece, idea, or theme."[98]

Examples 9.16 to 9.19 feature excerpts from the Piano Sonata in B-flat Major K. 333 that illustrate a variety of connections between aggregate completion and form. Example 9.16 shows the beginning of the development of the second movement in E-flat major, a passage that employs high concentrations of chromatic notes along with duple and triple cross rhythms in a gesture seemingly designed to throw the listener off balance. (Mozart was fond of starting a development section in this way; another example is the corresponding section in the last movement of the G-minor symphony discussed earlier.) In

this passage all but one of the twelve tones—B-natural—have
been heard by the third beat of m. 32.[99] Thereafter, in mm. 35–36,
the progression turns more diatonic in order to stabilize F minor. The
missing B-natural is not introduced until m. 37, where its unexpected
and conspicuous appearance in the melody signals the beginning of a
chromatic ascending sequence in the bass that leads to the tonicization
of A-flat major (the subdominant of the tonic key). After m. 39, with
its resolution to C, B-natural drops out for a considerable length of
time. The development is brought to a close by means of a stepwise
bass descent connecting A-flat with B-flat, the dominant. Significantly,
B-flat is immediately preceded in the bass by C-flat, the enharmonic
equivalent of B-natural, which has been absent for eight measures.
The enharmonic substitution of C-flat effectively dissolves the tension
inherent in the B-natural and creates a large-scale reciprocal relation

Example 9.16   Mozart, Piano Sonata in B♭ Major, K. 333 (1783–84) ii, mm. 31– 48

that in a sense "frames" the main body of the development section: B-natural–C (mm. 37–39) balanced by C-flat–B-flat (mm. 47–48). The liquidation of tension through enharmonic substitution is a device frequently found in association with formal articulation in Mozart's music.

Example 9.17 shows the cadenza from the sonata-rondo finale of the Sonata K. 333. A significant change is signaled in m. 174 by the shift to the parallel minor, effected by the chromatic substitution of D-flat for D-natural. This occurrence of D-flat completes an aggregate unfolded over a very large span of the movement, a section beginning with the return of the main theme in m. 111. In fact, the absence of D-flat until m. 174 is especially conspicuous, since the other chromatic elements have been introduced much earlier, within the short span of mm. 131–36. At the conclusion of the cadenza D-flat once again comes to the fore as the climactic melodic pitch in the fermata chord in m. 197. Thereafter, D-flat makes but one more appearance in the movement—at the very close of the cadenza (m. 198) within the tentative chromatically ascending gesture that leads to the return of the main theme. In this scale D-flat is followed immediately by D-natural, which in effect "corrects" the chromatic substitution that took place at the beginning of the cadenza. The reciprocal chromatic relations that thus frame the cadenza—D-natural–D-flat balanced by D-flat–D-natural—set off a section that constitutes an interpolation into the main body of the movement. Although one might conceive of going directly from the lead-in of mm. 170–71 to the coda beginning in m. 199, this cadenza is hardly an optional addition to the form, for it lends emphasis to the single chromatic element that would otherwise be absent for the latter half of the movement.

The process of aggregate completion is intimately involved in the articulation of form throughout this finale. The main theme of the rondo is itself quite diatonic, admitting a single chromatic note, E-natural, as a fleeting passing tone. The subsidiary themes and episodes that connect restatements of the refrain are consequently the vehicles for chromaticism in the piece. Thus, in the intial aggregate formation in the movement, the remaining chromatic elements are not introduced until the arrival of a second theme in mm. 24–36. Even after the second theme has closed, one chromatic note, G-sharp, remains to be heard. This note is introduced in the brief transitional phrase (mm. 36–40) that returns to the refrain. Because this transition involves the completion of the aggregate and features as well the highest chromatic concentration in the piece thus far, the effect of the subsequent restatement of the diatonic refrain is to wipe clean the chromatic slate and begin the process anew. The next return

268

Example 9.17   Mozart, Piano Sonata K. 333, iii, mm. 170–78, mm. 197–98

of the refrain, in m. 111, achieves the same effect. Indeed, the preceding transitional phrase includes an entire ascending chromatic scale filling in the octave on the dominant—the most direct assertion of the chromatic aggregate in the composition. In the material intervening between the statements of the refrain in mm. 41 and 111, there is one other significant form-defining completion: the A-flat in m. 75 completes the aggregate formed over the span begun in m. 41, occurring as the critical seventh of a dominant cadencing to E-flat major with the arrival of a new theme in m. 76. This section is framed by the reciprocal chromatic relations F–F-sharp (in the melody in mm. 60–61) and G-flat–F (in the bass in mm.101–2).

The concentration of chromatic elements in Mozart's music varies greatly from composition to composition. Certain pieces employ the full aggregate almost from the start. (See, for instance, the opening of the Quartet K. 428 shown in examples 9.4 and 9.5) The first movement of the Sonata K. 333, on the other hand, manifests a rather low chromatic density. Only one chromatic element (E-natural) is involved in the presentation of the main theme. Another (B-natural) is introduced in the bridge to the second theme, and two more (C-sharp and F-sharp) occur in the course of the second theme itself. The final remaining chromaticism, G-sharp, enters at the beginning of the closing material (m. 40; see ex. 9.18). While this note receives negligible attention in the exposition, its enharmonic equivalent serves a pivotal role in both the development and the recapitulation. The shift from F major to F minor near the beginning of the development (m. 71; see ex. 9.19) launches the turbulent passage that comprises the main material of this section. The A-flat–A-natural voice leading in the two preceding measures (mm. 69–70) hints at this change, and alludes as well to the G-sharp–A motion from which this chromaticism originated in the exposition (ex. 9.18). In the recapitulation A-flat marks the crucial turn in the bridge material which keeps the harmony, as required, in the region of the tonic (m. 105). Throughout the closing section of the movement A-flat occurs frequently in conjunction with harmonic turns toward the subdominant. (See, for example, the final three measures.)

In the third movement of the Sonata K. 333, G-sharp is the subject of comparable chromatic play. As noted in our earlier discussion of this movement, G-sharp is the last chromatic tone to enter (m. 37); in fact it occurs in the same register and voice-leading situation as its initial entrance in the first movement. It then completes the next aggregate formation in m. 75. In the final measures of the coda A-flat is emphasized (as the seventh of the applied dominant of E-flat major) in a fashion very reminiscent of the close of the first movement. While the lowered seventh is quite conventional in such contexts as codas,

Example 9.18 Mozart, Piano Sonata K. 333, i, mm. 39–40

Example 9.19 Mozart, Piano Sonata K. 333, i, mm. 68–71

the frequent focus on the G-sharp/A-flat chromatic element at significant formal junctures in both the first and third movements of the sonata would seem to indicate that this chromaticism fulfills a motivic function lending coherence to the work as a whole.

The first movement of the Piano Sonata in G Major K. 283 similarly manifests a low chromatic density. The main theme is entirely diatonic, and the first chromatic element, F-natural, is not introduced until the bridge to the second theme (m. 18; see ex. 9.26). The final chromatic element, A-sharp, enters only once, six measures before the end of the exposition (m. 48), as an unaccented passing sixteenth note. This pitch does not appear at all in the development section and in the recapitulation only three times (mm. 101, 106, and 116). It is therefore difficult to make a case for aggregate completion as a formal principle in the overall form of the movement. Nonetheless, the principle does seem to apply in certain more local situations in the piece. For instance, in the closing group the passage in mm. 115–16 contains every pitch except F-natural, a pitch emphasized in mm. 118–20 (after one measure of pure diatonic harmony) in the closing melodic gesture, F-natural–E–F-sharp–G (see ex. 9.27).

Although Mozart's standard practice with regard to aggregate formation appears to have been a gradual exposition of the twelve chromatic tones in strategic steps or stages, one encounters problematic passages where all but one or two chromatic elements are present within a certain span, and yet the remaining tones are not to be found in that general vicinity. Such situations raise the question of whether aggregates can be identified across larger musical spans and whether the process can be interrupted by intervening materials that have nothing to do with a particular unfolding of the chromatic aggregate. Examples 9.20 and 9.21 illustrate two such problems. Example 9.20 shows a portion of the closing materials of the finale of the Piano Sonata in F Major K. 332. Through m. 225, ten of the chromatic elements are present—all but E-flat and F-sharp. If Mozart had followed the corresponding close of the exposition of this movement, the piece would in fact end with the tonic in m. 226 (with perhaps several confirming repetitions of that chord). Instead, he deceptively opens up the progression again with the applied dominant of B-flat major in m. 227, which supplies the missing E-flat in the high melodic register. At this point only F-sharp remains to be heard, yet Mozart does not include this pitch in the remainder of the movement. Looking back through the score, we find that the nearest F-sharp or, rather, G-flat occurs in m. 196, in the midst of a rather densely chromatic harmonization of a contrasting tune in the parallel minor. Because this element is enclosed within its own chromatic field (it contributes to the formation of an aggregate within a different musical span), and because the sudden diatonic burst of F major in m. 200 appears to clean the slate and signal the beginning of a new aggregate formation, one is not satisfied that this G-flat is sufficiently associated with the elements of the final aggregate to render it complete. The problem of completion is solved in this instance only when one takes into account the possibility of repeating the latter half of the movement, for in so doing one returns to m. 91, where F-sharp is a powerful chromatic agent through m. 99 (see ex. 9.21). (In fact, this passage features both E-flat and F-sharp, the two elements missing from the closing material shown in example 9.20.) In effect, the process of aggregate formation demands this repetition. The second time around, of course, the final aggregate remains incomplete, a situation inherent in the employment of this special technique.

272

Example 9.20   Mozart, Piano Sonata in F Major K. 332 (1781–83), iii, mm. 215–32

Example 9.21   Mozart, Piano Sonata K. 332, iii, mm. 91–100

Example 9.22 shows a chromatic passage from the exposition of the first movement of the Piano Sonata K. 333 that contains every pitch except G-sharp. Just several measures before this phrase G-sharp appears for the first time (m. 40; see ex. 9.18), completing the first aggregate of the piece, as has been described above. Because this G-sharp marks a completion, it is somewhat problematic to associate it with the succeeding aggregate as well. If one looks ahead for the next occurrence of this chromaticism, the only candidate within the exposition itself is the passing melodic A-flat in m. 60 (see ex. 9.23). At first this A-flat may seem too innocuous to effect the completion of an aggregate. Upon closer scrutiny, however, this pitch, in its relation with the melodic A-natural on the downbeat of m. 61, proves to bear the seeds of the dramatic shift to F minor in the development, discussed in conjunction with example 9.19. One might well consider the aggregate in question to remain incomplete within the exposition, creating a tension that continues into the development and is resolved only upon the arrival of the strong A-flat in m. 71. The more long-range, "nonadjacent" aggregate completions observed in examples 9.20–9.23 indicate that aggregate formation may occur in intricate ways and be a powerful force for continuity and coherence in large-scale musical forms.

Example 9.22   Mozart, Piano Sonata K. 333, i, mm. 46–50

  In discussing previous examples we have occasionally alluded to the motivic function of a chromatic pitch relation, and it is indeed true that such relations are often important factors of coherence, even among movements of a multimovement composition. A straightforward case in point is the Piano Sonata K. 280, where E-flat is a focal chromatic element in the first movement, stated conspicuously in the first phrase of the theme itself (see ex. 9.35). Although it receives little emphasis elsewhere in the first movement, E-flat surfaces importantly at the beginning of the development of the finale (see ex. 9.15), and is touched upon once again, perhaps by way of an allusion, in the closing material of this movement (ex. 9.24). Since E-flat occurs naturally in both the tonic key of the second movement (F minor) and especially its relative major, it is more difficult to evaluate its motivic significance there; but in light of the appearances of E-flat in the outer movements, it does seem as if certain presentations of E-flat in the middle movement—for instance its unaccompanied statement at the beginning of the second part (m. 25)—resonate motivically with occurrences of E-flat in the outer movements (see ex. 9.25).
  The Piano Sonata in G Major K. 283 is similarly unified by motivic play focusing on the lowered seventh scale degree, F-natural, and its diatonic counterpart, F-sharp. Instances of this play are shown in examples 9.26 to 9.30 (see also ex. 9.11). Several of these examples have been discussed previously, so they should require little further comment here. Particularly noteworthy is the emphasis on F-natural in the theme of the second movement, shown here in its last appearance at the close (see ex. 9.28). While in the movements in G major F-natural is typically "corrected" to F-sharp, in the C-major context of the second movement the reverse situation applies.

Example 9.23   Mozart, Piano Sonata K. 333, i, mm. 60–62

Example 9.24   Mozart, Piano Sonata K. 280, iii, mm. 177–83

Example 9.25   Mozart, Piano Sonata K. 280, ii, mm. 25–28

Example 9.26   Mozart, Piano Sonata K. 283, i, mm. 16–20

Example 9.27   Mozart, Piano Sonata K. 283, i, mm. 118–20

Example 9.28   Mozart, Piano Sonata K. 283, ii, mm. 38–39

Example 9.29   Mozart, Piano Sonata K. 283, iii, mm. 25–28

Example 9.30   Mozart, Piano Sonata K. 283, iii, mm. 103–7

As a final example of motivic connection I cite the second movement of the Piano Sonata in A Minor K. 310, in particular the dramatic
shift from C major to C minor at the beginning of the development
section (see ex. 9.31). This progression is precisely the reverse of a shift
from C minor to C major that takes place at the arrival of the second
theme in the exposition of the first movement (ex. 9.32). (Here C minor
does not occur as a tonic, but its imminent arrival is strongly implied
by the E-flat in the six-four harmony.) The play between E-flat and E-
natural, the crux of these modal shifts, constitutes an expansion of the
thematic D-sharp–E appoggiatura introduced with startling effect at
the very outset of the piece (ex. 9.33). It is not surprising to find an
important shift from C major to C minor in the finale of the sonata as
well (see ex. 9.34).

What is most interesting in these examples of motivic chromaticism
is that correspondences exist between various presentations of particular pitches (or their enharmonic or octave equivalents) without
regard to their harmonic settings or key contexts. And often correspondences are especially strong between presentations of a pitch in
a specific register (that is, recurrences of a particular frequency). These
observations suggest that Mozart was acutely sensitive to the absolute
quality of each individual pitch, a quality that resides in its physical
attributes (frequency and timbre) and exists apart from the various
scale-degree functions it might fulfill. This conclusion would bear out
the teachings of musicians contemporary with Mozart, including
Vogler, who claimed to discriminate among the notes of the chromatic
scale on the basis of their individual characters. Such a refined sensi-

Example 9.31   Mozart, Piano Sonata K. 310, ii, mm. 32–37

Example 9.32   Mozart, Piano Sonata K. 310, i, mm. 18–23

Example 9.33   Mozart, Piano Sonata K. 310, i, mm. 1–2

Allegro maestoso

Example 9.34   Mozart, Piano Sonata K. 310, iii, mm. 25–32

tivity could come about in part through the tactile sensation of playing on the keyboard or on another instrument, an especially important aspect of improvisation. But in the case of a musical intellect such as Mozart's, one hardly need attempt to ascribe this awareness of pitch to any particular origin. Indeed, it would be difficult to imagine that he did not have such a grasp of the chromatic universe.

As intimated in portions of the preceding discussion, chromaticism in eighteenth-century practice is closely connected with processes of phrase structure and periodicity. A clear example occurs in the finale of the Sonata K. 310, where an interpolation of chromatic material interrupts and thus postpones the final cadence of the work (see ex. 9.13). It is possible to imagine a simple A-minor harmony, like that actually found in the last measure of the work (m. 252), following directly upon the dominant in m. 225, although its arrival at this point would certainly be abrupt and perfunctory. Instead of the expected tonic, Mozart substituted the chromatically saturated ascending sequence that we have already discussed, a device that heightens the sense of urgency with which we expect the tonic. (Subsequently, at points where a solid tonic could occur—mm. 233, 239, and 245—it is stated in a high register or in an otherwise weak disposition.) In a composition where four-measure phrases predominate in a manner quite unusual for a piece by Mozart, the seven-measure span given to the chromatic phrase (mm. 226–32) generates tension and a feeling of disjuncture, hurtling us forward into the final phrases of the piece (mm. 233–52). The gesture is designed in every way to arouse excitement and to throw us off balance.

Chromaticism can affect phrase structure in more subtle ways, as is illustrated by the main theme of the first movement of the Piano Sonata K. 280 (ex. 9.35). We have already seen that the melodic E-flat in m. 3 exerts a strong pull downward from F to D. As the phrase continues, it is necessary to correct this note to its diatonic form, E-natural. It appears that the purpose of the two-measure phrase in mm. 5–6, set off from the phrases before and after by its *piano* dynamic, is to make this correction: the inner part D–E–F in mm. 4–6 is thus a direct response to the descending third in the melody in mm. 3–4. The chromaticism in m. 3 has in a sense generated an initial phrase of six (4 + 2) measures—a phrase that, were it not for the appearance of E-flat, might have conformed to the Classical norm of the four-measure phrase. The six-measure antecedent phrase in turn demands a special kind of consequent. For this purpose Mozart creates an approximate balance by means of a seven-measure (3 + 3 + 1) consequent phrase derived from a more basic four-measure idea in the following manner: after the first three measures of the consequent (mm. 7–9), these measures are repeated with slight variation, displacing the tonic expected in m. 10, but finally cadencing in m. 13. If the cadential tonic is regarded as the beginning of the next phrase, then the initial theme proves to be symmetrically apportioned into two six-measure phrases. Example 9.36 shows a hypothetical (and relatively uninteresting) eight-measure phrase that might have occurred had the lowered seventh not been introduced in m. 3.

Example 9.35   Mozart, Piano Sonata K. 280, i, mm. 1–13

Example 9.36   Mozart, Piano Sonata K. 280, i,
hypothetical diatonic version of main theme

Although the E-flat is the source of certain motivic correspondences in the Sonata K. 280 (discussed in conjunction with examples 9.24 and 9.25), it is not consistently exploited throughout the work. The truth of this observation becomes clear when one compares this piece to the Sonata K. 332 in the same key, the opening of which is given in example 9.37. Here Mozart begins with a theme based on the same E-flat–E-natural chromatic relation, but seizes upon it, playing its motivic significance for all its worth. Actually, as in the exposition of the Sonata K. 280's first movement, the appearance of E-flat in the main theme is apparently inconsequential. It is the only chromatic element in the first twenty-one measures, a span embracing the main theme and a second idea in the tonic (mm. 11–20), and it is presented only in m. 2 as part of a left-hand arpeggiation figure. But as in the Sonata K. 280, the F–D descending third brought about by the E-flat requires and receives the response of a third ascending through E-natural back to F (mm. 3–5). This motion, somewhat concealed by octave displacement, is among the features demonstrated in the sketch of the main theme given in example 9.38. In contrast to Mozart's theme in the Sonata K. 280, in the Sonata K. 332 he waxed expansive in mm. 5–9, elaborating upon the subject of descending and ascending thirds in a wonderful imitative passage that extends the harmony of m. 5 but does not carry forward the basic progression. The phrase is brought to a close in mm. 9–12 with a consequent phrase that might well have been stated directly following m. 4. Example 9.39 shows a simple diatonic eight-measure phrase that might be said to underlie Mozart's twelve-measure theme. Since the subject of the phrase extension in mm. 5–9 was generated by the lowered seventh, E-flat, this chromaticism is at the heart of Mozart's theme. The lyrical expansiveness of this theme is highlighted by its juxtaposition with the light and humorous, entirely diatonic eight-measure phrase in mm. 12–20. This jaunty second idea in the tonic—a highly unusual structural feature—is in fact quite comparable to the simple phrase (in ex. 9.39) underlying the main theme, and may be interpreted as the alter ego of the theme itself.

The abrupt entry of the first conspicuous chromaticism in the piece, the C-sharp in doubled octaves in m. 22, signals the beginning of the bridge to the second theme. In this transition four-measure phrases are the norm, with all five nondiatonic elements making strategic entrances. The last chromatic element to enter, F-sharp, is introduced as the critical raised sixth of the German sixth chord in mm. 35–36, a dramatic high point that occurs in conjunction with an extension of the four-measure phrase in mm. 31–34 to six measures. The bridge culminates with the assertion of G major, the secondary dominant. The strong presence of E-flat throughout the latter part of the bridge leads us to expect a cadence to C minor, the minor dominant. With the

282

Example 9.37 Mozart, Piano Sonata K. 332, i, mm. 1–56

Example 9.38 Mozart, Piano Sonata K. 332, i, mm. 1–12

Example 9.39 Mozart, Piano Sonata K. 332, i,
hypothetical diatonic version of main theme

arrival of the second theme, however, Mozart corrected the E-flat to E-natural, a maneuver that corresponds, of course, to the voice leading of the first phrase of the main theme. This relation surfaces within the second theme itself as the D-sharp–E decoration of the third of C major, most evident in the appoggiaturas in mm. 49 and 55. The subsequent sequential episode (mm. 56–70) is framed by reciprocal chromatic conversions from E-natural to E-flat in m. 58 and E-flat to E-natural with the arrival of the closing material after m. 70.

The thorough inspection of chromaticism in this movement may be left to the interested reader. For our purposes, it is sufficient to call attention to some particularly important moments involved in chromatic motivic correspondences. After a full sixteen-measure period in diatonic C major, the development shifts to the parallel minor beginning an episode comparable to that in mm. 56–70 of the exposition. The development leads ultimately in m. 123 (see ex. 9.40) to the major mediant of F major, an A-major harmony that incorporates C-sharp, the crucial chromatic element that instigated the motion away from the tonic in the exposition. In the measures that follow, the harmony undergoes a process of "dechromaticization" in which the restoration of C-natural is particularly critical—a process reciprocal with that of the bridge of the exposition. (Note the familiar shift from major to parallel minor in m. 127.) Because the second and closing themes must be recapitulated in the tonic at the end of the piece, the chromatic relations formerly associated with these themes are changed. It is noteworthy that as a result of transposition to the tonic the only chromatic element present in this material in the last twenty-four measures of the movement is C-sharp, a pitch that in the final phrase (ex. 9.41) resonates particularly strongly with its initial presentation. Important instances of the E-natural/E-flat relation are found at the beginning of the second movement and in mm. 12–14, 48–51, and 91–94 of the third, and should require no further comment. The crucial arrival of E-flat at the conclusion of the finale has already been discussed in conjunction with example 9.20.

Example 9.40   Mozart, Piano Sonata K. 332, i, mm. 122–33

Example 9.41   Mozart, Piano Sonata K. 332, i, mm. 226–29

As a final observation concerning the first movement of the Sonata K. 332, we note the prevalence of the sixteen-measure period as a norm. Most clearly manifested in the clear-cut phrasing of the second theme (mm. 41–56) and the opening period of the development (mm. 94–111), the sixteen-measure structure may be identified as a basis of virtually every period in the piece. If one considers the twelve-bar main theme an extension of an eight-measure phrase, then that phrase together with the "alter ego" tonic phrase in mm. 12–22—itself an eight-measure phrase extended to ten by repetitions of the cadence in mm. 20–22—is an extension of a sixteen-measure period in the tonic. The bridge section (mm. 23–40) is eighteen measures in length, which are subdivided 4 + 4 + 4 (+ 2) + 4, with the two-measure extension of the third phrase occurring in conjunction with the climactic augmented sixth chord, as previously discussed. Following the second theme is an episode of fifteen measures divided 4 + 7 + 4. Compared to a norm of sixteen measures, the odd length is the result of a rhythmic compaction in the central phrase, with the progression of mm. 64–65 compressing into two measures what would have ordinarily taken three. The closing material (mm. 71–93) comprises twenty-three measures, resulting from the overlap of materials of sixteen and eight measures at m. 86. The sixteen-measure phrase does not constitute a basic unit, however, but rather the expansion of an eight-measure idea, which might be explained as follows (with extensions shown in parentheses): 4 (+ 2) + 4 (+ [1 + 2 + 2 + 1]). Thus the closing material, too, is based on a sixteen-measure norm. What is most relevant with regard to our topic is that, with the exception of the closing material, in every case just mentioned the extension of phrases is intimately connected with chromaticism, and this relation continues throughout the piece.[100]

To conclude this investigation of chromaticism in the Classical style, I shall comment on two much-discussed excerpts from Mozart's chamber music—the opening of the "Dissonance" Quartet K. 465 and the first period of the Quintet in C Major K. 515—in the hope that the analytical approach offered here will provide some new insight into the complexities that have continued to strain theoretical systems up to the present. The famous opening of Mozart's Quartet K. 465 is shown in example 9.42. The key of this work provides an important frame of reference for understanding the introduction to the first movement— one that has generally been overlooked in the innumerable discussions of this passage in the literature. The tendency to treat the opening as if it is a separate entity with its own key of C minor, although understandable, has been the source of much confusion. Perhaps the most important question for comprehending this introduction in its proper role as part of a larger composition is: Which notes are the

"right" notes, and which are the "wrong" ones?—or, more properly:
Which pitches are the diatonic elements, which the chromatic?

Example 9.42   Mozart, Quartet in C Major K. 465 (1785), i, mm. 1–26

I shall argue that, in order to understand the full implications of Mozart's use of chromaticism in this introduction, we must hear it in C major. True, at the outset the preponderance of the evidence points to the minor mode. Thus the first violin's A-natural in m. 2 is heard by the informed listener as a purposefully selected nonharmonic tone. But is it not possible that this tone is in fact diatonic, that the viola and second violin (which after all are playing the traditionally subsidiary middle parts) have introduced elements of doubt and confusion that divert the listener from the ultimate goal of the work?

From the perspective of C major, the opening presents a curious reversal, for the first four-measure phrase contains every nondiatonic note but lacks two diatonic elements, F and E, the latter particularly critical as the third scale degree that would define the major mode. These missing notes are introduced soon after, in m. 6, but at this point E serves as a lower auxiliary to F. A good deal of the drama of the introduction is focused on E-natural and its gradual attainment of the status of a diatonic element of the key. It appears for the first time as a stable pitch as the resolution of F in the melody on the downbeat of

m. 14, but is immediately displaced by E-flat on the second beat of the measure. In the expanded dominant that closes the introduction (mm. 16–22), although E-flat is stressed at first as part of an applied diminished seventh chord, it is ultimately displaced by E-natural treated as a lower auxiliary to F. The listener might well expect the resolution of this F, the added seventh of the dominant harmony, to take place prominently at the beginning of the main theme, which follows immediately. Mozart allowed a certain tension between F and E to continue throughout this theme, however, postponing a definitive melodic resolution until the F–E appoggiatura over the closing tonic harmony in m. 44. The play about the natural third scale degree thus appears to be basic not only to the main theme but to the introduction as well, explored in diatonic and chromatic terms respectively.

The play revolving about A-natural and A-flat, the diatonic and chromatic versions of the sixth scale degree in C major, is likewise a motive that is worked out in a variety of ways in all four movements of the quartet, frequently with specific reference to the original (a^2) register of A-natural. In the main theme of the first movement A-natural is the high point of the first four-measure phrase (m. 26), stated as a straightforward appoggiatura that recalls the initial gesture of the introduction, a much less secure presentation of the A as upper auxiliary to G. Throughout the exposition A-natural continues to receive attention (see, for instance, mm. 71 and 93), and is most poignantly juxtaposed in a cross relation with A-flat just before the development (mm. 103–4) in an unmistakable allusion to the events of the introduction (see ex. 9.43). As would be expected, the development exploits the chromatic and diatonic aspects of the sixth scale degree. Perhaps most telling, however, is the understated final phrase of the movement, where the diatonic A prevails, with A-flat converted by this point to a fleeting chromatic passing tone, G-sharp (mm. 241–46; ex. 9.44).

Example 9.43 Mozart, Quartet K. 465, i, mm. 103–7

290

Example 9.44   Mozart, Quartet K. 465, i, mm. 241– 46

Example 9.45   Mozart, Quartet K. 465, iv, mm. 30–34

Example 9.46   Mozart, Quartet K. 465, iv, mm. 192–98

There are many other manifestations of the A–A-flat dichotomy in the remaining movements of the Quartet K. 465. It will suffice here to mention some particularly important appearances. In the second movement A-natural is given the strongest possible support as the mediant in the key of F major. Its chromatic counterpart is the focus of attention in an episode in the parallel minor toward the conclusion of the movement (mm. 93–101). The Menuetto (in C major) features many prominent appearances of A, often highlighted by means of a G-sharp–A appoggiatura. The Trio (in C minor), on the other hand, exploits A-flat. The cello line at the end of the Trio makes explicit the play with A–A-flat. In the finale the chromatic slide from G to A through G-sharp in the final phrase of the main theme (mm. 31–32) puts the relation in perspective (see ex. 9.45). The development, true to the pattern established in the middle sections of the preceding movements, once again explores the chromatic aspect of the sixth scale degree, but ends in mm. 196–98 with a diatonic reaffirmation in the first violin's insistent repetitions of the A–G appoggiatura figure (ex. 9.46). Appearing in the tonic in the recapitulation, the second theme emphasizes A-natural in its contours (mm. 258–91). The ensuing chromatic episode, with its emphasis on the lowered submediant harmony, provides A-flat with its last consonant setting in the piece. In the coda this chromatic element, in either of its spellings as A-flat or G-sharp, virtually evaporates. Mozart could now make light of the A–G–F-sharp–G melodic turn from the opening of the quartet (mm. 382–86), going so far as to embellish G with its diatonic upper neighbor in the joyously warbling trills of mm. 388–91 and 401–4 (see ex. 9.47). It is clear that the time of doubt is past; the diatonic scale is victorious.

This overview of the motivic strategy of the composition makes it evident that the introduction to the first movement sets up tensions between diatonic and chromatic elements with virtually unprecedented directness and drama. Returning to the introduction, we can now examine the relations between the dissonant chromatic events and the underlying diatonic framework, and the effect of these relations on periodicity as well. Example 9.48 provides a sketch of the essential voice leading of the introduction (see graph a). The outstanding features demonstrated in the sketch are the chromatic unfolding of the tonic from its root position to its first inversion during the first twelve measures, followed by two successive authentic cadences on the tonic supporting a stepwise descent through the fifth of the scale in the melody in mm. 13–23. A similar descending unfolding of the fifth takes place in the upper voice in mm. 1–12, participating in a voice-

Example 9.47   Mozart, Quartet K. 465, iv, mm. 378–94

leading pattern with the bass: 5–6, 5–6, 6, 6, 6. This pattern is actually the means for expanding the progression from I to I⁶. The sketch also reveals a certain squareness in the phrasing of the introduction. The four-measure phrase appears to be the basic unit of periodicity, with this unit observed quite strictly throughout. This is particularly true if the fermata chords in mm. 22 are interpreted as having the value of one measure each, actually a reasonable account of how their durations would be performed. The twenty-four-measure period that is thereby defined up to and including the cadence to the Allegro is divided symmetrically into two twelve-measure phrases articulated at the point of completion of the unfolding to the minor tonic sixth chord (m. 12).

Graph b of example 9.48 shows a basic diatonic structure that could be said to underlie the introduction. This structure is shown here in the context of a hypothetical eight-measure phrase, squarely divided 4 + 4, given in a durational reduction with the quarter note equivalent to one written measure. As can be seen in the alignment of the sketches in the two graphs, we have regarded the patterned unfolding of the tonic in the first twelve measures as an expansion of a simple tonic chord that might well be accorded much less time. All the significant chromatic ideas of the piece are introduced in the course of this opening twelve-measure tonic expansion, and are only echoed in condensed

Example 9.48   Mozart, Quartet K. 465, i, mm. 1–23, sketches

forms in the remaining twelve measures. In the latter half of the period, too, the diatonic scale, as represented by E-natural, may be observed to win out gradually over the chromatic.

One chromatic event in the basic voice leading of the first phrase occurs out of structural necessity and acts in a sense as a catalyst to the chromaticism that pervades the passage. I refer to the bass B-flat in m. 5, which marks a crucial change at the point when the 5–6 progression is repeated, producing a sequential descending progression. Had the diatonic B-natural been retained here in the bass, the tendency of this tone, in conjunction with the melodic F-natural, would have been to resolve back to C so as to support the mediant in the melody. The chromatic B-flat seems necessary, or at least highly desirable, in order to initiate the bass descent. Mozart followed through on the implications of this gesture, allowing the bass to descend chromatically as far as the dominant. With a decisive quickening of the pace in mm. 9–12 (as measured with regard to the descending parallel sixths of the underlying voice leading), the bass descends diatonically from the fifth to the third degree of the scale, but to the minor third. It is as if the chromaticism precipitated by the lowering of B to B-flat has automatically led the harmony into the minor region. One might say that the idea of the bass descent from tonic root to altered third has generated the chromaticism and in turn the modal mixture of the introduction.[101] The chromaticism originates at a level of structure less fundamental than that of the diatonic underpinning, and its use here is clearly connected with the extension of phrases beyond normal lengths.

To explore more deeply the effects of chromaticism on periodicity, we move finally to the famous opening period of the first movement of the Quintet in C Major K. 515, Mozart's most expansive movement of chamber music. The score of this excerpt is given in example 9.49. This passage contains a wonderful illustration of how Mozart delighted in juxtaposing thickly chromatic and purely diatonic passages. The sequential passage in mm. 34–37 presents all twelve tones of the chromatic scale in the closest concentration of the period, while the phrase immediately following (mm. 38–39) is diatonic simplicity itself.[102]

The chromatic saturation of mm. 34–37 might well indicate that the process of aggregate completion is important elsewhere in the passage, and indeed this is the case in the first phrase of the period (mm. 1–20), in which the nondiatonic elements of C major are introduced at strategic points. In m. 4, the first chromatic note, F-sharp, appears in the melodic turn. The next two, C-sharp and B-flat, enter as elements of the diminished seventh appoggiatura chord in m. 15, which marks the first significant departure from the pattern of events thus far. In m. 17, G-sharp is introduced as the bass of a conspicuously syncopated diminished seventh chord effecting a deceptive cadence. The only nondiatonic element remaining to be heard is E-flat, which Mozart reserved for the dramatic shift to the parallel minor at the beginning of the second phrase (m. 21). The C-minor harmony thus initiates a new phrase while at the same time completing the process of chromatic unfolding underlying the first phrase.

The remainder of the first period is divided into at least two sections on the basis of aggregate completion. The entire chromatic scale is employed in the thirteen-measure phrase preceding the sequential progression in mm. 34–37, although F-sharp, A-flat, and A-natural occur here only as elements of the melodic turns about G. One might thus consider this phrase (mm. 21–33) as a complete unfolding of the aggregate, but it seems preferable to regard the full chromaticism of the following sequence as the culmination of the process begun in m. 21. After the point of greatest chromatic density in the period is reached, the slate is wiped clean by the pure diatonicism of mm. 38–39. In mm. 40–41, however, chromaticisms begin to filter in once again, first as decorations of the plagal cadence, then through the much more powerful chromatic assertion in m. 43 on the part of the highly unusual D-flat six-four chord. With the deceptive cadence in m. 46, the phrase comes to a moment of relative repose, but despite the conspicuous chromaticisms the entire aggregate has not been completed up to this point. A single note, B-flat, remains to be heard. The subject from mm. 41–43 appears once again, but this time it is developed and extended over an A-flat pedal beginning in m. 48. The first violin repeats the subject several times in ascending stepwise sequence, reaching B-flat as the local melodic apex in m. 51. This long-awaited pitch is then emphasized as an appoggiatura tone in each of the other parts in mm. 53–54.

While on the broadest level the B-flat in m. 51 completes an aggregate that began in m. 38, another process of aggregate formation takes place within the context of the final phrase of the period, beginning with the upbeat to m. 47. This process is reciprocal with that of the first phrase of the period (mm. 1–20). In the first phrase the process of aggregate completion involves the gradual introduction of the nondiatonic elements into a field in which the diatonic elements clearly have priority. In a reverse procedure, the chromatic elements at first predominate in the last phrase, and two diatonic elements, B-natural and E-natural, are withheld until the cadence in mm. 55–57. Postponing these crucial pitches—the key-defining leading tone and the mode-defining third scale degree—until the very end heightens the contrast between the diatonic and chromatic aspects of the key and maximizes the effect of attaining a long-sought goal.

Example 9.49   Mozart, Quintet in C Major K. 515 (1787), i, mm. 1–57

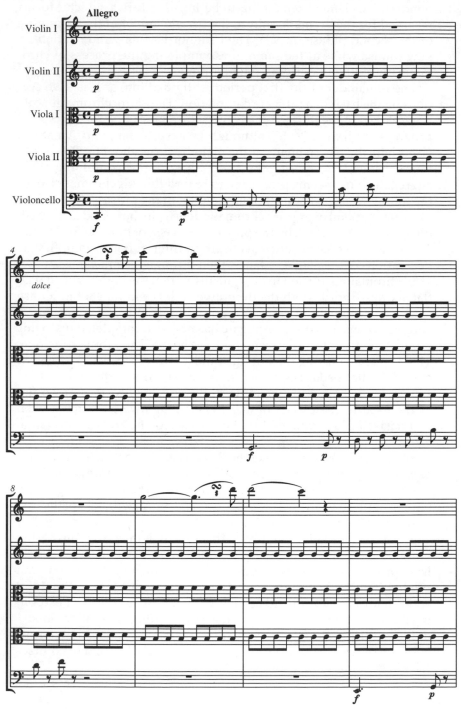

298

The chromatic tension of the period reaches its peak with the German sixth chord in m. 54 that directly precedes the cadence. At this point several chromatic relations are highlighted. The bass A-flat, essentially sustained as a pedal since m. 48, has in fact just been "decorated" by its diatonic equivalent, A-natural, in the bass in m. 52. The first violin's high E-flat, the apex of the phrase (which links with the same pitch at the beginning of the second large division of the period, m. 23), is juxtaposed against the E-natural that wins out at the cadence.

The central diatonic-chromatic opposition of the period is that between F and F-sharp, the natural and raised versions of the fourth scale degree. The F-sharp, the first chromaticism of the piece, which was introduced in the seemingly trivial melodic turn about G in m. 4, returns climactically at the end of the period (mm. 53–54) in the same register and leads to G, fulfilling at last the ascending tendency of the melody evident from the beginning. The contrasting descending tendency of the diatonic F-natural, evident in both the bass motion in mm. 16–19 and the melody in m. 17 and mm. 42–46, receives special emphasis in the plagal material in mm. 38–39. The diatonic-chromatic conflict is particularly critical in mm. 52–53, when F-natural is raised to F-sharp in order to effect the definitive melodic ascent to the fifth scale degree.

The chromatic play described above results in a grand expansion of, and deviation from, the normal phrase structure of a period in Classical music. The tendency toward expansion has already been reflected in the famous five-measure phrases at the opening, which are rhythmically derived from four-measure phrases. (Mozart provided the basis for comparison at the beginning of the development [m. 152ff.], where this main material is stated in normal four-measure groupings.) Example 9.50 contains two sketches demonstrating the basic voice leading and normal periodic organization over the fifty-seven measures of the period. Graph a shows the essential diatonic harmony and voice leading of the passage in the context of a normal eight-measure period divided into two four-measure phrases. (The whole-note value here corresponds to the duration of a regular four-measure phrase.) Graph b shows the approximate relative duration of each harmony as it occurs in the basic structure of the composition, with the quarter note equal to four measures. The integers in this second graph specify the actual number of measures in which each diatonic function is structurally effective. It becomes clear that the second large phrase of the period is rhythmically an augmentation of the first (roughly double in length). This expansion is based primarily on prolongations of the tonic and subdominant through elaborate voice exchanges. Remarkably, each of these prolongations occupies seven-

Example 9.50   Mozart, Quintet K. 515, i, mm. 1–57, sketches

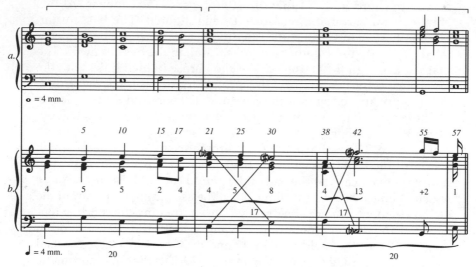

teen measures, creating an unexpectedly precise balance. Because the length of the tonic prolongation in mm. 21–37 approximately matches that of the opening phrase (mm. 1–20), the arrival at the subdominant in m. 38—one of the most dramatic moments in the piece—seems to mark the beginning of another section, one that could be understood as the third section of a tripartite form. This final section is in fact twenty measures in length, balanced exactly with the initial phrase.

The expansion that takes place in the second phrase results from a systematic exploitation of the chromatic elements introduced with relative simplicity in the first. In the initial phrase the chromatic elements occur in conjunction with the motivic turning figure or rather ordinary diminished seventh chords functioning as applied dominants of diatonic harmonies. In the latter phrase Mozart gave free rein to chromaticism of the most fanciful sort. Particularly effective are the chromatic voice exchanges within the tonic and subdominant harmonies, in which chromatic equivalents are juxtaposed as in false relations:

* * *

Our exploration of these works by Mozart has disclosed a use of chromaticism that is far from "accidental." This music is most definitely not, however, a "world in which the twelve notes hold sway," as Webern and Schoenberg found in certain of Bach's compositions. On the contrary, chromatic practice in Classical music depends on the consistent hierarchical distinction between diatonic and nondiatonic elements. In no sense does chromaticism contradict or even attenuate tonal structure; rather, it exists as another dimension of musical form, in that the finest of tonal nuances are played out in motivic relations that may penetrate to the farthest reaches of musical space. In the sense that chromaticism is a basis for motivic structure, it might be considered of secondary importance in relation to the fundamental structure defined by tonality. Yet we have observed many instances in which the completion of the full chromatic aggregate coincides with a major point of formal articulation. For Mozart, as for later generations of composers, the universe of twelve tones seems to have exerted a powerful influence, rendering musical statements of fewer than twelve pitches in a sense structurally deficient, dependent upon other statements to provide the sense of resolution achieved through a complete chromatic unfolding.[103]

The reason why Schoenberg and Schenker insisted on the importance of chromaticism within tonality has become clear. The most vital aspects of music—the strategy and indeed the very subject matter of the musical argument—often reside in the types of diatonic-chromatic oppositions that we have explored. Chromatic relations have a direct bearing on large-scale form, and the various extensions and elisions of phrases that give Classical music its incredible energy are frequently connected with the development of a chromatic motive. Indeed, the unique rhetorical power of Classical music results from its accommodation of chromatic explorations, maintaining all the while a clear distinction between diatonic and nondiatonic elements.[104]

Notes

1. Johann Philipp Kirnberger, *The Art of Strict Musical Composition*, trans. David Beach and Jurgen Thym (New Haven, 1982), 14.
2. Ibid., 24. Kirnberger's A is tempered to the ratio of 161/270, as opposed to the natural ratio of 3/5.
3. Floyd K. Grave and Margaret G. Grave, *In Praise of Harmony: The Teachings of Abbé Georg Joseph Vogler* (Lincoln, Neb., 1987), 20–22.
4. Heinrich Christoph Koch, *Versuch einer Anleitung zur Composition* (1782–93; reprint ed., Hildesheim, 1969), 1:38–39.
5. Kirnberger, *The Art of Strict Musical Composition*, 60n.

6. Charles Rosen argued to the contrary in his *The Classical Style: Haydn, Mozart, Beethoven* (New York, 1971), 27.

7. Heinrich Christoph Koch, *Musikalisches Lexikon* (1802; reprint ed., Hildesheim, 1964), 1501. Kirnberger insisted that even in the case of keyboard music with twelve fixed pitch classes, the listener infers enharmonic differentiations; see Kirnberger, *The Art of Strict Musical Composition*, 372.

8. Grave, *In Praise of Harmony*, 42–43.

9. Carl Philipp Emanuel Bach, *Essay on the True Art of Playing Keyboard Instruments*, trans. William J. Mitchell (New York, 1949), 434; see also Koch, *Versuch* 1:76.

10. Kirnberger, *The Art of Strict Musical Composition*, 368.

11. See for instance C. P. E. Bach, *Essay on the True Art*, 435.

12. See for instance ibid., 438; Kirnberger, *The Art of Strict Musical Composition*, 47–48; and Vogler, discussed in Grave, *In Praise of Harmony*, 38.

13. See his demonstration of modulations among all diatonic harmonies; Kirnberger, *The Art of Strict Musical Composition*, 131.

14. Grave, *In Praise of Harmony*, 62–63.

15. Ibid., 62–63, 66.

16. C.P.E. Bach, *Essay on the True Art*, 436–38.

17. Ibid., 438.

18. Ibid., 434.

19. Kirnberger, *The Art of Strict Musical Composition*, 149.

20. Ibid., 356.

21. Ibid., 152.

22. Ibid.

23. Ibid., 297–306. Other theorists discussed the use of modulation in text setting as well. See for instance Koch, *Versuch* 2:104, and Vogler, discussed in Grave, *In Praise of Harmony*, 191.

24. Kirnberger, *The Art of Strict Musical Composition*, 142–43.

25. Ibid., 353–54.

26. Koch, *Versuch* 1:76: "In the course of a melody a tone may by chance be raised a chromatic half step, in part to give the melody more gracefulness and animation, but sometimes also to make a rapid and unusual modulation into a remote key." ("In dem Laufe einer Melodie wird oft ein Ton zufällig um einen chromatischen halben Ton erhöhet, theils um der Melodie mehr Zierlichkeit und Schwung zu geben, theils aber auch zuweilen um eine geschwinde und ungewöhnliche Ausweichung in eine fremde Tonart zu machen.")

27. Kirnberger, *The Art of Strict Musical Composition*, 368.

28. Koch's diatonicism is evident in such examples as no. 392, but may be due in part to the fact that he intended these examples for the beginning composer. Heinrich Christoph Koch, *Introductory Essay on Composition: The Mechanical Rules of Melody, Sections 3 and 4*, trans. Nancy Kovaleff Baker (New Haven, 1983), 230–33.

29. Ibid., 241–44 ex. 403 and 176–77 ex. 364.

30. Ibid., 198.

31. Ibid., 234; but note that Koch stipulates *related* keys.

32. Ibid., 199.

33. "Im galanten Stile bekannte chromatische Satz"; Koch, *Versuch* 1:192–93.

34. Vogler, *Betrachtungen der Mannheimer Tonschule* (1778–81; reprint ed., Hildesheim, 1974), text 3:165–66 (reprint, 179–80); music 4:418.

35. "So führt das Schiksal uns hieher,/ Um uns vielleicht noch grausamer zu trennen!"

36. Kirnberger, *The Art of Strict Musical Composition*, 368.

37. The eighth chapter of Kirnberger's treatise is entitled in the original German "Von der Modulation in entfernte Tonarten, und von plötzlichen Ausweichungen." "Ausschweifung" is found in the article from Johann Georg Sulzer's *Allgemeine Theorie der schönen Künste* (Leipzig, 1771 and 1774), cited in Koch's *Versuch* 3:303.

38. Kirnberger, *The Art of Strict Musical Composition*, 371; he stated that in ascending lines chromatic elements should occur only on weak beats, whereas in descending lines they properly occur on strong beats. Mozart playfully broke such rules in the theme of the Menuetto from his Quartet in G Major K. 387.

39. Kirnberger, *The Art of Strict Musical Composition*, 407.

40. Koch, *Introductory Essay*, 104.

41. See for instance ibid., 161 exx. 356–57.

42. Ibid., 177 ex. 364, and 241 ex. 403.

43. Ibid., 76–78 ex. 226.

44. Grave, *In Praise of Harmony*, 64–66.

45. "Daher muss bei dem angehenden Tonsetzer auch in diesem Stücke das Studium guter Partituren den Mangel der Theorie ersetzen"; Koch, *Versuch* 3:38.

46. Aside from the prevailing Darwinism in the air at the turn of the century, there was ample precedent for Schoenberg's evolutionary point of view in nineteenth-century music history and theory. In the *Traité complet de la théorie et de la pratique de l'harmonie* (Brussels and Paris, 1844), François-Joseph Fétis described four phases in the history of music, from unitonic to omnitonic—that is, from modality to free chromatic modulation. His analysis anticipated aspects of Schoenberg's and Webern's account of the history of harmony, although Fétis believed that each phase resulted not so much from progress as from mere change.

47. Anton Webern, *The Path to the New Music*, ed. Willi Reich, trans. Leo Black (Bryn Mawr, 1963), 36–37.

48. Arnold Schoenberg, *Style and Idea: Selected Writings of Arnold Schoenberg*, ed. Leonard Stein, trans. Leo Black, rev. paperback ed. (Berkeley, 1984), 127.

49. Webern, *The Path to the New Music*, 17.

50. Schoenberg, *Style and Idea*, 216–17.

51. Ibid., 173.

52. Ibid., 395.

53. Ibid., 415–16.

54. Ibid., 409.

55. Ibid., 174.

56. Ibid., 268–69, 374–75.

57. Ibid., 286.

58. Ibid., 137.

59. Schoenberg observed that Bach and other masters gave free rein to chromaticism especially in pieces labeled "fantasia," signifying a "lack of restraint and a freedom in the manner of expression, permissible in our day only perhaps in dreams; in dreams of future fulfilment; in dreams of a possibility of expression which has no regard for the perceptive faculties of a contemporary audience; where one may speak with kindred spirits in the language of intuition and know that one is understood if one uses the speech of the imagination—of fantasy." See *Style and Idea*, 274. One can well imagine that Schoenberg felt Bach to be a kindred spirit communicating through his music across the centuries.

60. Ibid., 393.

61. Ibid.; Schoenberg was careful to explain that in this fugue "the Comes consists of only eleven different tones, and of the twelve repetitions and transpositions, only seven are complete, while five omit one or two of the twelve tones."

62. Webern, *The Path to the New Music*, 29.

63. Ibid., 36.

64. Arnold Schoenberg, *Theory of Harmony*, trans. Roy E. Carter (Berkeley, 1978), 370.

65. Webern, *The Path to the New Music*, 44, 50.

66. Ibid., 50.

67. Ibid., 51.

68. Schoenberg, *Style and Idea*, 375.

69. Webern, *The Path to the New Music*, 34; presumably his emphasis.

70. Ibid., 29.

71. For a fine evaluation of Schenker's contribution to the theory of chromaticism, see Matthew Brown, "The Diatonic and Chromatic in Schenker's Theory of Harmonic Relations," *Journal of Music Theory* 30 (1986): 1–33.

72. Heinrich Schenker, *Harmony*, ed. Oswald Jonas, trans. Elisabeth Mann Borgese (Chicago and London, 1954), 256. Outside of direct quotations from this work, I have replaced the translator's term "tonicalization" with the now more standard "tonicization."

73. Ibid., 272–73.

74. Schoenberg, *Theory of Harmony*, 185.

75. Ibid., 427–28.

76. Schoenberg, *Style and Idea*, 277.

77. Schenker, *Harmony*, 110–11.

78. Ibid., 301.

79. Heinrich Schenker, *Free Composition (Der freie Satz), Vol. 3 of New Musical Theories and Fantasies*, trans. Ernst Oster (New York, 1979), 1: 40–41.

80. Schoenberg, *Theory of Harmony*, 360–65.

81. Ibid., 387.

82. See for instance Koch, *Introductory Essay*, 84.

83. Schenker, *Harmony*, 288–89.

84. Schoenberg, *Style and Idea*, 277–78.

85. Ibid., 278; the order of these sentences excerpted from the text has been reversed in order better to convey the meaning in the context of the present discussion.

86. Schenker, *Free Composition* 1:41.

87. Ibid. 1: 70.

88. Ibid. 1:100, and 2:fig. 119.7; for more on Schenker's concept of motive, see Charles Burkhart, "Schenker's 'Motivic Parallelisms,'" *Journal of Music Theory* 22 (1978): 145–75.

89. Patricia Carpenter, "*Grundgestalt* as Tonal Function," *Music Theory Spectrum* 5 (1983): 15–16.

90. Schoenberg, *Style and Idea*, 223.

91. Ibid., 395.

92. Webern, *The Path to the New Music*, 22–23.

93. Carpenter, "*Grundgestalt* as Tonal Function," 17–18.

94. Grave, *In Praise of Harmony*, 62.

95. Found in Wolfgang Amadeus Mozart, *Symphony in G Minor K. 550*, ed. Nathan Broder, Norton Critical Scores (New York, 1967), 99–100.

96. Do not B-flat (m. 124) and G-sharp (m. 132), the bass pitches at the beginning and end of the passage, serve as auxiliaries to the important bass A (mm. 135–40) that progresses by fifth to D? Schenker understood the passage as implying a chain of diminished seventh chords based on a root progression by ascending fifth. See his *Harmony*, 196.

97. Schenker, *Harmony*, 289.

98. Webern, *The Path to the New Music*, 51.

99. Prior to the passage shown in the example, B-natural makes three appearances, in mm. 7, 19, and 28. In m. 19 it serves as a chromatic passing tone connecting B-flat and C in a middle voice, and in the other measures it occurs in a melodic appoggiatura to C. These latter instances seem especially to foreshadow the more dramatic appoggiatura in m. 39.

100. It should be mentioned that the actual lengths of the periods of this movement stand in good proportion with one another. The main theme and bridge sections total forty measures, precisely the length of the development section (from m. 94 up to and including the cadence to the tonic in m. 133). The material of the latter half of the exposition (comprising the second episode and the closing material) in theory occupies forty measures, but actually occupies only thirty-eight measures because of the modifications discussed above.

101. There can be no doubt that Mozart was experimenting with the structural repercussions of such bass motions at this time. Only months after composing this quartet in January 1785, he wrote the Fantasy in C Minor K. 475, which begins with a similar chromatic bass descent (with altogether different results).

102. The chromatic sequence is a perfect example of the chromatic progression that, according to Koch, was popular in the galant style (see note 33 above).

103. In James M. Baker, "Chromaticism in Mozart's 'Jupiter' Symphony" (to be published in the *Kongress-Berichtes "Internationaler Mozart-Kongress," Salzburg 1991*), the theories set forth in the present essay are applied in a detailed analysis of a single major work, with special attention to chromaticism as a unifying factor.

104. Once composers began to blur this distinction, as Mozart dared to do for a few measures at the beginning of the Quartet K. 465, the opportunity to conduct a Classically organized argument was lost. This, of course, was a sacrifice Romantic composers were more than willing to make.

TEN

Momigny's *Type de la Musique* and a Treatise in the Making

IAN BENT

N.B.: To assist the memory, I earlier classified major 3ds and 6ths together under the name "imperfect consonances: category 1," and minor 3ds and 6ths under the name "imperfect consonances: category 2." However, in the interests of greater precision, I now abandon my initial idea, envisioning that I shall classify these intervals in their own right, following a more rigorous analysis of the effects that they produce.
—Jérôme-Joseph de Momigny,
Cours complet d'harmonie et de composition, 132.

A change of heart, openly admitted by a theorist in mid-treatise, is to say the least striking. The present essay concerns the general notion of consistency in scientifically based theory, and examines the commonly held presumption that a work of theory is unitary in conception. The distinction in mode of writing that we make between "book" and "serial publication" is, it suggests, to some extent artificial and might be better understood in terms of an intermediate modality called "formative writing." While touching upon scientific and literary works, this essay focuses primarily on the formulation of music theory, and it takes the remarkable case of Jérôme-Joseph de Momigny's *Cours complet d'harmonie et de composition* of 1803–5[1]—in which the above curious *nota bene* appears—as its exemplification. In so doing, it first traces three specific theoretical issues (classification of consonant and dissonant intervals, primacy of harmonic over melodic materials, and primogeniture of the 3d over the 5th), making a bibliographical excursion in order to reconstruct the writing process of the *Cours complet*; it next turns to Momigny's handling of the minor mode with respect to the major before raising broader issues of scientific method and publishing practice; finally, it discusses Momigny's faltering faith in the status of the 11th and 13th as intervals within the harmonic series, in addressing the question of inconsistency.

Creating Categories: Consonance and Dissonance

The *nota bene* quoted at the head of this essay marks the partial discarding of a classification of diatonic intervals set up some one hundred pages earlier. This earlier classification encompassed not all intervals but only those that occurred within what Momigny called his *Type de la Musique* (translated here as "Model")—a succession of pitches extracted from the harmonic series as he understood it, and presented as a sequence of piled-up 3ds, the basis for which will be discussed later in this essay. This Model, as measured from its second note (i.e., second harmonic), represented a steady gradation from absolute consonance to maximum dissonance and back (pp. 36–37). In graph form, this may be demonstrated as in example 10.1.

Momigny's initial classification encompassed all the intervals that occurred between any two notes in this sequence. Where major and minor alternatives existed in the Model as a whole, those constructed over the first and second notes took precedence: consonant intervals were designated "first-class" and dissonant intervals "first-degree" if falling within the octave, "second-degree" if falling outside. Hence the major 3d and the major 6th were "first-class" consonances, the minor 7th was a "first-degree" dissonance, the major 9th a "second-degree" dissonance. Of those constructed over the third note and not already present over the first and second notes, consonant intervals were designated "second-class," dissonant "third-degree." Thus the minor 3d (B–d) and the minor 6th (B–g) were "second-class" consonances, the minor 9th (B–c^1) was a "third-degree" dissonance. Finally, over the fifth note there arose the major 7th, and this was accorded "fourth-degree" dissonance. Consonant intervals as a whole were

Example 10.1

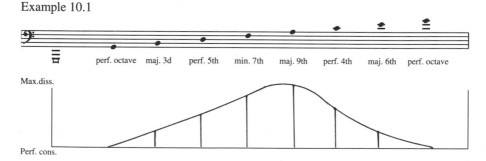

perf. octave   maj. 3d   perf. 5th   min. 7th   maj. 9th   perf. 4th   maj. 6th   perf. octave

Max.diss.

Perf. cons.

Table 10.1.

CONSONANT INTERVALS

perfect octave:	perfect consonance	
major 3d/6th:	imperfect consonance: first-class	} first degree of diminution
minor 3d/6th:	imperfect consonance: second-class	of consonance
perfect 5th:	half-consonance	} second degree of diminu-tion of consonance

DISSONANT INTERVALS

perfect 4th:	half-dissonance	
diminished 5th:	leading-tone dissonance	
augmented 4th/tritone:	leading-tone dissonance inverted	
minor 7th:	dissonance: first-degree	
major 9th:	dissonance: second-degree	
minor 9th:	dissonance: third-degree	
major 7th:	dissonance: fourth-degree	maximum dissonance

---

further subdivided at a higher level into "degrees of diminution of consonance." After scrutinizing all intervals constructed over all of the first eight notes of the Model (G_1–e^1: replicating the sequence above e^1 up to c^3 for this purpose), he set out his resultant classification schematically, skewed because of the absence of 2ds in the Model. Table 10.1 is a tabulation of the text of pages 40–41 and music examples of plates 3 L–M).

Momigny offered two cryptic maxims for this classification: (1) "plus un intervalle dissonnant est rapproché, et plus il est dissonnant"; and (2) "une consonnance rapprochée *d'une* octave, est plus consonnante" (p. 41). If the latter is taken to mean "the closer a consonant interval is *to the first octave in the Model*," and to refer only to noninverted consonances, then it serves to justify the greater consonance of the first octave (perfect) over the 3d (imperfect), and the 3d over the 5th (half), but fails to deal at the lower level with that of the major 3d over the minor. Momigny followed the maxim with the words: "The octave becomes unison, and forms a uni-sonance. The 6th becomes 3d, which is more consonant than the 6th" (p. 41). If this is intended to qualify rather than supplement the maxim, then the maxim itself must instead mean that, of two mutually inverted forms of an interval, the one closer to the first octave is the more consonant, giving higher status to the unison over the octave and the 3d over the 6th, but failing to reflect his view of the perfect 5th over the 4th.

The first of the two maxims, if taken to apply only to the uninverted intervals of Momigny's Model (i.e., the 7ths and 9ths, centering as they do around the octave), may signify that "the closer an interval comes *to the higher octave*, the more dissonant it becomes." This would appear

to be the implication of the words that follow this maxim: "The 7ths and 9ths, brought closer to the point of contact, to the point at which they touch and collide, are much more dissonant than otherwise"; but they continue: "The inverted diminished 5th (which is the tritone) is much more dissonant than the noninverted"—and this does not conform to the maxim (p. 41). Alternatively, Momigny's maxim and following words may imply that when the 7ths are inverted, and the 9ths narrowed by octave displacement, they reach the "point of contact" as 2ds and are deemed "much more dissonant." In this light, the augmented 4th is "closer" than diminished 5th—in conceptual terms, at least—and is indeed deemed more dissonant.

Further obscurity is cast by a discussion six pages later. After a detailed treatment of triads and of 7th and 9th chords, Momigny remarked: "Simple consonances and dissonances do not invert further because they then change their nature" (p. 47). Plate 5 E (see ex. 10.2) is cited in support of this remark. (Consonant intervals are here rep-

Example 10.2

resented by a pair of void note heads, dissonant intervals by a pair of solid note heads, half-dissonant intervals by one of each, and half-consonant intervals inconsistently by a pair of void note heads.) Because it is limited to those intervals that are projected by the notes of the Model (set out in scale order) over the octave of the fundamental, in direct and inverted form, it automatically excludes the augmented 4th, diminished 5th, major 7th, and minor 9th. Otherwise its terminology conforms precisely to that of table 10.1, save that the minor 7th is termed "*simple* dissonance: first-degree." In addition, however, the major 2d is included—as a direct interval, as the inversion of the minor 7th, and as the octave contraction of the major 9th—and is in each case termed "double dissonance: first-degree." The minor 2d, had it been shown, would logically have been termed "double dissonance: second-degree."

Changing Formulations:
Consonance/Dissonance, Harmony/Melody

Having briefly examined Momigny's initial classification of diatonic intervals, as set out by him on pages 36–41 of the *Cours complet*, we can now return to the curious *nota bene*, quoted at the head of this essay. How far-reaching is Momigny's disclaimer at this point? And why should he suddenly have entered such a disclaimer, having taken the trouble to state his classification so fully?

In answer to the first question, what Momigny "abandoned" was the classification of 3ds and 6ths into two "classes" of imperfect consonance, and of 7ths and 9ths into four "degrees" of dissonance (and with it that of dissonances into simple and double). The rest of the initial classification system remains more or less intact. Henceforward for the remainder of the *Cours complet* the octave retains its status as the sole perfect consonance, 3ds and 6ths theirs as imperfect consonances (octaves, 3ds, and 6ths being classed together as "true consonances"),[2] the perfect 5th and 4th theirs as half-consonance and half-dissonance, and diminished 5ths, augmented 4ths (the qualifier "leading tone" now discarded), and 7ths theirs as dissonances (see table 10.2, p. 328).

Why should Momigny have "abandoned" what he had been at pains to express? Perhaps for pedagogical reasons? Momigny did on occasion change his formulation of a topic for these reasons. He gave an "Avertissement" to this effect:

Warning

Despite the fact that my system differs in essential ways
from all of those that have, one after another, been entertained hitherto, I restrict myself, more often than not, to
expounding them as if they had already been generally
accepted. However, I shall be sure to offer remarks at the
end of each cahier designed to eliminate any doubts that
may arise. Being more concisely stated in this way, my
principles will establish themselves better in the minds of
my readers; and those who have never studied any of the
existing systems will not be held up by discussions arising
from each issue. (p. 35)

Nonetheless, this plainly does not apply in the present case, since the
initial formulation is discarded rather than amplified.

This change of formulation is by no means the only one that Momigny
introduced during the course of his treatise. For example, initially he
established the primacy of harmonic over melodic materials. Both
derive from nature: they are different ways of viewing the spectrum
of the vibrating string. However, whereas harmony, constructed in
piled-up 3ds, is present at its source in nature, melody, in the form of
the scale, must be derived by reordering. Thus the string, vibrating in
up to fourteen parts, is summarized as follows:

This is the one true Model of the musical system, which,
excluding unisons, and considered as harmony, is G, G, B,
D, G, B, D, F, A, C, E; and excluding octaves is G, B, D, F, A,
C, E.

Considered simply as melody, this model presents the
system in the order G, A, B, C, D, E, F.

This is the fecund source from which I shall cause all the
great principles, unknown or misunderstood, to spring.
(p. 13)

Momigny detailed his derivation of the scale more clearly thus:

The true scale is *G, A, B, C, D, E, F*.

It is produced by the opening sequence of *tones* of the
musical system, in terms of harmony. These are the octaves
of the notes G, B, D, F, which form it concurrently with the
closing *tones* of the harmonic system, A, C, E, which are
intercalated between these octaves.

It is immediately apparent from the *tones* produced by
the generative string that harmony is given us by nature,
and that it is the elder sister of melody. (p. 25)

Example 10.3

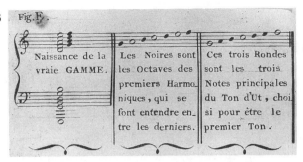

Example 10.4

Thus the scale (hence melody), while derived from harmony by the projection of one segment of the harmonic system upon another, was at the same time "[the scale] of nature," and "nature herself furnishes proof of it."[3]

When, however, he later returned to the matter, his account of the origin of melody became subtly altered. Offering a "Table of Harmonic Generation" (plates 14 C–E, of which only 14 C is reproduced here as example 10.4), he commented that "harmony is seen to be a succession of 3ds, of which three arise before melody, which does not itself begin until after the F, with the octave of the fundamental G" (p. 130).

While example 10.4, in preserving the distinction between void and solid note heads made by example 10.3 (which took care to state that the void note heads g, b, d¹, f¹ representing octaves "are heard between" the void note heads a, c¹, e¹), is not inconsistent with that earlier representation, text and example together embody a small but significant shift of emphasis. Melody now no longer results from a reordering of nature, but is directly present *in* nature; and this is borne out by the series of fractions 4/8, 4/9, 4/10, 4/11, 4/12, 4/13, 4/14.

Shifting Positions: Acoustical Issues

It is appropriate at this point to clarify the physical bases of Momigny's theory. Like Rameau, Momigny believed that the origin of harmony and melody lay in "the different sounds distinguished in the resonance of a sonorous body . . . the unique principle of music, of its theory, and of its practice."[4] Thus Momigny declared: "I admit as principle only that which is furnished by the resonance of the sonorous body" (p. [iii]). Momigny was, however, at pains to distance himself from Rameau. He signaled this distance terminologically: "What Rameau has called the sonorous body, I call *Type musical*, in other words, the generation of different sounds produced by a single instrumental string, set at one and the same time in vibration and in resonance" (p. 10). He dissociated himself from Rameau at the opening of his preface:

> It is emphatically not the system of *Rameau*, or the principles of *Fux* titivated, elucidated, or mutilated, that I am about to offer to the public, but a *new theory* established on the true interpretation of Nature, on the analysis of good practical works, in which I admit as principle only that which is furnished directly by the resonance of the sonorous body, *correctly heard*, and only that which is at the same time sanctioned by the ear, buttressed by the reason and authority of the greatest masters. (p. [iii])

One aspect of this declaration cannot concern us here, great though its interest is: namely, the implied allegation that Rameau had disregarded what musical masterworks themselves had to offer him as evidence for his theory ("on the analysis of good practical works"), as regards both the qualities and the errors of their composers ("buttressed by the reason and authority of the greatest masters"; see also p. iv), preferring instead the abstract world of mathematics.[5] It is indeed one of the distinguishing features of Momigny's *Cours complet*, constituting a significant legacy for scholars today, that the treatise contains many analyses of works (in part or whole) by C.P.E. Bach, J.S. Bach, Beethoven, Clementi, Handel, Haydn, Momigny himself, and Mozart, notably the extended analyses of the first movements of Mozart's String Quartet in D Minor K. 421/417b and Haydn's "Drum Roll" Symphony in E-flat Major, No. 103.

What does concern us is his imputation that Rameau had (*a*) interpreted Nature falsely, (*b*) heard the harmonic spectrum incorrectly, and (*c*) admitted into his theory elements not supported by aural evidence. Of these, (*a*) and (*b*) refer in part to Rameau's frequently stated belief that only three distinct pitches are distinguishable by ear in the sonorous body—the fundamental and its perfect 12th and major 17th (third and fifth harmonics), i.e., the tonic, and the compound perfect 5th and major 3d;[6] moreover, that while "the sonorous body when activated divides into an infinite number of parts called *aliquots* or *submultiples* that vibrate, even resonate, of all these parts" the ear distinguishes "only the 12th, double 5th, and the 17th, triple major 3d," not even the octaves of the fundamental ("Nouvelles réflexions" in *Code*, 193–94); and in particular that the seventh harmonic (the minor

21st, or compound minor 7th) is "si foible [weak, or flat] qu'il vous échappera sans doute," and that the seventh, eleventh and thirteenth harmonics are "toujours faux" (*Génération harmonique*, 10–11, 61–62). Imputation (*b*) must also refer to Rameau's contention that dissonance is not aurally detectable in the sonorous body (*Nouveau système*, 55), and arises only in harmonic constructs involving a fourth "term." Imputation (*c*) above may refer to Rameau's belief that a sonorous body can emit "vibrations slower than those of the total body," which "serve . . . to fortify in the ear the sound that occasions them" (*Génération harmonique*, 5).

With all these contentions Momigny took issue, and in so doing he allied himself against the strict adherents of Rameau ("those such as d'Alembert, Béthizy, Abbé Roussier, and later MM. Langlé, Rodolphe, Catel . . . a modern-day Tower of Babel"; "Discours préliminaire," 26), and with a sparser lineage of theorists who sought reform from within the Rameau tradition—theorists who, far from denying the natural origins of music, wished to give them fuller credit. This lineage included Charles Levens, Tremolet, Jean-Adam Serre (1704–88), Charles-Louis-Denis Ballière de Laissement (1729–1800), Jamard (b. ca. 1720), and Abbé Jean-Étienne Feytou (1742–1816). Levens's *Abrégé* of 1743[7] had defined a scale based on the harmonic series direct and inverted, in which the seventh harmonic played an integral role, and Serre's *Essais* of 1753 had argued against Rameau and for the audibility of the seventh harmonic over the higher-order partials.[8] Ballière's *Théorie de la musique* of 1764 rejected Rameau's view of the seventh, eleventh, and thirteenth harmonics, asserting that it was the musician's principles were "false" rather than Nature, and setting out the first twenty harmonics over the fundamental C (including B-flat, B-natural, C-sharp, D-sharp) as affecting the "expérience fondamentale."[9] Ballière's diagrammatic representation of the sonorous body as an inverted triangle marked off by horizontal *étages* (see fig. 10.1) bears a marked resemblance to Momigny's later triangular diagrams in the *Cours complet, La seule vraie théorie*, and the second volume of the *Encyclopédie méthodique: musique* (see fig. 10.2).[10] Ballière attributed this conceptualization of the propagation of sound as (by analogy with the cones of light waves) a sphere calibrated by intermediary spheres penetrated by many cones to the English inventor-physicist Francis Hauksbee the Elder (d. ca. 1713).[11] Ballière followed Tremolet in giving a separate syllable, *za*, to the minor 7th of the seventh harmonic,[12] the resultant scale comprising not seven but eight tones to the octave. As the self-sufficiency of their names implies, *za* and *si* were considered discrete diatonic components of the scale rather than mutual alternatives. Jamard's *Recherches* of 1769 took over this system, defining the eighth through sixteenth harmonics as the "échelle

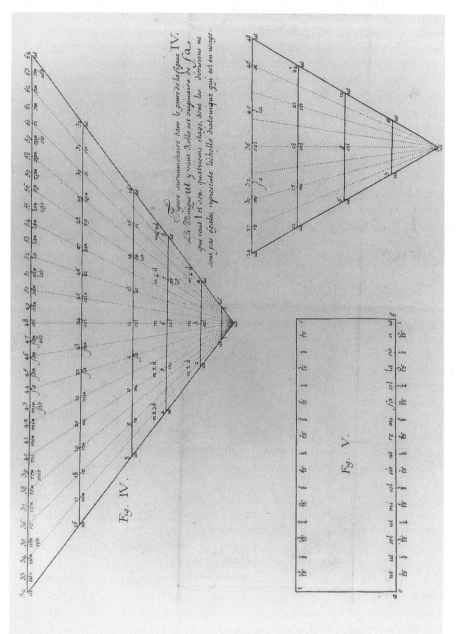

Figure10.1　Diagram from Ballière's *Théorie de la musique*.

TABLEAU DE LA RÉSONNANCE DU CORPS SONORE,
EN *UT* MODE MAJEUR.

32 *sol.*

31 *fa* ♯ X.

30 *fu* ♯.

29 *fa* X.

28 *fa.*

27 *mi* ♯.

26 *mi.*

25 *ré* ♯

24 *ré.*

23 *ut* ♯.

22 *ut.*

21 *si* ♯.

20 *si.*

19 *la* ♯.

18 *la.*

17 *sol* ♯.

16 *sol sol sol sol sol sol sol sol sol sol sol sol sol sol sol sol.*

Genre chromatique. 15 *fa* ♯ *fa* ♯ *fa* ♯ *fa* ♯ *fa* ♯ *fa* ♯ *fa* ♯ *fa* ♯ *fa* ♯ *fa* ♯ *fa* ♯ *fa* ♯ *fa* ♯ *fa* ♯.

14 *fa fa fa fa fa fa fa fa fa fa fa fa fa.*

— Mi faux. 13 *mi mi mi mi mi mi mi mi mi mi mi mi mi.*

12 *ré ré ré ré ré ré ré ré ré ré ré ré.*

Ut trop haut. 11 *ut ut ut ut ut ut ut ut ut ut ut ut.*

10 *si si si si si si si si si si.*

9 *la la la la la la la la la.*

8 *sol sol sol sol sol sol sol sol.* (*)

Fa trop bas. 7 *fa fa fa fa fa fa fa.*

6 *ré ré ré ré ré ré.*

5 *si si si si si* tierce majeure de la double octave.

4 *sol sol sol sol* double octave.

3 *ré ré ré* quinte de l'octave.

2 *sol sol* octave.

Corde génératrice résonnant dans toute son étendue................. } 1 SOL dominante.

(*) Le type de la mélodie diatonique commence à ce *sol*, & finit au *fa* au-dessus.

Figure 10.2   Momigny's Diagram in *Encyclopédie méthodique: musique*.

diatonique": *ut, re, mi, fa, sol, la, za, si, ut*.[13] Feytou's system likewise adopted an eight-note scale, but with the thirteenth harmonic labeled *ta*, and the seventh and fourteenth harmonics *la* with the syllable printed upside down.[14]

Momigny, influenced by the analogy between the colors of the visual spectrum and the tones of the aural spectrum (an analogy suggested by Isaac Newton himself),[15] adhered to a scale of seven tones but opted for inclusion of the minor 7th as the final element. A precedent for this had been supplied by Ballière, who quoted the *Journal encyclopédique* for March 1762 as stating that the scale C, D, E, F, G, A, B-flat was more easily derivable from Nature than one with B-natural.[16] Momigny solved the contingent problem of the absence of the leading tone by what was undoubtedly his largest single leap of the imagination: "It is not the tonic that generates all the tones of the scale, but the *dominant*" (p. 14). This was his "secret, wrested from Nature." Perhaps this idea was prompted by Serre, who had posited that whereas the tonic was the "son principal" of a key, it was the subdominant that was the generator—"this subdominant is, so to speak, the root [*racine*], the physical basis of the mode, the generator or fundamental tone, albeit it is not the principal tone or the tonic."[17] In one single stroke, Momigny (*a*) established the gamut of C as G, A, B-natural, C, D, E, F (pp. 25–26), with the tonic at the midpoint instead of the extremity, thereby reconciling his form of the mode with that of the Greeks and Guido d'Arezzo; (*b*) identified the "corde génératrice" of the key of C as G, thereby (in his eyes) eliminating the necessity for three generators as posited by Rameau, and imbuing the musical system with true unity; and (*c*) acknowledged the audible presence of dissonance within the sonorous body itself, thereby prompting the classification with which this essay began.

These, then, are the physical justifications of Momigny's theory. With them in mind, let us turn to a further issue in which Momigny betrayed changes of formulation during the course of his treatise. Initially, in order to establish the "primogeniture" of the major 3d over the perfect 5th, Momigny had to posit (pp. 11–13) that a string vibrates not only in its five separate fifths but compositely as two-fifths of the total string length (yielding the major 3d above the first harmonic). He even posited its vibration as four-fifths (yielding the major 3d immediately above the fundamental) and as two-thirds; however, at the time that he came to engrave the supporting music examples (plates 1 D–Q) something prevented him from incorporating these latter two proportions. And in presentation of the system as a whole (pp. 11–13), all aliquot parts other than the fifth of the string were said to vibrate only singly. Later, when summarizing this material, he extended the principle:

Instead of representing the octave as 1/2 it has to be designated by 2/4 (for two fourths taken together make a half), the 3d above it by 2/5, the 5th by 2/6, the 7th by 2/7, and so forth. It is quite straightforward for the 3d, being lowered by an octave, and the string length that produces it being double what is assigned in established theories, to be represented by 2/5 instead of 1/5. In order to reduce everything to the same numerator [*Dénominateur*], it is clear that the 5th should be represented by 2/6 instead of 1/3. The 7th, an octave lower, is naturally represented by 2/7 instead of 1/7. (pp. 91–92)

While extending vibration in two parts to everything from the fourth upwards, he avoided applying it retroactively to the third, and so contrived to maintain the "primogeniture" of the 3d over the 5th. However, when returning to the matter on page 129, he reformulated the principle, picking up his earlier idea, positing that all aliquot parts vibrated not only singly and compositely in each pair of those parts but also, where possible, compositely in fours—and this of course neatly excluded the third part, i.e., the 5th. This formulation is illustrated in plate 14 C (ex. 10.4), in which it is imperative to realize that the first note is the fundamental.

Chapter 14 is entitled "General Recapitulation of the Foregoing." This is the third time that the earliest material has been summarized and reviewed, and it seems clear that Momigny used this chapter to adjust his position on certain aspects of his theory. It is important not to overstate these adjustments. For example, while initially explaining the scale as a reordering of the sounds in nature, Momigny was aware that the vibrating string divided into "a great many more shorter string lengths" than fourteen parts (pp. 13–14); and he later made it plain that

> Just as the *generative string* subdivides (1) into diatonic major and minor 3ds and (2) into diatonic major and minor 2ds, it later subdivides into chromatic major and minor 2ds. Nor does the string, infinitely subdivisible as it is, or apparently infinitely so, limit itself to that; but we ourselves are obliged to stop at that point. . . . [Whereas] the microscope comes to the aid of the eye, nothing other than long experience and assiduous attention comes to the aid of the ear. (p. 86)

Indeed, he seems to have had a fleeting vision at this point of a world of microtones in which our ears functioned as "high-quality microscopes," such that "we would need to learn all over again how to hear."

For all the shifting of position, what the *Cours complet* presents, then, is not an inherently inconsistent theory but rather a theory in the process of development. How can this be so in a single treatise—even more puzzling, within one volume of a treatise? To answer this, we need to make a bibliographical excursion.

Writing Theory by Installments: The Cours complet

The *Journal des débats* was a Parisian newspaper founded in 1789 as the official organ of the États Généraux (which became the newly formed Assemblée Nationale in June 1789, at the French Revolution). It was the *Congressional Record,* or the *Hansard,* of the French government; although it lost this status in the interim, its full title in the 1800s can be translated *Journal of the Proceedings and Statutes of the Legislature and of the Acts of Government.*[18] It was published daily including Sundays. Each of its four pages (for it was by that time a single broadsheet folded once to make folio format) was divided three-quarters of the way down. The top three-quarters held the political news; the bottom quarter was entitled "Feuilleton du *Journal des débats,*" reporting the daily events of the Parisian theaters and opera, presenting reviews, and even offering a fashion column. The bottom right corner of page 4 displayed announcements of newly published and forthcoming books. There, on 4 May 1803, we read the following announcement:

> *Complete Course in Harmony and Composition,* following a new theory based on incontestable principles, taken direct from Nature, in agreement with all good practical works, ancient and modern, and made available, in all its clarity, to the world at large, with the epigraph:
> "In the realm of the fine arts, licenses exist solely because presumptuous persons with a smattering of erudition have been in unseemly haste to erect the pillars of Hercules."
> by J.-J. Momigny.
> This Work, comprising about 300 pages in large octavo, with a great many plates for the examples, all incorporated into the text, will be issued in twelve parts, month by month, commencing with the coming month of *Prairial* [21 May–19 June 1803].
> The price is 24Fr. to subscribers, 50 to others. This can be paid at only 6Fr. a time in order to receive the goods with delivery free of charge.
> Paris, *chez* Momigny, Boulevard Montmartre and facing the rue Montmartre, no. 31.[19]

The publishing history of Momigny's treatise is a fascinating puzzle in itself.[20] Momigny was to change his plan of publication before even the first installment was released, for on the reverse of the 1803 title page there appears an "Avertissement":

> I had announced in the *Journal des débats* that the examples for this work would all be incorporated into the text, because at the time I was counting on engraving the entire book. Having since come to the opinion that it would be more agreeable set in type, I have decided to place all the examples in a single volume of plates. This work, which was to have comprised a single volume in large octavo, will now consist of three volumes, namely two of text and one of plates. This enlargement will have no effect on the subscription price, which is 24Fr., a quarter of which is due on subscription. It will appear in twelve parts of varying extents, commencing during *Messidor* [20 June–19 July]. In order to satisfy the impatience of some of my subscribers, I shall, if I can, speed up the issuing of this work.[21]

The recto of this title page conforms closely to that of the original *Journal des débats* announcement, including the "epigraph." Put another way, the announcement was evidently a draft for the title page; and the epigraph, now identified as a quotation from the "Discours préliminaire," had meanwhile itself undergone slight redrafting.[22] This title page is dated "AN XI. (1803.)." The intersection of the eleventh year of the French republican calendar and the Christian calendar's 1803 yields a time frame for the dated title page of 1 January–23 September 1803.

Momigny provided separate title pages for the second and third volumes, and these in turn furnish us with further information. That of the third volume is engraved and contained within a rule-frame. The wording of its title conforms precisely to that of the 1803 title page of the first volume, as do Momigny's address and the date given below the frame as "AN XI * 1803." The epigraph is absent, and in its place is a device, the price, and the name of the engraver. The title page is integral to the first gathering of plates, twenty-four pages in all, which supplies plates 1–7. These are precisely the music examples required for the first two cahiers.[23] From this we might infer that the first gathering of plates was issued with the second cahier of the text.

The first cahier had "just been issued" by 27 August 1803, on which date Cocatrix reported:

> It will comprise three volumes in large octavo, two of text or discourse, and one of plates or examples.
> It will appear in twelve parts, at least one part each month,

more rapidly if possible, commencing from the first day of *Thermidor* [20 July 1803], and will be dispatched by post.
Cahier 1 has been issued.[24]

The "Discours préliminaire" is referred to in a second announcement appearing in the *Journal des débats* on 14 September 1803, unashamedly advertising the work and its author, but failing to reflect the new makeup by describing it as:

... one volume in octavo. ...

His work is eminently readable, even for those who are not born musicians. The author is an enlightened man, if one may judge from the "Preliminary Discourse," which embodies highly ingenious ideas on the nature of harmony. He clearly seeks to come close to the style of the great masters, and to lead his reader along the path of truth and beauty. A historical note on the progress that music has made in the modern age cannot fail to be of lively interest to lovers of music: if the author has a fault, it is that he pushes his enthusiasm for his art a little too far. This *Course of Harmony* deserves a favorable reception by the public, as presenting the authentic formulation of the musical system and having as its goal the perfection of the art itself.[25]

The gathering of plates next in sequence (pp. 25–48 = plates 8–18) supplies exactly the examples required for cahier 3 of the text (pp. 97–160, signed 7–10). This must have been issued between 14 September 1803 and 17 January 1804, for on that date a further announcement appeared in the *Journal des débats*, stating the format and makeup correctly as:

Three volumes in octavo, two of text and one of examples. Price: 24Fr. It is appearing by cahier of four leaves at a time;

and declaring:

Cahier 4 is in press. ...

The plan of this work is vast and methodical, the ideas are great and luminous, and it is hoped that it will satisfy the needs of professors and lovers of music who have long been waiting for a really well-written book on this subject—something that has never been encompassed before in its entirety.[26]

The next two gatherings of plates (pp. 49–72 = plates 19–23; pp. 73–100 = plates 24–28), supply the examples required for the fourth and fifth cahiers of the text (pp. 161–224, signed 11–14; pp. 225–88, signed 15–18). It is possible that these two gatherings of plates were issued together.[27] So far, the gatherings of plates have comprised three of twelve leaves followed by one of fourteen leaves. The next comprises sixteen leaves (pp. 101–32 = plates 29–30A), and supplies the residue of examples needed for cahier 6 of text, itself 50 percent longer than the regular thirty-two-leaf unit (pp. 289–[384], signed 19–24). With this issue, volume 1 was completed.

The following leaf of volume 3 is signed "Second volume de planches" (and thereafter every other leaf as "2ᵈ. volume." or "Second volume." through to page 165), as if Momigny were contemplating dividing the plates into two volumes, making a four-volume work in all. However, he did not furnish a title page for a second volume of plates, as he did at the corresponding point in the text. The title page of volume 2 conforms to the 1803 title page of volume 1, save that it is dated "AN XIII. (1805.)," a dating that places it in the time frame 1 January–22 September 1805.

Volume 2 of text is made up of twenty regular eight-leaf gatherings (signed [25]–44; 320pp. = pp. 385–704), including the "Dictionnaire et table des matières" (pp. 668–704) as integral, concluded by a noninte-gral four-leaf gathering (signed 45; 8pp. = pp. 705–[12]) devoted to the "Table raisonnée des chapitres" (pp. 705–11). With the beginning of volume 2, the cahier system disappears from the signatures; gather-ings 26 and 27 are signed "Tome II.," but gatherings 28–45 are signed by number alone.

Had the original publication schedule been followed, volume 2 would have been sent to subscribers in six further cahiers, each accom-panied with its associated plates. All the bibliographical evidence suggests, however, that volume 2 was instead sent to subscribers as a single issue, presumably accompanied by the entire suite of plates (pp. 109–314). Whereas in volume 1 each cahier begins a new chapter (save for cahier 6, which is one leaf displaced from a chapter heading), in volume 2 not a single one of the nineteen gatherings presenting the body of the treatise (i.e., gatherings 25–43) coincides with a chapter heading. Whereas the plates for volume 1 were carefully planned so that each cahier began with a new plate and figure A, and the plates for each cahier made up a gathering, there is no semblance of such rational planning for volume 2.[28] However, if volume 2 was indeed issued as a single unit, and its plates likewise, it was nonetheless sup-plied unbound, since a footnote to the concluding summary of volume 2 states:

> I have numbered the chapters and pages in sequence [from volume 1], so as to facilitate the binding of volumes 1 and

> 2 in one if that should be thought more convenient for study-
> ing the *Course*, given that there is only one table of contents,
> and only one dictionary, which does double duty as a sub-
> ject index. (p. 661)

Direct support for the above construction comes from the most
surprising quarter: the article "Opéra (grand)" in the *Encyclopédie
méthodique: musique* (vol. 2, cols. 231b–33a), in the midst of which appears a lengthy account of the personal relations between Grétry and
Momigny. Grétry advised the latter to "stick by the first volume [of the
Cours complet]; the second is much inferior," to which a footnote tells
us: "This work had appeared by installments, the first volume in cahiers
of three or four gatherings, and the last [i.e., volume 2] all at one time."
The contributor of this article was, needless to say, Momigny himself.
Internal support comes also from within the *Cours complet* (vol. 2, p.
653), which speaks of two years' rethinking that "set back the entire
publication of the work" (see the following section).

It is difficult to determine whether Momigny intended a distinction
between "grand in-8°" (the format stated in the *Journal des débats* of 4
May 1803, the reverse title page, and Cocatrix for 27 August 1803) and
"in-8°" (that stated in the *Journal des débats* for 14 September 1803 and
17 January 1804).[29] Even so, from the fact that what was initially announced as encompassing "about 300 pages" with music examples
"incorporated into the text" ultimately became 712 pages without music
examples plus 314 pages of plates, we can deduce that the treatise was
far from complete when Momigny embarked on the printing of
cahier 1.

Momigny reissued the work in 1806, and again in 1808, with no
significant changes.

Moving the Foundations: Formative Writing

We can now reconstruct the probable sequence of events with regard
to Momigny's theoretical formulations. For example, his initial attempt to find acoustical justification for the "primogeniture" of 3d
over 5th came in the *Cours complet*, pp. 11–13, pages that form part of
cahier 1, issued between 4 May and 27 August 1803. His second formulation, extending the principle that aliquot parts of a string vibrate in
pairs as well as singly, came on pages 91–92, which fall at the end of
cahier 2, issued probably by 14 September 1803. The fact that the plates
for the discussion in cahier 1 match not the formulation on pages 11–
13 but that on pages 91–92 accords with our earlier deduction that the
plates for cahiers 1–2 were issued at the same time as the text of cahier
2. His third formulation, by which aliquot parts vibrate not only in

pairs but also wherever possible in quadruples also, occurs on page 129, which is part of cahier 3, issued between 14 September 1803 and 17 January 1804.

We can thus surmise that the abandonment of the classification of 3ds and 6ths into two categories of consonance, occurring as it did in the third gathering of cahier 3 (p. 132), reflected Momigny's rethinking of the subject, and very likely also readers' reactions to cahier 1. There are signs of his having had second thoughts even before the beginning of cahier 3. Appended to cahier 2, on pages 84–96, is a series of "Observations," supplementary to the cahier itself and unsupported by plates. The latter part of this returns to the classification of intervals, offering "an infallible means of recognizing a consonance: i.e., when it can be can inverted without ceasing to be consonant." This recursive definition is designed, while including the octave, 3ds, and 6ths, to exclude the perfect 5th. A vestige of the old subclassification exists: while there is only one perfect consonance and only one half-consonance, there are several imperfect consonances, "because that which is imperfect admits of plurality and degrees" (p. 93).

Nor does the process of reformulation end at page 132. On the contrary, Momigny constructed two subsequent independent classificatory schemes, one that arranges intervals along a continuum between maximum unity (octave) and maximum variety or plurality (minor 2d: pp. 446ff. and 646), and another that categorizes intervals into harmonic and nonharmonic or melodic (pp. 450–53), developing a concept, not synonymous with "consonance," that he called "harmoniousness" (p. 650). What is more, these reformulations seem to have advanced further during the fifteen years after completion of the *Cours complet*, for Momigny supplied the *Encyclopédie méthodique: musique* (vol. 2, cols. 474a–510b) with an article, "Système de J.J. de Momigny," in which he returned to the matter with fresh maxims such as the following, which maps harmoniousness onto variety: "Moins les intervalles directs de l'échelle de la variété sont grands, & plus ils sont harmonieux," by which the diminished 5th and diminished 7th are both deemed more harmonious than the minor 7th. There is no space here to pursue these reformulations. But how did Momigny react when he arrived at the general summation of his *Cours complet* (pp. 637–67) and was confronted with representing his own original, now partly discredited classification? Table 10.2 is a tabulation of the "Récapitulation" that he offered. While broadly isomorphic with table 10.1, although dispensing with the discarded subclassifications, it is subtly amplified, first by the incorporation of inverse intervals, and second by the mapping onto it of the later harmonic/nonharmonic categorization. In supplying inversions it now incorporates all dia-

Table 10.2.

Direct	Inverted
CONSONANT—HARMONIC	
perfect octave: perfect consonance	unison
major 3d	minor 6th
minor 3d	major 6th
CONSONANT—NONHARMONIC	
perfect 5th: half-consonance	perfect 4th: half-dissonance
DISSONANT—HARMONIC	
diminished 5th: *sans contact*	< augmented 4th
minor 7th	< major 2d below: *en contact*
major 9th	[<] major 2d above: *en contact*
minor 9th	< minor 2d [above]: *en contact:* max. diss.
DISSONANT—NONHARMONIC	
major 7th	
all other intervals	

< signifies that the dissonance level of the inversion is greater than that of the direct interval.

tonic intervals by name, and so rids the previous classification of certain asymmetries. It also provides clarification of the earlier cryptic "points of contact," telling us for example that "the major 2d below is much harsher than the [minor] 7th, because it is a dissonance *en contact*" (p. 645). Moreover, between the minor 3d/major 6th and the perfect 5th/4th it interpolates the following remark, which serves to clarify the distinction between harmonic and nonharmonic:

> These [i.e., octave, major and minor 3ds and 6ths] are the sole consonances. All other intervals are not real consonances, since the two notes that comprise them do not have a true *ensemble* and do not form a unique *tout*, but two distinct *touts*, one more or less subordinated to the other. (p. 644)

If this extended reformulation of the consonant/dissonant classification shows that Momigny's rethinking process continued right through to the simultaneously produced volume 2, then his handling of the minor mode demonstrates this fact at its most dramatic. Momigny had devoted an entire chapter to the status of minor: chapter 23, pp. 199–224, falling in cahier 4 (pp. 161–224), which must have been issued some time shortly after 17 January 1804. There he rejected Rameau's several explanations for the origin of minor, and also that of d'Alembert, and treated it—according to his later account of events (pp. 652–53)—as "nothing more than the major mode with the 3d and the 6th lowered by a half step, these being considered chromatic in genus." However, he subsequently saw the error of his ways, and

> in an effort ultimately to avoid brushing any difficulties under the carpet, rather wishing to tackle and overcome them all, I searched for and discovered . . . the *grand système musical*. As a result, the reader should turn for the minor mode not to chapter 23 but to chapter 34, a chapter that I wrote after two further years' meditation, and that set back the entire publication of the work. (p. 653)

How frustrating to commit oneself irrevocably on so central a topic, in an eponymous chapter, only to revoke one's treatment before even the table of contents is printed. Such are the trials of publication by installment. Chapter 34, entitled "The Logic of Music: the *grand système musical* embodying the three genera not separately but together," does not discuss the minor mode as such, but sets out Momigny's new system of key comprising twenty-seven tones, of which the central seven are diatonic, the two flanking sets of five are chromatic, and the two outer sets of five enharmonic. Surprisingly brief, it occupies pages 435–42, thus falling into volume 2, issued between 1 January and 22 September 1805. (Momigny's "two years" evidently reflect an element of hyperbole.)

Such changes of heart hardly fill the modern reader with respect. A book, after all, is a unitary work; internal consistency is the least we may expect of it. Failing that, how is the reader to verify the arguments? Especially in a cumulative argument of this type, in which the physical basis of music is established first, then the framework of consonance and dissonance set in place, then formulations of mode and scale, harmony, melody, and rhythm provided, and so forth—in a progression of this type, is it not intolerable that the foundations should be moved to suit the superstructure? It is as if Wittgenstein, in the *Tractatus Logico-Philosophicus* (1922), had changed his view of the relationship between "object" and "state of affairs" by the time he reached propositions, and again by the time he came to address the limitations of language.

For an author to revise his views between publications is another matter. Any scientist, any scholar may do that. Very few move as unerringly forward as Albert Einstein. For most, each publication is a separate quantum of theoretical formulation. The scientist may reposition himself, may even recant previously held opinions. So in music, we allow that Rameau should have changed his account of the origin of minor, or the status of the subdominant, several times between 1722 and 1760—we may even applaud the single-mindedness with which he constantly sought the truth.

The book is one mode of writing; serial publication is another. That Schenker's formulation of the *Urlinie*, for example, changed during the lifetime of his journal *Der Tonwille* (1921–24) seems acceptable. A periodical is a set of publications formally associated (by a common title page, by a promise to publish at regular intervals, by the contractual agreement of a subscription), yet substantially discrete. Even when of single authorship (as in the periodicals of Mattheson, Mizler, Marpurg, Vogler, and others), each issue is essentially independent. Writers have often used the periodical as a forum for theoretical exposition (*Der Tonwille* and *Das Meisterwerk in der Musik* were Schenker's workbench between 1921 and 1930); revision of basic tenets is acceptable, indeed quite natural, in this context.

As for Momigny, he too changed his views between publications. Thus, in *La seule vraie théorie* of 1821, while maintaining the precedence of the major 3d over the perfect 5th, he abandoned his theoretical justification by resonance at two-fifths and four-fifths of string length (pp. 26–29). The physical evidence, he now conceded, was to the contrary: "The 5th and the 4th rank before the 3d and the 6th [in the resonance of the sonorous body], which fact runs clearly counter to [the] gradation . . . of the true scale of consonance" (p. 27). In other words, his claim for the 3d and the 6th over the 5th was still "precedence," but was now no longer "primogeniture." To this extent, he forfeited the grounding of his theory in natural phenomena. Instead, he invoked the evidence of "the ear, and of every piece of music in two or more parts." The argument at this point digresses into pure music-theoretical politics, with the École Royale de Musique and the Académie des Sciences figuring along with Charles-Simon Catel, Antoine Reicha, and even Rameau himself. The argument for natural origins could of course now be turned from the physical phenomenon of resonance to the psychological one of consonance and harmoniousness, buttressed by the aesthetic values of unity and variety, but in the process the high ground of rationalism was clearly ceded:

> Nothing is more philosophical, nothing conforms more to reason, than to seek the ordered scale of consonance and dissonance in the generation of tones; but not to renounce this system, chimerical and obviously false as it is . . . is to reveal that one has the ears of Midas,[30] or . . . that one is not prepared to trust one's judgment in the matter. (p. 27)

It is not surprising, then, to find that by 1821 Momigny had again changed his classification of intervals. He now gave "definitively the order of harmonic intervals according to their degree of harmony" as: (1) minor 3d, (2) major 3d, (3) minor 6th, (4) major 6th, (5) diminished 5th, (6) augmented 4th, (7) perfect 5th, (8) diminished 7th, (9) minor

7th, (10) perfect 4th, (11) augmented 2d, (12) major 2d. The unison now emerged as direct, the octave as inverted. New maxims were devised: "Plus un intervalle harmonique, direct, est petit, plus ses deux termes ont d'unité" and its inverse, "Plus un intervalle harmonique, renversé, est grand, plus il a d'unité" (pp. 47–48). These again mark a shift of criteria from the physical to the psychological.

We can excuse these changes, made sixteen years after the completion of the *Cours complet*. Can we as willingly condone those made during the composition of the *Cours complet*, between 1803 and 1805? Consider a somewhat similar case. *Natura non facit saltum* (Nature does not make leaps), the hypothesis whereby the evolution of species takes place "by insensibly fine gradations," was a principle fundamental to Darwin's *Origin of Species*.[31] The *Origin* had been written under great pressure, in the space of eight months in 1859, in order to establish Darwin's claim to the conception of natural selection, and came under heavy criticism not only from hostile scientists and theologians, but also from fellow evolutionists. Over the course of five further editions of the book, even the stubborn Darwin responded to these criticisms by making modifications (most particularly in the fifth and sixth editions, 1869 and 1872), and these not only greatly increased its length but also in certain respects sacrificed its internal consistency. Thus *Natura non facit saltum*, a cornerstone of the initial theory, having been subject to attack on many grounds (such as gaps in the fossil record, and calculations as to the age of the earth), became compromised through Darwin's revisions. One scholar has said: "By persistently altering the basic structure of the first *Origin*, rather than writing up afresh his much altered views, Darwin made it difficult to gauge the full extent of his changes and the implications they held for the theory as a whole."[32]

With only slight alterations, these words could be applied to Momigny's *Cours complet*. The comparison may be thought impertinent. I certainly do not intend to equate the stature of the *Cours complet* with that of the *Origin*, nor to liken the self-justifying Momigny with the ever-humble Darwin. True, Darwin's changes were made slowly and cautiously over a period of thirteen years of continuing research. Those of Momigny were made over a mere two-year period. Darwin's theory did appear whole in its first version, albeit often obscurely and ambiguously expressed, and made its historic impact in that form. That of Momigny embodied its changeabilities within its first completed edition. However, the comparison does have some relevance. Momigny probably rushed into print before he was ready. Although he was revising his views not in subsequent editions but in subsequent installments of the same edition, he was nonetheless adjusting his theory after having committed himself to print in one and the same work; and the result was unquestionably an undermining of the initial position of his theory, and a destabilizing of the whole. The analogy with Hugo Riemann's successive revampings of books (many of which began life as *Katechismus der* . . . , later to become *Vademecum der* . . . , and finally *Handbuch der* . . . as they were revised and upgraded) would perhaps be crass, but that with the first edition of A.B. Marx's *Lehre von der musikalischen Komposition* is not inappropriate. Marx's account of sonata form at the end of volume 2 (1838) was subsequently wholly superseded by his vastly longer account in volume 3 of the same edition (1845); yet he suffers no ignominy in our minds for having made that major change.

A more pertinent analogy lies perhaps with the novels of Charles Dickens, all fifteen of which were published serially. *Nicholas Nickleby*, for example, appeared in twenty monthly installments of three or four chapters each between April 1838 and October 1839 in *Bentley's Miscellany*, before being published in book form in 1839. Dickens, moreover, actually wrote them serially; that is, each monthly episode was typically not ready until ten days before it was due in press. "He saw none of his novels as a completed whole until after the last installment was written. Hence he could not revise."[33] Dickens developed strategies for dealing with the problems of serial publication. Despite his mastery of the medium, there are examples of plots turning out in ways that surprised him, of novels that grew from stories, of breaks in structure, loose ends, and inconsistencies of detail. Dickens evidently relied a great deal on his memory of earlier installments, and this resulted in unintended changes of character and misattributions of actions. These discontinuities never seriously threaten the integrity of the whole as they do that of Momigny's *Cours complet*; and doubtless the criteria for consistency apply differently as between a work of fiction and one of theoretical discourse. The fact remains, however, that these novels, while now having the semblance of unitary works, were in reality the products of periodic publication and display many signs of their mode of issue.

We can perhaps best interpret Momigny as caught on the horns of a number of dilemmas: dilemmas as to publishing procedure, as to the nature of his readership, as to scientific method. First, having given the impression at the outset that the work was already complete, he was undoubtedly still writing, like Dickens, while the publication schedule was under way. Put another way, he had given out that the work was unitary when in fact it was serial. Behind this lies the fact that Momigny was his own publisher, having established a music printing and publishing house on his arrival in Paris in 1800 and maintained it until 1828. He published all his own theoretical works and compositions, and a large catalogue of compositions by other composers.[34] Indeed, the report of the Institut National of 17 September 1808 backhandedly offered "recognition to him who has devoted his time to writing [the *Cours complet*] and his fortune to publishing it" (*La seule vraie théorie*, p. v). Being his own publisher afforded him liberties both of operation and of marketing not normally available to an author, liberties he perhaps should not have allowed himself.

Second, whereas the titles of Rameau, Serre, Ballière, Jamard, and others bore such words as "théorie," "traité," "système," "démonstration," "principes," Momigny's symptomatically bears the word "cours"—self-declaredly a practical manual, a work of pedagogy—and "complet" to boot; i.e., it covers the full range of practical subjects, including counterpoint, fugue, canon, and figured bass. Inspired with a mission not only to rewrite music theory but also to reform contemporary methods of musical instruction, he perhaps sought to do too much in one work. His diverse readerships needed different modes of discourse; the result suffered from a certain schizophrenia—a practical work that was too academic, a scientific work that was too personal and informal.

Third, he was working according to Cartesian methodology, which required him not only rely on self-evident truths, to reduce his problems to as many parts as necessary, and to arrange his material in order from simplest to most complex, but also "everywhere to make such complete enumerations and such general reviews [as to] be sure to have omitted nothing."[35] It was perhaps this very procedure, the frequent retracing of one's steps in every detail, sometimes appearing as a "récapitulation," that prompted Momigny's periodic adjustments, thus exposing the allegedly unitary but actually serial nature of the publication. Quintessentially Cartesian too were the rejection of all previous authority and received knowledge (including the clamorous disowning of Rameau, Jamard, and Feytou), the recourse to first principles, and the dogmatism, the air of arrogance, that tended to result from this intellectual frame of mind. The end product is a work whose every statement purports to be definitive, whereas many a one turns out in due course to be heuristic—"mobile theory," one might call it. Rameau too was dogmatic in his theoretical works, but he took care not to wrongfoot himself in the way that Momigny unfortunately did.

It is worth, nonetheless, toying with a distinction between genuinely inconsistent theoretical writing, and what we might call "formative writing" in the *Cours complet*. Formative writing is writing that moves consistently forward, correct with itself at any one moment but not necessarily correct with its own past—like a focal-plane shutter in a camera, during whose time of travel the image in front of it may slightly change, and so which records an image that is vertically correct but laterally distorted. Momigny did not in general recant his own past statements (our opening *nota bene* and the case of the minor mode were exceptions); he moved unconsciously forward, his rationalist ego intact. The result is often surprisingly free from any real inconsistency.

Doubting One's Ears: Audibility of the Eleventh and Thirteenth Harmonics

A final example will illustrate this claim. It concerns Momigny's handling of one important issue: the sense in which the intervals of the 11th and 13th can be said to be present in the Model as the eleventh and thirteenth harmonics. In cahier 2 (p. 49), Momigny formulated an idea that was the confluence of two earlier notions, both of which we have already encountered: first, that the generative source of a key is its dominant rather than its tonic; second, that the intervals of the 11th and 13th are constituents of the *Type de la Musique*.

One virtue of the dominant generator, he argued, is that it provides an inherent archetype for tonal motion. Whereas Rameau's tonic generator offered only the tonic triad, "inert in nature, lacking movement," the dominant generator offers a dynamic process. As the first three notes of Momigny's Model, with octaves excluded, are traversed, the dominant triad (G, B, D) is etched out, in equilibrium; "from the moment the fourth note [F] arrives, that equilibrium is upset, motion is set in train, and the need for a second chord is sensed"; that need is intensified as the fifth note [A] arrives; after which the tonic triad (C, E, G) is delineated, "satisfying this pressing need, and reestablishing the equilibrium." "This," Momigny concluded, "is in absolute conformity with the nature of man and all created beings." The second equilibrium, he declared, is all the stronger for the intervention of a keen sense of need aroused by the addition of F and A to G, B, D (p. 49).

Such an archetype, resting on a phenomenon perceived as universal—equilibrium established, upset, then restored, transformed and stronger—resembles the Hegelian triad of thesis-antithesis-synthesis, and to some slight degree anticipates Moritz Hauptmann's formulation of 1853.[36] Momigny's formulation contains one obvious logical defect: his Model, with octaves excluded, comprises seven notes, whereas his archetype demands eight. The final G is anomalous. Momigny blurred the issue by using the following sequence of terms: first "a perfect triad (G, B, D)," then "the fourth harmonic note (G, B, D, F)," then "at the fifth tone (G, B, D, F, A)," and finally "the perfect triad of the tonic (C, E, G)." In this way the anomaly of the eighth term is never addressed. The fifteenth was, of course, present in the Model with its octaves, but it is not, even so, the first octave to follow the thirteenth.

The fifteenth apart, Momigny was clearly bothered by the status of the eleventh and thirteenth. At first he spoke with confidence of their acoustical presence, even their audibility:

> Few musicians are capable of distinguishing more than three or four of these different tones, leaving aside octaves. I myself can readily distinguish five: G, B, D, F, A, but only with difficulty the sixth and seventh: C, E—not just because they are weaker, but also because the octaves of the earlier tones intercalate themselves among them, masking them, so to speak, or at least diverting attention to themselves. (p. 14)

In cahier 3 (p. 128) he maintained this stance, stating: "There are seven principal notes, all deriving from the resonance of a single string, having the natural property of dividing by 3ds: as G, B, d, f, a, c^1, e^1. . . . It takes highly practiced ears to hear these tones arising all at the same time from the division of one and the same string." Much later, in volume 2—effectively cahier 7, issued in 1805—he formulated the matter differently, and in so doing he partly returned to the old battleground between his own and Rameau's views of the detectable presence of dissonance in the sonorous body. The audibility of the first five notes is "incontestable" (p. 483); that of the remainder needs greater caution:

> Less in accordance with the ear than with reasoning, we have stated that in addition to the five notes G, B, D, F, A the single string G also produces the sixth and seventh notes, C and E.
>
> But albeit this reasoning is based on the analogy of the seven primary colors to the seven primary diatonic notes, and thus on the notion that the seven notes must have a single identical origin or source, we have to agree that these two latter tones elude the ear, whether because they are too weak in themselves and are masked by the octaves of the first five tones, or whether because the string genuinely does not generate more than five notes and their octaves. I am less inclined toward the latter, because I believe I have heard these last two notes sometimes myself, though very rarely. (p. 484)

And yet two paragraphs later he used the inaudible status of eleventh and thirteenth as the basis for his next contention: "Just as we distinguish no more than five distinct notes in a vibrating string, plus their octaves, so too we may not introduce more than five distinct notes into a chord, all a 3d apart" (p. 485). His last word on the matter in this treatise is:

> As to the eleventh and thirteenth, they elude everybody's ear, and it is less *de auditu* that I posit them than by analogy and reasoning, although I believe myself to have heard them several times. (p. 639)

There are three logical possibilities: the eleventh and thirteenth are either audible acoustical fact, or inaudible acoustical fact, or purely rational notion. In his original declarations (pp. 14 and 128) Momigny asserted the first of these possibilities (albeit the second effectively applied to those with unpracticed ears). He therefore did not entertain the third possibility. Later he shifted ground to open up all three possibilities; and in his final statement he renounced the first possibility ("elles échappent à toutes les oreilles") and seemingly favored the third over the second possibility ("c'est moins *de auditu* que je les y suppose . . . que par raisonnement et analogie").

Throughout this entire chain of discussion, there is no inconsistency of thought. The analogy to which Momigny refers in the last two statements is established at the very outset:

> The phenomenon of the decomposition of light, discovered by Newton, presents nothing more remarkable or more astonishing than that of harmonic generation. Everyone knows that a shaft of sunlight, decomposed with the aid of a prism, produces seven primary colors, in the following order: red, orange, yellow, green, blue, indigo or purple, and violet. In just the same way, a string on the piano or violoncello, or any sounding body, produces seven distinct tones, plus the octaves of these sounds. (p. 10)

Moreover, Momigny's declarations of his own hearing ability remain consistent. They simply function differently on different occasions. At first they provide evidence for undoubted acoustical audibility, later evidence for one of three alternative systems; finally they constitute the bewildered shake of the head of a man who *thought* he had heard them ("quoique je croie les avoir entendues plusieurs fois").

When all is said and done, perhaps the problem of the *Cours complet* comes down to one simple thing: a desire on Momigny's part to establish himself, as soon as possible after his arrival in Paris in 1800, as the foremost music theorist of his day. Viewed in this light, his setting up as printer and publisher provided the practical means to pursue this desire, while his announcement of the *Cours complet* was in effect the issuing of a public challenge. From then on, he was for two years working against his own deadlines. If so, then he surely fell prey to the danger, as Descartes warned us, that befalls those who take their example from the histories of past ages: they are "betrayed into romantic extravagances, forming projects that exceed their powers."[37]

Notes

1. Title page to volume 1: COURS COMPLET | D'HARMONIE | ET DE COMPO-SITION, | D'après une théorie nouvelle et générale de la | Musique, basée sur des principes incontestables, | puisés dans la nature, d'accord avec tous les | bons ouvrages-pratiques anciens et modernes, et | mis, par leur clarté, à la portée de tout le monde. | Par Jérôme-Joseph DE MOMIGNY. | - | «Il n'est de licences dans les beaux-arts, que parce que | «des demi-savans présomptueux se sont trop hâtés de | «poser les colonnes d'Hercule.» | De Momigny, | Discours préliminaire de cet ouvrage. | - | - | A PARIS, | Chez [brace] De Momigny, au grand magasin de Musique et d'Ins- | trumens, boulevart et en face de la rue Montmartre, | n°.31; | Bailleul, imprimeur-libraire, rue Grange-Batelière, | n°. 3. | «==» | AN XI. (1803) | |

The authoritative study of Momigny, his life and career in politics, publishing, composition and theory, is Albert Palm, *Jérôme-Joseph de Momigny: Leben und Werk: Ein Beitrag zur Geschichte der Musiktheorie im 19. Jahrhundert* (Cologne, 1969), to which the present study is much indebted.

2. "véritables Consonnances"; e.g., ibid., 150, where the unison is included.

3. Ibid., 26. Momigny had a vested interest in deriving the scale (*gamme*) in this form, since he maintained that the scale (*a*) contains the tonic at its midpoint rather than at its outer limits, (*b*) is constructed of two overlapping diatonic tetrachords of which the tonic forms the fulcrum: G, A, B, C :: C, D, E, F (ibid., 26–29). This he extends by two further notes to produce G, A, B, C, D, E, F, G, A, "a series which I call a 'voice'. . . . A melodic 'voice' is a series of conjunct tones, complete in itself, which can be sounded in succession while avoiding three whole tones" (84–85; Momigny's account of the origins of harmony and melody is first stated on 11–13, then summarized on 31–32, then resummarized on 84–86, and discussed further on 153).

4. Jean-Philippe Rameau, *Génération harmonique ou Traité de musique théorique et pratique* (Paris, 1737), iv (preface) and 162. See Deborah Hayes, "Rameau's Theory of Harmonic Generation: An Annotated Translation and Commentary" (Ph.D. diss., Stanford University, 1968). As is well known, Rameau learned of the harmonic spectrum, with its audible simultaneously sounding overtones arising as aliquot parts of a fundamental frequency (probably formulated for the first time by Joseph Sauveur (1653–1716), who presented it in his *Système général des intervalles des sons* in *Mémoires de mathématique et de physique* [1701], 299–366) after completing his *Traité de l'harmonie* (Paris, 1722). Rameau first incorporated it into his theory in the *Nouveau système de musique théorique* (Paris, 1726), esp. iii (preface) and 17–18, retaining it thereafter as the central unifying principle of his theory, generalized as "Le principe de tout est un," "Nouvelles réflexions sur le principe sonore," in *Code de musique pratique, ou Méthodes pour apprendre de la musique . . . avec des nouvelles réflexions sur le principe sonore* (Paris, 1760), 185.

5. This allegation is not wholly true: in his *Nouveau système*, Rameau had quoted *in extenso* a monologue from act 2, scene 5, of Lully's *Armide*, setting out vocal line, continuo bass, and fundamental bass on three parallel staves as exemplification of types of root movement (pp. 80–90), and returned to it in *Observations sur notre instinct pour la musique* (Paris, 1754), 70–125, and *Code de musique pratique*, 168–69; and he

devoted chapter 23 of his *Nouveau système* entirely to "Examples of Errors Arising in the Figurings of Corelli's [*XII Sonate a Violino Solo*] Op. 5 [Rome, 1700]," in which he quoted seventeen passages for criticism and correction. See E. Cynthia Verba, "The Development of Rameau's Thoughts on Modulation and Chromatics," *Journal of the American Musicological Society* 26 (1973): 69–91.

6. Rameau, *Nouveau système*, iii, and 17–20; *Génération harmonique*, [v], 10–11, and 27–28; *Démonstration du principe de l'harmonie* (Paris, 1750), vi–ix and 15; *Nouvelles réflexions de M. Rameau sur sa Démonstration du principe de l'harmonie* (Paris, 1752), 3–4; and elsewhere.

7. I have been unable to consult Levens, *Abrégé des règles de l'harmonie* (Bordeaux, 1743), so have been dependent on François-Joseph Fétis's account, *Biographie universelle*, 2d ed., vol. 5 (Paris, 1863), 291. On the precursors of Momigny, see also Palm, *Jérôme-Joseph de Momigny*, 111.

8. J.-A. Serre, *Essais sur les principes de l'harmonie* (Paris, 1753), 44–48 and 117–19.

9. C.-L.-D. Ballière, *Théorie de la musique* (Paris and Rouen, 1764), 1 and 4–5.

10. Momigny, *Cours complet*, vol. 3, plates 1 C–Q; *La seule vraie théorie de la musique . . . ou Moyen le plus court pour devenir mélodiste, harmoniste, contrepointiste et compositeur* (Paris, 1821; reprint ed., Geneva, 1980), 26, 36; *Encyclopédie méthodique: musique*, ed. N.E. Framéry and P.L. Ginguené, vol. 2 (Paris, 1818), 488.

11. Ballière, *Théorie de la musique*, 13. See Francis Hauksbee the Elder, *Physico-Mechanical Experiments on Various Subjects* (London, 1709; 2d ed., 1719). Ballière had seen this work in translation, *Expériences physico-méchaniques sur différens sujets* (Paris, 1754), 2:317: "If the sonorous body is located at the center of a sphere, then all the conical pyramids that comprise that sphere, calibrated at different distances [from the center] can be seen as having circular bases whose areas increase as the square of their diameters or of the radii of the sphere." This passage is translated from the French edition, since I have been unable to locate it in either English edition. (Plate 6, fig. 37, illustrates this.)

12. On Tremolet's paper "Règles nouvelles de la musique," presented to the Académie des Sciences in 1749, see Albert Cohen, *Music in the French Royal Academy of Sciences* (Princeton, 1981), 88–89.

13. [T.] Jamard, *Recherches sur la théorie de la musique* (Paris and Rouen, 1769), 8, 40–41, and 49–50.

14. Feytou first presented this system verbally to the Académie des Sciences in 1787; see Cohen, *Music in the French Royal Academy of Sciences*, 89. It was presumably this theory that appeared as Feytou's contributions to the *Encyclopédie méthodique: musique*, vol. 1 (Paris, 1791), principally cols. 131–57 ("Basse fondamentale") and 475–85 ("Échelle"). In volume 2, cols. 462–74, Momigny provided articles on the systems of Jamard and Feytou with his own refutations.

15. See Cohen, *Music in the French Royal Academy of Sciences*, 31; analogies between light and sound in Newton's *Opticks or a Treatise of the Reflections, Refractions, Inflections & Colours of Light* (1704); see 4th ed., with intro. by E.T. Whittaker (London, 1931), 284 "as the Cube-Roots of the Squares of the lengths of a Chord, which sound the Notes of the Eight, sol, la, fa, sol, la, mi, fa, sol, with all their intermediate degrees answering to the Colours of those Rays, according to the Analogy described in the seventh Experiment of the second Part of the first Book"; see also 125, 126–27, 225, and 345–46.

16. Ballière, *Théorie de la musique*, 5–6; I have been unable to consult the quoted item.

17. See Serre, *Essais*, 52 and 120–21; however, I know of no evidence that Momigny was acquainted with Serre's work.

18. *Journal des débats et loix de pouvoir législatif et des actes du gouvernement*. The first

volume is entitled *États-Généraux, ou Récit de ce qui s'est passé aux États-Généraux, depuis le 5 Mai 1789, jusqu'au 17 Juin suivant, époque à laquelle les Communes se sont consituées en ASSEMBLÉE NATIONALE.* Initially in small format, the paper adopted larger format in May 1802.

19. *Journal des débats*, 14 Floréal an 11. Mercredi 4 Mai 1803, p. 4.

20. It has been sketched (and much of the above material cited) by Palm, *Jérôme-Joseph de Momigny*, 336–39, who does not, however, attempt a detailed account of the issuing by installments.

21. The reverse of the title page without dedication (see note 1 above). Palm (ibid., 336–37) hypothesized that this title page was "attached to the first eight issues, probably about the middle of 1804," citing a copy extant in the Bibliothèque Nationale, Paris. He failed to realize that it was integral to the first cahier and must therefore have been issued at the outset of the publication schedule.

22. In the title, "une théorie nouvelle" has become "une théorie nouvelle et générale de la Musique," "ouvrages pratiques" is now hyphenated, and "par sa clarté" has become "par leur clarté." The epigraph, originally beginning "Il n'y a de licences dans les beaux-arts que parce que," now begins "Il n'est de licences dans les beaux-arts, que parce que." This epigraph is a quotation from the *Cours complet*, 10. See note 1 above for transcription of the full title page of volume 1.

23. Cahier 1, sixty-four pages in four gatherings (signed [1]–4), comprises the preliminary pages and the entire "Discours préliminaire" (pp.[i]–viii and 9–32) and pp. 1–32 of the *Cours complet* itself; cahier 2, again sixty-four pages in four gatherings (signed 3–6), comprises pp. 33–96. Plate 1 A is referred to on p. 10 of the *Cours complet*, and plate 7 M on p. 83.

24. *Correspondance des amateurs musiciens, rédigée par le Cit. Cocatrix, Amateur* (Paris, 1802–5; reprint ed., Geneva, 1972), 9 Fructidor an IV, No. 40, 27 Août 1803, p. 2.

25. *Journal des débats*, 27 Fructidor an 11. Mercredi 14 Septembre 1803, p. 4.

26. *Journal des débats*, 26 Nivôse an 12. Mardi 17 Janvier 1804, p. 4.

27. In my possession is an incomplete copy of the *Cours complet* that is of considerable bibliographical interest. It contains portions of volumes 1 and 3. Of volume 1, it has the preliminary pages, the whole of the "Discours préliminaire" (32pp.), and pp. 1–96 of the *Cours complet*. Its title page is the earliest for volume 1, namely that discussed above and transcribed in note 1, dated 1803, bearing the "Avertissement" discussed earlier on its reverse. Of volume 3 it has pp. 1–100, including the earliest title page, namely the engraved counterpart described above, dated 1803. The whole has been stabbed and bound in a soft cover of pink marbled paper, and a paper label on the front cover has, in an early nineteenth-century hand, the words "Cours complet d'Harmonie — J.J. De Momigny." Pages are in all cases untrimmed, leaving the physical structure of the book clearly visible. It is noticeable that the plates for cahiers 4 and 5, pp. 49–72 and 73–100, all on a paper with a common watermark different from that of the previous gathering, conform in every way, suggesting that they were issued together. This fragmentary item amounts to cahiers 1–2 of text, accompanied by the plates for cahiers 1–5, and represents an incompletely preserved or perhaps discontinued subscription, volume 1 thus as it was around September 1803, volume 3 as presumably sometime in mid-1804. There is, however, evidence that at least cahier 3 was at some time in the hands of the owner.

28. The plates for gathering 25 comprise exactly twelve leaves, and this may perhaps suggest that Momigny adhered to his rational plan as he began laying out the plate material for volume 2. If so, that plan was evidently soon abandoned. More to the point, those twelve leaves contain the development and recapitulation of the first movement of Mozart's String Quartet in D Minor K. 421/417b. The plates for the first movement of Haydn's Symphony No.103 comprise twenty-four leaves, and may form

two gatherings; but they are not coincident with gatherings of the text (text gatherings 37–38 refer to plates 45R–47C).

29. E.J. LaBarre, *Dictionary and Encyclopaedia of Paper and Paper-Making with Equivalents of the Technical Terms in French, German, Dutch, Italian, Spanish and Swedish*, 2d ed., rev. and enl. (Amsterdam, 1952), 247, stated that "when preceded by 'large', the deviations from the basic size vary from one inch to four inches (being on one occasion the same)." Such deviations operate on measurements of the unfolded sheet, and would reduce by a factor of eight on the folded octavo leaf. He included "grand" and "de grand format" in his list of French adjectives (246 and note). Since, however, "grand" was not used by Momigny in conjunction with a named size, I know no way of ascertaining what he had in mind.

30. Ears of Midas: in a musical contest between Apollo and the satyr Marsyas, Midas decided against Apollo, whereupon Apollo changed Midas's ears into those of an ass.

31. Darwin relates "that old canon in natural history of 'Natura non facit saltum'" to bodily organs in chapter 6 of the first edition, "Difficulties on Theory," and then to instincts in chapter 7, "Instincts": see *The Origin of Species by Means of Natural Sciences, or The Preservation of Favoured Races in the Struggle for Life* (London, 1859), ed. J.W. Burrow (Harmondsworth, 1968, reprinted 1985), 223–24, 236–37, 263.

32. Peter J. Vorzimmer, *Charles Darwin, the Years of Controversy: The "Origin of Species" and Its Critics, 1859–82* (Philadelphia, 1970), 233. "The fact that the *Origin* increased in size with each new edition, and that in the fifth edition alone nearly half of all the sentences had been either altered or deleted, signifies the structural weakness that had afflicted [it]"; ibid., 222. Compare, for example, the opening paragraph of chapter 15 in the sixth edition with the corresponding passage in chapter 14 of the first edition, to gauge the shift of position. The differences among the six editions of the *Origin* are meticulously documented in Morse Peckham, ed., *The Origin of Species by Charles Darwin: A Variorum Text* (Philadelphia, 1959). See also Jacques Barzun, *Darwin, Marx, Wagner: Critique of a Heritage* (London, 1942).

33. A.C. Coolidge, Jr., *Charles Dickens as Serial Novelist* (Ames, Iowa, 1967), 50. Ten of the novels were serialized monthly, five weekly. On inconsistencies, see ibid., 89–95. Other novelists who published first in serial form include Thackeray, Trollope, George Eliot, Hardy, and Flaubert.

34. Palm, *Jérôme-Joseph de Momigny*, 334, speaks of "some 750 titles by altogether 153 composers, plus 15 anonymous works." See also ibid., 35–37, 80–83, and 333.

35. René Descartes, *Discours de la méthode*, part 2, ed. Étienne Gilson (Paris, 1964), 70–71; see Descartes, *"Discourse on Method" and the "Meditations,"* trans. F.E. Sutcliffe (Harmondsworth, 1968), 41.

36. Hauptmann first adumbrated his Hegelian triad, in terms of "unity" (*Einssein*), "duality" (*Getrenntsein*), and "conjunction" (*Verbindung*), in the course of his *Erläuterungen zu Joh. Sebastian Bachs "Kunst der Fuge,"* [J.S. Bach:] *Oeuvres complettes*, ed. Carl Czerny et al., supp. vol. to vol. 3 (Leipzig: C.F. Peters, Bureau de Musique, 1841), p. 8a (an English translation of this work appears in the present author's forthcoming *Music Analysis in the Nineteenth Century*, Cambridge Readings in the Literature of Music). He subsequently presented his fully formed theory in *Die Natur der Harmonik und Metrik* (Leipzig, 1853; 2d ed., 1873; English trans., 1888).

37. René Descartes, *Philosophical Writings*, trans. N.K. Smith (London, 1952), 120.

ELEVEN

Normality and Disruption in Beethoven's Bagatelle Op. 119, No. 8

CHRISTOPHER HATCH

Not long ago Michael Cherlin had occasion to describe two different ways of thinking about musical significance:

> By one model, significance roughly correlates to dramatic impact: any musical event that is disruptive, distinctive, or surprising becomes significant. . . .
>
> The alternative model is based on normative procedures or expectations, and it emphasizes relatively simple paradigms that underlie structural coherence. . . . [M]usically significant events are those that impart significance to events that cannot stand on their own. . . .
>
> Now it is obvious that music works by playing off the two kinds of significance . . . one against the other.[1]

These remarks have the ring of truth about them, for every listener has experienced how regularity and fulfilled expectations, on the one hand, and salient disturbances, on the other, coexist in music. As for scholars and performers, interpretations with respect to what is musically normal and what is exceptional inform their thinking through and through. Whether consciously or not, still inescapably the theorist, the musicologist, and the practicing musician all make decisions based on an application of Cherlin's two kinds of significance. Such decisions at their best are not purely intuitive. They have both historical and theoretical dimensions, which themselves merge at times, as a close study of any given work could reveal. In this essay investigation focuses on Beethoven's Op. 119, no. 8, a twenty-measure bagatelle in C major (ex. 11.1), which has previously been discussed by Edward T. Cone and Lawrence Kramer from two quite different perspectives.[2]

That both modes of significance are present in a work does not mean that they are equally easy to recognize or to pin down in words.

342

Example 11.1

The unusual event can leap from its surroundings. In Op. 119, no. 8, the B-flat strikingly introduced in m. 9, for instance, is just such an event. Contrariwise, what constitutes the establishment of norms is a more open question, to which answers may be sought in a number of places. Some regularizing procedures are adequately dealt with by reference to happenings within the piece; others would be insufficiently grounded without explanations drawn from the greater worlds of theory and practice, both past and present.[3]

In this connection one ought to consider the function of musical repetition. While many problems in defining what is normal can be solved only through a knowledge of conventional compositional procedures or of prescriptive theory, an immediate repetition, whether it be long or short, has a normative component that is created locally, purely inside the work. Where the repetition is inexact or even obscure, the repeated elements will still have acquired some normalizing force. (This force is not limited, however, to explaining "events that cannot stand on their own.")

Several passages in Op. 119, no. 8, show signs of hidden repetition, and none more interestingly than those that involve the B-flat in m. 9. These particular direct repetitions occur only when the repeat marks are obeyed.[4] When mm. 1–3 follow mm. 7–8, the chords marked x, y, and z in ex. example 11.2 recur in somewhat altered guise, as does the rising line G–G-sharp–A. In m. 2 a further A-sharp is reached. Thus when m. 9 in its turn comes right after m. 8, the likelihood is strong that the exposed B-flat will momentarily be taken for an A-sharp and only gain its function as B-flat with the entrance of F-natural and D in m. 10. On its first appearance the disruptive power of the B-flat operates twice: as an unexpected note and as a note whose presumed identity is reinterpreted.

The second time m. 9 is heard it follows the C-major chord of m. 20 and so is more readily acclimated to what has come before.[5] Moreover, mm. 18–20 have featured a melodic line that mm. 9–12, when repeated, give out again in distorted form (see exx. 11.3a and 11.3b). The precedents laid down in mm. 18–20 and adhered to in mm. 9–11 include an implicit meter—duple in one case, triple in the other—that is suddenly truncated at B-flat by stress on a weak beat.

The paired passages—mm. 1–3 corresponding to mm. 7–8 and mm. 9–12 to mm. 18–20—are so located as to frame each reprise of the bagatelle's binary form. Another musical recurrence similarly frames the whole piece. The closing melody (mm. 18–20) represents a rhythmically contracted and intervallically expanded version of the opening melodic line (see exx. 11.3b and c). The initial move, G–A, reap-

Example 11.2

Example 11.3

a. mm. 8–11

b. mm. 18–20, 9

c. mm. 1–4

pears for the first time in mm. 18–19. In contradistinction to the rhyth-mic hastening of the last bars generally, the second G–A is cast in augmentation (♩ | ♫, wherein the G is repeated, instead of ♪♩).

The repetitions and recurrences mentioned thus far have been founded on a reassertion of the same pitches or pitch classes. But mm. 4–13 contain several repetitions that employ transposition. Most ob-vious perhaps is the repetition in mm. 5–8 of elements from the open-ing phrase, including parallel thirds between the outer voices and a statement of the melody from mm.1–4, now in a migrant form that passes the line from voice to voice (see ex. 11.4). These restatements at the fifth up or fourth down are joined with a transposition of elements at the fourth up (see ex. 11.5). This hint of a subdominant transposition

Example 11.4
mm. 1–4

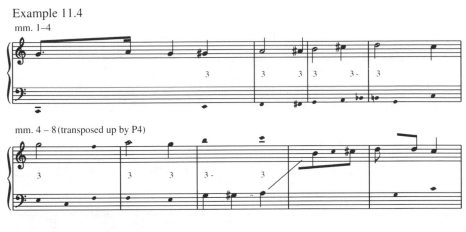

mm. 4 – 8 (transposed up by P4)

Example 11.5
a. mm. 2–4 (transposed up by P4)

b. m. 4ff.

of mm. 1–4 is worth pointing out only in light of the later modulation to the key of F major (mm. 9–12). Such a reading could be supported by noting how the "alto" in mm. 1–5 trails the rise of the top voice at the fifth below beginning with the third beat of m. 1; by this interpretation the F-sharp–G in m. 5 can acquire the same scale-degree positions (sharp 1–2) as the C-sharp–D in mm. 3–4. That the key of F major is in the offing may be demonstrated through a counterfactual example (the latter half of example 11.5b), which by making a cadence on F starts to overlap the content of the bagatelle's twelfth measure.

The phrase that would be omitted by this elision (mm. 9–12) outlines a fairly clear repetition of mm. 4–8 at the major second below (see ex. 11.6). As a result of this parallelism the disturbing B-flat of m. 9

Example 11.6

a. mm. 4–9

b. mm. 8–12 (transposed up by M2)

conditions the listener to expect the comparable A-flat in m. 12; both notes lie three half steps above the cadential notes, G and F respectively, just secured at the end of the preceding phrase. Yet an observer could be justified in thinking that mm. 9–12 constitute a "digression" and stand "opposed" to the bagetelle's first section, especially in their diatonicism.[6] In fact, the details of mm. 9–12 almost schematically separate the agents that convey the two kinds of significance described by Cherlin; the unexpected diatonicism and the changes introduced at m. 9 in the textural and rhythmic spheres offset and complement the reuse of an already familiar harmonic and melodic progression.

In the earlier examples, too, transposition embraced both harmonic and melodic components. Does the bagatelle offer any instances of purely linear-motivic transposition? Although Lawrence Kramer finds the piece to be an epitome of "utterly relaxed lyricism,"[7] its rich part writing, finally surfacing in the contrapuntal exchanges of mm. 13–15, suggests the possibility of tight motivic construction. Perhaps the four-note group in the top voice that moves to a melodic apex in mm. 5–6 can be considered a normative motivic cell. The pattern—falling second, rising third, and rising second—subsequently appears in various permutations on different scale degrees and sometimes with inserted notes (see ex. 11.7). Its links with two almost identical scale-step progressions, 6–5–4–2 and 6–5–2–4, reinforce its status as a primary motivic building block. Whereas mm. 5–6 contain the most prominent and direct expression that the motive attains, certain linear activities in mm. 1–4 will have drawn attention to the figure's emerging significance (see the lowest two staves at the left in ex. 11.7).

The four-note motive does not wed itself to any one rhythmic configuration. Of course, entirely apart from such motives and other pitch-determined ingredients, rhythm everywhere acts to establish norms and create disturbances. Were it feasible in so short an essay as this, one could set about exploring how the rhythmic regularity and metric conformity of the melody in mm. 2–7 quickly encounters dissolution in the upcoming bars. The role of the rhythmically rushed and metrically displaced cadences throughout might likewise be appraised. At all events, the rhythmic life of any piece readily lends itself to a bifocal analysis utilizing Cherlin's two categories.

Yet, be it in connection with rhythm or in connection with pitch, the determination of what is unexpected and what normal does not always come easily. The content of mm. 1–4 provides a case in point. Kramer singles out three "augmented triads," one in each of the first three measures; he discusses them as though they were conspicuous features of the phrase.[8] At the same time, a diatonic simplification can supply a voice-leading model from which the true augmented triads of mm. 1 and 2 derive their significance (see ex. 11.8). The diatonic scheme retains the rising parallel thirds along with two inner voices whose behavior seems bent on avoiding forbidden parallel fifths.[9] When chromatic alteration and half-step passing tones enter in at the points marked *5 in the example, they produce the augmented triads and the related chord in m. 3.

A question remains as to whether this chromaticized version of a diatonic plan is in fact something out of the ordinary. Here one can consult theory books from Beethoven's time in the hope that they may settle the issue. Their evidence suggests that this chromaticism is largely run-of-the mill; paired outer voices rising by half steps and augmented triads created by similar ascending lines appear in several examples found in treatises by Emanuel Aloys Foerster, Johann Georg Albrechtsberger, and Gottfried Weber (see exx. 11.9a and 11.9b).[10] The theorists' formulas do not, however, go on to generate the pitch complex that falls on the last beat of m. 3. Perhaps the line between the distinctive and the customary should fall between this simultaneity and the simple augmented triads, rather than between the augmented triads and their surroundings, as Kramer's critique implies. In other words, these triads may establish a pattern from which the third beat of m. 3 deviates.

Turning again to the B-flat of m. 9, one may hope to situate this singular feature of the bagatelle in a regularizing theoretical context, to explain it by reference to normative procedures that reside outside the confines of the piece. Here Albrechtsberger and his prescriptive illustrations may be of help. In demonstrating how to carry out a

Example 11.7
mm. 1–9

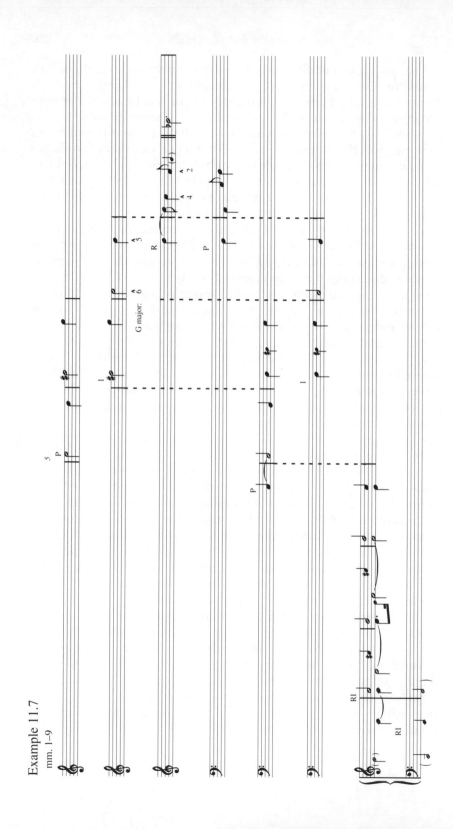

Example 11.7 (cont.)

mm. 11–20

Example 11.8

) indicates P5

Example 11.9

a.

b.

modulation that moves the tonic down by a whole step, Albrechtsberger shows a procedure like Beethoven's modulation in m. 8ff.[11] The progression hinges on altering a triad's quality from major to minor; in the bagatelle a G-major chord (in m. 8), which has acted as a tonic, becomes—according to one interpretation[12]—a G-minor triad (m. 9) that then serves as supertonic in the key of F major.

A more encompassing pattern might better explain these events, that is, give a fuller account of what lies behind them. If the disruptive B-flat and its ultimate resolution to A are taken as a clue, a chromatic half-step descent all the way to G can be recognized as a structural melodic entity in mm. 8–14, with a subsequent emphasizing of the terminal note through the move A-natural–G (mm. 15–16; see ex. 11.10c). A theorist of Beethoven's day might assign to the notes C–B–B-flat–A a four-chord harmonization like those in examples 11.10d and 11.10e, or to the notes B-flat–A–A-flat–G a harmonization like the one in example 11.10f.[13] The more extensive circumstances in the bagatelle exploit a harmonic progression that at once echoes the theorists' models and expands upon them in parallel musical statements set out in the keys of G major and F major, respectively (ex. 11.10g).

The cross relation between B-natural and B-flat, which is stressed in Op. 119, no. 8, is certainly not entailed by the underlying chromatic

Example 11.10

line. Yet the Beethovenian treatment of these notes has its precedents in both theory and practice. Such a cross relation sometimes arises where the harmonic support given the chromatic descent differs markedly from that in Op. 119, no. 8 (see exx. 11.10a and 11.10b).[14]

Devotees of Beethoven will notice that the harmonies in mm. 8–16 of the bagatelle recall some of the composer's most striking thoughts, specifically the openings of the piano sonatas Op. 31, no. 1, and Op. 53, the "Waldstein,"[15] and the beginning of the second movement of Op. 59, no. 1 (the first "Razumovsky" quartet). The beginning of Mozart's "Dissonance" Quartet K. 465 should also come to mind, and in this opening the friction between the seventh and lowered seventh scale degrees is again given weight.[16] Each of these pieces begins with a repetition carried out exactly at the whole step below. The bagatelle, on the contrary, disguises the repetition and situates the descent about halfway through the piece.

Surprisingly, the chromatic descent of mm. 8–16 does have a firm, if hidden alliance with the work's opening, since in slow motion it retraces the first seven notes of the melody (mm. 1–3) run backwards. What has gone up quickly comes down with deliberation. At the same time, a reinterpretation has taken place in the matter of metric location. The chromatically inflected notes, which have occurred on the weak, third beats when they rise, acquire metric strength when they fall. This procedure is in keeping with the advice of at least one eighteenth-century theorist; as James Baker points out elsewhere in this volume, Johann Philipp Kirnberger recommended off-the-beat positioning for rising chromaticism and the reverse for falling chromaticism.[17]

The shifting harmony that begins in m. 8 is not tied to, but precedes, the work's most irregular deployment of phrase lengths. After m. 12 the phrasing departs from a symmetry that has strictly governed the first eight bars and to which the next four have also adhered. Measures 13–20 combine their novel phrase lengths with unprecedentedly imitative texture. To show the polyphonic interplay, the phrasing might be outlined on two levels as demonstrated in example 11.11.

Example 11.11

The unit of seven bars in the top voice can be normalized according to the theories of Heinrich Christoph Koch and described using his terminology. A four-measure phrase that starts with a complete "incise" of two measures might be posited (see ex. 11.12b). Koch allows for the immediate but varied repetition of an incise, which yields a six-bar unit (see ex. 11.12c). He also permits the repetition of single measures, and he illustrates how two voices—one transposed by an octave—can function in a repeat (for the equivalent in Op. 119, no. 8, see ex. 11.12d).[18] To apply this second technique within an already repeated incise is to go beyond Koch's guidelines, but his pedagogical writings do point to certain norms operating within the unusual phrase construction of mm. 13–20.

As to the overall form of Op. 119, no. 8, that is, as to the way it works out its binary design, two aspects making no dramatic impact may nevertheless cause puzzlement. One involves the exceptional choice of the subdominant key as the one that prevails in the passage from the cadence in the dominant (here G major, m. 8) to the final return of the work's all-controlling tonic key (here C major). Koch recognizes the subdominant as an appropriate key for a passage in this position. He recommends that it end on a half cadence, which in the bagatelle would mean on C major as the dominant chord in the key of F major; in his example the cadential chord is addressed by a half-diminished harmony founded on the half step below its root.[19] Koch states as a general principle that where the return of the tonic key is not immediately preceded by a phrase that closes on the dominant of that key, the precedent phrase "must be formed so that it loses its completeness and is bound more closely with the following section."[20] An inspection of the bagatelle will confirm that both the harmony and the phrasing of mm. 12–16 roughly agree with Koch's requirements.

The other cause for puzzlement concerns the apparent absence from the piece of a recapitulatory phrase or two. But, even aside from the framing function of mm. 1–2 and 19–20, which has been spoken of above, the problem is illusory. Edward T. Cone has explained the recapitulatory nature of mm. 13–18 and demonstrated their congruence with mm. 3–8.[21] In m. 17 the rising parallel thirds in eighth notes likewise refer back to the slower thirds that mount through the first four measures. The four eighth notes D through G in m. 18 also quote those in m. 4. Finally, rhythmic motives appearing toward the close of the work recall earlier occurrences, reshaped by augmentation and diminution (see ex. 11.13).[22] A listener anticipates some sort of recapitulation simply on the basis of an acquaintance with the related

Example 11.12

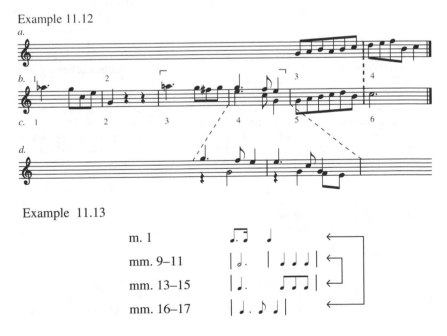

Example 11.13

repertory. This bagatelle by Beethoven satisfies such an anticipation, though not in the way that limited definitions of recapitulation might suggest.

All the foregoing observations about Op. 119, no. 8, have been abetted by Michael Cherlin's distinction between two kinds of musical significance and are intended, on the one hand, to highlight the peculiar moments and irregularities of the piece and, on the other, to search out normal, more elemental patterns behind these events. This sampling of varied approaches goes only so far. It does not result in criticism or analysis, though critics and analysts could profitably marshal such observations as preparation for their more specialized undertakings. A commentary like this one does, however, share with both criticism and analysis an essential trait—an unwavering focus on the piece at hand. In these endeavors the work of music theorists, past and present, can be exploited to sharpen this focus. In fact, recourse to theory along with a knowledge of historically relevant compositions is much needed lest the observer be surprised by what is ordinary or oblivious to what is normative.

Notes

1. Michael Cherlin, "Why We Got into Analysis and What to Get Out of It," *Theory and Practice: Journal of the Music Theory Society of New York State* 11 (1986): 70. For comments on the uses and misuses of the concept of the normative, see Leo Treitler, *Music and the Historical Imagination* (Cambridge, Mass., 1989), 72–74.

2. Edward T. Cone, "Beethoven's Experiments in Composition: The Late Bagatelles," in Alan Tyson, ed., *Beethoven Studies 2* (London, 1977), 89–92; Lawrence Kramer, *Music and Poetry: The Nineteenth Century and After* (Berkeley, 1984), 11–15. Example 11.1 above reproduces Op. 119, no. 8, in the form in which it has been readied by Professor Glenn Stanley of the University of Connecticut for an edition of Beethoven's bagatelles prepared for C.F. Peters of Leipzig.

3. Here "within the piece" will mean within the single bagatelle. A different perspective would prevail if the eleven bagatelles of Op. 119 were seen as a cycle rather than a collection of individual pieces. On the question of whether Op. 119 is a cycle or a collection, see Cone, "Beethoven's Experiments," 84–85; Jürgen Uhde, *Beethovens Klaviermusik*, 2d ed., vol. 1, *Klavierstücke und Variationen* (Stuttgart, 1980), 135–36; and Barry Cooper, "Beethoven's Portfolio of Bagatelles," *Journal of the Royal Musical Association* 112, no. 2 (1986–87): 208–22.

4. The consequences of taking the repeats in Op. 119, no. 8, might be studied in light of Beethoven's careful composition of first and second endings in some of the other late bagatelles, a topic touched on in Cooper, "Beethoven's Portfolio," 214–15.

5. See Cone, "Beethoven's Experiments," 92.

6. Ibid., 89.

7. Kramer, *Music and Poetry*, 13.

8. Ibid.

9. For similar schematic examples of rising progressions that alternate six-three and five-three chords, see Carl Philipp Emanuel Bach, *Versuch über die wahre Art das Klavier zu spielen* (1753–62; reprint ed., Leipzig, 1976), part 2, 49–50; trans. by William

J. Mitchell as *Essay on the True Art of Playing Keyboard Instruments* (New York, 1949), 213–14 figs. 252 and 253. The theorists considered relevant to the purposes of the present study include both contemporaries of Beethoven and writers whose treatises were in circulation during the composer's formative years.

10. Example 11.9a is from Emanuel Aloys Förster, *Anleitung zur Generalbass* (Vienna, 1823), as given in Robert W. Wason, *Fundamental Bass Theory in Nineteenth Century Vienna* (Ann Arbor, 1983), 41. Example 11.9b is from Johann Georg Albrechtsberger, *Collected Writings on Thorough-Bass, Harmony and Composition, for Self-Instruction* (London, 1855), 57 ex. 360. See also ibid., 18 ex. 96; Gottfried Weber, *Versuch einer geordneten Theorie der Tonsezkunst* [*sic*] *zum Selbstunterricht mit Anmerkungen für Gelehrtere* (Mainz, 1817–21), *Notenheft*, ex. 278; Bach, *Versuch*, part 2, 65 ex., and *Essay*, 225 fig. 278.

11. Albrechtsberger, *Collected Writings*, 65 ex. 461.

12. See Cone, "Beethoven's Experiments," 91–92.

13. Examples 11.10d and 11.10f: cf. Bach, *Versuch*, part 2, 76 ex., and *Essay*, 234 fig. 257. Examples 11.10d and 11.10e: cf. Weber, *Versuch*, vol. 4, exx. 434a and 433a, respectively. For ex. 11.10e, see also the example from Heinrich Christoph Koch printed as ex. 9.7 "fig. 11" in James M. Baker's contribution to the present volume, p. 245. For some uses by Beethoven of such a progression as ex. 11.10d, see Christopher Hatch, "Ideas in Common: The *Liederkreis* and Other Works by Beethoven," in Edmond Strainchamps, Maria Rika Maniates, and Christopher Hatch, eds., *Music and Civilization: Essays in Honor of Paul Henry Lang* (New York, 1984), 60.

14. Example 11.10a is taken from Mozart's Violin and Piano Sonata in G Major K. 379, second movement, first variation (transposed up by a perfect fourth); ex. 10b is taken from Heinrich Christoph Koch, *Versuch einer Anleitung zur Composition* (1782–93; reprint ed., Hildesheim, 1969), 3:142 ex.; trans. in part by Nancy Kovaleff Baker as *Introductory Essay on Composition: The Mechanical Rules of Melody, Sections 3 and 4* (New Haven, 1983), 124 ex. 284 (transposed down by a perfect fifth).

15. The opening of the "Waldstein" Sonata, which places the chromatic descent in the bass, is printed as ex. 16.2 in Lee A. Rothfarb's contribution to the present volume, p. 460. The chromatic move of the bass down from the tonic note to the dominant is that of the seventeenth-century *lamento* bass. Beethoven uses this bass as the foundation for the theme of his Thirty-two Variations on an Original Theme WoO 80. Theoretical models that resemble Beethoven's harmonic treatment of a descending chromatic bass line in these variations and in the "Waldstein" Sonata are found in Bach, *Versuch*, part 2, exx. on 56, 201, 221, and 329, and *Essay*, 219 fig. 264, 334 fig. 408aa, 350 fig. 419, and 433 fig. 472.

16. See James M. Baker's contribution to the present volume, pp. 287–88 ex. 9.42.

17. Ibid., p. 305 n. 38.

18. Varied repetition of an "incise": Koch, *Versuch* 3:175–78, and *Introductory Essay*, 139–41. Repetition of a measure with octave transposition: Koch, *Versuch* 3:162, and *Introductory Essay*, 133. Example 11.11a above shows the actual melodic close of Op. 119, no. 8, a close of the sort Koch terms a "feminine ending." Beethoven's harmonic treatment of this close is one that the theorist would find "improper" (Koch, *Versuch* 2:399–400, and *Introductory Essay*, 27–28). For a full-scale study of the relation of Koch's theories to the practices of another master composer, see Elaine Sisman, "Small and Expanded Forms: Koch's Model and Haydn's Music," *Musical Quarterly* 68 (1982): 444–75.

19. Koch, *Versuch* 3:91–92 ex., and *Introductory Essay*, 99–100 ex. 249.

20. Koch, *Versuch* 3:92, and *Introductory Essay*, 100.

21. Cone, "Beethoven's Experiments," 89–90.

22. See Uhde, *Beethovens Klaviermusik* 1:163, where the opening three-note rhythmic figure is said to be "loosened" in the figure introduced in m. 13.

TWELVE

Coda as Culmination: The First Movement of the "Eroica" Symphony

Robert P. Morgan

In his 1860 essay "Music of the Future," Wagner considers the construction of the first movement of a Beethoven symphony in light of the genre's origins in dance music:

> Here the actual dance melody is broken up into its smallest elements, each of which, consisting often of only two tones, is made interesting and expressive through at times a predominantly rhythmic, at times a predominantly harmonic significance. These elements then combine into ever-changing groups, at times expanding like a torrent in logical sequence, at times breaking up in a whirl, but always bound together by such a plastic motion that the listener cannot escape their influence for a single moment. . . . The completely new result of this procedure was the stretching out of the melody through the richest possible development of all its motives to a large, continuous musical span, nothing other than a single, totally unified melody.[1]

Wagner here illuminates an essential feature of the Beethoven sonata form, one closely linked to his own compositional inclinations, to be sure, but also tied to a more general aesthetic idea whose musical manifestations had become evident well before his time (not least in Beethoven): that temporal forms are "organic," possessing an evolutionary character that makes their every moment a consequence of the preceding one, with the entire structure unfolding toward a final, predetermined conclusion.

In Wagner's words, an entire movement becomes a single melody. Quite correctly he stresses "the completely new result of this procedure," for it entails a very different conception of musical form from that of the eighteenth century. Notions of symmetrical balance, of distinct formal functions such as exposition and development, of well-differentiated degrees of stability and instability, of similarity and contrast, yield to an ideal of continuous musical evolution.

Although Beethoven did not abandon sonata form, his rethinking of it in more organic terms as a dynamically evolving process leading toward a moment of final culmination fundamentally affected both the structural and expressive features of his work. In seizing upon this facet of Beethoven's music, Wagner could of course interpret it as a milestone on the stylistic path toward his own. Whatever the historical limitations of Wagner's view, however, it emphasizes important aspects of Beethoven's oeuvre that may be overlooked, or at least underplayed, when approached from a more traditional, less historically sensitive formal perspective. Above all, it focuses light on what is new about Beethoven's codas; for only there does Wagner's "melody" come to an end, its ultimate course and direction finally revealed.

* * *

More recently our understanding of Beethoven's codas has benefited from an unusually lucid discussion in the form of a friendly exchange between two of our most perceptive musical commentators: Charles Rosen and Joseph Kerman. Although Rosen and Kerman have not addressed each other directly in this exchange, each frequently refers to the other, often borrowing insights as points of departure for new ideas. The give and take has been cordial, reflecting mutual respect and admiration even at moments of occasional disagreement. In view of the bitter acrimony that now attends so many colloquies in the field, this one has been notable for both its courtesy and its enlightenment.

The exchange initiated in 1980 with Kerman's highly favorable assessment of Rosen's *Sonata Forms*, when the reviewer noted a "lacuna—almost bizarre in a seemingly methodical book of 350 pages on sonata forms": the absence of "any sustained discussion of the sonata-form coda."[2] Shortly afterwards, Kerman published his wide-ranging "Notes on Beethoven's Codas," presumably to help fill the "lacuna" noted in Rosen's book.[3] (Following an opening paragraph on the paucity of literature on the coda, Kerman again mentions Rosen's "conspicuous disappointment" in this connection.) The final installment appears in a substantial new chapter on codas added to the revised edition of *Sonata Forms*, Rosen's own response to Kerman, whose article he mentions frequently and appreciatively.[4] At fifty-six pages the new chapter is by far the longest in the book, almost equal to the three on exposition, development, and recapitulation combined.

Beethoven's "Eroica" has been especially favored in the discussion. Although Rosen does not refer to it in his new chapter, the first movement, particularly its coda, figures prominently elsewhere in *Sonata*

Forms, as well as in Kerman's review and article. Indeed, Rosen's remark on the "reestablishment of symmetrical equilibrium" at the end of the symphony's first movement, through "an incredibly long passage that does nothing but repeat a V–I cadence over and over again in E-flat major,"[5] seems to have first restimulated Kerman's thoughts on codas. In his review, noting Rosen's "rare and rather revealing slip," Kerman observes that the passage in question, far from simply repeating, "does nothing less than resolve the main theme," thereby "providing an emotional resolution, or rather an apotheosis . . . so different in spirit and form from the symmetrical resolutions of Haydn and Mozart."[6]

This is provocative, holding the promise of a more dynamic conception of the end of the movement. Although Kerman says little else about the "Eroica" coda in his review, he returns to it in his article, allotting it more space than any other composition. Given his bold initial perception, however, the discussion is disappointingly tame, providing little explanation of how Beethoven actually achieves the "emotional apotheosis" of the movement's final moments.

At this point I would like to step in, a late and uninvited arrival in this exchange, to offer some additional thoughts on the "Eroica" movement, especially on the relationship of the coda to the music that precedes it—and in doing so, to keep Wagner's metaphor for the Beethoven symphonic movement firmly in mind.

* * *

Rosen's comment on the "Eroica" coda refers to the long, remarkably repetitious music heard near the movement's end (m. 631ff.), where a greatly simplified version of the opening theme, now with regular tonic-dominant alternations, is stated four times. In focusing on the "reestablishment of symmetrical equilibrium," he stresses the section's tonal function, as ballast for a movement that has a long and complex development and, even in its exposition and recapitulation, moves quickly away from the tonic. He is surely correct; tonal balance *is* reestablished here and, after so much waywardness, contributes significantly to the effect of "apotheosis." Kerman's objection stems from the conviction that the passage cannot be understood in purely tonal terms, that more than tonal resolution is at stake. He also is surely correct. But just what is at stake?

One of the points on which Rosen and Kerman agree is that codas must be understood in terms of previous events: Rosen refers to the coda of the finale of the Eighth Symphony as "the goal of the entire movement, as required by the material,"[7] and Kerman asserts (with Wagnerian echoes) that the Beethoven sonata form is "the story of a theme—the first theme—and the exciting last chapter of that story is told in the coda."[8] The assumption is clear: as the last thing heard, the coda takes care of previously unsettled business.

Our understanding of the "Eroica" coda, then, depends upon our comprehension of the entire movement, above all the history of its "first theme." Both authors remark on this theme's peculiarities and their significance for the music's future course—e.g., its "drift away from the tonic . . . at the opening" (Rosen), and its "harmonic, rhythmic, and registral uncertainties" (Kerman).[9] But they do not note what seems to me its most remarkable aspect: the fundamentally orchestral conception of the first thematic group as a whole. Indeed, the overall shape of this music is so heavily dominated by "textural" considerations—including choice of instruments, spacing, registration, density, volume, and the like—that one wonders if the word "theme" really applies at all. From a strictly conventional point of view, there is no theme, that is, no fixed melodic unit representing a stable, repeatable whole. When the opening material returns, it is always fundamentally transformed (except for the repeat of the exposition), both its integrity and functional role within the sonata form thereby compromised. This is a new kind of Beethovenian opening, inherently developmental from the start.

The theme's predominantly textural conception is evident from its first measure, following the famous opening chords. The latter are usually viewed in terms of rhythmic-metric function,[10] but they have an equally important textural role, defining the full orchestral-registral space within which the movement will play itself out. The full-range, *forte* tonic, whose recurrences throughout the movement (cf. mm. 1–2, 37–40, 75–76, 398, 430–43, 548–51, and 689–91) have an almost "motivic" character, supplies a frame against which the unconventional low-register cello opening is contrasted. The sudden reduction in resources and power is drastic (and also "motivic"—the first of many such drops in the piece), creating a special kind of tightly wound tension that gradually recoils in the opening thematic statement (mm. 3–45). Like the crouch preceding a leap, the sudden retrenchment at m. 3 gives rise to an extended release of accumulating energy, a process that becomes perhaps the central structural agent for the entire movement, reappearing throughout in ever-changing forms and contexts, of which those associated with the first theme are the most critical, but by no means the only, representatives.

One function of the first group is to reestablish through progressive additions the full range and texture of the opening chords. Example 12.1 provides a sketch of the section's registral evolution, focusing primarily on the statements of the basic motivic material of mm. 3–6, whose reappearances in different octaves largely account for the registral development. (These are indicated, in "shorthand," by three boxed notes taken from the head of the motive.) There are three main thematic segments, indicated on the sketch by arabic numerals, each formed by statements of the basic motive (only the first in each segment is complete, the others being two-measure fragments). The first segment is preceded by the opening *tutti* chords, and the second and third are separated by an extended dominant buildup (indicated by the roman numeral V in the sketch).

Following the initial cello motivic statement, the thematic focus cuts away from the lower register to the syncopated violin figure two octaves higher (m. 7), expanding the registral space and initiating the second half of the first thematic unit. Although this phrase is unique among all the formal units found in the three thematic segments in not being directly derived from the opening motivic idea (its syncopated rhythm, however, is of major significance for the movement), it has the important function of juxtaposing against the cello's low opening the higher octave that will become the principal motivic register for the second segment (mm. 15–23). There it is carried first by clarinet (mm. 15–18), then by first violin (mm. 19–20), and finally by flute (mm. 21–22), as the main motive, treated developmentally, moves upward in fragmented sequential repetitions toward the dominant. The intensification of the already registrally unstable opening is heightened by shifting doublings on each motivic statement, which lend the segment a notably "scattered" texture: one octave higher and lower in flute and horn (mm. 15–18, the flute cutting off at m. 17); two and three octaves lower in cello and bass (mm. 19–20); and one and two octaves lower in clarinet and bassoon (mm. 21–22).

With the arrival on the dominant at m. 23, a more heavily scored "preparatory" dominant prolongation builds toward the third thematic segment, increasing tension by delaying tonal resolution, by syncopation, and by motivic fragmentation: four-measure units become two measures, then one measure, followed by a dissolution combined with a dramatic registral expansion outward in both directions, *crescendo* (mm. 35–36). The third thematic segment bursts in on the crest of this expansion as a climactic goal (m. 37), *fortissimo* and *tutti* (instruments have been introduced progressively throughout the section, with trumpets saved for this point), reestablishing the tonic and full registral expanse of the opening chords. The basic motive, now doubled in all five octaves encompassed by the opening chord, receives a final massive statement, capping the entire thematic development.

This final segment then breaks up almost immediately. Following

Example 12.1

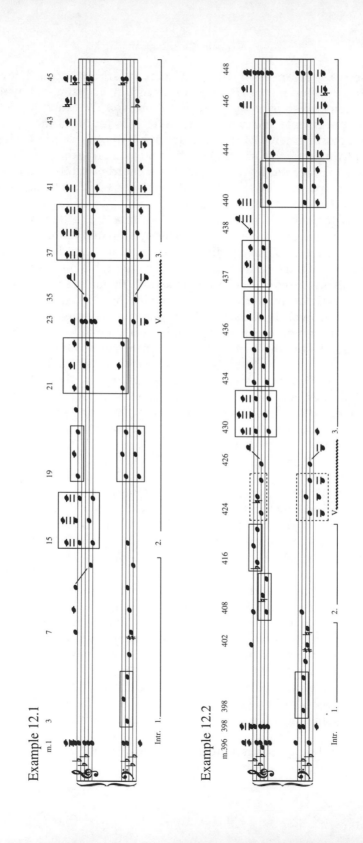

Example 12.2

the first motivic statement (mm. 37–40), it moves through a fragmentary motivic sequence, confined to the lower three octaves (mm. 41–42), before modulating quickly to V of V (m. 45). There a drastic reduction of forces, reminiscent of m. 3 but here overlapping within a single measure, articulates the beginning of the next formal phase, the transition to the second group.

The entire first group thus encompasses a single "textural" process: the reestablishment of the opening *tutti* through a series of stages, each designed to open up new octaves through motivic explorations within the previously defined full registral space. Coupled with a dynamic increase from *piano* to *fortissimo*, plus steadily increasing orchestral and textural density, the process culminates with the total saturation of the available space, reflected in the five-octave motivic doubling. It then breaks up quickly, allowing a new process of expansion to begin.

This is a new, fundamentally developmental kind of "first theme," which will require equally new treatment within the sonata-form format, as is confirmed when the section reappears in the recapitulation. There the first group's reprise takes a fundamentally new course, though it preserves the essential integrative feature of its original form: a dynamic traversal of the full registral space over three thematic segments. Again a low-register opening (mm. 398–408) is followed by a more fragmented restatement introducing new registers and pulling away from the tonic (mm. 408–24), leading to a dominant prolongation (mm. 424–29), and culminating in a final *tutti* return (mm. 430–48), the whole accompanied by increases in dynamics and textual density.

The differences are nevertheless notable. The opening *tutti* chords, now on V, overlap with the dominant prolongation preceding the reprise, their previously latent "upbeat" character made explicit, and emphasized by a *crescendo*, timpani roll, and eighth- and sixteenth-note string figuration. The "downbeat" is supplied by a third, tonic chord, corresponding to the ones in mm. 1–2. The textural reduction to the low cello opening is even more abrupt than before, overlapping with this chord. Critical thematic differences develop in the theme's fifth measure, where an E-natural leads to the now-modulating second thematic segment, the famous F-major/D-flat-major horn-flute episode of mm. 408–24.

This section receives considerable attention from Rosen and Kerman, who see it as a moment of relaxation: in words quoted approvingly by Kerman, Rosen notes that "all genuine harmonic motion appears to stop: the dynamics, *piano* and *dolce*, reflect the cessation of harmonic energy."[11] Accordingly, he stresses the "delicacy" and "exoticism" of this remarkable moment of apparent calm. Yet when compared to what has already transpired, this moment must also be understood as one of considerable surprise. Two previous passages are critical: most obviously, the corresponding point in the exposition, where after a tonic-oriented first section the second thematic segment develops forcefully—tonally, motivically, registrally, orchestrally, and dynamically—toward the dominant (mm. 17–23); and more immediately, the dramatic V–I reinterpretation of the introductory chords in the reprise (mm. 396–98), where the "letdown" associated with the sudden reduction of texture for the cello entry is even more pronounced than in the exposition.

Since the first group in the exposition was designed to build up gradually from the cello opening, its return in the recapitulation will presumably "justify" this extraordinary drop. In light of this, the failure of the second thematic segment (mm. 408–24) to provide the expected expansion—indeed, its very qualities of "delicacy" and "exoticism"—produces a significant second "letdown." The strange, unfocused quality of this almost parenthetical passage, subverting the expected developmental thrust of the principal thematic material, far from being simply a moment of relaxation and repose, brims with tension.

Its apparent failure to press forward is further exacerbated by the long dominant prolongation preceding the recapitulation, where there is also a radical reduction of musical content. The prolongation ends with the sudden *tutti crescendo* on the introductory chords (mm. 396–98), seeming to encapsulate the underlying idea of the entire first group in a single gesture. Because of what follows, however, the *crescendo* only increases tension, anticipating an idea that then threatens not to materialize.

Beethoven sets up this foil, of course, to overcome it, to bring the music back on course after it has seemingly lost its way and thus heighten the original effect. The horn-flute episode leads to a dominant prolongation (m. 424), as did the second thematic segment in the exposition (m. 23), but the prolongation is significantly rewritten to compensate for the now-depleted level of energy. Instead of beginning *piano* and rising to *fortissimo*, it begins *pianissimo*, that is, still softer than the horn-flute episode. It is also more obviously motivic than before, with a new, dominant-oriented version of the basic idea that accelerates and then dissolves after three measures, giving way to the faster eighth-note figuration and a four-measure *crescendo* and outward registral expansion similar to those features at mm. 35–36.

Whereas previously this expansion led to the third and final *fortissimo* thematic statement, here it leads to a reworked return of the *second* segment (previously replaced by the horn-flute segment), now *forte* and in full textural array (m. 430). All of the registral-orchestral instability associated with the passage in the exposition is gone. And now it forms only the first part of a two-phased thematic segment that links the original second and third segments into a single, continuous unit: its rising motivic sequences and increasing dynamics (*più forte*, m. 436) lead without break to the return of the climactic third statement, *fortissimo* (m. 440). The culminating third segment has thus become a more extended event, itself expansive in its first half.

The registral distribution of the main motive throughout the section, indicated in example 12.2, is markedly different from that of the exposition, especially the extended final segments. The motivic statements rise in register during the first two segments (cf. mm. 398, 408, and 416), a direction temporarily reversed by the more heavily scored dominant prolongation at m. 424 (the motive associated with this essentially nonthematic segment is placed in a broken-lined box in the sketch). But the latter's rising motion leads on to a three-octave motivic doubling in the highest register that opens the third segment (m. 430), culminating the overall upward direction to this point. Although the first flute soon abandons the motive, removing the top octave doubling, the upward expansion continues in the first violin, which ascends through rising sequential figures, pushing all the way up to a-flat^3 (m. 439)—the highest string note yet—before resolving to a pedal g^3 for the final thematic statement (m. 440).

For this climactic statement the principal motive appears in the three lower octaves only, a reduction from the corresponding five-octave statement in the exposition. Yet the climactic effect is even more pronounced. In response to the massive buildup provided by the preceding music, high violin writing, *fortissimo* dynamic (now with added *sforzandi*), thematic use of the horns and trumpets (limited to an accompanimental role in the previous measures), and remarkably dense, rhythmically active orchestral texture combine to provide an image of rare sonic power. This final moment then breaks up as quickly as before, moving to V at m. 448 with a sudden drop in intensity corresponding to m. 45.

The first group thus reaffirms its role in the exposition, but in a significantly more complex and dramatic form. The thrust toward the final culmination is delayed by a more episodic second segment, in compensation for which there is a more extended two-phased climactic statement. The first group does not simply return; it goes beyond, exceeding its previous level of intensity.

This brings me back to the coda passage discussed by Rosen and Kerman, where the opening thematic material and the dynamic processes associated with the first group reappear, now in an unprecedentedly direct and straightforward form, for a third and final statement. Once again a single-register motivic opening (here in middle register) expands toward a final *tutti*, but now in an unbroken, inexorable succession of developmental increments. What was achieved before only with seeming difficulty, with moments of diversion, uncertainty, and waiting, is accomplished with supreme confidence and purpose. This music knows exactly where it is going and the most direct path to get there (underscored by the running eighth-note figures accompanying the thematic material).

The motivic material is reworked in several critical ways. First, the opening thematic idea is recast so that, instead of falling to C-sharp as in m. 7 (a move that brought such far-reaching tonal, formal and expressive consequences), it stays resolutely within the tonic triad. This creates a more inclosed four-measure group (mm. 631–34) that generates a corresponding dominant response (mm. 635–38), producing a tonally unstable (I–V) but rhythmically balanced (4 + 4) eight-measure unit designed to fall back on itself, thereby initiating its own "circular" repetition (the basis for Rosen's "incredibly long passage that does nothing but repeat a V–I cadence"). To this extent the theme is "normalized," a term favored by Rosen and Kerman for such final simplifications.

The four circular repetitions of this eight-measure unit (mm. 631–62) bring about a final "textural *crescendo*" analogous to those of the exposition and recapitulation, though progressing in more regular incremental stages and involving not only the treatment of the main thematic material but the registral distance separating this material from the accompanimental sixteenth- and eighth-note figures, as well as the loudness, density, and overall complexity of the total texture. Once again a final *tutti* emerges (m. 647, becoming still more emphatic at m. 655), but now one that represents the last link in an unbroken, four-phased thematic unfolding (thus extending the idea of the re–capitulation's two-phased third segment). Everything extraneous to the developmental thrust is omitted.

In summary, the placement of three different, yet closely related thematic blocks associated with the principal motive at strategic points in the movement, the first at the beginning and the last at the end, anchors the entire structure and controls its overall course. Indeed, one might say that these segments supply at least the outline for the "whole story": each carries the plot forward in a new, yet consistent direction, and the last (as we shall see) ties together various disconnected threads. To that extent the movement conforms to Kerman's "story of a theme," with the coda statement representing his "exciting final chapter."

* * *

In his Beethoven article Kerman points out that "in the technical language of sonata form 'coda' is the one term that does not refer (however imperfectly) to a musical function, but merely to a position." He counters by suggesting that certain codas—notably middle-period Beethoven ones—have a "resolving" function that is both tonal and thematic in nature:

> Again and again there seems to be some kind of instability, discontinuity, or thrust in the first theme which is removed in the coda. The aberration may be linear, harmonic, rhythmic, registral, or textural, but in any case the coda has a function over and above that of "saturating the ear with the tonic chord," in Rosen's phrase. In addition to this harmonic function it has a thematic function that can be described or, rather, suggested by words such as "normalization," "resolution," "expansion," "release," "completion," and "fulfillment."[12]

This is helpful, and properly elaborated could offer a significant contribution to our understanding of Classical formal processes. It also tells us something important about one aspect of the "Eroica" coda's outcome, but only one aspect, and one that could easily lead to misplaced emphasis. For although the final "apotheosis" clearly "resolves" some features of the basic thematic material, it by no means resolves them all. Indeed, in a critical sense the music remains expansive—and thus developmental—right up to the close.

Moreover, one needs to be wary about the appropriateness of the formal functions designated by the other sonata-form terms. One of the most characteristic aspects of Beethoven's music in the early years of the nineteenth century is precisely its subversion of such conventional functions. The opening section of the "Eroica," for example, is deeply developmental, as much so as it is expository, setting the example for a movement that will be consistently expansive throughout, opening up new areas of exploration rather than confirming old ones. The music is "dynamic" through and through, not only in opposing strongly contrasting formal units (characteristic of the Classical style in general) but in structuring those units in a consistently open-ended manner. The "Eroica" leans toward "continuous development," though certainly not to a degree that entirely eradicates traditional sonata-form functions. These remain in force, but only barely, having been significantly adjusted under the demands of a new expansiveness.

The role of the "Eroica" coda and its closing thematic apotheosis must therefore be interpreted within this consistently developmental context, and any consideration of "thematic resolution" acknowledge the expanding framework of the whole. Thus if the third of the three principal thematic sections is said to supply the "exciting final chapter" of Kerman's "story of a theme," the stress should be placed on "exciting," on continuing development, and not just on "resolution." This closing thematic gesture would be quite different—"unheroic," in fact—if its developmental precedents were ignored. (Such a possibility threatened in the horn-flute episode of the recapitulation, but there the episodic character only temporarily derailed forward progress, as we have seen, being ultimately appropriated to intensify the subsequent thrust.)

Thus, although the removal of all tonal and thematic deflections at the close creates a kind of resolution, it also allows the other musical parameters—the "textural" ones that have played such an important part in the previous statements—to come even more emphatically to the fore. These remain as developmental as ever, projecting a process of expansive evolution that, for the first time, is direct and uninterrupted. Kerman, then, is fundamentally mistaken, it seems to me, in remarking with reference to this passage that "when Beethoven fashions a characteristic, joyous litany-cum-*crescendo* out of his main theme he is no more 'developing' it than he would be if he were to make cadential phrases out of it in Mozart's manner."[13]

* * *

The story of the "Eroica" is not just "the story of its (main) theme," moreover, but of all of its contents. The other segments have significant consequences for the main thematic statements, and the full story can be appreciated only in the interaction of them all.

The second theme seems at first glance notably conventional; strongly contrasting in rhythm, texture, and character, it appears to form a moment of relative repose within the expansive whole. Yet it is immediately put off balance by beginning "too soon," on the very next quarter note after the *fortissimo* downbeat cadential arrival in m. 83; and its essentially steady quarter-note rhythm extends without break the driving quarter-note motion of the brass that pushed toward the cadence in the previous two measures. The more stable, lyrical character of the tune is, moreover, quickly dissipated, first by the relatively developmental sequential continuation of its initial four-measure phrase; and then, more drastically, by the failure of a full "consequent" phrase to appear after an eight-measure "antecedent" (mm. 83–90).

The sequential repeat of the closing eighth-note figure of the first eight-measure phrase at the beginning of the second (cf. m. 90, violin, oboe, and bassoon, and m. 91, flute), joined with an unexpected turn to minor (also m. 91), tips the listener that things are perhaps less simple than they seemed. Then the new phrase modulates immediately toward the lowered major mediant (mm. 91–94), after which it seems to self-destruct: a pair of sequentially repeated motivic fragments (mm. 95–99) appear, in radical registral opposition (recalling the first group), leading to a weak half cadence on V of V (m. 99), the tonal basis for yet another segment of textural-dynamic *crescendo*. The contrasting theme as well becomes party to the underlying developmental processes.

So does the famous "new" theme introduced in the development section (m. 284), in certain respects reminiscent of the second theme. It too has predominant quarter-note motion and appears as a moment of apparent calm within an otherwise charged context. And its entrance is also "too soon," following without pause a major downbeat cadence and extending its quarter-note motion. Here, in addition, rhythmic instability is heightened by quarter-note syncopations (first violin); and the melody modulates abruptly in the last measure of its first phrase, leading to the subdominant (A minor) and a sequential repetition (m. 292). The repetition also modulates in its final measure, this time to C major and the return of the principal motivic material. The theme is thus inherently unstable (and becomes even more so in subsequent statements).

Rosen stresses, as have others, the relationship of this theme to the original form of the principal motivic idea, focusing especially on the contour of the cello's countermelody (ex. 12.3a).[14] A more immediate relationship exists between the oboe theme itself and the form the principal motive assumes in its occurrences in the development at mm. 186–93 and 198–205—that is, the form heard just before the appearance of the new theme. The main motive's conversion to minor anticipates the new theme's mode, and the new contour and overall interval succession correspond closely to those of the latter; both themes contain two balancing subphrases, the second answering the first on the dominant and extending its upward motion, beginning on the second scale degree rather than the first (ex. 12.3b).

The significance of this connection becomes fully evident in the

Example 12.3

coda, when the E-minor development theme returns at m. 581, just before the final, climactic appearance of the principal motive. The latter is not immediately derived from the original version of the main motive, but from the development-section version just discussed, whose formal layout—two four-measure phrases, the first on the tonic and second on the dominant—exactly mirrors that of the climactic theme (ex. 12.3c), the first two measures of each subphrase being identical except for mode and transposition. This connection is underlined by the slightly altered reappearance of the development-section version, in major, at the beginning of the coda (m. 565).

The main difference between these two versions of the principal thematic material is that the four-measure phrases of the climactic one end on the upper fifth degree (a change anticipated first in the development, in the major-mode variation at m. 300ff., and more closely in the reprise, in the flute-horn episode of the recapitulation, where the association is emphasized by the use of solo horn, the same instrument that begins the climactic statement).[15] The new phrase ending serves to bring the original motive into yet closer correspondence with the E-minor theme from the development (ex. 12.3d). The coda return of the latter, first in F minor (m. 581ff.), then in E-flat minor (m. 589ff.), thus anticipates the outline of the climactic theme. The E-flat-minor restatement, shortly preceding the climactic theme's first entrance, does so at identical pitch level (though not mode), while the F-minor/E-flat-minor relationship of the two statements adumbrates the recurring E-flat–F alternations of the initial notes of the climactic theme's two four-measure subphrases. The strong sense of release, of thematic and modal clarification, when the outline of the minor theme gives way to that of the closely related major theme, makes its own significant contribution to the final apotheosis.

The "new" theme, then, is part and parcel of the movement's overall course, intimately tied to the continuing search for the main theme's culminating form. The close correspondences between development and coda, often noted, are consequently more than a matter of thematic balances, paired against those of the exposition and recapitulation, but form part of the long-range preparation for the final thematic consummation.

Nor are the coda's materials entirely derived from the development. The final form of the theme is closely linked with the *tutti* material that announces the close of the exposition at mm. 109–16, sharing its triadic motivic base, alternation of balancing tonic and dominant subphrases (only two measures each in the closing section), and circular repetition. Since this closing material returns in the recapitulation (m. 512ff.), all but one of the four principal sections end with related material, the last two linked by tonic key.

There are, in addition, three "expansive" segments not yet discussed, whose recurrences throughout the movement create important long-range associations. Their local function is essentially "preparatory," rather than thematic; they lead either to an important thematic entrance or to a climactic cadence.

Two of the three form closely related dominant prolongations. The first, the prolongation from the first group beginning at m. 23, has been briefly discussed. In addition to its tonal function, it has three essential features: motivic echoes of the principal motive (the rising arpeggiated figures in the first violin, mm. 28–32), syncopation, and a final registral expansion outward in both directions. The second appears at m. 99, as part of the second group, prolonging V of B-flat and leading to the *tutti* material that announces the closing section at m. 109. Like the first, it contains syncopation (mm. 99–101) and expands in register, moving outward in both directions in its final two measures. (As part of the second group, however, it does not refer to the principal motive.)

Although this second segment recurs only once, in the essentially literal, transposed return of the second group in the recapitulation, the first one has a more active life, reappearing in varied form at several points throughout the movement. It occurs twice in the development, both times extended and elaborated: at mm. 248–79, where it begins off the dominant but leads to the dominant prolongation of E that precedes the first appearance of the "new" theme; and at mm. 338–66, where it initiates the long dominant prolongation preceding the recapitulation. In both instances the final registral expansion is omitted, replaced by an abrupt drop in energy with the arrival of the dominant prolongation (mm. 280 and 366 respectively).

This music does not return in the recapitulation (as we have seen), but is replaced by the related yet distinct material at mm. 424–29.[16] Its replacement, part of the extensive first-group transformations, plus its failure to reach fruition in its development-section appearances, takes on added significance in the coda. There the passage is brought back at m. 603 to prepare the opening of the final thematic statement. Since the latter begins at a low level of intensity, however, once again the segment fails to reach full expansion. After increasing in loudness to m. 621, it loses dynamic power, while the syncopated motive dissolves into a succession of accompanimental octaves. This produces a smooth link to the opening of the final thematic section (aided by the overlapping eighth-note figuration, introduced near the beginning of the coda but heard only intermittently to this point). The final thematic segment thus articulates the only soft opening in the movement that does not coincide with an abrupt drop in energy, but only a gradual one.

This preparatory segment has one additional appearance: at the very end of the coda, mm. 685–88, that is, *after* the circular repetitions of the final thematic thrust. There it leads triumphantly and uncontested to the closing tonic of the movement, the first time it has managed to reach full fruition since its first appearance in the exposition. The final resolution thus provides a far-ranging, as well as immediate, release.

Before considering the third of these preparatory segments, we must return to the final thematic statement and consider its contribution to the closing cadence. Its circular repetitions are not themselves, in fact, cadential at all (despite Rosen's remark about repeating V–I cadences), since they are designed to return to the tonic only in generating a repetition. That is, they are essentially open-ended, so that closure can be attained only by breaking the cycle.[17] This finally happens at m. 663, when the fourth eight-measure unit gives way to an extended cadential passage (mm. 663–73), signaled by the cessation of the accompanimental figure, and during which the first violin pushes up again to a-flat^3 (m. 668), matching the registral extreme of the first-group climax in the recapitulation, before descending to the tonic at m. 673.

Beethoven does not end with this cadence either. There is a final push toward the still more emphatic, confirming close at mm. 689–91, with which the movement actually closes. The first arrival (m. 673) brings another overlapping point associated with a sudden drop in tension, joined with the return of the not-yet-discussed third "preparatory" segment (mm. 673–80). Like the two previously considered, this one spans large portions of the movement and shares their registrally expansive, harmonically static quality. Unlike those, however, it does not prolong a dominant but a tonic, from which it eventually departs. It has appeared twice previously, each time initiating a passage leading to the second theme (mm. 57–65 in the exposition, mm. 460–68 in the recapitulation). As in the coda, these are associated with major points of structural arrival (i.e., the first cadence on the dominant in the exposition, the corresponding tonic return in the recapitulation), coupled with a sudden drop of energy.

The passage is designed gradually to restore the suddenly reduced energy level, and in a way with which we are now familiar: dynamic *crescendo*, accumulation of instruments, accelerating rhythm, registral expansion outward. In the exposition and recapitulation, this culminates with a deflection toward III of the prevailing key (m. 65 and m.

468), bringing about a brief developmental diversion (mm. 65–83 and 468–86) before the cadence preceding the entrance of the second theme. Unlike the other two expansive segments, then, this one does not lead immediately to a climactic cadence, but to a climactic dissonance, associated with the diminished VII⁷ of III chords at mm. 65 and 468.

When the passage recurs at the end of the coda (again on the tonic), it is changed in only one respect: it leads to the dominant (m. 681) instead of to the diminished VII⁷ of III. Once attained, the dominant expands upward (mm. 681–84), yet again to a-flat³ in the first violin, in a syncopated, arpeggiated top-voice motion clearly derived from the upward arpeggiations of the music from m. 23 (compare especially the first violin line, mm. 28–30 and 681–84), a relationship that is immediately confirmed by the more literal final recurrence discussed above of the material from m. 23 (mm. 685–88). The latter, now shorn of all complications (except syncopations) and with its expansive quality concentrated entirely in the first violin's rising motivic argeggiations, echoes the previous arpeggiation (cf. mm. 681–84 and 685–88), the two joining together to supply a balancing eight-measure V–I conclusion for the eight-measure I–V passage beginning at m. 673. The concluding cadence thus supplies an extraordinary moment of synthesis and culmination: the material from m. 57, finally dominant directed, receives a "long-range resolution,"[18] and, directly linked with the m. 23 segment, joins material from both thematic groups in a final, emphatic gesture.

The function of the repeating eight-measure thematic units is thus not cadential but developmental; they supply the dynamic thrust that builds to the *tutti* of the cadential progression proper (mm. 663–73). That cadence, subverted by the sudden dynamic drop at m. 673 (the last of so many in the movement), triggers a final, confirming cadential expansion that provides the formal synthesis and long-range resolution just discussed. Only then is "resolution" achieved.

***

Wagner's metaphorical interpretation of the Beethoven symphonic movement as a single melody, my point of departure, seems remarkably apt when read in light of the formal attributes of the "Eroica." The original motivic idea, in itself incomplete and fragmentary, returns in different guises throughout, delineating a gradually unfolding shape that eventually encompasses the whole. The other formal segments—notably the new theme in the development section and the various expanding preparatory segments—all share in determining the specific course of this unfolding.

But perhaps the most telling feature with regard to Wagner's meta-phor is that the various processes initiated at or near the opening reach conclusion only at the end. This is most evident in the principal motive itself, whose final shape emerges only in its last appear-ance near the end of the coda, but also in such long-range connections as the resolution of the passage from m. 57 in the final measures of the symphony, and in the synthesis of this music with the analogously expanding passage from the second group.

In his slightly earlier essay on Liszt's symphonic poems, Wagner, writing in a more polemical vein in support of Liszt against the detrac-tors of program music, criticizes Beethoven for remaining too closely tied to the dance basis of symphonic music. Beethoven clings to *Wechsel* (change)—to contrast and repetition—at the expense of *Entwicklung* (development)—the continuous unfolding of a dramatic idea. Wagner then offers his famous criticism of the *Leonore* Overture No. 3 for ob-serving the convention of recapitulation:

> Whoever has eyes to see will recognize precisely in this great overture how detrimental it was for the master to retain the traditional form. For can anyone capable of un-derstanding such a work not admit that I am right in iden-tifying its weakness as the repetition of the first part follow-ing the middle section, which distorts the idea of the work to the point of incomprehensibility; and all the more since in all other parts, and especially at the end, the dramatic development can be recognized as the master's sole deter-minant? Whoever is sufficiently unbiased and has the sense to realize this will have to admit that it could only have been avoided by completely giving up the recapitulation and thus also the overture form—the original, embryonic, symphonic dance form—and that from this would have come the point of departure for the construction of a new form.[19]

Here Wagner's bias, governed as much by his own compositional inclinations as by Liszt's, gets the better of his judgment. Yet his view of the movement as tending toward (even when not achiev-ing) uninterrupted development—in aesthetic terms, as tending toward organicism—tells us something essential about this mu-sic, above all, its reflection of one of the major philosophical currents of the time. Although Beethoven has indeed retained eighteenth-century sonata-form conventions, he has reshaped them fundamentally under the pressures of a more consistently develop-mental conception. Characterized elsewhere by Wagner as "this most significant composition . . . with which the composer first set out fully in his own individual direction,"[20] the "Eroica" is to that extent already the "music of the future."

Notes

1. Richard Wagner, "Zukunftsmusik," *Gesammelte Schriften und Dichtungen* (Leipzig, 1887–88), 7:127.

2. Joseph Kerman, "Theme and Variations," *New York Review of Books*, 23 October 1980, 52.

3. Joseph Kerman, "Notes on Beethoven's Codas," in Alan Tyson, ed., *Beethoven Studies 3* (Cambridge, 1982), 141–59.

4. Charles Rosen, *Sonata Forms*, rev. ed. (New York, 1988), 297–352.

5. Ibid., 355.

6. Kerman, "Theme and Variations," 52.

7. Rosen, *Sonata Forms*, 331.

8. Kerman, "Notes on Beethoven's Codas," 150.

9. Rosen, *The Classical Style: Haydn, Mozart, Beethoven* (New York, 1971), 68; Kerman "Notes on Beethoven's Codas," 150.

10. Among others by Rosen himself, in *The Classical Style*, 350; see also Edward T. Cone, *Musical Form and Musical Performance* (New York, 1968), 23.

11. Rosen, *Sonata Forms*, 293.

12. Kerman, "Notes on Beethoven's Codas," 149.

13. Ibid., 152.

14. Rosen, *The Classical Style*, 393. See also Heinrich Schenker, "Beethovens Dritte Sinfonie zum erstenmal in ihrem wahren Inhalt dargestellt," *Das Meisterwerk in der Musik*, vol. 3 (Munich, 1930), 50.

15. In this instance, then, the more developmental circular version of the theme "normalizes" the more placid one heard earlier.

16. Though the form that the principal motive assumes here is derived from the second appearance of this material in the development section, m. 338ff., the passage is missing one essential component: the rising, syncopated arpeggiation figure featured prominently in all previous appearances.

17. There is thus no cadential overlap here—that is, a cadence coinciding with a new beginning. The second four-measure phrase is not designed, and is therefore unable, to lead to a strong conclusion, as is apparent if one imagines the effect of ending after one of the circular repeats. Again, the role of the eight-measure units is expansive, not contractive.

18. This phrase is borrowed from Lewis Lockwood, "*Eroica* Perspectives: Strategy and Design in the First Movement," in Tyson, *Beethoven Studies 3*, 105. Lockwood, recognizing the critical formal significance of the various nonthematic segments, points out that the three statements of material first heard at m. 57 appear in essentially final form in Beethoven's earliest continuity drafts, suggesting that their "role in the larger strategy may have emerged at a relatively early stage of planning" (104).

19. Wagner, "Über Franz Liszt's symphonische Dichtungen," *Gesammelte Schriften* 5:190.

20. Wagner, "Beethovens heroische Symphonie," ibid., 186.

THIRTEEN

Symmetry and Symmetrical Inversion in Turn-of-the-Century Theory and Practice

DAVID W. BERNSTEIN

> Symmetry is one of the simplest principles: to the right of the axis there is the same thing (in equal distances, in equal amounts, etc.) as to the left of the axis. Inversion and the principle of mirror and retrograde are basically the same. Their advantage, in addition to easier comprehensibilty, is that they offer a new *Gestalt* that in reality has the same inner relationships, only in inverted order or direction.[1]

The above quotation states a principal assumption of Schoenberg's twelve-tone system: a given twelve-tone row and its inversion, retrograde, and retrograde inversion are equivalent representations of the same musical idea. Similar concerns are echoed elsewhere in Schoenberg's theoretical writings. For example, in a lecture treating the theoretical basis of his twelve-tone system, Schoenberg described a concept that he termed "absolute musical space."[2] This notion disavows both absolute upwards and downwards as well as backwards and forwards in musical space. In other words, our musical intellect, according to Schoenberg, recognizes an equivalence between a succession of tones and its reversed or inverted order. When applied to the twelve-tone system, this equivalence may be shown by an example (ex. 13.1) taken from Schoenberg's essay "Composition with Twelve Tones."[3] The relationship between the basic set and its three "mirror" forms is once again depicted as symmetrical, based on a correspondence of notes about a vertical and horizontal axis.

Discussions of symmetry are not new to the literature concerned with twentieth-century music. Schoenberg's own preoccupation with symmetry extended far beyond the relationship between the basic set and its three forms and was in fact an essential structural element in his tonal and nontonal music.[4] Symmetry has likewise been crucial in the music of other composers. For example, Webern's predilection for

Example 13.1

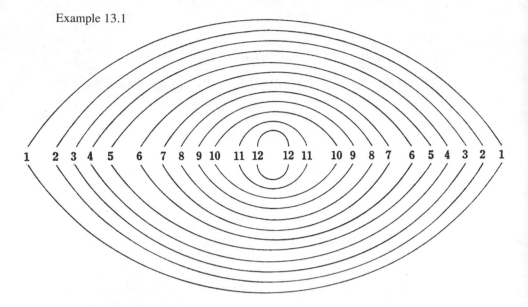

the palindrome is only symptomatic of his employment of symmetrical structure throughout the fabric of his music.[5] Moreover, symmetry is a prominent stylistic feature in the music of Berg, Bartók, and Stravinsky.[6] In more recent times both Milton Babbitt's and George Perle's extensions of Schoenberg's twelve-tone system rely upon structural symmetries.[7]

Symmetry and the various compositional operations associated with it have provided many twentieth-century composers with a means of constructing coherent pitch and interval relationships in the absence of diatonic tonality. The historical basis for this stylistic development in part lies in the tonal music of the nineteenth and early twentieth centuries. Recently, several analytical studies have illustrated that symmetry based upon the partitioning of the octave into equal segments is present in the music of Beethoven, Schubert, Chopin, Wagner, Liszt, and Mahler.[8] However, our historical understanding of this development, viewed only in these terms, is incomplete. In this essay I will demonstrate that the symmetries so often present in both twentieth-century theory and practice also evolved from several important currents in the intellectual history and, in particular, the music theory of the late nineteenth and early twentieth centuries.

Symmetry has been a preoccupation of many thinkers and artists quite apart from twentieth-century composers and music theorists. Interest in symmetry can be traced back to the philosophy, mathematics, and aesthetics of the ancient Greeks. During the nineteenth and early twentieth centuries, however, the theory of symmetry took its modern scientific form, appearing throughout diverse scientific disciplines.[9] It became manifest in areas such as biology, group theory, physics, and crystallography. Ernst Haeckel's studies of symmetries in the animal and plant kingdoms,[10] the investigations of Felix Klein and Sophus Lie concerning symmetrical structure and its relationship to group theory,[11] Pierre Curie's formulation of a principle of symmetry in physics,[12] and E.S. Federov's theories concerning symmetry and its application to crystallography[13] are a few noteworthy examples. In fact, it has been suggested that of all the scientific innovations that arose during the nineteenth century the concept of symmetry was to have the most profound impact upon twentieth-century science.[14]

No discussion of symmetry in nineteenth-century science would be complete without at least a brief mention of Goethe's scientific writings.[15] An important notion applied throughout these works is his concept of "polarity." Goethe found polar relationships throughout a wide variety of natural phenomena. Polarities of light and dark played a critical role in his *Farbenlehre*. Similarly, the diastolic and systolic beating of the heart, the contraction and expansion of leaf forms, acidification and deacidification and magnetism, were for Goethe examples of a duality of opposites present throughout nature.[16] Of particular interest to the present study is Goethe's discussion of polarity in music:

> Major and minor as the polarity in the theory of tone. The basic principle of both: the major key created by climbing, by an acceleration upward, by an upward extension of all intervals; the minor key by falling, by an acceleration downward. (The minor scale extended upwards would have to become a major scale.)
> Development of this contrast as the basis for all music.[17]

Described in this passage is the symmetrical relationship between major and minor—an idea that, as we shall see below, took root in the theoretical writings of Moritz Hauptmann[18] and was developed by subsequent generations of German theorists in the late nineteenth and early twentieth centuries.

The importance of symmetry to nineteenth-century scientists was not without parallels in the discipline of music theory. Nineteenth-century theorists sought symmetrical structure in all sorts of musical phenomena. This parallelism between music theory and science was all but inevitable during a period in which the positivistic philosophy of Ernst Haeckel, Wilhelm Wundt, Ernst Mach, and others was a dominating force. Positivism recognized the validity of scientific knowledge only, rejecting all things not demonstrable by empirical means. The emphasis placed by positivistic philosophy on a rational, nonchaotic, and scientifically justified *Weltanschauung* inspired music theorists as well as scientists in their search for symmetries, since the logical consistency of such phenomena was easily reconcilable with the positivistic world view.

German music theorists at the turn of the twentieth century were obsessed with symmetrical structure. Their interest in symmetry may be traced back to the development of an important movement in German harmonic theory that took place during the second half of the nineteenth century—namely, harmonic dualism. The bilateral symmetry, manifest in the symmetrical relationship between the major and minor triads, was a buttress of dualistic harmonic theory. Hugo Riemann, perhaps dualism's most fervent proponent, explained that the major and minor triads are symmetrically related, the major consisting of a perfect fifth and a major third above the fundamental and the minor triad formed by the same intervals below. As can be seen in example 13.2, this model is bilaterally symmetrical; the major chord is a mirror image of the minor and vice versa.

Example 13.2

Throughout most of his career, Riemann sought an acoustical foundation for his theory in the undertone series.[19] A given complex musical tone, for Riemann, engendered both an overtone and a symmetrically related undertone series. The symmetry inherent in the dualistic model of the *Klang* not only supplied an "acoustical" foundation for the symmetrical relationship between major and minor, but also served as a basis for Riemann's theory of tonal function, harmonic progression, and chordal generation, and for his definition of consonance and dissonance. Riemann's theory of tonal function reduces the multiplicity of chordal relations to three primary *Klänge*: Tonic (T), Dominant (D), and Subdominant (S). This group of relationships, according to Riemann, has an acoustical explanation, since the fundamental of a given *Klang* (apart from those overtones and undertones that are its octave equivalent) is most closely related to its overtone and undertone a twelfth above and below respectively. Similarly, Riemann's fascination with symmetrical structure is apparent in his approach to harmonic progression. Each unit of harmonic motion is explained according to his dualistic model of the *Klang*. For example, a progression from the tonic triad in major to the minor subdominant triad—an instance of what Riemann called a "turn of harmony" (*Wechselwirkung*)—inverts the tonic triad. The root of the tonic becomes the fifth or what Riemann termed the prime of the minor subdominant, below which a major third and perfect fifth are generated.

According to Riemann, dualism was introduced into nineteenth-century music theory by Moritz Hauptmann. In his *Die Natur der Harmonik und Metrik* (1853), Hauptmann provided a dialectical explanation for the major triad. He proposed the model given here as example 13.3a, in which the roman numerals I, II, and III represent unity, duality, and the union of duality and unity, respectively. The major triad consists of the union in the major third of the dialectically opposed root and fifth.

Example 13.3

	a.	C	E	G		b.	F	A♭	C
		I	III	II			II	III	I

Hauptmann derived the minor triad logically as an antithesis or negation of the major. As can be seen by referring to example 13.3b, the minor *Klang* consists of the union in the minor third of the dialectically opposed fifth and root. Thus, in a certain sense, the major and minor triads in Hauptmann's theory are inversionally related, since the dialectical representation of the one is a "mirror image" of the other. This led Riemann to consider Hauptmann a dualist whose theory was grounded in a logical rather than an acoustical basis.

Several scholars have noted that Riemann's claim may in fact be based upon a misrepresentation of Hauptmann's system.[20] This view is substantiated by several passages in Hauptmann's own writings in which he denied that the minor triad is actually perceived from the "top" down.[21] In considering the minor triad as the logical antithesis of the major harmony, Hauptmann supplied this additional explanation for the minor triad:

> The determinations of the intervals of the triad have been taken hitherto as starting from a positive unity, a Root, to which the Fifth and Third are referred. They may also be thought of in an opposite sense. If the first may be expressed by saying that a note has a Fifth and Third, then the opposite meaning will lie in a note being a Fifth and Third.[22]

In these terms, the fifth of an F-minor triad, for example, is both the third of A-flat and the fifth of F—a derivation that contradicts the dualistic model of the *Klang* wherein the minor chord is generated from the fifth down and not upwards from its root and third. In fact, Hauptmann's double foundation for the minor triad later became the basis for harmonic monism—a movement in late nineteenth-century German harmonic theory that directly challenged the dualism of Riemann and his followers. Nevertheless, deciding whether or not Hauptmann was a dualist cannot alter the fact that his theory influenced the development of harmonic dualism in the latter half of the nineteenth century.

Riemann traced the evolution of harmonic dualism from Hauptmann to Arthur von Oettingen. In fact, Oettingen's earliest treatise, *Harmoniesystem in dualer Entwickelung* (1866), may very well have been a primary influence shaping Riemann's dualistic theory. Moreover, Oettingen's two lesser-known treatises, *Das duale Harmoniesystem* and *Die Grundlage der Musikwissenschaft und das duale Reininstrument*, both of which appeared after 1900, are perhaps the most systematic expression of dualistic theory ever written.

Oettingen, like Hauptmann before him, advocated a system of tuning based upon pure fifths and pure major thirds. He arranged these intervals into a table reproduced here as example 13.4.[23] Series of pure fifths appear on horizontal axes, pure thirds on vertical axes. The difference of a syntonic comma (81:80 or approximately 22 cents), such as that between an F-sharp generated by projecting four moves of pure fifths from D and an F-sharp a pure major third above D, is designated by a horizontal line. A note with a horizontal line above is a comma lower than the same note without a line. A line drawn below a given note indicates that the note is a comma higher than the same note without a line. It is apparent that his system is not merely symmetrical, but symmetrical around D, the axis of inversion of a diatonic system

Example 13.4

Buchstaben-Tonschrift.

−8	−7	−6	−5	−4	−3	−2	−1	0	1+	2+	3+	4+	5+	6+	7+	8+	
d̄	ā	ē	h̄	f̄is	c̄is	ḡis	d̄is	āis	ēis	h̄is	f̄isis	c̄isis	ḡisis	d̄isis	āisis	ēisis	+ II
b̄	f̄	c̄	ḡ	d̄	ā	ē	h̄	f̄is	c̄is	ḡis	d̄is	āis	ēis	h̄is	f̄isis	c̄isis	+ I
ges	des	as	es	b	f	c	g	d	a	e	h	fis	cis	gis	dis	ais	0
eses	bb	fes	ces	ges	des	as	es	b̲	f̲	c̲	g̲	d̲	a̲	e̲	h̲	fi̲s	− I
ceses	geses	deses	asas	eses	bb	fes	ces	ges	des	as	es	b̲	f̲	c̲	g̲	d̲	− II

Example 13.5

lacking both sharps and flats. Oettingen attempted to demonstrate the practical application of his tuning system by several analyses of works, including compositions by C.P.E. Bach, Mozart, Haydn, Liszt, Wagner, and Reger.[24] He also constructed a keyboard instrument with fifty-three notes to the octave according to his tuning system.[25]

Oettingen's theory of harmony rests on the capacity of the elements of a *Klang* to have either a common fundamental or a common overtone. He named these two attributes "tonicity" and "phonicity."[26] The major triad is "tonic," since its constituents have a common fundamental, while the minor triad is "phonic," since its members all possess a common overtone. As an example of the latter, in a C-minor triad G is an overtone of C, E-flat, and G. Example 13.5 illustrates Oettingen's model of the *Klang*, which anticipated Riemann's and is also symmetrical.

The symmetry inherent in Oettingen's representation of the *Klang* is even more pervasive than in Riemann's. For Oettingen, each *Klang* has both a tonic fundamental and a phonic overtone. Example 13.6 illustrates this principle with respect to both a D–major and a G-minor triad—that is, tonic and phonic *Klänge* based on D. (Examples 13.6 and 13.7 should both be read in the bass clef. The curious notation of flats and sharps is indicative of Oettingen's pure tuning.) The black notes in the upper and lower portions of example 13.6 represent segments of the undertone and overtone series generated by each chord tone. The major *Klang* on D has a tonic fundamental D because, as can be seen by referring to the lower left of example 13.6, it is the closest common undertone. Similarly, as shown in the upper right of example 13.6, the phonic overtone of the D-major triad is C-sharp since it is the closest common overtone of D, F-sharp, and A. The situation for the minor *Klang* is the exact opposite. The phonic overtone D appears in the upper left, the tonic fundamental, E-flat, in the lower right. Oettingen explained that the G-minor *Klang* is phonically consonant and tonically dissonant because its tonic fundamental E-flat is not a member of the G-minor triad. Conversely, the D-major *Klang* is tonically consonant and phonically dissonant since its phonic overtone, C-sharp, is not a chord tone of the D-major triad.

Oettingen also examined the tonicity and phonicity of intervallic consonance. The phonic overtones and tonic fundamentals of the intervals contained within a D-major *Klang* are illustrated in example 13.7. The tonic fundamentals appear on the lower staff, the phonic overtones on the upper staff. Oettingen observed that in each case the phonic overtone and tonic fundamental are exactly the same distance from the generating interval. For example, the fifth D–A engenders a phonic overtone an octave above the A and a tonic fundamental an

Example 13.6

Phonische Kon-
sonanz von $d°$

Phonische Dis-
kordanz von $d+$

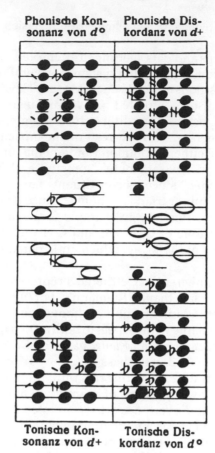

Tonische Kon-
sonanz von $d+$

Tonische Dis-
kordanz von $d°$

Example 13.7

Konsonanz-Amphibolie der Intervalle von $d°$:

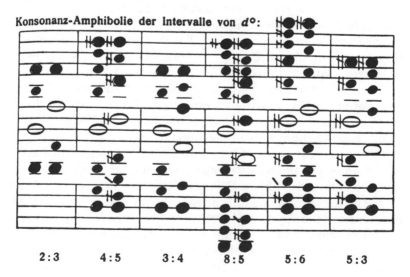

2 : 3   4 : 5   3 : 4   8 : 5   5 : 6   5 : 3

octave below the D. Oettingen called this symmetrical relationship "amphibolic consonance" (*Amphibolie*),[27] noting that this twofold equivalence is characteristic of music in two voices. As may be seen by referring once again to example 13.6, the phonic overtone and tonic fundamental of a triad are not symmetrically located. Oettingen claimed, therefore, that triads entail a degree of symmetrical imbalance and thus are less consonant than intervals. He explained that this phenomenon provided a theoretical justification for the tendency in older music to conclude a composition on an open fifth.[28]

Oettingen's ideas with respect to symmetry were not limited to his representation of the *Klang*. His notions of "tonicity" and "phonicity" became what he called a "dual" basis for the definition of consonance, chord construction, and progression.

> The inner duality or "twofoldedness" of harmony also permits an outer, dual, i.e., a twofold-opposite form of development of the harmonic system that makes itself known in a symmetrical construction of all tone structures and chord progressions.[29]

Oettingen stated that in a given system based on C, the fifths above and below, that is, F and G, are the most closely related to C. However, if these notes represent *Klänge*, they are ambiguous, since each may be considered as either a fundamental or a "phonic" overtone. Oettingen termed these two possibilities "tonality" (*Tonalität*) and "phonality" (*Phonalität*). As seen in example 13.8a, in tonality F, C, and G are fundamentals, in phonality the same notes are "phonic" overtones. (The "+" and "o" stand for tonic and phonic *Klänge* respectively.) As might be expected, the two models are symmetrically related.

Example 13.8

a. F–a–c C–e–g G–b–d
or
F+–C+–G+
tonality

b♭–d♭–F f–a♭–C c–e♭–G
or
F°–C°–G°
phonality

b. C+: C, D, E, D, F, G, A, B, C
C°: C, D♭, E♭, F, G, A♭, B♭, C

Tonality and phonality provided Oettingen with a symmetrical derivation for the major and minor scales. As illustrated in example 13.8b, the major scale when inverted yields the Phrygian mode. Oet tingen observed that although his Phrygian version of minor had been in use during the past and was also employed in non-Western music, it was essentially neglected by European composers.[30] He claimed, however, that a return to phonality was in progress. To support his contention, Oettingen cited an excerpt from Beethoven's *Egmont* Overture (ex. 13.9a). According to Oettingen, the overture proceeds from F minor to C minor. Oettingen considered C minor to be a phonality based on G (ex. 13.9b). He asserted that Beethoven was intuitively aware of this derivation, since the composer emphasized the G–A-flat in the basses, cellos, and violas.[31] Oettingen pointed out that even with the appearance of the dominant seventh chord on G in mm. 4–7, the G–A-flat is still retained by the violas.

Example 13.9

a.

b.　　　　G⁰　　G, A♭, B♭, C, D, E♭, F, G

Oettingen also examined symmetrically equivalent cadential progressions (exx. 13.10 and 13.11).[32] He noted that the phonic overtone must always be in the upper voice in the last chord in order to avoid an incomplete-sounding progression such as that resulting from the six-four chord at the end of example 13.11b.[33] The progressions in examples 13.10 and 13.11 are mirror images of each other inverted around D—the axis of symmetry for the "white note" diatonic system. Furthermore, Oettingen presented these examples in the bass clef because the notes are also visually symmetrical around D.

Despite its popularity, harmonic dualism did not go uncriticized. A major stumbling block was that the symmetrical relationships generated by the system looked fine on paper but were not audible. This flaw was pinpointed by an early twentieth-century German theorist,

Example 13.10

in ton. -e :

in phon. -$\bar{e}$:

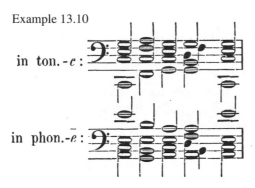

Example 13.11

a.

b.

Example 13.12

Georg Capellen.[34] Capellen wrote a short monograph[35] and an article[36] both criticizing Riemann's theory. He explained that the ear

> rejects the inversion that is noticeable by the eye, since it hears all the tones in a simultaneity from the bottom up (in terms of the fundamental) according to the law of gravity, which is also valid in music. *The external difference in direction entails a more profound difference in type.*[37]

This view formed the basis for Capellen's repudiation of harmonic dualism. The symmetrical relationship between the major and minor *Klänge* is not aurally perceptible and is therefore invalid.

The same idea had been expressed some years earlier by the scientist and philosopher Ernst Mach. Mach's empiricism was so rigorous that he adamantly denied the existence of atoms for the simple reason that they cannot be perceived by the naked eye. It is thus not surprising that he was also critical of dualistic harmonic theory on perceptual grounds. In a short article[38] and in a book entitled *Beiträge zur Analyse der Empfindungen*,[39] which was extremely popular in Vienna at the turn of the twentieth century,[40] Mach explained that bilateral symmetry was perceptible visually, but in many cases not aurally. Mach, whose discussion of symmetry was cited by the German psychologist Carl Stumpf,[41] directed his criticisms against Oettingen. He maintained that the ear notices little or nothing of the symmetrical relationships between the harmonies given here as example 13.12 because

> a reversal of musical sounds conditions no repetition of sensations. If we had an ear for height and an ear for depth, just as we have an eye for right and an eye for left, we should also find that symmetrical sound structures existed for our auditory organs.[42]

Mach's conclusions must sound a bit severe, especially to those engaged in the analysis of nontonal music, where inversional equivalence like that illustrated in example 13.12 is often an important assumption. Both Mach's and Capellen's critiques, however, were directed toward the irreconcilable differences between the symmetries engendered by harmonic dualism and a musical practice based upon tonal syntax. For example, Capellen cited Riemann's representation of the I–IV–V–I progression in major and its symmetrically equivalent version in minor (ex. 13.13a). Capellen could not accept the contention that these progressions are equivalent since, considered in terms of root progression (i.e., from the bass up), they are dissimilar.

Capellen accepted Riemann's expansion of the same cadential progression in major by adding a major sixth and minor seventh to the subdominant and dominant, respectively—Riemann's so-called "characteristic dissonances." However, he criticized Riemann's claim that there is a symmetrically equivalent progression in minor. Example 13.13b illustrates the major and minor versions of the progression. In minor, the addition of the dissonant tones is reversed: the dominant is expanded by the addition of a sixth below, the subdominant by a seventh below. Although the two progressions are inversionally equivalent, they are not, in Capellen's view, functionally analogous. Capellen concluded that Riemann's obsession with symmetry had led him to produce harmonic progressions in the minor mode that were incommensurate with actual musical practice.

Example 13.13

Despite his opposition to harmonic dualism, Capellen's own theory of harmony incorporated symmetrical relations. Capellen's theory began with what he considered an acoustically validated major ninth chord. His model of tonality was based on the intervals of this *Naturklang*: third, fifth, seventh, and ninth. Reducing the latter two intervals to major seconds via octave transposition, Capellen incorporated these intervals into a symmetrical model that is given here as example 13.14b. Relationships of a major second are located on the vertical axis. The diagonal lines mark out fifth relations. Finally, major third relations occur on successive apexes on the left and right.

In labeling the components of his model, Capellen adopted a somewhat bizarre notational system in reaction against the scale-degree notation utilized by Simon Sechter and his followers and against the symbols of Riemannian function theory (ex. 13.14a). Accordingly, the tonic, dominant, and subdominant became *Mittel-* (M), *Rechts-* (R), and *Linksklänge* (L). *Ober-* (O) and *Unterklang* (U) signify relations of a

Example 13.14

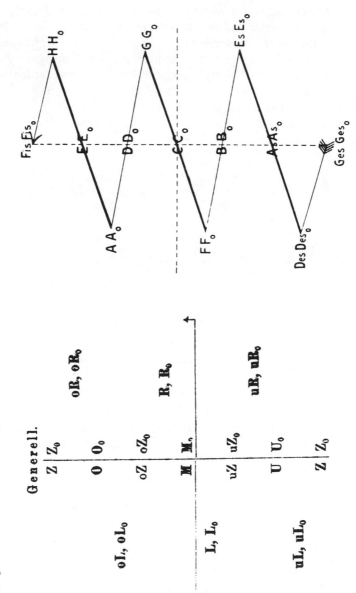

major third above and below the *Mittelklang* respectively. *Ober-Rechts-* (oR) and *unter-Rechtsklänge* (uR) are a major third above and below the dominant. Similarly, *ober-Links-* (oL) and *unter-Linksklänge* (uL) are a major third above and below the subdominant. *Zwischenklänge* (Z) are a tritone above and below the *Mittelklang*. Finally, *ober-Zwischen-* (oZ) and *unter-Zwischenklänge* (uZ) are a major second above and below the *Mittelklang*.[43] A less idiosyncratic letter notation is given in example 13.14b. Following a notational convention initiated by Oettingen, minor triads are indicated by a subscript "o".

Capellen admitted that the tonic triad and the chords a fifth below and above combine to form the most basic expression of a key. However, his theory of harmony generated the entire chromatic from a single *Naturklang* and did not require the use of these chords to articulate a coherent tonality. The musical examples found in his *Fortschrittliche Harmonie- und Melodielehre* (1908) indicate that he believed symmetry could help to establish tonal coherence. For instance, example 13.15 shows a symmetrical progression taken from this work based on the partitioning of the octave into major thirds.

Example 13.15

Capellen claimed to have discovered a compositional manifestation of symmetry in the opening two phrases of the *Tristan* Prelude. Example 13.16 illustrates his analysis of this passage.[44] We should note here that Capellen, like many of his contemporaries, did not view the G-sharp in m. 2 as a chord tone and thus labeled

Example 13.16   Wagner, *Tristan und Isolde*

the *Tristan* chord as a dominant seventh chord with a lowered fifth—
B/D-sharp/F-natural/A.[45] He claimed that his notational system
clearly represented the harmonic sequence found in the passage. In
example 13.16 both the appropriate roman numerals and Capellen's
symbols are given. (In the latter a dot indicates a lowered chord tone.)
The sequence is not strict because U (or VI) becomes O (or III). However, since U and O are symmetrically located with respect to the tonic
(or *Mittelklang*)—that is, the former root is a major third below its tonic
and the latter a major third above—this change manifests inversional
properties in the passage. Thus Capellen's claims, although lacking
the analytical rigor required by theorists today, are certainly of historical interest, especially in view of the many more recent discussions
concerning symmetry in the *Tristan* Prelude.[46]

An additional example of the importance of symmetry to Capellen's
harmonic theory is manifest in what he termed the reciprocal relationship between the fundamental of a chord and the resultant combination tone produced by its overtones. Capellen demonstrated that by
silently depressing a low C at the piano and briefly striking a C-major
triad above, the low C as well as the C-major chord would sound. He
asserted that the low C vibrates because it is a combination tone produced by the C-major triad. The C-major triad is in turn a result of the
combination tone because the latter contains this chord among its
overtones. Today, combination tones are generally thought of as subjective phenomena, the result of a nonlinear distortion in our hearing
mechanism. Capellen's combination tone is produced by the piano
and is an actual sound stimulus that creates sympathetic vibrations at
the pitch of undamped low C. His understanding of this phenomenon
was probably taken from Helmholtz, who also considered cases in
which combination tones are not generated solely within the ear.[47] The
existence of a combination tone not only enabled Capellen to give
acoustical justification to fundamental notes not present on the musical surface but also illustrated the presence of symmetry in the structure of the *Klang* without recourse to harmonic dualism and its spuri-
ous undertone theory.

Capellen's fascination with symmetrical relationships, such as those
he found in the *Tristan* Prelude, as well as the essential role that symmetry played within his theory of harmony in general, may seem to
contradict his rejection of the various symmetrical relationships that
underlie dualistic harmonic theory. Capellen's conception of tonality,
like that of Riemann, clearly places him within the tradition of German function theory. Tonality, in these terms, is expressed by root
relationships around a given tonal center. The logic of a given progression is governed by the tonal function of its constituent harmonies

or, in other words, how the root of each chord in the progression relates to the tonic. For Capellen, the root of a chord invariably determined the chord's constituent tones from the bottom up, in accordance with the natural model presented by the overtone series. This view permitted a conception of tonality, not unlike Riemann's, in which the tonic is a central axis about which the remaining harmonic functions are symmetrically disposed. It did not allow, however, for such inversional equivalence as that between the major and minor triads, since symmetries of this type contradict what Capellen called the "musical law of gravity," a premise basic to all tonal music. Indeed, the symmetries recognized by Riemann seem more appropriate for nontonal music—music in which there is no *a priori* assumption of functional relations based upon chordal roots. Thus Capellen's refutation of harmonic dualism suggests that he understood how an emphasis on symmetrical structure could lead to the decline of the tonal system—a historical process that ironically was to culminate only a few years after the publication of his writings criticizing Riemann.

As well as being a focus of theoretical speculation, symmetry also provided turn-of-the-century theorists with a means of expanding compositional technique. This practical branch of theory was concerned with the procedure of symmetrical inversion, a term coined by Bernhard Ziehn[48] and also discussed by Capellen[49] and Hermann Schröder.[50]

Ziehn claimed to have arrived at symmetrical inversion from a study of contrapuntal practice from the Renaissance to the present.[51] According to Ziehn, symmetrical inversion was derived from an older contrapuntal technique called *contrarium reversum*, which consisted of the melodic and contrapuntal inversion of one or more voices. Example 13.17 illustrates the technique in an exercise taken from Zarlino's *Le istitutioni harmoniche* (1558).[52] The contrapuntal lines in this example are strict melodic inversions of each other. Moreover, they are both inversionally symmetrical around a D axis. The special status of the note D as an axis of inversion was known as early as the Renaissance and continued to provide a basis for contrapuntal exercises in strict melodic inversion during the seventeenth, eighteenth, and nineteenth centuries.[53] Georg Capellen attributed the nineteenth-century origins of this idea to Simon Sechter. In his *Die Grundsätze der musikalischen Komposition* (1853–54), Sechter described a technique that he termed *doppelten Kontrapunkt in der melodischen Gegenbewegung*. This entailed contrapuntal and strict melodic inversion in two, three, or four voices (ex. 13.18a).[54] As may be seen in example 13.18b, he demonstrated that *melodische Gegenbewegung* converging into a D axis produces strict inversion.[55]

394

Example 13.17

Example 13.18

Sechter's method is the same as that which Ziehn termed symmetrical inversion. Ziehn explained that due to tonal (and in other cases modal) exigencies *contrarium reversum* did not always require strict melodic inversion. For instance, example 13.19 is taken from Bach's *The Art of Fugue.*[56] Although the lower voice is inversionally related to the upper voice, we should note that the melodic inversion in the lower voice is inexact in mm. 7, 11, and 12. Symmetrical inversion constituted a chromatic expansion of *contrarium reversum*, allowing not only for the precise inversion of contrapuntal lines, but also for the inversion of entire compositions. Ziehn's technique, like that of his predecessors, was based upon inversion around an axis of symmetry that Ziehn referred to as a tonal center. Any note may serve as an axis, but the inversional relationships around D (as well as its inversional complement A-flat) are those most clearly recognizable on the piano keyboard. Example 13.20a illustrates a symmetrical inversion of the chromatic scale and a series of symmetrically related triads and seventh chords. Example 13.20b contains the symmetrical inversion of a setting of a theme derived from the letters BACH. In both cases the symmetrical inversion is around a D axis.

Ziehn maintained that symmetrical inversion was a means by which contrapuntal and harmonic practice could be extended. In fact, Ziehn's influence is apparent in several of Busoni's works such as his *Fantasia Contrappuntistica*, which was finished in 1910, the year the composer met with Ziehn in America. Ziehn also proposed that symmetrical inversion be used for the development of piano technique, particularly that suitable to modern music.[57] He composed exercises using symmetrical inversion for pianists who wanted to attain equal facility in the right and left hands.

Hermann Schröder[58] was a violinist and theorist whose efforts were concerned with providing a scientific basis for the existence of the undertone series.[59] Although, as we shall see, Schröder's treatise *Die symmetrische Umkehrung in der Musik* (1902) was surrounded by controversy, it remains the most extensive work written on the subject. He also delivered a lecture on symmetrical inversion to the Berlin chapter of the International Musical Society.[60] Schröder explained that symmetrical inversion had its roots in both musical practice and the theoretical literature. He considered it a manifestation of harmonic dualism, and attributed its development in modern times to Hauptmann, Oettingen, Riemann, Oskar Fleischer, and Ziehn.[61] Schröder claimed that his contribution would make symmetrical inversion applicable to modern compositional technique.

Schröder began, as had Riemann before him, with the dualistic interpretation of the *Klang*:

We find in the tone the *Klang* with its aliquot parts, which
serves as the basis of our tone system, and in the symmetrical inversion of the *Klang* column, the perfect opposite.[62]

As can be seen in example 13.21, Schröder's representation of the *Klang*
did not stop at the major and minor triads but continued even beyond
the thirty-second partial and undertone. At one point he argued that
the undertones, although not obviously present, are "latent" and can
be demonstrated mechanically.[63] Schröder admitted that a natural basis
for the undertone series had not yet been fully established, though he
looked forward to its discovery.[64]

Proceeding from a preliminary discussion of the over- and undertone series, Schröder's treatise painstakingly examines the symmetrical inversion of scales, melodies, chords, harmonic progressions, and
ultimately entire compositions. It demonstrates that the symmetrical
inversion of the major scale and the various forms of the minor generates the liturgical modes.[65] For example, the inversion of the major
scale yields the Phrygian mode. Schröder found the inversion of the
diatonic and liturgical mode systems more interesting than the inversion of chromatic materials. He realized that, when inverted, diatonic
configurations engender a change of quality, such as the inverted major
chord becoming minor or the inverted major scale becoming Phrygian.
On the other hand, the chromatic scale does not produce a change of
quality under the same operation. This opinion points to an essential
difference between Ziehn's conception of symmetrical inversion and
Schröder's, since Ziehn's interests lay in the application of the technique to chromatic music.

Schröder's explication of the symmetrical inversion of the chromatic scale led him to several formulations that are strikingly similar
to those found in contemporary twelve-tone theory. He observed that
the symmetrical inversion and transposition of the chromatic scale
may be described according to an axis of inversion. For example, a
chromatic scale starting on C and its symmetrical inversion transposed down a major second are symmetrical around a B-natural axis
(ex. 13.22). Schröder called this axis a *phonische Mittelpunkt*, adapting
the term from Oettingen's *Phonalität*. Today, inversionally related
twelve-tone rows are often examined according to just such an axis of
symmetry. This procedure has proved to be especially useful for the
analysis of Schoenberg's music, his later twelve-tone works in particular.[66] Schröder also noted that the twelve transpositions of symmetrically related chromatic scales may be divided into two classes, depending on whether they are symmetrical around a single note or a

Example 13.19

CANON per Augmentationem, contrario motu

Example 13.20

Example 13. 21

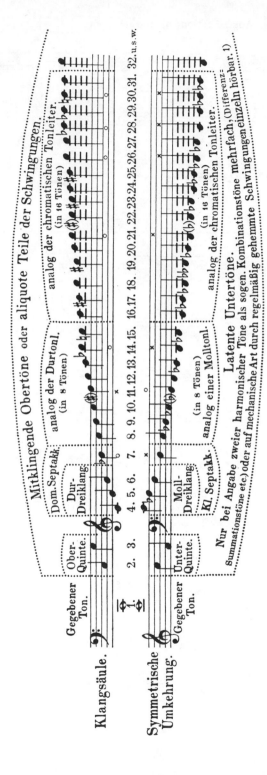

Example 13.22

dyad (exx. 13.23a and 13.23b).[67] He observed that, when considered with respect to the vertical dyads formed by inversion, the two groups of symmetrically related scales have unique harmonic properties.[68] Once again, his discussion foreshadows contemporary twelve-tone theory, in which the same two groups of inversionally related twelve-tone scales are differentiated according to "odd" and "even" dyadic sums.[69]

Ziehn was outraged by the appearance of Schröder's monograph on symmetrical inversion.[70] In addition to citing many inaccuracies contained in Schröder's treatise, Ziehn accused him of stealing his idea of symmetrical inversion. He claimed that Schröder was introduced to the concept by one of Ziehn's pupils, the organist and composer Wilhelm Mittelschulte.[71] Ziehn insisted that the technique was entirely his own creation and was not found earlier in either practice or theory. He maintained that the limitations of the liturgical modes, as well as an incomplete knowledge of chromaticism, had impeded the development of *contrarium reversum* so that it did not always produce strict inversion. In addition, he objected to Schröder's contention that symmetrical inversion had roots in the history of harmonic dualism. The quasi-scientific inquiries of such theorists as Oettingen had little to offer the practical musician.[72] According to Ziehn, the masterpieces of music, not the laws of physics, provided the basis for a science of music.[73] He noted that although Riemann's model of tonality was based on a symmetrical relationship, he did not provide even a passing comment concerning symmetrical inversion in his *Lehrbuch des Kontrapunkts* (1888).[74] Ziehn stubbornly asserted that he alone had developed the older technique into symmetrical inversion.

Despite its alleged "borrowing" and historical inaccuracies, Schröder's treatise is an interesting contribution to the history of music theory. It not only anticipated later developments, but also provided a link between the history of harmonic dualism and symmetrical inversion. Yet Ziehn was not alone in attacking Schröder's monograph. Georg Capellen reviewed the treatise in an article that was first published in 1903 and later appeared as the third section of his treatise *Die Zukunft der Musiktheorie* (1905).[75] Capellen's criticisms were directed toward Schröder's acceptance of harmonic dualism. As Capellen had

Example 13.23

argued elsewhere, the symmetrical relationship between the major and minor *Klänge* was to be faulted on perceptual grounds. He contended that this relationship, when extended to melodies, harmonic progressions, or entire compositions, is likewise invalid:

> If, as the author maintains, the symmetrical inversion of a composition really was a "natural mirror image," a "negative," a "reverse and dark side," then the identity with the original, without supplementation and variation, must be perceived by the ear in the same way that the eye perceives a mirror image.[76]

Capellen believed he saw a logical flaw in Schröder's reasoning. Although Schröder began with the dualistic interpretation of the *Klang*, he recognized that symmetrical inversion often affected a change in quality. Capellen maintained that this acknowledgment actually con-

Example 13.23 cont.

stituted a refutation of harmonic dualism, since dualism posited an equivalence relationship between symmetrically related structures.

Capellen also objected to the practical application of symmetrical inversion and cited Schröder's symmetrical inversion of the first prelude from Bach's *Well-Tempered Clavier* as a case in point. The first few measures of Schröder's version are reproduced along with the original in example 13.24.[77] In rejecting the symmetrical inversion of this piece, Capellen explained that the procedure did not produce a viable musical work for many reasons: he singled out the irregular handling of six-four chords and the disruption of large-scale key relations, as well as the uncharacteristic leaps in the soprano voice.[78] Capellen conceded, however, that elsewhere Schröder did discuss the modifications necessary when inverting a given work, and in this relative sense Capellen accepted symmetrical inversion.

Example 13.24

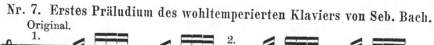

* * *

In conclusion, German theorists under the omnipresent influence of Hauptmann and Helmholtz sought to create elegant theoretical systems that were, in most cases, both logically unified and empirically verifiable. Throughout this period a fascination with symmetrical structure was a recurrent theme. This phenomenon, however, did not take place in isolation. The efforts of music theorists were certainly motivated by the rise of a modern theory of symmetry in several fields and undoubtedly fueled by the emphasis placed on scientific knowledge by the positivistic world view.

The preoccupation with symmetry shared by Ziehn, Capellen, and Schröder was largely an outgrowth of the dualistic harmonic theories of their predecessors: Hauptmann, Riemann, and Oettingen. Despite his critical stance contra Riemann, Capellen's theory of harmony was largely an attempt to reconcile Riemannian function theory with musical practice. Similarly, although Ziehn disavowed speculative harmonic theory, it seems that his interests in symmetrical inversion were also inspired by the evolution of late nineteenth-century dualistic harmonic theory.

Finally, it is clear that in several instances turn-of-the-century music theorists either anticipated important stylistic developments or contributed directly to the evolution of twentieth-century musical practice. For instance, Schröder's discussion of axes of inversion foreshadowed compositional techniques employed by Schoenberg and others, as well as the theoretical formulation of these techniques by Milton Babbitt and David Lewin. Ironically, the type of inversional equivalence repudiated by Capellen on the grounds that it contradicted the basic premises of the tonal system later became an essential component of nontonal musical syntax. It is more difficult to establish a concrete relationship between theory and musical practice. It appears, however, that the labor of theorists in exploring the structural potentials of the tonal system did not go unnoticed by composers. Ziehn's influence on Busoni, which has been briefly mentioned here, is well documented in the literature.[79] Far more significant is Schoenberg's historical position in relation to these matters. Although the acceptance of harmonic dualism as a theoretical foundation of the tonal system for the most part ended with Riemann, the symmetries so fervently promulgated by turn-of-the-century theorists were reapplied by Schoenberg and other twentieth-century composers in a context that was unfettered by the limitations of tonal syntax and did not require the verification of empirical science. Indeed, Schoenberg's conception of an "absolute musical space" did not originate in a vacuum. It was the logical development of theoretical principles associated with the evolution of late nineteenth- and early twentieth-century German harmonic theory.

Notes

1. Arnold Schoenberg, "Der musikalische Gedanke und die Logik, Technik, und Kunst seiner Darstellung" (manuscript housed at the Arnold Schoenberg Institute in Los Angeles), 61: "*Sym[m]etrie* ist eines der einfachsten Prinzipien: rechts von der Achse befindet sich dasselbe (in gleichen Abständen, in gleichen Massen etc.) wie links von der Achse. Das Prinzip des Spiegels, des Krebs, und die Umkehrung sind im Grund auch dasselbe. [para.] Ihr Vorteil ist, nebst leichter Fasslichkeit, dass sie

doch eine neue Gestalt darbieten die in Wirklichkeit die gleichen inneren Verhältnisse hat nur in umgekehrter Reihenfolge oder Richtung." The publication of an edition and translation of the entire manuscript, by Patricia Carpenter and Severine Neff, is forthcoming and will be entitled *The Musical Idea and the Logic, Technique, and Art of Its Presentation: A Theoretical Manuscript by Arnold Schoenberg* (Columbia University Press).

2. Claudio Spies, "'Vortrag / 12 T K / Princeton,'" *Perspectives of New Music* 13 (Fall–Winter 1974): 81ff.

3. Arnold Schoenberg, "Composition with Twelve Tones," *Style and Idea*, ed. Leonard Stein (London, 1975), 214–45.

4. David Lewin, "Inversional Balance as an Organizing Force in Schoenberg's Music and Thought," *Perspectives of New Music* 6 (Spring–Summer 1967): 1–21.

5. See, for example, Bruce Archibald, "Some Thoughts on Symmetry in Early Webern: Op. 5, no. 2," *Perspectives of New Music* 10 (Spring–Summer 1972): 159–63; and Leland Smith, "Composition and Precomposition in the Music of Webern," in Hans Moldenhauer and Demar Irvine, eds., *Anton Webern: Perspectives* (Seattle, 1966), 86–101.

6. George Perle, "Berg's Master Array of the Interval Cycles," *Musical Quarterly* 63 (1977): 1–30; idem, "Symmetrical Formations in the String Quartets of Béla Bartók," *Music Review* 16 (1955): 300–312; Elliott Antokoletz, *The Music of Béla Bartók* (Berkeley, 1984); and Arthur Berger, "Problems of Pitch Organization in Stravinsky," *Perspectives of New Music* 2 (Fall 1963): 27ff.

7. Milton Babbitt, "Twelve-Tone Invariants as Compositional Determinants," *Musical Quarterly* 46 (1960): 246–59; and idem, "Set Structure as a Compositional Determinant," *Journal of Music Theory* 5 (1961): 72–94. George Perle, *Twelve-Tone Tonality* (Berkeley, 1977).

8. See, for example, Richard Taruskin, "Chernomor to Kashchei: Harmonic Sorcery; or, Stravinsky's 'Angle,'" *Journal of the American Musicological Society* 38 (Spring 1985): 73–142. Taruskin, while tracing the origination of the octatonic scale from the early nineteenth century through Liszt and Rimsky-Korsakov to Stravinsky, provides a number of interesting examples of the symmetrical partitioning of the octave in the music of Schubert and Liszt. A Schenkerian approach to partitioning by equal thirds may be found in Gregory Michael Proctor, "Technical Bases for Nineteenth-Century Chromatic Tonality: A Study in Chromaticism" (Ph.D. diss., Princeton University, 1978), and Howard Cinnamon, "Tonic Arpeggiation and Successive Equal Third Relations as Elements of Tonal Evolution in the Music of Franz Liszt," *Music Theory Spectrum* 8 (1986): 1–24. See also Felix Salzer and Carl Schachter, *Counterpoint in Composition* (New York, 1969), 217–20, for examples in the music of Schubert, Chopin, and Wagner. For a discussion of partitioning by equal thirds in Mahler's Ninth Symphony, see Christopher Lewis, *Tonal Coherence in Mahler's Ninth Symphony*, Studies in Musicology, no. 79 (Ann Arbor, 1984).

9. For general discussions of the theory of symmetry, see Hermann Weyl, *Symmetry* (Princeton, 1952); A.V. Shubnikov and V.A. Kosick, *Symmetry in Science and Art*, trans. G.D. Archard (New York and London, 1974); A.V. Shubnikov and N.V. Belov, *Colored Symmetry*, trans. Jack Itzkoff and Jack Gollob (New York, 1964); and the special issue on symmetry, *Studium Generale* 2 (1949): 203–278.

10. Ernst Haeckel, *Kunstformen der Natur*, 10 vols. (Leipzig, 1899–1904).

11. I.M. Yaglom, *Felix Klein and Sophus Lie: Evolution of the Idea of Symmetry in the Nineteenth Century*, trans. Sergei Sossinsky, ed. Hardy Grant and Abe Shenitzer (Boston, 1988).

12. Pierre Curie, "Sur la symétrie," in his *Oeuvres* (Paris, 1884).

13. For a list of Federov's writings and other important works on symmetry, see Shubnikov and Belov, *Colored Symmetry*, 249–60. The discoveries of Federov and his predecessors influenced the work of the Dutch artist M.C. Escher. See Caroline H. MacGillavry, *Fantasy and Symmetry: The Periodic Drawings of M.C. Escher* (New York, 1976). Escher's work, which often is based on complex symmetrical relationships, may have also been influenced by Koloman Moser and the Viennese secessionist movement in the decorative arts at the turn the century. See M.L. Teuber, "Perceptual Theory and Ambiguity in the Work of M.C. Escher," in H.S.M. Coxeter et al., eds., *M.C. Escher: Art and Science* (New York, 1986), 166–67.

14. Yaglom, *Felix Klein and Sophus Lie*, v.

15. Johann Wolfgang von Goethe, *Scientific Studies*, ed. and trans. Douglas Miller (New York, 1983).

16. Ibid., xiv.

17. Ibid., 302. This excerpt is from a brief outline entitled "Theory of Tone," which Goethe drafted with Karl Friedrich Zelter (ibid., 338).

18. The influence of Goethe's scientific writings on Hauptmann is discussed in Wilhelm Seidel, *Über Rhythmustheorien der Neuzeit* (Bern, 1975), 157.

19. A discussion of Riemann's theories as well as a list of his theoretical writings can be found in William C. Mickelsen, *Hugo Riemann's Theory of Harmony, with The History of Harmonic Theory, Book III, by Hugo Riemann*, trans. and ed., William C. Mickelsen (Lincoln, Neb., 1977).

20. Mark McCune, "Moritz Hauptmann: *Ein Haupt Mann* in Nineteenth-Century Music Theory," *Indiana Theory Review* 7, no. 2 (Winter 1986): 1–28, and Peter Rummenhöller, *Musiktheoretisches Denken im 19. Jahrhundert*, Studien zur Musikgeschichte des 19. Jahrhunderts, vol. 12 (Regensburg, 1967), 80–81.

21. Moritz Hauptmann, *Opuscula* (Leipzig, 1874), 54, and idem, *Briefe von Moritz Hauptmann, Kantor und Musikdirektor an der Thomasschule zu Leipzig, an Franz Hauser*, ed. Alfred Schöne, vol. 2 (Leipzig, 1871), 276.

22. Moritz Hauptmann, *The Nature of Harmony and Metre*, ed. and trans. W.E. Heathcote (London, 1888), 14.

23. Oettingen's table has been recently referred to as a *Tonnetz*. See Martin Vogel, "Arthur v. Oettingen und der harmonische Dualismus," in Martin Vogel, ed., *Beiträge zur Musiktheorie des 19. Jahrhunderts* (Regensburg, 1966), 114ff. Vogel traces this particular arrangement of fifths and thirds to Leonhard Euler; see Martin Vogel, "Die Musikschriften Leonhard Eulers," *Euleri Opera Omnia*, series 3, vols. 11/12 (Zurich, 1960), lx. For a history of the *Tonnetz* as it pertains to the development of German *Funktionstheorie* after Riemann, see Renate Imig, *Systeme der Funktionsbeziechnung in den Harmonielehren seit Hugo Riemann*, Orpheus Schriftenreihe zu Grundfragen der Musik, vol. 9 (Düsseldorf, 1970).

24. Arthur von Oettingen, *Das duale Harmoniesystem* (Leipzig, 1913), 113ff.

25. Ibid., 266ff., and idem, *Die Grundlage der Musikwissenschaft und das duale Reininstrument*, Abhandlungen der mathematisch-physichen Klasse der kgl. sächsischen Gesellschaft der Wissenschaften, vol. 34 (1916).

26. Arthur von Oettingen, *Harmoniesystem in dualer Entwickelung* (Dorpat and Leipzig, 1866), 31–33.

27. Oettingen, *Das duale Harmoniesystem*, 35.

28. Ibid., 37.

29. Oettingen, *Harmoniesystem in dualer Entwickelung*, iv: "Die innere Dualität oder Zweifaltigkeit der Harmonie gestattet auch für das Harmoniesystem eine äussere, duale, d.h. zweifaltig-gegensätzliche Form der Entwickelung, die in einem symmetrischen Bau aller Tongebilde und Klangfolgen sich kund thut."

30. Ibid., 82.

31. Ibid., 95.

32. Ibid., 74.

33. Ibid., 75.

34. For a detailed exposition of his ideas, see David W. Bernstein, "The Harmonic Theory of Georg Capellen" (Ph.D. diss., Columbia University, 1986).

35. Georg Capellen, *Die Zukunft der Musiktheorie (Dualismus oder "Monismus"?) und ihre Einwirkung auf dem Praxis* (Leipzig, 1905).

36. Georg Capellen, "Die Unmöglichkeit und Überflüssigkeit der dualistischen Molltheorie Riemann's," *Neue Zeitschrift für Musik* 97 (1901): 529–31, 541–43, 553–55, 569–72, 585–87, 601–3, and 617–19.

37. Capellen, *Die Zukunft der Musiktheorie*, 74: "lehnt aber überhaupt die dem Auge bemerkbare Kopfstellung ab, da es nach dem auch in der Musik gültigen Gesetz der Schwere alle Töne im Zusammenklänge von unten nach oben (im Grundbasssine) hört. *Der äusserliche Unterschied in der Richtung vertieft sich also zum Unterschiede in der Art.*"

38. Ernst Mach, "On Symmetry," in his *Popular Scientific Lectures*, trans. Thomas J. McCormack (1893; La Salle, Ill., 1986), 89–106.

39. Ernst Mach, *Beiträge zur Analyse der Empfindungen* (Prague, 1885), trans. C.M. Williams as *Contributions to the Analysis of the Sensations* (1890; La Salle, Ill., 1986), 125–27.

40. Hilde Spiel, *Vienna's Golden Autumn, 1866–1938* (New York, 1987), 133–34.

41. Carl Stumpf, *Konsonanz und Dissonanz*, Beiträge zur Akustik und Musikwissenschaft, vol. 1 (Leipzig, 1898), 99.

42. Mach, "On Symmetry," 103.

43. This terminology was employed in Capellen's *Die musikalische Akustik* (Leipzig, 1902) and was later revised in his *Fortschrittliche Harmonie- und Melodielehre* (Leipzig, 1908).

44. Georg Capellen, "Harmonik und Melodik bei Richard Wagner," *Bayreuther Blätter* 25 (1902): 11.

45. See David W. Bernstein, "Georg Capellen on *Tristan und Isolde*: Analytical Systems in Conflict at the Turn of the Twentieth Century," *Theoria* 4 (1989): 34–62.

46. For modern discussions of symmetry in *Tristan und Isolde*, see Benjamin Boretz, "Meta-Variations, Part IV: Analytic Fallout (I) ," *Perspectives of New Music* 11 (Fall–Winter 1977): 159–72; Edward T. Cone, "'Yet Once More, Ye Laurels,'" *Perspectives of New Music* 14 (Spring–Summer/Fall–Winter 1976): 294–306; John Rahn, *Basic Atonal Theory* (New York, 1980), 78; and Milton Babbitt, *Words about Music,* ed. Stephen Dembski and Joseph N. Straus (Madison, 1987), 146–51.

47. Hermann von Helmholtz, *On the Sensations of Tone*, trans. Alexander J. Ellis (1862; reprint ed., New York, 1954), 153.

48. Bernhard Ziehn, *Harmonie- und Modulationslehre* (Berlin, 1887); idem, "Über die symmetrische Umkehrung," *Gesammelte Aufsätze zur Geschichte und Theorie der Musik* (Chicago, 1927), 186–217; and idem, *Canonic Studies: A New Technique in Composition* (New York, 1912; reprint ed., Ronald Stevenson ed., New York, 1977). For discussions of Ziehn's life and writings, see Hans Joachim Moser, *Bernhard Ziehn (1845–1912): Der deutsch-amerikanische Musiktheoretiker* (Bayreuth, 1950), and Winthrop Sargeant, "Bernhard Ziehn, Precursor," *Musical Quarterly* 19 (1933): 169–77. A more recent examination of Ziehn's theories may be found in Severine Neff, "Otto Luening (1900–) and the Theories of Bernhard Ziehn (1845–1912)," *Current Musicology* 39 (1985): 21–41.

49. Capellen, *Die Zukunft der Musiktheorie*, 72–79.

50. Hermann Schröder, *Die symmetrische Umkehrung in der Musik*, Publikationen der International Musikgesellschaft, Beihefte, vol. 8 (Leipzig, 1902).

51. Ziehn, "Über die symmetrische Umkehrung," 186–217.

52. Gioseffo Zarlino, *Le istitutioni harmoniche* (Venice, 1558), part 3, trans. Guy A. Marco and Claude V. Palisca as *The Art of Counterpoint* (New Haven, 1968), 133.

53. See Alfred Mann, *The Study of Fugue* (London, 1958), 44. The works Mann mentioned include Giovanni Maria Bononcini's *Musico prattico* (Bologna, 1673), Johann Joseph Fux's *Gradus ad Parnassum* (Venice, 1725), Friedrich Wilhelm Marpurg's *Abhandlung von der Fuge* (Berlin, 1753–54), and Ernst Friedrich Richter's *Lehrbuch der Fuge* (Leipzig, 1859).

54. Simon Sechter, *Die Grundsätze der musikalischen Komposition*, vol. 3 (Leipzig, 1854), 316.

55. Ibid., 306.

56. Schröder, *Die symmetrische Umkehrung in der Musik*, 2–3.

57. Bernhard Ziehn, *System der Uebungen für Klavierspieler* (Berlin, 1881).

58. *Musik in Geschichte und Gegenwart*, s.v. "Schröder, Hermann."

59. Hermann Schröder, *Untersuchungen über die sympathetischen Klänge der Geigen-Instrumente* (Leipzig, 1900).

60. *Zeitschrift der International Musikgesellschaft* 3 (1901–2): 126.

61. Schröder, *Die symmetrische Umkehrung in der Musik*, 4.

62. Ibid.: "Wir finden in dem Tone den Klang mit seinen aliquoten Teilen, welcher unserem Tonsystem als Basis diente, und in der symmetrischen Umkehrung der Klangsäule den vollkommenen Gegensatz."

63. Ibid., 5.

64. Ibid., 34.

65. Ibid., 7.

66. For example, see David Lewin, "A Study of Hexachord Levels in Schoenberg's Violin Fantasy," *Perspectives of New Music* 6 (Fall–Winter 1967): 18–32.

67. Schröder, *Die symmetrische Umkehrung in der Musik*, 16–17.

68. Ibid., 16–17.

69. Babbitt, "Twelve-Tone Invariants," 246–59.

70. Ziehn, "Über die symmetrische Umkehrung," 186f.

71. Ibid., 194.

72. Ibid., 197–98.

73. Ziehn, *Canonic Studies*, 10.

74. Ziehn, "Über die symmetrische Umkehrung," 198.

75. Georg Capellen, "Über die symmetrische Umkehrung," *Neue Zeitschrift für Musik* 99 (January 1903): 49–52; idem, *Die Zukunft der Musiktheorie*, 72–79.

76. Capellen, *Die Zukunft der Musiktheorie*, 73–74: "Wäre die symmetrische Umkehrung eines Satzes wirklich wie Verfasser behauptet, ein "Natur-Spiegelbild", ein "Negativ", eine "Kehr- und Schattenseite", so müsste die Identität mit dem Original, ohne dass Änderungen und Ergänzungen nötig sind, vom Ohre aufgefasst werden, wie bei Spiegelbildern vom Auge."

77. Schröder, *Die symmetrische Umkehrung in der Musik*, 86–87.

78. Capellen, *Die Zukunft der Musiktheorie*, 75.

79. For example, see Antony Beaumont, *Busoni the Composer* (Bloomington, Ind., 1985), 161–64.

FOURTEEN

Schoenberg and Goethe: Organicism and Analysis

SEVERINE NEFF

> *Alle Gestalten sind ähnlich, und keine gleichet der andern;*
> *Und so deutet das Chor auf ein geheimes Gesetz,*
> *Auf ein heiliges Rätsel.*
>
> —Johann Wolfgang von Goethe,
> *Die Metamorphose der Pflanzen*[1]

"I believe Goethe would be quite satisfied with me,"[2] Arnold Schoenberg wrote in his sketchbook upon discovering the set for the third movement of his Wind Quintet Op. 26. Goethe's exceptionally powerful influence on Schoenberg was crystallized in 1934 in his major unfinished theoretical work, "Der musikalische Gedanke und die Logik, Technik, und Kunst seiner Darstellung."[3] This manuscript adopts the terminology and epistemology of Goethe's comparatively neglected scientific work.[4] The importance of this work for the Second Viennese School is further illustrated by Anton Webern's remarks:

> A theme is presented. It is varied . . . all the rest is based on that one idea; it is the prime form. The most astounding things happen, but it is still always the same.
>
> Now you see what I am driving at—Goethe's *Urpflanze*: the root is actually nothing other than the stem, the leaf in turn is nothing other than the blossom; all variations of the same idea.[5]

Nothing could be more indicative of the holistic, organic model that is the basis of all Schoenberg's analytical thought, and nothing could be further from the mechanistic, logical-postivist model that is the basis of much contemporary theoretical thought on Schoenberg.

My thesis is that Schoenberg's theoretical writings must be evaluated in the context of his intellectual tradition: organicism as redefined by Goethe. The first section of this study discusses how Goethe's holistic epistemology leads to particular concepts of organic function. The second section shows how Schoenberg adopted Goethe's thought in his concepts of *Monotonalität, Hauptmotiv, Grundgestalt*, and "tonal problem." A third and final section demonstrates how Schoenberg's concepts analytically apply to Schubert's *Der Wegweiser*, song no. 20 from *Winterreise*.

Goethe and the Organic Model

The concept of the organic unity of an artwork was initially articulated in Plato's *Phaedrus*: "A composition should be like a living being, with a body of its own, as it were, and neither headless nor feetless, with a middle and with members adapted to each other and to the whole."[6] Aristotle's concept of organic form gives primacy to a whole that is more than the sum of its parts. Plotinus added the criterion that an alteration of a part, whether by size, addition, or removal, involves the alteration of the whole.[7] Ancient philosophy was reclaimed in eighteenth-century Germany by Immanuel Kant. Kant's student and Goethe's friend, the poet and dramatist Friedrich Schiller, wrote: "Music in its highest refinement must be a *Gestalt*."[8]

Within this tradition Goethe was unique in that he was not only a discerner of form; he was a maker of an immense variety of forms, both literary and scientific.[9] His ideas of artistic and natural forms were strongly integrated. Goethe's "poetic mind does indeed constitute the interest of his scientific work, not because he thinks as a poet when he is supposed to be thinking as a scientist—he moves freely between both these modes of thought—but because his extensive firsthand experience in the two spheres makes him uniquely qualified to evolve a conception of form embracing both art and nature."[10]

Goethe studied botany, optics, meteorology, anatomy, osteology, biology, chemistry, physics, and geology. Except for his identification of the intermaxillary bone in the human jaw, his scientific contributions are now considered relics. Only his decision to observe natural process through transformation as opposed to classification remains interesting in a Darwinian sense.[11] The harsh criticism of Goethe's work by the scientific community focuses on a single point. Goethe did not believe in the mathematical quantification of cause and effect, the traditional mechanism for *Erklärung* or explanation in science. Instead, he valued organic, holistic thinking as the highest and primary state:

> The comprehensive [thinkers] whom vanity might call cre-
> ators, are productive in the highest degree. Since they start
> with ideas, they express the *unity of the whole*, and it may
> then become nature's job to fit itself somehow into this idea.[12]
> (Italics added.)

This way of thinking led to a specific type of scientific analysis in
which a hypothesis was *not* generated out of quantified "cause and
effect" statements. In holistic thinking, cause and effect are identical:
the part does not "cause" the whole; it exists as or *presents* a formal
aspect of the whole: "Nature has neither core nor outer rind, being all
things at once."[13]

At this point it will be helpful to refer to table 14.1a, which summarizes the main concepts of Goethe's scientific thought discussed in this
essay. The left column of this table presents Goethe's general vocabulary of organicism; the right column presents his corresponding vocabulary in botany. Goethe never developed his concepts solely in the
abstract. Therefore, the following discussion will focus on botany, one
field in which Goethe developed his ideas quite completely. It is crucial to realize throughout this discussion that the methods applied to
botany can also be applied to color, to anatomy or, most crucially, to
art.

Goethe's organic hypotheses grew out of a type of thinking process
called *Anschauung* or "intuitive contemplation": "a combination of
mediate knowledge *about* with the immediacy of knowledge *of*."[14] The
goal of *Anschauung* was the "archetype" or *Urphänomen*: an imagined
synthesis of all instances of a given phenomenon. A practical example
of *Anschauung* can be seen in Goethe's study of botany. For a decade
Goethe collected countless species of plants, drawing their forms and
taking note of their common functions. Goethe, however illogically,
claimed that the *imagined* synthesis of this material produced in his
mind's eye an abstract vision reflecting the potential contents and
form of all plants: the hypothesis of the *Urpflanze*, the archetypal plant.[15]

The nature of the *Urpflanze* became the focus of Goethe's first encounter with Schiller. As a schooled philosopher, Schiller called
Goethe's *Urpflanze* a Platonic idea or universal—"plantness" existing
unchanged, beyond time, space, rest, motion, and number. As an artist, Goethe disagreed. How could an abstract entity such as the idea,
by definition without specific content or form, be presented in an object
that existed with content and form in space and time? How could this
universal be presented in the particular? Goethe insisted instead that
the *Urpflanze* was simultaneously both concept and experience: the

Table 14.1.

a. Goethe's Epistemology		*b.* Schoenberg's Adaptation of Goethe
Anschauung ["intuitive contemplation"]	*Anschauung* ["intuitive contemplation"]	*Anschauung* ["intuitive contemplation"]
Urphänomen ["archetype"]	*Urpflanze* ["archetypal plant"]	*Monotonalität* ["monotonality"]
		Grundton ["fundamental"] in nature
		Tonic in art
Bildung/Umbildung ["formation"/"transformation"]	*Bildung/Umbildung* ["formation"/"transformation"]	*Bildung/Umbildung* ["formation"/"transformation"]
Der innere Kern ["inner nucleus"]	*Blatt* ["Leaf form"]	*Hauptmotiv* or "tonal problem" ["basic motive"]
vis centrifuga ["centrifugal force"]	Outward growth	Centrifugal force: motion from tonic
vis centripeta ["centripetal force"]	Inward and upward growth	Centripetal force: motion to tonic
Funktion ["function"]	Cotyledon, leaf, petal, stem	Functioning parts: statement, transition, contrast, retransition, final section, coda
Gestalt	Individual plant *Gestalt*	Individual piece

Grundgestalt ["basic configuration"]

imagined object, containing all his past and present empirical observations, the conclusion of *Anschauung*. He said of ideas, "I can see them with my eyes."[16]

After positing the archetype or *Urphänomen*, Goethe's next step concerned how the individual object, the single manifestation of the archetype, demonstrated a network of coherence within it. For Goethe such study of the functioning parts within a whole was the study of *Bildung* (formation) and *Umbildung* (transformation). Both *Bildung* and *Umbildung* are based on the root *Bild* (picture, model, image). The understanding of formation and growth is thus a process of picturing gradations of change in the mind's eye paralleling the method of *Anschauung* itself: "What is alike in idea may manifest itself in empirical reality as alike, or similar, or even totally unalike and dissimilar: this gives rise to the ever-changing life of nature."[17] For Goethe the specific plant *Gestalt* was generated out of varied changes of the same *innere Kern* (inner nucleus): the *Blatt* (leaf form).

Goethe's drawings of individual plants (see fig. 14.1) emphasize the transformations of the leaf form into the functioning parts of the plant: cotelydon and petal.[18] According to Goethe, such transformation of the *Blatt* is achieved through two opposing forces, the centripetal and the centrifugal:

> The idea of metamorphosis deserves great reverence, but it is also a most dangerous gift from above. It leads to formlessness; it destroys knowledge, dissolves it. It is like the *vis centrifuga* and would be lost in the infinite if it had no counterweight: here I mean the drive for specific character, the stubborn persistence of things which have finally attained reality. This is a *vis centripeta* which remains basically untouched by any external factor.[19]

In the plant *Gestalt* the centrifugal force is the outward growth into diverse structures such as cotyledon or leaf. The centripetal force is manifested by the inward motion toward the single and continuous structure of stem. The balance between these two forces characterizes and molds the individual plant *Gestalt*.

For Goethe the centrifugal and centripetal forces thus shape a *hierarchy* of changing parts within the whole:

> The less perfect the creation, the more its parts are alike or similar and the more they resemble the whole. . . . The more similar the parts, the less they will be subordinated to one another. Subordination of parts indicates a more perfect creation.[20]

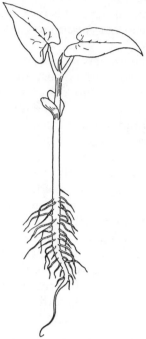

Figure 14.1   Goethe's drawing illustrating the homology of
the cotyledon and leaf.

The "subordination of parts" within a hierarchical structure inevitably results in the idea of function. Parts within the whole become "forms of function which reciprocally determine each other and unite into a system of dependencies."[21] Goethe was able to consider such a functional hierarchy because, like all organic thinkers, he presupposed a network of connection between parts "joined from the outset." Such a connection was presupposed by definition because any concept of wholeness presumed an interrelatedness between parts. For the organic thinker a function is then a presupposition of relationship between part and whole that presents a hierarchy of subordinate parts within the whole. Returning to Webern's words, we can now understand the comparison of musical theme and *Blatt* as a description of functional hierarchy: "The root is actually nothing other than the stem, the leaf in turn is nothing other than the blossom; all variations of the same idea."

Schoenberg's Adoption of Goethe's Epistemology for His Analytical Method

Schoenberg, like Goethe, believed that "our finest ability [is] the ability to receive an impression of totality."[22] This impression is a matter of experience as well as intellect: "In the intellectual realm everything is preliminary, even if it is right."[23] For Schoenberg conceptual knowledge thus existed in the experience of the object: "Therefore, whenever I theorize, it is less important whether these theories be right than whether they be useful as comparisons to clarify the object and to give the study perspective."[24]

These viewpoints determined Schoenberg's opinion that a general theory of music "should start with the subject . . . the sense of hearing."[25] However, this was impossible without a cogent theory of perception: "Unsurmountable difficulties lie in the way of analysis of the impression if the observing subject is now taken as the point of departure for inquiry."[26] As a result, he adopted an epistemological method close to Goethe's *Anschauung*. (See table 14.1b, which summarizes Schoenberg's analytical concepts.) Just as Goethe studied innumerable species of plants, Schoenberg studied innumerable pieces and the craft used to create them. His concern was never *Erklärung* but always, as pointed out in the title of his 1934 "Gedanke" manuscript, *Darstellung*—the organic *presentation* of material that enabled the whole to be comprehensible to the listener.

Schoenberg's perceptions about tonal pieces coalesced late in his career into an *Urphänomen* called *Monotonalität*:

> According to this principle, every digression from the tonic is considered to be still within the tonality, whether directly or indirectly, closely or remotely related. In other words, there is only *one tonality* in a piece, and every segment considered as another tonality is only a region, a harmonic contrast within that tonality.[27]

Schoenberg understood *Monotonalität* as an *Urphänomen* functioning in both nature and art. The natural basis of *Monotonalität* is the *Grundton*, the fundamental of the overtone series. In the artistic realm the *Grundton* is understood to be the tonic, and the overtones, the regions of the tonic. Schoenberg himself explained that

> the primitive ear hears the *Grundton* as irreducible, but physics recognizes it to be complex. In the meantime, however, musicians discovered that it is *capable of continuation*, i.e. that *movement is latent within it*. That problems are concealed in it, problems that clash with one another, that the *Grundton* lives and seeks to propagate itself.[28]

Like Goethe's *Urpflanze*, which contains the functional potential of all possible plant forms, Schoenberg's concept of *Monotonalität* presents the functional potential of all tonal pieces. It is what Schoenberg considered a scientific model, that is, one that "must try to include all conceivable cases."[29] Schoenberg's hypothesis of *Monotonalität* is illustrated in the major and minor charts of the regions; an extended version of the latter appears in table 14.2a.

The major and minor charts of the regions have a detailed inner structure built on the traditional key relationships: vertically, the circle of fifths; horizontally, relative and parallel minor relations. As David Lewin observed, the design is symmetrical: the sharp and flat regions form polar opposites around the central tonic.[30] Schoenberg's theory includes further functional classifications that determine distances from the tonic (see table 14.2b).[31] "Direct and Close" regions are those that share six or seven pitches with it. The next groupings, "Indirect but Close" and "Indirect," have tonics that are related to those of a previous grouping by the alteration of a major-minor (or minor-major) relation (M to m or m to M).[32] The "Indirect and Remote" and "Distant" regions are related to a previous grouping either through functions of the subdominant minor region (e.g., sd/SD/subT), or through fifth relations or substitution (e.g., sharp sm to m, S/T to Np).

During his determination of the hypothesis *Monotonalität*, Schoenberg also considered the problem of *Bildung* and *Umbildung*: the tonic needed to be made "capable of continuation" in time through structures analogous to Goethe's *Blatt*. The structures Schoenberg identified are the *Motiv* and the *Grundgestalt*, both difficult terms to define precisely.

Schoenberg left us only one, highly general definition for *Grundgestalt*, which is found in the "Gedanke" manuscript of 1934–36:

> *"Grundgestalten"* are those *Gestalten* that (if possible) occur repeatedly within an entire piece and to which derived *Gestalten* are traceable. (Formerly, this was called the motive, but that is a very superficial designation; for *Gestalten* and *Grundgestalten* are usually comprised of several motive forms; while the motive is *at any one time the smallest part*.)[33]

Schoenberg's student Josef Rufer interpreted such general statements as describing the first phrase of a piece establishing a characteristic sound and usually asserting the tonic.[34] In this study I adopt Rufer's interpretation.

In his extant writings Schoenberg gave several different definitions for *Motiv*. In 1917, 1934, and 1943 he defined a *Motiv* as a "unit which contains one or more features of interval and rhythm whose presence is manifested in constant use throughout a piece."[35] In the *Harmonielehre* (1911), when commenting on Brahms's Third Symphony, he distinguished between a *Motiv* and a *Hauptmotiv*, the latter being the structure that is directly analogous to Goethe's *Blatt*.[36] I take the *Hauptmotiv* to be the first interval of a work whose later multiple functional

Table 14.2.

---

a. Minor Chart of the Regions

np	Np	subt	subT	v	D	♯m	♯M		Fifths
subtsm	subtSM	m	M	t	T	♯sm	♯SM		
		sm	SM	sd	SD	dor	S/T	♯subt	♯subT	Relative/parallel minor
			Np						

Abbreviations

T means tonic	SM means submediant major
D means dominant	M means mediant major
SD means subdominant	Np means Neapolitan
t means tonic minor	dor means Dorian
sd means subdominant minor	S/T means supertonic
v means five-minor	subt means subtonic minor
sm means submediant minor	subT means subtonic major
mm means mediant minor	

[*N.B.* All symbols in capitals refer to major keys; those in small letters to minor keys.]

Chart in G Minor

a♭	A♭	f	F	d	D	b	B		
d♭	D♭	b♭	B♭	g	G	e	E		
		e♭	E♭	c	C	a	A	f♯	F♯
			A♭						

b. Functional Classification of the Minor Chart of the Regions
[letters on the chart read G minor as tonic]

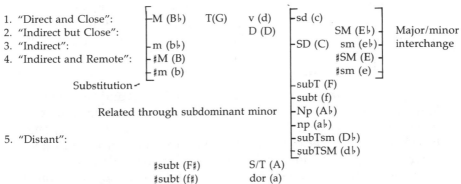

1. "Direct and Close": —M (B♭)   T(G)   v (d)   ⌐sd (c)
2. "Indirect but Close":   D (D)   SM (E♭) ⌐   Major/minor
3. "Indirect":   —m (b♭)   —SD (C)   sm (e♭)—   interchange
4. "Indirect and Remote": — ♯M (B)   ♯SM (E) —
                           — ♯m (b)   ♯sm (e) —

        Substitution⌐

                                               —subT (F)
                                               —subt (f)
        Related through subdominant minor   —Np (A♭)
                                               —np (a♭)
5. "Distant":   —subTsm (D♭)
                                               —subTSM (d♭)

                    ♯subt (F♯)   S/T (A)
                    ♯subt (f♯)   dor (a)

reinterpretations in light of *Monotonalität* can generate the composition's tonal form.

   In later studies such as the "Gedanke" manuscript of 1934, Schoenberg described what I call the first chromatic version of the *Hauptmotiv* as the "tonal problem" stated either in the *Grundgestalt* itself or in a subsequent reinterpretation.[37] Adopting Goethe's terminology, Schoenberg considers the "tonal problem" as that which makes a tonic "capable of continuation" through its inherent centrifugal motion. For an organicist such a motion to outlying regions literally creates a problem because it contradicts the unity of the tonal center. In any piece this outward motion must be turned back toward the tonal center by a corresponding centripetal force, solving the problem and thus shaping the form of the piece. In Schoenberg's words, each composition raises

> a question, puts up a problem, which in the course of the piece has to be answered, resolved, carried through. It has to be carried through many contradictory situation [sic]; it has to be developed by drawing consequences from what it postulates . . . and all this might lead to a conclusion, a pronunciamento.[38]

For Schoenberg the motivic transformations of the *Grundgestalt* and the "tonal problem" thus produce the functioning parts of a piece: its tonal form. The statement of a theme introduces the relationships of the *Grundgestalt* and sets up the "tonal problem." This "problem" demands expansion and continuation to regions away from the tonic, thus creating a transition. Eventually a contrast is likely to take shape, containing the most tonally distant reinterpretation of the opening material, the climax of the centrifugal force. But this inevitably leads to a retransition as the centripetal force begins to overcome the centrifugal force. The final section or coda eliminates all centrifugal tendencies of the "tonal problem," reinterpreting both the material of the *Grundgestalt* and the "tonal problem" in the tonic. Thus in a truly organic work the opening already presents the form of the whole.[39]

Interpretation of Schoenberg's Analytical Method

Though Schoenberg demonstrated the *Grundgestalt* and "tonal problem" in his classroom teaching, unfortunately he did not illustrate these concepts in a complete analysis.[40] Therefore contemporary analysts have to interpret and reconstruct his procedures from more general or incomplete comments. The following analysis of *Der Wegweiser* is an attempt to illustrate Schoenberg's analytical methods as applied to a complete piece. We shall find that the choice of chromatic pitches and regional references in this work can be profoundly illuminated by Schoenberg's ideas.

The song consists of a piano introduction and four sections corresponding to the four stanzas of the poem. A regional chart of the piece appears in table 14.3 The first and third sections are almost identical, moving to the "Indirect and Remote" region of the subtonic minor; the second, in the tonic major, leads to a piano interlude modulating back

Table 14.3.   Regional Chart of *Der Wegweiser*

Piano Introduction:	mm. 1–5	tonic	
Stanza One:	mm. 5–12	tonic	
	mm. 13–16	subtonic minor	"Indirect and Remote"
	mm. 16–20	tonic	
Stanza Two:	mm. 21–26	tonic major	"Direct and Close"
	mm. 27–34	submediant minor	"Indirect"
	mm. 35–39	tonic	
Stanza Three:	mm. 40–47	tonic	
	mm. 48–52	subtonic minor	"Indirect and Remote"
	mm. 53–54	tonic	
Stanza Four:	"roving" between:		
	mm. 55–58	tonic	
	mm. 59–63	subtonic minor	"Indirect and Remote"
	mm. 63–64	subtonic minor's submediant	"Distant"
	mm. 65–83	tonic	

to the minor; the fourth section functions as a coda whose "roving" harmony sums up the issues of the "tonal problem" created as early as m. 3.[41] My analytical focus in following the progress of the song will be the "tonal problem" that is functionally "carried through many contradictory situations," developed, and finally dissolved through reinterpretion in the tonic.

THE "GRUNDGESTALT" AND THE "TONAL PROBLEM"

The five-measure piano introduction is divided into a two-measure diatonic antecedent and a three-measure chromatic consequent, both closing on the tonic. The diatonic antecedent functions as the *Grundgestalt* (see ex. 14.1a). It introduces the characteristic marchlike surface rhythm of four eighth notes and the equally characteristic horizontal motion of linearized ascending thirds (motives *m* and *m1*) and nonlinearized descending thirds (motives *n* and *n1*). The vertical sixths resulting from these motions may be designated motives *x*, *y*, and *z*—*x* and *y* being major sixths and *z*, a minor sixth.

The consequent phrase preserves most surface rhythms of the *Grundgestalt* but alters its pitch motive (see ex. 14.1b). The phrase is introduced by a C–D–E-flat bass line (mm. 2–3) that parallels the rhythm of motive *m* and as a result can be understood as a registrally disjunct extension of *m* to flat 6; this is the first *reinterpretation* of the *Grundgestalt* and the *Hauptmotiv* or motive *m*. In the meantime (see ex. 14.1c), the

420

Example 14.1

Was ver-

a. Pitch motives of the *Grundgestalt*

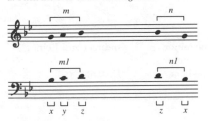

b. Extension of motive *m* to flat 6

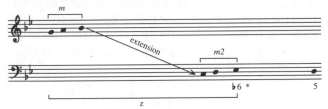

c. Extension of motive *m1*: the "tonal problem"

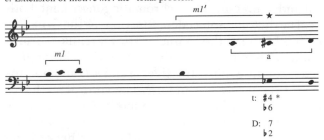

*Numbers refer to scale degrees, not to figured bass notation.

tenor resumes motive *m1* across phrase groups and chromaticizes the ascent from C to D. The part of *m1* in the consequent phrase shapes the "new" motive form *a*. The C-sharp of motive *a* coincides with the bass E-flat producing an augmented sixth chord that resolves to the cadential dominant. While the C-sharp–E-flat would no doubt be considered a surface phenomenon in a Schenkerian analysis, for Schoenberg the juxtaposition of C-sharp and E-flat is the "tonal problem," the reinterpretation of the *Hauptmotiv*, the crucial first chromatic interval leading away from the tonic, the first manifestation of a centrifugal motion. The C-sharp is sharp 4 of the tonic, sharp 7 of the dominant; the E-flat is flat 6 of the tonic, flat 2 of the dominant; both are the results of motivic extension. These scale degrees and their reinterpretations will present the functional progress of the work, guiding the piece into "distant" regions beyond the subtonic minor and ultimately back to the tonic.

The "Tonal Problem" Reinterpreted in Motive "A"

The flat 6 relation of the "tonal problem" is reiterated in the bass line 1–flat 6 across mm. 1–11 and finally as a direct interval from mm. 10–11 (see ex. 14.2a). The chromatic descent from E-flat begun in m. 11 incorporates two presentations of the inversion of motive *a* [*a(I)*] and generates two minor sixths (*z*), G–E-flat and descending D-flat–F, whose parallelism recalls motives *x* and *y* in the *Grundgestalt*. Note that D-flat is flat 6 of the subtonic region, just as E-flat is flat 6 of the tonic. However, D-flat is also the enharmonic equivalent of sharp 4 in the tonic. To move from one region to another, Schubert thus functionally reinterpreted the pitches of the "tonal problem."

As to the alto line, its presentation of motive *a* (inverted) echoes that of the bass line. Such presentations proliferate: in mm. 11–12 the alto reads A-flat–G–F-sharp, flat 2–1–sharp 7 of the tonic minor. This is followed in mm. 13–14 by G-flat–F–E, flat 2–1–sharp 7 of the subtonic minor (see ex. 14.2b). In a functional sense they recall the dominant interpretation of the "tonal problem" in m. 3.

Beginning in m. 11, the extension of the same alto line then moves to the tonic region through another inversion of motive *a*, which functionally reinterprets the pitches of the "tonal problem." The note E-flat, the flat 7 of the subtonic minor, is reinterpreted as flat 6 of the tonic. Note that the presentation of the inversion of motive *a* in mm. 16–17 (7–flat 7–6 in the subtonic) is also the functional inversion of motive *a* at the *Hauptmotiv*, read as 7–sharp 7–8 of the dominant. Moreover, example 14.3 shows how the tenor transition to the parallel tonic major, A–B-flat–B (mm. 20–22), is another presentation of motive *a* recalling the triadic major/minor shift in m. 17.

Example 14.2

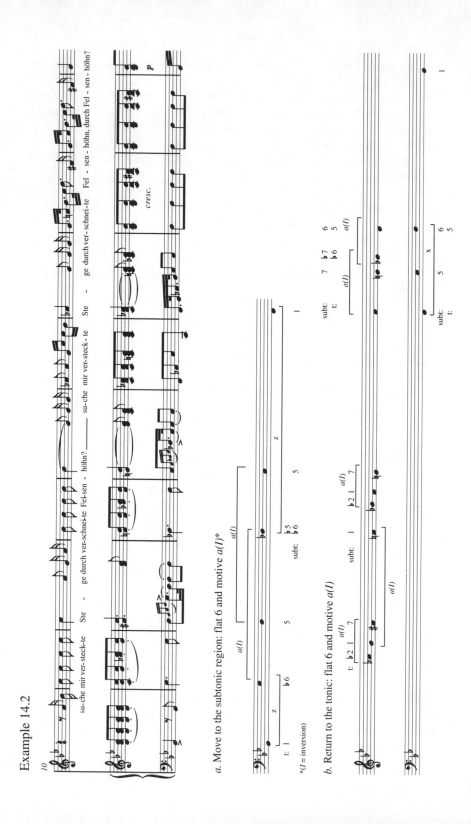

a. Move to the subtonic region: flat 6 and motive *a(I)**

*(I = inversion)

b. Return to the tonic: flat 6 and motive *a(I)*

Example 14.3 Major-minor shifts

Example 14.4 "Tonal problem" in the submediant region

Example 14.5   Return to the "tonal problem"

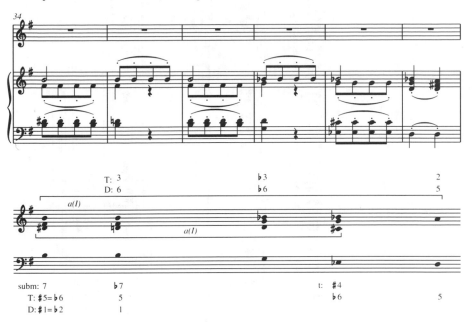

The second stanza moves from the tonic major to the "indirect but close" region of the submediant (m. 27) through the reinterpretation of motive *a* as D–D-sharp–E (5–sharp 5–6 in the tonic, 7–sharp 7–1 in the submediant minor; see ex. 14.4). The note D-sharp is the enharmonic equivalent of E-flat, flat 6 in the tonic, and the progression is in turn a deceptive cadence to flat submediant of the submediant. Moreover, the end of this stanza juxtaposes the flat 6 and sharp 4 of the submediant; C and A-sharp correspond to E-flat and C-sharp, the pitches of the "tonal problem."

The following piano interlude moves back to the tonic minor by reversing the A–B-flat–B progression that first led to the tonic major in mm. 19–21 (see ex. 14.5). The soprano B–B-flat–A is paralleled by the tenor D-sharp–D–C-sharp, which starkly insists on the actual pitches of the "problem." The interlude ends with the same augmented sixth and dominant as the first statement of the "tonal problem," but now they form only a half cadence: the dominant is left hanging, setting the stage for a virtually exact recapitulation of the first stanza.

Example 14.6

a. The inversion between the alto in mm. 11–17
and the bass in mm. 57–62

b. Flat 6 becomes sharp 4

Flat 6 Becomes Sharp 4 in Root-Function Harmonies

The fourth and final stanza reflects the text by introducing a chromatic succession on a rising bass, beginning on sharp 4 and going through flat 6 (C-sharp–D–E-flat) but now continuing to rise chromatically through an inversion of the alto line of mm. 11–17 (see ex. 14.6a). In this inversion, however, Schubert skipped the F-sharp of the rising chromatic line, emphasizing this change by the descent of a minor seventh before renewing his chromatic ascent with G–G-sharp–A (see ex. 14.6b). The lack of F-sharp allows mm. 60–62 to be registered most easily in the subtonic minor, mm. 57–58 in the tonic minor.

The subtonic minor region culminates on a triad built on flat 6 spelled enharmonically as C-sharp–E–G-sharp (m. 63; see ex. 14.6b), which is also interpreted on sharp 4 of the tonic! In this retransition the two functions of the "tonal problem" sharp 4 and flat 6 thus have fused harmonically—a consummate organic procedure. Furthermore, as a tonic, this chord actually resolves to its own flat submediant, which is equivalent to the dominant of the dominant,[42] thus bringing the progression back to the tonic region.

The "Tonal Problem" Dissolves

The final two chromatic progressions of the work steadily eliminate the features of the "tonal problem" by emphasizing the subdominant harmony for the first time in the piece (see exx. 14.7a and 14.7b). Here C-sharp and E-flat occur only in the context of their substitutes, C and E, which incorporate them into the diatonic framework of the rising melodic minor scale. The cadence in mm. 76–77 retains another version of the "tonal problem," A-flat–G–F-sharp (flat 2–1–sharp 7), but this too is eliminated in the final cadence where A-flat is replaced by A (see ex. 14.7b). At the same time, the thirds in the voice (B-flat–G, A–F-sharp) serve as a final reminder of the opening motives m and m1 of the *Grundgestalt*, now followed not by a "tonal problem," but by the diatonic simplicity of the final tonic chords.

My analysis using Schoenberg's methods has shown how the functional manipulations of the "tonal problem," E-flat–C-sharp, have presented the moves to regions other than the tonic as well as the return to the tonic, thus shaping the song's tonal form. This form is organic: all relationships not only reflect a reinterpretation of the "tonal problem" but are hewn with respect to the motives or transformed motives and the *Hauptmotiv* introduced in the *Grundgestalt*. Both the *Grundgestalt* and the "tonal problem" encapsulate certain potentials of *Monotonalität* that are then realized and resolved in the actual song.

Example 14.7 Dissolution of the "tonal problem"

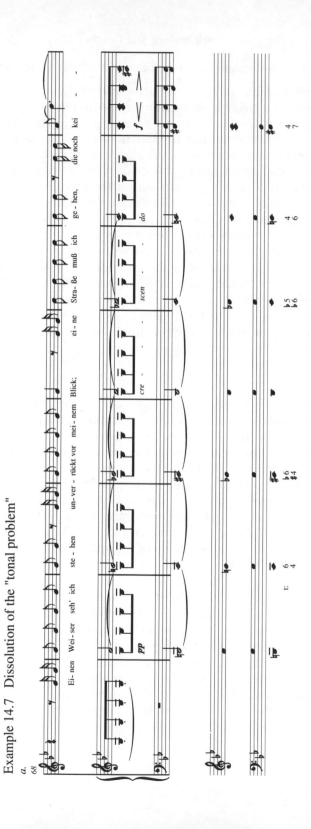

Such insights can be clarified only by the use of the analytical methods developed by Schoenberg. The true nature of his methods is becoming clear as we study his crucial "Gedanke" manuscripts, which provide the philosophical underpinning for his point of view. We now can appreciate the intellectual tradition of Goethe within which Schoenberg worked, thus demonstrating at the same time the originality of his analytical methods. The "tonal problem" is an especially suggestive and original analytical idea that can yield distinctive insights, different from those offered by that other great organic tradition of music analysis initiated by Heinrich Schenker. Schoenberg's methods of analysis remain a largely untapped resource for theorists to interpret, though Schoenberg's creative work left him little time for written analysis as such. As has been said of Goethe, Schoenberg was not only "a discerner of form, he was a maker of it."

Notes

1. "All shapes are akin and none is quite alike the other; /So to a secret law surely that chorus must point, /To a sacred enigma." In Johann Wolfgang von Goethe, *Selected Poems*, ed. Christopher Middleton (Boston, 1983), 154–55.

2. "Ich glaube, Goethe müsste ganz zufrieden mit mir sein": see Skizzenbuch V, manuscript no. 525, Arnold Schoenberg Institute, Los Angeles, which is reproduced in Leonard Stein, "The Journal and the Institute," *Journal of the Arnold Schoenberg Institute* 1, no. 1 (1976): 5, and commented on in "Letters to the Editor," *Journal of the Arnold Schoenberg Institute* 1, no. 2 (1977): 181–90.

3. The 1934–36 "Gedanke" manuscript appears in four loose-leaf notebooks left uncatalogued in Schoenberg's own bibliographical system and housed at the Arnold Schoenberg Institute. An edition and translation by Patricia Carpenter and Severine Neff of the work is forthcoming in *The Musical Idea and the Logic, Technique, and Art of Its Presentation: A Theoretical Manuscript by Arnold Schoenberg* (Columbia University Press).

4. It is interesting that one of the few analytical works in Schoenberg's surviving library is an application of Goethe's scientific concepts to motivic development in Beethoven: Fritz Cassirer, *Beethoven und die Gestalt* (Berlin, 1925). Unfortunately, this text is not annotated by Schoenberg. He does mention the work in a list of theoretical books that "interest him": see Arnold Schoenberg, *Letters*, ed. Erwin Stein (New York, 1964), 207.

Like Goethe, Schoenberg also wrote on nature and animals, comments curiously omitted in Josef Rufer's catalogue *The Works of Arnold Schoenberg*, trans. Dika Newlin (London, 1959): e.g., Schoenberg's manuscript no. 238, "Mathematik" (Mathematics); no. 216e, "Sprache der Tiere" (Language of Animals). Other texts like the "Vorwort" (Preface) and "Prinzipien des Aufbaus" (Principles of Construction) in the "Gedanke" manuscript emphasize the difference between art and science; but at the same time, Schoenberg's analytical vocabulary includes "Liquidation" and "Motiv," which he derived from chemistry and physics: see undated manuscript "Form," no. 180 under "Articles, Essays," in Josef Rufer's catalogue. Like Goethe, Schoenberg also investigated meteorology, keeping a diary on cloud formations and transformations, which he believed would predict the course of the First World War; for a transcription and edition, see Paul A. Pisk, "War-Clouds Diary by Arnold Schoenberg," *Journal of the Arnold Schoenberg Institute* 9, no. 1 (1937): 53–77.

Schoenberg, like Goethe, was a visual artist. In the "Gedanke" manuscript there is a large sketch of an eye, a favorite subject of Schoenberg the painter. For Goethe the eye was the most crucial organ for scientific investigation. The *Bild* (image, model) was the focal point of his studies of *Bildung* (formation) and *Umbildung* (transformation).

5. The quotation is from a 1932 letter from Webern to Schoenberg transcribed and translated in Ursula Rauchhaupt, ed., *Schoenberg, Webern, Berg: The String Quartets: A Documentary Study* (Hamburg, 1971), 31. See also Barbara Zuber, "Reihe, Gesetz, Urpflanze, Nomos," in Heinz-Klaus Metzer and Riehn Rainer, eds., *Anton Webern* (Munich, 1984), 304–36; and Angelika Abel, *Die Zwölftontechnik Weberns und Goethes Methodik der Farbenlehre: Zur Kompositionstheorie und Ästhetik der Neuen Wiener Schule*, Beihefte zum Archiv für Musikwissenschaft, no. 19 (Wiesbaden, 1982).

6. Plato, *Phaedrus*, trans. W.C. Helmbold and W.G. Rabinowitz (New York, 1956), 53.

7. See G.N. Giordano Orsini, *Organic Unity in Ancient and Later Poetics* (Carbondale, Ill., 1975), 90.

8. "Die Musik in ihrer höchsten Veredlung muss Gestalt werden:" cited in Cassirer, *Beethoven und die Gestalt*, 2. For a brief history of organicism related to music, see Ruth Solie, "The Living Work," *19th-Century Music* 4, no. 2 (1980): 147–56.

9. Elizabeth M. Wilkinson, "Goethe's Conception of Form," in *Goethe: A Collection of Critical Essays*, ed. Victor Lange (Englewood Cliffs, N.J., 1968), 116.

10. Ibid., 116–17.

11. Eighteenth-century botany was heavily dependent on the mechanistic systematizations and classifications of Linnaeus. A consideration of underlying, changing patterns of natural processes offered a fresh point of view. This school of Goethe and fellow botanists-biologists such as Lorenz Oken is termed *Naturphilosophie*. The intel-

lectual focus of *Naturphilosophie* was termed *Morphologie* by Goethe. See Charles Singer, *A History of Biology to about the Year 1900: A General Introduction to the Study of Living Things*, 3d rev. ed.(London, 1959), 215–22. For a partial English translation of the scientific works, see Johann Wolfgang von Goethe, *Scientific Studies*, ed. and trans. Douglas Miller (New York, 1988). For evaluations of Goethe's scientific work, see Sir Charles Sherrington, *Goethe on Nature and Science* (Cambridge, 1942), 23–24; and Agnes Arber, "Goethe's Botany: *The Metamorphosis of Plants* (1790) and Tobler's *Ode to Nature* (1782)," *Chronica Botanica* 10 (1946): 68. Goethe's own answer to his critics is *Venetian Epigram, No. 77* (see Goethe, *Selected Poems*, 127):

> So you dabble in botany, optics? How can you, a poet?
> Don't you feel better employed touching a sensitive heart?
> Oh, those sensitive hearts. Any charlatan knows how to touch them.
> No, let my one joy be this, Nature, to touch upon you!

   12. Goethe, "Excerpt from Studies for a Physiology of Plants,'" *Scientific Studies*, 73–74. The original is in idem, *Sämtliche Werke*, vol. 24, *Schriften zur Morphologie*, ed. Dorothea Kühn (Frankfurt am Main, 1987), 351.
   13. Goethe, "True Enough: To the Physicist," *Selected Poems*, 237. The manner of explication through presentation also can be shown in Schenkerian theory. For example, the existence of a diminution between the foreground and middleground levels of a piece shows no cause and effect between levels: it shows the "presentation" of the diminution. For a specific discussion of "presentation" and diminution, see Thomas Clifton, "An Application of Goethe's Concept of *Steigerung* to the Morphology of Diminution," *Journal of Music Theory* 14, no. 2 (1970): 165–89; Gary W. Don, "Goethe and Schenker," *In Theory Only* 10, no. 8 (1988): 1–14; and William Pastille, "Music and Morphology: Goethe's Influence on Schenker's Thought," in Hedi Siegel, ed., *Schenker Studies* (Cambridge, 1990), 29–44.
   14. Arber, "Goethe's Botany," 85. For comments on *Anschauung*, see Goethe, "Judgment through Intuitive Perception," "Analysis and Synthesis," "The Purpose Set Forth (from *On Morphology*)," in his *Scientific Studies*, 31, 49, and 63. The originals appear in Goethe, *Sämtliche Werke*, vol. 24. For discussions of Goethe's epistemology, see Humphrey Trevelyan, "Goethe as Thinker," in William Rose, ed., *Essays on Goethe* (London, 1949); Karl Viëtor, *Goethe the Thinker* (Cambridge, Mass., 1950); also Wilkinson, "Goethe's Concept of Form," 123. For a philosophical evaluation, see Ernst Cassirer, *The Problem of Knowledge* (New Haven, 1950), 145. Cassirer saw Goethe's position as unique in Western philosophy.
   15. Wilkinson, "Goethe's Concept of Form," 123. A translation and commentary on *Versuch die Metamorphose der Pflanzen zu erklären* appears in Arber, "Goethe's Botany," 90–155; for the original text, see Goethe, *Sämtliche Werke* 24:109–51.
   16. Cited in Peter Salm, *The Poem as Plant: A Biological View of Goethe's "Faust"* (Cleveland, 1971), 15.
   17. See Goethe, *Scientific Studies*, 65; the original appears in idem, *Sämtliche Werke* 24:392.
   18. The drawings are from Singer, *History of Biology*, 391. For the reference to *Kern*, see Goethe, *Scientific Studies*, 55: "The structure in its final form is, as it were, the inner nucleus molded in various ways by the characteristics of the outer element." The original text appears in idem, *Sämtliche Werke* 24:212.
   19. See Goethe, "Problems," in his *Scientific Studies*, 43; the original text is in Goethe, *Sämtliche Werke* 24:582.
   20. Goethe, *Scientific Studies*, 64; the original text is in idem, *Sämtliche Werke* 24:393.

21. Arnolds Grava, *A Structural Inquiry into the Symbolic Representation of Ideas* (Paris, 1969), 27. For a philosophical discussion of organic function, see Ernst Cassirer, *Substance and Function* (New York, 1953), esp. 17.

22. Arnold Schoenberg, "Gustav Mahler," in his *Style and Idea*, ed. Leonard Stein, trans. Leo Black (New York, 1975), 449.

23. Schoenberg, "Gedanke" manuscript (see note 3 above), 156: "Auf Geistesgefiet ist alles nur Vorstufe, auch wenn es richtig."

24. Arnold Schoenberg, *Theory of Harmony*, trans. Roy E. Carter (Berkeley, 1978), 18. See idem, *Harmonielehre* (Vienna, 1911), 16.

25. Schoenberg, *Harmonielehre*, 16.

26. Ibid., 15.

27. Arnold Schoenberg, *Structural Functions of Harmony*, ed. Leonard Stein, rev. ed. (New York, 1969), 19. The original version of the chart of the regions appears in idem, "Gedanke" manuscript (see note 3 above) as an insert in the essay "Construktionelle Funktions der Harmonie" (Constructive Functions of Harmony).

28. Schoenberg, *Theory of Harmony*, 313, and idem, *Harmonielehre*, 350.

29. Schoenberg, "Prinzipien des Aufbaus" (Principles of Construction), "Gedanke" manuscript, 217.

30. David Lewin, "Inversional Balance as an Organizing Force in Schoenberg's Music and Thought," *Perspectives of New Music* 6, no. 2 (1968): 3–4.

31. Schoenberg, *Structural Functions*, 30 and 68–69. I have extended the minor chart of the regions to outlying regions.

32. The columns on my example are intended to show derivations. For a discussion of major-minor interchange, see ibid., 51.

33. Schoenberg, "Gedanke" manuscript, 42: "*Grundgestalten* sind solche Gestalten, welche (womöglich) im ganzen Stück immer wieder auftreten und auf welche abgeleitete Gestalten zurückführbar sind. [Man hat früher das Motiv so genannt; das ist aber eine sehr oberflächliche Bezeichnung; denn Gestalten und Grundgestalten sind meist aus mehreren Motivformen zusammengesetzt; das Motiv aber ist der *jeweils kleinste* Teil.]" The bracketed sentence is Schoenberg's annotation of his own text.

34. Josef Rufer, *Composition with Twelve Tones*, trans. Humphrey Searle (Westport, Conn., 1954), 32. See also idem, "Begriff und Funktion der Grundgestalt," *Bericht über den 1. Kongress der Internationalen Schönberg-Gesellschaft*, ed. Rudolf Stephan (Vienna, 1974), 173–79.

35. Arnold Schoenberg, *Models for Beginners in Composition* (New York, 1943), 15. See also "*Zusammenhang, Kontrapunkt, Instrumentation, Formenlehre*," entered in "Unfinished Theoretical Manuscript, No. 2" in Rufer, *Works of Schoenberg*, 136 and housed at the Arnold Schoenberg Institute. The manuscript reads: "[A] musical motive is a sounding, rhythmicized phenomenon that, by its (possibly varied) repetitions in the course of a piece of music, is capable of creating the impression that it is the material of the piece." ("Musikalisches Motiv ist eine tönende rhythmisierte Erscheinung, welche durch ihre [eventuell variierten] Wiederholungen im Verlaufe eines Musikstückes den Anschein zu erwecken vermag, als ob sie dessen Material sei.")

36. Schoenberg, *Theory of Harmony*, 164: "When Brahms introduces the second theme of his Third Symphony (F major [first movement]) in the key of A major, it is not because one 'can introduce' the second theme as well in the key of the mediant. It is rather the consequence of the principal motive of the bass melody (harmonic connection!) F–A-flat (third and fourth measures), whose many repetitions, derivations, and variations finally make it necessary, as a temporary high point, for the progression F–A-flat to expand to the progression F–A (F, the initial key, A, the key of the second theme). Thus, the basic motive is given by the initial key and the key of the second theme." See idem, *Harmonielehre*, 187.

Note that the term *Hauptmotiv* is synonymous with *Grundmotiv* or "basic motive," which Schoenberg most extensively described in the unpublished comment "Zur Terminologie der Formenlehre" (On the Terminology for the Theory of Form), the manuscript classified "Mus 66" by Schoenberg and housed at the Arnold Schoenberg Institute.

The idea of a motive instigating a motion and formal consequences is also generally alluded to in Schoenberg, "*Zusammenhang, Kontrapunkt, Instrumentation, Formenlehre.*" Schoenberg generally described a motive as "something that gives rise to a motion. *A motion is that change in a state of rest which turns into its opposite.* Thus one can compare the motive with a driving force." (". . . etwas das zu einer Bewegung Anlass giebt. *Eine Bewegung ist jene Veränderung eines Ruhezustandes, die ihn in sein Gegenteil verkehrt.* Man kann somit das Motiv mit einer treibenden Kraft vergleichen.")

37. The "tonal problem" is discussed in Schoenberg, "Gedanke" manuscript, 15–16, 17, 35, and 89–91. See also P. Murray Dineen, "Problems of Tonality: Schoenberg and the Concept of Tonal Expression" (Ph.D. diss., Columbia University, 1988), chap. 10.

For Schoenberg's specific use of the terms "centrifugal" and "centripetal," see Arnold Schoenberg, "Prinzipien des Aufbaus," "Gedanke" manuscript, 223.

38. From an undated English manuscript left uncatalogued by Schoenberg. The comment begins: "My Subject: Beauty and Logic in Music." See Jean and Jesper Christensen, *From Schoenberg's Literary Legacy: A Catalog of Neglected Items* (Detroit, 1988), 99.

39. For a discussion of formal parts of a piece, see the following from Schoenberg, "Gedanke" manuscript: "Kontrast" (Contrast), 199; "Feste Formung" (Stable Form), 21; "Lockere Formung" (Loose Form), 27; "Gesetze der Fasslichkeit" (Laws of Comprehensibility), 55; "Die Gesetze des musikalischen Zusammenhangs" (Laws of Coherence), 65. See also idem, *Fundamentals of Musical Composition* (London, 1967), chaps. 18 and 20.

40. For documentation of Schoenberg's classroom teaching, see Gerald Strang Collection, Arnold Schoenberg Institute. For an application of an analytical methodology that takes Schoenberg's "tonal problem" into account, see Patricia Carpenter, "*Grundgestalt* as Tonal Function," *Music Theory Spectrum* 3 (1983): 15–38.

41. "Roving" harmony references many regions but does not definitively assert any one; see Schoenberg, *Structural Functions*, 3.

42. Schoenberg would call this chord a transformation on the second degree: ♯. The slash indicates a transformation chord.

FIFTEEN

The Contrapuntal Combination: Schoenberg's Old Hat

P. Murray Dineen

Andrew Porter, describing Schoenberg's concept of basic shape, tells the following anecdote:

> There is a story of Schoenberg's picking up a hat, turning it about in front of his pupils, and explaining: "You see, this is a hat, whether I look at it from above, from below, from the front, from behind, from the left, from the right, it always remains a hat, though it may look one thing from above and another from below."[1]

Using his hat to represent a musical work, Schoenberg was trying, I think, to convey the notion of a multifaceted musical space. His point: from different perspectives or even obscured, an object retains its identity, be it a hat or a piece of music. Music, like hats, is multifaceted. It follows that the experience of music can be spatial; one can know a piece from the perspectives of its many faces—from many locations in a musical space—which fuse into a whole:

> As I learn to know [a piece of music], I know it as a thing, quite apart from any single experience of it. I can "walk around it", so to speak, and am very much aware of its "other side". And if I know it well, I certainly know what it "looks like" as a whole, as if from a single point of view.[2]

Schoenberg's concept of the contrapuntal combination stems from this notion of a multifaceted musical experience. For Schoenberg the combination of a subject with various counterpoints expresses the totality of a contrapuntal composition; each new counterpoint provides a new perspective on its subject, as does every turn of Schoenberg's hat. To know a contrapuntal composition well is to know all the combinations of subject and counterpoints—all the subject's

435

facets and hence its shape from various contrapuntal perspectives—
and to know this completely, as if from one unified perspective.

In prose, Schoenberg used the term *contrapuntal combination* in his
characteristically aphoristic style, a style that unfortunately left many
suggestive thoughts only tentatively defined. The essay "Bach," included in the collection of essays titled *Style and Idea*, provides the
clearest definition of this term.[3] At the heart of a Bach fugue lies a basic
combination, from which stem various derived combinations of subject with counterpoints or countersubjects: "There is a basic combination which is the source of all combinations" (*SI*, 397). In the fugue, this
combination is "unraveled"—disassembled and reassembled to produce various component combinations:

> Contrapuntal composition . . . [produces] its material
> by . . . a procedure rather to be called *unravelling* [*Abwick-
> lung*]. That is, a basic configuration or combination taken
> asunder and reassembled in a different order contains ev-
> erything which will later produce a different sound than
> that of the original formulation. Thus, a canon of two or
> more voices can be written in one single line, yet furnishes
> various sounds. If multiple counterpoints are applied, a
> combination of three voices, invertible in the octave, tenth
> and twelfth, offers so many combinations that even longer
> pieces can be derived from it.
>
> According to this theory, one should not expect that new
> themes occur in such fugues, but that there is a basic com-
> bination which is the source of all combinations. (*SI*, 397)

I shall refer to this procedure of assembling subject and countersubjects by the term *envelopment*, as if a subject were wrapped or enveloped in successive counterpoints.[4] And I shall define the contrapuntal
combination as the sum of a basic combination and the various envel-
oping combinations derived from it during the course of a piece. A
contrapuntal combination can be represented by placing the basic
combination on staves and aligning the derived combinations above
or below it.

To understand the concept of contrapuntal combination, one must
know that for Schoenberg counterpoint meant the combination of
motives,[5] especially the "invertible combination"—invertible
counterpoint. As he put it: "Real counterpoint is based on invertible
combinations."[6] Species counterpoint is but a preparation for "real
counterpoint."[7]

Real counterpoint, for Schoenberg, also presumes an independence
of parts. Contrapuntal parts are not governed by a preconceived chordal

harmony proceeding from a notion of scale degrees and root progressions.[8] Nor do individual parts in a contrapuntal composition "develop" thematic material by varying or altering thematic features—by "developing variation," as Schoenberg called it.[9] Instead subjects and countersubjects remain largely unaltered, unvaried, and in this sense undeveloped.

Schoenberg refined the definition of *contrapuntal combination* by relating the term to a style of music—polyphony from the time of J.S. Bach—and by contrasting this style with its successor, homophony. For Schoenberg, Bach's time shows a marked change in musical styles and compositional techniques, from Renaissance polyphony to Classical homophony, from the style of contrapuntal combination and the technique of envelopment or unraveling to the style of accompanied homophony and the technique of developing variation:[10]

> While Bach still was living a new musical style came into being out of which there later grew the style of the Viennese Classicists, the style of homophonic-melodic composition, or, as I call it, the style of Developing Variation. (*SI*, 115)

Bach was at home in both styles, an able practitioner of both techniques. Schoenberg heralded Bach as "the first to introduce just that technique . . . of 'developing variation'" (*SI*, 118) that succeeded the technique of contrapuntal envelopment. I sense, however, that in Schoenberg's eyes Bach was above all the master of counterpoint, who elevated the complex style of Renaissance polyphony to new heights.

The distinction in style Schoenberg drew between polyphony and homophony proceeds from two distinct concepts of harmony, linear and vertical—a linear concept according to which harmony derives from the coincidence of independent linear parts, and a vertical concept of harmonies built above chordal roots. The concept of harmony derived from independent linear parts is appropriate to the contrapuntal combination, while the concept of root-progression harmony is not:

> As many theorists of the older school state, harmony is achieved through the intelligent motion of independent parts which lend each other color and meaning by their vertical changes. According to that consideration harmony, embellished by moving parts but bound to degrees, could not, on the one hand, fulfill this task, while, on the other hand, the necessary development of harmony, which is provoked by the basic problems of moving progressions, could never be brought into accord with the demands of independent parts.[11]

Thus, for Schoenberg, counterpoint is based on the combination of lines (especially combination through invertible counterpoint), to which root-progression harmony is extraneous. The totality of a piece of contrapuntal music is expressed in the multifaceted combination of the subject and all the various countersubjects or counterpoints that enfold it. We know such a piece—much as Schoenberg's students knew his hat—by viewing its subject from the various perspectives of these countersubjects and counterpoints, these forming a total, unified perspective. This is an older technique of composition—Schoenberg's old hat, as it were—compared with the newer techniques of developing variation and, as we shall see below, twelve-tone composition.

The contrapuntal combination may be illustrated by an analysis of Bach's Fugue in G Minor from the second book of the *Well-Tempered Clavier*, a fugue well known for its invertible counterpoint. To begin, I shall set forth a contrapuntal combination—the subject enveloped by the various manifestations of its countersubject. In the interest of clarity, the subject and countersubject have been reduced to a chain of sixths and thirds, as set forth in the lower system of example 15.1. (The combination in this example is that of answer and countersubject in mm. 5–8.)

It is possible that Bach tested invertible combination of his subject and countersubject at various intervals. Example 15.2 lists the combinations that appear in the fugue, as well as their inversions. (The two sections of the example, a and b, are based on the combination of subject and countersubject in mm. 9–12. This combination appears at the bottom of each section, at the correct pitch level. Other combinations in the example have been transposed from the score, to show more clearly the procedure of inversion.) In the first section,

Example 15.1   J.S. Bach, Fugue in G minor, *Well-Tempered Clavier*, book 2, mm. 5–8

Example 15.2   The contrapuntal combination

Example 15.2 (cont.)

countersubjects appear inverted above subject; in the second section, subjects appear inverted above countersubject.[12]

The two lowest staves of each section, which are joined by a brace, constitute the basic combination. Note that the upper of each pair of staves is the locus or fulcrum of inversion—the fixed point around which the bottom staff is inverted. In each section the inversions are numbered successively upward from the bottom. When I refer to combination a1, I mean the combination of countersubject a1 and the subject beneath it; combination b2 combines subject b2 and the countersubject beneath it. Combinations a1 and b1 derive from inversion at the octave; a2 and b2 from inversion at the tenth; a3 and b3, inversion at the twelfth; and a4 and b4, inversion at the thirteenth.[13] Example 15.2 contains the complete contrapuntal combination of the fugue. Bach's task (this following Schoenberg's thought) was to break apart the total combination—the sum of the two sections of the example—and express it successively in individual combinations, a form more readily available to his listener.

A casual glance at the interval content of this example will produce interesting observations, among these that inversion reverses or retrogrades successions of intervals. Speaking solely in terms of intervals, one may observe that any combination in the first section has a complementary retrograde form in the second—the two combinations sharing a common interval of inversion. Combination b2 retrogrades a2 (both are produced by inversion at the tenth), b3 retrogrades a3 (inversion at the twelfth), and b4 retrogrades a4 (inversion at the thirteenth).

The temporal and spatial aspects of contrapuntal combination are intriguing. First of all, the total combination must be broken apart and "unraveled" through time to be expressed concretely. It would be impossible to hear and to know all the combinations if they were heard simultaneously. Bach's task was to unravel the total combination strand by strand through time. Does this not suggest that the total combination is nontemporal, or *pre*temporal (pardon the oxymoron), lying outside the measure of a piece? In other words, the combination awaits the procedure of unraveling to become known to the listener in time. The real essence of the fugue is timeless in a most literal sense.[14]

Secondly, and solely in terms of interval succession, is there no referential combination, since any given combination is at one and the same time the retrograde of another combination and the inversion of yet another? As example 15.2 shows, the basic combination of one section is a form derived by inversion of the other. In this respect, there is nothing intrinsic to any given combination that distinguishes it as referential from another, thus no intrinsically basic combination, no prime form. The same holds if we consider retrograded interval succession. Because of this retrogression, is there then no intrinsic, definite beginning or end to a particular combination, the end of one being the beginning of another under inversion? If so, it follows that there is no right or wrong side up; the subject is not predisposed to sit either above or below the countersubject. Thus the contrapuntal combination is nontemporal and spatially abstract, as opposed to its concrete, temporal realization (or reification) in the fugue.

In order to show something of the total combination unraveling, broken down into its components, in the G-minor fugue, let me pursue a spatial metaphor. The subject may be viewed from the perspective of its various countersubjects, much as one might look at Schoenberg's hat from his students' perspectives. In mm. 9–12, combination b1, from the perspective of the countersubject the subject lies above me, with the contrapuntal interval of a third nearest (see ex. 15.3). It is as if I held Schoenberg's hat above and faced its front—figuratively, the interval of a third. In mm. 13–16, the countersubject is inverted at the octave so the subject lies below me and the interval succession is retrograded—the interval of a sixth appears first (this is combination a1; see ex. 15.4). It is as if I put Schoenberg's hat below me and, while doing so, turned it laterally 180 degrees so as to look at it from the back—the interval of a sixth. In mm. 20–23, combination b1 returns, and the hat is restored to its original position. In mm. 20–23, another combination, however, emerges tentatively, a combination with the interval succession fifth to octave (see ex. 15.5). This new combination (b2) appears distinctly in mm. 45–48; it doubles combination b1 at the third, thus yielding the double succession of intervals fifth and third to octave and sixth (see ex. 15.6). Following my metaphor, this double combination creates a sense of depth, as if the hat were in perspective above me—the closeness of its brim (the intervals of a third to a sixth) and the distance of its crown (fifth to octave).[15]

In mm. 51–54, a multiple combination appears (see exx. 15.7a–c): the subject is doubled in sixths, the countersubject in thirds. There are two successions of a third to a sixth (combination b1), one accompa-

Example 15.3   J.S. Bach, Fugue in G minor, mm. 9–12

442

Example 15.4
mm. 13–16

Example 15.5
mm. 20–23

Example 15.6
mm. 45–48

Example 15.7
mm. 51–54

Example 15.8
mm. 59–62

nied by the succession of a fifth to an octave (b2) and the other by a new combination (b4, invertible at the thirteenth), octave to fourth. Here my metaphor has reached its useful limit, for I have a fourfold combination—two hats, each seen from two vantage points.

How remarkable, then, to encounter in mm. 59–62 a combination of equal complexity (ex. 15.8). It contains retrogrades of mm. 51–54: the

444 P. Murray Dineen

succession of third to sixth of mm. 51–54 becomes sixth to third (combination b1 becomes a1); fifth to octave becomes octave to fifth (b2 becomes a2) and appears twice. And a new combination, tenth to seventh (a3), surfaces. Here, surely, the total combination is only partly unraveled, and we get a glimpse of the abstract whole.

* * *

Schoenberg drew a distinction between his concept of counterpoint and concepts set forth by his contemporaries such as Ernst Kurth, whose "linear counterpoint" he derided.[16] For Schoenberg, Kurth's linear counterpoint grew from a concern with individual rather than combined lines, with the horizontal dimension rather than the vertical. Such a concept was anathema to Schoenberg, for whom counterpoint meant not individual lines but lines in combination: "The individual line explains nothing about the whole and gives no indication why this one line should appear at the same time as others. . . . Only the relationship of several rows to one another, the vertical aspect of the line, gives them their significance!" (SI, 296).

Schoenberg did not relate the concepts of contrapuntal combination and twelve-tone composition in his writings. He apparently conceived of a twelve-tone work as being essentially homophonic; contrapuntal imitation served only in deriving subordinate voices:

> The meaning of composing in imitative style [in twelve-tone composition] is not the same as it is in counterpoint. [Imitation] is only one of the ways of adding a coherent accompaniment, or subordinate voices, to the main theme, whose character it thus helps to express more intensively. (SI, 235)

This last sentence differentiates between principal and subordinate voices, a distinction foreign to contrapuntal combination. Describing twelve-tone composition, Schoenberg found that "the combination as such . . . is entirely outside the discussion as an element in the process of composition" (SI, 208). Indeed, twelve-tone composition with a contrapuntal combination based on the row and its derived forms would be too facile. Since in twelve-tone composition there is nothing comparable to dissonance, which provides the main criteria for selecting counterpoints in tonal counterpoint, nothing could be excluded from a twelve-tone combination for lack of suitability. The realization of the composer's idea would be too easily won in a twelve-tone contrapuntal combination. As Schoenberg put it: "Even the writing of whole fugues is a little too easy under these circumstances" (SI, 248).

Despite these distinctions, there is still a comparison to be made between contrapuntal and twelve-tone composition in terms of musical space. As is the case with the contrapuntal combination, Schoenberg's method of composing with twelve tones also stems from the notion of a multifaceted musical experience. Like knowing a contrapuntal combination, to know a twelve-tone composition well is to know all the row forms used, and to know these from the all-embracing perspective of the so-called magic square, or row matrix.

When writing on Bach and invertible counterpoint, Schoenberg spoke of a basic combination—subject and countersubject—from which other combinations are derived, these forming a totality called the contrapuntal combination. His derivation of a row matrix from a basic twelve-tone row is strikingly similar, especially in terms of the unified spatial experience to be gained from a twelve-tone work. To know such a work well, perhaps we should also know something of Schoenberg's thoughts on the contrapuntal combination, and in doing so let history inform our theory.

Perhaps the contrapuntal combination sheds some light on the famous Schoenberg aphorism: *"The two-or-more-dimensional space in which musical ideas are presented is a unit"* (SI, 220; from the essay "Composition with Twelve Tones [1]"). The same questions about top and bottom, front and back, can be asked of the row matrix, the total combination of prime and all derived forms of the twelve-tone row. In the essay just cited, Schoenberg asserted that the various dimensions of musical space—the various perspectives of a musical subject—form a unity, as if one locates a work in space according to a single, all-embracing perspective, a "unit." This conception establishes no privileged or absolute, referential point of view in twelve-tone composition, but instead considers the so-called prime, inversion, and retrograde as complementary and hence equal perspectives comprised by our vision of the whole: *"The unity of musical space demands an absolute and unitary perception. In this space . . . there is no absolute down, no right or left, forward or backward. Every musical configuration, every movement of tones has to be comprehended primarily as a mutual relation of sounds"* (SI, 223).[17]

Schoenberg was presumably trying to illustrate this unitary notion of musical space as he turned his hat before his students. In the essay on twelve-tone composition, he similarly used other objects as examples to show that identity is not tied to a single position in space:

> To the imaginative and creative faculty, relations in the material sphere are as independent from directions or planes as material objects are, in their sphere, to our perceptive

faculties. Just as our mind always recognizes, for instance, a knife, a bottle or a watch, regardless of its position, and can reproduce it in the imagination in every possible position, even so a musical creator's mind can operate subconsciously with a row of tones, regardless of their direction, regardless of the way in which a mirror might show the mutual relations, which remain a given quality. (*SI*, 223)

The twelve-tone composition, like a fugue, may also be seen as the unraveling of an abstract combination—the contrapuntal combination presupposing the same multidimensional spatial unity as does the twelve-tone composition. In other words, a fugue and a twelve-tone work both combine a multitude of spatial perspectives into one absolute unity—in the case of the fugue, the total combination, while in the case of the twelve-tone work, the row matrix.

As I have suggested, the experience of a musical work as a multi-faceted combination holds both for a contrapuntal combination such as a fugue and for twelve-tone composition, despite Schoenberg's apparent distinctions. To know a twelve-tone work well is to know all combinations of prime forms, inversions, and retrogrades used, much as in a Bach fugue one knows all combinations of subject and countersubject. In both cases, the composer would map out an abstract tonal space: on the one hand, a prime row extended through transposition and inversion to form a row matrix; on the other, a basic combination of subject and countersubject enveloped to form a contrapuntal combination.

There are essential differences, of course, between Bach's fugue and Schoenberg's twelve-tone compositions. Bach preferred (in this fugue) inversion by transposition, not mirror inversion. And Bach's combinations are governed constantly by the strictures of dissonance treatment, while the combination of twelve-tone rows is not.

Despite these differences, the tonal space of Bach's fugue and that of a twelve-tone composition are similar. Ultimately, they are both nontemporal: nothing intrinsically favors either a row or its retrograde, or a particular contrapuntal combination and its retrograde, as referential. Both tonal spaces are abstract and unitary: there is no absolute point of reference, no favored row form or combination. Prime row and basic contrapuntal combination are determined extrinsically by order of appearance in the piece. In both fugue and twelve-tone composition the composer makes temporally manifest this abstract idea of a unitary tonal space by presenting the row matrix or combination in successive (and thus more salient) component rows or combinations. We sense the abstract unity of the tonal space as we come to know the work and fuse these various facets together.

In summary, a twelve-tone composition—like a fugue—is an un-raveling of an abstract combination, Schoenberg's new hat, as it were, turning before us. And in Schoenberg's conception of a twelve-tone work and his appreciation of Bach, we find both a fascinating histori-cal interpretation and a unique theoretical perspective that demon-strates structural similarities between works separated by nearly two centuries.

Notes

1. Andrew Porter, "Modern German Chamber Music," in Alec Robertson, ed., *Chamber Music* (Harmondsworth, 1957), 397–98. See Erwin Stein, "New Formal Prin-ciples," in his *Orpheus in New Guises*, trans. Hans Keller (London, 1953), 63; also Anton Webern, "The Path to Twelve-Note Composition (Lecture 7, 26 February 1932)," in his *The Path to the New Music*, ed. Willi Reich, trans. Leo Black (Bryn Mawr, 1963), 53: "An ash-tray, seen from all sides, is always the same, and yet different. So an idea should be presented in the most multifarious way possible."

2. Patricia Carpenter, "The Musical Object," *Current Musicology* 5 (1967): 64. For the purposes of this paper, I shall use the following as a working definition of space: "Space may be concretely experienced as immediate, personal, dynamic—place in relation to me, extension as matter of things I can touch or as background for things I see or a motion I make. As it is differentiated from me and my own bodily orienta-tion, it becomes more abstractly conceived—mediate, impersonal, static—hyposta-sized into a unified space of places. Ultimately, it is the abstract possibility of exten-sion itself—continuous, boundless, homogeneous, a continuum in which all things have a place." Idem, "Aspects of Musical Space," in Eugene Narmour and Ruth A. Solie, eds., *Explorations in Music, the Arts, and Ideas: Essays in Honor of Leonard B. Meyer* (Stuyvesant, 1988), 344.

3. Arnold Schoenberg, *Style and Idea,* ed. Leonard Stein, trans. Leo Black (Berkeley, 1984), 393–97. Subsequent references to this source in both the text and notes are abbreviated *SI*. See also the following: Rudolph Stephan, "Schönbergs Entwurf über das Komponieren mit selbständigen Stimmen," *Archiv für Musikwissenschaft* 29 (1972): 239–56, which contains a facsimile of Schoenberg's outline (dated 1911) for a text in contrapuntal composition proposed to Universal Edition; Josef Rufer's preface to Arnold Schoenberg, *30 Kanons*, ed. J. Rufer, trans. P. Branscombe (Kassel, 1963), v–viii, and Schoenberg's canons therein.

4. The term *envelopment* was suggested by Patricia Carpenter.

5. "Counterpoint: the study of the art of voice leading with respect to motivic combination." Arnold Schoenberg, *Harmonielehre*, 3d ed. (Vienna, 1922), translated by Roy E. Carter as *Theory of Harmony* (Berkeley, 1978), 13.

6. Arnold Schoenberg, *Fundamentals of Musical Composition* (London, 1967), 125.

7. Arnold Schoenberg, *Preliminary Exercises in Counterpoint* (London, 1963).

8. Schoenberg does refer, however, to scale degrees as chordal roots in contrapun-tal exercises in *Preliminary Exercises*. See parts 2 and 3 passim.

9. See Walter Frisch, *Brahms and the Principle of Developing Variation* (Berkeley, 1984). Frisch compares developing variation with the contrapuntal combination on p. 2.

10. Style is to be distinguished from idea. Schoenberg did so with the example of a pair of pliers: the idea of increased power gained by leverage around a fulcrum is realized in the two arms of a pair of pliers, which are joined at the middle around a

fulcrum. Pliers may eventually become obsolete, but the idea of leverage is eternal: "The tool itself may fall into disuse, but the idea behind it can never become obsolete. And therein lies the difference between a mere style and a real idea" (*SI*, 123).

We might think of the "idea" as the basic combination—or, as I shall show, the notion of an absolute musical space—which is realized stylistically in Bach's fugue. Josef Rufer wrote in *Schoenberg, 30 Kanons*, vi–vii, of a "polymorphous" canon that "admits of a large number of imitative repetitions of the basic part," these being "variations of an idea" (*Variationen einer Idee*), which reveal the "riches of content" (*Inhalt*).

11. Schoenberg, *Preliminary Exercises*, 222.

12. I could have expressed this in a single section, with my present second section replaced by a lower extension of table 1, such that countersubjects appear in various transpositions below the subject. In this sense, the subject would be truly enveloped by countersubjects both above and below. My present arrangement, which assumes inversion of the subject around a fixed countersubject, allows for greater ease of comparison between particular combinations.

13. Combination a4 is not realized in the piece and hence b4 is not in truth an inversion but rather a noninverting transposition of the countersubject. I have included inversion at the thirteenth, however, for the sake of completeness.

14. "The fugue . . . , as it is epitomized by Bach, uses a frame . . . to freeze the forces in order to project a certain heightened moment as if 'forever.' Again the whole of the fugue is 'all there' in its initial theme—a basic combination of figures which never change, much like pieces of a mosaic; it is a subject that 'takes time' to be demonstrated in all its different aspects. Repetition here cannot be separated from a process of penetration, analysis, and explication; it eliminates time. . . . Bach's idea of fugue is in a sense timeless; ultimately it must be grasped outside of time." Patricia Carpenter, "Musical Form Regained," *Journal of Philosophy* 62, no. 2 (1965): 46.

"Each musical composition embodies a system of interrelationships that is, to a significant extent, independent of the time within which the composition unfolds. And anyone wishing to understand these relationships will find it necessary to compare musical segments that are widely separated within the actual sequence of the work. Music analysts thus find it useful, at least at some stage of their work, to view a composition as a fixed set of synchronic connections, independent of their specific temporal location. If, as in the physical sciences, one thinks of space as an ordering of individual events in relation to one another rather than as an absolute physical medium, then clearly the spatial model is eminently, and inescapably, applicable to music." Robert P. Morgan, "Musical Time/Musical Space," *Critical Inquiry* 6 (Spring 1980): 529.

15. Combination b2 is in fact preceded in mm. 47–50 by its inversion, a2, with the requisite retrogression of intervals.

16. Ernst Kurth, *Grundlagen des linearen Kontrapunkts: Bachs melodische Polyphonie*, 5th ed. (Bern, 1956).

17. "Fundamentally every point in this space is capable of becoming the ideal vantage point of the observer, the vantage point for the 'view'; there is no single, predetermined or fixed point from which the directions could be determined in a particular case or to which they could be referred. That which is right, left, etc., changes with the point occupied in space. 'Absolute', therefore, in the sense of independent, unrestricted, released from every tie (certainly from the tie to a fixed reference point in space): specifically, not relative." Regina Busch, "On the Horizontal and Vertical Presentation of Musical Ideas and on Musical Space (I)," trans. Michael Graubart, *Tempo*, no. 154 (September 1985): 8.

SIXTEEN

The "New Education" and Music Theory, 1900–1925

LEE A. ROTHFARB

Consciously or unconsciously, music theorists of the past have adopted various ideological premises for their work. Names such as Rameau, Marx, Hauptmann, Helmholtz, and Riemann come to mind.[1] In addition to ideological premises, a theorist's intended audience and objectives affect the style and methodology of their work. Hauptmann's *Die Natur der Harmonik und Metrik* (1853), for example, which is explicitly *not* intended as a guide to composition, differs by nature from A.B. Marx's *Lehre von der musikalischen Komposition* (1837–47), which, in attempting to unite intellect (*Geist*) and action (*That*), *is* intended as a guide to composition.[2] Both theorists have roots in Hegelian idealism, but their expressions of it, and their intended audiences and goals, differ fundamentally.

We can also identify intellectual stimuli that affected music theory in the early twentieth century. For example, the theorists of the time were interested in psychology, which was then a young and intriguing field. Gestalt psychology in particular appealed to musicians because of its holistic approach to perception. The anti-positivistic spirit of the day, stressing inner life and unconscious processes, reinforced the interest in psychological questions.[3]

In addition to specific intellectual currents, a more general cultural phenomenon also affected music theory: the educational reform movement of the two decades preceding World War I. The idea that events in public education affected music theory may at first seem unusual. When we consider, however, that the early twentieth-century reforms in education extended beyond core subjects, such as mathematics and science, especially to education in the arts, and further that certain contemporary music theorists taught in settings other than universities and conservatories (e.g., in secondary schools and newly launched continuing education programs for adults), it is not surprising to find

449

that some music-theoretical writings reflect their authors' experiences in institutions other than the academy. Hermann
Kretzschmar (1848–1924) and one of his best-known students,
Arnold Schering (1877–1941), for example, were active outside the university in the early stages of their careers. Both
Kretzschmar and Schering published works that grew out of
activities in continuing education programs, in Kretzschmar's
case also out of his work as a conductor. Moreover, Kretzschmar was
an important advocate of reforms in music education in public
schools. The composer-theorist and distinguished journalist August
Halm (1869–1929) was a renowned pedagogue whose writings influenced both music education and music criticism in the early twentieth century. Halm fostered an aesthetic viewpoint different from
that of Kretzschmar and Schering, and so advocated a different educational philosophy.[4] Ernst Kurth (1886–1946), a university professor and author of landmark monographs on the music of Bach,
Wagner, and Bruckner, followed Halm's approach. In order to understand the motivation and outlook of these authors' theoretical writings, we must first discuss the educational reform movement in the
decades around 1900.[5]

   In 1890, Julius Langbehn (1851–1907), disillusioned by liberalism's
failure to bring about cultural and social rebirth, accused the ossified
educational system of hastening cultural decline. At the very beginning of his immensely popular *Rembrandt als Erzieher*, Langbehn remarked sarcastically, "Germany is full of people who wear glasses,
either actually or in spirit."[6] He questioned the efficacy and value of
perpetuating abstract knowledge detached from practical and spiritual needs. "German education," he argued, "which has for so long
risen to abstraction and distinction, must now come back down to the
simple and concrete, otherwise it could quickly change over into too
shrill a voice."[7] Education had become preoccupied with esoterica,
indifferent to personal development, and antithetical to anything that
might stimulate innate curiosity and sustain natural enthusiasm for
learning.

   Educators who visited German schools in the decades around 1900
confirm Langbehn's accusations. John T. Prince and William H. Winch,
for instance, reporting on their visits around 1890 and 1900, tell of
drab, bare-walled classrooms where the only pictures displayed were
those of Luther and the emperor.[8] Asked about the neglect of visual
stimuli, German teachers answered soberly that students no longer
notice what they see all the time. Teachers responded to Winch's sug-
gestions for a less theoretical approach to science by saying that a
"hands-on" method would take too much time in an already overbur-

dened curriculum.[9] Thomas Alexander and Beryl Parker report having had similar experiences in the course of their travels around 1910.[10]

Young, idealistic teachers at the turn of the century rebelled against such methods. They rejected the politicization and functionalization of education as intellectually stifling. To reformers, contemporary society was mechanized and artificial enough without perpetuating methods that reinforced these qualities. Change was a natural process to progressives, who saw educational reform as part of a larger plan for cultural and moral renewal in Germany, while conservatives fought to preserve the status quo. Changes had been introduced as early as the 1870s and 1880s, but they affected more the structure than the substance and style of education. The reformers of the 1890s and early 1900s were concerned with material and method, and above all with the ultimate meaning, the significance, of what students learned in the classroom.

It would take us too far afield to discuss all the reforms that make up the so-called New Education. We are concerned here with those reforms that pertain to education in the arts, and with how their underlying ideas affected certain music-theoretical writings of the time. After discussing the premises of the New Education, we will review selected music analyses that arose from the spirit of the New Education.[11]

* * *

Like any far-reaching and influential "movement," the New Education was diverse in its local features and agendas, and varied in the specific application of its principles. Still, there are a few fundamental traits that run through its regional manifestations. Foremost among these is the deliberate focus on the child *as child*, and not as a proto-adult. This attitude gave the movement a slogan: *Vom Kinde aus!* (Begin with the child!). Broadly understood, this phrase embraces the spirit and method of the New Education.[12] It meant that childhood is to be viewed as a distinctive, unrepeatable, independent stage in life, and not merely as a prelude to adulthood. In contrast to the old rote-and-recitation method, the reformers stressed the need to promote children's spontaneity (*Selbsttätigkeit*) and to avoid choking off that spontaneity from the start with fact mongering. Central to the New Education was letting the child's native talents evolve naturally (*entfalten "lassen"*) in a casual but thoughtfully directed manner. Removing obstacles, presenting opportunities, awakening thought processes, in short, preparing the ground for learning and leaving the rest to natural intellectual development—these were the keys. The student was thus no longer considered a mere receptor and repository of knowledge but rather a discoverer and creator. The child was seen as a type of "artist," whose creativity and originality the teacher would unlock and cultivate.[13]

In order for students to develop their natural abilities, education itself had to proceed naturally, i.e., not through studying pictures or learning historical and scientific facts. Rather, the New Education stressed direct, personal experience. Students studied history by visiting historical sites and monuments and by acting out plays, learned about agriculture by visiting and working on farms, learned about trades and commerce by observing and working alongside craftsmen, and studied geography and topography by taking field trips. Real-life experiences would make learning more meaningful, reformers argued, leading to a genuine understanding of the subject matter, and so foster critical judgment and synthetic thinking.[14] Acquiring culture at the source, by active experience, was a hallmark of the New Education.

Such a program could not easily be realized in public schools. In addition to problems of financing and implementing such ideas with large numbers of students, there was the predictable resistance from "old school" conservatives. Reformers got around these problems by founding private schools. School communities were formed, often called "free schools" to emphasize independence. These communities typically withdrew to idyllic country and woodland settings to escape industrialized areas and the superficialities of society. "Free schools" were governed by a collective body of teachers, students, and parents. Daily business was handled by a director, or "leader," often the school's founder, whose educational philosophy set the tone for both learning and living. Many "free schools" were founded, built, and operated in such a communal fashion. In throwing off the yoke of the empire's authoritarianism, the New Education would be democratic, at least ideally.[15]

As explained earlier, the New Education stimulated ideological and methodological revisions in the teaching of all subjects. Not surprisingly, education in the arts was especially susceptible to these ideas. The goals of language, drawing, and music teachers coincided naturally with those of the New Education: fostering spontaneity, imagination, and creativity. In *Rembrandt als Erzieher*, an inspiration for many reformers, Langbehn did after all have the arts primarily in mind as the basis for reforms. In contrast to those who saw science and technology as the focus of human activity, Langbehn saw the arts as its focus, and the source of cultural revitalization and sustenance.[16]

Alfred Lichtwark (1852–1914), a school teacher and later director of the Hamburg Art Museum, was the leading spokesman for educational reform in the arts. He was a key organizer of three national arts education conferences, the last of which focused on music and physical training (Hamburg, 1905). The conferences brought together artists, educators, *and* laypersons, in keeping with the idea that revising arts education should benefit society as a whole, not just a select, talented few. For Lichtwark and his followers the arts were more than decoration or diversion. According to his plan, a revised understanding and appreciation for the arts would stimulate a new way of thinking and living. In the large scheme of things new forms of education in the arts would bring a cultural renaissance. The demand for arts education does not arise as an isolated phenomenon; "from the very outset," Lichtwark declared, "it is inseparably linked with the contemporaneous call . . . for a moral renewal of our life. The two areas cannot be separated."[17]

Music educators of the time realized that reforms in music education were necessary and that they were linked to the cultural elevation of society as a whole. In a booklet entitled *Musikalische Zeitfragen* (1903), Hermann Kretzschmar analyzed contemporary problems. Looking back at the nineteenth century, he saw a lamentable decline in the popular cultivation of art music that was, curiously, in inverse proportion both to the tremendous growth of education for professional musicians and to the artistic achievements of German composers. He concluded that music education for the folk had received too little attention: "Music must above all be secure in the folk, in receptiveness and understanding; music must evolve its power and benefits based on a well-supervised involvement with music. Only then can one argue over composers and trends in compositional practice."[18]

In order to instill a musical consciousness in the folk, Kretzschmar advocated a revised approach to singing instruction and also proposed a program of basic training in music aesthetics. By this he meant training in "musical hermeneutics," that is, in interpreting the meaning of musical events and how they combine to form a whole. Kretzschmar published two essays that laid the groundwork for such training. It would be a means for understanding the content (*Inhalt*) of musical artworks, and would be based on a new form of the doctrine of affections.[19] In proposing hermeneutic analysis, Kretzschmar intended to remedy the failings of music education.[20]

Contrary to Eduard Hanslick's formalist outlook, Kretzschmar held that instrumental music contains "a general spiritual content [*geistiger Inhalt*], for which the particular musical form serves as a husk and shell." A trained person will be able "not only to feel [this content] but also to sketch it in words . . . at least in its essential parts." The task of hermeneutics, then, is "to distill the affects from the tones and to lay out the structure of their development. . . . Whoever penetrates past the tones and sonic forms to the affects elevates the sensuous pleasure, the formal work, to a spiritual activity." To his formalist-minded contemporaries Kretzschmar declared: "The understanding of formal structure is only an intermediate stage. Forms are means of expression. That which is expressed is something spiritual."[21]

Kretzschmar introduces hermeneutic analysis by interpreting the content of intervals, motives, melodic variations, rhythms, harmonies, and simple chord progressions. Once small contexts are interpreted—a theme, for instance—the rest follows naturally, since "the task of discerning the meaning of four hundred measures is essentially no different from revealing the meaning of four or eight bars . . . For the whole is the sum of individual passages."[22]

In his second article on hermeneutics, Kretzschmar illustrates how his ideas might apply to a whole piece. Extending and refining work from the first article, he first interprets the subject of the Fugue in C Major from J.S. Bach's *Well-Tempered Clavier*, book 1 (ex. 16.1). According to Kretzschmar, the cautious but deliberate ascent of a fourth at the head of the subject (c^1–f^1), together with the quick descent at the tail, give the theme a "melancholy" content. The two "energetic" ascending fourth leaps (e^1–a^1, d^1–g^1) strive to overcome that affect. This miniature struggle within the subject becomes the formal content of the fugue as a whole: the gradual triumph of energetic determination over melancholy resignation.

Kretzschmar divides this example into two sections, mm. 1–6 and 7–14, each containing an unsuccessful attempt to overcome the affect. In the first attempt the soprano sweeps up to g^2 (m. 4) but then sinks back, along with the other voices (m. 5). In the second attempt an energetic stretto renews the effort to break free (m. 7). The soprano climbs up to a peak by sequential repetition of the tail motive up a whole step (m. 8). However, the companion voice in the *stretto* (tenor) fails to follow through with the ascending sequence. The tenor stalls on e^1 (m. 8), and the effort founders on a poignant dissonance at the downbeat of m. 9. The modulation to A minor thwarts the enterprise altogether and dashes hopes of breaking the affect (mm. 11–14).

Kretzschmar gives a listener some insight into the formal processes in the first half of the fugue by referring to readily perceivable phenomena like melodic direction and register (mm. 4–5), imitation and poignant dissonance (mm. 7–9), and modulation to a minor key.[23] If we look more closely at mm. 1–14, we can identify several technical phenomena that support his hermeneutic analysis. For example, the ascent from the first to the fourth scale degree at the beginning of the subject hints at subdominant harmony, which is less "energetic" than

455

Example 16.1   J.S. Bach, Fugue in C Major, *Well-Tempered Clavier,* book 1, mm. 1–14

a typical outline from the first to the fifth degree, and perhaps explains Kretzschmar's "melancholy" affect. The descending resolution from f^1 to e^1 in m. 1 could imply a plagal progression, IV–I, which again has a less energetic effect than would have resulted if f^1 had ascended to g^1, implying an active IV–V progression. Kretzschmar finesses these details by pointing to conspicuous features that invite dramatization and require little technical commentary. In explaining the buildup in m. 4 and the downswing in m. 5, he might have referred to the f-sharp–g2 at the registral peak (V/V–V), and to the entrance of b-flat (V^7/IV–IV) during the downswing. Those events imply an intensification of energy toward the dominant and then a slackening toward the subdominant. Further, we might point out the dissonances on each tied sixteenth note of the subject in mm. 8–9 (compared with consonances at analogous spots in mm. 3, 5, and 6), heighten the *stretto* and contribute to the overall intensification. Finally, the b^2–f^2 augmented fourth in the soprano between mm. 8 and 9, leading into Kretzschmar's e^1–f^2 "crisis" on the downbeat of m. 9, would have reinforced the view of an abortive attempt to break the affect. Since none of these details is theoretically "advanced," Kretzschmar may have thought them suitable for elementary training in the aesthetics of form, for they would not burden the analysis with too many technicalities. For a music amateur, Kretzschmar's analysis is both intelligible and sufficient.

Kretzschmar's emphasis on spiritual content rather than on form, and on the necessity to "feel" that content, agrees with fundamental ideas advocated by the New Education, specifically, that learning should be based on direct experience and the activity of imagination. Further, the rejection of purely formalistic analysis encourages spontaneity and creativity, two other New Education ideals. Hearing musical forms as expression is different from hearing them as syntactic processes. In focusing on the spiritual content of musical artworks, hermeneutic analysis is "experiential" in nature.

Arnold Schering expanded and refined Kretzschmar's notion of hermeneutic analysis. A few ideas from Schering's early publications are worthy of special attention here because, like those in his mentor's articles on hermeneutics, the ideas arose from a desire to educate the public in the inner workings of music, and because Schering also bases his analytical method on direct experience and creative imagination. One of Schering's earliest books, *Musikalische Bildung und Erziehung zum musikalischen Hören* (1911), is the published version of an adult education course given in Leipzig. Its purpose was "to initiate a larger music-loving public to the nature of the language of music, and to musical enjoyment."[24] The book appeals not to reason alone, Schering explains, but mainly to active feeling (*regsames Gefühl*) and to the mental experience (*seelische Erfahrung*) of readers.

The greater part of *Musikalsiche Bildung* interprets the affective meaning of individual musical elements. The first part of the book outlines an analytical approach based on the psychological law of tension and release, the "true fundamental law of all musical stimuli."[25] Intervals become the "bearers of certain emotional qualities." Intervals combine to form motives, and these in turn create melodies. Chords, as products of voice leading, contain stored energy and thus strive in one direction or another. Forms are the fluid, collective expression of contrasting forces, which imbue a work with an internal, processive logic. An analysis portrays musical processes as a drama of forces and counterforces (*Kräfteschauspiel*), where the coordination of all musical elements is a "manifestation of the one grand, fundamental relationship of tension and release, . . . the ultimate relationship from which all music derives."[26] After establishing the conceptual framework and interpretive mechanisms, Schering offers six model analyses, which range from a dramatization of the Prelude and Fugue in G Minor from the *Well-Tempered Clavier*, book 1, to a discussion of rhythm and meter in Schumann's *Träumerei*.[27]

Three years after *Musikalische Bildung*, Schering published a short essay that defines the purpose of hermeneutic analysis. Like Kretzschmar, who had spoken of an "orientation" toward a work, Schering speaks of a preparation for "bringing to consciousness in the fullest and most vivid way imaginable the aesthetic ideas manifest in a piece of music, thus providing the listener with the greatest possible psychic resonance." He calls for a scientific theory of the "statics and dynamics" of tone processes and speculates that such a theory will reveal those processes to be "nothing more than the reflection of the statics and dynamics of our mental life."[28]

Unlike Kretzschmar, Schering was not directly involved in educational reform. However, Schering's *Musikalische Bildung* does aim at achieving the same goals as those of reform pedagogy in music: raising the musical-cultural consciousness of the folk by providing amateurs with a path to greater musical understanding. Like Kretzschmar, Schering minimizes technicalities and, like the early twentieth-century educational reformers, stresses the experiential aspect of learning.[29]

Although Schering and, especially, Kretzschmar did involve themselves in education of amateurs, both men worked primarily in academies, where they trained professional musicians and scholars. Schering only briefly turned his attention to music education for the folk. The bulk of their writings was intended for the professional music community. August Halm, by contrast, wrote with the amateur in mind. He is remembered for his lifelong commitment, as author and composer, to educating music amateurs and enthusiasts. He was a recognized leader in music education and an inspiration to the youth music movement. From 1914 to 1918 he trained teachers in a southern German institute at Esslingen. Although Halm's writings are rarely mentioned today, in the early twentieth century his numerous essays were widely read and his three monographs generally acclaimed.[30] He was acknowledged as "one of the most significant musical personalities to initiate a new outlook on the artwork and the artistic process," and was eulogized as a musical "truth seeker" and eloquent "herald" of that truth.[31]

From 1906 to 1910, and again from 1920 to 1929, Halm was the head music instructor and resident composer at the Free School Community in Wickersdorf, a small village in the Thuringian Forest, about twenty-five miles south of Weimar. Gustav Wyneken (1875–1965), an outspoken, controversial educational philosopher and cofounder of the school, proclaimed Wickersdorf a model of reform pedagogy and, moreover, a cradle of social and cultural reform.[32] Music was for the neo-Romantic Idealist Wyneken the purest expression of the "objective spirit." As such, music was the symbol of Wickersdorf's educational mission and the hub of its life.[33] In this attitude Halm and Wyneken were in complete philosophical agreement.

The main musical event at the school and the climax of each week was Halm's musical lecture demonstration (*Konzertrede*). These lectures addressed various formal and aesthetic matters as illustrated in pieces Halm played on the piano. The talks were largely nontechnical, without, however, lapsing into hermeneutic narratives. Halm approached music strictly as music. He cautioned against surrendering to its ancillary psychological effects and against seeking a "fictitious content behind musical utterance . . . as if the meaning of music could lie in something other than the music."[34] According to Halm, art does not "put a magnifying glass in [one's] hand so that, contemplating the self, one can revel in vanity." His goal was to disclose the form, the "only truly communicable element" and "the purpose of the spiritual effort," based solely on intramusical processes.[35]

Asked about the purpose of his lectures and books, Halm replied that he hoped to create a good public through education. He was committed to giving music enthusiasts literature of high quality and substance.[36] Technical literature addressed too narrow an audience, according to Halm, while popular literature lacked substance and, worse, misled readers. Aspiring music amateurs were

Halm's intended audience.[37] His paramount purpose was restoring the then-derogatory epithet "dilettante" to respectability, and his analyses were written with that goal in mind. By creating an audience of true dilettantes, Halm hoped to reunite the composer with the public, the two having become estranged in the late nineteenth century because of the gradual decline of true education (*Bildung*) and concomitant growth of specialized, technical training (*Ausbildung*).[38]

Many of Halm's published analytical discussions are revisions of his Wickersdorf lecture demonstrations. By reviewing his interpretation of parts of Beethoven's "Waldstein" Sonata, first movement, we can get an idea of his style of analysis.[39] Halm does not provide a complete analysis and, given the limited training of his audience, bypasses many details. Nevertheless, by using a minimum of theoretical apparatus he is able to illuminate what are for him essential processes that build formal logic. With a unique blend of artistic sensitivity and eloquence Halm establishes a midpoint between program-note poetics and scholarly science.

The context of Halm's remarks on the "Waldstein" is a generalization that harmony is "the impelling and supporting force of the development and structure" in music, and that harmony should thus be the "foremost subject of music instruction."[40] He demonstrates his point by explaining the unusual harmonic events in mm. 1–20 (see ex. 16.2): the unexpected shift from G major to B-flat major in mm. 4–5, and the analogous shift from G major to D minor in mm. 17–18. Both spots are to his ear disjunctive, even the second spot, despite the fifth relation in the second instance. Hearing mm. 1–7 in literal succession, Halm says, will not yield the harmonic logic of the passage. In order to make sense out of the harmonic relationships, we must hear functionally, not just "forward" (successively) but "backward" as well. Listening to the events successively, we encounter the move from I to V. When we encounter B-flat major, and then its dominant, rather than relating the G-major to the B-flat-major chord (a forward hearing), we hear backward to the I–V progression in C major, and thus understand mm. 5–7 as an imitation of mm. 1–3. The functional hearing is I–V in C major, followed by I–V in B-flat major, and the harmonic succession from G to B-flat becomes nonfunctional, like Riemann's "dead" intervals at junctures between melodic phrases.

The B-flat–F progression, despite its retroauditive logic, introduces a tonal disturbance nevertheless, and so raises the expectation of restoring tonal balance with a return to C major. The V^7 in mm. 9–11 reorients the tonal disposition and heightens the expectation of a return to C major, which is essential to the dynamic-formal unfolding. The allusion to C minor (mm. 7–13), recalling the B-flat detour, makes

Example 16.2   Beethoven, "Waldstein" Sonata, i, mm. 1–21

the return to C major truly satisfying. In Halm's view a dynamic process has occurred: an opening of tonal space with I–V in C major, a retroauditively understood intrusion of I–V in B-flat major, a reorientation toward C but in the opposite mode, a suspenseful half cadence (m. 13), and a satisfying resolution of harmonic-formal tension at the return of C major in m. 14.

The modified repeat at m. 14 of the opening events further heightens the dynamic unfolding. The low-register block chords of mm. 1–2 are transposed up an octave and transformed into a *tremolo*. Analogous to mm. 1–7, Halm hears mm. 14–21 as I–V in C major followed by I–V in D minor. That hearing involves both a local and a broader retroauditive interpretation. Locally, mm. 14–17 condition our understanding of mm. 18–21; more broadly, mm. 1–8 condition our understanding of mm. 14–21. The broader hearing is crucial because it makes us aware of the overarching dynamic intensification in mm. 1–21, and further: while mm. 1–8 descend from C to B-flat, mm. 14–21 *ascend* from C to D minor, and then on to E major.[41]

Having traced the harmonic and resultant dynamic-formal logic in the first section of the exposition, Halm examines the first section of the recapitulation (ex. 16.3). He interprets the surprising A-flat in m. 168, the sequence ending on a pause on B-flat, and the subsequent detour into E-flat major as formally necessary. The series of distant

Example 16.3 "Waldstein" Sonata, i, mm. 166–76

tonalities explored in the development and the expansive, compensatory dominant pedal in the retransition discharge their cumulative energies into the recapitulation, causing the harmony to overshoot its goal. The result is a harmonic reflex, a gradual dissipation of the energy during the detour in mm. 168–73, which leads to the return of C major in m. 174. While the unexpected events in mm. 168–170, together with their aftermath in mm. 171–73, would have been dynamically unmotivated and thus inappropriate in the exposition, they are logically necessary in the recapitulation, given the dynamic curve of the development and retransition.

Unlike Kretzschmar and Schering, Halm avoids emotionalizing musical events and, unlike Paul Bekker, he avoids anthropomorphizing them as well. Instead, Halm *dynamicizes* them. "The dynamic activity, the drama of the dynamics," he says, "is wholly sufficient for me, is for me also the truly concrete aspect."[42] Musical events embody dynamic qualities for Halm, but only as intramusical, cross-referential elements for creating form. In this sense Halm is a formalist. Further, in adhering strictly to musical events as heard, in accounting for their momentary dynamic properties as well as for their retro- and pro-auditive influences, he can be considered an early musical "phenomenologist."[43] His distinction as a pedagogue and analyst lies in his ability to achieve substantive musical insights with relatively simple analytical tools, and to communicate those insights in an engaging discourse accessible to a broad public.

Halm's writings influenced a generation of audiences, music amateurs, and music educators. His influence may not have been as strong in university circles, but his ideology and style of analysis did have a profound effect on the Bern professor Ernst Kurth, Halm's successor at Wickersdorf. Before taking a faculty position at the University of Bern, Kurth taught for one year at the Free School of Wickersdorf and became immersed in its culture. Looking back on the time he spent at Wickersdorf, Kurth wrote:

> For me it was a stimulating and momentous time. My activity at the University of Bern remains strongly influenced by the culture and outlook of the whole intellectual life [*Geistesleben*] at the Free School Community, despite the fact that the scholarly activity brought with it other objectives. It is precisely in this regard, though, that I hope not to have obscured the intellectual and cultural outlook that pervades the incomparably lively intellectual climate [*Geistigkeit*] of the Free School Community.[44]

Kurth's published analyses derive from the Wickersdorf *Weltan-*

schauung: music as a pure expression of the human spirit, to be experienced directly. Over the course of his career, Kurth translated this experiential attitude toward music into a psychological approach to analysis in which variously shaped melodic and harmonic configurations and, formally, undulatory tiers (*Wellenschichten*) are interpreted as sonically manifest psychic tension and motion.

> The central task of all music theory is to observe the *transformation of certain tension processes into sounds*. Only in this way is it possible to awaken, even in theoretical reflection, an empathy and internal sympathetic resonance with the animated *creative* forces, and so to restore once again the connection, long since torn asunder, between theory and art.[45]

Like Halm, Kurth focuses on dynamic processes in music, but while Halm interprets them phenomenologically, Kurth interprets them psychologically.[46]

Despite their differences in analytical orientation, the two theorists are similar in many ways. Like Halm, Kurth minimized analytical esoterica in order to reach a broad audience and to maximize the musical experience. Further, both men preferred flexible, narrative analysis to systematized analysis. Unlike some of their well-known contemporaries (e.g., Riemann and Schenker), neither developed an analytical system. Instead of devising attendant analytical tools and formulating a theoretical system, they focus on intra-opus interpretation. For Halm and Kurth the goal of analysis was to determine the dynamic function of interdependent musical components and so to reveal the unfolding logic of the whole.[47]

Above all, Halm and Kurth are linked by their roots in New Education ideology and methodology, and by their concern for musical *Bildung* rather than *Ausbildung*. Kurth implies his concern for *Bildung* in the above-cited quotation when he refers to the intellectual life at Wickersdorf. His commitment to educating a broad public manifests itself explicitly in his *Bruckner* monograph (1925). As in the Wickersdorf lecture demonstrations modeled after Halm, in *Bruckner* Kurth seeks to make the discussion understandable for laypersons by clarifying technical concepts in the course of the analytical commentary. At one point Kurth even remarks that "amateurs often have one of many advantages of impartiality over professional musicians" in grasping Bruckner's formal logic, implying that too much musical intellectualizing can hinder a genuine understanding of music.[48]

* * *

The New Education challenged teachers to reexamine the substance, style, and, crucially, the significance of their endeavors. Teachers of classical studies, for instance, felt the challenge particularly strongly. Why, reformers asked, devote years to learning about ancient history and cultures and thereby slight modern German (or European) history and culture?[49] Whatever the subject matter, however, educating the child as child (vom Kinde aus) meant implementing appropriate teaching strategies to make learning meaningful and, above all, effective in students' lives.

Kretzschmar, Schering, Halm, and Kurth responded to the challenges in different ways. Faced with choosing between simplified professional training, which often cheapens music with superficialities, and a full professional training, which can obscure music with complexities, they developed alternatives. "Deficient technical training [Ausbildung]," Halm affirms, "does not amount to education [Bildung]."[50] Familiar theoretical "systems" and formalistic analysis were deemed arbitrary or too confining in their biases and results.[51] The emphasis on harmonic and metric syntax in traditional analytical practices shifted in the newer approaches to dynamic-formal syntax, interpreted along hermeneutic, phenomenological, or psychological lines.

Like reformers in public education, the theorists discussed in this essay emphasized independent, creative thinking in the effort to understand music. They considered the results of conventional analysis merely the basis for interpretation, not the interpretation itself. Parsing harmonic-contrapuntal syntax was thus only a prelude to, or an implicit background for, genuine analysis: determining formal propriety and functionality of musical events. The meaning of musical elements and events, as data of experience, was central for the reformers in music theory.

In a study of nineteenth-century "music-theoretical thinking," Peter Rummenhöller breaks down the epistemological bases of music theories into several components: conceptual framework (Theoriebegriff, e.g., idealistic, positivistic), methodology (Verfahrensweise, e.g., inductive, deductive), analytical premises (Grundlegung, e.g., step or function theory, dualistic or monistic), systematization (Aufbau), and expression (Ausprägung).[52] Important as these components are for understanding the epistemological roots of theories, they do not take into account their sociological roots. While Heinrich Schenker's writings, for example, grew out of extensive activities as a performer, editor, and analyst, they were motivated sociologically, too, by the author's contempt for shallow dilettantism and his dismay at aesthetic ignorance. Schenker railed against the dilettante. Halm, on the other hand, valued the dilettante and tried steadfastly to restore dilettantism to its rightful status. These contrasting views of the dilettante illustrate as clearly as any technical distinctions the underlying differences between Schenker and Halm as theorists. More importantly, however, their attitudes highlight the significance of a sociological bias inherent in a theory. Schenker, an elitist, blames and flees the dilettantes; Halm, a populist, courts and tries to rescue them.[53]

The first decades of the twentieth century were a time of various "isms" and "movements." Caught up in a prevailing *Zeitgeist* of renewal, the reformers of the day saw themselves as missionaries of social and cultural revival. Educators felt an especially strong sense of mission because the results of their enterprise could significantly affect the values of subsequent generations. Music educators concerned with a broader public, and not only, or even primarily, with a select group of professionals, originated modes of analysis that emphasized interpretation of music as experienced. Given the oft-encountered student antipathy toward formalized theory and analysis, especially in the early stages of training, one wonders whether an appropriately modified New Education approach might not benefit such studies today.

Notes

1. Several writers have studied connections between intellectual history and music theory. Sources with a broad perspective include Carl Dahlhaus, *Die Musiktheorie im 18. und 19. Jahrhundert, erster Teil: Grundzüge einer Systematik*, Geschichte der Musiktheorie, vol. 10 (Darmstadt, 1984), and Peter Rummenhöller, *Musiktheoretisches Denken im 19. Jahrhundert; Studien zur Musikgeschichte des 19. Jahrhunderts*, vol. 12 (Regensburg, 1967). Other studies investigate the intellectual sources of a single theorist's ideas, for example, William A. Pastille, "*Ursatz*: The Musical Philosophy of Heinrich Schenker" (Ph.D. diss., Cornell University, 1985), and Lee A. Rothfarb, *Ernst Kurth as Theorist and Analyst* (Philadelphia, 1988), 1–30. Americans have been less interested in this aspect of music theory than European scholars.

2. Moritz Hauptmann, *The Nature of Harmony and Metre*, ed. and trans. W.E. Heathcote (London, 1888; orig. Leipzig, 1853), xxxix: "We shall . . . assume acquaintance with the general field of practical music, as a whole and in its particular parts. . . . For our intention is not to instruct in these things upon the lines of their outward occurrence or their use in art, or with a view to these." Adolf Bernhard Marx, *Die Lehre von der musikalischen Komposition*, 2d ed., vol. 1 (Leipzig, 1841), 9: "The theory of composition is a theory of art; it should give us the *skill* [*Können*] (for art takes its name from skill [*ars*]), the action [*That*], not the mere *knowledge* [*Wissen*]. The composition student certainly may not satisfy himself with understanding and knowing everything contained in a theory; he must be able to *produce it himself.*"

3. I have discussed some connections between psychology and music theory in "Ernst Kurth's *Die Voraussetzungen der theoretischen Harmonik* and the Beginnings of Music Psychology," *Theoria* 4 (1989): 10–33. Henry Stuart Hughes discusses anti-posi-

tivism in the early twentieth century in chapter 2 of his *Society and Consciousness: The Reorientation of European Social Thought, 1890–1930* (New York, 1976), 33–66.

4. Siegfried Schmaltzriedt surveys leading ideas in Halm's work and provides a selection of his publications in *Von Form und Sinn der Musik* (Wiesbaden, 1978). The ideas of Kretzschmar, Schering, and Halm will be discussed later in the present essay.

5. James C. Albisetti studies the late nineteenth-century background of early twentieth-century reforms in his *Secondary School Reform in Imperial Germany* (Princeton, 1983). Sources on reform pedagogy in the early 1900s are cited in notes below.

6. "The whole of current education is historical, Alexandrian, backward-looking; it looks less to creating new values than to registering old values." Julius Langbehn, *Rembrandt als Erzieher, von einem Deutschen* (Leipzig, 1890), 1.

7. Ibid., 167. "The current German scholar's education," Langbehn declared, "must become a German folk education" (ibid., 182). The significance of Langbehn's *Rembrandt als Erzieher* is discussed in Wolfgang Scheibe, *Die reformpädagogische Bewegung 1900–1932: Eine einführende Darstellung* (Weinheim, 1969), 6–11.

8. John T. Prince, *Methods of Instruction and Organization of the Schools of Germany* (Boston, 1892), 13–14. William H. Winch, *Notes on German Schools, with Special Relation to Curriculum and Methods of Teaching* (London, 1904), 20. Winch is referring to a visit to a school in Leipzig.

9. Winch, *Notes on German Schools*, 22.

10. Thomas Alexander and Beryl Parker, *The New Education in the German Republic* (New York, 1929), 3–4. Alexander and Parker describe how students sprang "stiffly to attention" upon visits by the principal or guests, and recall the "sharp, strained, high-pitched voices . . . shouting out answers to questions or reciting memorized lessons." Teachers impressed them as being serious autocrats "profoundly conscious of [their] responsibility to the nation and king."

11. Lest I simplify the picture of German educational reform too greatly in an attempt to correlate it with developments in theory in the early 1900s, I must point out that various reforms were introduced in Germany from the 1870s on. Reforms were enacted in the wake of the unification of Germany in 1871. Georg Kerschensteiner's *Arbeitsschule* (activity school), organized in 1880, revised curricula to strengthen values and character in an increasingly industrialized society, and inspired many imitators up through around 1910 (Dortmund, Dresden, Augsburg, Leipzig, Hamburg, etc.). We are not concerned with those events. Sources that discuss reforms before the 1890s are Friedrich Paulsen, *German Education Past and Present*, trans. T. Lorenz (London, 1908), 244–69; Alexander and Parker, *New Education*, 119–23; and Albisetti, *Secondary School Reform*. Our concern in the following paragraphs is the experimental schools that began to appear around 1900 in Germany and were modeled after Cecil Reddie's Abbotsholme School, founded at Derbyshire, England, in 1889.

12. The Swedish educator Ellen Key (1849–1926) set the tone for reformers in her book *The Century of the Child* (1900; German trans., 1902), which explores the ramifications of the slogan *Vom Kinde aus*. Key's book went through sixty editions.

13. Wolfgang Scheibe summarizes some premises of educational reform in the early twentieth century in his *Reformpädagogische Bewegung*, 51–80. See also Frederick Roman, *The New Education in Europe* (London, 1924), 206–9; and William Boyd and Wyatt Rawson, *The Story of the New Education* (London, 1965), 1–56. Rawson briefly characterizes the New Education on pages viii–ix. Dennis Shirley's qualifying paper for the Harvard Graduate School of Education, "Paul Geheeb's Leadership of the Odenwaldschule, 1910–1930" (1987), summarizes the background and main tenets of German reform pedagogy in the first twenty-five pages.

14. This all sounds idealistic, to be sure. Public school systems could not possibly realize such a program. Still, some public school systems did designate certain grade

levels to try out modified versions of programs initiated in private schools. The major innovations came from country boarding schools (*Landerziehungsheime*), which, being freer of bureaucratic control than public schools, could implement such programs.

15. Actually, since experimental schools of this period were largely private and thus accessible primarily to those with sufficient financial means, they were democratic only in a limited sense.

16. "All higher intellectual powers gravitate toward the concept of art. . . . If the concept of art, which logically belongs at the forefront of human existence, is actually placed there, then the task of a genuine education is realized." From *Rembrandt als Erzieher*, cited in Scheibe, *Reformpädagogische Bewegung*, 140.

17. Alfred Lichtwark, *Das Bild des Deutschen*, quoted in Scheibe, *Reformpädagogische Bewegung*, 140–41. The statement comes from Lichtwark's keynote address at the opening conference. The other two conferences were on graphic arts (Dresden, 1901) and language arts (Weimar, 1903). Alexander and Parker discuss Lichtwark and the arts education movement in *The New Education*, 96–116. See also Herman Nohl, *Die pädagogische Bewegung in Deutschland und ihre Theorie*, 2d ed. (Frankfurt am Main, 1935), 38–50, and Scheibe, *Reformpädagogische Bewegung*, 139–43.

18. Hermann Kretzschmar, *Musikalische Zeitfragen* (Leipzig, 1903), 4. Of the many criticisms and remedies that Kretzschmar discusses, he is most adamant about the teaching of singing in schools. He laments that for all the time spent, the results are meager. Students were taught singing by rote and consequently could not read music well. Time was spent mainly on learning patriotic and folk songs, or traditional hymns. No foundation was laid for mature musical understanding or enjoyment. Prince (*Methods of Instruction*, 176–79) and Winch (*Notes on German Schools*, 255–64) confirm Kretzschmar's assertions about the students' inability to read music.

19. Hermann Kretzschmar, "Anregungen zur Förderung musikalischer Hermeneutik," *Jahrbuch der Musikbibliothek Peters* 2 (1902): 45–66; and "Neue Anregungen zur Förderung musikalischer Hermeneutik: Satzästhetik," *Jahrbuch der Musikbibliothek Peters* 12 (1905): 75–86. The two essays are reprinted in Kretzschmar's *Gesammelte Aufsätze*, vol. 2 (Leipzig, 1911), 168–92 and 280–93. A translation of the first seven pages of Kretzschmar's first article is included in Bojan Bujic's *Music in European Thought, 1851–1912* (Cambridge, 1988), 114–20. Werner Braun discusses Kretzschmar's background and comments on the two essays in his "Kretzschmars Hermeneutik," in Carl Dahlhaus, ed., *Beiträge zur musikalischen Hermeneutik*, Studien zur Musikgeschichte des 19. Jahrhunderts, vol. 43 (Regensburg, 1975), 33–39.

20. Kretzschmar, "Neue Anregungen," 76: "Music instruction and public provisions have taken a direction that has greatly increased the dangers of a merely mechanical involvement with art, and of a fanciful, obscure involvement that goes to the other extreme." Kretzschmar means that both strictly formalistic and "poetic" analyses are inadequate. Hermeneutic analysis would provide the necessary "orientation" to a work (ibid., 76).

21. Kretzschmar, "Anregungen," 51 and 53. In the preface to the *Gesammelte Aufsätze*, vol. 2, Kretzschmar says that his ideas for hermeneutic analysis derive from his experiences as a conductor, when subscribers requested that he provide explanatory introductions to unfamiliar or difficult works. Kretzschmar's concert-hall guides are revised versions of such introductions (Kretzschmar, *Gesammelte Aufsätze* 2:v; idem, *Führer durch den Konzertsaal*, 2d ed. [Leipzig, 1891], iii).

22. Kretzschmar, "Anregungen," 63–64. Also: "According to the laws of addition, a whole composition must be explainable [by interpreting individual motivic figures]" (ibid., 49). Gestalt psychology would of course dispute Kretzschmar's additive thesis.

23. Kretzschmar, "Neue Anregungen," 76–79.

24. Arnold Schering, *Musikalische Bildung und Erziehung zum musikalischen Hören* (Leipzig, 1911), preface.

25. Ibid., 15 and 22.

26. Ibid., 49 (intervals); 50 (motives); 56, 61, and 69 (chords); 63 (form); 78 (coordination).

27. Ibid., 98–158. Other pieces include Mendelssohn's Op. 53, no. 2, from the *Songs without Words*, and Mozart's Fantasy in D Minor K. 397.

28. Arnold Schering, "Zur Grundlegung der musikalischen Hermeneutik," *Zeitschrift für Aesthetik und allgemeine Kunstwissenschaft* 9 (1914): 168 and 173.

29. Schering carried his analytical method to extremes in his later studies of Beethoven. Schering's career is discussed and his work evaluated in Arno Forchert, "Scherings Beethovendeutung und ihre methodischen Voraussetzungen," *Beiträge zur musikalischen Hermeneutik*, 41–52.

30. Note 4 above cites Siegfried Schmaltzriedt's edition of Halm, *Von Form und Sinn der Musik*. Halm's main works are *Von zwei Kulturen der Musik* (Munich, 1913; 3d ed., Stuttgart, 1947); *Die Symphonie Anton Bruckners* (Munich, 1914; rev. ed., 1923; reprint ed., Hildesheim, 1975); and *Beethoven* (Leipzig, 1927). Halm also published a *Harmonielehre* (Leipzig, 1900); a collection of essays entitled *Von Grenzen und Ländern der Musik* (Munich, 1916), and an *Einführung in die Musik* (Berlin, 1926; reprint ed., Darmstadt, 1966). Walter Gerstenberg gives a biographical sketch of Halm in his "Der Musiker August Halm," *Jahrbuch des Archivs der deutschen Jugendbewegung* 1 (1969): 18–22.

31. Hugo J. Kinzel, "Musik als geistige Macht: August Halm zum Gedächtnis," *Neue Zeitschrift für Musik* 115 (1954): 90. Hans Berchtold, "August Halm und sein Werk," *Schweizerische Musikzeitung* 69, no. 11 (1929): 409. In a review of Halm's *Von zwei Kulturen*, Fritz Jöde (1887–1970), an eminent music educator and a leading spokesman for the youth music movement, lauded the author's "extraordinary pedagogical abilities," and wished for Halm's work "the broadest dissemination in musical circles, which so desperately need a form of music pedagogy that truly goes into depth" (*"Von zwei Kulturen der Musik," Der Wanderer* 7 [1916], reprinted in *Die deutsche Jugendmusikbewegung in Dokumenten ihrer Zeit*, comp. Wilhelm Scholz and Waltraut Jonas-Corrier et al. [Wolfenbüttel, 1980], 70). Hilmar Höckner discusses Halm's significance as a music educator in his *Die Musik in der deutschen Jugendbewegung* (Wolfenbüttel, 1927), 63–94. Hellmuth Lungershausen reviews Halm's influence on training of teachers in his "Auswirkungen Halmscher Gedankengänge in der neuen musikalischen Lehrerbildung," *Singgemeinde*, vol. 3 (1931), reprinted in *Die deutsche Jugendmusikbewegung*, 690–92.

32. There is a wealth of literature on the Wickersdorf school, and on Wyneken. Brief introductions may be found in Scheibe, *Reformpädagogische Bewegung*, 113–14; Alexander and Parker, *New Education*, 198–201; Nohl, *Pädagogische Bewegung*, 82–84); Alfred Knopf, *Wickersdorf einst und jetzt* (Jena, 1938), 68–74; and Fritz Karsen, *Deutsche Versuchsschulen der Gegenwart* (Leipzig, 1925), 74–84. Wyneken himself gives lengthy accounts of the philosophy behind Wickersdorf and of its activities in his *Wickersdorf* (Lauenberg, 1922), and in two Wickersdorf yearbooks (Jena, 1908, 1909). Wyneken's career is summarized in Heinrich Kupffer, "Gustav Wyneken: Leben und Werk," *Jahrbuch des Archivs der deutschen Jugendbewegung* 2 (1970): 23–32.

33. Wyneken, *Wickersdorf*, 103.

34. August Halm, "Musikalische Bildung," *Wickersdorfer Jahrbuch 1909–10* (Jena, 1911), 63; reprinted in idem, *Von Form und Sinn*, 220. "One ought not to take the psychological element in music for the logical element" ("Humor und Musik," *Von Grenzen und Ländern*, 111). If the composer's mental state is the ultimate guarantor of quality in musical art, then, Halm remarks facetiously, "the psychiatrist is declared

the rightful judge of music" ("Unsere Zeit und Beethoven," *Die Rheinlande* 11 [1911]: 60; in idem, *Von Form und Sinn*, 153). See also Wyneken, *Wickersdorf*, 105.

35. Halm, "Musikalische Erziehung," *Neue Deutsche Schule* 1, no. 2 (1906); reprinted in idem, *Von Form und Sinn*, 203; see also idem, "Reden bei Gelegenheit musikalischer Vorträge," *Wickersdorfer Jahrbuch 1908* (Jena, 1909), 67. The "Reden" essay is an introduction to another entitled "Über die Variation" (*Jahrbuch 1908*, 68–88). Together they give a good picture of Halm's mode of thought and analysis. Concerning hermeneutic analysis, Halm says, "It was really an error that the hermeneuticist wanted to predispose the public to certain feelings. What each person feels need not be stated. And when feelings diverge, then nothing can be stated" (*Beethoven*, 66).

36. Wyneken says this in his introduction to the third edition of Halm, *Von zwei Kulturen*, xiv. . See also Wyneken, *Wickersdorf*, 109.

37. Fritz Jöde, "*Von zwei Kulturen*," in *Die deutsche Jugendmusikbewegung*, 70: "Some may have the impression that, in Halm's work, it is only a matter of discussing musicological issues, which are irrelevant for the cultivated [*gebildete*] nonmusician. No evaluation could be more incorrect. Halm does not primarily address professional musicians at all. Rather, he aims at serving today's ever increasing need, precisely outside of this [professional] circle, for insight into the essence of music." Years after publishing *Von zwei Kulturen*, Halm wrote "We came ever closer to music for musicians and further away from music for amateurs. Music was more and more for the experts, just as once religion was entrusted to the priests, until someone found the courage to proclaim the teachings of the priesthood. For us such a reformation is necessary in music. And the music clergy, compelled by the reformation, would have to change and renew itself" (August Halm, "Gegenwart und Zukunft der Musik," *Das hohe Ufer*, vol. 2 [1920], reprinted in idem, *Von Form und Sinn*, 253).

38. Halm distinguishes between *Bildung* and *Ausbildung* in "Musikalische Bildung," 48 reprinted in idem, *Von Form und Sinn*, 211. Concerning the dilettante, he says, "The customary method of having people engage in 'some music,'—i.e., giving the aspiring dilettante the same training as the future professional musician, but reduced in quality and terminated at a lower level—this method has proven itself bad enough. The epithet 'dilettante' owes its connotation of atrophy, error, feebleness, and . . . even of annoyance, and the epithet public its connotation of antagonism or stupidity, to that method. . . . The school and only the school can cause the two epithets to regain a good reputation" (ibid.).

39. Halm, "Musikalische Bildung," 50–53, reprinted in idem, *Von Form und Sinn*, 212–14. Halm repeats the "Waldstein" analysis in *Von zwei Kulturen*, 107–10. Other representative analyses are of the development section of Beethoven's "Pastoral" Symphony, and of his "Tempest" Sonata, first movement, both in *Von zwei Kulturen* (39–69 and 81–117). Wyneken points out that the content of some of Halm's early lecture demonstrations ended up in the first few Wickersdorf yearbooks and in *Von zwei Kulturen* (Wyneken, "Die Musik an der Freien Schulgemeinde Wickersdorf," in *Die deutsche Jugendmusikbewegung*, 630; idem, *Wickersdorf*, 107; idem, *Der Gedankenkreis der Freienschulgemeinde* [Leipzig, 1913], 18; Halm, *Von zwei Kulturen*, 3d ed., xiv). Some of the material in Halm's *Beethoven* and *Einführung in die Musik* no doubt comes from his lecture demonstrations in the post-1920 period.

40. Halm, "Musikalische Bildung," 49–50; reprinted in idem, *Von Form und Sinn*, 212. By instruction in harmony Halm did not mean training in strict four-part voice leading, but rather learning to "feel and understand the effects" of harmony.

41. Halm, "Musikalische Bildung," 51–52; reprinted in idem, *Von Form und Sinn*, 213. Note that in the key of C major, both B-flat major and D minor represent "dark" chords of the subdominant region, the former further removed and the latter closer to C major, appropriate to the dynamic-formal curve. E represents a "brighter," domi-

nant region. The formal curve thus gradually intensifies, from a distant to a near subdominant region and ultimately to a distant dominant region.

42. Halm, *Einführung in die Musik*, 139. Halm says this in connection with comments he makes about the ending of the first movement of Beethoven's Piano Sonata Op. 81a.

43. In an article that outlines a phenomenological basis for understanding music, Arthur W. Cohn mentions Halm as an innovator of a phenomenological aesthetics ("Das musikalische Verständnis: Neue Ziele," *Zeitschrift für Musikwissenschaft* 4 [1921]: 135). Hans Mersmann, however, one of the first writers to explore extensively the idea of a phenomenology of music in its historical and analytical implications, characterizes Halm's works as being pre-phenomenological ("Versuch einer Phänomenologie der Musik," *Zeitschrift für Musikwissenschaft* 5 [1922–23]: 227: "liegen . . . oberhalb der phänomenologischen Probleme"). Halm may not have worked out a music phenomenology systematically or ideologically, as Mersmann did, but his analytical premises and goals agree fully with Mersmann's. In another article on music phenomenology Mersmann, like Halm, identifies the content of music as the "sum of its tectonic forces" and specifies the task of music phenomenology as understanding "the phenomena of the artwork as an evolution of elemental forces" (Hans Mersmann, "Zur Phänomenologie der Musik," *Zeitschrift für Aesthetik und allgemeine Kunstwissenschaft* 19 [1925]: 378 and 377).

44. Höckner, *Die Musik in der deutschen Jugendbewegung*, 93–94. I have written about Kurth's Wickersdorf experience and Halm's influence on Kurth in my *Ernst Kurth as Theorist and Analyst*, 4–5, 8–9, and 222–23. Kurth and Halm corresponded regularly until the latter's death in 1929. Incredibly, they met only once.

45 Ernst Kurth, *Romantische Harmonik und ihre Krise in Wagners "Tristan,"* 3d ed. (Berlin, 1923; reprint ed., Hildesheim, 1968), 2.

46. Note 34 above cites Halm's opinion of psychologically based analysis. Kurth's writings culminate in his *Musikpsychologie* (Berlin, 1931).

47. In their quest to understand form as an unfolding dynamic narrative, Kurth and Halm are forerunners of Wallace Berry's approach to analysis in his *Structural Functions in Music* (Englewood Cliffs, N.J., 1976). Berry lays the groundwork for his explorations of tonal, textural, and rhythmic structures in the introduction (pp. 1–26). Significantly, Berry agrees with Kurth and Halm in believing that "a great deal of understanding of musical process, in its essential terms, [is] accessible to the involved *layman or amateur* [emphasis added]. Indeed, many of the most persuasive factors in musical effect and function are delineative of shapes and processes that can be demonstrated, given necessary theoretical and analytical calculations, relatively simply" (ibid., 3).

48. Ernst Kurth, *Bruckner*, vol. 1 (Berlin, 1925; reprint ed., Hildesheim, 1971), vii and 283. The book grew out of Kurth's open lectures at the University of Bern, as well as out of talks given at informal gatherings of amateurs and educators in the Bern area. Kurth grants that he had to assume some basic knowledge of his readers, but goes on to say that certain discussions of harmony "can be skipped by readers lacking the requisite training with no loss to the overall intelligibility" (ibid., vii).

49. At the 1890 conference on education, no less than Kaiser Wilhelm himself criticized the emphasis on classical studies. See Albisetti, *Secondary School Reform*, 140.

50. Halm, "Musikalische Bildung," 48; reprinted in idem, *Von Form und Sinn*, 211. Heinrich Schenker also argued against poor music-theoretical instruction, but his writings differ greatly from those of Halm (Heinrich Schenker, *Counterpoint*, vol. 1 [1910], trans. John Rothgeb and Jürgen Thym, ed. John Rothgeb [New York, 1987],

xxiii–xxv; idem, *Free Composition* [1935], trans. and ed. Ernst Oster [New York, 1979], xxii–xxiii). See note 53 below.

51. Recall Arnold Schoenberg's indictment of theory and the exasperated outburst "These systems!" in his *Harmonielehre* (Vienna, 1911), 5. In the spirit of Husserl's watchword *zu den Sachen* (to the things), some music theorists of the day tried "to get away from the primacy of theories, of concepts and symbols," as did Husserl, in order to establish "immediate contact with the intuited data of experience" (Herbert Spiegelberg, *Doing Phenomenology* [The Hague, 1975], 15).

52. Rummenhöller, *Musiktheoretisches Denken*, 8.

53. Heinrich Schenker, *Counterpoint* 1:xviii–xx. In a review of Schenker's editions of the Beethoven sonatas, Halm differentiates himself from Schenker, whose "strongly esoteric approach . . . addresses only musicians, the knowledgeable and able, so that . . . the image of a musical folk, or even a public [*Gefolge*], has no place" (August Halm, "Heinrich Schenker," *Die Freie Schulgemeinde* 8 [1917]: 15). Scheibe discusses the demand in the early twentieth century for qualitative nonspecialist adult education in his *Reformpädagogische Bewegung*, 361.

SEVENTEEN

Harmony as a Determinant of Structure in Webern's Variations for Orchestra

GRAHAM H. PHIPPS

On 3 May 1941, Anton Webern sent a photocopy of his newly completed Variations for Orchestra to Willi Reich together with an explanatory letter. The purpose of the letter was to provide instructions for his friend, who in turn was to present the score of the Variations personally to the Swiss conductor Paul Sacher. Webern hoped that this would lead to a first performance of the work under Sacher's baton in Basel. Reich's presentation would need to be particularly effective; after all, Sacher had recently rejected Webern's Cantata No. 1, Op. 29.[1] Webern began by advising his friend: "I should like very briefly to tell you a little about the work, so that you have an an effective counter to possible objections and can throw at least a certain amount of light."[2]

As preparation for Reich's meeting with Sacher, Webern's letter is interesting in that it provides information on: (1) his own musical style, (2) the form of the Variations, and (3) two musical ideas from which the entire work is drawn. His discussion of these points thus provides us with a compelling basis for an investigation into one of his mature compositions.

Regarding his style, Webern observed:

> Now you would have to say unequivocally: this is music (mine) that's in fact based *just as much* on the laws achieved by musical presentation *after* the Netherlanders; that doesn't reject the development that came then, but tries on the contrary to continue it into the future, and doesn't aim to return to the past. What kind of *style*, then? I believe, again, a new one. Exactly following natural law in its material, as the earlier, preceding forms followed tonality; that's to say, *building* a tonality, but one that uses the possibilities offered by the nature of sound in a different way, namely on the basis of a system that does "relate only to each other" (as Arnold has put it) the twelve different notes customary in

Western music up to now, but doesn't on that account (I should add to clarify things) ignore the rules of order provided by the nature of sound—namely the relationship of the overtones to a fundamental. Anyway it's impossible to ignore them, if there is still to be *meaningful* expression in sound! But nobody, really, is going to assert that we don't want that! So: a style, whose material is of that kind, and whose formal construction *relates the two possible types of presentation to each other.*[3]

According to this description, Webern saw his own twelve-tone music not as a rejection of an older musical practice, but as a projection of possibilities inherent in that older style.[4] The new style that he described builds a new tonality by combining the possibilities of the older, established relationship of fundamental and its overtones with a new method of presentation, that of the twelve-note series.[5]

If Webern's comments are taken literally, his remarks about the relevance of the fundamental and its overtones in his twelve-tone music mean that the tradition of harmony derived from the overtone series is one of the basic ingredients of that repertory. It follows that harmonies are to be understood as tertian, that chord roots are determined as lower pitches of vertical thirds and fifths and as upper pitches of vertical sixths and fourths, that chord successions are derived from the overtone series, that the "tonal" form of a composition is related to its harmonic structure, and that none of the above considerations is negated by employment of the serial method.

With regard to musical form, Webern thought of his work in terms of the Classical sonata with its characteristic phrase structure:

The "theme" of the Variations extends to the first double bar; it is conceived as a period, but is "introductory" in character. Six variations follow (each one to the next double bar). The first bringing the first subject (so to speak) of the overture (andante-form), which unfolds in full; the second the bridge-passage, the third the second subject, the fourth the recapitulation of the first subject—for it's an andante-form!— but in a developing manner, the fifth, repeating the manner of the introduction and bridge-passage, leads to the Coda; sixth variation.[6]

In the context of the Classical sonata the terms "first subject," "bridge passage," and "second subject" refer to a formal scheme in which traditional harmonic relationships play a formative role. Thus, Webern's explanation sparks one's imagination: was he referring here to Classical tonal paradigms as well as thematic ones? Such an interpretation seems especially plausible in light of his remarks about fundamentals and their overtones.

The letter to Reich also addresses the disposition and nature of the tone row in the Variations. Webern wrote:

> Now everything that occurs in the piece is based on the two ideas given in the first and second bars (double bass and oboe!). But it's reduced still more, since the second shape (oboe) is itself retrograde; the second two notes are the cancrizan of the first two, but rhythmically augmented. They are followed on the trombone, by a repetition of the first shape (double-bass), but in diminution! And in cancrizan as to motives and intervals. That's how my row is constructed— it's contained in these thrice four notes.[7]

As our examination will show, Webern's "two ideas" are presented in the opening measures as familiar tertian sonorities, so that, just as Webern described in his commentary to Reich, two methods of presentation have been combined: serial organization and the traditonal relationship of fundamentals with their overtones.

These three citations from Webern's letter to Reich, together with our observations on their embodiment in the work itself, raise several questions for today's music theorist. How can a harmonic concept founded on the relations of a fundamental to its overtones apply in serial music, where it is generally thought that the order of pitches organizes the "tonal" environment? Are not the simultaneities in this style merely "accidents" whose origins should be understood in terms of the series? How can a serially ordered pitch-class system and a traditional harmonically generated pitch-class system coexist within a single composition?

To answer these questions, we must first examine the music itself. From directly intelligible impressions that the music provides and with the support of statements by the composer, I shall attempt to explain the role that harmony plays in articulating the structure of this masterwork.

***

In keeping with his explanations for Reich, Webern wrote at the top of his first page of sketches for the Variations: "Theme: periodically constructed in phrase like parts; repetition in a new form."[8] This suggestion of Classical phrase structure is borne out in the sketches; at m. 10 Webern wrote *Nachsatz* to indicate the division in the theme (mm. 1–20). In example 17.1 the antecedent phrase is shown as a two-voice canon, which is the way that the theme appears in the sketches.[9] The two ideas described by Webern as the basis of the entire composition comprise the first eight pitches of the *dux* as given in the example. Although both ideas are presented in a linear manner, they may be easily heard as chords.

Example 17.1   The canon in Weber's theme, mm. 1–9

The vertical disposition of pitches in the first motive (m. 1 in the double bass) has the root as the lowest note, with a minor third, a major seventh, and a major ninth appearing in ascending order above it. The combination of minor third and major seventh above a root is a common chordal type in early twentieth-century music. Hindemith uses it as a focal sonority in the fourth movement of his *Kleine Kammermusik* for winds, Op. 24, no. 2, and Schoenberg uses it to announce the beginning of the second song from his *Book of the Hanging Gardens*, Op. 15. Webern's "chord" simply adds the major ninth to this sound and leaves out the fifth of the chord.

The chord formed by the disposition of pitches of the second motive (m. 2 in the oboe) may, at first glance, seem to be closely related to the first chord. In the initial vertical dispositions of the two chords, the lower three pitches form identical pitch-class sets, and the upper two pitches form a minor third in the first instance and a major sixth in the second. Application of an overtone theory to these chords, however, shows them to be quite different. Whereas the first is in root position, the second is in first inversion.

This second chord, also a familiar sonority in literature of the early twentieth century, comprises root, perfect fifth, and major and minor thirds sounding together. Usually in this major-minor chord the third of the major triad appears in a lower octave than that of the minor, so that one might say the vertical disposition of its thirds reflects the order of overtones above a fundamental. Bartók, for example, uses the same vertical disposition of the major-minor triad throughout the first movement of his Second String Quartet (see ex. 17.2). Throughout this essay the two chords will be referred to either as minor-ninth chord and major-minor triad or as x and y chords, respectively.[10]

Because of its symmetrical properties, the tone row of the Variations has only two forms, prime and inversion.[11] Example 17.3 shows that in both forms, the outer tetrachords are x chords and the middle tetrachord is a y chord. In the case of prime set forms ordinal pitches 2, 5, and 9 serve as roots of chords, whereas in the case of inverted set forms ordinal pitches 4, 8, and 11 serve as roots. If ordinal pitch 1 is considered 0 transposition level, the "chord progressions" are represented by the transposition numbers 1, 2, 8 for primes and 9, 3, 2 for inversions. Thus, in prime forms the root succession is by ascending half step followed by tritone; in inverted forms it is by tritone followed by descending half step.

Webern's notation sometimes obscures the rhythmic relationships. To clarify these relationships, I have adopted a numerical procedure in which each duration is represented by the number of thirty-second-note values between articulations; internal rests are counted as belonging to the previous note value. In these terms the numbers for the two motives that Webern described are 8848 and 3126, respectively. A method for describing these two rhythmic motives is important to our analysis because it provides a way to show how Webern uses these rhythms to reinforce salient harmonic relationships throughout the work. Table 17.1 shows chord roots and types, rhythmic identities, and timbral assignments for each of the four-note motives in both the antecedent and consequent phrases of the theme. In the theme a special relationship is formed between B-flat and F by means of three pairs of x chords built on these roots (see above). These six chords are comprehensibly connected by the low range they occupy and by their spacing, which always creates a root-position chord whose third, seventh, and ninth are located in this ascending order above the bass. In the consequent phrase of the *dux*, the inner voices of the F chords sound in a lower octave than do those of the B-flat chords. What results from this are vertical dispositions that mirror each other. When the F and B-flat chords appear a second time in the consequent phrase of the *dux*, each retains its earlier rhythm along with its vertical arrangement, but they exchange places with regard to complementary timbres (strings vs. brass) and serial order. The third pair of B-flat and F chords, which enters in the consequent phrase of the *comes*, for the first time presents

Example 17.2 Triad with major and minor thirds sounding simultaneously, in
Bartók, Second String Quartet, i, mm. 38–41

Example 17.3 Chordal disposition of the tetrachords in P-0 and I-0 set forms
in Webern's Variations

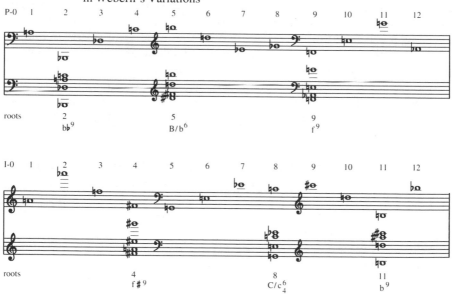

Table 17.1.   Chords, Rhythms, and Timbres in Webern's "Theme"

Antecedent Phrase:

chord roots:	*dux:*	$b\flat^9$	B/b^6	f^9	$f\sharp^9$	C/c_4^6	b^9
	comes:		b^9		C/c_4^6		$f\sharp^9$
rhythms:	*dux:*	8848	3126	4244	4424	6248	8488
	comes:		3124		4422		8484
timbres:	*dux:*	double bass	oboe	trombone	violin	bass clar.	violin
	comes:		viola		cello		harp & double bass

Consequent Phrase:

chord roots:	*dux:*	f^9	B/b^6	$b\flat^9$	b^9	C/c_4^6	$f\sharp^9$
	comes:	$f\sharp^9$	C/c_4^6	b^9	$b\flat^9$	B/b^6	f^9
rhythms:	*dux:*	4244	3126	8848	8488	6248	4424
	comes:	4242	×	8848	×	6244	×
timbres:	*dux:*	cello	flute, oboe, clar.	tuba	violin	bass clar.	violin
	comes:	tuba, trombone	strings	harp, viola	brass	oboe	brass

the chords as simultaneities. No longer can there be any doubt about chord identity as the brass choir plays a resolution of b-flat⁹ to f⁹.

As to the other x chords in the theme, the four b⁹ and f-sharp⁹ chords in the *dux* resemble those of B-flat and F with respect to spacing and contrast with them in timbre and range, since they are all scored for violin. In the *comes* the two f-sharp⁹ chords have less tonal significance. They appear in first inversion, contrast with each other in register and timbre, and have rhythms merely derivative of the basic rhythm for x chords.[12]

The two b⁹ chords in the *comes* differ both from one another and from the rest of the x chords in the theme. The second of these b⁹ chords has the ninth in the bass, though it uses the x rhythm. The other b⁹ chord (m. 2) establishes a new relationship: the viola presents it simultaneously with a y harmony, a B/b⁶ chord played by the oboe. Each appears in the 3126 rhythm that will be associated with y chords. But the tie between these two chords is established even more strongly when the b^2–d^2 pitches that announce the y chord in the *dux* are imitated in the same octave as the highest pitches of the x chord of the *comes*. This exact pitch-register correspondence may, in fact, account for the different positioning of the x chord on B in m. 2 of the *comes*. The y chords on B are found in the consequent phrase with characteristic y rhythms.

The only remaining chordal formation in the theme is a *y* chord on
C. It appears always in second inversion and with the major third sounding below the minor third. In the *dux* it appears once in each phrase in
the bass clarinet using the *y* rhythm. In the *comes* it appears in a complementary bass-register timbre (strings)— in the antecedent phrase in *x*
rhythm, and in the consequent phrase as a chord.

Thus Webern used two familiar and easily comprehended chord
types in his theme to establish connections within the harmonic complex B-flat–B–F and its transposition up by semitone. This complex is
a common part of early twentieth-century musical language. For example, the same progression appears at the end of the development
and the beginning of the recapitulation in the first movement of Ravel's
String Quartet (ex. 17.4), where the dominant, C, is followed by its
tritone equivalent, F-sharp, before resolving to the tonic, F.[13] By putting

Example 17.4   Succession of chord roots at the recapitulation in the
                first movement of Ravel's String Quartet

together two semitone-related transpositions of this complex in his theme, Webern presented a model rich in harmonic possibilities for subsequent variation.

***

The first variation (mm. 21–55), which Webern termed the "first subject," lacks the aurally identifiable division into antecedent and consequent phrases that was found in the theme. The texture is that of two melodic lines with chordal accompaniment. Within the two–voice canon, the *dux* comprises a melodic presentation of the first and third tetrachords from prime forms in which the last two ordinal pitches of each row map onto ordinal pitches 1 and 2 of another prime set that is a whole tone lower. Thus, a sequence of four row presentations connects P-0 to P-10 to P-8 to P-6, bringing about a large-scale motion by tritone. This melodic line is accompanied by the respective retrograde forms of the same rows in a succession of twelve chords so that the melodic tetrachords, presenting x chords in a linear fashion, are accompanied by a series of vertical x chords that move in a progression of descending perfect fifths from an initial F chord to a concluding E chord. All the x chords in this succession of verticalities appear in root position; as a result, they are easily comprehended and may be said to recall the x chords that appeared in the theme. The progression of x chords is interspersed with a series of y chords moving down by step from B to F. Hence, the x chords recall the perfect fifth relations, B-flat–F and F-sharp–B in the theme, whereas the y chords reinforce the tonal structure of the variation with its fourfold sequence.

Despite this variation's appearance as a continuous single phrase, the disposition of rows in the *dux* and *comes* is like that found in the theme. That is, the antecedent phrase of the first variation comprises P-0 and P-10 in the *dux* and RI-0 in the *comes*—beginning with a reiteration of the tonal relations of the theme, but ending with a new relationship— and the consequent phrase introduces a completely new family of harmonic relationships. The following illustrates the tonal relationships found in the first variation. As in example 17.3, all the four-note melodic presentations are expressed as chords (table 17.2).

A comparison of the canonic structure of the first variation (ex. 17.5) with that of the theme (ex. 17.1) will show that the *dux* here has weaker harmonic definition than before. Although this melodic line in the first variation consists entirely of presentations of x chords, their notes have in every instance been vertically redistributed so that chordal identities cannot be so easily grasped. Only three of the four-note cells appear in root position, and in these representations, one (c-sharp^9) has the seventh sounding below the third, while the other two (f-sharp^9 and e^9)

Table 17.2.   Harmonic Organization of Webern's First Variation

Antecedent Phrase:								
chord roots: *dux:*	$b\flat^9$		f^9	$a\flat^9$			$e\flat^9$	$f\sharp^9$
accompaniment:	f^9	B/b^6	$b\flat^9$	$e\flat^9$		A/a^6	$a\flat^9$	$c\sharp^9$
comes:	b^9				C/c^6_4	$f\sharp^9$	a^9	
Consequent Phrase:								
chord roots: *dux:*	$c\sharp^9$	e^9		b^9				
accompaniment:	G/g^6_4	$f\sharp^9$	b^9	F/f	e^9			
comes:	$B\flat/b\flat^6$	e^9	g^9	$A\flat/a\flat^6_4$	g^9			

have both the ninth and seventh sounding below the third. Despite its loss of harmonic comprehensibility, this line maintains a logical harmonic pattern that alternates root movement by upward fifth with that of upward third—the two types characterized by Schoenberg as weak successions[14]—connecting the same beginning and ending harmonies (b-flat^9 and b^9) that were found in the *dux* of the theme.

Similarly, harmonic identities are obscured in much of the *comes*. Only the first and last chords (b^9 and d^9) appear in root position, and of these two, only the b^9 appears with the original disposition of root, third, seventh, and ninth in ascending order. In this variation attention is called to B in two ways:

1. As in the theme, the *comes* presents a b^9 chord simultaneously with a B/b^6 in the *dux* (mm. 24–26). Here again B and D sound in the same register in both chords; however, unlike the corresponding notes in m. 2 of the theme, these two notes are in the middle of the vertical sonority. Hence the linkage between the two chords is not so readily perceived. This lessened comprehensibility is partially compensated for by the 3126 rhythm and string timbre assigned to the b^9 chord; these qualities serve to recall the viola entry of the same chord from the corresponding *comes* in the theme.

2. The linear representation of b^9 that concludes the *dux* begins with its first two notes in the violin, the same instrument that plays the b^9 at the beginning of the *comes*. This connection is emphasized by the b^2 tonic accent that announces the final four-note cell of the *dux*. (See m. 51 of the score.)

Apart from the connections between B chords, the harmonic focus of the first variation has definitely shifted to the chordal accompaniment with its double progression of downward fifth in the x chords and downward whole tone in the y chords. Even here harmonic identity in some of the x chords is weakened; although all appear in root position, three of them (b-flat^9, c-sharp^9, and f-sharp^9) have the seventh sounding below the third. The vertical rearrangement of these chords matches the positionings of the seventh in the corresponding b-flat^9, c-sharp^9, and f-sharp^9 chords in the melodic *dux* line.

Example 17.5   The canon in Webern's first variation, mm. 21–39

Antecedent

***

In the manner of a "bridge passage," as Webern has described his second variation (mm. 56–73), the motivic identities of the four-note cells are neutralized.[15] In place of the distinctive rhythmic figures 8848 and 3126 for x and y chords respectively, the "bridge passage" comprises a double series of chords played as vertical simultaneities. *Dux* and *comes* both consist of a series of sixteen chords followed by one four-note melodic presentation.

Although this variation is shorter than either of the preceding sections, it includes twice as many forms of the row. The *dux* begins with the familiar b^9 chord, here the first tetrachord of the row form (RI-0) that began the *comes* in both the theme and the first variation. Since the pitch-class content of the final tetrachord of RI-0 is the same as that of the first tetrachord of RI-7—although the notes occur in different orders—a vertical presentation allows a mapping procedure of prime versions of the melody moving by perfect fifth. The *dux*, representing eight such mapped-on row presentations, consists of a series of seventeen chords in which an upward cycle of fifths occurs in both x and y chords. The *comes*, derived from eight similarly mapped-on presentations of the inverted melody, consists of a series of seventeen chords in a downward cycle of fifths. Table 17.3 shows the harmonic organization of this variation. The first thirteen chords in each series, when taken together, constitute a palindrome starting and ending with simultaneous b^9 and f^9 chords. Two g-sharp^9 x chords appear "imitatively," with the same voicing and temporal values, at the center of the palindrome—the first in the *dux* played by violins, the second at the same octave in the *comes* played by viola and cello. The palindromic aspect of this canon is reflected most clearly in the chords that surround the g-sharp chord in imitation. The two x chords on either side of the g-sharp^9 chord have the same durational value (equivalent to five eighth notes); the c-sharp^9 chords of mm. 60 (*dux*) and 65 (*comes*) are scored identically for brass, and the e-flat^9 chords in the same measures are scored identically for woodwinds. This mirroring technique allows the two canonic lines to merge temporarily. At the outer extremes of the palindrome, although the pitch content of the chords is "imitative" in

Table 17.3.　Harmonic Organization of Webern's Second Variation

DUX:	B	(C)	F♯	(G)	C♯	(D)	G♯	(A)	E♭	(E)	B♭	(B)	F	(F♯)	C	(C♯)	G
COMES:	F	(B)	B♭	(E)	E♭	(A)	G♯	(D)	C♯	(G)	F♯	(C)	B	(F)	E	(B♭)	A

Roots of x chords are shown without parentheses; those of y chords are shown with parentheses.

retrograde, scoring and rhythmic values do not coincide exactly. Thus the continuation of the retrograde cycle past the end of the palindrome is the natural outcome of a procedure in which the two lines are gradually achieving some degree of individuality. Part of the rhythmic property from the theme and the first variation is reassigned to the last chord in each cycle. Ending this double cycle of fifths on simultaneous g^9 and a^9 chords leads smoothly to the next variation.

**

Webern's third variation, his "second subject" (mm. 74–109), demonstrates in a particular way the relevance of his characterization of the Variations as a developmental form. To be sure, this variation still uses the two four-note motives in ways that suggest a traditional harmonic interpretation, and it is divided into antecedent and consequent phrases in a manner suggestive of a "second subject." Yet there is another aspect of Webern's tone row that has special importance for this variation, helping not only to articulate its internal tonal organization, but also to establish it as a real "second subject" by making use of a traditonal tonal plan common to the mainstream of the 1930s and 1940s. This aspect of the row, as yet unremarked either in Webern's own writings or in the secondary literature, is directly related to the occasion for his letter to Reich from which I have quoted above.

Whether or not Webern's composition was in some way influenced by Sacher's rejection of his Cantata No. 1,[16] the first pages of the manuscript for the Variations contain an unmistakable reference to a work recently premiered with great success by Sacher in the Stadt Casino in Basel—Bartók's *Music for Strings, Percussion, and Celesta*. Example 17.6 shows Webern's first sketches for the Variations, taken from page 48 of the fourth sketchbook. The first line of musical notation in this sketch, dated 15 April 1940, represents his initial conception of the row, beginning with the five-note motive A–B-flat–D-flat–C–B (the same notes with which Bartók's piece begins), following that with a tritone transposition of the motive, and concluding with the remaining two pitches of the twelve-note chromatic (another tritone, A-flat–D). On the following day, as the second line of the sketch Webern adjusted the row to its final form: the initial five-note motive, a perfect-fifth transposition of it as ordinal pitches 6–10 (beginning on D), and the first two notes of a third presentation starting on G as the eleventh ordinal pitch. Even though the sketches indicate that Webern thought of his row as three four-note groups, the raw material may be described as a series of sequential presentations of Bartók's five-note motive moving by upward fourth. The third line of Webern's sketch shows a four-note cell in the bass register (later to be the first motive of the work) followed by an-

Example 17.6 Webern's first sketches for the Variations

15.IV.40

Thema: Period 1. zusammengesetzt mit satzartigen Theilen. Wiederholung in neuer Form

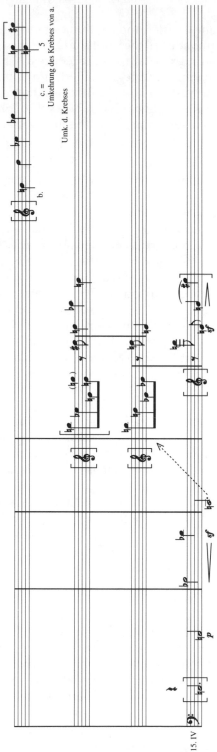

other four-note cell in the treble register. Here he used the earlier version of his row, the one with the five-note motive beginning on E-flat as ordinal pitches 6–10; the second four-note cell is revised on the next line of the sketch to conform with his final conception of the row.

Both of Webern's conceptions of the row honor Bartók's realizations of his motive in that the first movement of the *Music for Strings, Percussion, and Celesta* involves a dramatic large-scale motion by tritone from A (in m. 1) to E-flat (at the climax in m. 56), while at the movement's local level the motive appears in successive imitative entries that move by perfect fifth. In his theme and first two variations, Webern used the Bartók melodic cell in a series of statements of a particular harmonic complex that employs these two intervals. Beyond this point, however, one is hard pressed to find connections between the two works. (If one is looking for a composition that draws upon Bartók's motive in a comprehensible manner, Stravinsky's *In Memoriam Dylan Thomas* would seem a better choice.)

But Webern's third variation may persuade us that the Bartók source served a more fundamental role in the work's tonal organization than we might have suspected from our study of the theme and first two variations. Whereas each of these sections of the work can be described in terms of a single serial procedure—presentation of the family of row forms at 0 transpositional level in the theme, and mapping by whole tone and by fifth, respectively, in the two variations—the third variation presents several different serial relationships in rapid succession. It begins as a two-voice canon in contrary motion at the tritone. The first linear connection of rows recalls the mapping technique of the first variation in that ordinal pitch 11 in both the *dux* and the *comes* becomes the first ordinal pitch of the next row form. But here a different technique is used. Instead of mapping one row to the next, ordinal pitches 11 and 12 of the first series are followed by a row form that inverts this cell as its first and second ordinal pitches. If one considers Webern's row purely in terms of its pitch organization—i.e., as a projection of fifth-related statements of the Bartók quotation—the melodic organization in this passage might be described as two statements of the Bartók cell (ordinal pitches 1–5 and 6–10), a false beginning of a third statement (ordinal pitches 11–12), followed by inverted statements of the cell. This manner of connecting rows is not pursued throughout the variation. One can say only that rows are related each to the next in the respective voices of the canon by common tone or by semitone. Table 17.4 illustrates these connections.

In this variation Webern maintained the four-note cells from the earlier sections of the work while introducing new rhythmic figures. The practice of identifying the four-note cell with a single timbre is altered in two ways (see ex. 17.7):

Table 17.4.   Connections between Rows in
Webern's Third Variation

Antecedent Phrase: mm. 74–91	
dux:	I-3 to P-5 (11 of I-3 = 1 of P-5)
comes:	P-9 to I-7 (11 of P-9 = 1 of I-7)
	I-7 to RI-7 (common tone)
Consequent Phrase:	
dux:	P-7 to R-7 (common tone)
	R-7 to P-6 (12 of R-7 = 2 of P-6)
	P-6 to P-5 (common tone)
comes:	P-6 to R-6 (common tone)

Table 17.5.   Harmonic Organization of Webern's Third Variation

Antecedent Phrase:												
dux:	A	(E♭)	D	E♭			(E)		B♭			
comes:	G	(A♭)	D	C♯	(G)	F♯	F♯	(G)	C♯			
Consequent Phrase:												
dux:	F	(F♯)	C	C	(F♯)	F	E	(F)	B	E♭	(E)	B♭
comes:	E			(F)			B		B		(F)	E

Roots of *y* chords are shown in parentheses.

1. The new rhythmic figure, which is introduced with the first cell of the *comes* in mm. 74–75, presents the first pitch as a quarter note in one timbre, and the remaining three pitches as consecutive sixteenth notes in another timbre with three sixteenth rests separating the two elements. (The figure of three sixteenth notes in m. 74 outlines a chord in a conventional manner, from the root upward; when combined with the long note F-sharp in m. 74, a root position g^9 chord sounds in the characteristic disposition of an *x* chord.)

2. On two occasions (*dux*, mm. 78–87, and *comes*, mm. 91–99), two consecutive four-note cells are played by the same instrument. In the second pair of cells the Bartók motive can be heard distinctly as the first five pitches played by the trumpet. Despite some shifts in octave register, the motive is made accessible through use of a single timbre—especially to anyone aware of the omnipresent quality of the Bartók source in the Variations.

But it is the harmony that gives one the clearest sense of organization in this variation. Table 17.5 shows the harmonic structure of the variation. Four features of harmonic organization can thus be observed:

1. The third variation begins with the same harmonies that ended the second variation, but in opposite lines. Thus the *comes* begins this variation by continuing the mapping procedure of the previous *dux*, and the *dux* similarly continues the mapping procedure of the previous *comes*.

Example 17.7 The canon in Webern's third variation, mm. 74–109

This point further justifies Webern's description of the second variation as a "bridge passage."

2. The third harmony in each voice is d^9. This chord represents the end point of the projected chordal pattern from the second variation and, as such, matches the g-sharp^9 chords of m. 63 previously mentioned. Although in mm. 78–81 these d^9 chords are presented in a linear manner, the impression here is again that two lines are merging, especially since three of the four pitches sound in the same octave register. The impression of merging lines is enhanced by the silences in the *dux* that allow the intervening pitches of the *comes* to complete the chord.

3. In similar manner, a b^9 chord occurs simultaneously in both lines at mm. 102–4 in the consequent phrase. Here both voices have the same octave register, rhythmic figure, and vertical arrangement; only the serial order differs. Agogic stress on B and D recalls the connections between these two notes found at the beginning of the theme and of the first variation.

4. The final chord of the *dux* is the familiar first chord of the theme, b-flat^9.

These observations indicate how tonal comprehensibility is gained through harmonic ties with past events. The harmonic agreements on d^9 and b^9 chords recall a prominent imitative moment from m. 2 of the theme. The appearance of new rhythmic shapes and the shift of tonal focus from the B-flat–F of the theme and first variation to D and B justify Webern's description of this variation as the "second subject."

From the evidence cited above, one could already regard this as the "Bartók variation," with a melodically comprehensible quotation and serial manipulations drawn from the five-note motive. In Bartók's composition the most dramatic arrival is surely the one on E-flat in m. 56, where a succession of imitative entries—spiraling alternately upward and downward by fifth from the initial A—converge. In other circumstances the E-flat of m. 56 might be considered a tritone equivalent to the A at the beginning of the movement; here the E-flat is the "point of furthest remove."[17] This term, originially applied to development sections of eighteenth-century movements, is frequently transferred to expository sections of developmental forms in early twentieth-century literature.

Webern's third variation conforms with this common harmonic procedure in two ways:

1. The harmonic succession E–B-flat is prominent in this variation. It appears as the final "tonal" resolution in the *dux* of the antecedent phrase, where the E/e harmony in the first violin is followed by a b-flat^9 chord in the flute (mm. 88–91). In a more obvious way the simultaneity E–B-flat is created by the two *x* harmonies having these roots at the end of the variation (mm. 107–9). This harmonic tritone relationship is dra-

matized both in the course of remembrance at the local level and as a large-scale event in the Variations. The b-flat^9 that concludes the *dux* recalls the *comes* entry that begins this variation (mm. 74–75), where its rhythmic figure was introduced. In both instances the concluding figure of three sixteenth notes is taken by the clarinet. But there are significant differences: in mm. 74–75, the clarinet outlines the chord upward from the root, and the long note played by the cello supplies the seventh; in mm. 107–9, by contrast, the clarinet outlines only the upper notes of the chord, and the trumpet supplies the root on the long note. The use of the trumpet for the root recalls the b-flat^9 chord in the brass at m. 20, which ends the theme. Pairing this b-flat^9 chord with an e^9 chord in the harp emphasizes the tritone relation between the two like sonorities and suggests a large-scale tritone connection between the double-bass b-flat^9 of m. 1 and a related string instrumentation of the e^9 chord.

2. Bartók's A–E-flat is referred to in a clearly comprehensible fashion. The E-flat in the harp at the end of this variation appears simultaneously in the double bass as a note that will be sustained to begin the fourth variation. Hence, the use of registral extremes and timbral association links A and E-flat in a way that recalls the dramatic link between these two pitch classes in Bartók's composition.

***

Webern characterized his fourth variation (mm. 109–34) as "the recapitulation of the first subject . . . but in a developing manner." More than any other section of this work, this variation appears to lack tonal focus. It may be described as a four-voice canon or, more accurately, as two overlapping canons at the whole tone (see ex. 17.8).

While rhythmic groupings suggest the pairings shown in the example, the pitch materials suggest another organization: four parallel statements of an inverted melody using mapping techniques from the first variation. In contrast to the *retrogression* of *x* chords—alternating upward fifth with upward third—in the melodic lines of the first variation, employment of inverted set forms in the fourth brings about a similar *progression* of *x* chords. In this instance, however, unlike the *dux* of the first variation, ordinal pitch cell 5–8 is included in the melodic lines, placing *y* chords between the fifth-related pairs of each set form. But this progression of *x* chords and upward step movement of *y* chords seems to be obliterated by the canonic texture, so that each chord sounds in a cluster of four simultaneous transposition levels at $t = 0, 1, 2,$ and 3. Harmonic comprehensibility would appear impossible amid such contrapuntal conflict.

Other factors, however, can influence the situation. The most obvi-

Example 17.8   The canon in Webern's fourth variation, mm. 109–15

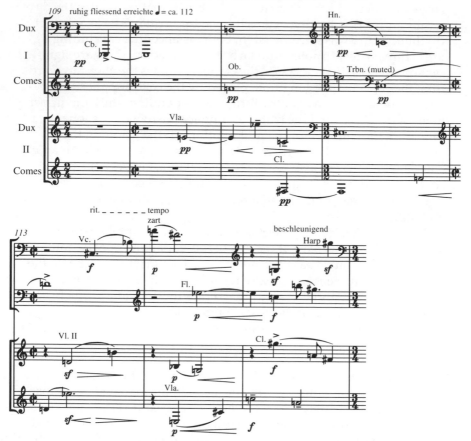

ous of these is the resolution of G to C in the timpani: first a roll on G for the length of four quarter notes (mm. 122–23), and then the quarter note C (m. 133). Despite the nine-measure space between these two pitches, the resolution is prominent here because the timpani plays so seldom in the Variations; in fact this is the only variation that contains two different timpani pitches. The resolution is, of course, a conventional one, commonly found in timpani parts at "tonal" points of arrival in eighteenth- and nineteenth-century music. The traditional meaning of this resolution in a development section almost always has something to do with dominant function. Thus its occurrence here suggests further refinements to our interpretations of earlier events.

If one recalls (1) the B-flat–F resolution at the beginning of the theme, (2) the f⁹ chord in the brass at the end of the theme, and (3) the persistent F in the timpani of that variation—the whole-note roll in the *comes* at the

Table 17.6.   Harmonic Organization of Webern's Fourth Variation

	1	2	3	4	5	6	7	8	9	10	11	12
Dux:	C	(F♯)	F	D	(A♭)	G	E	(B♭)	A	F♯	(C)	B
Comes:	D	(A♭)	G	E	(B♭)	A	F♯	(C)	B	G♯	(D)	C♯
Dux:	C♯	(G)	F♯	E♭	(A)	A♭	F	(B)	B♭	G	(C♯)	C
Comes:	E♭	(A)	A♭	F	(B)	B♭	G	(C♯)	C	A	(E♭)	D

Roots of *y* chords are shown in parentheses. Boldfaced letters indicate chords in root position.

end of the antecedent phrase (m. 37) and the repeated root of the *y* chord in mm. 48–50—then the G–C resolution in the fourth variation can be an important articulator of the form. If F represents the tonic in the "first subject," then the G–C resolution suggests the type of return that conventionally occurs in a development.

Some other aural evidence backs up this assertion. From the beginning of the Variations, harmonies have been introduced in root position. In fact, harmonic comprehensibility might be equated with the presence of root-position chords, especially of *x* chords. These root-position chords have appeared sometimes as simultaneities and sometimes in linear form. In the fourth variation each canonic line comprises the twelve chords, as shown in table 17.6. Here we see that root-position G chords dominate this complex contrapuntal texture. They appear first in positions 2 and 3, from which they "resolve" by upward fifth (to D) or downward step (to F); then in positions 6 and 7, the latter accompanied by a similar sonority a whole tone lower on F; then in position 10, accompanied by the same sonority a whole tone higher on A, with both chords resolving by downward fifth (to C and D, respectively). The G–C resolution is confirmed in position 12, where an *x* chord on C sounds. Thus, what may be the most harmonically comprehensible aspect of the respective canonic lines confirms the aurally more accessible G–C resolution of the timpani.

***

If the resolution of G to C that ends the fourth variation has any relevance for the structure of the Variations, then one might expect some reference to F at the beginning of the fifth variation, perhaps a reprise of the theme or the first variation with their B-flat to F resolutions. Failing such a tonal reference, the prominent G and C could appear to be merely "accidents" of serial presentation.

Webern's references are not so direct, however. Although B-flat–F references do not appear as such, the fifth variation (mm. 135–45) does, in fact, begin with an unmistakable reference to the theme. The first four variations having introduced their varied characterizations of the theme's basic material, the fifth variation begins with what sounds like a subdominant version of the *dux* from m. 1, using similar timbre (viola replacing double bass) and rhythm (8488 replacing 8848). Although this presentation of P-5 clearly refers to the *dux* of the theme, registral differences in the *x* chords lessen its harmonic comprehensibility. In both *x* chords here the root is the highest pitch and the third the lowest. In contrast, the *y* chord in cell 5–8 of this row is an exact transposition of the first statement of this motive (m. 2).

Another factor that could diminish the comprehensibility of this passage is the new relationship between *dux* and *comes*. Had the transpositional model been followed literally, the *comes* would have entered with P-6, placing an *x* chord with an E root directly under the *y* chord on E in the flute. Instead, the *comes* uses I-6, thereby placing a c^9 chord directly under the flute's E-natural. The immediate effect is to disturb the possibility of harmonic identification with the theme. This impression is offset by means of synthesis: the *comes* in this passage adopts the chordal mapping procedure from the second variation, rather than the melodic imitative procedure from the *comes* of the theme. In this way a rapid succession of chords, c^9–F-sharp/f-sharp^6–f^9–B/b^6, underlies the 5–8 cell in the *dux*. As a result of combining these aspects of the theme and the second variation, b-flat^9 chords appear next in both successions. A harmonic concordance is evident here as the *dux* and *comes*, each imitating the other, share the same vertical disposition of this *x* chord and provide the high B-flat^3 with a tonic accent. In fact, the two lines have merged on the very chord that opened the Variations, although in a different register.

The b-flat^9 chords of mm. 139–40 occur at the end of the antecedent phrase of the fifth variation. At the same time, two new lines enter with the inverted row forms on G and G-flat, respectively—i.e., I-10 and I-9. This second canon makes use of the chordal mapping procedure from the second variation and, in so doing, lines up vertical correspondences between the d^9 and D/d^6 chords in m. 143 and a linear representation of a g^9 chord with a G/g^6 chord in mm. 143–44. Also of interest are the harmonic contents of mm. 140–41, where the first canon sounding against the *dux* of the second canon brings about a harmonic juxtaposition of b-flat^9 and B/b^6 chords like that at the beginning of the theme and the first variation. The other important tonal event in this variation occurs at the end where the two *comes* lines present f-sharp^9 chords. (Here it is interesting to observe, that the F-sharp and F exchange registers while the other two pitches remain in the same register.) The vertical alignment of all the harmonic groups in this variation is shown in table 17.7. The end of the antecedent phrase and the beginning of the consequent are marked by tonal concurrences on B-flat and B, respec-

Table 17.7.   Harmonic Organization of Webern's Fifth Variation

Antecedent Phrase:							
dux:	e♭⁹	E/e⁶		b♭⁹			
comes:		C⁹ F♯/f♯⁶ f⁹ B/b⁶		b♭⁹			
Consequent Phrase:							
I: *dux:*		b⁹		F/f⁶			e⁹
comes:		b⁹		C/c⁶			f♯⁹
II: *dux:*	e⁹	B♭/b♭⁶		E♭/e♭⁶	d⁹	A♭/a♭⁶	g⁹
comes:	e♭⁹	A/a⁶	a♭⁹		D/d⁶	d♭⁹	G/g⁶ f♯⁹

tively (note the absolute correspondence in register within each chord), just as a similar concurrence on F-sharp ends the variation. With the exception of the F that the events of the previous variation might have led us to expect, the tonal pillars that had articulated the beginnings of both phrases of the theme appear in corresponding positions in this variation. Hence, Webern's description of the variation as recapitulatory is borne out in harmonic terms.

***

Webern's "coda," his sixth variation (mm. 146–80), introduces several new elements into the contrapuntal texture. Since the harmonic vocabulary in the expository and recapitulatory sections has been limited to two chord types, identified as such through timbral and rhythmic associations and employed in a limited pattern of harmonic successions, the sudden appearance of new chord types in some of the same timbral groupings might appear to upset the harmonic balance. On the contrary, the particular way in which the "coda" uses these new chord types provides a clinching argument for our thesis that harmony, more than any other element, articulates the form of the Variations.

The occasion for the new chord types is the following: P-7, P-10, and P-9 are combined with I-1 as soprano, alto, tenor, and bass lines of a four-voice canon, given in ex. 17.9 as Webern wrote it on four staves in his sketchbook. Measures 146–62 constitute the antecedent phrase, in which each canonic line presents one complete row statement with its last two pitches mapped on to the first ten pitches of a second row. Although this is a serial disposition familiar from the expository first variation and the recapitulatory fourth variation, the rhythmic and timbral groupings are quite different here. In fact, harmonic comprehensibility in the individual lines of this phrase has been obscured by these two factors: ordinal pitch cells 1–4 and 9–12 are not presented with the familiar 8848 family of rhythms nor are they assigned to a single timbre. Although ordinal pitch cell 5–8 retains its characteristic rhythm in this phrase, its vertical positioning now locates the third of the minor triad below that of the major.

Example 17.9 The canon in Webern's sixth variation, mm. 146–80

Antecedent

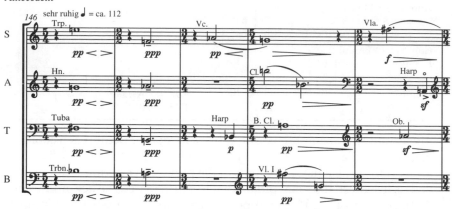

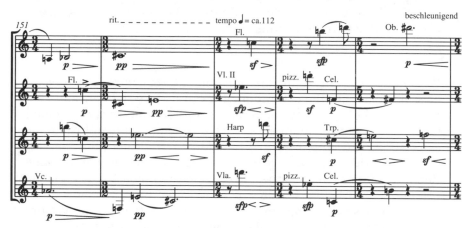

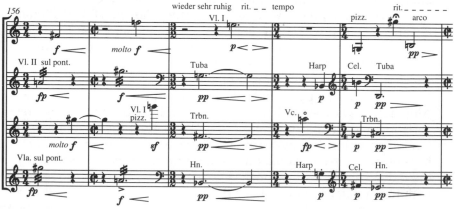

Consequent

As shown in example 17.9, the variation begins with a new chordal sonority composed of the respective first pitches of the four canonic lines; it is scored for a familiar timbre of brass instruments, heretofore reserved for simultaneities of *x* or *y* chords. The chord at m. 146, although new to this composition, has a tertian disposition common in nineteenth- and early twentieth-century music, consisting of root, major third, minor seventh, and minor ninth. It might be understood as a variant of the *x* chord, one in which the qualities of the third, seventh, and ninth above the bass have been changed. Accordingly, this F-sharp^9 chord is related in a conventional harmonic sense to the f-sharp^9 chords with which the *comes* lines concluded the fifth variation. Hence, the connection between the final two variations is much more harmonic than serial.

But the changes at the beginning of this "coda" have a significance far beyond that derived from its connection to the previous variation. They bring about a grand summation of the salient harmonic features of the whole composition; that is, they fulfill the Classical tonal function of a coda. The tonal role of this "coda" may be summarized as follows.

By means of the F-sharp chord in m. 146, this antecedent phrase shifts the harmonic focus away from the individual line to strictly vertical combinations of the four canonic lines. Despite its new method of defining harmonies, the phrase contains six chords—the normative number as established in the antecedent phrase of the theme and employed in the first, second, and fourth variations, where antecedent-consequent phrase pairing has previously occurred. These chords may be explained in terms of the chordal successions in the theme and their derivatives from the first five variations.

Since the first harmony of the "coda" is F-sharp, one of two root successions might be expected—either F-sharp–C–B or F-sharp–G–C-sharp. Although the particulars have been changed, the succession of six chords in this antecedent phrase retains essential harmonic features from the second of these possibilities and combines them with another element that supplies an important harmonic event missing from the preceding variation.

The F-sharp–G–C-sharp succession is suggested by the relationship between the initial F-sharp^9 and the second chord (see ex. 17.9, m. 147). The latter has some obvious attributes of an x chord on G, since it presents G as a possible root in the bass, with minor seventh and minor ninth above. That is to say, it contains all the components of the preceding F-sharp^9 chord except for the third above the bass, which is replaced by a major ninth. The third chord in the succession (m. 158) repeats the F-sharp^9 now in inversion, with both third and ninth sounding below the root. The first three chords, thus described, are essentially F-sharp–G–F-sharp.

The next two chords complete a chord complex that suggests the expected F-sharp–G–C-sharp prototype. The first of these chords, the fourth in the overall succession (m. 160), consists of only three different pitches. Like the G chord, it contains a root in the bass, plus seventh and ninth—in this instance major seventh and minor ninth—and lacks a third. By analogy with the other chords in this phrase, it is a D chord. The fifth chord (m. 161) is subject to different interpretations. Its disposition, with C-sharp in the bass and the minor third and major seventh above, suggests another x chord on C-sharp, though this interpretation is somewhat undermined by the B-flat in the top voice.

The overall effect of these five chords is one of a succession F-sharp–

G–D–C-sharp in which the second and last elements contain disturbing notes, A-natural and B-flat, respectively. Taken by itself, this progression could be a derivative of the expected prototype. The added D root simply projects another perfect fifth relationship within the chord complex. The note D is also an important secondary pitch class in its own right within this composition, as we have already discovered.

But what about the disturbing added notes? Although the A–F–A-flat combination of pitches above the bass note G in the second chord may be explained as one seventh and two ninths above the root, as given above, we might also see this combination of pitches as a suggestion of an F chord with both major and minor third. This alternative is especially compelling when one considers the extraneous B-flat in the C-sharp chord.

Taken together, these two "disturbances" remind one of the B-flat–F "resolution" that was the first harmonic gesture of the theme. Two factors enhance this possibility:

1. The G–C motion at the end of the fourth variation has set up an expectation of a "resolution" to F, especially when past F and B-flat events are taken into account. Further, the expected F was the only one of the structural notes from the theme that did not appear in the fifth variation. Therefore, references in the "coda" to F and its relationship to B-flat, however secondary they may appear, fulfill the harmonic expectations set up by the conventional timpani resolution of the fourth variation.

2. The sixth chord in the succession of the antecedent phrase in the "coda" (m. 162)—a chord that we have not yet discussed—confirms some of our expectations regarding F. It may be described as a normative combination of C and F functions, with F and its major third plus C and its major seventh. In this way the six–chord succession makes a double harmonic impression—one of suggesting the normative chord complex, and another of completing the recapitulation of tonal functions that occurred in the expository theme and first three variations.

If the "coda" is seen purely in terms of its serial organization, there appears to be no break in continuity between antecedent and consequent; m. 163 simply continues the four-voice canon, employing the same mapping procedure as the antecedent phrase. The ear, however, recognizes a marked change from the final chord of the antecedent phrase in m. 162—composed of the respective tenth ordinal pitches of four different set forms—and the return of four-note linear cells that restate in contrapuntal texture the familiar 8848 and 3126 rhythms and their derivatives. As a result of this change, the three four-note cells in each of the canonic lines once again assume the harmonic identities that were assigned to them in the theme. These harmonies are shown in table 17.8.

Table 17.8.   Harmonic Organization in the Consequent Phrase of Webern's Sixth Variation

Soprano:	$c\sharp^9$	D/d_4^6	$g\sharp^9$			b^9			C/c_4^6		$f\sharp^9$
Alto:	e^9	F/f^6	b^9			d^9			Eb/eb^6		a^9
Tenor:	eb^9	E/e	bb^9	eb^7	f^9	bb_{+5}^7	c^7	$C\sharp/c\sharp^6$	g^9	Ab/ab^6	d^9
Bass:	b^9	F/f^6	e^9	d^7	a^7	Eb/eb^6	f_{+5}^7	Ab/ab^6	g^9	$C\sharp/c\sharp^6$	c^9

Since the soprano and alto lines maintain the same mapping procedure throughout this consequent phrase, they also outline the same six-chord succession that occurred in the first variation. A sense both of harmonic connection with the antecedent phrase and of harmonic completion is evident in the soprano line. Its c-sharp⁹ chord, outlined in mm. 163–64, confirms the C-sharp implications from the end of the antecedent phrase. The melodic disposition taken from the "first subject" brings about a return to RI-0 in m. 168, with its "tonic-level" restatement from both the beginning of the *comes* and the conclusion of the *dux* of the theme. Thus the harmonic content at the conclusion of the theme and the "coda" is identical in their respective soprano lines.

But harmonic return in the "coda" is not confined to the soprano line. Webern underscored it with a new variant derived from the second variation. The soprano return to B-flat in the clarinet (m. 168) is anticipated (in m. 167) by the familiar b-flat⁹ chord scored for brass choir and taken from a return of the P-0 set form. At this point the tenor line begins to use the chordal mapping procedure of the second variation, but with an important change. Following the *x* chord in m. 167, the viola plays a three-note chord in which pitch 5 (B-natural) does not appear. This ordinal pitch is taken as a common tone with the B-natural of the alto line (note 9 in P-6); Webern used arrows in his sketches to show that the alto B-natural is shared by the tenor line. This deletion from the chordal sonority causes the expected B/b⁶ chord to sound as an e–flat⁷ chord, containing the minor third and major seventh that have been associated previously with *x* chords. The deletion thus not only changes the progression, but also transforms a *y* chord into a quasi-*x* chord. As a result of this one alteration in the tenor line the chordal succession that surrounds the clarinet entry on B-flat is b-flat⁹–e-flat⁷–f⁹; and the following chord, by means of the same procedure, suggests an *x* chord on B-flat—with root, augmented fifth, and major seventh. In this way the chordal progression accompanying the soprano B-flat entry is a succession of *x* chords that provide the conventional cadential pattern I–IV–V–I in B-flat.

Even the final chordal identities in the four canonic lines have particular relevance to the harmonic language of this composition. Since the alto lies either a major sixth below or a minor third above the soprano line, parallel b⁹ and d⁹ harmonies are formed where the clarinet enters on B-flat in mm. 168–73. Although the vertical positioning of the pitches in the b^9 of the soprano somewhat obscures the harmony, there is an obvious tonal reference between the double-bass D in mm. 170–71 of the soprano and the timpani and bass clarinet in m. 172 of the alto. Once again, the timpani articulates an important harmonic function: as the root of the chord, it aids the comprehensibility of the d^9 chord in the alto. This fact calls attention to the alto resolution, d^9–E-flat/e-flat–a^9. In the tenor line the series of chords is followed by a concluding linear d^9 chord announced by the trumpet in m. 179. Thus D, a pitch that received secondary emphasis in m. 2 of the theme and primary emphasis in the third variation, contributes to part of Webern's tonal summation in the "coda." It sounds in the tenor at the end with its dominant in the alto, and the entire complex of x chords, presented as they are in linear fashion, outlines a D major-minor seventh chord-of-chords.

***

In the Variations for Orchestra Webern's method of presenting his harmonic language makes it directly accessible to the sensitive and attentive listener. By introducing at the outset two short, rhythmically distinct melodic motives that can be easily identified as familiar tertian chords from the repertory of the 1930s and 1940s, Webern prepares his audience for events that are commonly associated with these harmonies. Timbral and rhythmic similarities connecting perfect-fifth transpositions of these chords at the local level encourage the listener to project his traditional tonal values into the larger architecture of the Variations. Webern also provides reinforcement of traditional tonal expectations: the harmonic successions in the antecedent and consequent phrases conform with common tonal paradigms of the 1930s and 1940s. Harmonic relationships between the larger architectural units, i.e., the theme and the individual variations, can then be heard as realizations of the harmonic language established from the beginning of the work. Even those harmonic connections that seem obscure are in every instance derived from common harmonic procedures that can be readily heard and easily grasped. Thus, a harmonic analysis of the Variations illustrates Schoenberg's contention that "there can be no doubt that after two centuries of development of homophonic forms and a very complex harmony, the musical thoughts of our time are not contrapuntal but melodic-homophonic-harmonic."[18]

　　In this work Webern took no liberties with the serial order of pitches. Therefore an analysis that accounts for the serial organization of its constituent parts will describe its structure accurately. Yet there is something incomplete in such an analysis precisely because the musical reasons for connections between different row forms cannot be adequately expressed in terms of the series alone. Set theory can be more informative in that it identifies the appearances of like interval collections, e.g., the x and y chords described in this essay. But the underlying assumption of set theory, that traditional tonal relationships do not exist in this music, makes it impossible to account for many of the musical events in this work. Although helpful for gathering information, these theories can provide only a partial basis for understanding the Variations.

As we have seen, both Schoenberg and Webern advocated a traditional understanding of music built upon harmonic thinking that derives directly from the Classical tradition. Their comments along this line are persuasive encouragement for the thorough harmonic investigation of the Second Viennese repertory. Our examination of Webern's Variations illustrates the advantages of this kind of evaluation and shows that the twelve-tone method is only a means toward an end[19]—in this composition, toward a harmonic organization that is entirely logical in terms of contemporary musical practice and readily accessible to the listener.

Notes

1. The circumstances of Webern's correspondence with Sacher in regard to Cantata No. 1 are recounted in Hans and Rosaleen Moldenhauer, *Anton von Webern: A Chronicle of His Life and Work* (New York, 1979), 566–67. See also pp. 689–90 for a discussion of their correspondence regarding the Variations.

2. Anton Webern, *The Path to the New Music*, ed. Willi Reich, trans. Leo Black (Bryn Mawr, 1963), 61.

3. Ibid.

4. Compare this statement by Webern with Allen Forte's assertion: "In 1908 a profound change in music was initiated when Arnold Schoenberg began composing his 'George Lieder' Op. 15. In this work he deliberately relinquished the traditional system of tonality, which had been the basis of musical syntax for the previous two hundred and fifty years. Subsequently, Schoenberg, Anton Webern, Alban Berg, and a number of other composers created the large repertory known as atonal music." *The Structure of Atonal Music* (New Haven, 1973), ix.

5. In an earlier letter to Reich, dated 3 March 1941, Webern wrote of his Variations: "The presentation is horizontal as to form, vertical in all other respects." Webern, *The Path to the New Music*, 60.

6. Ibid., 62.

7. Ibid.

8. Webern's original text reads: "Theme: Periodl. zusammengesetzt mit satzartigen Theilen. Wiederholung in neuer Form." In Moldenhauer, *Anton von Webern*, 568, the word "satzartig" is given the misleading translation "motivic."

9. Examples 17.1 and 17.5–17.8 below are my combination of two elements: (1) The

choirbook format (SATB) adopts the procedure that Webern used in his sketchbook; it shows the individual canonic lines rather than the separate instrumental lines. (2) The pitches and rhythms in my examples are those from the published score; there are many instances in the sketches where octave register, orchestrational details, and rhythms differ substantially from those in the published score. Thus the actual source of these examples is the published score, but the method of presentation is that of the sketches.

10. Forte set numbers for these two chords are 4-3 and 4-17, respectively. Since the premise of this essay is that the traditional connotations of these chords play a forma-tive role in Webern's Variations, I have chosen to use traditional chord labels rather than Forte's set numbers. Compare the findings of my study with his discussion in *The Structure of Atonal Music*, 1, in which he states: "The repertory of atonal music is characterized by the occurrence of pitches in novel combinations, as well as by the occurrence of familiar pitch combinations in unfamiliar environments." See also note 4 above.

11. Since the prime and retrograde inversion of this row are identical, as are the inversion and the retrograde, there are only twenty-four forms. Thus every row has two possible labels. In regard to this possibility, note that the prime form beginning on B-flat is given the label RI-0 and not P-1. This label is the one used by Webern in his sketches. It suggests a "home key" relationship between the rows of the *dux* and *comes* in the theme.

12. In this discussion augmentations, diminutions, and retrogrades are regarded as derivatives. Accordingly, the derivatives of the basic *x* rhythm, 8848, that are used by Webern are 8488, 4424, 4244, 2212, and 2122; those of the basic *y* rhythm, 3126, are 6213, 624-12, and 12-426. In addition, it may be noticed that in some instances the final note in an imitating *comes* lacks its full value.

13. For a discussion of this idea, see Graham H. Phipps, "The Tritone as an Equiva-lency: A Contextual Perspective for Approaching Schoenberg's Music," *Journal of Musicology* 4, no. 1 (Winter 1985–86): 51–69.

14. The other categories that Schoenberg gave are "strong" downward fifths or downward thirds and "superstrong" upward or downward seconds. See Arnold Schoenberg, *Theory of Harmony*, trans. Roy E. Carter (Berkeley, 1978), 115–23.

15. Arnold Schoenberg, *Models for Beginners in Composition*, ed. Leonard Stein, 3d ed. (Los Angeles, 1972), 56–57, illustrates how "the constant neglect" of motivic elements "neutralizes" its basic obligations. The method of getting rid of these obligations he defines as "liquidation."

16. See note 1 above.

17. A historical discussion of this concept is given in Leonard Ratner, *Classic Music: Expression, Form, and Style* (New York, 1980), 225–27.

18. This comment was one of the key points made by Arnold Schoenberg in his first intended preface for *Preliminary Exercises in Counterpoint*, ed. Leonard Stein (London, 1963), 222.

19 . Schoenberg characteristically referred to his as a "method of composition with twelve notes." In so doing, he eschewed use of the term *system* to explain his music. Particularly in his *Theory of Harmony*, 7–12, he explained the shortcomings of systems and concluded: "Art propagates itself through works of art and not through aesthetic laws."

EIGHTEEN

"The Fantasy Can Be Critically Examined": Composition and Theory in the Thought of Stefan Wolpe

AUSTIN CLARKSON

The music and the speech about music of a composer arise from the same creative source, and so we expect that each will shed light on the other.[1] But the relationship varies greatly, depending on whether the composer takes language and music to be distinctive or intimately related systems of communication. Some describe the antecedent conditions (the pretext) and the context of a piece, some give an objective account of structural and other technical features of the music, and others compose in speech an almost poetic analogue to the music.[2] Each position articulates a particular relationship between music and speech about music. At one end of the spectrum language is a medium for objectifying and transcending music, and at the other language is a medium for subjectifying and embodying music. Each will result in a distinctive theory of music with particular value systems both for music and for speech about music. When the composer's speech about music deals with structure, technique, and form, it will be construed from the transcendent position as a theory of music, but when it concerns contextual, intuitive, and imaginal factors it will be bracketed as extramusical, programmatic, impressionistic, or mentalistic. But if a composer explicitly holds the embodied position and argues that these factors should be included in the theory of music, are we not obliged to incorporate them if we wish to construe responsibly his or her paradigm of musical meaning? And so it is with Stefan Wolpe, who argued that the theory of music must deal with fantasy. A lecture he gave in Kassel in 1957 begins: "The fantasy can be critically examined." We shall return to it below.

The composer's music and his theory of music have joint custody of his creativity: "Listening is do-it-yourself composing. Composing is speculative listening."[3] Now one leads the way, now the other. They must be taken together in order to formulate the composer's paradigm of musical meaning.[4] For Stefan Wolpe music and speech about music were intimately connected, and he expressed himself fluently and vividly in both. His language is rich in feeling, metaphor, wit, and plays on words, and he often composed fanciful visual arrangements of words on the page. On occasion he also wrote poetry and set his own texts to music. So for Wolpe language was a medium of creative expression very close to music. This attitude to language carried through to the program notes he wrote for his compositions. He related the images and feelings that motivated a piece, but he also went into structural aspects of the music expressed in both technical and figurative language. In some of his lectures he addressed technical issues in detail, specifying the pitch structures and compositional processes of particular pieces.[5] Many of Wolpe's lectures are profusely illustrated with musical examples specially composed for the purpose, so that music and language form an integral fabric, each commenting on, analogizing, and amplifying the other.[6] For Wolpe music and speech about music share a broad common ground or, as Seeger put it, a high degree of homology.[7] By maximizing the area of homology between the domains of music and speech about music, Wolpe condensed musical fact and value, concept and percept, algorithm and image into an extraordinarily rich and complex medium of discourse. Because his music and speech about music were linked so closely, interpretation is difficult but rewarding. I shall attempt to construe Wolpe's paradigm of musical meaning by considering together a piece of music and a lecture, both composed in the same year.

The last major phase of Wolpe's creative life, which extended from 1959 to 1970, was inaugurated with a piece for piano and a lecture on his poetics of music. The lecture "Thinking Twice"[8] was given at the University of California at Los Angeles in the spring of 1959 and again that summer at Darmstadt, while the composition *Form for Piano*[9] was premiered by David Tudor in New York on 22 May of the same year.

Form is a single movement of some three minutes' duration. The bare facts can be summarized briefly. The piece begins with an image consisting of six pitches given in even quarter notes, "Remote and restless." I shall call this image 1 (see ex. 18.9). The six-note group is a closed, self-contained image that functions in the piece as: (1) an ordered motive that recurs once at t0; (2) an unordered hexachord I shall denote as N that appears in many diverse images at t0 and t5; (3) the complementary hexachord Ñ in many diverse images at t0 and t5; and (4) an aggregate of N plus Ñ at t5. The pitch materials are restricted, but because the hexachords are usually unordered, there is a remarkable variety of shapes. The piece consists of a series of some forty images that are juxtaposed to produce a high degree of contrast. For instance, images 2 and 3 freely reorder N to create strong contrasts with image 1 (see ex. 18.9). The complementary hexachord Ñ interrupts in m. 4 with a trill image (image 4), followed by an explosion of quickly rising chords. Two-thirds of the way through the piece hexachords N and Ñ are superimposed in images of climactic intensity. Thereafter N and Ñ appear alternately at t5 until just before the end, when N (t0) in the original ordered form returns *ppp*. The final image combines N plus Ñ (t5) in a crumbling image that is a characteristic Wolpe close.

In 1957 Wolpe wrote to a friend: "I have finished a cycle of four works—a concept of doing, inventing, and realizing. After this I'll start anew on a different plane."[10] The first piece in the new style was *Form*, which marks a radical break with his previous style,[11] by introducing a new principle to replace developing variation, namely, the principle of the conjunction of opposites. This is discussed in the program note he wrote for a performance of *Form* in 1964:

> Whereas the previous pieces were based upon closed relationships between consecutive events utilizing the art of infinite grades of transition, in the *Form for Piano* the art of molding opposites into adjacent situations becomes the main concern. In that sense the great degree of opposites becomes released, and the old relationships become rarer and stranger. In a way, it leads to the elimination of the principle of opposites as being opposed and makes the most opposite the most likely adjacent. Opposites become complementary and allow the infinite and instant conversion of line into lines, into sounds, into varying quantities of action, from much to nothing, from nothing to little, from little to scarcely anything, from scarcely anything to a conjuring plenty of abandon. Since opposites become adjacencies, the modes of opposite expression as hard and soft, wild and tame, flowing and hesitant, etc., all these modes become self-inclusive. The piece feeds its own totality and brings everything into its focus.[12]

The principle of conjoined opposites was for Wolpe a concept of formal process that would replace the principle of developing variation. By conjoined opposites he meant sequences of images marked by nongradual contrasts of qualities (nothing, little, much; hard, soft; wild, tame), textures (line to lines; lines to sounds),[13] and gestures (flowing, hesitant). Notations in the score used by the pianist Irma Wolpe Rademacher give additional clues regarding certain structural relations and personal associations.[14] The local and global structures should thus be expressed in terms that integrate more abstract relations with regional properties of the imagery. Wolpe was striving for a music that would bring together within a piece with limited pitch materials the widest possible spectrum of expressive and structural contents. But now we should turn to the lecture "Thinking Twice" for a fuller understanding of Wolpe's new paradigm.

The lecture sets the framework for his new way of "doing, inventing, and realizing" by appraising contemporary trends that differed from his own aesthetic. He looked askance at integral serialism, aleatoric music, and the historical inheritance of developing variation, pointing out the differences he had with these paradigms. He then proceeded to present a wide range of concepts: opposites, the "discontinuum," varying the speed of pitch circulation with the tempo of structural transformation, "constellatory space," "organic modes or generic sets," and so forth.

The lecture begins with a kind of epigraph:

No one can blur the evidence of the light's ravishing speed.
No one can dissuade an apple from falling,
as no one has the strength to withhold his breath.[15]

The three declarations are rich in metaphor, blurring the boundary between cognitive and imaginal knowing. The quasi-poetic language invites readers to lower their mental level from that of the focused awareness of scientific discourse to that which is receptive to fantasy. Wolpe thus induces the reader to do a cognitive double take, which is perhaps what he means by the title "Thinking Twice."

Let me try to paraphrase these opening lines:

The forces of nature both physical and physiological—light, gravity, the need to breathe—are the ground of human existence. We ignore these forces and the laws that govern them at our peril, for they rule our music making and our thinking about music.

The lecture continues:
"Thinking Twice," paragraph 1:

Laws of nature can't be bent into modifying the nature of laws, but one can sit out history and its yesterday's implications. Many have tried so. But, having taken their judgments for granted, they find themselves confronted by the turntables of history, and, being like waves that try to stick to the ground, they fight, or give up, or wither away. The better among them are dissatisfied by the images of their art, which have become flat and dull. [See ex. 18.1]

Paragraph 1 paraphrased:
Humans cannot manipulate the laws of nature, but history is an artifact that can be altered.[16] Historical principles are as mutable as the

record that is revolving on a turntable. Those who try to hold onto
historical traditions and fail to adapt to new conditions are engaged in
a futile struggle. They are like waves that try to stay in one place instead
of going with the flow of the tide. Those who disengage themselves
from the constraints of tradition find that the old sounds are no longer
interesting. Example 18.1, Wolpe's first illustration, provides a musical
gloss with a languid phrase in which overstuffed dominants are under-
laid by tired intervals falling in the bass.
"Thinking Twice," paragraph 2:

> One has to practice one's art with a knowing sense of its
> radical nature. Because substance is radical (as the nerves
> are, and the mind that attests to the making of substance)
> one is touched, initiated, formed by experiencing the traces,
> pressures, compressions of musical substance. This substance
> behaves with all its fierce contractions, interhinging the se-
> quences of tones into cogent levels of shapes, interlapping
> them into internalized, center-bound, concentric rows of
> pitches, pitch-aggregates, of sounds, of sound-aggregates.
> [See ex. 18.2]

Paragraph 2 paraphrased:
    The artist's creativity is rooted in an intimate relationship with the
musical material itself. The composer is not an omnipotent artificer
manipulating inert matter, but a collaborator with sound material, which

Example 18.1

Example 18.2

is a living substance. The composer establishes a relationship with the material that allows a reciprocal exchange of energy, sensations, and formative concepts. The power of the artist to form the material is matched by the power of the material to form the artist. There should be no separation between mind and material—material is informed with mind, mind with material. Thus the material can be observed to manifest various types of actions. The first action is one that focuses inward, centering, compressing, and contracting; while the second expands, rarefies, unfocuses, and releases.

Wolpe composed a musical image for each of these actions and inserted the music within the sentences of the text to create a mixed genre of discourse that combines music with speech about music in a continuous flow. We shall stay with these first two paragraphs, as they have important implications for Wolpe's theory of music. But first we must examine more closely the second musical example. If we rescore example 18.2 (Wolpe's second illustration) onto four staves, the structure of the image emerges more clearly (ex. 18.3). The rescored version reveals that the image is composed of six trichords plus the lone pitch a^2, which serves to close the twelve-tone chromatic circuit. The six trichordal shapes are constructed from the four unordered pitch-class sets given in example 18.4a. Wolpe referred to pitch-class (pc) sets in this lecture as "autonomous fragments" of the twelve-tone set, that is, segments of the set that are free to separate from the serial ordering and behave autonomously through rearrangement and transposition. Trichords A and B do just that (see ex. 18.4a). The four pc sets are all transpositions of the unordered pitch-class set [0, 1, 2], which has a complement of intervals made up of seconds only (two minor and one major). As pc set [0, 1, 2] comprises the smallest intervals, it affords an image of compression and contraction. When the four [0, 1, 2] trichords are taken together, they constitute a derived set consisting of eleven tones of a twelve-tone aggregate, of which the twelfth pc is A. In Wolpe's example two of the pc sets are ordered on the horizontal axis—trichord $A2$ is the retrograde of trichord $A1$, and trichord $B2$ is the retrograde of trichord $B1$. Such mirror symmetries serve the action of focusing and centering, and the overlapping in *stretto* supports the image of "fierce contraction."

But Wolpe's theory of composition was at this time also concerned with ordering musical shapes on the vertical axis in order to structure musical space, and he had been developing a system of vertical intervallic proportions since about 1950. He wrote a lecture on the system in 1959 and delivered it at Dartington Hall in England in the summer of that year.[17] If we apply his system to these examples, we can see that Wolpe disposed the four pc sets A, B, C, and D by means of a core vertical structure consisting of a major seventh enclosing a minor sev-

Example 18.3

Example 18.4   *a.* Unordered pitch-class sets

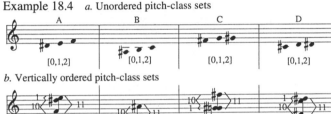

b. Vertically ordered pitch-class sets

enth and minor second (ex. 18.4b). Jonathan Bernard has developed a notation for such vertical orderings, which for this structure is [1][10].[18] There are two possible rotations of this vertical structure: one with the minor second below (as in *B* and *C*), the other with the minor second above (as in *A* and *D*). These "proportions" (the term Wolpe used for such vertically ordered structures) can be rotated or inverted in various ways. In this example *B* is a rotation of *A*, and *D* is a rotation of *C*. Wolpe reinforced the quality of this image ("internalized, center-bound, concentric") by confining it to a single basic vertical structure and keeping it within a range of less than two octaves.

Now to the third paragraph of "Thinking Twice":

> It [musical substance] also behaves as an outwardly spreading, extensively trajecting force, impulse-driven, eccentric, in full release of width, of an outside spatial dimension, of furtherness and farness. The substance affirms the double-content of nature: to be core and inwardly held, to be form and mould which are extended into and outwardly grasped. [See ex. 18.5]

Paragraph 3 paraphrased:

Example 18.5 (Wolpe's third illustration) contrasts with example 18.2 in almost every respect. The pitch material, which also constitutes a twelve-tone aggregate, consists of five trichords, four of which are versions of pc set [0, 1, 5] (see exx. 18.6 and 18.7). Trichord *A* forms pc set [0, 1, 4], which is contained within a major third rather than a perfect fourth.[19] By contrast with pc set [0, 1, 2] of example 18.2, the pc set of

Example 18.5

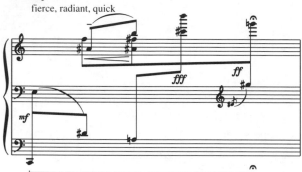

Example 18.6

Example 18.7   *a.* Unordered pitch-class sets

b. Vertically ordered pitch-class sets

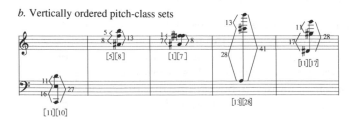

example 18.5 [0, 1, 5] includes each of the three basic interval types (seconds, thirds, and fourths) and thus has the greatest possible diversity of intervallic resources for a trichord.[20] The horizontal disposition of these trichordal pc sets displays none of the regularity and symmetry found in example 18.2. Every shape is different in number of notes, horizontal contour, and spatial proportion, although shapes A, B, D, and E do have in common a rising motion (see ex. 18.7a). In example 18.5, the vertical orderings (see ex. 18.7b) vary from very wide (D) to very narrow (C), they are asymmetrical, and they fill a large space of five octaves. The vertical orderings of A and E are almost identical, but their rhythmic orderings differ. Dynamics, tempo, and the performance indications provide additional means of contrasting the images. The dynamic range in example 18.2 from *piano* to *forte* is narrower than example 18.5, which goes from *mf* to *fff*. And the tempo changes from "slow" to "quick." The performance indication for example 18.2 is "inwardly" and for example 18.5 is "fierce, radiant." All in all, the analysis of these two examples supports the opposition Wolpe wished to draw between an image that is "internalized, center-bound, concentric" and one that is "outwardly spreading, extensively trajecting . . . , impulse-driven, eccentric."

It is remarkable that the opposition Wolpe drew between these two fundamental images finds an exact analogy in Rudolf Laban's pioneering theory of movement. Laban introduced his analysis of movement with a fundamental distinction between two actions, one that flows from the periphery of the space surrounding the body inward to the center, and another that flows from the center of the body outward. He called them "gathering" and "scattering" actions, respectively. "Gathering can be seen in bringing something toward the center of the body, while scattering can be observed in pushing something away from the center of the body."[21] The parallels between Laban's gathering action and Wolpe's second illustration and Laban's scattering action and Wolpe's third illustration are illuminating. Wolpe did not know of Laban's analysis of movement, but his intuitive grasp of the fundamentals of gesture suggests that an "effort-shape" analysis of Wolpe's music would be appropriate.[22]

Laban analyzed and notated physical movement according to the dimensions of time, space, and weight, where time ranges from sudden to sustained, space is traversed directly or indirectly, and weight is strong or light. By combining these parameters Laban obtained eight effort actions, which he labeled: punch, slash, dab, flick, press, wring, glide, and float.[23] He added a fourth dimension, flow, which ranges from free to bound. It would intensify the gathering action to play it with bound flow, and the scattering action with free flow.

To continue with the fourth paragraph of "Thinking Twice":

> These are basic manifestations of musical substance, and one's attitude must remain ever alerted by examining rigorously and without fear how much history one carries along with oneself, and whether this load, in effect, interferes with a radical attack on all genuinely fresh musical problems. The less history is repeated, the more unique is the moment's time and all that rests wholly on the moment's total dedication. A moment will crystallize as history after it has existed within all its momentary actuality. Then truly will the moment be rallied into the vast depths of time which history is: the ever-restored and ever-advancing moment.[24]

Paragraph 4 paraphrased:

Unless one is aware of the musical structures and values one has inherited from the past, one may be unable to experience newly emerging ideas. One must free oneself from the fetters of received styles and genres in order to be open to active fantasy. When one is fully open to the present moment and formulates the musical images that arise, those images will take their place in the fabric of history. The present must be redeemed at every moment in order for history to be meaningful.

This is a key formulation that Wolpe reprised at the end of the lecture:

> If the use of what belongs to the content-making of earlier times offers organic sensations of an extreme kind, then the intercourse of conceptually different events will convey to us history's only worthwhile actuality: the ever-restored and ever-advancing moment.[25]

The lecture implies a theory of creativity that holds that knowledge from the past cannot solve all present problems, and that we must be open to the new knowledge that fantasy offers up at each moment of time. It is a theory of creativity that places as much value on understanding the goal-directed aspects of the musical image as on knowing its antecedent conditions.

Let us now return to *Form*. So far we have found that Wolpe's new paradigm involves the conjoining of opposed images that are formed from a restricted choice of pitch, durational, and timbral materials. But what of the global aspects of the organization of *Form*? In "Thinking Twice" he wrote: "The form must be ripped endlessly open and self-renewed by interacting extremes of opposites. There is nothing to develop because everything is already there in reach of one's ears. If one has enough milk in the house, one doesn't go to the grocery store."[26] Indeed, taken together, the forty or so images in *Form* can be thought of as a congeries of diverse and continuously available items, like a market well stocked with the necessities of life. The forces needed to make so many different items cohere are generated not from familiar rhetorical strategies of exposition, complication, crisis, and release, but from the tensions generated from the juxtapositon of strongly contrasted images. The images may be grouped in period-like structures (for example, the eight in example 18.9 form a group), but from one image to the next there is a high degree of tension. Opposed images follow upon each other rapidly, hence transitions are almost instantaneous and take place silently in the brief spaces between images. Each image takes up no more than two or three measures, but because the gestures are strongly contrasted, the spaces between the images that allow for the transition are highly charged. This accords with Laban's observation that it is not possible to modulate gradually between effort actions that are directly opposed (for example, from punch to float, or from press to flick). There must be an instant's pause in which to shift from one to the next. In this way the piece gains its formative tension from a succession of discrete, characteristic, and strongly marked images that cover a wide range of shapes and textures, colors, gestures, and affects.[27]

On the level of pitch processes image 1 states hexachord N [0, 1, 2, 3, 5, 6] as an ordered motive (see ex. 18.9), consisting of two statements of the trichord [0, 2, 5]: A-flat, F, B-flat, and A, G, E. The complementary hexachord Ñ [0, 1, 2, 3, 4, 7] appears in m. 4, but not in the ordered form. Ñ has the same interval vector as N,[28] but the trichord Wolpe selected for image 4 is [0, 1, 2], which contains only seconds. Thus image 4 can be expected to make a strong contrast with the previous three. Indeed, images 1, 2, 3, 6, 7, 8 (derived primarily from N) bear a fundamental resemblance to the scattering action of example 18.5, and images 4 and 5 (from hexachord Ñ) resemble the gathering action of example 18.2. Hexachord Ñ does not occur in an ordered form until near the end of the piece (mm. 50–52), although it is associated at times with the narrow, focused image of mm. 3–4. The transposed versions dominate the second half of the piece. A hushed recurrence of the original, untransposed form of hexachord N near the end evokes the nostalgia of a half-remembered image after so much diversity. The concept of reprise is not totally absent from *Form*, and makes its appearance increasingly frequently in Wolpe's late works.

Let us now examine the first page of *Form* in more detail. It can be seen to contain eight successive images separated by brief silences. (The images are numbered consecutively below each system of example 18.9.)

Image 1. Hexachord N is introduced (m. 1) as a series of quarter notes in the manner of an alto or soprano voice announcing a subject. The even, quiet tones are in a narrow range; the gesture is floating (sustained time, light weight, indirect space); the performance indication "remote and restless" suggests an undercurrent of disquiet. The succession of two trichords [0, 2, 5] provides a lateral symmetry of two groups with the vertical proportion [2][3], the second group an inversion of the first.[29] The lateral symmetry is reinforced by the vertical symmetry of a descending tritone span (B-flat, E) centered about G. This image is bounded, contained, balanced, centered, and quiet, but tense with potentialities. It is germinal matter that is both formed and unformed. It states itself and evokes its complement. It can create concrete internal references through reprise, but it is not limited to that role.

Image 2. In Wolpe's earlier style such an opening statement would have led to a process of developing variation, as in the Symphony (1956), but the second image cancels that possibility. Hexachord N is reordered to emphasize trichord [0, 1, 4]. The gesture—a punch (sudden time, strong weight, direct space)—is in maximum contrast to the float gesture of image 1. The spatial proportion is asymmetrical, opening up to a span of 3 1/2 octaves, which is still bounded by the notes B-flat and E.

The vertical structures shown in example 18.8 are instances of one of the principal spatial proportions of the piece, a seventh or ninth either enclosing or subtending a third. That this vertical structure is a fundamental element of the design is confirmed by the words "kleinste Gegenstand" (minimal structure) written above m. 37 in Irma Wolpe Rademacher's hand, where a seventh subtends a third in the spatial proportion [3][11]. The structure in example 18.8a can be read as a ninth above a third above a compound ninth. Similarly, the structure in example 18.8b, read from the top down, is a ninth enclosing a third, above a ninth enclosing a third. Wolpe distinguished between symmetrical and asymmetrical proportions; thus example 18.8a is asymmetrical, whereas example 18.8b is symmetrical (the structure on pitch E is parallel to the structure on pitch f). Image 2 thus conjoins symmetrical and asymmetrical spatial proportions with contrasted dynamics and uneven rhythmic divisions. It is a hammer blow with a rebounding echo that explodes the cool, flat surface of image 1.

Example 18.8

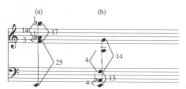

Example 18.9 *Form*, mm. 1–10

Image 3. Hexachord N is reordered anew at a slightly faster tempo. This image returns to a narrow line as in image 1, but now with a nervously indirect rising motion enlivened by an offbeat and brusque counterpoint that splits image 1 into contrasting elements for the right and left hands. It is questioning, conflicted.

Image 4. A few notes from the complementary hexachord Ñ emphasize trichord [0, 1, 2]. The space shrinks abruptly from 4 1/2 octaves to the interval of a second on C^1. The pitch circulation is now frozen and lethargic with the pedal allowing overtones to ring hollowly. The gesture is shrinking, spaceless, weightless, disembodied. The affect, hesitant, remote, dormant.

Image 5. Hexachord Ñ is given complete, slowing down to the initial tempo. Dense chords rise energetically in a strong, rising, pressing gesture (sustained, heavy, direct). A trichord [0, 2, 5] from hexachord N adds interfering elements from the complementary hexachord to make a dense, seven-note cluster. The affect is aggressive, impatient.

Image 6. A scattering action ramifies through five octaves. Compare image 6 with the scattering action of example 18.5 from "Thinking Twice." As in that image, dispersion and centripetal motion are underlined by the use of four different trichords: [0, 1, 2], [0, 1, 4], [0, 2, 5], and [0, 2, 7]. The asymmetrical vertical proportions are saturated by ninths and thirds. Varied dynamics place some pitch elements in the background, others in the foreground. The affect is expansive, joyous, exuberant.

Image 7. This image recalls the shape and gesture of image 5. The vertical sonority of image 5 is rotated to begin image 7 with a dense, heavy cluster sinking downward. The trichord [0, 1, 4], disposed in the proportion [9][11], occupies the bass register. The gesture is gathering, but off balance. The affect is withdrawn.

Image 8. This image hooks onto the end of image 7, with multiple echoes and refractions of the trichord E, E-flat, C [0, 1, 4], which radiates into the tenor register. The image is rarefied, occupying a wide space with large intervals, subsiding, and releasing. Tension ebbs as the image closes with a cadential pause on the dyad G–A, an open major ninth, the core vertical structure of the piece. G is reiterated while the pianist stops the string with the finger, bringing a fresh timbre to mark the end of the opening frame of eight images. The affect is soothing, affirming.

This approach to the opening of *Form* has attempted to bring the structural and expressive aspects of the musical image into close connection. It respects the importance Wolpe gave in his program notes to textures, qualities, and gestures for creating opposing images. Having established the place of the image at the core of Wolpe's paradigm of musical meaning, we can now address his notion that the theory of music must make room for fantasy. Let us return to the lecture he gave at Kassel in 1957:

> The fantasy can be critically examined. The recurrence of its tendencies makes it possible to investigate it [fantasy] critically. The problem [of analyzing fantasy] can be grounded and formulated in theoretical propositions. Fantasy can only be properly apprehended by theory if its extraordinary diversity is acknowledged and if the impossible is included as a theoretical possibility. The study of botany must be as beautiful (and fragrant) as a flower; the theory of music must be as manifold and exciting as the musical imagination itself. When the fantasy is controlled by a theoretical concept, then the imaginal becomes estranged from theory. This imbalance brings a compensatory reward. Sometimes it is better to know than to invent. Sometimes all knowledge fails, and only the creative vision and imagination remain as the residue of the suffering of understanding the (essential) principle. Fantasy rises and sets—as fast as light. Art consists in incessantly flowing structures.[30]

In this opening paragraph Wolpe declares that the products of the fantasy exhibit regularities that make it possible to incorporate a theory of fantasy into the theory of music. A theory of fantasy must not only deal with the extraordinary diversity of the products of fantasy; it must also reckon with the fact that fantasy is the source of what was hitherto unknown. For Wolpe the new is not merely a novel rearrangement of known contents of consciousness. A theory of music that does not deal with fantasy is inadequate to man's creative instinct, which can produce the hitherto unforseeable, impossible, and unimaginable. Wolpe does not deny the value of cognitive analyses of music, but he insists that music theory must be adequate to the full power and range of the imagination. When reason fails, it is the creative imagination that persists.

Since Wolpe's paradigm of meaning calls for incorporating fantasy into the theory of music, we must develop the concept of fantasy more fully. Fantasy is generally regarded as the product of the faculty of the imagination, but the imagination is variously defined. By some it is taken as a special faculty of the mind and by others as the reproductive activity of the mind in general. On the former view imagination is the product of intellection, a special function of cognition; on the latter it is the product of the creative instinct. Wolpe places imagination and the products of fantasy at the core of creative activity, and so his paradigm is compatible with a theory of fantasy that grounds it in the primary process of the unconscious. This accords with the theory of fantasy developed by C.G. Jung, who defined *fantasm* as follows:

> [The *fantasm* is] a complex of ideas that is distinguished from other such complexes by the fact that it has no objective referent. Although it may originally be based on memory-images of actual experiences, its content refers to no external reality; it is merely the output of creative psychic activity, a manifestation or product of a combination of energized psychic elements. In so far as psychic energy can be voluntarily directed, a fantasy can be consciously and intentionally produced, either as a whole or at least in part. In the former case it is nothing but a combination of *conscious elements*. . . . [In the latter case] fantasy is either set in motion by an intuitive attitude of expectation, or it is an irruption of *unconscious* contents into consciousness. [31]

It would seem clear that Wolpe's concept of fantasy falls within Jung's latter category of fantasms that irrupt into consciousness from the unconscious. Wolpe does not seek to control fantasy, but is content to stand by and observe its manifestations.

Jung then proceeds to distinguish two types of fantasy, the active and the passive:

> Whereas passive fantasy not infrequently bears a morbid stamp or at least shows some trace of abnormality, active fantasy is one of the highest forms of psychic activity. For here the conscious and the unconscious personality of the subject flow together into a common product in which both are united. Such a fantasy can be the highest expression of the unity of a man's individuality, and it may even create that individuality by giving perfect expression to its unity. . . . Passive fantasy, therefore, is always in need of conscious *criticism*, lest it merely reinforce the standpoint of the unconscious opposite. Whereas active fantasy, as the product of a conscious attitude *not* opposed to the unconscious, and of unconscious processes not opposed but merely compensatory to consciousness, does not require criticism so much as *understanding*.[32]

Wolpe uses the term *fantasy* in the sense of Jung's active fantasy, where the conscious mind directly participates with the unconscious to release imagery that informs the current situation with new insights. Wolpe illustrates his notion of active fantasy as follows:

> One doesn't need to sit on the moon if one can write a poem
> about it with the twitch of one's senses. One is there where
> one directs onself to be. On the back of a bird, inside of an
> apple, dancing on the sun's ray, speaking to Machaut, and
> holding the skeleton's hand of the incredible Cézanne—there
> is what there was and what there isn't is also.[33]

By taking a positive attitude to the fantasy Wolpe does not reduce it to
unwanted products of the unconscious, but rather affirms it as the revelation of the artist's highest individuality. The consequence for a theory
of music that incorporates active fantasy is that it should proceed by
understanding (*Verstehen*) as well as by explanation (*Erklären*), by analogy, metaphor, and personification, as well as by deduction from rules
and laws.

Understanding music in relation to the active fantasy brings us to the
problem of incorporating fantasy into a rational theoretical paradigm.
Jung indicated dissatisfaction with reductive explanations of psychological phenomena that seek the causes of fantasy images in past experience alone. Fantasy, according to Jung, also has a prospective, goal-
oriented meaning as well as a causal explanation. The fantasy looks
forward as well as backward. Jung pointed to the fact that in everyday
experience we accept that a person's opinion is not simply a product of
previous opinions expressed by others, but is a statement of that
individual's aims and intentions. Thus a teleological and not merely a
retrospective standpoint is introduced into an explanation of the opinion. If this is the case for conscious contents, Jung argued, then there is
no reason not to apply a goal-directed perspective to the explanation of
fantasy and the contents of the unconscious, since the unconscious can
be empirically shown to supply new knowledge that compensates for
the conscious attitude.[34] Summing up his definition of fantasy, he wrote:

> A fantasy needs to be understood both causally and purpo-
> sively. Causally interpreted, it seems like a *symptom* of a
> physiological or personal state, the outcome of antecedent
> events. Purposively interpreted, it seems like a *symbol*,[35] seek-
> ing to characterize a definite goal with the help of the mate-
> rial at hand, or trace out a line of future psychological devel-
> opment. Because active fantasy is the chief mark of the artistic
> mentality, the artist is not just a *reproducer* of appearances,
> but a creator and educator, for his works have the value of
> symbols that adumbrate lines of future development.[36]

Jung's understanding of the prophetic role of the artist distinguishes
his psychology from those psychologies of creativity that seek to reduce art to the products of past experience or of known contents of

consciousness. And so we can look to Jung to support the paradigm of a music theory that attempts to deal with the prospective meaning of the musical image. Wolpe appears to concur when he enjoins us:

> Don't get backed too much into a reality that has fashioned your senses with too many realistic claims. When art promises you this sort of reliability, this sort of prognostic security, drop it. It is good to know how not to know how much one is knowing. One should know about all the structures of fantasy and all the fantasies of structures, and mix surprise and enigma, magic and shock, intelligence and abandon, form and antiform.[37]

Perhaps Wolpe toyed with the idea of titling his piece *Form and Antiform*.

To elaborate further Wolpe's new paradigm we could continue to let his music and his speech about music gloss each other as we have attempted here. We can listen to *Form* and be delighted by its audacious beauty, and we can read "Thinking Twice" and be intrigued by Wolpe's poetics of music. To understand and explain Wolpe's thought calls for taking his music and his speech about music together as a complex, polyphonic medium of discourse with common roots in unconscious processes, but with variegated branches in his music and lectures. Since for Wolpe the world of rational sense experience was enlivened and disconcerted by active fantasy, the theory of his music must be formed likewise.

Notes

1. Cf. Charles Seeger, "Speech, Music, and Speech about Music," in his *Studies in Musicology, 1935–1975* (Berkeley, 1977), 16–30.

2. Cf. Austin Clarkson, "Text and Pretext in the Interpretation of Contemporary Music," *Report of the Twelfth Congress of the International Musicological Society, Berkeley, 1977* (Kassel, 1981), 768.

3. Benjamin Boretz, "The Logic of What?" *Journal of Music Theory* 33, no. 1 (1989): 107.

4. For a discussion of paradigms of meaning, see Austin Clarkson, "Myths of Meaning: An Archetypal Perspective on Ethnomusicological Paradigms," in Robert Witmer, ed., *Ethnomusicology in Canada*, CanMus Documents, no. 5 (Toronto, 1990).

5. See Stefan Wolpe, "Über neue (und nicht so neue) Musik in Amerika," *Journal of Music Theory* 28, no. 1 (1984): 1–45.

6. Stefan Wolpe, "Thoughts on Pitch (1952)," *Perspectives of New Music* 17 (1979): 28–57; idem, "Any Bunch of Notes (1953)," *Perspectives of New Music* 21 (1982–83): 295–310; and idem, "Proportionen (1960)," in Matthew Greenbaum, "Stefan Wolpe's 'Proportions': A Translation and Commentary" (Ph.D. diss., City University of New York, 1983).

7. Speaking about another system of communication (music) "must be conducted mainly in terms of speech-music analogy, allowing for indeterminate amounts of homology and heterology." Seeger, "Speech," 16.

8. Stefan Wolpe, "Thinking Twice," in Elliott Schwartz and Barney Childs, eds., *Contemporary Composers on Contemporary Music* (New York, 1967), 275.

9. Edition Tonos, 1962. The first page of the score is given in example 18.9. Recorded by Robert Miller on Composers Recording Inc., SD 306, and Russell Sherman on New World Records, NW 308.

10. Unpublished letter to Irma Jurist Neverov, dated Berlin, 5 May 1957. The four pieces are Enactments for Three Pianos (1953), Piece for Oboe, Cello, Percussion, and Piano (1955), Symphony (1956), and Quintet with Voice (1957).

11. Cf. Edward Levy, "Stefan Wolpe, for His Sixtieth Birthday," *Perspectives of New Music*, 2 no. 1 (Fall–Winter 1963): 51–65;. reprinted in Benjamin Boretz and Edward T. Cone, eds., *Perspectives on American Composers* (New York, 1971), 185.

12. Notes spoken by the composer at a concert of his works at the Frances Parker School Auditorium, Chicago, 24 April 1964.

13. "Sounds" probably is Wolpe's English for the German "Klänge," meaning "sonorities" or "chords."

14. Irma Wolpe Rademacher wrote down a number of comments that Wolpe made about the images in the music while he coached her in performing the piece. For example: "gradual crystallization, rudimentary form accumulation" (m. 36), "ganz fremd" (m. 37), "kleinste Gegenstand" (over bar line between mm. 36–37), "canonic correspondences" (m. 40), "ominous destruction (swamp)" (m. 41), "dawn" (m. 42). She related that "swamp" referred to a terrifying childhood experience Wolpe had when he was caught in quicksand.

15. Wolpe, "Thinking Twice," 275.

16. The chiasmus "laws of nature"/"nature of laws" is a typical Wolpean word play. His speech, like his music, is rich in inversions, reversions, retrogrades, and accumulations of images.

17. Stefan Wolpe, "Notes on Proportions," unpublished. The next year he developed the theory of proportions in a lecture given at Darmstadt, "Über Proportionen." See Greenbaum, "Wolpe's 'Proportions.'"

18. Jonathan Bernard, *The Music of Edgard Varèse* (New Haven, 1987), chap. 2.

19. Wolpe may have injected a different pc set in order to create more diversity, but it was probably in order to include pc C, which closes the chromatic circuit.

20. Wolpe classified pc sets according their content of basic interval types. Among trichords there are three with seconds only ([0, 1, 2],[0, 1, 3], [0, 2, 4]), one with seconds and thirds ([0, 1, 4]), one with thirds only ([0, 4, 8]), two with thirds and fourths ([0, 3, 6], [0, 3, 7]), one with seconds and fourths ([0, 2, 7]), and three with seconds, thirds, and fourths ([0, 1, 5], [0, 2, 5], [0, 2, 6]). His nomenclature for pc sets utilized the generic designations of seconds, thirds, fourths.

21. Rudolf Laban, *The Mastery of Movement* (Boston, 1971), 91.

22. Of course, Laban's categories of movement analysis can be applied to many styles and types of music with a well-defined gestic vocabulary.

23. For an introduction to the effort-shape analysis of movement, see Cecily Dell, *A Primer for Movement Description* (New York, 1977). Punch, for example, combines sudden time, direct space, and strong weight. The opposite action is float, which combines sustained time, indirect space, and light weight.

24. Wolpe, "Thinking Twice," 276.

25. Ibid., 307.

26. Ibid., 302–3.

27. Cf. Morton Feldman: "A modular construction could be the basis for organic development, however I use it to see that patterns are 'complete' in themselves and in no need of development, only of extension." *Morton Feldman Essays*, ed. Walter Zimmermann (Kerpen, 1985), 131. Feldman was a student of Wolpe in the late 1940s.

A comparison between Wolpe's notion of a steady state of opposed images and Feldman's modular constructions would be worth developing.

28. The two hexachords N and Ñ have been named by Allen Forte 6-Z3 and 6-Z36, respectively. There are fifteen such pairs of hexachords that differ in structure but are identical in interval content. Forte has named such sets Z-related sets. See his *The Structure of Atonal Music* (New Haven, 1973), 21–22.

29. The notation of vertical interval structures follows the method developed by Bernard (see his *Varèse*, chap. 3.) There is not space here to develop Wolpe's technique of spatial proportions, which has some similarities to that of Varèse.

30. The lecture was given at the Staatliche Akademie, Kassel, in 1957. It begins: "Die Phantasie lässt sich kritisch beobachten. Die Wiederkehr ihrer Tendenzen lässt sich kritisch prüfen. Das Problem wird in den theoretischen Lösungen verankert und formuliert. Die Phantasie erkennt sich in der Theorie, die gut ist nur dann, wenn sie den Problemen ihre grösste Varietät zusichert und das Unmögliche als theoretische Möglichkeit propagiert and miteinschliesst. Die Botanik soll so schön sein (und duftend) wie die Blume; die Theorie der Musik so vielgründig and aufregend wie die musikalische Phantasie selbst. Dort, wo die theoretische Konzeption die Phantasie dirigiert, dort wächst auch die Phantasie über ebendiese Theorie hinaus. Diese Ungleichheit wird zum gegenseitigen Geschenk. Manchesmal ist es besser zu wissen als zu erfinden. Manchesmal misslingt alles Wissen, und nur die schöpferischer Anschauung und Einbildung bleiben als Rest einer Qual, das (eigene) Prinzip zu verstehen. Die Phantasie reisst auf und setzt—schnell wie das Licht. Die Kunst summiert in fortwährenden, fortführenden Gliederungen." The lecture is unpublished.

31. C.G. Jung, *Psychological Types*, trans. of *Psychologische Typen* (1921) by H.G. Baynes in Jung, *Collected Works*, vol. 6 (Princeton, 1971), 427.

32. Ibid., 428–29.

33. Wolpe, "Thinking Twice," 303.

34. Cf. C.A. Meier, *The Unconscious in Its Empirical Manifestations*, trans. Eugene Rolfe (Boston, 1984), chap. 1.

35. Jung distinguished 'symbol' from 'sign'. A sign stands for a known thing, whereas a symbol formulates an essential unconscious factor. The symbol is composed not only of rational but also of irrational data. The emergence of a symbol into consciousness requires a suspension of the will. Thus the symbol is the best possible formulation of a relatively unknown thing, which cannot for that reason be more clearly or character-istically represented. See Jung, *Psychological Types*, 474–75.

36. Ibid., 432.

37. Wolpe, "Thinking Twice," 303.

NINETEEN

The Traditions Revisited: Stravinsky's *Requiem Canticles* as Russian Music

RICHARD TARUSKIN

I have spoken Russian all my life, I think in Russian, my way of express-
ing myself is Russian. Perhaps this is not immediately apparent in my
music, but it is latent there, a part of its hidden nature.
                        —Igor Stravinsky, in *Komsomolskaia pravda*,
                                                27 September 1962

It is well established by now that Igor Stravinsky's deeply ingrained habits of Russian thinking and hearing continued to tell on the music of his last period, even on its serial procedures. Pieter van den Toorn has shown how frequently the "Russian" [0, 2, 3, 5] tetrachord and especially the octatonic-specific [0, 1, 3, 4] tetrachord crop up in Stravinskian rows, and also how Stravinsky continued to rely on the accumulated experience of fifty years' octatonic routine when it came to navigating his path from row form to row form in such early serial pieces as *Agon* and *Canticum sacrum*.[1] With reference to the riper twelve-tone works, Milton Babbitt has revealed the startling persistence of [0, 3, 6, 9] and [0, 4, 8] symmetry as governors of "centricity" in music constructed according to Stravinsky's technique of hexachordal transposition and cyclic permutation ("rotation").[2] Such findings, more persuasively than any previously offered, testify to the essential continuity underlying what seemed Stravinsky's radical style-break of the early fifties.

***

It seems appropriate, then, to consider Stravinsky's last major work, the *Requiem Canticles*, not only in light of these recent analytical observations, but also in light of a very suggestive remark by Nicolas Nabokov, an old comrade from the Diaghilev days, who had remained close to Stravinsky despite his estrangement from the music of the last period. To Nabokov, as to most of Stravinsky's older acquaintances, the serial music "with a few exceptions [had] seemed remote and forbidding." But then all at once:

> Toward the very end of Stravinsky's life something changed. He wrote a piece, his last grand piece of music, the *Requiem Canticles*. Though in it he used the novel devices of serial technique, he somehow overpowered them. It was immediately, instinctively, totally lovable to me. I was able without any effort to penetrate into the essence of its tragic beauty. I was as fully taken and shaken by it as I used to be in the thirties and forties by every new composition of Stravinsky.[3]

In part this reaction must be attributable to sentiment: an aged, infirm composer at work on a Requiem can mean only one thing. "*He* and *we* knew he was writing it for himself," Vera Stravinsky said to Robert Craft as they were planning the music for her husband's funeral.[4] By comparison with its immediate predecessors, from *Movements* for piano and orchestra (1959) to the orchestral Variations (1964), the *Requiem Canticles* are moreover strikingly direct and uncomplicated in texture and rhythm. They are homophonic and pulsatile in the old Stravinsky manner. "What a shock," wrote an early reviewer, "after the intense, controlled densities of the marvelously inventive Variations to hear the almost ingenuous repeated-note fives of the Requiem Prelude!"[5] Gesturally the work is vivid, at times even obvious, with its tolling bells in the Postlude, suggestive of a church or a chiming clock, or the murmuring voices in the "Libera me," where, in Craft's words, "the music leaves the concert hall and actually becomes part of a Requiem service."[6] For a composer whose music is so constantly labeled "hieratic" and compared with "ritual," the *Requiem Canticles* could hardly have seemed more typical, not to say stereotypical, in its conception.

On the self-referential surface the piece fairly reeks with nostalgia, quite belying the commonly expressed opinion that "Stravinsky kept no key to the past."[7] Those tolling bells in the Postlude recall a whole gamut of Stravinskiana, from the ending of *Svadebka* (the only previous Stravinsky composition to employ *campane*, the orchestral tubular chimes), to the graveyard scene in *The Rake's Progress*.[8] The *falsobordone* in the "Libera me" is a direct throwback to Stravinsky's 1932 setting of the Orthodox creed—and so is the actual harmony, ingeniously contrived to emphasize "liturgical" open fifths, octaves, and triads despite its strictly serial derivation (each chord being a verticalization of a transposed and "rotated" hexachord).[9] The litanic refrain harmony in the Interlude, consisting of a repeated chord always enunciated by flutes and horns (with timpani) in long-short pairs, is such an obvious reference to the *Symphonies of Wind Instruments* of 1920 that it is a wonder no critic or analyst seems yet to have reported the fact (the more so as the *Symphonies* shared the program with the "Requicles" on the latter's première performance at Princeton, 8 October 1966). Beyond these surface resemblances, Pierre Souvtchinsky has reflected on the *Svadebka*-like conclusion in a way that penetrates a bit beneath: it is "one of those endings, like that of *Les Noces*, which do not end, or end in infinity. And this is where Stravinsky adds a dimension to Western music."[10]

A quintessentially Stravinskian "immobility" pervades the *Requiem Canticles* and unquestionably refers back to the composer's familiar early manner. The static punctuating chords in the Interlude, already mentioned, are an example of this; but so is the habitual Stravinskian "stutter"—oscillation between contiguous pitches or simultaneities— that persists in the serial music, even across the boundaries between set forms (and nowhere more so than in the *Canticles*). (See ex. 19.1.)

These are among the features that make the *Requiem Canticles* so uncommonly accessible to anyone who knows and cherishes Stravinsky's "Russian" style. Just as surely, though, they are features incidental at best to row technique, and in some cases a bit at odds with it. Even with due recognition of the importance, to a composer like Stravinsky, of overcoming the "resistance" of his materials, it is neither a satisfying view of his serial music, nor one calculated to affirm its integrity, that sees what is personal and characteristic in the music as the result of license or sly contrivance rather than as organic fruit of the method. The "Libera me," especially, seems a strangely aberrant case if Stravinsky is thought to have, by dint of elaborate strategy, somehow wrested from the serial method a kind of harmony he might have composed without effort or qualm at an earlier phase of his career. That is why it is important to look further, to uncover the even more essentially "Russian" features of the *Requiem Canticles* that are embedded deeply in its set structures, and that may be brought to analytical consciousness only by probing Stravinsky's own characteristic and highly personal serial procedures.

Example 19.1 *Requiem Canticles*

a. "Exaudi," mm. 67–69 (chorus only)

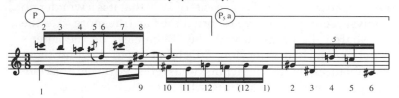

o – ra – ti – o – nem   me – – am,

b. "Dies irae," mm. 88–89 (flutes and xylophone only)

c. "Tuba mirum," mm. 125–35 (bass soloist and bassoon)

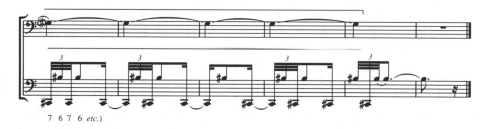

(Tu) – – ba   mi – rum,   tu – – ba   mi – ru – (u)m.

7 6 7 6 *etc.*)

d. "Lacrimosa," mm. 245–47

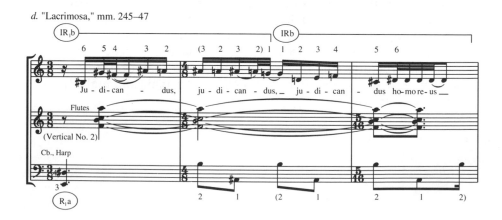

Ju – di – can – dus,   ju – di – can – dus, _   ju – di – can – dus ho – mo re – us _

Flutes

(Vertical No. 2)

Cb., Harp

***

Although dodecaphony, in Stravinsky's own (dictated and edited) words, represented a rebirth of "rhythmic polyphony" and "melodic or intervallic construction" following the exhaustion of the "period of harmonic discovery,"[11] and though (in unedited conversation with a British journalist) Stravinsky the fledgling serialist declared himself to be "absolutely contrapunctical, like very few Russian composers even of the past,"[12] the fact remains that his late serial music is the most essentially harmonic—in the literal, vertical, chordal sense of the word— of any that lies within the borders of the dodecaphonic realm. Nor did he ever deny it: the 1959 *Conversations* abound in confessional remarks to the effect that "I compose vertically and that is, in one sense at least, to compose tonally"; that "I hear harmonically, of course, and I compose in the same way I always have"; and that his serial music was not only composed, but "intended to be heard vertically."[13] As will become clear in the necessarily brief and telegraphic description that follows of Stravinsky's methods of "composing vertically," they continued, even in his latest phase, to mark him as a Russian musical thinker, and point up deep-seated connections with his earlier—indeed his earliest— musical and technical predilections.

This cannot be the place for a basic exposition of Stravinsky's late serial method.[14] Its most peculiar feature, possibly acquired in the first instance by studying certain compositions and theoretical writings by his Los Angeles neighbor Ernst Krenek,[15] consisted in partitioning the twelve-note series into two hexachords, which are then transposed in sequence by each of the intervals they contain. The standard way of effecting this sequence of transpositions is by "rotating" (cyclically permuting) the hexachord so that each of the five transpositions will commence with the next order position in the series, transposed to the pitch of the first. So much Stravinsky may have picked up from Krenek. The operation about to be described, however, is uniquely Stravinskian.[16] When an array of hexachordal transposition-rotations is arranged as a square, as in example 19.2, the columns reading up and down will yield five chords (plus a generating unison at the left, marked "0"). These chords, "verticals" in Stravinsky's nomenclature, consist of the collections of tones that stand in each respective order position within the six "rotated" hexachords. As harmonic constructs they are only very tenuously related to the original series. In particular they have little or nothing to do with the series qua series—that is, a temporally unfolding sequence or succession of intervals—and therefore have a rather ambiguous status as serial phenomena.

In what is surely the shrewdest comment to date on this innovation of Stravinsky's, Milton Babbitt has noted that if the "'verticals' . . . have no predecessors in serial or preserial composition," they nevertheless have distinct "attitudinal" antecedents in Russian music. Citing Rimsky-Korsakov and Scriabin, Babbitt speaks of the Russian propensity for conceiving harmony in such a way that "the 'chord' is regarded more as a thing-in-itself, a collection, even as a spatial and temporal ordering of pitches, than in its tonally functional role," i.e., within a directed progression.[17]

The "attitude" Babbitt describes, of course, is a manifestation of the same "inorganic" or "anti-organic" formal sensibility one can observe in Stravinsky's music since the time of his early piano sonata, always a distinguishing characteristic of the St. Petersburg strain of Russian music in which he had been fostered. Tchaikovsky, though his description is framed as damagingly as he could manage, had put his finger on it as early as 1880:

> What is the so-called New Russian School but the cult of varied and pungent harmonies, of original orchestral combinations and every kind of purely external effect? Musical ideas give place to this or that union of sounds. Formerly there was composition, creation; now (with few exceptions) there is only research and contrivance.[18]

Example 19.2

a. Set 1 IRa, rotation transpositions

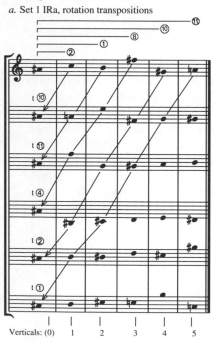

b. Set 2 IRa, rotation transpositions

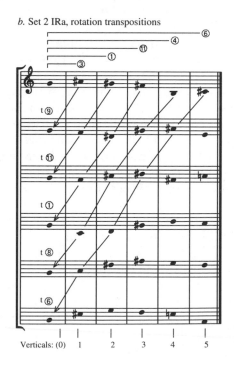

to right

rete and
anner of
e from a
eral, and

ete array of
erted retro-
verted retro-
icals used in

ls (computed
the intervallic
s (or, in math-
. This leads to
other context,
ansposition-ro-
nd the generat-
a tone center—
e. That is to say,
given in example
" pitch class A-
so arrange them-

Io-historical description of the decline and
and of the place of harmony within his
es perfectly both with Tchaikovsky's com-
ight:

a doctrine dealing with chords and
a brilliant but short history. This
gradually abandoned their direct
nce and began to seduce with the
ir harmonic effects. . . . When I
rmonically" I mean to use the
ithout reference to chord rela-

rence to chordal relations can only
ic entities, products of "research
d, or as Babbitt has put it, self-
hinks immediately of Scriabin's
hord, the "Auguries" chord in
vinsky chords that have been

se, as sonorous object,
e was not exclusively
d in a different hier-
er than as anteced-
unmistakable, and
the successive
he notion of asso-
y coherent" har-

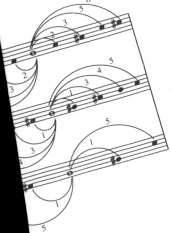

way to characterize
e octatonically in-
No. 7, the mirror
ately symmetrical
ulations through
ctitious harmonic
nd specific way—
"cadence" of th
nosa." The lat
stra) derive
of twelve
mns in
exa

sounded one element at a time, moving systematically from left
across the board. "Associative harmony" indeed.

But of course there is more to it than that. Just how conc
specific the relationship was between Stravinsky's earliest m
harmonic research and contrivance and his latest will emerg
few technical observations on the nature of "verticals" in ge
those in the *Requiem Canticles* in particular.

***

To return for a moment to example 19.2, it shows the compl
transposition-rotations for the first hexachord of the inv
grade in each of the two sets used in the *Canticles*.[21] The inv
grade has chosen for illustration because most of the vert
the piece happen to have been derived from it.

As will be readily observed by comparing the interval
in semitones) of the transpositions with those making up
content of the hexachords, the former are the inversion
ematical terms, the complements to sum 12) of the latte
the interesting situation, described by Babbitt in an
whereby the verticals produced by any hexachordal tr
tation will invariably be arranged symmetrically arou
ing ("0") pitch class, which thus assumes the role of
"center" being construed here in the most literal sens
verticals 1 + 5, 2 + 4, and 3 (self-inverting) in the array
19.2a can be symmetrically displayed around the "
sharp, while their counterparts in example 19.2b wil
selves around "0" pitch class G (see ex. 19.3).[22]

Example 19.3   Symmetrical structure of verticals

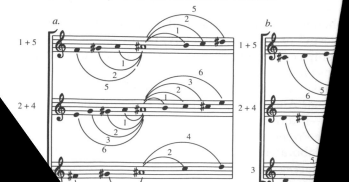

Babbitt calls this phenomenon a "bonus . . . apparently unanticipated by Stravinsky."[23] On the contrary, it is hard to imagine what more
powerful motive there could have been for Stravinsky to explore
Krenek's transposition-rotation technique in the first place than its
potential for yielding inversionally symmetrical harmonies, including
some Stravinskian perennials. It was a new entrée into what was for
him the most familiar and congenial harmonic terrain of all. In fact, it
expanded the potential vocabulary of symmetrical harmonic constructs
to which Stravinsky had structurally meaningful access, and offered a
new perspective on those symmetrical pitch collections—whole tone
and of course, especially, octatonic—that had furnished the stylistic
bedrock of Stravinsky's "Russian" music.

The self-inverting "middle" vertical (position 3) in each of the
hexachords displayed in example 19.2 is none other than a French sixth
chord, the only collection common to the whole-tone and octatonic
scales. What is more, the actual pitch-class content of the two chords is
identical, testifying to the close relationship between the two sets from
which they derive. Nor will it be missed that the tetrachords on either
side of the pivot in the sum of verticals 1 + 5 in example 19.3b are [0, 1,
3, 4] octatonic half-scales. The [0, 1, 3, 4] tetrachord, moreover, is the
self-inverting "middle" vertical produced by the complementary
hexachord of series 1, and the sum of verticals 1 + 5 in that hexachord
yields the complete octatonic collection. Let it be also entered as evidence that vertical 1 in example 19.2a is a conspicuous subset of the
octatonically referable *Petrushka* chord, and that when added to its reciprocal, vertical 5 (which is of course the inversion of the subset in
question), it yields a six-note subset of the octatonic collection.

The abundance of traditionally Stravinskian material the *Requiem
Canticles* sets generate upon hexachordal transposition-rotation seems
little short of astonishing. Just an unanticipated "bonus"? Hardly; it
arises out of a strong octatonic/whole-tone bias that is built into the
structure of the sets themselves. The close structural relationship between the two sets has been often remarked in the literature. It has
always posed something of a riddle: If the two sets are indeed so close,
why were they both needed to compose the piece?[24] Let us defer the
answer for now—there *will* be an answer—and consider the sets in light
of their referential content.

In both sets, five notes in each hexachord refer to a single octatonic
collection (see ex. 19.4). The disposition is reciprocal: hexachords 1a
and 2b refer to collection 3, their opposite numbers to collection 2. The
opening [0, 5, 11] trichord of hexachord 2a, moreover, is one intimately
associated with Stravinsky's earlier octatonic and octatonic-diatonic
usages.[25]

Example 19.4   Octatonic affinities of the
               Requiem Canticles hexachords

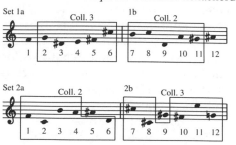

These referential proclivities are very strongly asserted on the chordal surface of the Prelude to the *Canticles*. The pulsing harmonies in that movement are derived from a simple traversal of set 2, conjoined with its retrograde, so that the piece both begins and ends with the first trichord of the set, as shown in example 19.4. The first unbroken series of these pulses (mm. 1–7) is built on the first hexachord—with the exception of note 5, the "odd" note (i.e., the single pitch class that is not referable to collection 2). Instead, the pitch class in question, A-sharp, is partitioned out to initiate the violin solo in m. 4. The partition invests the A-sharp with a double function: it simultaneously occupies the fifth position in the first hexachord of set 2 (hexachord 2a in the terminology of Stravinsky's serial charts as reproduced by Claudio Spies and adapted in example 19.4) and the first position in the first rotation-transposition of the opening hexachord of the same row's retrograde form (R_1a) at the further transposition of a tritone. That is evidently why Stravinsky resorted to R_1a to furnish the pitch sequence for the violin solo in mm. 4–7. It is practically the sole instance in the *Requiem Canticles* of what is in any case a great rarity in Stravinsky's serial music: viz., the transposition of a "rotated" hexachord to a pitch level that is not the product of the rotation operation itself. The anomaly can only be explained, it seems, by the need to partition the "foreign" pitch out of the pulsing prelude chords, leaving them wholly referable to the octatonic collection, and therefore "Stravinskian" in a way that a Nabokov (or a Haieff, or a Markevitch) could readily recognize and appreciate.

Besides the emphatic [0, 5, 11] chord—which, in a fashion that fairly parodies the "Augures printanières" from *The Rite*, is repeated thirty-two times to bring the Prelude to a conclusion (and which will resurface to stand alone in the choral echoes of the "Dies irae" outbursts in mm. 83–84 and 98–102)—two other harmonies of long-standing Stravinskian pedigree are highlighted in the course of the brief opening movement. The accompanying pulses in mm. 25–33 (a total of forty-four iterations) comprise positions 1–4 in hexachord 2b (in context, positions 3–6 of the retrograde series), which as an aggregate yield the anhemitonic [0, 2, 5, 7] tetrachord of *Petrushka*'s opening "fairground" harmony (ex. 19.5a). After a silent bar the pulse is resumed (mm. 35–46) with the last note of hexachord Ra plus the first two pitches of Rb (in terms of example 19.4 these are positions 5–7 in set 2), which combine to form the major-minor trichord [0, 3, 4] (ex. 19.5b). (Both the tetrachord and the trichord, be it noted, have impeccable octatonic credentials.) Between the notes of the [0, 3, 4] chord and those of the concluding [0, 5, 11] chord (ex. 19.5c), the series provides an intervening A (order position 4). Stravinsky nonchalantly omitted it, perhaps condoning the ploy on the grounds that the scamped pitch occurs several times in the melodic parts running above. Can one doubt that he was bent on ferreting out "associative harmonies" calculated to evoke a shock of recognition from connoisseurs of his "Russian" idiom?

Example 19.5   Harmonies derived from
set 2 retrograde in Prelude

a. mm. 25–33

b. mm. 36–46   *c.* mm. 47–54

The "Lacrimosa" is at once the movement most thoroughly composed out of transposition-rotations (involving the two IR—inverted retrograde—hexachords and the resultant verticals as shown in example 19.2) and, by no means coincidentally, the one most saturated with traditional octatonic sonorities. The vocal line begins with the retrograde of the fifth transposition-rotation of the "b" hexachord (that is to say, at the lower right extremity of the chart from which Stravinsky worked), and snakes its way up through the array before switching over to the "a" hexachord and snaking its way down.[26] Hexachord IR$_5$b has its "odd" (octatonically nonreferable) note at the beginning, which perhaps explains why Stravinsky started at the end. Until the sixth note, then, the vocal line in the "Lacrimosa" is referable to collection 2, and so are the accompanying "vertical" in the flutes and the bass note in the double bass and harp (the latter derived from the untransposed "a" hexachord of the retrograde). Moreover, the first four notes of the voice hexachord make up the [0, 1, 3, 4] octatonic tetrachord, presented— just as it was, forty-three years earlier, in the "Tema" of the *Octuor* variations—as a third [0, 4] filled in by a second [1, 3]. Stravinsky underscored this reminiscence with a characteristic "stutter" (ex. 19.6).

At m. 232, both the voice part and the bass move to pitches referable to collection 3, as are, mostly, the pitches in the accompanying flute vertical. The harmony produced, in fact, is nothing else than a *Petrushka* chord (excepting only the E-sharp in the piccolo, which however can be referred back to collection 2). The bridging passage for the trombones at m. 234 (derived from I_1a) exactly duplicates the pitch content of the preceding vocal phrase, with the odd note similarly placed, so that we have in effect a return to collection 2. The next combination (m. 235), consisting of IR_4b in the voice, vertical no. 3 (from IRb) in the flutes, and notes 1–4 of Ra in the bass instruments, juxtaposes collection 3 melody with collection 2 harmony (cf. Stravinsky's older practice—indeed, Rimsky-Korsakov's practice—of juxtaposing octatonic "harmony" and "melody" scales).[27] And so it goes. The music in example 19.6 could almost have come out of *Zvezdolikii*.

Example 19.6 Octatonic analysis of "Lacrimosa," opening

***

Alongside the "verticals" technique described by Babbitt and others, first employed in the *Movements*, and best exemplified within the *Requiem Canticles* by the "Lacrimosa," there is another type of vertical construction in the *Requiem Canticles* that is unique to that composition, and even more explicit in its symmetrical-centric properties, since it makes actual what is only virtual in the usual verticals technique: namely, literal pitch-class centricity as (in Babbitt's words) "the compositional point of convergence of all the symmetries."[28] As a serial operation it is so artless that no analyst approaching Stravinsky from a Schoenbergian perspective has dreamed of looking for it, yet it perfectly epitomizes Stravinsky's brand of "twelve-tone tonality."

At three points in the *Requiem Canticles* Stravinsky generated passages of four-part chordal harmony by simply running the basic untransposed forms of the complete set concurrently. The first of these takes place near the end of the first choral movement, the "Exaudi" (mm. 71–76). Series 1 in its prime form (P) is set against its own retrograde (R), the retrograde of its inversion (RI), and the peculiarly Stravinskian "retrograde of the inverted retrograde" (R/IR), this last only differing from what Stravinsky called the inversion by its pitch level (in this case it stands a major second lower than the inversion, in formal language at t10). In terms of Stravinsky's serial charts as reproduced by Claudio Spies,[29] these forms correspond to the P and the R read left to right, and to the I and the IR read right to left (see ex. 19.7, in which the set forms are distinguished by the shape of their note heads: round for P, square for R, triangular for RI, and diamond for R/IR).

Since we are dealing simultaneously with two inversionally related pairs (P and R/IR; R and RI) and with two reversibly related pairs (P and R; RI and R/IR), a situation like the one Babbitt has described with respect to verticals again arises: symmetrically placed columns yield sums with inversionally-reversibly symmetrical intervallic content. But since there was no uniform starting point at "0," there is consequently no single axis of symmetry. And since there are an even number of elements, there is no "middle vertical" that is itself inevitably self-inverting (though many of the individual columns do fortuitously produce such collections). Furthermore, while some of the sum collections (namely, those referable to the whole-tone scales) have single axes of symmetry corresponding variously to the starting points of P and R, conditions are such that there is nothing to prevent the axis of symmetry from being a semitone pair (what George Perle calls an "odd axis").[30] Under such circumstances there is no global pitch center (though A-sharp is contextually singled out as the pitch class of priority in the present case: the passage quoted is followed by one in which whole sequences of regular "verticals" produced by the IRa hexachord are sounded in succession over A-sharp, held as a pedal).

The next instance of the concurrent-set-forms device is an especially interesting one, since it accounts for the generation of the static *Sympho-*

Example 19.7 "Exaudi": the last choral phrase (mm. 71–76) analyzed

a. The row forms

b. Their simultaneous deployment

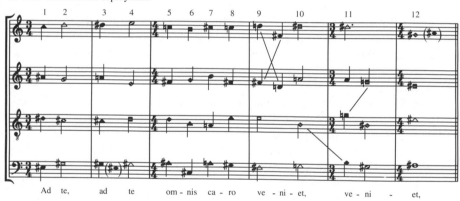

Ad te, ad te om - nis ca - ro ve - ni - et, ve - ni - et,

c. Symmetrical sums

nies-like chord at the beginning of the Interlude. It has been claimed, by those eager to connect Stravinsky's serial technique with Schoenberg's, that this six-note chord is the sum of the initial trichord of set 1 and the transposition of its inversion at the fourth.[31] However prevalent and potent in Schoenberg's music, the technique of combining inversionally related hexachords at transpositions that yield twelve-tone aggregates (what Babbitt has christened "combinatoriality") was never exploited by Stravinsky, who was, in his concern for pitch centricity, extremely chary of transpositions generated by any means other than his own hexachordal rotation technique. There is no evidence that Stravinsky was even aware of Schoenberg's "combinatorial" practice. The refrain chord in the Interlude is generated by a fourfold array of basic functions that is even simpler than the one from the "Exaudi." It is merely a matter of the concurrence of the P, R, I, and IR forms of set 1, just as they are found on the basic serial chart (ex. 19.8; note heads differentiated as before).

In this case the simultaneities have been fudged to a degree, so as to obtain a greater number of whole-tone chords than would otherwise have arisen. Since the only difference between this array and the preceding one involves the order of presentation of the third and fourth row forms, not their content, the sum collections are just what they were the first time. Again, as there is no controlling "0" pitch class, there is no inherent center. Only the multiple repetitions of the refrain chord serve factitiously to "tonicize" it.

Previous writers have claimed that only in the Interlude did Stravinsky at once display both of the sets that inform the *Requiem Canticles*, and have made much of what they perceived to be the symmetrical deployment of the two sets around that central movement.[32] In fact the harmonies in the Postlude are derived from the sets in combination as well. Not only does this make the Postlude a fitting harmonic summary, but it also enabled Stravinsky to generate strings of as many as eleven harmonies derived from a single "0" pitch class, all of them consequently disposable around a single axis of symmetry—a single, literal center.

Thus, the eleven tolling chords in mm. 290–92 consist of the vertical concatenation of both primes and both inversions (exx. 19.9a–19.9c). Given the similarity of the two sets, we have a near-palindromic matrix of (by definition) self-inverting harmonies symmetrically disposed around the F that starts each of the row forms on its way, which Stravinsky treated as a pedal, the way he had treated the "0" pitch classes that control the hexachordal verticals in other movements. Only by deploying in tandem a pair of sets with a common starting point could Stravinsky have generated such an impressive array of self-inverting

540

Example 19.8   Opening of Interlude analyzed

a. The row forms

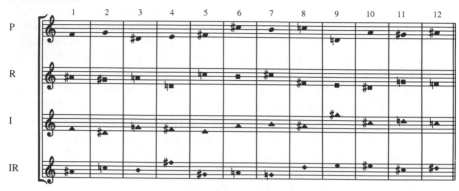

b. The refrain chord
(mm. 136–39)

c. Simultaneous deployment of all row forms in mm. 140–43

(positions 1 / 2)

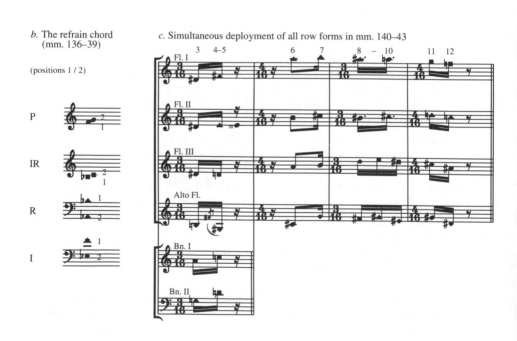

Example 19.9   Simultaneous deployment of two sets in Postlude, mm. 289–92

a. The row forms

b. Bell chords analyzed

c. Their symmetrical disposition around F

harmonies—minor seventh chords, augmented triads, whole-tone segments, French sixths, diminished triads and sevenths, plus others without common-practice standing—all motivated by a new syntax governing their "contextual coherence" or "association," as Babbitt would
say. And that must be the reason why there are two different sets in the
Requiem Canticles to begin with. It was a *reprise de contact* with a style of
writing that had formed the backbone of Stravinsky's true "Russian"
music—that is to say, the music he actually wrote in Russia—as comparison with a well-known passage in *The Firebird* will remind us (ex.
19.10).

Example 19.10   The *Firebird*, fig. 4, "Apparition de l'oiseau de feu," reduced
and analyzed to show symmetrical disposition of harmonies

The sequence of chords at mm. 295–97 derives from the simultaneous deployment of the retrogrades and inverted retrogrades. The
first notes in each series are omitted so that the sequence can once again
number eleven chords in keeping with the numerological ground plan.
Had Stravinsky chosen the retrograde inversion rather than the inverted retrograde (the difference is t10 in the case of set 1 and t4 in the
case of set 2), he would have merely reproduced the chord sequence in
example 19.9 in reverse order. Instead he produced a noncentric and
not consistently symmetrical concatenation that he felt the need arbitrarily to adjust at various points so as to improve the harmony; he
actually substituted the second hexachord of the set 1 inversion for that
of the inverted retrograde, so that the "second line" in example 19.11
actually doubles back on itself (at t2) at the midpoint. It follows, of
course, that under these rather loose harmonic conditions the G-sharp
pedal no longer plays any inherently structural role. No longer a true
center, it seems to have been selected simply to match the lowest pitch
of the first chord (see ex. 19.11).

Example 19.11 Simultaneous deployment of two sets in Postlude, mm. 294–97
a. The row forms

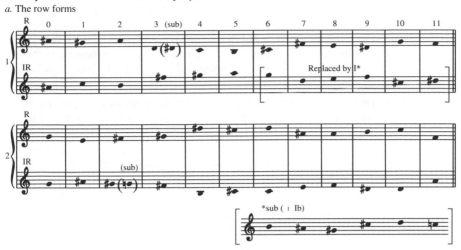

b. Bell chords analyzed

c. Their collectional affinities

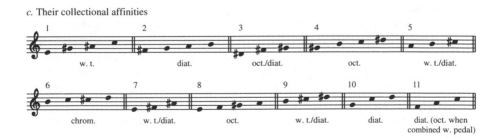

The final string of quarter-note tolling chords (mm. 300–302) is derived from the untransposed primes and retrogrades and therefore describes a perfect (though in the event arbitrarily telescoped and otherwise modified) palindrome. When the pedal B-sharp (C) is added to those verticals in the palindrome that do not already contain it, three pairs can be formed that yield inversionally symmetrical displays either around the pedal or around a central axis dyad (ex. 19.12).

Is it mere coincidence that verticals 4 and 5 in example 19.12, omitted from the actual chord progression at m. 300, very nearly correspond in pitch-class content to the seven-member whole-note chord at the beginning of the Postlude? Probably so, for there is another way of accounting for that chord and its fellows at mm. 294, 299, and 304–5, the so-called "chords of death."[33] They are combinations of hexachordal verticals referable to sets 1 and 2. Referring back to example 19.2, we recall that the "a" hexachords of both sets share the all-important self-inverting middle vertical, and that the latter is a subset of octatonic collection 2. If one of these verticals were rotated on an [0, 3, 6, 9] axis (in keeping, let us say, with the progression from pedal F at the beginning of the Postlude to pedal G-sharp at m. 294), the collection would be exhausted. The opening "chord of death," meanwhile, is in fact made up of seven of the eight pitch classes in collection 2 (only B is missing). It seems reasonable, then, to consider it the product of such a rotation, and beyond that, as Stravinsky's fond (and in this funerary context, touching) farewell to the pitch field that had served him so long and so fruitfully.

The second "chord of death" is made up of six out of the nine pitch classes found in the two second-position verticals in example 19.2. The third chord (m. 299) is the most massive, consisting of eight different pitch classes. They are all present and accounted for (with a single remainder) if the first-position vertical from the "a" hexachord of set 1 is combined with the corresponding vertical derived from the "b" hexachord of set 2. The fourth chord (m. 304) is wholly contained within the third-position vertical in the set 2b array (plus the B-sharp pedal). Finally, the enigmatic four-note chord that represents the point of intersection between the series of "chords of death" and that of the "tolling bells" in the very last measure of the piece, exactly corresponds in pitch-class content with the first-position vertical in the set 2a array, as already illustrated in example 19.2. Example 19.13 summarizes these derivations.

Whenever possible, Stravinsky voiced these chords in ways that emphasized triadic partitions at their tops and wide spacings at the bottoms, suggesting harmonically stable roots. He was once again, at the very end of his career, up to the same tricks of *trompe-d'oreille* "poly-

Example 19.12   Simultaneous deployment of two sets in Postlude, mm. 299–302

a. The row forms

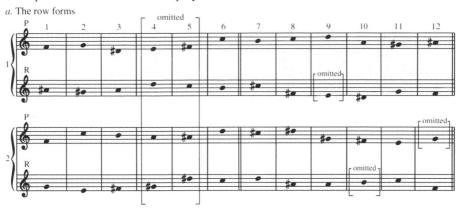

b. Bell chords analyzed

c. Symmetrical sums

Example 19.13   Derivation of "chords of death"

a. "Middle vertical" of the "a" hexachord (*cf.* ex. 19.3)
referred to collection 2 and compared with the chord
at m. 289

b. Chord at m. 294 compared with the second-position
"vertical" of set 1, hexachord a (i.e., hexachord 1a),
and first-position vertical of set 2, hexachord b
(hexachord 2b)

c. Chord at m. 299 compared with the first-position
"vertical" hexachord 1. (*cf. Petrushka* chord) and
first-position "vertical" of hexachord 2b

d. Chord at m. 304 compared with the third-position
"vertical" of hexachord 2b

e. Chord at m. 305 compared with the first-position
"vertical" of hexachord 2a

harmony" he had employed in the period of his first fame. Like those
earlier "polychords," of which the one named after *Petrushka* remains
the most famous, the "chords of death" in the *Requiem Canticles* are
precisely the sort of thing Babbitt so perceptively described as
"attitudinally Russian": chords as "things-in-themselves," as "sonorous objects." They are farewell "kisses of the earth," and the composition in which they so surprisingly appear must surely be the most
attitudinally Russian twelve-tone music ever composed.

***

Stravinsky's elaborately verticalized serial technique was something
he guarded during his lifetime as if it were some kind of Beliaev-circle
guild secret.[34] Yet, as already intimated, it is possible to wonder whether

his serialism was in the final analysis much more than a marriage of convenience or one made for appearances' sake, or whether, had he world enough and time, Stravinsky might have found a more direct and theoretically better integrated route to the technique that produced his final style. For it is precisely the principle of intervallic order—the most fundamental serial principle of them all—that seems least relevant to Stravinsky's goals and predilections. Never did he exhibit the least interest in exploring the twelve-tone aggregate "contrapunctically," whether by partitions, by juxtapositions of combinatorial row forms, or by "derivation" (i.e., the Webernian technique of embedding within the twelve-tone series trichords or tetrachords that are themselves related in intervallic contour). His hexachordally based (at times, as in the *Introitus* of 1965, even tetrachordally based) twelve-tone music shows a far greater affinity for what the pre-Schoenbergian atonalist Hauer would have called *Tropen* than for the Schoenbergian concept of a *Reihe*. When one observes him—in *Abraham and Isaac*, for example, as well as in the "Lacrimosa" from the *Canticles*—threading his strangely dogged and mechanistic way through his rotation charts in all directions, up, down, and from side to side, one cannot escape the conclusion that Stravinsky's concept of serialism really had little to do with maintaining an intervallic succession, and everything to do with the perpetual arrangement and rearrangement of a fixed set of intervals around a center (and someone really should make a study to determine why that center was so often F!).

In short, Stravinsky succeeded, just as Nabokov said he did, in "overpowering" the serial method—or rather, foiling it. He figured out how to wheedle and cajole from it a new brand of the symmetrically disposed centric but not tonally functional music for which, as Arthur Berger was first to point out, Stravinsky had a long-standing and stylistically determinant affinity.[35] In the terms of his *Poetics of Music*, he had found a new source of *complexes sonores*—complexes that now took the form of magic boxes: six-by-six intervallic arrays through which paths could be traced omnidirectionally, and which could thus lead to new and interesting tonal "polarities." In effect, Stravinsky was feeling his way to a kind of "twelve-tone tonality," in some ways comparable to that formulated half a dozen years after his death by George Perle. Because his approach was instinctive and in many ways irrelevant to the Schoenbergian technique he thought he was adopting, his methods were often cumbersome and—from the perspective of the analyst if not that of the listener—disconcertingly arbitrary. In the *Requiem Canticles*, though, he found his way at last to the "second simplicity" he had achieved in the music of his "Russian" years. The dauntless octogenarian had achieved a new and inspiring breakthrough to simplicity, immediately perceived as such by Nabokov and the many others for whom the *Requiem Canticles* formed the great exception among Stravinsky's late serial pieces.

And it was not only due to whatever backward glances the *Canticles* embodied. One cannot shake the impression that in this last major work Stravinsky was standing on the threshold of what could have been a new period—a new "Russian period," if you please—that might have seen him cast off his excess Schoenbergian or Krenekite baggage and find his way to a settled and integrated idiom, one in which a newly refined and simplified technical means more nearly suited his creative ends.

At the age of eighty-four, then, Stravinsky was still a restless young composer, a newly young composer in fact, feeling his way toward a future. The more we learn about this inexhaustible musical phoenix, the stronger the analytical lens we train on his work, and the deeper our historical perspective, the clearer become the connections between his pasts and his futures. He loved to hint at the presence of "serial tendencies" in *The Firebird*.[36] And they are surely there. But we may point just as surely to hints of *The Firebird* in his serialism.

Notes

1. Pieter Van den Toorn, *The Music of Igor Stravinsky* (New Haven, 1983), 402–26; also the discussion of the *Epitaphaim* (1959) on 433–35.

2. See Milton Babbitt, "Order, Symmetry, and Centricity in Late Stravinsky," in Jann Pasler, ed., *Confronting Stravinsky: Man, Musician, and Modernist* (Berkeley, 1986), 247–61, especially the tables on 252, 254, and 258, with their striking vertical alignments of zeros, nines, and threes at the beginnings of hexachords (in *Movements*) and of zeros, fours, and eights plus octave-bisecting zeros and sixes (in the double-rowed *Requiem Canticles*).

3. Nicolas Nabokov, *Bagazh* (New York, 1975), 179.

4. Robert Craft, *Stravinsky: Chronicle of a Friendship, 1948–1971* (New York, 1972), 377.

5. Eric Salzman, "Current Chronicle: Princeton," *Musical Quarterly* 53 (1967): 81–83.

6. Craft, *Chronicle*, 377.

7. Ernst Roth, "A Great Mind and a Great Spirit," *Tempo*, no. 81 (Summer 1967), 4.

8. Louis Andriessen and Elmer Schönberger took this evocative resonance as the springboard for an analysis of the Postlude's numerology that is both fascinating and moving (*The Apollonian Clockwork* [Oxford, 1988], chap. 2). Unfortunately, it is also inaccurate. The climactic christological observation—that the "strokes of the clock" and the "chord of death" come together for the first and only time in the last measure, at the thirty-third stroke of the clock and the thirty-third beat of the last section of the piece ("Wasn't there someone who died after 33 years?")—is based on a faulty count; the coincidence occurs on either the twenty-eighth or the thirty-first beat (depending on whether one starts to count the last section from m. 298, a silent bar, or m. 299), not the thirty-third. The thirty-third beat is the last in the piece, and contains no attacks.

9. See Claudio Spies, "Notes on Stravinsky's Requiem Settings," in Benjamin Boretz and Edward T. Cone, eds., *Perspectives on Schoenberg and Stravinsky* (Princeton, 1968), 249.

10. Craft, *Chronicle,* 329.

11. Igor Stravinsky and Robert Craft, *Conversations with Igor Stravinsky* (Garden City, N.Y., 1959), 121; reprint ed. (Berkeley, 1980), 108.

12. Arthur Jacobs, "Talking with Igor Stravinsky," *Radio Times,* 21 May 1954, 8.

13. Stravinsky and Craft, *Conversations,* 22; reprint, 24–25.

14. A good general introduction to the subject may be found in Van den Toorn, *The Music of Igor Stravinsky,* chap. 14 (pp. 427–55), which contains detailed analyses of parts of *The Flood* and *Abraham and Isaac.* Briefer but especially lucid is the opening discussion in Paul Schulyer Phillips, "The Enigma of *Variations*: A Study of Stravinsky's Final Work for Orchestra," *Music Analysis* 3 (1984): 69–89. Milton Babbitt's more elliptical analyses of *Movements* in *Confronting Stravinsky* (see note 2 above) and in "Stravinsky's Verticals and Schoenberg's Diagonals: A Twist of Fate," Ethan Haimo and Paul Johnson, eds., *Stravinsky Retrospectives* [Lincoln, Neb., 1987], 15–35, may then be tackled. The centric implications of Stravinsky's methods are explored in Charles Wuorinen and Jeffrey Kresky, "On the Significance of Stravinsky's Last Works," *Confronting Stravinsky,* 262–70.

15 . See Babbitt, "Stravinsky's Verticals," 19–20; also Catherine Hogan, "*Threni*: Stravinsky's Debt to Krenek," *Tempo,* no. 141 (1982), 22–25.

16. It has since been taken up by such composers as Oliver Knussen and Charles Wuorinen. The latter has included a primitive didactic exposition of it in his textbook *Simple Composition* (New York, 1979), 105–9.

17. Babbitt, "Stravinsky's Verticals," 19.

18. To N.F. von Meck, 18/(30) July 1880 (Modeste Tchaikovsky, *The Life and Letters of Peter Ilich Tchaikovsky,* ed. Rosa Newmarch [New York, 1973], 382).

19. Stravinsky and Craft, *Conversations,* 121; reprint, 108–9.

20. Babbitt, "Stravinsky's Verticals," 19.

21. The two sets are apportioned in the work as follows: "Exaudi," "Rex tremendae," and "Lacrimosa" are based on series 1; the Prelude, "Dies irae," "Tuba mirum," and "Libera me" are based on series 2. As will be demonstrated in detail below, the Interlude and Postlude make use of both sets, the former in alternation, the latter in simultaneous deployment.

22. For a formal description of the procedure, demonstrating how inversional symmetry is an immanent function of the transpositional and permutational operations employed, see Milton Babbitt, "Contemporary Music Composition and Music Theory as Contemporary Intellectual History," in Barry S. Brook et al., eds., *Perspectives in Musicology* (New York, 1972), 166–67.

23. Babbitt, "Order, Symmetry, and Centricity," 259.

24. Spies, "Notes," 233–34 (Spies speculated that set 1 was "a remedial addition" to offset the "deficiencies" of set 2); also see Babbitt, "Order, Symmetry, and Centricity," 255 and 258–59.

25. For a discussion of its formative bearing on the harmony of *The Rite of Spring,* see Van den Toorn, *The Music of Igor Stravinsky,* 100ff.; also idem, *Stravinsky and "The Rite of Spring"* (Berkeley, 1987), 145ff. The same trichord (often combined with its inversion to produce the symmetrical tetrachord [0, 5, 6, 11]) is also a seminal harmonic construct in the music of Bartók (see Leo Treitler, "Harmonic Procedure in the Fourth Quartet of Béla Bartók," *Journal of Music Theory* 3 [1959]: 292–98; also George Perle, "Symmetrical Formations in the String Quartets of Béla Bartók," *Music Review* 16 [1955]: 300–312) and Schoenberg (see any bar of *Erwartung*).

26. For a complete description of this process, see Spies, "Notes," 245–48, with reference to the chart of rotations and verticals on p. 236.

27. See Richard Taruskin, "Chernomor to Kashchei: Harmonic Sorcery; or, Stravinsky's 'Angle,'" *Journal of the American Musicological Society* 38 (1985): 104–5.

28. Babbitt, "Stravinsky's Verticals," 30.

29. Spies, "Notes," 236.

30. George Perle, *Twelve-Tone Tonality* (Berkeley, 1977), 7–8.

31. E.g., Spies, "Notes," 245.

32. Ibid., 234; Babbitt, "Order, Symmetry, and Centricity," 255; idem, "Stravinsky's Verticals," 31 and 34: "[Stravinsky's] last large composition, *Requiem Canticles*, reveals two sets, whose appearances are symmetrically distributed around the Interlude, the centerpiece of the main body of the work, where the two sets appear, and simultaneously once, at the center of the centerpiece." Craft's lengthy analytical caption to fig. 268 in *A Stravinsky Scrapbook, 1940–1971* (London, 1983), which shows a draft of the Postlude, while correctly stating that both series appear in it, is otherwise unaccountably inaccurate and irrelevant.

33. For the name, see Craft, *Chronicle*, 415.

34. A single laconic analytical example reproduced in Craft, *A Stravinsky Scrapbook*, 120, is his only known attempt to explicate his procedures technically.

35. In the exordium to his article "Problems of Pitch Organization in Stravinsky" *Perspectives in New Music* 2, no. 1 (Fall–Winter 1963): 11–42 (reprinted in Boretz and Cone, *Perspectives on Schoenberg and Stravinsky*,123–55), Berger had called for a "new branch of theory" that might begin to deal adequately with music that is "centric (i.e. organized in terms of tone center) but not tonally functional."

36. Igor Stravinsky, *Expositions and Developments* (Garden City, N.Y., 1962), 151; reprint ed. (Berkeley, 1981), 133.

Contributors

JAMES M. BAKER is professor of music and chair of the Department of Music at Brown University. His varied writings on music theory investigate both tonal and post-tonal analytical problems.

IAN BENT is Anne Parsons Bender professor of music at Columbia University. He has written and edited numerous publications that pertain to the history of theory.

DAVID W. BERNSTEIN is assistant professor of music at Mills College. His published studies on German and Austrian theorists concentrate primarily on the period around 1900.

THOMAS CHRISTENSEN is associate professor of music theory at the University of Iowa. His publications have often been devoted to French music theory of the eighteenth century, especially the work of Jean-Philippe Rameau.

AUSTIN CLARKSON is professor of music at York University. An expert on the music of Stefan Wolpe, he has also written on the psychology and philosophy of music.

P. MURRAY DINEEN is assistant professor of music at the University of Ottawa. His scholarly essays have sought to clarify aspects of Schoenberg's theory.

CHRISTOPHER HATCH taught at Columbia University from 1953 to 1991. His articles include analyses of works by nineteenth-century composers, principally Beethoven.

EDWARD A. LIPPMAN is professor emeritus of music at Columbia University. The diverse topics of his books and articles lie mostly within the philosophy of music.

MARIA RIKA MANIATES is assistant dean of graduate studies at the University of Toronto. Among the subjects of her many publications are Mannerism and the writings of Nicola Vicentino.

ROBERT P. MORGAN is professor of music at Yale University. He specializes in nineteenth- and twentieth-century music history, theory, and analysis.

SEVERINE NEFF is associate professor of music at the College-Conservatory of Music, University of Cincinnati. As author and editor, she has been much involved in Schoenberg studies.

LEEMAN L. PERKINS is professor of music at Columbia University. His publications deal largely with the theory and the history of Renaissance music.

GRAHAM H. PHIPPS is professor of music at North Texas State University. He has given special attention to studying the Second Viennese School as well as the history of German and Austrian music theory from 1750 on.

BENITO V. RIVERA is associate professor of music in the School of Music at Indiana University. The subjects of his scholarship range in time from the Middle Ages to the nineteenth century.

LEE A. ROTHFARB is Gardner Cowles associate professor of the humanities at Harvard University. His publications are concerned with early twentieth-century theorists, Ernst Kurth in particular.

ERNEST H. SANDERS is professor emeritus of music at Columbia University. His writings have addressed a wide variety of issues relating to music of the Gothic era.

PETER N. SCHUBERT is assistant professor of music at McGill University. His papers and articles have presented analyses of both Renaissance and twentieth-century compositions.

EDMOND STRAINCHAMPS is associate professor of music at the State University of New York, Buffalo. His publications focus on early seventeenth-century music and musicians.

RICHARD TARUSKIN is professor of music at the University of California, Berkeley. He has written extensively on Renaissance music, on Russian music, and on Stravinsky's life and works.

Index

Academies and confraternities, Florentine, 190
Achillini, Claudio, 153
Acoustics and perception of music: as
components of music theory, 12–13,
218, 219, 228, 230, 315–21, 330, 334–36;
status of undertones, 380, 388, 395–96.
See also Harmonic dualism; Overtone
series
Aesthetics: "authentistic," 22–23; defini-
tion of, 217; place of, in music theory,
217–31 passim; training in, 453
Aiguino, Illuminato: modal theory of, 2,
103–6, 118–21
Albrechtsberger, Johann Georg, 31, 347,
350
Alembert, Jean le Rond d', 13, 317, 328
Alexander, Thomas, 451
Analyses of complete pieces: Bach, *Well-
Tempered Clavier*, book 2, G-minor
Fugue, 438–44; Beethoven, bagatelle
Op. 119, no. 8, 341–54; Beethoven,
"Eroica" Symphony, first movement,
360–74; Okeghem, *Missa cuiusvis toni*,
65–69; Palestrina, motet *Dies sanctificatus*, 118–32; Schubert, *Der Wegweiser*,
418–27; Stravinsky, *Requiem Canticles*,
525–48; Webern, Variations for Orchestra, 475–502; Willaert, madrigal *O invidia*, 82–88; Wolpe, *Form* for piano, 506–
7, 514–18
Analysis of music: Bottrigari's, Vicentino's, and Zarlino's approach to, 161–
65; designed for amateurs, 453, 456–
59, 462–65; hermeneutic, 31–33, 454,
456–57; historical components in, 3–6,

20–22; impossibility of objective historical, 22–26, 32–33; Kerman's advice on,
21; Momigny's inclination toward, 316;
scope of, 231; Tomlinson's advice on,
21; Treitler's recommendations on, 21–
22
Analytical methods: Capellen's, exemplified, 391–92; derived from Wagner's
writings, 357–58, 360–76; governed by
contextual, intuitive, and imaginal factors, 506–18; Halm's, exemplified, 459,
461–62; of investigating Classical chromaticism, 258–302; Kretzschmar's, exemplified, 454, 456; Kurth's, described,
463; Oettingen's, exemplified, 386;
Schenker's, exemplified, 256–57;
Schering's, described, 456–57; Schoenberg's, applied to Schubert, 418–27;
surveyed, 3–6. *See also* Pitch-class sets;
Twelve-tone methods
Anonymous IV, 41, 42, 44
Aristides Quintilianus, extract from *On
Music*, 220–21
Aristotle and Pseudo-Aristotle, 139, 142,
145, 149, 150, 218, 231, 410
Aristoxenus, 140, 149, 150, 166, 169,
220; extract from *Harmonic Elements*,
218–19
Arrighetti, Lodovico, 189
Arrivabene, Andrea, 139
Artusi, Giovanni Maria, 137, 150, 151,
154, 156, 160–61, 194, 206, 210; polemi-
cal attacks by, quoted, 141, 143, 145,
174; quarrel with Bottrigari, 140–49,
152
Augustine, Saint, 221